Lecture Notes in Computer S

Commenced Publication in 1973
Founding and Former Series Editors:
Gerhard Goos, Juris Hartmanis, and Jan van Leeuwen

Shigeo Sugimoto   Jane Hunter
Andreas Rauber   Atsuyuki Morishima (Eds.)

Digital Libraries: Achievements, Challenges and Opportunities

9th International Conference on
Asian Digital Libraries, ICADL 2006
Kyoto, Japan, November 27-30, 2006
Proceedings

 Springer

Volume Editors

Shigeo Sugimoto
Research Center for Knowledge Communities
University of Tsukuba
Ibaraki 305-8550, Japan
E-mail: sugimoto@slis.tsukuba.ac.jp

Jane Hunter
School of Information Technology and Electrical Engineering
The University of Queensland QLD
4072, Australia
E-mail: jane@itee.uq.edu.au

Andreas Rauber
Department of Software Technology and Interactive Systems
Vienna University of Technology
Vienna, Austria
E-mail: rauber@ifs.tuwien.ac.at

Atsuyuki Morishima
Research Center for Knowledge Communities
University of Tsukuba
Ibaraki 305-8550, Japan
E-mail: mori@slis.tsukuba.ac.jp

Library of Congress Control Number: 2006936076

CR Subject Classification (1998): H.3, H.2, H.4.3, H.5, J.7, D.2, J.1, I.7

LNCS Sublibrary: SL 3 – Information Systems and Application, incl. Internet/Web
and HCI

ISSN   0302-9743
ISBN-10   3-540-49375-1 Springer Berlin Heidelberg New York
ISBN-13   978-3-540-49375-4 Springer Berlin Heidelberg New York

Springer is a part of Springer Science+Business Media

springer.com

© Springer-Verlag Berlin Heidelberg 2006
Printed in Germany

Typesetting: Camera-ready by author, data conversion by Scientific Publishing Services, Chennai, India
Printed on acid-free paper   SPIN: 11931584   06/3142   5 4 3 2 1 0

Preface

The International Conference on Asian Digital Libraries (ICADL) was born in Hong Kong in 1998 and hosted in Taipei (1999), Seoul (2000), Bangalore (2001), Singapore (2002), Kuala Lumpur (2003), Shanghai (2004) and Bangkok (2005). ICADL 2006 held in Kyoto, Japan was the 9th of the ICADL series. ICADL has been recognized as an important event for the digital library communities not only in Asia but also globally. The primary mission of ICADL, like the Joint Conference on Digital Libraries (JCDL) and European Conference on Digital Libraries (ECDL), is to serve as a forum for exchange of new advanced technologies and ideas among researchers and practitioners. In addition, ICADL as a conference based in Asia is an important event not only for people in developed countries but also in developing countries where there is large diversity in culture, language and development.

ICADL 2006 received 170 paper submissions from 23 countries. Every submission was reviewed by at least three reviewers. The Program Committee selected 46 full papers and 14 short papers based on the quality and contribution to digital library research. ICADL as well as JCDL and ECDL cover a wide range of information technologies for digital libraries as well as the human and social aspects of digital libraries. The topics of the papers in the proceedings include information extraction, information retrieval, metadata, architectures for digital libraries and archives, ontologies, information seeking, cultural heritage and e-learning.

The Program Committee accepted six papers as posters from those submitted primarily by authors from developing countries in Asia. In general, it is difficult for authors in developing countries to get their papers accepted in major digital library conferences. Through this new category in ICADL, the Program Co-chairs hope to enable Asian authors to present their works to the global community and to inform the global community of activities in Asia.

ICADL 2006 is proud of our distinguished keynote and invited speakers. Their experiences, activities and perspectives for the future are very valuable to the global digital library community. ICADL 2006 organized a special program as a showcase of national DL activities in Asia and Japan and invited several important institutions and organizations.

We would like to express our special thanks to Katsumi Tanaka and all members of the Organizing Committee of ICADL 2006. We would like to express our special thanks to Eepeng Lim, Shalini Urs, Hsinchun Chen, Ching-chih Chen, Edward A. Fox and all members of the Steering Committee of ICADL who encouraged us to organize ICADL 2006. We would like to thank our Program Committee members and reviewers for their excellent work. Last but not least,

we would like to thank all of the authors who submitted their papers to ICADL
2006.

November 2006   Shigeo Sugimoto
                                                         Jane Hunter
                                                       Andreas Rauber
                                                     Atsuyuki Morishima

Organization

Honorary Conference Chair

Makoto Nagao (NICT, Japan)

General Chair

Katsumi Tanaka (Kyoto University, Japan)

Program Committee Co-chairs

Jane Hunter (University of Queensland, Australia)
Andreas Rauber (Vienna University of Technology, Austria)
Shigeo Sugimoto (University of Tsukuba, Japan)

Finance Chair

Masatoshi Yoshikawa (Kyoto University, Japan)

Publication Chair

Atsuyuki Morishima (University of Tsukuba, Japan)

Publicity Co-chairs

Taro Tezuka (Kyoto University, Japan)
Kenji Hatano (Doshisha University, Japan)

Local Arrangements Co-chairs

Satoshi Oyama (Kyoto University, Japan)
Akira Maeda (Ritsumeikan University, Japan)

ICADL Steering Committee Chair

Ee-Peng Lim (NTU, Singapore)

Program Committee

Robert Allen (Drexel, USA)
Toshiyuki Amagasa (University of Tsukuba, Japan)
Chutiporn Anutariya (Shinawatra University, Thailand)
Thomas Baker (DCMI/University of Goettingen, Germany)
Jose Borbinha (IST/INESC-ID, Portugal)

Liddy Nevile (La Trobe University, Australia)
Paul Nieuwenhuysen (Vrije Universiteit Brussel, Belgium)
Pimrumpai Premsmit (Chulalongkorn University, Thailand)
Somporn Puttapithakporn (STOU, Thailand)
Edie Rasmussen (UBC, Canada)
Andreas Rauber (Vienna University of Technology, Austria)
S. Sadagopan (IIIT-B, India)
Tetsuo Sakaguchi (University of Tsukuba, Japan)
Hideyasu Sasaki (Ritsumeikan University, Japan)
Michael Seadle (Michigan State University, USA)
Praditta Siripan (NSTDA, Thailand)
Ingeborg Solvberg (NTNU, Norway)
Ohm Sornil (NIDA, Thailand)
Shigeo Sugimoto (University of Tsukuba, Japan)
Atsuhiro Takasu (NII, Japan)
Yin-Leng Theng (NTU, Singapore)
Shalini Urs (University of Mysore, India)
Stuart Weibel (OCLC, USA)
Ian Witten (Waikato University, New Zealand)
Vilas Wuwongse (AIT, Thailand)
Christopher C. Yang (CUHK, Hong Kong SAR)
Masatoshi Yoshikawa (Kyoto University, Japan)
Marcia Lei Zeng (Kent State University, USA)

External Reviewers

Ahmed Abbasi
Aixin Sun
Alexander Zadorin
Claus-Peter Klas
Daning Hu
David Bainbridge
David Milne
David Nichols
Fabrizio Falchi
Hsin-Min Lu
Ingo Frommholz

Jiexun Li
Julie Allinson
Kathryn Hempstalk
Leonardo Candela
Matthew Dailey
Maxim Gubin
Michael Maslov
Nichalin Suakkaphong
Olena Medelyan
Qing Li
Rob Schumaker

Robert Neumayer
Ronald Schroeter
Saadia Malik
Siddharth Kaza
Stephan Strodl
Tianjun Fu
Tiziano Fagni
Xin Li

Sponsoring Institutions

The 21st Century Center of Excellence Program "Informatics Research Center for Development of Knowledge Society Infrastructure," Graduate School of Informatics, Kyoto University, Japan

Research Center for Knowledge Communities, Graduate School of Library, Information, and Media Studies, University of Tsukuba, Japan

Table of Contents

Keynote and Invited Talks

Advanced Digital Archives

Digital Libraries and Learning

Distributed Repositories

Information Extraction

Personalization for Digital Libraries

Information Retrieval

Metadata

Digital Libraries and Archives Architecture

Multimedia Resource Retrieval and Organization

Organizing Knowledge

Semistructured Data/XML

Information Seeking in Digital Archives

Information Organization

Short Papers

Poster Papers

National and Regional Projects on Digital Libraries and Archives

The Age of Content and Knowledge Processing

Makoto Nagao

National Institute of Information and Communications Technology,
4-2-1 Nukui-Kitamachi, Koganei, Tokyo 184-8795 Japan

Internet has become an indispensable infra-structure on the earth with more and more high speed digital information services provided year by year. Correspondingly, a wide variety of content is created, stored and distributed. This includes not only text but also speeches, music, pictures and videos. On the Internet, an unbelievably large amount of content of every kind is accessible from anywhere in the world, and a smart, intelligent information retrieval system has become major priority. People are not satisfied with the current retrieval systems. In Japan there are research and development projects for new generation retrieval systems, where a central issue is how to guarantee the trustworthiness and the authenticity of the retrieved information. Another serious issue is that content on the Internet is not organized systematically, and is not necessarily suitable for everybody to use. Self organization of varieties of information into a knowledge system will be another important technology to be developed in the future. Digital libraries that provide reliable content with rich related information using relatively simple access methods act as a kind of standard reference to establish technologies to solve the issues above. Because the scope of information access is all over the world, multilingual machine translation is an indispensable technology. The paper will discuss these problems by surveying the state of the art of content and knowledge processing.

S. Sugimoto et al. (Eds.): ICADL 2006, LNCS 4312, p. 1, 2006.
© Springer-Verlag Berlin Heidelberg 2006

Cyber Science Infrastructure and Scholarly Information for the Promotion of e-Science in Japan

Jun Adachi

National Institute of Informatics
2-1-2 Hitotsubashi, Chiyoda-ku, Tokyo 101-8430, Japan
adachi@nii.ac.jp

1 Introduction

Cyberinfrastructure is now considered crucial in many countries, not only for advancing scientific researches but also for promoting educational activities based on digital contents such as scholarly databases, e-journals and coursewares in higher education. The Cyber Science Infrastructure (CSI) is one of such initiatives which was launched in Japan. In this talk, the current activities in CSI will be described, putting emphasis on scholarly information sharing and dissemination.

CSI is a new initiative aiming at a comprehensive framework in which Japanese universities and research institutions are collaboratively constructing an IT-based environment for boosting scientific research and educational activities. Various preceding initiatives are reorganized and included in CSI, such as the national research grid initiative, the university PKI and authentication system initiative, and projects related to academic and scholarly information sharing and dissemination, as well as the project for a next-generation high-speed network.

CSI was launched in late 2004 as a collaborative effort of leading universities, research institutions and the National Institute of Informatics (NII).

2 CSI as Next-Generation Scholarly Environment

NII is an inter-university research institution that was established in April 2000 to conduct comprehensive research on informatics. The institute is also been assigned a pivotal role in developing a scholarly information and networking infrastructure for Japanese universities. Therefore, NII also has a service operation arm for networking and proving databases.

The followings are three goals that NII considers indispensable for the Japanese research community:

- Design and deployment of a next-generation high-speed network for research institutions and universities and the operation of this network as a stable infrastructure for research and higher education,

S. Sugimoto et al. (Eds.): ICADL 2006, LNCS 4312, pp. 2–3, 2006.

- Development of scholarly databases and digital libraries, enabling the dissemination of scholarly information from universities, and
- Promotion of informatics research jointly undertaken with universities.

Since the achievement of these goals is NII's most important mission, NII has integrated its preceding activities for developing information infrastructures into the Cyber Science Infrastructure (CSI) initiative, incorporating researchers and universities outside NII who share these three goals.

In 2005, the CSI initiative obtained support from MEXT (the Ministry of Education, Culture, Sports, Science and Technology) and the Council for Science and Technology Policy of the Japanese government.

Currently, CSI includes the following specific initiatives and projects:

- Deployment of SINET3 using 40 Gbps optical network,
- Initiative for University PKI and authentication system Development,
- National research grid initiative,
- Provision of academic and scholarly information.

3 Academic and Scholarly Information in CSI

NII has been providing a wide range of scholarly information mainly for university researchers and students. In April 2005, NII launched GeNii as a unified portal of databases on various scholarly subjects. GeNii currently offers four services: CiNii, Webcat Plus, KAKEN, and NII-DBR. Among these, CiNii is an integration of Citation Index of Japanese scholarly articles in Japanese society journals and university bulletins with electronic full-text.

The university libraries' consortia and NII jointly operate and e-journal repository called NII-REO. The repository ensures long term access to e-journals that are indispensable for academic research and education. Last year, we successfully acquired large-scale archival digital articles from Springer-Verlag and Oxford University Press journals, which go back to the 19th century. NII and university libraries are planning to add more titles to this digital archive of scholarly e-journals.

In recent years, more and more university libraries are considering to install their institutional repositories for dissemination of academic information. NII started a collaborative project with universities, aiming at deployment and coordination of institutional repositories in Japan. In 2006, 57 universities are participating in this project.

4 Concluding Remarks

The Cyber Science Infrastructure (CSI) is a new initiative for evolving Japan's scholarly information infrastructure. In CSI, sharing of electronic resources is promoted, and the dissemination of scholarly information originating from universities are strongly encouraged. CSI could be regarded as a new model of distributed and virtual digital library in the future academic environment.

Working Together in Developing Library and Information Science Education in the Asia Pacific

Schubert Foo, Christopher S.G. Khoo,
Abdus Sattar Chaudhry, and Shaheen Majid

Division of Information Studies
School of Communication and Information
Nanyang Technological University
Singapore 637718
{assfoo, assgkhoo, aschaudhry, asmajid}@ntu.edu.sg

Abstract. Ongoing initiatives that offer potential collaboration and cooperation among LIS educators, particularly in the Asia Pacific context, are identified and discussed. By no means being exhaustive, these areas include hosting and participating in workshops, symposiums and conferences; implementing a portal for education; developing a repository of learning objects and resources; assuring quality through accreditation; and promoting and sustaining research and scholarship. These are highlighted with the aim to foster and promote dialogue among LIS educators, researchers and practitioners, and to engender participation in these activities. Collectively, these areas lay a foundation to create an informal network to improve information exchange and dissemination, knowledge sharing and creation, and research collaboration, thereby helping to further improve and ensure high standards of LIS education, practice and research in the region.

1 Introduction

The emergence of the Web Wide Web and the networked information society has changed the landscape and roles of information professionals dramatically. Six challenges have been identified by Johnson (1998) facing these professionals: assisting users deal with information overload through higher selectivity and screening; high level of technical skills to manage new information and communication technologies (ICTs); competition with other professionals for positions in increasingly converged library, information and computing services; need for new skills drawn from those traditionally seen as separate sectors of the information industry such as publishing; higher level of skills for teaching and facilitating information literacy; and the ability to work with other people. Against this backdrop, we have seen library and information schools rise to the challenge to train such a new breed of information professionals by reinventing themselves and engaging in the revision of their LIS curricula, rightly recognising the lack of expertise in traditional LIS departments and thereby fostering and creating collaboration and cooperation opportunities with other departments to offer new specialisms within the framework of a generalist programme of education. Beyond this, these departments have extended their reach beyond the

S. Sugimoto et al. (Eds.): ICADL 2006, LNCS 4312, pp. 4–11, 2006.

institution into national and international boundaries. In the Asia Pacific region, we have begun to witness pockets of activities by LIS educators to enhance and promote collaboration to deal with this increasing demand of educating competent information professionals for the future. Typical activities would include the hosting of seminars, symposiums, workshops and conferences; making available learning and teaching resources; collaborative research and scholarship; improving quality of education through information sharing and accreditation.

This paper attempts to outline some of these activities along these lines with the aim to further engage and promote dialogue among LIS educators, practitioners, researchers, and to engender participation, either formally or informally, to further develop these activities to reach a higher plane of quality that would benefit all educators, students and LIS professionals alike.

2 Workshops, Symposiums and Conferences

In 2004, the Research Center for Knowledge Communities (RCKC), University of Tsukuba organised an international symposium on digital libraries and knowledge communities in networked information society in cooperation with the National Science Foundation (NSF, USA), DELOS Network of Excellence on Digital Libraries (DELOS, EU) and the Japan Society of Library and Information Science (University of Tsukuba, 2004). In 2006, the symposium focused on new directions for information science education in the networked information society. In this March 2006 symposium, speakers from North America and Asia-Pacific countries gathered to share information and ideas, and provided updates of new directions for education for the future (University of Tsukuba, 2006). Institutions represented at the symposium included the University of Pittsburgh (US), University of Michigan (US), University of British Columbia (Canada), National Taiwan University (Taiwan), Nanyang Technological University (Singapore), Monash University (Australia), University of Tokyo (Japan), Khon Kaen University (Thailand) and Sookmyung Women's University (Korea).

In essence, the three pillars of information, namely, people (society), technology (IT) and information (LIS and related disciplines) seems to be an acceptable framework and way forward to inculcate the skills and competencies of future information professionals. LIS schools working in collaboration with other schools and disciplines is clearly an upward trend to recognise the diversity of needs in the marketplace. Opportunities for growth still prevail – examples include archives management, records management, and knowledge management. Interesting discussions on the "I" schools versus the "L" schools continue to prevail as we grapple with the new future. A more structured approach in the form of the LIPER (Library and Information Professionals Education Reform) project in Japan is an attempt to restructure the Japanese LIS education and training system to tackle the current state of LIS education that takes the current forms of *shiso* training (public libraries), *shisho-kyoyu* training (school libraries) and graduate LIS education. Information, which is now widely acknowledged as a key commodity by industries, businesses, governments and universities is an enabling resource to fuel research to tackle global priorities to advance knowledge and understanding, ensuring economic and cultural prosperity, and providing safety and security. Online proceedings of the symposium will eventually be made available at the symposium's website.

Another related conference in LIS education and practice in 2006 is the inaugural *Asia-Pacific Conference on Library and Information Education and Practice* (A-LIEP) conference that was held at Nanyang Technological University in April (NTU, 2006). The conference was organised by NTU's Division of Information Studies in collaboration with the Department of Information Science, University of Malaya (UM), and NTU Library. Traditionally, the LIS profession in Asia-Pacific has often looked to the West for ideas and leadership without realising the growing wealth of valuable developments, innovations and expertise in the own yard of countries in Asia-Pacific. Each country exhibits its own history of LIS education and research, shaped by socio-economic, political and cultural factors. As a result, LIS education and research in Asia-Pacific exhibit a wide variety of characters, flavors and areas of strength. The conference provided a platform for each country to tell its story of LIS, engender dialogue and knowledge sharing, and pave the way for greater collaboration and cooperation among LIS educators and researchers in the Asia-Pacific as well as globally. The conference saw an exciting gathering of more than 200 LIS professors and professionals from 20 countries, including the presidents of the American Society for Information Science and Technology (ASIST), Australian Library and Information Association (ALIA) and the Library Association of Singapore (LAS), as well as representatives from the American Library Association (ALA), Association for Library and Information Science Education (ALISE) and International Federation of Library Associations (IFLA), and many deans and heads of Information departments across the Asia-Pacific region, North America and Europe (Khoo, Singh & Chaudhry, 2006). In addition, a pre-conference meeting on accreditation of LIS programmes in Asia was held with representatives from several countries and LIS associations. An update of the 2006 Tsukuba's symposium that was highlighted previously was also given by Professor Shigeo Sugimoto (Symposium's Organising Chair) as an introduction to the final panel discussion that was attended by all conference participants. A number of regional collaborative projects were initiated at the conference including developing a Web portal and learning objects repository for LIS education in Asia, and a regional accreditation scheme for LIS education. These will be further elaborated in subsequent sections of this paper. Proposals were also received from Taiwan and Japan to host the second and third A-LIEP conferences in future.

A-LIEP is akin to ICADL (International Conference of Asian Digital Libraries) which had its initial roots in Hong Kong in 1998 as an event to invite international participation focusing on and highlighting digital libraries, related technologies and issues especially in the Asian region. Professor Hsinchun Chen from the University of Arizona, who first initiated this conference, has seen it mature annually to its current 9th current meeting in Kyoto, Japan. ICADL is now firmly established as one of the three key international digital library conferences around the world, the other two being the IEEE/ACM JCDL (Joint Digital Library Conference) and ECDL (European Digital Library Conference). Over the years, ICADL have been hosted by major Asian cities that included Taipei (Taiwan), Seoul (South Korea), Bangalore (India), Singapore, Kuala Lumpur (Malaysia), Shanghai (China) and Bangkok (Thailand). We are indeed hopeful that A-LIEP will be nurtured in the same way through the support and collaboration of LIS educators and practitioners in Asia-Pacific so that it can truly make its mark and serve as an important platform to congregate LIS educators and professionals together to jointly advance and improve the LIS education and practice landscape.

3 Portal for LIS Education and Development

A portal for LIS education known as LISEA (Library and Information Science Education in Asia) located at http://www.ntu.edu.sg/sci/lisea was to be set up after A-LIEP conference to promote resource sharing among LIS educators and researchers after the conference. The portal will be developed jointly by the Division of Information Studies at NTU and the Department of Information Science at UM. The objectives of this portal are fourfold:

1. To provide a gateway to LIS education programmes in Asia—including a directory of LIS schools and programs, and faculty members.
2. To provide a forum for LIS educators—including a listserv, a blog and a news service.
3. To serve as a learning repository and exchange for LIS education—including a repository of teaching materials contributed by LIS schools and educators
4. To serve as a digital library of LIS publications, papers and reports—including a bibliography of papers published by LIS educators in Asia, and papers on LIS education in Asia.

Work is currently ongoing in the design and development of the portal, accumulating and editing the contents for publication and in developing public relations to publicise this collaborative effort to obtain commitment, support and contributions from LIS education and research communities. The portal, when completed, will serve as a very important repository of information, gateway to learning and teaching resources, an invaluable platform to discuss and deliberate current and emerging issues, and sharing of best practices. The portal is also expected to house information about key research projects in the region, continuing education programmes, conferences, job advertisements, and so on.

4 Development of Repository of Learning Objects

A repository of learning resources is currently being developed at the Division of Information Studies at NTU with a view to facilitate and promote sharing of teaching resources by LIS education programs in Asia. This forms part of the functionality of LISEA portal (Section 3). The main issues in this development pertain to content creation, management and organisation, as well as accessibility and usability of resources in the repository (Chaudhry *et. al.*, 2006). At a more detailed level, it encompasses the resolution of quality, size and format of learning objects; metadata, vocabulary, and taxonomy considerations; and repository system, interface; and accessibility policies and mechanisms. While many of these issues are still being researched to date, the developers envisage a phased development approach that will gradually render the full repository functionality over time. When completed, the repository is expected to yield a host of significant benefits (Chaudhry *et. al.*, 2006):

- LIS instructors who are teaching a particular subject for the first time will benefit from hindsight the different perspectives/approaches that other instructors have taken in teaching the subject, the level of details covered for different topics, amount of material that can be covered in a certain amount of time, types of activities used to enhanced learning and evaluation methods. Course development time is expected to be reduced by re-using the learning objects and customising it to distinct needs.
- LIS instructors who are already teaching the particular course will likewise benefit from alerts to new developments and emerging topics that are being covered by other instructors. Instructors can also search for supplementary materials, for example, diagrams, illustrations, exercises/tutorials and class activities, to enhance student learning.
- LIS students will find the repository useful as a resource base for supplementary readings, tutorials, assessment and examination questions, term papers, and dissertation topics. The repository can help expand their horizon of learning and sharing, ideas generation, and aid identification of topics for their term papers and dissertation research.
- LIS professionals can use the repository for e-learning in new and emerging areas on the assumption that the learning objects on the subject are detailed and comprehensive enough.

The key to the success of this repository hinges on both the technologically and usability aspects of the platform, and more importantly, on the content development and use by a sustainable (and growing) pool of participants who can achieve a win-win situation in contributing and using the repository. More information on the issues that are currently been addressed by the development team on the repository can be found in the paper by Chaudhry *et. al.* (2006).

5 Quality Assurance Through Accreditation

The topic of quality assurance through some form of accreditation schemes augurs both positive and negative inclinations. While proponents of the scheme see the real worth and value of the scheme, a mark of achievement of the standing of one's programme, and the overall confidence in the education process, the dissidents view this as a means of parochialism and protectionism so as to achieve competitive advantage by this group of accredited members. While the reality of the situation is true on both sides, accreditation will no doubt enhance the quality of education and acceptability of degrees, and create mobility among professionals. Currently, there are no accreditation schemes for most parts of Asia Pacific except for Australian library schools through ALIA. As such, there is a need for LIS departments in this part of the world to embrace this aspect of development for the future.

Arising from a first study about a regional accreditation scheme by Majid, Chaudhry, Foo, and Logan (2002), it has subsequently evolved into a proposal at the CONSAL (Congress of South East Asian Librarians) Conference in 2003 in Brunei (Khoo, Majid & Chaudhry, 2003). In the proposal, the accreditation standards of ALA, ALIA, IFLA and Chartered Institute of Library and Information Professionals (CILIP, UK) were examined and guidelines provided in these standards were adjusted with respect to the Southeast Asian context. Issues related to implementation of a regional accreditation system were discussed in two later library conferences, namely, ICADL in Bangkok in 2005, and A-LIEP in Singapore in 2006. At the last meeting in Singapore, it was proposed that further discussions should continue with various stakeholders to further refine the scheme and to seek collaboration with other accreditation bodies. This is in view of the differing perceptions from different LIS schools whose education systems are different from one another. In this instance, accreditation at different levels may prove more appropriate. These levels include recognition, assessment, endorsement, and accreditation.

It is expected that some countries would be able to use the accreditation guidelines for securing adequate resources and may not pursue formal accreditation. Additionally, ongoing engagement with international forums like IFLA, ALA, ALISE, etc. is expected to be useful for quality improvement, and ultimately, establishing a system for accreditation in this part of the world.

6 Research and Scholarship

The networked information society has spurred and spawned many important areas of researches that need to be tackled. In examining the research trends and developments of digital libraries in the Asia Pacific region, Theng and Foo (2005) noted the emerging individuals and groups of digital library researchers in a number of Asia Pacific countries who are well plugged into the global digital library community, collaborating with established researchers, fostering new initiatives, making good research progress, reporting findings in scholarly journals and conferences, and making significant contributions in the global digital library research agenda. The diversity and richness in heritage, culture, languages and practices across Asia Pacific, including that of LIS education poses real challenges and opportunities for further research, but especially in areas of cross-cultural and cross-lingual research. A truly useful LIS portal would encompass the provision of solutions or reporting findings to such challenges for the communities it serve.

Rigorous research and scholarship must continue to prevail among educators and researchers in order to make LIS course offerings and education more up-to-date, relevant and challenging for students, in contributing towards knowledge, and sharing findings that can have impact globally. An example would be the need to seek a reliable and affordable long term solution to the digital preservation problem – to manage and preserve the digitally born materials that are growing substantially. Other potential areas of research include web archiving, information and media literacy, health and medical literacy, environment scanning, knowledge sharing, e-books or resources, and others. To this end, we need businesses and governments' support to fund such research to maintain the intellectual and cultural heritage of countries, and to create a global network of researchers who have common research interests. Likewise, creating a network of LIS educators and professionals to foster collaboration and cooperation is an important agenda that needs to fostered and nurtured.

Other opportunities in the area of research and scholarship include the establishment of awards, scholarships or visiting programmes for faculty/researcher/student exchanges, inter-institutional joint research projects, and others. These activities can aid the development of a vibrant research culture and produce relevant and significant research outcomes for the region. For example, the School of Communication and Information at NTU currently offers four Asian Communication Resource Centre (ACRC) research fellowship awards annually for research in communication and information from an Asian perspective. These fellowships aim to encourage researchers to benefit from the rich resources of ACRC and to have the opportunity to engage and interact with faculty of the School and AMIC (Asian Media Information and Communication Centre) researchers; encourage more in-depth research in areas of communication, information and ICT in Asia; and promote cooperation among communication and information professionals in the region (ACRC, 2006).

7 Conclusion

This paper has described a number of areas that present opportunities for collaboration among LIS educators, practitioners and researchers. While we are still largely at an early stage to make a significant impact on global LIS education, we need to start somewhere and the continued efforts, commitment and advocacy work done by many individuals and groups are important first steps for us to reach the long term final ultimate goal of being equal leaders of education to our counterparts outside the region.

A loose bottom-up structure to create an informal network organisation appears to be the logical direction for the formative stages of this effort. At the same time, we should also be mindful of what we can learn from others who have matured into more structured formal networks with established policies and processes. Examples of such international networks in higher education in Asia Pacific are APHERN (Asia Pacific Higher Education Research Network - http://www.aprim.net/aphern/aphern.htm) launched in Bangkok in 1995, and CERNET (Chinese Education and Research Network - http://www.edu.cn/HomePage/english/index.shtml) for the Chinese region launched in 1995.

In their research in international networks for higher education, Ottewill, Riddy & Fill (2005) noted that only by sharing experiences and ideas can progress be made. They cited a number of distinct contributions of such collaboration and cooperation: (1) information exchange and dissemination through conferences and workshops, hosting discussion boards or online seminars, gateways to information, and access of educational resources; (2) knowledge creation through sponsorship of research and development; (3) contribution to processes of policy making and implementation; (4) fostering a culture of cross-national dialogue and collaboration for individuals and institutions. This last point is modeled after the values of mutuality, respect and open mindedness. When taken collectively, they add towards the sources of stimulation and support for educators. They help complement national sources and can serve to revitalise academic communities. They also pointed out issues and challenges and suggested characteristics that can be used to assess network effectiveness. While we are still a long way off in realising such formal networks and the way to effectively manage them, their contributions can certainly serve as motivators for educators, practitioners and researchers in Asia Pacific to take concrete first steps to make commitments to improving LIS education through a renewed urgency of collaboration and cooperation. Establishing a forum of LIS educators in Asia, promoting knowledge sharing for improved LIS education through repositories of teaching materials, and furthering the quality improvement efforts through regional accreditation schemes and other initiatives seem to be steps in the right direction.

References

1. Asian Communication Resource Centre (2006). ACRC Fellowship Award. Available at: http://www.ntu.edu.sg/sci/research/acrc.html (accessed 8 September 2006)
2. Chaudhry, A., Khoo, C.S.G., Theng, Y.L., & Halim, A. (2006). Issues in developing a repository of learning objects for LIS education in Asia. *Proceedings of the World Library and Information Congress: 72nd IFLA General Conference and Council*, August 20-24, Seoul, Korea.
3. Johnson, I.M. (1998). Challenges in developing professionals for the "information society": and some responses by the British schools of librarianship and information studies, *Library Review*, 47(3), 52-59.
4. Khoo, C, Majid, S., & Chaudhry, A. (2003). Developing an accreditation system for LIS professional education programmes in Southeast Asia: Issues and perspectives. *Malaysian Journal of Library & Information Science*, 8(2).
5. Khoo, S.G.C., Singh, D., & Chaudhry, A. (Eds) (2006). *Proceedings of the Asia-Pacific Conference on Library & Information Education and Practice 2006* (A-LIEP2006), Singapore, April 3-6.
6. Majid, S., Chaudhry, A., Foo, S., & Logan, E. (2002). Accreditation of library and information studies programmes in Southeast Asia: A proposed model. *Singapore Journal of Library and Information Management, 32*, 58-59.
7. Nanyang Technological University (2006). Asia-Pacific Conference on Library & Information Education and Practice 2006 (A-LIEP2006): Preparing Information Professionals for Leadership in the New Age. Available at: http://www.ntu.edu.sg/sci/A%2DLIEP/ (accessed 8 September 2006)
8. Ottewill, R., Riddy, P., & Fill, K. (2005). International networks in higher education: realising their potential?, *On the Horizon*, 13(3), 138-147.
9. Foo, S., & Theng, Y.L. (2005). A snapshot of digital library development: The way forward in the Asia Pacific. in Theng, Y.L, & Foo, S. (Eds.), *Design and Usability of Digital Libraries: Case Studies in the Asia Pacific*, Idea Group Publishing, Hershey, PA, 351-370.
10. University of Tsukuba (2004). International Symposium on Digital Libraries and Knowledge Communities in Networked Information Society (DLKC'04). Available at: http://www.kc.tsukuba.ac.jp/dlkc/ (accessed 8 September 2006).
11. University of Tsukuba (2006). Annual Symposium of the Research Center for Knowledge Communities: New Directions for Information Science Education in the Networked Information Society. Available at: http://www.kc.tsukuba.ac.jp/symposium2006/Site/KC%20Symposium.html (accessed 8 September 2006).

Annotating the Web Archives – An Exploration of Web Archives Cataloging and Semantic Web

Paul H.J. Wu, Adrian K.H. Heok, and Ichsan P. Tamsir

Nanyang Technological University
31 Nanyang Link
{hjwu, heok0001, ichsan}@ntu.edu.sg

Abstract. Despite the success of Internet access via search technology, it has become increasing plain that such a mode is inadequate when applied to holdings in a Web Archives. A greater amount of relevant contextual information is essential in accessing Web Archives. The degree of relevance of the contextual information has to be customized to suit research on culture and heritage study over time. Information scientists have long been struggling to find a system that can help them organize Web Archives so that users can have access to complete and coherent collections. In this paper, we demonstrated how annotation, more than just an intuitive way of expressing one's thoughts on the materials under study, is in fact an appropriate tool for cataloging web archives in order to ensure a high quality of access for users. After a demonstration of access to archived web materials, we recommended a way of organizing web archives based on several design principles for a web annotation system that preserves the evidence and context of the cataloging process. Only by adhering to these principles can web archives cataloging be said to have incorporated the collaborative cataloging ideals of the semantic web movement. Implementing our web annotation system will help ensure better quality archives with more evidence and contextual information preserved within the system.

Keywords: Web Annotation, Web Archives, Semantic Web, Collaborative Cataloging, Evidence and Context.

1 Introduction

Web users are accustomed to instant access to information with the success of Web search technology. However, the same cannot be said of Web archives. There have been increasing interests in re-looking at more complex information architecture for leverage, such as taxonomy, metadata, ontology, and the integration of different modes of access, including searching, browsing and routing. This paper examines a particular case for accessing web archives which contains complex materials that can serve distinct communities, including social scientists and historians. We present a perspective that web sites are more than mere publications. They should be seen as evidence of the cultural activities of contemporary society. As such, its collection

S. Sugimoto et al. (Eds.): ICADL 2006, LNCS 4312, pp. 12–21, 2006.
© Springer-Verlag Berlin Heidelberg 2006

should be managed differently, as an archive would it holdings, preserving the contextual evidence of its content. In a previous paper [1], we demonstrated a bibliographic approach to cataloging web archives and showed how metadata produced by web annotation can serve as points of access to web archives. In that paper, a short survey of the various library web archives models around the world also points to a pressing inadequacy in the available methods of organizing their materials. These usually employ the use of "bibliocentric" cataloguing that treats each website as an entity without relationship to the other materials in the collection. This is because the contextual and provenancial information of these collections, which are essential for social scientists and historians to understand, are not made apparent, with much of the information being buried deep within the archives. A more suitable model being developed as the Arizona Model [2], where archival principles of provenance and original order are adopted, may prove more useful in presenting a web archives' holding to facilitate knowledge discovery. The technological challenge then becomes one of how web annotation can be effectively extended to help organize contextual and provenancial relationship based on bibliographic metadata. We explained the need for these requirements with a concrete case in Section 2 from a post-custodian approach.

In Section 3, a context-aware web annotation system, termed the Web Annotation for Web Intelligence (or WAWI), is introduced. One that ensures the capture of evidence and contextual information of web archives catalog. The WAWI web annotation system is part of a joint project between the National Library Board of Singapore and Nanyang Technological University to catalog and archive Singapore websites. Before explaining how context-aware annotation works, we reviewed and distinguished a difference between annotation systems. The first group is context-less and the other is context-aware annotations. Context-less annotation does not provide the relationship between the metadata and that of the content from the web material (the context with which the metadata content is describing). Thus, it is difficult to verify whether the metadata annotated is consistent with the web content by a third party not involved in the original annotation. Without such verification, the evidence of the metadata may be compromised and rendered not usable as historical data because the authenticity of such web archives records must be preserved over time. Context-aware annotation establishes the relationship between the metadata, the content of the web material and the social context in which the content was produced. A context-aware annotation system can thus help librarians ensure the quality of the records more effectively by being able to (1) relate semantic content in the metadata to web content; (2) render agreement, disagreement and different granularity of evidence; (3) provide flexible and precise annotation of the evidence; and (4) relate ontology to metadata in a relational metadata. Such a system is also congruent with the tagging movement, such as Technorati, Flickr and del.icio.us, which itself reflects a growing trend that tries to leverage collective efforts to organize materials on the Internet, aspiring to one which approximates a Semantic web. Such collaborative efforts are essential to Web 2.0 and the semantic web, a context-aware annotation system will facilitate the assurance of quality in these efforts. Evidence within an inconsistency resolution mechanism like Wikipedia can be invoked to resolve discrepancy immediately or preserve them for future resolution.

2 Post-custodian Approach to Web Archives Cataloging and the Semantic Web

As mentioned, the Semantic Web, specifically the tagging movement, allows actors other than the creator of the web materials to structure meaning to the materials. This collaborative approach in organizing information has been shared by professional archivists in the development of the Records Continuum Theory (RCT) for organizing records and archives [5]. RCT challenges the custodial role of the archives. It advocates that, in a post-custodial paradigm, archivists must become more than mere physical caretakers and take on the role of identifying, controlling and making valuable electronic records accessible to society at large. Similarly in the context of a web archives, the web archivist should take on a more proactive role in transforming the Web Archives into a "Semantic" Web Archives. In the current Web environment, public users should also be encouraged to collaboratively semanticize the web, as exemplified by the participants of the Tagging movement.

In an attempt to illustrate how contextually organized materials can facilitate access to holdings in a web archives, we shall use the example of the website of the Ministry of Manpower (MOM) in Singapore (www.mom.gov.sg).

The Ministry of Manpower's mission is to achieve a globally competitive workforce and great workplace, for a cohesive society and a secure economic future for all Singaporeans. One of the ways it sets out to accomplish this aim is the setting up of an Occupational Safety and Health (OSH) Division that promotes OSH at the national level. It works with employers, employees and all other stakeholders to identify, assess, and manage workplace safety and health risks so as to eliminate death, injury and ill-health. The department within the OSH Division focusing on the reduction of safety and health hazards is the OSH Inspectorate. It does so by providing advice and guidance through inspections of workplaces, investigating accidents and enforcing the relevant laws.

Here is a scenario of how a public policy scholar interested in examining how the Ministry of Manpower in Singapore handled an industrial accident, specifically the Nicoll Highway Collapse Incident.

Being an industrial accident, the OSH Inspectorate was the agency legislated to oversee investigations. To review the events from a government's point of view, the scholar can visit the OSH group of documents. He will be pointed to files containing the various public communication activities[1]. These files include speeches by the minister (in parliament for the amendment of the Factories Act), commission reports, press release, and even an FAQ. However, these files may not all be available from the current web site. This is because when events unfold the importance of information emanating from the government may change. Indeed by comparing the websites now and then in Figures 1a and 1b below:

---

[1] URL: http://www.mom.gov.sg/NewOSHFrameworkandInvestigationsonNicollHighwayCollapse

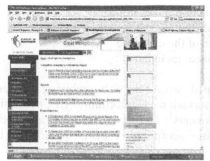

Fig. 1a. MOM circa 2004 from Web Archives

Fig. 1b. MOM circa 2006 in the current Web site

It was found that in the list of FAQ which was one of the key documents available in 2004 to help the public understand and interpret the information on the site was missing in 2006. However, with the creation of a web archives where such materials are organized into collectivities, changes in public communication patterns can be made more apparent.

Not only will researchers benefit from being able to accessed evidence of changing trends, but also ordinary citizens who want to find out about the accident at a latter date. All the helpful information is now no longer available at the live MOM website. He/She will now no longer be able to know learn via the FAQ, how the reports were being made and the various degrees of commissions that the government appoints. In addition, by relating the files to each other, one also discovers that not only MOM was involved but the Ministry of National Development (MND) and the Building and Construction Authority (BCA) were also involved in offering joint reports on the event. Their insights help molded new policies that come out of such reports and lead to the creation of a new OSH Framework.

With these, we observe context-aware web annotation is not only important for the current use of semantic web, but it is even more crucial for the lasting value of heritage and culture value of web materials. It then becomes crucial how the recordness of the materials in web archives has to be carried across time [6], [7]. Most of the current approaches surveyed in our last paper [1] on web archives cataloging have fallen short of the requirements to provide evidential and contextual organization to facilitate effective access.

3   Web Annotation System in Service of Web Archives Cataloging

As demonstrated in Section 2, a context-aware web annotation system can facilitate effective information discovery. In this section, we introduce the Web Annotation for Web Intelligence (WAWI) system. We will also demonstrate how the four design principles are implemented to achieve the objectives of preserving the evidence and context in cataloging and arranging web archives. They need to be able to

(1) Relate semantic content in the metadata to the web content
(2) Render agreement, disagreement and different granularities of evidence
(3) Provide flexible and precise annotation of the evidence
(4) Relate ontology to metadata in a relational metadata.

The WAWI annotation system is integrated with the web archiving platform developed by International Internet Preservation Consortium (IIPC)[2], which comprises web harvesting and access components[3]: Heritrix, Nutchwax, and Wera. The system architecture resulting from the incorporation of annotation in the cataloging process is shown in Fig. 2 below.

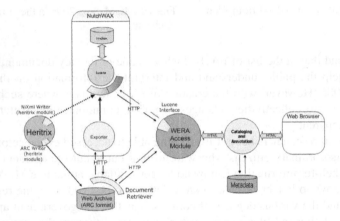

Fig. 2. WAWI annotation and cataloging system integrated with IIPC Web Archives platform

Please refer to [1] for further implementation details of WAWI system. Our discussion on design principles in the following shall reference Annotea [3] and CREAM [4] as model systems.

3.1 Relating Semantic Content of the Metadata to Web Content

As briefly mentioned in Section 1, there are two different kinds of annotation system: One provides the relationship between the semantic content of the metadata and the other does not. In a context-less annotation system such a relation is not provided. The opposite is true in a context-aware annotation system.

Examples of context-less annotation system developed in the web archives systems community can be found in [8] and [9]. In [8], annotated metadata was used for browsing; in [9], it was meant to be implemented as an automatic tagging system.

Context-aware annotation establishes the relationship between the metadata and the content of web material. The Annotea project in the WWW Semantic Web Consortium is an example of a context-aware system [3]. It provided relationship

---

[2] URL: http://www.netpreserve.org/about/index.php
[3] Heritrix URL: http://crawler.archive.org/; NutchWax URL: http://archive-access.sourceforge.net/projects/nutch/; Wera URL: http://archive-access.sourceforge.net/projects/wera/

between the semantic and the document content through its two properties: "annotates" and "context" in the namespace[4]. The WAWI annotation system adopted the Annotation Graph schema [10]. The resulting XML document fragments of those highlighted in Fig. 3 are presented below:

```
<annoschema id="{GUID0}" datecreated="23-09-2005" createdby="ichsan"
type="ontology" datemodified="" modifiedby=""
url="http://app.sgdi.gov.sg/listing.asp?agency_subtype=dept&agency_id=00
00000011">
<Division Title="OrganizationHealthSafty" id="{GUID1}" begin="566"
end="577" value=" Organizational Health and Safety" meta="Organizational
Safety and Health">
</Division>
<Division Title="ForeignManpwer" id="{GUID2}" begin="987" end="1004"
value="Foreign Manpower Policy" meta="Foreign Manpower Policy">
</Division>
</annoschema>
```

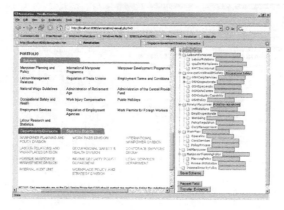

Fig. 3. Annotation Schema, an ontology reflecting the MOM organization chart, and its supporting web page at the Singapore Government Directory interactive (SGDi) (only partially shown)

Each annotation schema contains several annotation *attributes and elements*. The 'id' attribute contains the system generated unique id for the schema; the 'url' attribute denotes the web page that is annotated as support of the schema; other self-explanatory attributes include "datecreated", "datemodified", "modifiedby" and "createdby."

Each annotation element, such as **Division**, contain a 'begin' and an 'end' attribute, whose values are the *page coordinates* (see discussion in Section 3.3 below) of the text portion of the DOM tree of the webpage. The *value* attribute contains value as the text of the webpage that is delimited by the 'begin' and 'end' page coordinates, which was highlighted as evidence (or context in Annotea's term). The *meta* attribute contains the metadata that is assigned to the element that was supported by the evidence. In the MOM example discussed earlier, we created the annotation schema, an ontology, that relates to the MOM organization chart found in the SGDi Website.

---

[4] Defined at http://www.w3.org/2000/10/annotation-ns#

3.2 Rendering Agreement, Disagreement, and Different Granularity of Evidence

In Annotea, annotations are simply rendered as pencil symbols [3]. The pencil symbol model is limited as it can only indicate the starting point, but not the extent of the annotation. On the other hand, the AG model of annotation in WAWI encompasses the whole extent of the annotation. When disagreement and different granularities of evidence occur, various overlapping patterns of the extent will result. Therein lies a need for rendering complex patterns of annotation.

As demonstrated in Fig. 4, two disagreeing metadata records are shown by the overlapped annotation (evidence) of the OSH vision. With the highlighted patterns, the metadata records can then be verified and consolidated to a unified and agreeable metadata records as discussed in Section 1.

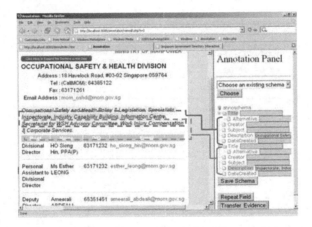

Fig. 4. Multiple-Evidence overlapping annotations in WAWI

3.3 Providing Flexible and Precise Annotation of the Evidence

Annotea uses Xpointer to define how annotation is related to the document. The location of the annotated text in the document is represented with Xpath. It uses the page element structure to point to a specific part of the document. However Xpointer can only point to the text at the element boundary; it does not point to a specific text position. In Annotea, the annotation does not include the extent of the annotation and is unable to point to the part that contains cross-boundary element. In our WAWI annotation system, the *page coordinate* approach was developed to provide these features. The page coordinate approach works by serializing the document as a sequence of text by omitting the document element structure. With this sequence of text as a coordinate, the precise position and extent of an annotation are recorded at the start and end positions of the text in the document.

3.4   Relate Ontology to Metadata in a Relational Metadata

As shown in Fig. 5, the OSH archived webpages circa 2004 has three metadata records corresponding to Speech, Press Releases, and FAQ files of OSH. The FAQ metadata record for the FAQ files of the webpage in Fig. 5 is demonstrated below; the 'url' and 'datecreated' attributes indicate that it was archived in 2004:

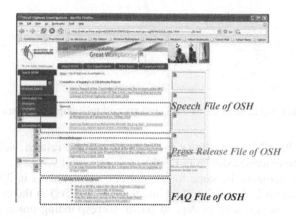

Fig. 5. Speech, Press Release, Frequently Asked Questions (FAQ) Files in the Web Archives of Occupation Safety and Health (OSH) Division of MOM circa 2004

```
<annoschema id="{guid}" type="metadata" datecreated="23-09-2004"
datemodified="23-09-2004" createdby="ichsan" modifiedby="ichsan"
url="http://web.archives/2004/www.mom.gov.sg/OSHD/">
  <ref>
        <nodeid>{GUID17}</nodeid>
        <nodename>FAQ File</nodename>
  </ref>
<annoElements>
        <Title id="1" begin="34" end="63" value="Nicoll Highway
Investigations" meta="Industrial Accident">
        </Title>
        <Subject id="4" begin="752" end="777" value="Frequently
Asked Questions" meta=" Frequently Asked Questions">
        </Subject>
</annoElements>
</annoschema>
```

Note that the additional <ref> element, like CREAM <ref> attribute [3], provided a pointer to the ontology "FAQ File" with {GUID17}. This is the additional relational metadata that links the metadata to the ontology. As shown in Fig. 6, each node of the ontology (displayed on the left-hand frame) has its corresponding metadata, which is displayed on the right-hand frame. The referring path to the "FAQ File" node above is then: "MOM → OccupationalHealthSafety → OSHInspectorate → IndustrialAccidents → NicollHighwayCollapse → FAQ".

Fig. 6. FAQ node in the MOM Ontology and its linking Metadata record

The "View Page" button allows the user to see the related web page with the metadata and the evidence shown in Fig 5.

The ontology remains the same for the current web archives in 2005 (Fig. 1b). As discussed in Section 2, despite the fact that there is no FAQ in the current web site, a user accessing it is still able to depend on its corresponding ontology to access the archived FAQ web materials, from 2004. This access allows the users to research on the various cultural and heritage concerns, including how Singapore's MOM conduct their public education program on the public hearing on OSH Inspectorate's committee reports.

4 Conclusion

Cataloging is a timeless and fundamental practice for organizing information regardless of the types of materials. However, the growth of the Internet continues to out-pace the speed of attempts to describe it. The emergence of the semantic web (or Web 2.0) then becomes an appealing solution, as it mobilizes the collective effort of the public to help "catalog the web." One of the most intuitive methods to transform a web into a semantic web is through web annotation. This paper proposes a context-aware web annotation system which can provides evidence and preserve context to the cataloged records of the materials within a web archives. It enumerates how such a system can help archivists ensure the quality of the records by being able to (1) Relate semantic content in the metadata to web contents; (2) Render agreement, disagreement and different granularities of evidence; (3) Provide flexible yet precise annotation of the evidence; and (4) Relate ontology to metadata in a relational metadata.. A review of existing web archive cataloging and access practices was carried out to assess whether the WAWI web annotation system was comparable in providing state-of-the-art ways of organizing web archives materials. By linking web archived and current materials via an ontology, we also concretely demonstrated how better quality access can be achieved to facilitate a historical understanding of a government's handling of accidents on a national scale. With evidence and context annotation in the cataloging process, the collaborative efforts of a community of users and archivists to maintain the catalogue is facilitated: Effectively opening up new horizons of creating web archives that is at once more research oriented, flexible in its approach, and in coping with the changing needs of users. All these are achieved with the archive still remaining robust enough to carry its holdings intact through time.

References

1. Wu, H-J Paul, Tamsir, P. I, Heok, K. Y. Adrian. Applying Context-Sensitive Web Annotation in Evidence-based, Collaborative Web Archives Cataloging, submitted to International Workshop on Archiving Web, 2006.
2. Pearce-Moses, R & Kaczmarek, J.: An Arizona Model for Preservation and Access of Web Documents. DttP: Documents to the People. 33:1. p.17-24 (2005)
3. Annotea: An Open RDF Infrastructure for Shared Web Annotations, *José Kahan, Marja-Riitta Koivunen, Eric Prud'Hommeaux, Ralph R. Swick* WWW10, May 1-5, 2001
4. Handschuh, S., Staab, S., Maedche, A., CREAM— Creating relational metadata with a component-based, ontology-driven annotation framework. Workshop on Knowledge Markup and Semantic Annotation at the First International Conference on Knowledge Capture (K-CAP'2001), Victoria, BC, Canada
5. Upward, F. (1998). Structuration Theory and Recordkeeping. Accessed on 5 Jun 06 at http://www.sims.monash.edu.au/research/rcrg/publications/recordscontinuum/fupp2.html4.
6. Wu, P. & Heok, A.: Is Web Archives A Misnomer – How Web Archives Can Become Digital Archives? In Khoo, C, Singh, D., & Chaudhry, A. (Eds) Proceedings of the Asia-Pacific Conference on Library & Information Education & Practice: Preparing Information Professionals for Leadership in the New Age, 298-350 (2006)
7. Wu, P. & Theng, Y.L.: Weblog Archives: Achieving the Recordness of Web Archiving. Proceedings in the Ninth International Cultural Heritage Informatics Meeting September 21 – 23, ICHIM 05, Paris (2005)
8. Steven M. Schneider, Kirsten Foot, Michele Kimpton, Gina Jones, Building Thematic Web Collections: Challenges and Experiences from the September 11 Web Archive and the Election 2002 Web Archive, http://bibnum.bnf.fr/ECDL/2003/proceedings.php?f=schneider
9. Charalampos Lampos, Magdalini Eirinaki, Darija Jevtuchova, Michalis Vazirgiannis Archiving the Greek Web, http://ww.iwaw.net/04/proceedings/Lampos.pdf
10. Bird, S. and Liberman, M.: Annotation Graphs as a Framework for Multidimensional Linguistic Data Analysis, In Proceedings of the ACL '99Workshop Towards Standards and Tools for Discourse Tagging, College Park, Md., 21 June, 1999, pages 1–10

Owlery: A Flexible Content Management System for "Growing Metadata" of Cultural Heritage Objects and Its Educational Use in the CEAX Project

Kenro Aihara[1,2], Taizo Yamada[1], Noriko Kando[1,2], Satoko Fujisawa[2],
Yusuke Uehara[3], Takayuki Baba[3], Shigemi Nagata[3], Takashi Tojo[4],
Tetsuhiko Awaji[4], and Jun Adachi[1]

[1] National Institute of Informatics
[2] Dept. of Informatics, the Graduate University for Advanced Studies
2-1-2 Hitotsubashi, Chiyoda-ku, Tokyo 101-8430, Japan
{kenro.aihara, t_yamada, kando, satoko, adachi}@nii.ac.jp
[3] Fujitsu Laboratories Ltd.
[4] Fujitsu Ltd.
1-1 Kamikodanaka 4-chome, Nakahara-ku, Kawasaki 211-8588, Japan
{yuehara, baba-t, NAGATA.Shigemi, tojo, awaji}@jp.fujitsu.com

Abstract. With the Educational use of Cultural heritage Archives and Cross(X) search (CEAX), we have investigated how to establish a framework for managing various kinds of information on cultural heritage objects and how to utilize them for educational purposes. To achieve this goal, we propose a conceptual framework in this paper called "Growing Metadata" and a flexible content management system called Owlery. Growing Metadata includes not only factual descriptions of objects but also various annotations about the objects, such as metadata for children, course materials prepared by school teachers, classroom reports, etc., and are reusable for search and educational purposes. Owlery is a software platform to create, share, utilize and reuse the Growing Metadata, and in which various metadata and annotations are managed in different levels of authenticity, authorship, and user groups. As a result of the experimental classes for 89 6th-grade children, our framework was found to be efficient and accepted by the content creators, like museum experts, content annotators and shool teachers.

1 Introduction

To globally share high-quality content on cultural heritage objects, we must consider to effectively associate objects with various levels of knowledgeable but subjective descriptions. The authors have been carried out this project which aims to reveal a methodology for managing content and utilizes it for educational purposes. We call it CEAX[1].

---

[1] CEAX stands for Educational use of Cultural heritage Archives and Cross(X) search.

S. Sugimoto et al. (Eds.): ICADL 2006, LNCS 4312, pp. 22–31, 2006.

We propose in this paper a conceptual framework called "Growing Metadata" and a flexible content management system called Owlery. Section 2 describes the background of this research and in Section 3, our framework is proposed. Then, Section 4 describes our systems for content management of cultural heritage objects and technical terms. An overview and the results from experimeital classes are shown in Section 5. Finally, a conclusion is given in Section 6.

2   Background and Related Work

2.1   Managing Metadata of Cultural Heritage Objects

The importance of the metadata is increased when the cultural heritage objects are digitized. For example, metadata can improve search effectiveness and usability of the search system by providing multiple access points and preserving the semantics and context of the objects. However, for management reasons, cultural heritage object metadata has its own difficulties and problems such as 1) diversified descriptions, 2) linking multiple versions of the same objects, and 3) readability for different user groups.

For the diversified descriptions, even titles can often be changed since they are given in rather recent time periods. In addition, the description of cultural heritage objects may differ in the principles, paradigms, viewpoints, and interpretation of each creator of the metadata and its users.

For multiple versions, digitized images and other related contents of objects are created for various purposes and different occasions by contents producers for different users with differing levels of quality and resolutions. Linking them together while maintaining your own contexts and differences, is critical for better usage of the contents.

Any other related materials, for example catalogs for exhibitions or auctions, textbooks, course materials prepared by school teachers, and even classroom reports by students or pupils can be kinds of metadata or annotations about the cultural heritage objects and are also useful, and can be considered variable contents if they properly managed to keeping their own contexts. In these ways, related metadata and contents are increasing and are being enhanced by various content creators. The problem of diversified descriptions increases in such environments.

Providing readable and understandable metadata and annotations for different user groups, such as non-experts, children, and users with different backgrounds, is particularly important for cultural heritage objects.

To address the above mentioned problems, we identify the following tasks:

- resolving the diversified descriptions
- implementation of a flexible content management mechanism
- content creation support systems
- adaptive levels of presentation

We propose in this paper a framework for cultural heritage object metadata called "Growing Metadata" and a system to manage the Growing Metadata in order to tackle these tasks.

2.2   Systems for Sharing Overall Content

For sharing content globally and managing it, metadata integration is recognized as one of the important issues[1]. The Semantic Web[2] which aims to make web pages understandable by computers, has been proposed and many applications based on the Semantic Web using a Resource Description Framework (RDF)[3,4] have also been proposed. One of the proposed systems is Piggy Bank[5]. Piggy Bank is a web browser extension that helps users to create Semantic Web content in their use of the existing web content. This research deals with one of the important issues of the Semantic Web: a bottleneck for producing Semantic Web content.

In addition, some content management systems (CMS) havae been proposed for instant web publishing, such as Wiki[6] and blog[7]. CMS enables users to not only create web content easily, but also make links to related content dynamically. Wikipedia[8], which is a Wiki-based free-content encyclopedia, can be used globally.

In the field of cultural heritage, it is important to keep in mind that many of the web pages may include not only knowledgeable explanations but also a variety of expressions, ambiguities, and even incorrect things. In fact, recall in general web search engines seems low because there is relatively less content than for general topics, although there are various expressions on even one concept.

We assume that it is essentially difficult to create ontology for this field, because it is hard to obtain an authorized consensus, other than experts' subjective opinions. Therefore, we have to consider a more flexible approach other than the Semantic Web, to manage the content, such as Semantic Blogging[9] and Semantic Wikipedia[10].

3   Framework of Growing Metadata

Table 1 (a) shows a typical example of metadata of the metadata of an object. Table 1 (b) shows a variety of titles of the "Haniwa Armored Man" from Table 1 (a). As shown in Table 1 (b), even one object may have various titles. For example, "埴輪", appearing in all the titles, means "Haniwa", which is an earthenware burial figure. Although "武人" means a warrior and an ordinarily educated Japanese person can understand it, another term, such as "兵士", is used nowadays in Japan instead. "挂甲" is also regarded as an unfamiliar term and it is difficult for even native Japanese speakers except an archaeologist to understand what it means. Titles that don't include "挂甲" inside them might be used for younger people, such as K-12 pupils; "Title 1", "Title 3", "Title 4", and "Title 7".

In the case of description, various descriptions can be written for even one object, as shown in Table 2. We would like to emphasize that each description has to be written for its own expected readers, such as experts, general adults, or children. We, therefore, must handle the descriptions for corresponding target readers. For example, "Description 1" from a catalog[11] seems to be written for

Table 1. Example of Metadata for "Haniwa Armored Man"

attribute	value
Item No.	J-36697
Title 1	[国宝] 埴輪武人
Title 2	Haniwa Armored Man
Place 1	太田市飯塚町出土品
Place 2	Object from site at Iizuka-cho, Ota-shi, Gunma
Period 1	古墳時代
Period 2	late Kofun period
Dimension 1	高 130.5

attribute	value
Title 3	武人の埴輪
Title 4	埴輪武人
Title 5	埴輪 挂甲をつけた武人
Title 6	埴輪 挂甲着用男子
Title 7	埴輪 武人
Title 8	埴輪 挂甲の武人

(a) Factual Data   (b) Various Titles

Table 2. Example of Descriptions about "Haniwa Armored Man"

Description 1	全身像。各部石膏復原。高 130.5。明茶褐色。胎土に砂粒・赤色粒を含む。冑には、三尾鉄表現がみられる。顔は粘土薄板貼付引伸ばし成形。台は断面楕円に近い隅丸胴張方形。透かしは上部両側に 1 対で円形、外面ハケ一部ナデ調整。赤彩は顔・靫・脚の小札にみられる。 (from [11])
Description 2	頬当 (ほおあて)・錣 (しころ) の付いた縦矧板鋲止衝角付冑 (たてはぎいたびょうどめしょうかくつきかぶと) と小札 (こざね) を革ひもで綴じた挂甲 (けいこう) に身を固め、両腕には籠手 (こて) をつけています。鞆 (とも) を巻いた左手は弓を執り、大刀の柄に右手をかけ、いまにも抜かんとする様相です。背中には矢を入れた靫 (ゆき) を背負っており、完全武装の東国武人の姿を表しています。人物埴輪の中でもきわめて優れた作品で、埴輪では唯一の国宝です。
Description 2 (en)	The haniwa warrior wears a visorless keeled helmet (J. tatehagi-ita byôdome shokakut-suki), a armor (J. keikô) which consists of small panels of iron (J. kozane) laced together with leather lace and puts the bracers (J. kote) on both forearms. His left hand bound with protecting tie (J. tomo) holds a bow while right hand holds a sword. He has an air to be going to revolt the sword. He puts the arrows in the quiver (J. yuki) on his back, and what is displayed is the shape of full-armed warrior in the eastern country. It is an extremely high-quality haniwa warrior and the only national treasure in haniwa.
Description 3	完全武装した東国の武人をかたどった埴輪です。ほお当て、首の後ろを保護する錣 (しころ) が付いた衝角付冑 (しょうかくつきかぶと) をかぶり、挂甲 (けいこう) とよばれる甲 (よろい) に身を固めています。両腕には、腕を保護する籠手 (こて) をつけています。左手に弓をもち、右手を大刀の柄にかけ、今にも抜こうとしているようです。背中には、矢を入れた靫 (ゆき) を背負っています。人物埴輪の中でもきわめて優れた作品で、埴輪ではただ一つの国宝です。
Description 3 (en)	It is a haniwa in the shape of the full-armed warrior in the eastern country. The haniwa warrior wears a visorless keeled helmet (J. shôkakutsuki) with cheek-guards and an armor called keikô. It puts the bracers (J. kote) on both forearms to protect them. The warrior's left hand holds a bow while his right hand holds a sword slung from his waist. It seems to be going to revolt the sword. He puts the arrows in the quiver (J. yuki) on his back. It is an extremely high-quality haniwa warrior and the only national treasure in haniwa.

experts, and "Description 3" is rewritten for children from "Description 2" for adults. In general, it is difficult to understand "Description 1", and it may also be hard even to read aloud to them. Another longer description about the object can be found on the Internet[12]. The authors suppose that the descriptions for a web page or a printed article may be able to be longer than the ones for an exhibition where visitors stop by and read them for a minute, even if the expected readers are adults.

Many of the existing global content management frameworks, such as the Semantic Web, assume that a global schema can be obtained, shared, and accepted by all concerned. Furthermore, it is necessary for all content creators to describe documents consistent with the conceptual schema. We, however, must not forget that people often consciously and unconsciously say incorrect things. The authors, therefore, make another approach to managing the content. The basic idea of our approach that descriptions are separated from the factual data, such as a unique identification number or its dimensions, as shown in Table 1 (a), in the metadata and associated with the related factual data or other descriptions, as opposed to the existing frameworks whose descriptions on each object are included within the metadata as well as in the factual data. Some typical factual data are the person, work, time, location, and organization.

In this paper, the term annotation will be used to refer to descriptions related to the content. Annotation includes various titles, descriptions about objects or terms, expressions of time period, location names, and so on.

We believe that our approach has the following advantages:

Dynamism of content repository. In our framework, basically any authorized user can append their own description, as well as blog or Wiki. The content repository gets dynamically *grown*, although existing frameworks [13,9,10] are based on a global schema, such as RDF.

Maintaining quality of content. As opposed to weblog or Wiki, our framework can maintain the content quality because our major content creators are experts, such as researchers or curators of museums. Our framework is open to general users, although a subject gateway approach[14] strictly controls its content.

Enhancing content to be searched. The content can be extended with associated descriptions and that helps it to be searched. For example, when the original title doesn't contain "武人", which is used as a search keyword, "埴輪挂甲着用男子" can be covered.

Association among contents. In the same manner as the advantage above, our framework gives dynamic links among related contents that share the same factual data. This advantage helps users to browse content archives.

Assistance for readers. Our framework gives links to technical terms stored in the repository automatically, like Wiki. When a user reads a description but it contains unknown technical terms, they can get help with it.

4 Systems for Content Management

4.1 Overview

Figure 1 illustrates our systems for content management based on Growing Metadata. The overall system consists of a content management system called Owlery (middle of the figure) and clients of Owlery (right and left).

We apply our systems for educational purposes. Therefore, there are several roles in our framework: experts from museums (bottom right), educators (middle right), learners (top right), a content management service provider (middle), and general users (left). Experts, such as curators of museums, use our client system, called Owlery Client, for authoring metadata and descriptions about cultural

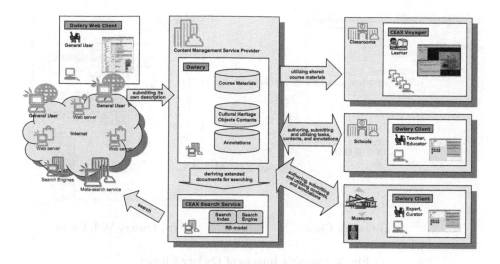

Fig. 1. Owlery and its Clients

heritage objects. Although educators also use the same client, they describe not only their own contents, such as neighboring historic sites, for classes but also tasks that must be prepared prior to a class. Tasks contain some metadata, such as objectives, dates, and subjects, and a content set as the course material to be used in the class. The content set will be used with another client, called CEAX Voyager, in the classroom by learners, under the guidance of the educator. On the other hand, genenral users can use our web-based client, called Owlery Web Client, to browse contents. Some users may append their own annotation.

4.2   Owlery: Content Management System

Owlery is our content management system and the core function of this framework. It stores the metadata of cultural heritage objects, annotations, and course materials declared by educators. The prototype system is implemented as Web Services on Apache Axis2 and Java and the data are managed by PostgreSQL.

Owlery has a CEAX Search Service, which gives flexible full text search functions based on an RS-model[15]. However, this is irrelevant to the main subject of this paper.

4.3   Clients of Owlery

Owlery Client. Owlery Client is a fully-functional client system for authoring, submitting, and utilizaing the contents of Owlery. Figure 2 (a) shows a snapshot image of Owlery Client, which contains the main window (back) and pop-up detailed information of a selected content. The main window has three panes: a search pane (left), an authoring pane (middle), and an information pane (right).

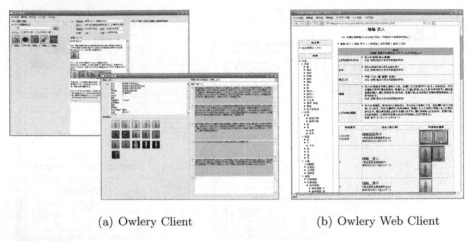

(a) Owlery Client   (b) Owlery Web Client

Fig. 2. Snapshot Images of Owlery Clients

A user can search objects, terms, and tasks in the search pane, while authoring their task in the middle. Information panes give useful information, such as suggestions related to the authored task and history of the creation of the content. In the detailed information window, they can declare their own description and select images and descriptions to be used in class.

Owlery Web Client. Owlery Web Client is a web-based client. Although some functions and its usability are less than with Owlery Client, it is easy to start using. Figure 2 (b) shows a snapshot image of the system. A directory tree is shown on the left, which is provided by an expert. Clickable links are designated in blue on the web page.

CEAX Voyager: Client for Supporting Discovery Learning. CEAX Voyager is an exploring tool for the contents of CEAX. It was designed for supporting guided discovery learning in classrooms. Users can view scattered object images in a two-dimensional space and zoom in on a selected image (Figure 3 (a)). It can highlight remarkable regions of images (indicated in the yellow box), as well as showing detailed information including descriptions.

In addition, the tool gives two computational functions: a graph layout and classification. The graph function coordinates images according to two axes selected by users (Figure 3 (b)). The classification function facilitates classifying objects into two categories semi-automatically. When a user wants to find some common factors of two groups or hidden relation amongst objects, they put a few exemplars into a corresponding segment, which is indicated by the two bottom regions in Figure 3 (c)). Next, the tool extracts common factors. However, the details of the classification is irrelevant to the main subject of this paper.

(a) Object Image and its Metadata and Description

(b) Graph Layout

(c) Classification

Fig. 3. Snapshot Images of CEAX Voyager

5   Feasibility Test

To reveal the feasibility of our approach, experimental classes were conducted using CEAX Voyager at an authentic elementary school in Nishi-Tokyo city. The learners were 89 6th-graders from three classes. The theme of the class, which was configured by the teachers in charge, was to discover the secrets of Haniwa. The teachers aimed to let pupils discover any secret, or hypotheses, by themselves and learn the process of discovering though abductive inference, verification, and presentation.

5.1   Data Set

In these experimental classes, we selected historic heritage objects from the Kofun period of Japan, which was from the late 4th to the 7th century A.D., including the national treasures of Japan owned by the Tokyo National Museum (TNM). We did this because Haniwa was supposed to be familiar to the pupils and TNM owns the largest collection of Haniwa in the world. First, an archaeologist described annotations for each object and technical term (e.g. "Description 2" of Table 2). Then, a science writer rewrote the annotations for the pupils (e.g. "Description 3" of Table 2). We prepared over 180 objects, 860 images, and 380 descriptions. From this collection, 291 images and corresponding annotations were selected to load into CEAX Voyager.

5.2   Results

In the classes, some of the supportive evidences for our approach were observed as follows:

Pupils were willing to read descriptions. The teachers and the authors had expected that pupils would not want to read descriptions about objects, because they usually tended to give up reading and lose concentration when

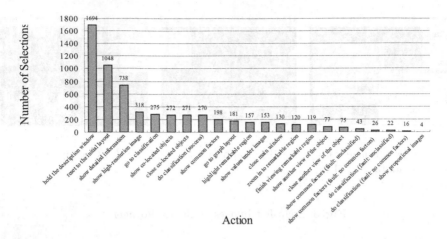

Fig. 4. Selection of Actions in Experimental Classes

unknown characters appeared. However, the teachers were surprised that the pupils got well-engaged with the beautiful images and tried to actively read descriptions about one object after another. In fact, the actions related to reading the descriptions were done much more than any of the other actions (Figure 4). The most selected action was "holding the description window" which facilitates visualizing the window that contains the descriptions.

Even descriptions for adults might be acceptable. We used some unrewritten descriptions, that is, descriptions for adults. Some pupils complained about the low readability of them, which we expected. However, some tried to read these descriptions even when unknown characters appeared.

In an interview with the teachers after the classes, they strongly agreed about the success of the tasks and the effectiveness of our systems and contents, although they couldn't get sufficient help from the usual search engines in the past. As a result, we believe that an appropriate form of expression for a description is necessary and our approach is feasible for this purpose.

6   Conclusion

This paper proposes a conceptual framework called Growing Metadata and a flexible content management system called Owlery. As a result of experimental classes that used the content and systems of our proposed framework, we found that the proposed framework is feasible for managing cultural heritage objects and utilizing it for educational purposes.

There are some future issues to consider and they are as follows:

– Automatic metadata extraction for importing external data
– Dynamically adapted description
– Usability testing of Owlery clients

Acknowledgments

The authors wish to express our gratitude to the Tokyo National Museum and Mr. Yoichi Inoue, Mr. Mitsuharu Iwasa, and Mr. Satoshi Tarashima for their valuable advice and permission to use the images and metadata of the museum.

Thanks are also due to Tanashi Elementary School of Nishi-Tokyo city for their cooperation with the experimental classes.

This study was supported in part by the Ministry of Education, Culture, Sports, Science, and Technolgy of Japan under the "Development of Fundamental Software Technologies for Digital Archives" program.

References

1. Bernstein, P.A.: Applying model management to classical meta data problems. In: Proceedings of the first Biennial Conference on Innovative Data Systems Research. (2003) 209–220
2. Berners-Lee, T., Hendler, J., Lassila, O.: The Semantic Web – a new form of web content that is meaningful to computers will unleash a revolution of new possibilities. Scientific American (2001)
3. Candan, S.K., Liu, H., Suvama, R.: Resource description framework: metadata and its applications. ACM SIGKDD Explorations Newsletter **3**(1) (2001) 6–19
4. World Wide Web Consortium (W3C): Resource description framework (RDF). (http://www.w3.org/RDF/)
5. Huynh, D., Mazzocchi, S., Karger, D.: Piggy Bank: Experience the semantic web inside your web browser. In: Proceedings of the fourth International Semantic Web Conference. (2005)
6. Canningham, W.: WikiWiki. http:/c2.com/cgi/wiki?WikiWikiWeb (2005)
7. : The blogosphere. In Rosenbloom, A., ed.: Communications of the ACM. Volume 47. (2004) 30–59
8. : Wikipedia. (http://en.wikipedia.org/)
9. Cayzer, S.: Semantic blogging and decentralized knowledge management. Communications of the ACM **47**(12) (2004) 47–52
10. Völkel, M., Krötzsch, M., Vrandecic, D., Haller, H., Studer, R.: Semantic Wikipedia. Proceedings of the 15th international conference on World Wide Web (2006) 585–594
11. Tokyo National Museum: Illustrated Catalogues of Tokyo National Museum – Objects from Proto-Historic Sites: Kanto District II. (1983)
12. Tokyo National Museum: Haniwa Armored Man. (http://www.emuseum.jp/cgi/pkihon.cgi?SyoID=7&ID=w123&SubID=s000)
13. Soo, V.W., Lee, C.Y., Li, C.C., Chen, S.L., Chen, C.c.: Automated semantic annotation and retrieval based on sharable ontology and case-based learning techniques. In: Proceedings of the 3rd ACM/IEEE-CS Joint Conference on Digital Libraries. (2003) 61–72
14. Wiseman, N.: International collaboration on subject based internet gateway. http://www.dlib.org/dlib/october98/10clips.html#GATEWAYS (1998)
15. Kanazawa, T., Aizawa, A., Takasu, A., Adachi, J.: The effects of the relevance-based superimposition model in cross-language information retrieval. In: Proceedings of the 5th European Conference on Research and Advanced Technology for Digital Libraries. (2001) 312–324

A Digital Library for Preservation of Folklore Crafts, Skills, and Rituals and Its Role in Folklore Education

Yung-Fu Chen[1], Po-Chou Chan[2,*], Kuo-Hsien Huang[2], and Hsuan-Hung Lin[2]

[1] Department of Health Services Management, China Medical University, Taichung 40402
yungfu@mail.cmu.edu.tw
[2] Department of Management Information Systems, Central Taiwan University of Science
and Technology, Taichung 40601 Taiwan, ROC
{bjjem, kshuang, shlin}@ctust.edu.tw

Abstract. The importance of folklore can be manifested by Alan Jabbour's speech in the 100th anniversary of American Folklore Society-"folklore reflects on the ancestral missions that have shapes us, the inherited values that we reflect and must radiate into the future". Currently, most of the digital preservation projects focus mainly on digitizing artifacts, in which the crafts of how to make them and skills of how to use them are neglected. Besides, folklore and religious rituals embed spiritual meanings. Step-by-step procedure of a ritual is not trivial for a people or a religion. The motivation of this project are manifested in three aspects: (1) folklore crafts, skills, and rituals play the same important roles in preserving our ancestor's wisdom in addition to folklore artifacts; (2) media richness facilitates learning of courses with high uncertainty and equivocality; and (3) e-learning with interactive videos gains more learner satisfaction than non-interactive and traditional classroom learning according to recent studies. In this paper, video clips are used for recording step-by-step crafts, skills, and rituals. The metadata used here are modified from our previous work regarding digital preservation of Taiwanese folklore artifacts by emphasizing the "Relation" element in linking individual steps together. A website served as an extension to digital library of folklore artifacts has been constructed to be used as an e-learning platform for folklore education in obligatory and higher education. The system not only constructs a digital library for folklore preservation but provides instructional interactive materials with media richness to support a more effective method for folklore education than non-interactive or traditional classroom learning.

1 Introduction

In recent years, digital content development with applications to the preservation of artifacts relating to the arts, languages, ecology, living styles, etc. has been studied and implemented worldwide [1,2]. Most of the digital contents emphasized artifacts rather than the craft in making or the skill in using these artifacts. Besides, folklore and religious rituals have their spiritual meaning that step-by-step procedure embeds

---

* To whom correspondence should be addressed.

S. Sugimoto et al. (Eds.): ICADL 2006, LNCS 4312, pp. 32–41, 2006.

significant meaning for a people or a religion. In this paper, as a preliminary study of digital content development for crafts, skills, and rituals, we applied the techniques of digital preservation, metadata, and E-learning to digitize folklore crafts, skills, and rituals for both preservation and online education. The same concept has been applied to digitize childcare standard operation procedures (SOPs) [3]. The SOPs mentioned here can also be referred to hospital operating procedures, experimental procedures for implementing scientific researches, or the processes of natural phenomena, such as photosynthesis in biology, reactions in biochemistry, hurricane generation in meteorology, etc. In contrast to general non-interactive e-learning and traditional classroom learning style, we proposed a metadata-based method for recording each step as a metadata record in which the title, description, associated digital media, and other related information are all included. Metadata format compatible with the Dublin core [1] was adopted, in which the "Relation" element contains two quantifiers, i.e. "Has Part" and "Is Part Of", is used to interlink between the main (parent) metadata record and its children metadata of individual steps.

The motivation and significance of this project are manifested in three aspects. First, in addition to folklore artifacts [2], folklore crafts, skills, and rituals play the same important roles in preserving our ancestor's wisdom. Second, media richness facilitates learning of courses with high uncertainty and equivocality [4]. Third, e-learning with interactive videos gains more learner satisfaction than non-interactive and traditional classroom learning according to recent studies [5].

1.1 Merits of Folklore and Folklore Education

The importance of folklore can be manifested by Alan Jabbour's speech in the 100th anniversary of American Folklore Society, which stated that "folklore reflects on the ancestral missions that have shapes us, the inherited values that we reflect and must radiate into the future" [6]. The word "folklore" may refer to unsubstantiated beliefs, legends, and customs, currently existing among the common people [7] or substantiated artifacts, crafts, skills, and rituals, widely governing the living style of the common people [2]. It can be stated that folklore customs take shape within a definite area, among a group of people in a collective environment. After a long period of settling and accumulation, during which the people can make their own choices and spur each other on a certain way of life, and then a certain mindset gradually emerge, which in turn lead to folk customs, religious beliefs, and value systems. People growing up in the same circle of folklore and customs will mutually understand each other, and will have the similar beliefs and share a worldview and a tacit understanding about many practices.

1.2 Folklore Artifacts and Their Relations to Folklore Crafts, Skills and Rituals

In general, folklore refers to the society and culture tradition of the common people and the customs practiced and beliefs held by the vast majority of people in the cultural mainstream that they have inherited from their ancestors, including legends, stories, religious beliefs, festivals, ancestor worship, taboos, ceremonies, leisure activities, music, singing, dance and so forth [2]. As a result, the value of folk artifacts, crafts, skills, and rituals lies in their demonstration of popular conceptions, life wisdom and the ancestral legacy hidden within the culture. Their basic value lies in their tight intermeshing of spirituality, psychology, and social mores; and their social functions and symbolic cultural meanings lie largely in their artistic and historical worth. In a previous investigation, we had finished content development and digital preservation of the Taiwanese folklore artifacts [2]. In this paper, we focus on the folklore craft in making and the skill and ritual in using these artifacts. For example, the craft in making puppets concerning wood sculpture, painting, clothing, and decoration, while the skill of using or playing the puppet in religious rituals regarding delicate finger operation, hand control, and arm and body movements.

Folklore objects and activities can be classified into four different types which include artifact, craft, skill, and ritual. One of our previous investigations focused only on digitization of folklore artifacts which are divided into ten categories [2]. In this paper, three types of folklore activities were added to make the folklore content and preservation more complete so that the spirits of folklore can be demonstrated more exhaustively. Table 1 shows the classifications and categories of the folklore artifacts and activities. An example of step-by-step demonstration of making puppet head is demonstrated in Table 2.

2 Materials and Methods

An artifact is related to static presentation of the folklore, which is usually an artwork produced by a craftsman, and eventually used as a tool in daily life or a utensil in a ritual. The skill refers to the use of artifacts skillfully in a ritual, daily life, or ceremony. Therefore, in this study, we classified the folklore objects and activities into four types, i.e. artifact, craft, skill, and ritual. The latter three types are referred to folklore activities embedding dynamic characteristics that can be delineated and recorded by step-by-step video clips.

Step-by-step folklore activities were demonstrated practically by the folklore specialists invited to participate in this study and the actions were taken by a professional photographer using a digital camcorder. The text and oral description of a folklore activity were done by a folklorist who majors in this specific activity. Video clips of individual steps were obtained by using the video editing software to edit a video sequence and saved as the Microsoft wmv and Apple Quicktime formats. These video clips were then combined with other related information and recorded using metadata format compatible with the Dublin core standard. Metadata designed based on the Taiwanese folklore artifacts [2] were extended to include folklore crafts, skills, and rituals.

2.1 Media Richness and Interactive Videos to Facilitate Learning

People generally acquire knowledge using different modalities and that individuals possess varying degrees of strength in each of them. In recent years, a great deal of research has been done on learning styles. Extensive research has been done concerning different learning styles or modalities [8,9]. Some students are visual learners, and others are auditory or kinesthetic learners. Some students learn globally, some analytically, some in a random fashion, while others learn sequentially. In a meta-analysis of learning and modalities study, Reiff [9] found that approximately 25% to 30% of students in a classroom are auditory learners, 25% to 30% are visual learners, and 15% are kinesthetic learners. Flaherty [8] reported that about 40% of students in K-12 consider themselves visual learners, 20% believe they are auditory, and 40% say they are kinesthetic learners. It is clear from these examples and many more found in numerous research articles, that although some students have strengths and weaknesses in certain modalities, most students learn with all their modalities [9].

Although different people have their individual strength for learning with various senses, the auditory and visual senses, manifested by video learning, seem to be more efficient for most people. More recent investigations showed that interactive videos are more effective than non-interactive videos [5]. It was also found that high media richness facilitates learning for courses with high uncertainty and equivocality, while it might cause distraction or loss of focus for courses with simple tasks [4]. Folklore artifacts, crafts, skills, and rituals embed abstract social, psychological, and spiritual concepts and sometimes unsubstantiated believes [7], they will definitely need high richness media to facilitate learning for learners with various age groups. In this paper, we apply metadata for constructing individual steps of the folklore crafts, skills, and rituals to support interactive multimedia environment emphasizing on interactive video for online folklore education.

2.2 Metadata Design and Webpage Implementation

In Table 2, an example of metadata showing individual steps of the procedure for delineating puppet head making is given. Each step in this table has a corresponding video segment. Additionally, a main (parent) metadata record is used to interlink with its related activity steps (children) by the "Relation" element proposed by the Dublin core, in which, as shown in Fig. 1, the element contains two Quantifiers; i.e., "Has Part" and "Is Part Of" for describing the sequential relation between the parent and

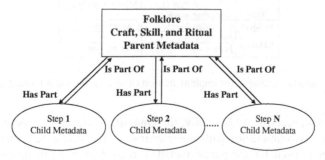

Fig. 1. Relationships between a parent metadata record and its children steps

Type	Collection Type	Folklore Artifact
	Sub Collection Type	Arts and Recreation
Title	**Budai Opera Puppet**	
	Classified Number	AARPU_00
	Content	Hand Puppet Theater
Subject	Situation and Function	Traditional Hand Puppet Theater has a very classical and refined flavor about it. It has seven major characters, including students, females, clowns, monks/nuns, children, miscellaneous and beasts
	Has Part	
Relation	Is Part Of	
	Reference Source	CACPU_00

↕ **Reference Relation**

Type	Collection Type	Folklore Craft
	Sub Collection Type	Artistic Carving
Title	**Taiwanese Hand Puppet Theater-The craft of making the puppet head**	
	Classified Number	CACPU_00
	Content	Hand Puppet Theater
Subject	Situation and Function	The head of the puppet is important as it gives it life and personality. The types of heads can be divided overall into "san gu" (lit. three bones) and "wu hsing" (lit. five forms). San gu refers to the brow, cheeks, and jaw bone, while wu hsing refers to the two eyes, two nostrils, and mouth. San gu and wu hsing endow the puppet it's own aesthetic beauty, personality, and emotions and feelings.
Relation	**Has Part**	CACPU_01, CACPU_02, CACPU_03, CACPU_04, CACPU_05, CACPU_06, CACPU_07, CACPU_08, CACPU_09, CACPU_10
	Is Part Of	
	Reference Source	AARPU_00

Is Part Of ↗   Is Part Of ↑   Is Part Of ↖

↙ Has Part   **Sequential Relation**   ......   ↘ Has Part

Type	Collection Type	Folklore Craft
	Sub Collection Type	Artistic Carving
Title	**Selecting wooden blanks**	
Subject	Classified Number	CACPU_01
Relation	Has Part	
	Is Part Of	CACPU_00

Type	Collection Type	Folklore Craft
	Sub Collection Type	Artistic Carving
Title	**Applying varnish and hair application**	
Subject	Classified Number	CACPU_10
Relation	Has Part	
	Is Part Of	CACPU_00

▼ Has Part

Type	Collection Type	Folklore Craft
	Sub Collection Type	Artistic Carving
Title	**Sculpting work**	
Subject	Classified Number	CACPU_02
Relation	Has Part	
	Is Part Of	CACPU_00

Fig. 2. A metadata example for implementation of sequential and reference relations

children metadata records. Additionally, the Quantifier "Reference source" is applied for expressing its relationship with other artifacts or folklore activities. The "Has Part" Qualifier is used for the parent metadata record to relate to its children steps, while the "Is Part Of" for the child steps to trace back to their parent.

A practical example describing the sequential relation and reference relation for the craft of making puppet head is shown in Fig. 2. With this mechanism, all the child steps can be tightly connected to their parent so that the ASP webpage design program can support flexible interaction between the users and the browsers for easy navigation. Also as shown in Fig. 2, the Quantifier "Sub-Collection Type" was added to the Element "Type" in the metadata proposed in [2]. A Microsoft SQL2000 server is built for handling database management and query. The web pages were designed using ASP.net.

3 Results

Figure 3 shows the homepage of the website supporting the digital preservation and online education for folklore crafts, skills, and rituals, where (a) shows the main metadata record in English and (b) in Chinese interfaces and descriptions. As depicted in the figure, the frame at the left allows the user to select the topics that he/she wants to browse. For each craft, skill, or ritual, a step-by-step video demonstration accompanied with either Chinese or English description can be selected by the 中文 (Chinese) or English button. The user can click Play button or click an icon related to its individual step to enter into step-by-step demonstration, as shown in Fig. 4. As demonstrated in this figure, the user can choose continuous play by clicking on the Continuous button or step-by-step play by selecting the desired step from the icons displayed at the bottom of the right frame, or using Previous or Next button to navigate sequentially. A user who intends to go back to the main metadata page (Fig. 3) can just click the Main button. For interoperation, web pages with XML format compatible to the Dublin core can be initiated by clicking the XML button.

4 Discussion and Conclusion

Jensen [10] noted that when more senses are involved in the learning process, a greater impression is made and the longer the information stays with the learners. An enriched environment creates a thicker cortex within the brain, more dendrite branching, more growth of spinal nervous, and larger cell bodies that lead to cells that communicate better. An enriched environment is multi-sensory so that people are able to see, hear, say and do as they learn. Fauth [11] and Jensen [10] indicated that people retain 10% of what they read, 20% of what they hear, 30% of what they see, 50% of what they see and hear at the same time, 70% of what they hear, see, and say, and 90% of what they hear, see, say, and do. Jensen [10] also noted that most people learn many things at the same time due to the abilities of their brains to process concurrently vast amounts of information, emotion, and awareness.

Einstein stated that he felt an idea first, and then experienced it through visual and kinesthetic images, before he was able to put the idea into words [12]. Diamond [13] demonstrated that enriching the learning environment changes the structure and ability of the brain's cerebral cortex.

Table 1. Categories and examples of Taiwanese folklore artifacts and activities. Refer to [2] for examples of folklore artifacts.

Collection Type	Sub-Collection Type	Example
Craft	Carving	Wooden utensil carving, bamboo utensil carving, leather carving, idol carving, puppet head carving, jade carving, etc.
	Weaving	Bamboo leave conical hat weaving, lantern weaving, tradition coir raincoat weaving, straw sandal weaving, Chinese macramé, "dark flower" weaving, xiangbao weaving, embroidery.
	Molding	Pottery, leather, dough figurines, candy blowing, glass, jiaozhi pottery, cutting and pasting, etc.
	Painting/ Dying	New Year's paintings, block print paintings, Taoist written incantations, Chinese opera face makeup, idol painting, painting of objects, cloth dying, plant dying, etc.
	Folk Culture Items	Calligraphy brush making, Chinese ink preparation, drum making, fan making, oil umbrella making, lacquerware making, papier mache making, kite making, top making, etc.
	Metal Objects Manufacturing	Gold objects, silver objects, tin objects, iron objects, bronze objects, etc.
	Special Crafts	Lion head making, miniature carving, micro carving, rice carving, brick carving, egg carving, hair carving, shell painting, etc.
Skill	Traditional Opera	Nanguan performances, beiguan performances, nanhu performances, bayin performances, erhu performances, dulcimer performances, pipa performances, bamboo flute performances, sheng (a reed pipe instrument) performances, etc.
	Musical Instrument Performances	Bajiajiang performances, Songjiang Battle Array performances, Cheguzhen performances, dance drumming array performances, bull fight dance performances, cloth horse dance performances, Taiwanese aboriginal dance performances, lion dance performances, etc.
	Dance Performances	Boxing performances, knife performances, spearplay performances, swordplay performances, staff performances, taichiquan performances, qigong performances, etc.
	Martial Art Performances	Top spinning performances, stilt performances, diablo performances, shuttlecock kicking performances, jump rope performances, Zhongkui dance performances, war drum performances, puppet performances, etc.
	Special Performances	Nanguan performances, beiguan performances, nanhu performances, bayin performances, erhu performances, dulcimer performances, pipa performances, bamboo flute performances, sheng (a reed pipe instrument) performances, etc.
Ritual	Religious Ceremonies	Buddhist, Taoist, Protestant, Catholic, Islam, and Yi Guan Dao ceremonies, etc.
	Belief Rituals	Venerating the Ruler of Heaven, the Earth God, Matzu, Buddha and ancestors, Avalokiteshvara, and Guan Gong, etc.
	Pray Ceremonies	Sending of the royal barge, the Jianjiao Ritual, the Raojing Ritual, the Incense Offering Ritual, the Gehuo Ritual, the Water Lantern Ritual, the Sky Lantern Festival, and the Qianggu Ceremony, etc.
	Celebrations and Festivals	New Years, Lantern Festival, Tomb Sweeping Day, Dragon Boat Festival, Ghost Month, Autumn Moon Festival, Winter Solstice, and Weiya (end of the year party), etc.
	Aboriginal Ceremonies	The Pas-taai Festival, the Harvest Festival, the Ear-Shooting Festival, the Flying Fish, the Eel Worshipping Festival, and the Qiandian Ceremony, etc.
	Special Ceremonies	Tossing Boabwei, divining by the Eight Diagrams, the soul leading ceremony, the Guanluoyin Ceremony, exorcising ceremonies, Antaisui Ceremony, etc.
Artifact		Clothing and Jewelry, Kitchenware and Dinnerware, Furnishings, Transportation, Arts and Recreation, Machinery and Tools, Religion and Religious Ceremonies, Aborigines, Study, Documents and Deeds.

Table 2. Step-by-step descriptions of the folklore craft for puppet head making

Step	Name	Description
CACPU_01	Selecting wooden blanks	The wood from Chinese Phoenix, red-bark oak, long-an, camphor trees are generally used in the making of blanks as they are hard but light, easy to carve, don't warp easily, and easy to manipulate because of their lightness. Wood blanks are soaked in water for three to four years before the carving work begins to make them durable and prevent them from rotting
CACPU_02	Sculpting work	The head of the puppet is first roughly etched into the wooden blank using an appropriately sized axe. A V-shape blade is first etched onto the wood carving tools such as slanted, round, and flat-edged knifes are used to define more clearly the san-gu (three bones) and wu-hsing (five shapes). Extra care must be paid to the shaping of the ears. The work of each craftsman is different.
CACPU_03	Refining work	After the rough carving is finished, the craftsman brings out the facial features, including the corners of the eyes and mouth, nostrils, philtrum, nasolabial furrows, and ear holes and lobes.
CACPU_04	Sanding	Coarse sandpaper is used several times to smooth the uneven inner and exterior surfaces of the doll.
CACPU_05	Paper covering	Ultra-fine, permeable tissue paper (also used in traditional Chinese painting) is affixed to the head with paste to cover the pores of the wood and to give it a "fleshed out" feeling when it is completed. Over time as the paint peels and reworking is needed, the paper is much easier to peel off.
CACPU_06	Applying sand-based plaster	The wood is painted with a mixture of finely filtered yellow sand and glue (3:1 ratio. They are boiled until they melt and combine). From five to eight layers are applied. After the paint is dry, the wood is carefully and repeatedly sanded down until it is smooth and free of coarse wood pores. From five to eight coats of plaster are needed.
CACPU_07	Smoothing the plaster surface	After the plaster is applied, the wood is dried naturally in the sun. Coarse and fine sand paper is then used to smooth out paintbrush and carving marks, leaving the wood smooth. The work is finished when there are no visible coarse wood pores.
CACPU_08	Lacquering	A mixture of colored powder and glue in 3:2 ratio is cooked together. From five to eight coats are applied to the now sanded and coated wooden blank.
CACPU_09	Applying face make-up	After the lacquer is applied, traditional paints are used to create the face pattern. It is used to make eyebrows, eye sockets, lips, wrinkles, commode (a traditional kind of head piece), and black hair.
CACPU_10	Applying varnish and hair application	Hair may be put into a bun or alternatively facial hair such a beard, moustache, or whiskers can be added depending on the age of the character. Either real hair or silk threads are dyed then affixed into prepared holes and affixed firmly into place using hot glue. The hair is styled based on the role it will play.

(a)   (b)

Fig. 3. Web pages for showing main (parent) metadata record of making puppet head with (a) English and (b) Chinese interfaces and descriptions

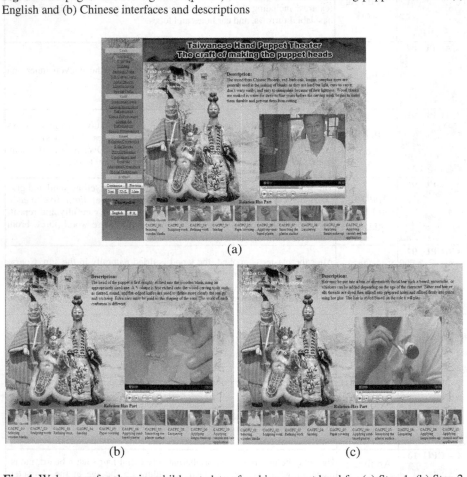

(a)

(b)   (c)

Fig. 4. Web pages for showing child metadata of making puppet head for (a) Step 1, (b) Step 2, and (c) Step 10, respectively

All the above psychological and educational theory and studies support interactive learning to be a more effective method for training of practical skills. In conclusion, in this preliminary study, digital preservation of folklore crafts, skill, and rituals using metadata has been proposed. The potential of using these materials with media richness and high interactivity for providing step-by-step demonstration of the task has been addressed. Metadata used for digital preservation of the Taiwanese folklore artefacts have been extended to accommodate folklore activities including crafts, skills, and rituals. The "Has Part" and "Is Part Of" identifiers in the "Relation" element are used to link the parent metadata record with its related children records for delineating sequential relation, while the "Reference" identifier used for linking among resources in the 4 categories. The system providing interactive learning and is expected to attain more effectiveness than the non-interactive learning [3,4,5]. Further large-scale investigation and evaluation will be done in our institutions. The proposed method will be also applied to preservation and education of folklore crafts, skills, and rituals in the near future.

References

1. Day, M.: Metadata-Mapping between Metadata Formats. Available at: http://ukolon.ac.uk/metadata/
2. Chan, P.C., Chen, Y.F., Huang, K.H., Lin H.H.: Digital Content Development of Taiwanese Folklore Artifacts. In: Fox, E.A., Neuhold, E.J., Premsmit, P., Wuwongse, V. (eds.): Digital Library: Implementing Strategies and Sharing Experiences. Lecture Notes in Computer Science, Vol. 3815. Springer-Verlag, Berlin Heidelberg (2005) 90-99
3. Wang, J.H.T., Chan, P.C., Chen, Y.F., Huang, K.H.: Implementation and Evaluation of Interactive Online Video Learning for Childcare SOPs. WSEAS Transations on Computers 5 (2006) 2799-2806.
4. Sun, P.C, Cheng, H.K.: The design of instructional multimedia in e-Learning: A media richness theory-based approach. Computers and Education (2006) In Press.
5. Zhang, D., Zhou, L., Briggs, R.O., Nunamarjer, J.F.: Instructional video in e-learning: Assessing the impact of interactive video on learning effectiveness. Information & Management 43 (2006) 15-27
6. Bronner, S.J.: The Meanings of Tradition: An Introduction. West. Folk. 59 (2000) 87-104
7. Randall M.: "Unsubstantiated belief": What we assume as truth, and how we use those assumptions. J. Am. Folk. 117 (2004) 288-295
8. Flaherty, G.: The learning curve: Why textbook teaching doesn't work for all kids. Teaching Today 67 (1992) 32-33
9. Reiff, J.C.: Learning styles: What research says to the teacher series. National Education Association, Washington, DC (1992)
10. Jensen, E.: Teaching with the brain in mind, The Association for Supervision and Curriculum Development, Alexandria, VA, (1998).
11. Fauth, B.: Linking the visual arts with drama, movement, and dance for the young child, In W. J. Stinson (Ed.), Moving and learning for the young child, American Alliance for Health, Physical Education, Recreation and Dance, Reston, VA, (1990)
12. National Dance Association: Dance education. A lifetime of experiences. Reston, VA: The American Alliance for Health, Physical Education, Recreation, and Dance. (1996)
13. M. Diamond, Enriching learning, Macmillan, NY, (1988).

A Digital Video Archive System of NDAP Taiwan

Hsiang-An Wang, Guey-Ching Chen, Chih-Yi Chiu, and Jan-Ming Ho

Institute of Information Science, Academia Sinica, Taipei, 115, Taiwan
{sawang, ching64, cychiu, hoho}@iis.sinica.edu.tw

Abstract. The National Digital Archives Program (NDAP), Taiwan has developed advanced technologies for managing digital video archives. The technologies enable us to build indexing systems for fast retrieval of digital video contents, and add values to the contents. This paper takes the Digital Museum of Taiwan's Social and Humanities Video Archive project as a case study to demonstrate the role of information science technologies in developing digital video archive systems and digitizing video and audio resources. By sharing our experience and the technologies developed in our research, we hope to provide digital content providers and researchers with guidelines for the design and development of digital video archive systems and value-added video/audio data.

Keywords: video archive, video content analysis, video index, video management.

1 Introduction

The National Digital Archives Program (NDAP) of Taiwan, which was launched on January 1, 2002, is sponsored by the National Science Council (NSC). The program's objective is to promote and coordinate the digitization and preservation of content at leading museums, archives, universities, research institutes, and other content holders in Taiwan [14].

The Digital Museum of Taiwan's Social and Humanities Video Archive is an applied research project of NDAP's video and audio archives. Its main purpose is to offer free public access to a digital library containing 3200 volumes (1600+ hours) of 16mm and Beta cam video footage. This video content was produced or collected by Daw-Ming Lee, at Taipei National University of the Arts (TNUA) [4] [10].

The archive is a collaborative project between TNUA and Institute of Information Science (IIS), Academic Sinica. TNUA is responsible for digitizing video/audio data, constructing metadata, user interfaces, and the visual presentation of information. Meanwhile, IIS is responsible for providing and integrating information technologies, and building metadata databases and management systems. IIS is also responsible for developing the following sub-systems: video/audio data format transformation, shot detection, metadata searching, audio searching, and the environment for the integration and distribution of data streaming.

The remainder of the paper is organized as follows. Section 2 describes related works. Section 3 describes the video archiving process. Section 4 details the system

S. Sugimoto et al. (Eds.): ICADL 2006, LNCS 4312, pp. 42–50, 2006.

architecture, its implementation, and addresses several implementation issues. Finally, we present our conclusions and indicate some future research directions in Section 5.

2 Related Works

Many digital archiving systems (DAS) have been developed since the mid 1990s. The goal of such systems is to provide user-friendly ways to save and present digital content so that users can retrieve and browse it easily.

Recently, there has been a rapid growth in video content produced by traditional means (e.g., news channels, educational content, entertainment media), and individuals. Consequently, many DAS have gradually extended their archived material from text/image content to video content. However, building a video archiving system is extremely challenging due to the size of the files and the content indexing problem. A number of researchers have presented various techniques for, and shared their experience in, building better video archiving systems.

The Informedia project [1] is famous for developing new technologies for video library systems. It uses a combination of speech, language, and image understanding to segment and index a linear video automatically. A speech recognizer is used to automatically transcribe a video soundtrack into text information, and a "video skimming" technique creates a video abstract that facilitates accelerated viewing of video sequences.

Another important video management project is IBM's CueVideo [5], which uses shot-boundary detection to summarize a video and extract key frames. It acquires spoken documents from videos via a speech recognition component, and the transcribed text is indexed to retrieve related audio/video clips.

In 2002, Marchionini and Geisler published the Open Video Digital Library (OVDL) [9], an integrated system that processes data for digital video archives. In this system, key frames are first extracted using MERIT software [12] and a Java program. Then, keywords are annotated, mainly manually, for the video and audio content. In addition, OVDL catalogs videos based on the attributes of genre, duration, color, and contributing organization. It also combines a number of key frames into a storyboard in order to present video content rapidly.

The Físchlár System [8] is an ongoing project that Dublin City University (Ireland) began developing in 1999. It utilizes advanced technologies for video management and analysis. First, it detects video shots via a shot-boundary detection module. Second, it deletes advertisements from the video shots obtained in the first step. In the third step, the system analyzes the content of remaining shots by spoken dialogue indexing, speech/music discrimination, face detection, anchorperson detection, shot clustering, and shot length cue, all of which are implemented based on the SVM algorithm. Finally, it applies the story-segment program to combine several shots into a story segment and saves the result in the database.

The systems and projects described above provide good guidelines for building a digital video library; however, they only process Western languages. Until recently, there has been a lack of techniques and experience for developing a video archiving system (e.g., a speech recognizer and a caption recognizer) for a Chinese environment. In this work, we report on such a system and release source code of two components, the watermark appending module and the format transformation module. The source code and executable program are available on the Open Source Software Foundry [15]. We discuss the components further in Section 3.2.

3 Video Archiving Process

Our video archiving process is divided into two stages. In the first stage, we choose an appropriate metadata standard to preserve the detailed description of our video file. The second stage is video digitization and content analysis, in which we digitize Betacam tapes into digital files and send the digital videos to the content analysis modules. This process reformats Betacam tapes into a digital format so they can be managed by our digital video archive system (DVAS).

3.1 Metadata Analysis

A number of video metadata standards have been proposed, for example, MPEG-7, developed by the Moving Picture Experts Group; the Standard Media Exchange Framework, developed by the BBC; the P/Meta Metadata Exchange Standard, developed by the European Broadcasting Union; the European CHronicles On-line project (ECHO), developed by the European Community [6]; and the Dublin Core application profile for digital video, promoted by the Video Development Initiative [16].

In our research, we initially used the Dublin Core metadata standard as a guideline to analyze the metadata. We found that, although the basic columns fulfill the needs of content description, the 15 columns defined by Dublin Core are not sufficient to describe all the content properties required in the management and archiving of audio and video content. Thus, in the second stage of our project, we used the metadata standard developed by ECHO as our guideline for metadata analysis because its definition of video metadata is more detailed than that of Dublin Core. The ECHO standard is an adaptation of the Functional Requirements for Bibliographic Records Model (FRBR Model) of the International Federation of Library Associations and Institutes (IFLA). We made minor modifications to the ECHO metadata standard in order to analyze, design, and develop the metadata management system for our digital archives and databases.

3.2 Video Digitization and Content Analysis

In this stage, we first transfer Betacam tapes to MPEG-2 files via a video capture card so that we can analyze, process, and preserve the video content at a later stage. Fig. 1 shows the video analysis and processing procedure, which is divided into six modules, namely: metadata injection, caption recognition/appending, voice recognition, shot detection, watermark appending, and format transformation. As these modules are all independent, users can utilize multiple computers to access different modules to reduce the processing time. In addition, all of these modules support batch operation to process a large number of video files in one operation.

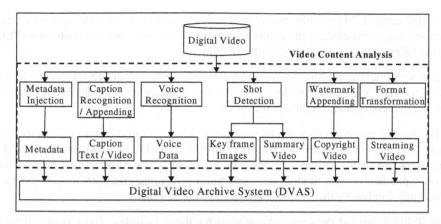

Fig. 1. The video analysis and processing procedure

1. The metadata injection system is a web system that is connected to the database system of DVAS. It allows a content provider to input metadata about a video via the user interface. The injected metadata is saved in the database and used to support DVAS when responding to users' keyword queries. To prevent misuse of the metadata by unauthorized people, the system contains a member authentication mechanism.

2. Caption recognition/appending. (i) The caption recognition module automatically retrieves the transcript from video content with captions if the content provider does not supply a transcript. Temporal information for indexing video content is also saved. A user can then use a keyword search to browse related video clips via the transcript and extra temporal information. In order to adapt to the general language of video files in Taiwan, this module focuses on processing Traditional-Chinese captions. The module was developed by joint cooperation between Chang et al. [7] and us. Its accuracy rate for recognition is over 90%. (ii) The caption appending module appends captions to a video from an external text file if users want to add captions to an uncaptioned video.

3. The voice recognition module is similar to the caption recognition module, but it processes the audio content of a video file. The module is developed via cooperation between Wang et al. [10][13] and our laboratory. It retrieves the transcript from the audio channel of the video, and saves it in DVAS. Users can use a keyword to search video content via the transcript, and then browse related video segments. This module, which focuses on processing Mandarin Chinese speech for videos, has an accuracy rate between 40% and 95%, depending on whether the voice data is noisy or clear.

4. The shot detection system performs shot detection on the MPEG1/2 files and outputs the analysis results as an XML file containing the temporal information about locations where scene content changes dramatically. We developed the technique of shot detection by cooperating with Shih et al. [2]. The video abstract extraction program extracts a n-second segment from each shot detected. It then combines these n-second segments into a *"Summary Video"*, which allows users to efficiently preview

the video content. Meanwhile, based on the shot detection results, the key frame extraction component extracts the appropriate frame from each shot to construct a JPEG format *"Key frame image"* file for static display.

5. The watermark appending module can embed an external image into every frame of a video file. A content provider can select a logo image and append it to a video to indicate ownership and discourage illegal use.

6. The format transformation module converts video data into different formats. For example, it can convert MPEG-2 files into MPEG-1, WMV, or RM formats. In addition, users can set up attributes for the output file, such as the frame size, bit rate and so on. Specifically, this module can generate a streaming file with a multi-bit rate format that can handle the various bandwidth of the Internet.

In Table 1, we list the time consumption for these modules. The testing environment is Windows XP with a P4 3.4G CPU and 1.5GB memory. The test data is 10 video files in MPEG2 format. The frame size of the files is 640*480, and the frame rate is 29.97 per second.

Table 1. The time cost of the video content analysis modules

Module	Time consumption rate (processing time / video duration)	Note
Caption recognition module	1.0 ~ 1.7	Depending on the number of captions
Caption appending module	0.60 ~ 0.63	
Voice recognition module	1.0 ~ 1.5	Depending on the number of video data
Shot detection module	0.7 ~ 1.0	Depending on the number of shots
Watermark appending module	0.65 ~ 0.70	
Format transformation module	0.7-0.9	The output format is WMV with 352*240 frame size; the bit-rate is 364K.

After analyzing and processing, the video content is stored in DVAS using different formats, including text, image and video files. DVAS manages the data, which can be edited, searched, browsed, and used when required. We describe DVAS in detail in the next section.

4 DVAS Architecture and Implementation

4.1 The Components and Workflow of DVAS

DVAS preserves video metadata and digital video data. To enable the general public to browse and search video content online, DVAS comprises a metadata database, a voice database, a video management and search system (VMSS), and a streaming server. Fig.2 illustrates the workflow of DVAS when responding to users' queries. The metadata database is responsible for saving injected metadata and the results of video caption recognition. The voice database is responsible for saving voice data obtained from the voice recognition module.

In DVAS, the VMSS provides capabilities for video management, such as metadata add/update/delete, and member authentication. It also provides a web query-interface and shows the query results obtained from the voice and metadata databases. To support real-time online viewing of videotapes, reduce the need for high network bandwidth, and protect intellectual property rights (i.e., prevent illegal copying), the DVAS utilizes a streaming server to play the video/audio content of videotapes.

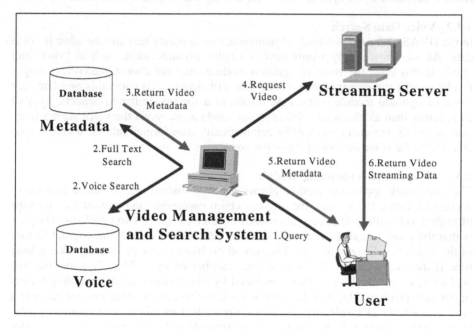

Fig. 2. The workflow of DVAS

4.2 The Implementation of DVAS

DVAS utilizes a 3-tier architecture: Apache and Tomcat Web programs serve as the application's server-tiers, and Oracle serves as the database-tier. We use the Linux Red Hat operating system for the server-tiers. The web pages were developed with JSP technology and Java Beans, and the video search engine was integrated with a streaming server for video/audio broadcasting. We use the Microsoft Media Server as the streaming server to publish WMV-format files. The hardware comprises two 1U servers with Intel Xeon processors to run VMSS and the streaming system. There is also a disk array that stores video abstracts and key frames as the total file size is 840 GB. Original videotapes are backed up with large tapes, because they are not accessed very often and the total file size is very large (over 8 TB).

4.3 Implementation Issues

4.3.1 Components for Video Content Analysis
We have already introduced several components for content analysis in Fig. 1. Each of these components is independent, so users can operate all or portion of them at the same time via several computers. In addition, all these components support batch operation, except the metadata injection system; thus users can deal with a large number of video files in one manipulation. As the components are independent, users can choose the minimum number of components to meet their requirements and easily reduce the processing time by using multiple computers. Furthermore, if the users have their own requirement for video content analysis, they can easily attach an external component to the system without modifying the original components.

4.3.2 Voice Data Search
In the DVAS, there are two kinds of metadata, one is purely text and the other is voice data. As we know, many words have a similar pronunciation, such as "two" and "too". In this case, the voice recognition module may not choose the correct output results so that the recognition accuracy rate will decline. To solve this problem, our voice recognition module outputs the results in a format similar to phonetic symbol data, rather than as characters. When a user sends a query via the voice search function in VMSS, the query text will be automatically transformed into the above format and sent to the voice database for comparison.

4.3.3 Watermark Appending Module
The watermark appending module allows users to embed a logo image into every frame of a video. In this way, the user can claim ownership and prevent illegal usage of his/her video files. Although this sounds efficient, it raises two problems. The first is that the result cannot be reversed, once the process is finished, the original frames of the video are changed forever. The second problem is that processing takes a long time if the user wants to deal with a large number of video files. To solve the two problems, we use the FLV format, developed by Micromedia, as the streaming format in our new platform. Because this format has a multi-layer architecture, we can add a new image layer into video frames in real-time when members of the general public browse video content. In this way, we can provide rights protection for video files without the above problems.

5 Conclusions and Future Work

The Digital Museum of Taiwan's Social and Humanities Video Archive project was established three years ago. It has developed from digitizing original negatives to the formulation, entry, management of metadata, and video searching. A complete workflow of digital archive applications has been established and verified, and the project has yielded productive research results. Besides above archive project, we also provide these technologies to Digital Archives of Formosan Aborigines program [3] and Government Information Office, Republic of China (Taiwan) video archive system (in building). The two projects are important archive projects, and have rich video data (2000+ hours). Through our techniques, they can easily build a video management system and then provide the video data to general public.

We now indicate some future research directions.

1. Improve the workflow of automatic digitization. Currently, certain steps, such as the selection of key frames, are sometimes performed manually in order to select an appropriate image. In the future, we will integrate different methods to streamline manual processing, which will reduce errors and improve the system's overall performance.

2. Improve the technology for voice searching, as the accuracy rate of voice recognition in video files is not very good because of speakers' accents and background noise.

3. Integrate video copy detection technologies for digital rights protection. Currently, users often add non-visible watermarks to protect digital rights, but this is very costly in terms of computing time. Also, watermarks spoil parts of a frame, and their robustness against attack is not sufficient to guarantee security. Thus, we are developing technologies that will automatically find a video's feature information. Then, based on that information, we can compare two videos quickly. If the two video's features match, we may infer that the original video was probably pirated.

4. Open our sources to the public. We have already released the source code and execution files of the video format transformation and video watermark appending tools via the Open Source Software Foundry (OSSF) Web site [15]. By continuing to open our sources, we expect that more people will become involved, thereby promoting the development of the digital video archive.

5. Integrate content-based retrieval techniques. Content-based visual retrieval has received a great deal of attention from researchers in recent years. Users can use visual cues, such as color, texture, shape, and motion, to search perceptually similar video clips. Therefore, the integration of text and content-based retrieval would provide a more flexible way for users to process queries.

The complete Digital Museum of Taiwan's Social and Humanities Video Archive project has a vast amount of high quality content and employs several techniques to process and present it. Due to space limitations, we have only described the technologies and system architecture of DAVS. Other topics, including video content, e-learning systems, the design of metadata, and the development of information science technologies have not been discussed in this paper. In the future, we will continue in-depth research and development of these areas in order to construct a more advanced digital library.

Acknowledgements

This research was supported in part by the National Science Council of Taiwan under NSC Grants: NSC 90-2750-H-119-230, NSC 91-2422-H-119-0601, and NSC 92-2422-H-119-091. The authors wish to thank the members of the Digital Archive Architecture Laboratory (DAAL) for their assistance in building systems, and developing and integrating core techniques.

References

1. Carnegie Mellon University, "Informedia, digital video understanding research", http://www.informedia.cs.cmu.edu/
2. C. C. Shih, H. Y. Mark Liao and H. R. Tyan "Shot Change Detection based on the Reynolds Transport Theorem", *Proc. Second IEEE Pacific Rim Conference on Multimedia*, pp. 819-824, Beijing, China, October 2001.
3. Digital Archives of Formosan Aborigines program, http://www.aborigines.sinica.edu.tw/
4. Digital Museum of Taiwan's Social and Humanities Video Archive, http://www.sinica.edu.tw/~video/intro/intro-year10-e.html
5. Dulce Ponceleon, Arnon Amir, Savitha Srinivasan, Tanveer Syeda-Mahmood, and Dragutin Petkovic, "CueVideo: Automated Multimedia Indexing and Retrieval", *ACM Multimedia '99* (Orlando, FL, Oct. 1999). p. 199.
6. European CHronicles On-line project, http://pc-erato2.iei.pi.cnr.it/echo/#
7. F. Chang, G. C. Chen, C. C. Lin, W. H. Lin "Caption analysis and recognition for building video indexing system", *ACM Multimedia Systems Journal,* 10 (4), pp. 344-355, 2005.
8. Físchlár System, http://www.fischlar.dcu.ie/
9. G. Marchionini and G. Geisler, "The Open Video Digital Library", D-Lib Magazine, Vol. 8, No. 12 (December 2002), http://www.open-video.org/
10. H. A. Wang, G. C. Chen, C. Y. Chiu, and Y.-C. Lin, "A case study on technologies of a digital video archive system", *2005 International Conference on Digital Archive Technologies*, pp.101-113, Taipei, Taiwan, June 2005.
11. H. M. Wang, S. S. Cheng, and Y. C. Chen "The SoVideo Mandarin Chinese Broadcast News Retrieval System," *International Journal of Speech Technology*, 7 (2), pp. 189-202, April 2004.
12. Maryland Engineering Research Internship Teams, http://www.ece.umd.edu/MERIT
13. M. F. Huang, K. T. Chen and H. M. Wang, "Towards Retrieval of Video Archives based on The Speech Content," in Proc. *International Symposium on Chinese Spoken Language Processing (ISCSLP2002)*, Taipei, Aug 2002.
14. National Digital Archives Program, Taiwan, http://www.ndap.org.tw/index_en.php
15. Open Source Software Foundry, http://rt.openfoundry.org/Foundry/
16. Video Development Initiative, "ViDe User's Guide: Dublin Core Application Profile for Digital Video", http://www.vide.net/workgroups/videoaccess/resources/vide_dc_userguide_20010909.pdf

A Research Project to Convert Chinese Traditional Calligraphic Paintings to SCORM-Compatible E-Learning Materials

Chao-chen Chen[1], Jian-hua Yeh[2], and Shun-hong Sie[3]

[1] Graduate Institute of Library and Information Studies,
National Taiwan Normal University
cc4073@cc.ntnu.edu.tw
[2] Depart of Computer and Information Science,
Aletheia University
au4290@email.au.edu.tw
[3] Department of Library and Information Science,
Fu Jen Catholic University
modify@ms37.hinet.net

Abstract. The research project presented in this paper aims to meet the need for courses in Chinese traditional calligraphic art through the use of digitalized paintings. Thus, this paper delineates vital aspects associated in converting such materials to e-formats and the platform on which digital archives and digital learning may become possible. Moreover, the construction of a platform for integrating digital content with e-learning creates a frontier, opening up new resources in Chinese traditional calligraphic painting instruction.

Keywords: SCORM, e-learning, contents package, learning objects, Chinese traditional calligraphic paintings.

1 Introduction

The raw materials used for this research project comes from a wide range of sources including: teachers' designs, existing media, internet websites, commercial databases, and, most significantly, digital archives. The major institutions having participated in the national digital archive plan since its initiation in 2001 are the National Palace Museum, National Museum of History, National Museum of Historic National Records, National Library, National Museum of Natural Sciences, Office of Historic Taiwan Records, Academia Sinica, and National Taiwan University. Digital content thus shared have traveled afar to the four corners of the country as its residents, regardless of their distance from the institutions, take advantage of such a resource in research and instruction.

However, for the digital archive content to be effectively used by learners in the e-environment requires them to be further treated with value-additions. This is due to the fact that the metadata format associated with those existing digital archive contents differs in various fundamental aspects from what is needed in an interactive learning

S. Sugimoto et al. (Eds.): ICADL 2006, LNCS 4312, pp. 51–60, 2006.

environment. That is to say, the perspective associated with and the practicality arising from dynamic instructional settings are such that they necessitate digital archive contents to be additionally processed for their conversion to a format readily to be used for teacher-student interactive activities. In the conversion process, the raw digital contents themselves, along with the metadata format, would be specifically treated accordingly to the requirements put forth by the e-learning environment.

This project is made all the more urgent and imperative, in view of the drift in the trend reflected in the new wave of reformation in Taiwan's school education. Evidenced is the lack of courses offered to teach Chinese traditional calligraphy and paintings in elementary, middle and high schools. Courses, which would introduce students to this distinctive art form and engage them in appreciating and learning it, have been scratched because their importance and value have not been stressed. This dire situation feeds a corresponding lack of interest among art schools/departments in colleges, who no longer put emphasis upon Chinese traditional calligraphy and painting in their entrance examinations and favor Western art forms instead. Exacerbating this lack of interest is the fact that beginners who are learning art usually find Chinese traditional calligraphy painting more difficult than Western art. Therefore, the overall picture is rather bleak insofar as the popularity of Chinese traditional art forms is concerned. To provide some impetus to interest in calligraphy painting, it is critical to make these art forms widely and readily accessible to teachers and students through interactive activities. This project means investing major efforts not only to digitally preserve this valuable component of our cultural heritage for future generations to enjoy but also to present them in a user-friendly form to invite people worldwide to learn, practice, and advance Chinese art forms.

The goal of this project is to convert both raw materials and packaged teaching materials into SCORM compatible formats so that they can be shared openly. Moreover, art teachers at every level in academia nation-wide will be given an explanation about the benefits of our project product; offered incentives to try out our internet resources; and invited to use our research product in their courseware design, lesson planning, and classroom activities. Some noted paintings by Zhang, Fu and Huang are used as samples to illustrate how the product of this project would operate and function in the e-learning environment. This SCORM project aims to present Chinese traditional calligraphic paintings in an e-format that enhances art teacher-student interactions, instills public appreciation for calligraphic art, and inspires world-wide desire to learn the art.

2 Ressearch Purposes and Method

The purpose of this research project is to integrate digital archival and digital learning by analyzing Chinese traditional calligraphic paintings held in the National Museum of History and transforming them into value-added contents ready to be utilized as a online resource for e-learning. Practically speaking, this project has three major interrelated parts.

(1)   To conduct investigation and surveys to determine the teacher-student needs regarding Chinese traditional calligraphic paintings.

(2)   To analyze approaches to convert Chinese traditional calligraphic paintings into shareable learning objects and metadata.

(3)   To construct a mechanism to convert between digital archive metadata and LOM metadata, and to establish a system to provide descriptions and package SCORM learning objects.

This research project employs the following in its methodology:

(1)   Interviews and panel discussions with scholars, experts, and teachers. This research has benefited from interviews and discussions with fourteen scholars in the field and top high school teachers, in order to gather from them critical information in the concerned areas. Several copies of teaching plans have resulted from this project.

(2)   Empirical Procedures. Based upon the above mentioned information and teaching plans, this project has designed lesson plans for demonstration. Raw archival materials have been analyzed and/or re-scanned to come up with learning materials. Administrative systems have been established to co-ordinate raw archival materials and lessons pool. Finally, this project invites teachers to share their input and come up with derivative lesson plans.

3   Results and Discussions

Based upon interviews and surveys, experiments, and lesson plans using Zhang, Fu, and Huang paintings, the research project has produced a collection of teaching materials in Flash format. Teachers and students using the teaching materials are encouraged to creatively make their own materials, so called derivative materials, by selecting parts and components from the collection and adapting them to their specific needs. Moreover, the research project has constructed an administrative system to integrate and co-ordinate Zhang-Fu-Huang paintings and teaching materials.

The following aspects of the research results are presented here below: Requirements Specified by Art Teachers for SCORM; Treatment of Learning Objects; Design and Description of X-System and X-Learning.

Requirements Specification

Scholars, experts, and teachers familiar with teaching art, expressed their requirements for the SCORM learning objects as follows:

(1)   Image resolution. Paintings are expected to be presented in high resolutions. When magnified, they should still have high image quality.

(2)   PowerPoint presentation format. For art teachers, the truth in the cliché comes pressing home: a picture is more than one thousand words. Accordingly, they

need PowerPoint presentations, which integrate well with other forms of e-learning resources, created with maximum possible clarity and flexibility.

(3)   Three important features:

(a) user-friendly. Even teachers who are relatively computer-illiterate should be able to use those materials.

(b) versatility. They would allow teachers to alter material contents in order to adapt materials for various settings.

(c) Classification labels based upon difficulty levels. Teaching materials should be classified as basic, intermediate, and advanced, so that teachers can have a preliminary index in their search for the right materials to use.

(4)   Rich metadata. With a comprehensive set of metadata, teaching materials can be dynamically sorted and presented as relating to particular themes and topics. This would improve on the rather dry and boring static presentations in the past. Moreover, Chinese traditional calligraphic paintings in their e-presentations could be linked to resources in other disciplines to achieve a comprehensive inter-disciplinary sharing.

(5)   Art teachers wish that Chinese traditional calligraphic paintings would infuse a breeze of humanism into our high-tech society and show a way to provide low-touch realities to our post-modern society, which is permeated by scientific/technological and materialistic ideologies.

Treatments of Learning Objects

Learning Objects are established according to the three aspects as follows.

(1)   Digitalizing originals and units. We planned to use the metadata already existing for Chinese traditional calligraphic paintings and dissect them in order to obtain sub-units from them. Yet, we found out that the units thus obtained proved to be too small to be practically useful. Therefore, we have to scan the entire corpus of 181 pieces, establishing the same number of metadata and JPG files for them. Including the sub-unit components thus produced in the process, a total of 694 files are netted. Those metadata have been incorporated into the original files, with additional descriptions attached.

(2)   Synchronizing metadata with LOM. A cross-reference table is established for those metadata files and LOM. This is due to the fact that National Museum of History first lacked those LOM files.

(3)   Categorizing the Learning Objects. In order to have those learning objects to be readily searched, we have those items categorized according to contents and techniques of those Chinese traditional calligraphic paintings.

Design and Description of X-System and X-Learning

Two functional modules are included in this research project. One is the archive system, also called X-System. The other is called X-Learning and converts metadata into LOM and SCORM packages. X-System to administer archives and X-Learning to administer modular designs. The relationships between X-System and X-Learning can be depicted by Fig. 1. This research project includes the X-System to co-ordinate various metadata and archives as well as to convert metadata files to LOM. Moreover, it packages learning objects for them to meet the standards of SCORM. In other words, we incorporate digital archives and digital learning into one system. Descriptions of the system explaining its function and structure are as follows:

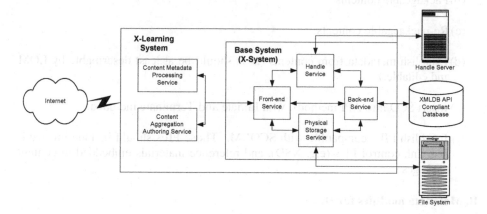

Fig. 1. The service architecture of X-Learning system

A. Infrastructural Needs

(1)   Digital Objects (DOs) stored in S-System can be described by more than two metadata formats.

(2)   The ability to deal with PIF. (Package Interchange File)

  (a) PIF storage.

  (b) Unzip PIF, release manifests, SCO, and assets.

(3)   Establish new PIFs.

  (a) Preview PIF contents (SCOs); preview DOs in X-System.

  (b) Select SCOs and DOs needed to borrow.

(c) Combine borrowed manifests with old ones to come up with new manifests.

(d) Preview integrated SCOs and Assets, and edit metadata.

(e) Insert API methods into SCO, including at least Initiate and Terminate.

(f) Package new manifests and SCOs into PIF transferable to LMS.

(4)   Practically speaking, the following functions should be available:

(a) Transfer ins and outs.

(b) Packageable contents.

(c) Re-packaegable contents.

(d) Establish metadata from contents (DOs should be at least describable by LOM and editable.)

(e) Insert SCO into API methods, with Initiate and Terminate included.

(f) Establish PIFs compatible with SCORM. Those PIFs should include imsmanifest.xml, control files (e.g. XSD), and reference materials embedded in content packages.

B. Metadata modules for Dos

(1)   Convert other metadata formats into LOM. (see Fig. 2)

(2)   If a DO is originally done for Learning Object (LO), it should be describable with LOM.

(3)   For LOs done for digital learning, their interfaces should be usable by DO makers to add some basic materials.

C. SCO and functions to insert applets

(1)   We can add to SCO API needed by standard SCORM 1.3.

(2)   We can use LOM to describe DO if it is SCO.

(3)   LO contained in digital learning materials should be open to additions from DO doers regarding basic information.

(4)   The system is capable to package assets into SCO in accordance with SCORM 1.3 CAM. (see Fig. 3)

Fig. 2. Mapping from archive metadata to LOM metadata in X-Learning system

Fig. 3. Authoring interface for packaging assets into SCO in X-Learning system

D. Content Aggregation (CA) Descriptions and Packages

(1)   The system is capable to package SCO and assets into CA in the standards set by SCORM 1.3 CAM. The constructed PIFs would include imsmanifest.xml, control files (e.g. XSD) and reference materials in content packages.

(2)   Metadata format from LOM can be used to describe CA.

E. Testing SCORM Packages

The fundamental goal of this research project is to convert archive items into learning objects. X-Learning system has such a capacity and can package files acceptable to other e-learning systems.

4 Conclusions

Some problems and insights discovered while converting Chinese traditional calligraphic painting archives into SCORM teaching materials are shared as follows:

(1) LOM has a column for categorization. However, the categorization systems available, including those used by the Chinese Library Science Association, Dewey system, and American Congress Library, do not lend themselves readily to those paintings. LOM is suitable for categorization needs arising from universally recognizable materials. Applying it to those paintings is like swinging a samurai sword to kill a chicken. Therefore, it has become necessary for us to come up with a new categorization scheme for Chinese traditional calligraphic paintings, in order to bring out their techniques and contents, as well as the knowledge and scopes involved. Such new categorization, however, entails subsequent maintenance work.

(2) The need to take new photos of the paintings. This tedious task of re-taking the photos becomes necessary due to the fact that, in the already existing archive photos, seals and inscriptions on the paintings are too tiny to be identified and analyzed. Taking new photos is something beyond our research's original scope; consequently, this research project took longer to complete than first planned. Based upon this experience, we recommend that all photographic works to be done on those paintings should include in their considerations the need for digital learning.

(3) The future need to incorporate paintings from other museums. This is to meet the goal of making available eventually of all the paintings to art teachers in SCORM formats, so that their creativity in coming up with instruction materials and aids will be further enhanced. Based upon this on-going need, we recommend that paintings from other major museums should be similarly processed and their SCORM materials integrated into the existing pool, so that eventually they are conveniently accessible to teachers.

(4) We strongly encourage teachers to make public and share the derivative materials they have developed. It is amazing how wonderfully their derivative works present themselves and lend to imaginative uses. Such public and open sharing would materialize a virtually limitless universe overflowing with quality courseware.

(5) An ultimate goal in producing SCORM materials is for them to be transform-
     able and hence reusable according to teachers' creative needs in different con-
     texts and approaches. What learning objects teachers need in their specific
     course designs varies significantly by the ideals to which they are inspired. It is
     critical, therefore, for teachers to have the resources needed to come up with the
     widest possible range of learning objects. How much they would be able to take
     advantage of resources available in a digital learning environment is determined
     in turn by the effectiveness of search, administration, and re-use functions. To
     be able to digitally de-construct and re-construct a painting in a way most con-
     ducive for such functions, needless to say, becomes an imperative task in
     SCORM material productions. We should aim to produce SCORM materials of
     such ready access and quality that they meet the challenges arising from the
     soaring spirit and soul of art teachers in their instructional activities. We will
     strive towards a seamlessly integrated e-learning environment utilizing all pos-
     sible digital hardware and software, so that teachers can be helped by SCORM
     to achieve the excellence they aim for in their instructions. Now, more than
     ever before, we are aware of the long way to go before we realize the maximum
     potentiality in SCORM.

References

1. ADL(2001). The SCORM Content Aggregation Model. V1.2 Retrieved Sept. 9, 2003,
    from http://www.adlnet.org/index.cfm?fuseaction=SCORDown
2. ADL(2004). The SCORM Content Aggregation Model. V1.3 Retrieved Feb. 5, 2004, from
    http://www.adlnet.org/index.cfm?fuseaction=SCORDown
3. Chew, L.K.(2003).eLearning Specifications for Distance Education. http://www.apan.net/
    home/organization/wgs/education/documents/shanghai8.pdf
4. Engelbrecht, J.C.(2003). SCORM Deployment Issues in an Enterprise Distributed Learn-
    ing Architecture. Retrieved Feb 20, 2004, from http://www.elearningguild.com/pdf/2/
    021803MGT-H.pdf
5. Griffith, R., & ADL Co-Lab Staff(2003). Learning Objects in Higher Education. Retrieved
    Jan. 12, 2004, from http://www.webct.com/service/ViewContent?contentID=16328050
6. Himes, F. & Wagner, E.D.(2002). Macromedia MX: Empowering Enterprise eLearning.
    Retrieved Jan. 12, 2004, from http://download.macromedia.com/pub/solutions/downloads/
    elearning/empower_enterprise.pdf
7. Heins, T., & Himes, F.(2002). Creating Learning Objects with Macromedia Flash MX.
    Retrieved Jan. 12, 2004, from http://download.macromedia.com/pub/solutions/downloads/
    elearning/flash_mxlo.pdf
8. Hodgins, W.(2000). The Future of Learning Objects. Retrieved Jan. 11, 2004, from http://
    www.reusability.org/read/chapters/hodgins.doc
9. IEEE(2002). Draft Standard for Learning Object Metadata. IEEE 1484.12.1-2002. Re-
    trieved Sept. 21, 2003, from http://ltsc.ieee.org/doc/wg12/LOM_1484_12_1_v1_Final_
    Draft.pdf
10. Learning Systems Architecture Lab(2003). SCORM Best Practices Guide for Content
    Developers(1st Edition). Retrieved Nov. 19, 2003 from http://www.lsal.cmu.edu/lsal/
    expertise/projects/developersguide/developersguide/guide-v1p0-20030228.pdf

11. Macromedia, Inc.(2001). Getting Started with eLearning Standards. Retrieved Sept. 8, 2003, from http://download.macromedia.com/pub/solutions/downloads/elearning/standards.pdf
12. Pasini, N. & Rehak, D.R.(2003). A Process Model for Applying Standards in Content Development. Retrieved Dec 19, 2003 from http://www.lsal.cmu.edu/lsal/expertise/papers/conference/edmedia2003/process20030625.pdf
13. Robert, M.(2002).A Strategy for eLearning Standards. Retrieved Sept. 16, 2003, from http://www.icaxon.com/elearning/elfebruary2002.html
14. Vladoiu, M.-M.(2003). Learning Objects Need Badly Instructional Digital Libraries Support. Retrieved Sept. 15, 2003, from http://www.vtex.lt/informatics_in_education/pdf/INFE020.pdf
15. Wiley, D.A.(2001). Connecting learning objects to instructional design theory: A definition, a metaphor, and a taxonomy. Retrieved Jan. 11, 2004, from http://reusability.org/read/chapters/wiley.doc
16. The MASIE Center(2002). Making Sense of Learning Specifications & Standards: A Decision Maker's Guide to their Adoption. Retrieved Sept. 8, 2003, from http://www.masie.com/standards/S3_ Guide.pdf
17. Home Page of Zhang, Fu, and Huang's Digital Learning Website. http://xsystem.glis.ntnu.edu.tw/xlm/
18. Home Page of X-System Learning. http://xsystem.glis.ntnu.edu.tw/learning/

Interdisciplinary Curriculum Development
for Digital Library Education

Seungwon Yang[1], Edward A. Fox[1],
Barbara M. Wildemuth[2], Jeffrey Pomerantz[2], and Sanghee Oh[2]

[1] Department of Computer Science, Virginia Tech,
Blacksburg, VA 24061 U.S.A.
+1 540-231-5113
{seungwon, fox}@vt.edu
[2] School of Information and Library Science, University of North Carolina – Chapel Hill,
Chapel Hill, NC 27599-3360 U.S.A.
+1 919-962-8366
wildem@ils.unc.edu
{jpom, shoh}@email.unc.edu

Abstract. The Virginia Tech (VT) Department of Computer Science (CS) and
the University of North Carolina at Chapel Hill (UNC-CH) School of Information and Library Science (LIS) are developing curricular materials for digital library (DL) education, appropriate for the CS and LIS communities. Educational
modules will be designed, based on input from the project advisory board,
Computing Curriculum 2001, the 5S framework, and workshop discussions.
These modules will be evaluated, first through expert inspection and, second,
through field testing. We are identifying and refining module definitions and
scopes, collecting related resources, developing a module template, and creating
example modules. These will be presented at the conference. The developed
curriculum should contribute to producing well-balanced digital librarians who
will graduate from CS or LIS programs.

Keywords: digital library, curriculum, 5S framework, education, CC2001.

1 Introduction

Contemporary human societies are inundated with enormous amounts of information.
To address the need for high quality, organized information, many digital libraries
(DLs) have been developed. However, there has not been much focus on education for
people who design and administer DLs compared to the investment in DLs. To solve
this problem, Virginia Tech's Department of Computer Science (VT CS) and the University of North Carolina at Chapel Hill School of Information and Library Science
(UNC SILS) have taken the first steps toward developing an interdisciplinary curriculum and collection of related resources for DL education [1]. Through a three-year
project,[1] we will define, develop, and test educational modules, guided by experts, the

---

[1] Funded by NSF Grant IIS-0535057 to VT and IIS-0535060 to UNC-CH for 2006-2008.

S. Sugimoto et al. (Eds.): ICADL 2006, LNCS 4312, pp. 61–70, 2006.
© Springer-Verlag Berlin Heidelberg 2006

Computing Curriculum 2001 [3, 4], the 5S framework [5, 6, 7], and analysis of existing DL course syllabi. Each module will include lesson plans, concept maps, exercises, demos, online resources, and a recommended reading list for both instructors and students. We encourage reuse, e.g., one- and two-semester DL courses can be based on selected modules.

Computer scientists working on DL areas tend to focus on the system side, while librarians, who administer digital libraries, generally put more emphasis on the service aspect of DLs. We expect our project will aid both CS and LIS students and instructors, as well as reduce the communication gap between the communities.

2 Foundations for Curriculum Development

To develop digital library modules and courses, standing on a solid foundation, we will follow a standard curriculum design model of analysis, design/development, and evaluation [2]. Currently, we are in the initial 'design' phase, identifying DL education modules and lessons. We have obtained expert guidance, since good module design requires a natural flow between modules and thorough understanding of DL courseware. Once the resulting modules are developed, they will be evaluated, first through inspection by experts in the area covered by the module, as well as by Ph.D. students attending JCDL doctoral consortia. Then, after revision based on the expert reviews, the modules will be evaluated as they are used to teach DL courses in CS and LIS.

To encourage active participation of DL researchers, we have presented papers in the 9th International Symposium on Electronic Theses and Dissertations, and the 6th ACM/IEEE-CS Joint Conference on Digital Libraries. In addition, we introduced the project in the workshop, 'Developing a Digital Libraries Education Program,' held right after the JCDL '06 conference. The organizers of the workshop plan to have a conference on DL education in 2007, and will involve our team in that activity.

As a theoretical foundation for our work, we have adopted the 5S framework [5, 6, 7], developed in the Digital Library Research Laboratory at Virginia Tech. The label "5S" refers to the five elements of this framework:

- Streams: all types of contents as well as communications and flows over networks, or into sensors, or sense perceptions (e.g., text, video, audio)
- Structures: organizational schemes including data structures, databases, and knowledge representations (e.g., catalog, metadata, hypertext)
- Spaces: 2D and 3D interfaces, GIS data, representations of documents and queries (e.g., interfaces, storage, vector/probabilistic/feature spaces)
- Scenarios: system states and events; also representations of situations of use by human users or machine processes, yielding services or transformations of data (e.g., searching, browsing, recommending)
- Societies: both software "service managers" and generic "actors", including (collaborating) human "users" (e.g., service managers, teachers, learners)

5S gives a formal framework (see [5, 7]) and a checklist for digital library development. We can say that a digital library has all the necessary components if all of the Ss are considered in its specification [6]. This 5S framework also can be used to describe the nature of and relationships among the DL modules in this project. Each DL module component can be explained by one or multiple Ss. The 5S framework helps us ensure that we have precise definitions of all key ideas in the modules, and that all important concepts in the DL field are covered.

In addition to the 5S framework, we used the ACM / IEEE-CS Computing Curriculum 2001 [3, 4] to design the basic structure of the module development. It covers a variety of areas, including Information Management. 'IM14. Digital libraries [elective]' explains topics and learning objectives regarding digital library education.

Since DL is a young and evolving field, and since education is primarily a human endeavor, we are engaging DL researchers and practitioners in designing the DL curricular framework. Currently we have an advisory board that includes colleagues from VT (10 people, mostly from Computer Science), UNC (13 people, mostly from Library and Information Science), and several other institutions. At two advisory board meetings already held (one at VT and one in conjunction with JCDL '06), we discussed module development, and received suggestions regarding resource preparation. Some instructors agreed to participate in module content development, providing access to their class materials, or to use their classes as part of the later evaluation in the field.

3 Digital Library Module Development

Initially 19 DL modules (components) have been identified [17]. They have been revised further to reflect the discussions at advisory board meetings. For example, some modules were integrated into others and new modules were added to ensure coverage of costing and economics, project management, and DL evaluation. Currently, we have designed a module template, and are developing the lessons in each module.

Fig. 1 shows the set of DL modules as well as one possible way of grouping them into a two-semester DL sequence. The benefit of this 'modular' design is that instructors can use the modules to create a course (or course sequence or program – or can make enhancements to existing courses) to exactly match their purposes. Instructors might create a course based on a single module if it contains enough resources. They also can plug a single or multiple modules into their current courses. For example, "Module 3-b: multimedia" can be extended into a course including various aspects of multimedia resource creation, management, and evaluation. (A draft design of module 3-b is explained in Section 3.3.) "Module 1: Overview" and "Module 10: DL Education & Research" can be used together as an introductory lecture in any type of course that deals with the theoretical and technical issues of DLs.

3.1 Digital Library Modules

In some cases, multiple modules will form a DL course, while in other cases one or more courses might deal with a particular module. For example, in LIS programs, there might be several courses related to services. A typical LIS program might have distinct courses to cover modules 7, Services; 7-a, Information needs, relevance, evaluation, effectiveness; 7-b, Search and search strategy, information seeking behavior,

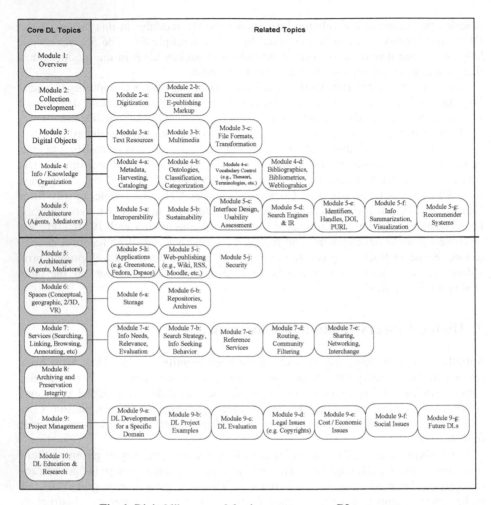

Fig. 1. Digital library modules in a two-semester DL sequence

user modeling, feedback; and 5-f, Information summarization, visualization. In CS, these topics might be covered in courses on information retrieval, human-computer interaction, and information visualization. Regarding DL architecture, for an LIS program the focus might be on DL design and management [15]. If the course is for CS students, the architecture module might focus on technical aspects of DLs. Thus, different versions of course modules may be needed for CS or LIS programs, and coverage might vary in accord with the level of students' knowledge.

To ensure this type of design, modules should be highly flexible and designed in detail. Each module should be decomposable into individual topics and their corresponding resources, so that some topics could be skipped or studied in different order. Clearly there will be revisions as we develop the content of each module and obtain feedback from experts and instructors. We will work to achieve wide coverage as well as balance between theory and practice, with various example digital libraries, and activities that involve use of many of the popular DL management systems.

3.2 Module Template Development

A module template was developed based on the educational experience of the research team, CC2001 [3, 4], and other resources [11, 12, 13]. The latest version of the template can be viewed online at http://curric.dlib.vt.edu/wiki/index.php/Module_template.

The current template design is as follows.

1. Module name
2. Level of effort required (in-class and out-of-class time required for students)
3. Learning objectives
4. Relationships with other modules (flow between modules)
5. 5S characteristics of the module
6. Prerequisite knowledge required (completion optional)
7. Introductory remedial instruction (completion optional; intended to address the prerequisite knowledge/skills required)
8. Resources (including all the resources in the 'Body of knowledge' section)
9. Body of knowledge (Theory + Practice):
    Topics might be skipped or studied in different orders
    For each topic:
    Theories and background knowledge of the topic
    Learning activities
    Presentation slides
    Interactive demo
    Resources
    - Textbooks (one or multiple chapters might be assigned)
    - Reference papers (relevant parts might be marked with SI tool [14])
    - Advanced reading
    Worksheets
10. Concept maps (created by students)
11. Exercises / Learning activities
12. Evaluation of learning outcomes
13. Glossary
14. Useful links

3.3 Module Preparation

The aim of module content development is to prepare high-quality study materials such as textbooks, reference papers, interactive demos, tutorials, and exercises (for evaluating students' understanding). There is more than one way to do this. Several advisory board experts expressed an interest in developing module examples with their class materials. Another way is to use publicly-available class materials. For example, we developed module 3-b (draft) based on Wake Forest University's 'Digital Media' curriculum materials [11]. These materials are based on work supported by the National Science Foundation.[2]

---

[2] NSF grants DUE-0127280 and DUE-0340969.

To provide study materials in good quality and quantity, we have been collecting and analyzing digital library course syllabi. We collected syllabi from DELOS member institutions in Europe (see Table 1) and retrieved resources such as textbooks, reference papers, online tutorials, software, and other documents (see Table 2).

Table 1. Selected DELOS member institutions with DL-related courses, and their resources listed (B = textbooks, reference books; P = reference papers, conference proceeding papers; O = online tutorials, articles)

Country	University/Institution	Course Title	B	P	O
Austria	Inst. for Info. Systems and Computer Media-IICM	Multimedia Information Systems 2	0	0	59
		Info. Visualisation	22	4	4
	Vienna Univ. of Technology	Info. Visualisierung	7	0	0
Czech Republic	Masaryk University of Brno	Informatics Colloquium	1	0	0
Germany	Max-Planck Institut für Informatik	Information Retrieval and Data Mining WS 05/06	18	0	0
Norway	Norwegian Univ. of Science and Technology	Information Retrieval	1	0	0

Table 2. Selected textbooks and reference books from the resources in Table 1

Topic	Title	Authors
Digital Library	From Gutenberg to Global Digital Libraries	Borgman, C.
Information Retrieval	Data Mining: Practical Machine Learning Tools and Techniques	Ian H. Witten, Eibe Frank
Archiving	Preserving Digital Information: Report of the Task Force on Archiving of Digital Information	Waters, D. et al.
Compression/ Indexing	Managing Gigabytes: Compressing and Indexing Documents and Images	Ian H. Witten
Database/ Multimedia	Multimedia Database Management Systems	G. Lu
Information Visualization	Information Visualization in Data Mining and Knowledge Discovery	Fayyad et al.

3.4 DL Literature and Syllabi Analyses

We also have analyzed published literature on DLs and readings assigned in courses on DLs. We used two corpora for the analysis of published literature: the complete runs of ACM Conference on Digital Libraries, JCDL, and D-Lib Magazine (Pomerantz et al., 2006). This analysis has identified that the greatest number of papers have been published on the topic of DL services and architecture, both in the conferences and in D-Lib. These results demonstrate that there are significant similarities within the literature on digital library across different venues. There are, however, shifts in topical coverage over the years.

For the analysis of course readings, we identified all materials assigned in DL courses in Library and Information Science programs accredited by the American Library Association (Pomerantz et al., in press). This analysis has identified the most frequently-assigned authors, books, journal articles, and journal titles in these courses. Additionally, like the analysis of published literature on DLs, this reading list analysis has identified that the greatest number of readings are assigned on the topics of project management and architecture. We are currently working on a similar analysis of reading lists from DL courses in Computer Science programs.

3.5 Example Modules (Draft)

While the DL modules are still in the early stages of development, a few examples may illustrate our conception of the finished modules. Fig. 2 shows a portion of the 'Body of Knowledge' for module 3-b: Multimedia, hypertext, and information access. It is based on Wake Forest University's work, "Digital Media Curriculum Development." The complete version can be viewed at http://curric.dlib.vt.edu/wiki/index. php/Module_3b.

---

5. Digital Audio Processing
- Pretest (grade does not count)
- Study online text **Chapter 5** but you can skip 5.5.4 and 5.5.5
- Carry out activities
  1. **Interactive tutorial on audio dithering** but note on the first question, there is a typo in that they want 64536 instead of the correct value, 65536.
  2. **Worksheet on audio dithering**, where you should turn in the Matlab log, but only do Exercises 1,2,3,4 and Question 1,2, and 6. Also, note the typo for Question 1 where "O" should be "Exercise 2."
  3. **Worksheet on digital audio file size and file transfer time**
  4. **Interactive tutorial on non-linear quantization and mu-law encoding**
  5. **Worksheet on non-linear quantization and mu-law encoding**
- Posttest (grade counts to demonstrate level of mastery)

Fig. 2. A portion of 'Body of Knowledge' section in module 10

In order to understand the topic, 'Digital Audio Processing,' students select the link and read some online text (in this case, chapter 5). They follow steps in the interactive tutorial created with Shockwave (see Fig. 3). Then they can check their level of understanding, solving the problems in worksheets. A score may be assigned to individual worksheets by the in\structor. In this type of module design, an instructor remains as an 'advisor' or a 'helper' as students study materials themselves.

Module 7-a, Information needs, relevance, evaluation/effectiveness, provides a different type of example (see Fig. 4). The complete module 7-a is at http://curric.dlib. vt.edu/wiki/index.php/Module_7a. Instead of using interactive tutorials or online book chapters, a selected list of reference papers are used (we are preparing this resource collection), including papers on different theoretical models of information seeking written by Wilson, Belkin and Vickery, Belkin, and Taylor. These and additional readings can be assigned to students and/or used by instructors in their preparation for teaching the module. The 'Outline of knowledge' closely follows the content of the

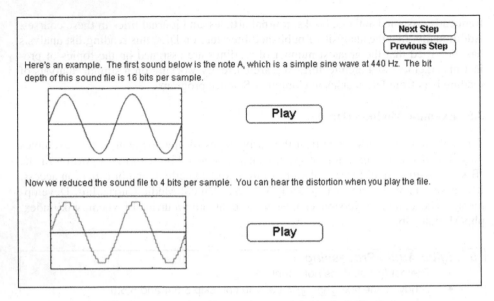

Fig. 3. An example of interactive tutorial, 'Audio Dithering'

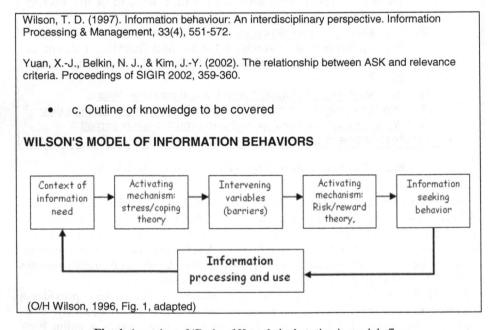

Fig. 4. A portion of 'Body of Knowledge' section in module 7-a

readings, and can be used as the basis for a lecture based on the given outline. Fig. 5 shows a 'Learning activity' within this module, in which students are asked to discuss the introduced topics in pairs.

Discussion activity: Personal experiences of an information need *To immediately follow the review of Wilson's generalized model of information behavior* Students in the class should be formed into pairs. In each pair, one student will interview the other. (This process should later be repeated, reversing roles.) The person being interviewed should be asked to recall a recent experience of having an information need. The interviewer should ask about the content of the information need, the context in which it arose, and the process through which it was pursued (successfully or unsuccessfully). The pair should then evaluate what was learned about this example of an information need and see if Wilson's model fully describes the process. Were there aspects of the information-seeking episode that are not covered in Wilson's model? Are there aspects of Wilson's model that did not occur during this information-seeking episode?

Fig. 5. A sample learning activity from module 14

4   Conclusion and Future Work

The collaborative VT-UNC DL curriculum development project is in the first of its three years, and module design is well underway, supported by the 5S framework and an analysis of CC 2001 and existing DL course syllabi. It is our hope that the international DL community will become involved in this interdisciplinary effort, and that its result will be improvement in the education of DL professionals.

References

1. Collaborative Research: Curriculum Development for Digital Library Education, 2006. Website URL is http://curric.dlib.vt.edu/wiki
2. Kent L. Gustafson and Robert Maribe Branch: Survey of Instructional Development Models (3rd ed.). Syracuse University, Syracuse, New York (1997)
3. CC2001, "Computing Curricula 2001 (Web Site)," vol. 2004: ACM and IEEE-CS, 2001. http://www.computer.org/education/cc2001
4. CC2001, "Computing Curricula 2001: Computer Science (IEEE Computer Society and Association for Computing Machinery Joint Task Force on Computing Curricula)," Journal on Educational Resources in Computing (JERIC), vol. 1, 2001. http://doi.acm.org/10.1145/384274.384275
5. M. A. Gonçalves, "Streams, Structures, Spaces, Scenarios, and Societies (5S): A Formal Digital Library Framework and Its Applications," Computer Science Doctoral Dissertation. Blacksburg, VA: Virginia Tech, 2004, 161 pages. http://scholar.lib.vt.edu/theses/available/etd-12052004-135923/unrestricted/MarcosDissertation.pdf
6. M. A. Gonçalves and E. A. Fox, "5SL - A Language for Declarative Specification and Generation of Digital Libraries," in Proc. JCDL'2002, Second ACM / IEEE-CS Joint Conference on Digital Libraries, July 14-18, G. Marchionini, Ed. Portland, Oregon, USA: ACM, 2002, pp. 263-272.

7. M. Gonçalves, E. Fox, L. Watson, and N. Kipp, "Streams, Structures, Spaces, Scenarios, Societies (5S): A Formal Model for Digital Libraries," ACM Transactions on Information Systems, vol. 22, pp. 270-312, 2004.

8. H. Suleman and E. A. Fox, "A Framework for Building Open Digital Libraries," D-Lib Magazine, vol. 7, 2001. http://www.dlib.org/dlib/december01/suleman/12suleman.html

9. H. Suleman, E. A. Fox, and M. Abrams, "Building Quality into a Digital Library," in Proceedings of the Fifth ACM Conference on Digital Libraries: DL '00, June 2-7, 2000, San Antonio, TX. New York: ACM Press, 2000.

10. Q. Zhu, "5SGraph: A Modeling Tool for Digital Libraries," Department of Computer Science MS thesis. Blacksburg: Virginia Tech, 2002. http://scholar.lib.vt.edu/theses/available/etd-11272002-21053

11. Yue-Ling Wong, Jennifer Burg, and Leah McCoy, "Integrated Digital Media Curriculum Development Project" Supported by the National Science Foundation under Grant No. DUE-0340969, from Jan 2004 - Dec 2006. The project homepage URL is http://digitalmedia.wfu.edu/project/digital-media-curriculum-development/textbased-index.html

12. Ze-Nian Li and Mark S. Drew, 2006, "Fundamentals of Multimedia" at http://www.cs.sfu.ca/mmbook/

13. Multimedia Systems course website, Department of Computer Science at University of Victoria, British Columbia, Canada, 2006. URL: http://www.csc.uvic.ca/courses/spring 2004/csc/461-561.html

14. The Superimposed Project at Virginia Tech, Blacksburg, VA, 2006. URL: http://si.dlib.vt.edu/

15. Youngok Choi and Edie Rasmussen, "What Do Digital Librarians Do?" in Proceedings of the Sixth ACM/IEEE-CS Joint Conference on Digital Libraries: JCDL '06, June 11-15, 2006, Chapel Hill, NC. USA: ACM, pp. 187-188.

16. Yongqing Ma, Warwick Clegg and Ann O'Brien, "Digital Library Education: The Current Status," in Proceedings of the Sixth ACM/IEEE-CS Joint Conference on Digital Libraries: JCDL '06, June 11-15, 2006, Chapel Hill, NC. USA: ACM, pp. 165-174.

17. Pomerantz, J., Wildemuth, B., Fox, E. A., & Yang, S. (2006). Curriculum Development for igital Libraries. In Proceedings of the 6th ACM/IEEE-CS Joint Conference on Digital Libraries (pp. 175-184). New York: Association for Computing Machinery.

18. Pomerantz, J., Oh, S., Yang, S., Fox, E. A., & Wildemuth, B. (in press). The Core: Digital Library Education in Library and Information Science Programs. D-Lib Magazine.

A Digital Resource Harvesting Approach for Distributed Heterogeneous Repositories

Yang Zhao and Airong Jiang

Tsinghua University Library
Beijing, China 100084
{zhaoyang, jiangar}@lib.tsinghua.edu.cn

Abstract. OAI-PMH has been widely adopted as a simple solution for harvesting the metadata of different repositories automatically. Harvesting digital resources described by the metadata is outside of the scope of the OAI-PMH data model. However, there are some growing needs to make resources, not only metadata, harvestable by an interoperable manner in the distributed heterogeneous environments. In this paper, we present the new approach of digital resource harvesting, which uses Message Queue-based communication mechanism as the datastream transfer method, and ensures the request and response message specification built on METS during the course of data transfer. The approach can harvest digital resources solely or synergically with OAI-PMH. A case study about this approach applied in CALIS_ETD digital library will be introduced in the end.

Keywords: OAI-PMH; Message Queue; Digital Resource Harvesting; METS.

1 Introduction

The Open Archives Protocol for Metadata Harvesting (OAI-PMH) has been widely adopted as a simple and powerful solution for metadata harvesting. There are many digital library systems and projects to use OAI-PMH to harvest metadata held by different repositories into central systems as a basis for building the value-added services, e.g., NDLTD, OAIster, NSDL, arXiv, etc. However, there are some growing needs to make resources, not only metadata, harvestable by an interoperable manner in the distributed heterogeneous environments. These needs are motivated by two major use cases. One is mainly for resource discovery in order to use content itself for providing value-added services of central systems, such as making full-text from different repositories searchable, or building browsing interfaces of high-quality thumbnail images. Another is mainly for resource preservation in central systems, such as harvesting digital contents from different repositories to the trusted central systems charged with storing and preserving safety copies of the contents. Both use cases have been discussed in the context of digital library projects, such as JISC FAIR in UK, DARE in Netherlands, DINI in Germany, NDIIPP in USA and so on [1].

Although OAI-PMH does not say anything about how to harvest digital resources described by the metadata, resource harvesting is associated with metadata harvesting

S. Sugimoto et al. (Eds.): ICADL 2006, LNCS 4312, pp. 71–80, 2006.

to some extent. For example, we can harvest resources according to the returned information of metadata harvesting or expand the scope of descriptive metadata to be more than just DC and similar bibliographic formats in order to be compatible with existing OAI-supported repositories. In nature, resource harvesting is more complex than metadata harvesting because of the complexity of digital resources that include many kinds of digital file formats (i.e., PDFs, GIFs, TIFFs, AVIs, etc.) or the ordered combination of many files (such as an E-book is made of many TIFF files).

There are some existing methods for indirectly harvesting digital resources. For example, the reference [1] puts forward to harvest resources within the OAI-PMH framework by means of complex and expressive metadata formats (i.e. SCORM, MPEG-21 DIDL or METS, etc.) to represent digital objects by embedding a base64 encoding or the network location of digital resources inside the wrapper XML document. However, it is difficult for a simple HTTP-based request-response to solve large datastream harvesting or transfer failures caused by the network congestion. References [2-3] emphasize on harvesting the network location of digital resources within the DC metadata record by some DC elements such as dc.format, dc.relation or dc.identifier. A separate process outside the scope of OAI-PMH collects the described resources from their network location. But this method does not provide the general mechanism for describing and gathering resources from their network location.

In order to make digital resource harvesting general and compatible with widely deployed OAI-supported repositories, and tackle many complicated problems caused by resource harvesting, we put forward an alternative approach to harvest digital resources in this paper. The proposed approach is based on METS (Metadata Encoding and Transmission Standard) that possesses sufficiently rigorous semantics to unambiguously express and describe both simple digital objects (consisting of a single datastream) and compound digital objects (consisting of multiple datastreams), which represent digital resources from different repositories. And the approach also discusses request-response communication mechanism based on MQ (Message Queue) between Data Providers (DPs) and Service Providers (SPs) for improving the security and efficiency of datastream exchange and transfer. The rest of the paper is as follows: Section 2 gives an overview of the approach. Section 3 introduces the implementation of the approach in the CALIS-ETD digital library. Section 4 gives the conclusion and future works.

2   An Overview of the Approach About Digital Resource Harvesting

Digital resource harvesting is concerned with some complicated problems, such as how to describe compound digital objects and their relationship, how to deal with transfer of large datastream representing digital resources and so on. Considering such complexity, the proposed approach discusses some key points about resource harvesting. We use MQ as the data transfer method in order to improve safety of data transfer and solve large datastream transfer. Also we ensure the message content specification during data transfer by MQ mechanism, which includes request message specification based on 5 verbs defined by CALIS (the China Academic Library & Information System) technology workgroup, and response message specification built on METS as complex object formats for accurately describing digital resources.

Like the OAI-PMH, we define two classes of participants including data providers (DPs) and service providers (SPs). DPs administer repositories that exposing digital resources. SPs harvest digital resources from DPS as a basis of building value-added services. MQ (Message Queue) applications are deployed and implemented between SPs and DPs in order to provide the two-way communication between them. Figure1 shows the architecture of digital resource harvesting. 1) When SP sends messages (request for resource harvesting) to DP, the MQ manger in DP puts request messages on message queue. 2) The message processing thread in DP is called whenever there is a new message on message queue, receives messages from the top of queue and orderly processes messages on queue one at a time.3) According to request messages, thread creates response message queue by communicating with metadata repository and digital object server in DP. Each response message consists of a XML document

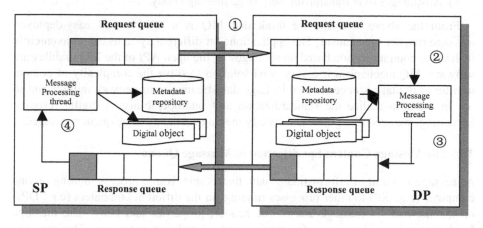

Fig. 1. Architecture of digital resource harvesting

format based on METS encoding schema that can describe and encapsulate digital resources and theirs metadata. 4) Finally, the message processing thread in SP read response messages and put digital resources and their metadata harvested into central metadata repository and digital object server. In the approach, message reception and message processing are decoupled and receiving a message takes very little time, even when processing the message may take significant time. This improves application responsiveness and guarantees that all messages are received.

2.1 Message Queue Transfer Mechanism

The message queue is reliable and asynchronous communication technology that enables applications on different systems to communicate with each other. With the message queue middleware software (such as OpenJMS or MSMQ), the process of building message queue applications between senders and receivers of message is simple and convenient. The application in senders uses the open API to create message on queue by allocating local memory and adding information to the message, such as timeout values, name of response queues and destination queues etc. The messages are sent through open API. The application in receivers uses the open API with queue identification information to receive and handle messages. MQ technology has following main features:

1) Synchronous or asynchronous communication: The applications can send request messages whether the receiving systems are available or not.
2) Reliable message transfer: MQ enables applications on different systems to communicate with each other even if systems and networks occasionally fail. MQ, using disk-based storage mechanisms and log-based recovery techniques, can ensure that messages get delivered as soon as connections are restored or applications and machines are restarted.
3) Advantages over transferring very large message body.

From the above analysis, we think that MQ is a reliable and easy-deployed message transfer mechanism. The applications on different systems can conveniently realize the communication based on messages by the open API of the MQ middleware software. MQ mechanism is a very good solution to solve the complexity of content transfer of digital resources caused by large datastream size or network failures and so on. In order to realize the standardization and interoperability of digital resource harvesting, we need to regulate and specify message content on the queue messages.

2.2 The Message Content Specification in Message Queue

A message is a unit of information or data that is sent from a process running on one computer (e.g., SP) to other processes running on the different computers (e.g., DPs) on the network. A message consists of header, properties and body. The message header contains values used for routing and identifying messages. The message properties provide additional information about data sent between SPs and DPs, for example, which processes create it, the time it is created etc. The message body contains data content of communications. In the approach, the message body mainly includes request and response content of resource harvesting between DPs and SPs. We specify and standardize content of the message body in the architecture of digital resources harvesting.

5 verbs were defined by CALIS for request of digital resource harvesting in message body. According to request, response content in message body is XML datastream based on METS schema to describe digital resources and their metadata. Table1 lists the functions of 5 verbs and their relationship with OAI-PMH, which can harvest digital resources solely or synergically with OAI-PMH. The former 3 verbs will cooperate with OAI metadata harvesting. Harvester of digital resources in SPs create request according to the information that OAI harvesters return, such as metadata datestamp or MetaID. The latter 2 verbs will lonely establish request of resource harvesting by digital object's ObjID or datastamp, and do not need to cooperate with harvesting based on OAI [4]. A MetaID can uniquely identify a digital resource and may include several ObjIDs, each of which represents the different files consisting of

a digital resource. For example, a scanned E-book has a MetaID and many ObjIDs to represent JPG files corresponding to each page of an E-book. For existing OAI framework, we only need add module of digital resource harvesting, rather than modify the existing OAI repository deployment.

Figure 2 demonstrates the request and response content in message body. The request in SP will send one of the 5 verbs to DP according to requirement of harvesting. DP processes request and send response messages to SP, which will handle harvested METS document. METS provides the expressive and accurate mechanism for representing both simple digital objects or compound digital objects, describing a variety of information pertaining to the datastream, such as descriptive, administrative and structural metadata, etc, and containing datastream by value embedding a base64 encoding of datastream or by reference embedding the network location of datastream inside the wapper XML document. So message response based on METS can provide the useful standard for harvesting and gathering of digital objects between DP and SP [5].

Table 1. 5 verbs for request message of digital resource harvesting

Verbs	Description of functions	Relationship with OAI
GetMetsItem	Get a digital object according to a metadata MetaID	Cooperating with OAI harvesting
GetMetsItems	Get a set of digital objects according to a set of metadata MetaIDs	
GetMetsItemByDate	Get a set of digital objects according to the specified datestamp bound	
GetObjMetsItem	Get a digital object according to a digital object's ObjID	Independently finishing harvesting tasks
GetObjMetsItems	Get a set of digital objects according to a set of digital object's ObjIDs	

3 A Case Study: Application of the Proposed Approach in CALIS-ETD Digital Library

3.1 General Information About CALIS-ETD Digital Library [6]

CALIS-ETD digital library is national digital library project funded by CALIS, and aims at making the electronic thesis and dissertation (ETD) resources become more readily and more completely available and speeding up technology and knowledge sharing. It is a distributed digital library system that consists of central CALIS-ETD system as SP and ETD resource repositories as DPs distributed in the member universities. The central CALIS-ETD system will centrally manage the ETD metadata or digital resources related to ETDs (such as first 16 pages of full-text ETDs, some technical datasheet, audio or video of ETDs, etc.) harvested from member universities. We cannot harvest full-text ETDs into central system because of the copyright restriction. The full-text search engine in the central system can abstract the index of ETDs (such as first 16 pages of full-text ETDs, etc.) harvested and enable them and metadata to be searchable. By the OPENURL or URN resolver, users in the central system can link obtained records to their corresponding full-text ETDs in member universities, whose access right is respectively controlled by each member university. We use the proposed approach based on the MQ transfer mechanism and message content specification based on METS to realize ETDs harvesting between the central system and 77 member universities of CALIS-ETD project.

Request message content

<? xml version="1.0" encoding="UTF-8">
<Mets>
  <MetsRequest>
    <verb>GetMetsItem</Verb>
    <MetaID>oai:calis.edu.cn:etd:student001
    </MetaID>

Request message content

```
<METS:fileSec>
  <METS:fileGrp>
  <METS:file       MIMETYPE="image/jpeg"       ID="Meta6_Obj1.Type1.format"
        SIZE="1024" USE="file 描述信息" ADMID="ADM1">
      <METS:FContent>
          <METS:binData>using base64-encoding</METS:binData>
      </METS:FContent>
  </METS:file>
  <METS:file MIMETYPE="PDF" ID="Meta6_Obj1.Type2.format" SIZE="1209"
        USE="file 描述信息">
      <METS:FLocat   LOCTYPE="OTHER"   OTHERLOCTYPE="CALISOID"
      xlink:href="urn:CALIS:0000-CollectionName/Meta6_Obj1.Type2.format" />
      <METS:Flocat                                           LOCTYPE="URL"
          xlink:href="http://www.calis.edu.cn/Collect/Meta6_Obj1_Type2.format" />
  </METS:file></METS:fileGrp>
  </METS:fileSec>
  <METS:structMap TYPE="leaf">
  <METS:div LABEL="元数据 6">
      <METS:div LABEL="对象 6-1" ORDER="1" TYPE="obj">
          <METS:fptr FILEID="Meta6_Obj1.Type1.format" />
          <METS:fptr FILEID="Meta6_Obj1.Type2.format" />
      </METS:div>
  </METS:div>
  </METS:structMap>
```

Fig. 2. The request and response content in message body

3.2 Module Design for Digital Resource Harvesting in Member Universities as DPs

To make ETD repositories in the member universities support resource harvesting, it is necessary to add the module of resource harvesting in order to support the message queue and METS message response mechanism. Figure 3 shows the main module for accomplishing functions of resource harvesting as DPs.

1) The listener thread will listen the message request queue from harvesters, resolve the request and put MetaIDs into the MetaID global List container in the memory queue manager. MetaID global List container will orderly get a MetaID from list and submit the MetaID to METS package creating thread, which transfer MetaID to the interface of repositories (databases) and digital object servers.

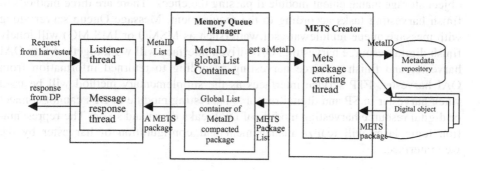

Fig. 3. The main module of digital resource harvesting as DP

2) METS package creating thread will create METS encoding datastream according to the returned information from repositories and digital object servers, which will be compacted for lessening the size of datastream. Each of compacted package of METS encoding datastream will be put in the global List container of MetaID compacted package in the memory queue manager. The message response thread will orderly send the METS compacted package representing digital resources as response messages to SP [4].

Most of member universities choose one of four types of commercial ETD repository systems that the project recommends as their local ETD repositories, which not only need to finish basic functions of managing ETDs, such as submitting, checking, cataloging, searching ETDs, etc, but also need to support OAI-PMH for metadata harvesting and the proposed approach for resource harvesting. For existing earlier ETD repositories that does not support resource harvesting, it is convenient to upgrade them to realize resource harvesting by installing plug-in because module of resource harvesting is independently designed and deployed [6].

3.3 Harvester Design in the Central System as SPs

The central system of CALIS_ETD digital library is developed in Java, using JDBC for database connectivity to ORACLE data source. The web interface is accomplished using Java servlets. Figure 4 shows main module of harvester. The storage layer centrally manages metadata and digital resources harvested from repositories in member universities by ORACLE Databases and digital object servers. The business logic layer is the core of harvester, which including several modules. DP registration module is charged with managing and maintaining the registration information of DPs in the member universities. Log module records log information of harvesting, such as how many records are harvested in certain time bound, what errors happened about harvesting, etc. The schema check module will examine correctness of METS packages, which will be put into the database by the digital object storage management module if passing the check. There are three methods to finish harvesting tasks according to the requirement. Message Queue server along with message queue middleware software (such as MSMQ or JMS MQ) will lonely finish digital resource harvesting. OAI-driven interface will work together with OAI harvester and finish resource harvesting according to returned information from OAI harvester. FTP service interfaces as the supplementary method will be used when harvester in SP and digital resource harvesting module in DPs cannot connect or digital resource harvesting module of DP breaks down and so on. The representation logic layer will realize management and configuration of harvester by the web interface.

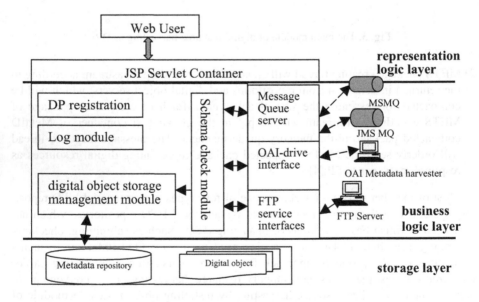

Fig. 4. The main module of harvester

The web configuration interface of harvester for creating tasks of resource harvesting is shown in Figure 5. The window of interface is divided into three parts. In the upper part, we can configure the time bound of harvesting tasks, automatic setup time of harvest tasks, running counts of each harvest task or timeout bound of harvesting. In the middle part, we may configure information related to DPs, such as repository names, IP addresses or service ports of DPs, etc. The lower part focuses on the information associated with MQ configuration, such as message queue name, MQ type and port of MQ service, etc.

3.4 Performance Evaluation of Harvesting

We take two phases to test the proposed approach and improve performance of resource harvesting. In the first phases, the main aim is to test feasibility of the approach by test programs to test prototype systems designed according to the proposed approach. The test uses the metadata and digital objects conforming to the specification required by the project, and is limited within small areas, which can ignore influence of network congestion or interruption. During the test, the approach is gradually amended and improved. In the second phases, we firstly choose about 20 member universities with better experience of managing ETDs and upgrade their existing ETD repositories or installing new ETD systems for supporting resource harvesting. Within two months, we have successfully harvested ETDs up to 60,000 records from repositories of about 20 member universities. The proposed approach is proved to be feasible. Of course, many problems are encountered during the course of real harvesting, such as unexpected interruption of harvest tasks or timeout error, poor data quality for lacking of better data validation mechanism, performance of harvesting partly influenced by capability of ETD repositories in DPs, frequent backend Oracle database down caused by synchronous running multi-tasks for harvesting, etc. So we need to gradually improve the performance of harvester in SP and ETD repositories in DPs according to problems that we have encountered.

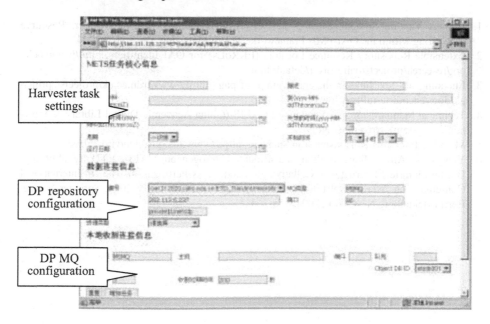

Fig. 5. The web configuration interface of harvester

4 Conclusion and Future Works

In this paper, we first analyze shortcomings of some existing methods of digital resource harvesting and put forward to an alternative approach about resource harvesting. The approach is based on the Message Queue transfer mechanism to ensure the security, reliability and efficiency of datastream transfer. We also specify and standardize message request specification including 5 verbs, and message response specification built on the METS encoding to describe complex digital resources, their metadata and relationship between them. Because of the flexibility and scalability of METS, the approach supports any types of digital resources from any distributed heterogeneous repositories. For example, the CALIS special resource digital library project also uses the approach to harvest the special Chinese resource from repositories of the member universities, such as rarebooks, ancient atlas, rubbings ancient genealogy and chorography and so on. And the approach, which is compatible with the well specified and widely applied OAI-PMH, make its deployment simple and general for existing OAI-PMH implementations.

Our work will continue in following some aspects. The first aspect will focus on improving performance of harvester, such as error warning, harvest interruption handle, detailed log and statistics analysis of harvested data and so on. The second aspect will be concerned with developing data quality check tool to verify and enhance the data quality of harvested digital resources.

References

1. Herbert Van de Sompel, Michael L. Nelson, Carl Lagoze, Simeon Warner. Resource Harvesting within the OAI-PMH Framework., D-Lib Magazine, December 2004
2. Extensible Repository Resource Locators (ERRoLs) for OAI Identifiers, http://www.oclc.org/research/projects/oairesolver/default.htm
3. Encoding full-text links in the eprint jump-off page, http://www.rdn.ac.uk/projects/eprints-uk/docs/encoding-fulltext-links/
4. Technical Standards & specifications of CALIS (China Academic Digital Library & Information System). November 2004.
5. Metadata Encoding & Transmission Standard, http://www.loc.gov/standards/mets/
6. Yang Zhao, Airong Jiang: Building a distributed heterogeneous CALIS_ETD digital library. Digital Libraries: International Collarboration and Cross-Fertilization. The 7th International Conference on Asia Digital Libraries. Shanghai, China, Dec 13-17 2004, Springer-Verlag, Berlin Heidelberg New York, 2004, 155-164.

Parallelising Harvesting

Hussein Suleman

Department of Computer Science, University of Cape Town
Private Bag, Rondebosch, 7701, South Africa
hussein@cs.uct.ac.za

Abstract. Metadata harvesting has become a common technique to transfer a stream of data from one metadata repository or digital library system to another. As collections of metadata, and their associated digital objects, grow in size, the ingest of these items at the destination archive can take a significant amount of time, depending on the type of indexing or post-processing that is required. This paper discusses an approach to parallelise the post-processing of data in a small cluster of machines or a multi-processor environment, while not increasing the burden on the source data provider. Performance tests have been carried out on varying architectures and the results indicate that this technique is indeed promising for some scenarios and can be extended to more computationally-intensive ingest procedures. In general, the technique presents a new approach for the construction of harvest-based distributed or component-based digital libraries, with better scalability than before.

1 Introduction

Digital library (DL) systems are rapidly growing in popularity as the technology matures and also because of the advocacy of groups such as the Open Access and Electronic Thesis and Dissertation communities. The effect of this popularity is that there are now more accessible collections, growing at relatively high rates - Lyman and Varian [10] estimated 5 exabytes of new digital information in 2002 alone!

There is a need for tools to manage these large and growing collections and meta-collections and make them accessible to the relevant audiences. However, these tools are not readily available and popular DL systems do not always scale appropriately [7] [6]. While much research has gone into the scalability of Web-delivered DL content (see, for example, [1]), access to services is only one dimension of the management tasks, which typically also include internal data processing for classification, preservation-related manipulation and ingest procedures.

At the same time, digital library tools need to be accessible to users and managers of collections of varying sizes. Keeping this in mind, this study has looked at how the current nature of harvesting of metadata, a popular first step in ingest mechanisms, can be recast to better scale with changes in underlying machine architectures. While harvesting is only one small part of a larger DL

S. Sugimoto et al. (Eds.): ICADL 2006, LNCS 4312, pp. 81–90, 2006.
© Springer-Verlag Berlin Heidelberg 2006

architecture, its operation can be parallelised with immediate benefits, without any changes to the data flow that may be needed when other services are parallelised.

2   Background

2.1   Metadata Harvesting

The Open Archives Initiative Protocol (OAI) created the Protocol for Metadata Harvesting (PMH) as a low barrier mechanism for computer systems to exchange metadata on a periodic basis [8] [9].

Metadata is encoded in XML and the exchanges happen as a layer over the HTTP protocol. The owner of the metadata is referred to as the data provider and the provider of services based on this data is referred to as the service provider. The act of transferring metadata from the data provider to the service provider is referred to as harvesting - thus the service provider operates a software tool called a harvester in order to initiate and control the process of harvesting metadata from the data provider.

Harvesting works as follows:

- The service provider executes its harvester to harvest metadata from a data provider. If metadata has not been harvested before, the harvester requests all metadata in a specified format.
- The data provider returns as much metadata as it can reasonably handle and sends back an opaque token, called a resumptionToken, to the harvester as a placeholder for more records.
- The harvester passes the records on to the service provider for ingest into the service provider's system.
- If the harvester encounters a resumptionToken at the end of the record stream, it sends a subsequent request to the data provider with this token as a parameter.
- The data provider sends back an additional chunk of records and a new token if necessary. This process continues in a cycle until all records have been transferred.
- When all records have been transferred, the harvester terminates its activities.
- At regular intervals afterwards, the service provider invokes the harvester to obtain records that have changed since the previous harvesting operation (by specifying the date of that operation). Every harvesting operation uses tokens as before to break up the responses into manageable pieces.

While this algorithm is partly sequential, some of the steps can clearly be carried out in parallel. Before the algorithm can be recast as a parallel one, it is necessary to investigate popular machine architectures that can support such parallelisation.

2.2   High Performance Computing

The following approaches to high performance (parallel) computing were considered for this work:

- Grid computing: refers to collaborative use of computers in a WAN or on the Internet to solve large problems. The EU-based DILIGENT project is investigating the adoption of grids for DL systems [4].
- Multi-processor/core machines: refers to single machines with multiple CPUs and/or multiple processing cores in each CPU. This is an ideal architecture for data-intensive operations such as indexing [1], but arbitrary scaling of the number of processors is usually not possible or prohibitively expensive.
- Beowulf cluster [3]: refers to a collection of machines all in the same location, connected to a high-speed LAN.

During the experimental phase, tests were conducted on a Beowulf cluster and a dual-CPU machine. Grid computing was not considered because of the requirement of a sufficiently fast underlying network, which is not available in the country where this research was conducted (and by extrapolation in some other countries where DL systems are used).

For the cluster it was also necessary to select an appropriate system software layer. openMosix [2] was chosen because it transparently makes a cluster appear as one large system, with no special programming or use of libraries. openMosix is a set of operating system tools that transparently migrate processes to balance the load across all nodes. It allows the use of standard System V IPC mechanisms (message queues, UNIX domain pairs, etc.) for synchronisation, therefore there would be no differences in the software that runs on openMosix, a multi-processor or a uniprocessor machine. In order to make best use of openMosix, however, software applications should be designed as a collaborating set of smaller processes (thus enabling migration of some of them). This technique is similarly an enabler for multi-CPU machines.

3   Parallel Harvesting

3.1   Basic Technique

Most data providers are production-mode digital library systems, with OAI-PMH support as an auxiliary service so processing multiple requests in parallel may be disallowed. Even if possible, there is no mechanism in OAI-PMH to request evenly-sized chunks of records - dates and sets may both be non-uniformly distributed within a collection. The only way to split a stream of records into reasonably-sized chunks is to rely on the data provider to do this by means of its resumptionToken mechanism.

In a parallel harvester, each process requests a chunk of records and passes the resumptionToken to an idle peer so it can get its own data and repeat the process until there are no more resumptionTokens.

A lightweight job scheduler serves not only to distribute harvesting jobs but also to intersperse those with post-harvesting data processing activities, wherever those can be parallelised as well, e.g., merging of sub-indices for a parallel-index-serial-query search engine.

Figure 1 illustrates the process of parallel harvesting and shows the various actors as described. In the illustration each process is depicted as being passed the token in sequence but in practice the scheduler will give the token to whichever node is currently idle (or randomly choose from among the idle nodes if more than one).

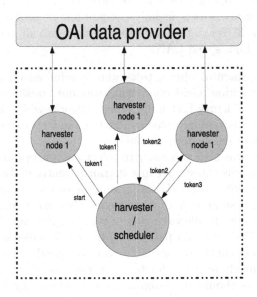

Fig. 1. Parallel harvester components and interaction

3.2   Distribution and Synchronisation

When harvesting begins, multiple processes are spawned(using fork). These processes are distributed as necessary to the various CPUs or cluster nodes (worker nodes) by the operating system, in a best effort to balance the load without application-specific information. Processes were chosen over threads because threads cannot be easily migrated in some parallel architectures.

The scheduler uses a work pool and processor farm approach to manage jobs [11]. The work pool is initialised to contain the usual first harvesting operation to obtain all records that have been changed since the date of the last harvest. The scheduler also maintains a set of flags to indicate which worker processes are busy. When there is at least one idle worker process and at least one job in the pool, the job is dispatched to the worker process (using a unix socket for communication). The worker process will then harvest the next chunk of data from the data provider and send the resumptionToken back to the scheduler as soon as it is obtained. The worker continues to process the data (e.g., create indices or reformat for ingestion) and sends a message to the scheduler when it is done with the job. The scheduler, in the meanwhile, could have signalled another worker process to deal with the new job that is in its pool. Thus, if the post-processing of data is time-consuming, the scheduler ensures that this is done in parallel, while the harvesting operations do not themselves overlap.

Figure 2 shows the overlapping of harvesting and processing operations in a parallel harvester, as compared to the traditional sequential harvester. Jobs with significant time spent on post-processing fare better in the parallel scenario.

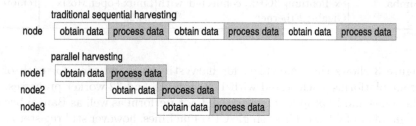

Fig. 2. Timing of sequential and parallel harvesting

4   Evaluation

In order to evaluate the efficiency of parallel harvesting, the platform was varied and tests were conducted for varying numbers of worker processes. Since the aim of this work was to support parallel harvesting irrespective of the underlying architecture, the operating system did all task allocation and/or migration implicitly.

Table 1 lists the different platforms used during testing and how they differed. The last column refers to whether or not the OAI-PMH data provider was on the same machine (if there was a single machine). Machine4 is so named because it is a single machine within the Simba cluster.

4.1   Typical Performance

First, each platform was tested with a harvester that performed inverted file indexing of the metadata, with each metadata chunk kept independent and the inverted files written to disk after processing. Indices were created for each metadata field as well as the whole record, and for individual stemmed and stopped words as well as the whole contents of each field. This is a typical first operation performed by the indexing portion of a search engine.

For the Machine4 and Simba platforms, the data was stored remotely using NFS. All other platforms stored the data locally.

Table 1. List of platforms, and their characteristics, used for experiments

Name	Machine Description	OS	Data Source
Laptop	Centrino 1.5GHz	Linux 2.6.12	local
Banzai Local	Dual Pentium 3GHz	FreeBSD 6.0	local
Banzai	Dual Pentium 3GHz	FreeBSD 6.0	remote
Machine4	Pentium 3GHz	Linux 2.4.26	remote
Simba	8x Pentium 3GHz, connected with Gigabit Ethernet	Linux+openMosix 2.4.26	remote

Figure 3 shows the time taken for harvesting and indexing for each of the different platforms, each tested with 1, 2, 4, 8, 16 and 32 worker processes.

Machine4 and Laptop, as expected, did not perform as well as Banzai because of the number of CPUs. These single CPU machines, however still register an improvement in performance when multiple processes are executed simultaneously, presumably because of the overlapping of IO with computation.

Banzai and Local Banzai take approximately half the time of their single CPU counterparts. When the number of processes increases drastically, Banzai performs better, probably due once again to Local Banzai having to serve its own data provider in addition to its harvesting and indexing operations.

Having 8 CPUs, it could be expected that Simba will provide the best performance at all times. However, the data communication when processes are migrated to other nodes takes its toll, especially when there are few processes and the load is not high. For a very small number of processes, openMosix has more idle processors than busy ones so spends a lot of time moving processes around, without taking into account that processes may have substantial data footprints as well. As the number of processes increases, it is easier for openMosix to spread the load and maintain this even spread without further migrations. Thus, for more than 4 processes, Simba outperforms the single CPU platforms but because of the data communication for process migration, remote disk access and synchronisation, the multi-CPU machine still outperforms the cluster-based solution.

4.2   Varying of Workload

The results of the first round of performance trials did not favour the cluster and it is hypothesised that this is because of a small workload and excessive remote data access. To test that the workload is in fact the reason why a dual-CPU machine outperforms an 8-node cluster, the workload was varied and additional tests were conducted.

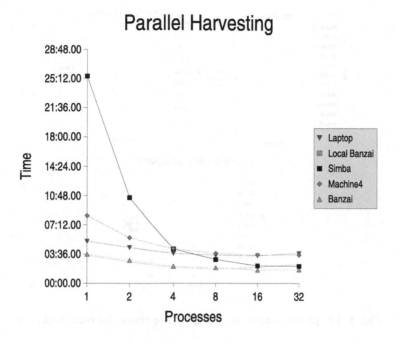

Fig. 3. Typical performance of different platforms for an indexing task

First, to remove any bias, only those platforms with remote data providers were considered. Then, the harvesters were set up to perform each of the following tasks on harvested data:

- index and commit to disk as before;
- index only; and
- index, perform some additional CPU-intensive calculations, and then commit indices to disk.

The results from these tests are shown in Figure 4. In the case of Indexing, Simba and Banzai perform equally well because the computational load is not high. With Indexing+Committing, Banzai outperforms Simba because of local disk access, as before. However, as the computional load is increased in the Indexing+Committing+Computing test, Simba begins to perform better than Banzai. This result shows that while disk-intensive operations may be better suited to a multi-CPU system, as the load of computational operations increases, a cluster of machines may offer a reasonable solution. From a digital library perspective, a cluster of machines may offer cost-effective possibilities for processing data for indexing, classification, automatic extraction, pattern detection and similar tasks.

Now, consider the data from this experiment depicted from the perspective of each machine rather than the tasks performed (see Figure 5). It is clear that

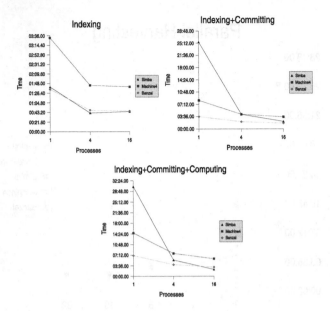

Fig. 4. Per-platform analysis of harvesting times, for each workload

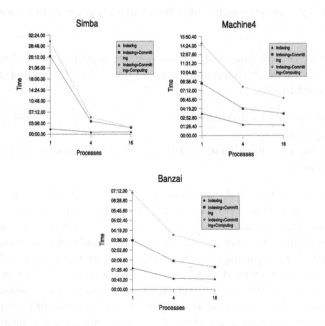

Fig. 5. Per-workload analysis of harvesting times, for each platform

a cluster of machines (Simba) has the advantage that for a sufficient number of processes, a higher computational load does not significantly increase the wallclock time. For the single processor and dual-processor machines, a higher computational load still results in a much higher processing time.

5   Conclusions

This work has begun to look at how existing digital library architectures can be made more scalable. The results naturally do not work for all scenarios and the performance may degrade in systems with large numbers of CPUs, for the given simple approach to parallelisation.

Nevertheless, the experimental validation shows that storage-intensive services can benefit from multi-processor machines, while computation-intensive services may work adequately on the more cost effective Beowulf clusters. In addition, the restructuring of OAI-PMH harvesters to include parallel network access and post-processing yields performance benefits on even single processor machines! In all cases, these gains were made purely by redesigning the harvester, without any modifications to the OAI-PMH and without adversely impacting the data provider. Also, the harvester is architected to work reasonably well on a single processor machine and easily scale up to make use of additional resources if they are available.

6   Future Work

For distributed digital library systems, these experiments have shown that there is benefit in paralleling even the most basic harvesting operation. The next step is to parallelise the various processing operations that take place within a digital library system, including indexing and querying. Early work with the parallel harvesting framework has shown that the scheduler can be used to manage multiple types of jobs simultaneously - thus some nodes could be harvesting and post-processing while others could be merging indices. For systems where multiple services require different processing operations, it is possible to use a computational pipeline, with each stage performing a particular operation.

There were some problems with data and process movement in openMosix. In looking at alternatives, the distribution of processes and data will depend on the specific data flow patterns of a digital library system. Dongarra et al. [5] emphasise that parallelism is only a part of the solution and that data flow must be considered. Further work is therefore needed to determine what the data flow patterns are and how best to optimise the distribution of processes, communication among processes and disk access patterns for typical DL services.

Eventually, in order to scale digital library systems arbitrarily, it may be necessary to rethink the fundamental nature of data storage, movement and processing in digital library systems. The OAI-PMH data provider enforces a notion of ownership or stewardship of data, but quickly becomes a bottleneck in large scale collections. Data ownership may need to be redefined in its relationship to data storage and locality so that scalable services have optimal access to data when needed.

Acknowledgements

This project was made possible by funding from University of Cape Town, NRF (Grant number: FA2005041200001), NRF-THRIP, Telkom and Siemens.

References

1. Andresen, Daniel, Tao Yang, Omar Egecioglu, Oscar H. Ibarra, and Terence R. Smith (1996), "Scalability Issues for High Performance Digital Libraries on the World Wide Web", Technical Report 1996-03, Department of Computer Science, University of California Santa Barbara, March 1996.
2. Bar, Moshe (2003), "openMosix, a Linux Kernel Extension for Single System Image Clustering", in Proceedings of Linux Kongress: 10th International Linux System Technology Conference, 15-16 October, Saarbrücken, Germany.
3. Brown, Robert G. (2004) Engineering a Beowulf-style Compute Cluster, Duke University Physics Department. Available http://www.phy.duke.edu/ rgb/Beowulf/beowulf_book/beowulf_book/index.html
4. Diligent (2006) A Digital Library Infrastructure on Grid Enabled Technology. Website http://www. diligentproject.org/
5. Dongarra, Jack, Ken Kennedy and Andy White (2003) "Introduction", in Jack Dongarra, Ian Foster, Geoffrey Fox, William Gropp, Ken Kennedy, Linda Torczon, Andy White (eds): Sourcebook of Parallel Computing, Morgan Kaufman, Amsterdam.
6. Haedstrom, Margaret (2003), "Research Challenges in Digital Archiving and Long-term Preservation", NSF Post Digital Library Futures Workshop, 15-17 June 2003, Cape Cod. Available http://www.sis.pitt.edu/ dlwkshop/paper_hedstrom.html
7. Imafouo, Amlie (2006), "A Scalability Survey in IR and DL", TCDL Bulletin, Volume 2, Issue 2. Available http://www.ieee-tcdl.org/Bulletin/v2n2/ imafouo/imafouo.html
8. Lagoze, Carl, and Herbert Van de Sompel (2001), "The Open Archives Initiative: Building a low-barrier interoperability framework", in Proceedings of the ACM-IEEE Joint Conference on Digital Libraries, Roanoke, VA, USA, 24-28 June 2001, pp. 54-62.
9. Lagoze, Carl, Herbert Van de Sompel, Michael Nelson and Simeon Warner (2002), The Open Archives Initiative Protocol for Metadata Harvesting – Version 2.0, Open Archives Initiative, June 2002. Available http://www.openarchives.org/OAI/2.0/ openarchivesprotocol.htm
10. Lyman, Peter, and Hal R. Varian (2003) How Much Information 2003?, University of California. Available http://www2.sims.berkeley.edu/research/projects/how-much-info-2003/index.htm
11. Wilkinson, Barry, and Michael Allen (1999) Parallel Programming: Techniques and Applications Using Networked Workstations and Parallel Computers, Prentice Hall, New Jersey.

Sibling Page Search by Page Examples

Hiroaki Ohshima, Satoshi Oyama, and Katsumi Tanaka

Department of Social Informatics, Graduate School of Informatics, Kyoto University
Yoshida-Honmachi, Sakyo, Kyoto 606-8501, Japan
TEL.: +81-75-753-5385; FAX: +81-75-753-4957
{ohshima, oyama, tanaka}@dl.kuis.kyoto-u.ac.jp

Abstract. We propose methods of searching Web pages that are "semantically" regarded as "siblings" with respect to given page examples.
That is, our approach aims to find pages that are similar in theme but
have different content from the given sample pages. We called this "sibling page search". The proposed search methods are different from conventional content-based similarity search for Web pages. Our approach
recommends Web pages whose "conceptual" classification category is the
same as that of the given sample pages, but whose content is different
from the sample pages. In this sense, our approach will be useful for
supporting a user's opportunistic search, meaning a search in which the
user's interest and intention are not fixed. The proposed methods were
implemented by computing the "common" and "unique" feature vectors
of the given sample pages, and by comparing those feature vectors with
each retrieved page. We evaluated our method for sibling page search, in
which our method was applied to test sets consisting of page collections
from the Open Directory Project (ODP).

1 Introduction

Web search has become a major way to obtain new information. When people
use a conventional Web search engine such as Google [1] or AltaVista [2], however,
they can only submit some query words to the search engine. When people are
studying a certain field comprehensively, they will submit some known words to
a Web search engine. Then, they need to check which search result pages contain
new content for them. In other words, in such situations, they try to find pages
that are related to the studying field but contain different content from what
they already know.

In this paper, we propose a method of searching Web pages that are "semantically" regarded as "siblings" with respect to given page examples. Here, the
user specifies some page examples as a query for the search. Our approach aims
to find pages that are similar in theme but have different contents from the given
sample pages. We call this approach "sibling page search".

The proposed approach is different from conventional content-based similarity
search for Web pages. It tries to recommend Web pages whose "conceptually"

---

[1] http://www.google.com/
[2] http://www.altavista.com/

S. Sugimoto et al. (Eds.): ICADL 2006, LNCS 4312, pp. 91–100, 2006.

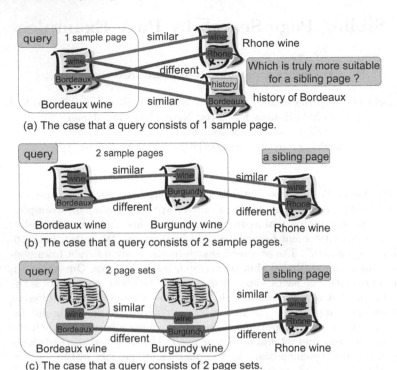

(a) The case that a query consists of 1 sample page.

(b) The case that a query consists of 2 sample pages.

(c) The case that a query consists of 2 page sets.

Fig. 1. The number of sample pages or page sets forming a query

classified category is the same as that of the given sample pages, but whose content is different from the sample pages. For example, when a user interested in wine and has already pages about "Bordeaux wine" and about "Burgundy wine", the user can throw these pages as a query for the search. Our approach will then find pages about such topics as "Rhone wine", which is another French wine but different from Bordeaux wine and Burgundy wine.

The proposed method was implemented by computing the "common" and "unique" feature vectors of the given sample pages, and then comparing those feature vectors with each retrieved page. We also evaluated our method, in which our method was applied to test sets consisting of page collections from the Open Directory Project (ODP).

2 Query Requirements for Sibling Page Search

A query for a "sibling page search" consists of sample pages which a user gives. Figure 1 shows three different cases of queries.

In case (a), the query consists of only one sample page about "Bordeaux wine". The sample page contains content about both "Bordeaux" and "wine". In this case, a page about "Rhone wine" might be a suitable sibling page for the query, but at the same time, a page about the "history of Bordeaux" might also be suitable. Here, it is difficult to determine which is truly more suitable.

Meanwhile, in case (b), the query consists of two sample pages about both "Bordeaux wine" and "Burgundy wine". In this case, it is possible to determine that "wine" is the common theme in both of pages and that "Bordeaux" and "Burgundy" are the different themes in each page. Therefore, it can be determined that a relevant page must contain content about "wine" and must not contain content about either "Bordeaux" or "Burgundy".

In case (c), the query consists of two page sets. When a page set is about "Bordeaux wine" and the other is about "Burgundy wine", the query can be treated in the same way as the case (b).

Consequently, a query needs to consist of two or more pages or two or more page sets. In this paper, we assume that a user's query consists of two or more page sets.

3   Sibling Page Search

3.1   Sibling Page Search Algorithm

In this paper, we use the vector space model [1] to retrieve sibling pages from user-selected page sets. When a user selects a collection $\{P_1, \ldots, P_n\}$ of page sets as a sibling page search query, the "sibling page" intuitively denotes a page that contains the "common" feature of $\{P_1, \ldots, P_n\}$ and that does not contain any "unique" feature of pages in $\{P_1, \ldots, P_n\}$.

The following is the rough sketch of our sibling page search algorithm:

1. Computing page-set feature vectors t_k from $P_k (1 \leq k \leq n)$. Each page-set feature vector t_k is computed by aggregating all the feature vectors of pages in P_k.
2. For $\{t_1, \ldots, t_n\}(n \geq 2)$, computing a vector c which represents "common" feature of $\{P_1, \ldots, P_n\}$.
3. For each $t_1, \ldots, t_n$, computing a vector $u_k (1 \leq k \leq n)$ which represents "unique" feature of P_k.
4. When a candidate page for a sibling page is obtained in some way, computing a feature vector d for the page.
5. Computing the similarity between the "common part vector" c and the candidate page vector d.
6. Computing the dissimilarity between each "unique part vector" $u_k (1 \leq k \leq n)$ and the candidate page vector d.
7. Computing the relevance of the candidate page using the similarity and the dissimilarities. The higher the similarity and the dissimilarities are, the higher the relevance becomes.

There are many possible methods of calculating these feature vectors. The following subsections describe two methods of computing t_k, three methods of computing c, and one method of computing u_k. Then, we define the relevance of a sibling page for a user's query.

3.2   Computing the Page Sets Vectors

The term frequency (TF) is often used for representing a page as a feature vector, but several different methods based on the TF can be considered. One such method, used in the SMART system [1], is based on the logarithm of the TF. We use both the normal TF (**N**) and the logarithm of the TF (**L**) to compute page set vectors. The values of the page set vector t_k for each term with methods (N) and (L) are defined as follows:

$$(N)\quad t_k(w_i) = \sum_{D_j \in P_k} tf(w_i, D_j), \tag{1}$$

$$(L)\quad t_k(w_i) = \log\left(1 + \sum_{D_j \in P_k} tf(w_i, D_j)\right), \tag{2}$$

where P_k is one of the page sets in the user's query, and $tf(w, D)$ is the number of a term w contained in a page D. For normalization, each element is divided by the maximum element in t_k, giving the normalized vector t'_k as follows:

$$t'_k(w_i) = \frac{t_k(w_i)}{t_k(w_{p_k})}, \tag{3}$$

where w_{p_k} is a term for which t_k has the maximum value in itself. We use t'_k as the page set vector.

3.3   Computing the Common Part Vector

The common part vector c is characterized by terms frequently appearing in all of the page set vectors. We use three methods in order to emphasize these commonly used terms: a method (**M**) to calculate the geometric mean of $t'_k(w_i)(1 \leq k \leq n)$, a method (**A**) to calculate the arithmetic mean of $t'_k(w_i)(1 \leq k \leq n)$, and a method (**L**) to take the minimum element from $t'_1(w_i), \cdots, t'_n(w_i)$, where n is the total number of page sets in the query. For each method, the value of c is obtained as follows:

$$(M)\quad c(w_i) = \sqrt[n]{\prod t'_k(w_i)}, \tag{4}$$

$$(A)\quad c(w_i) = \frac{\sum t'_k(w_i)}{n}, \tag{5}$$

$$(L)\quad c(w_i) = \min(t'_1(w_i), \ldots, t'_n(w_i)). \tag{6}$$

3.4   Computing the Unique Part Vectors

The unique part of the page set P_k is characterized by terms whose value in t_k is high but whose value in c is low. We define the unique part vector u_k as follows:

$$u_k(w_i) = \max\left(t'_k(w_i) - c(w_i), 0\right). \tag{7}$$

3.5   Definition of the Relevance

It is intuitively thought that a relevant page for a query contains the common part contents in all the page sets and does not contain any of the unique content of each page set. After representing a candidate page D as a feature vector $\boldsymbol{d}$, we quantify the relevance by using the similarity between $\boldsymbol{d}$ and $\boldsymbol{c}$ and the similarity between $\boldsymbol{d}$ and each $\boldsymbol{u}_k$.

First, in the same manner as computing the page set vectors, the feature vector $\boldsymbol{d}$ of a candidate page can be computed by using either the TF (**N**) or the logarithm of the TF (**L**). The formulas are as follows:

$$(\text{N})\quad \boldsymbol{d}(w_i) = tf(w_i, D), \tag{8}$$

$$(\text{L})\quad \boldsymbol{d}(w_i) = \log\left(1 + tf(w_i, D)\right) \tag{9}$$

The similarity between two vectors can be calculated by the cosine similarity. The cosine similarity between two vectors $\boldsymbol{v_1}$ and $\boldsymbol{v_2}$ is defined as follows:

$$\cos(\boldsymbol{v_1}, \boldsymbol{v_2}) = \frac{\sum_w (\boldsymbol{v_1}(w) \cdot \boldsymbol{v_2}(w))}{\sqrt{\sum_w \boldsymbol{v_1}(w)^2 \cdot \sum_w \boldsymbol{v_2}(w)^2}}. \tag{10}$$

When the vectors' directions are exactly the same, the cosine similarity takes the maximum value of 1; when their directions are perpendicular, it takes the minimum value of 0.

Using the cosine similarity, the similarity between $\boldsymbol{d}$ and $\boldsymbol{c}$, $Sim_c(D)$, is obtained as follows:

$$Sim_c(D) = \cos(\boldsymbol{c}, \boldsymbol{d}). \tag{11}$$

If a candidate page D is relevant as a sibling page, the unique part of D must be dissimilar to any $\boldsymbol{u}_k$. First, we get a feature vector which represents the unique part of D in same way to Formula (7):

$$\boldsymbol{d}_u(w_i) = \max\left(\boldsymbol{d}(w_i) - \boldsymbol{c}(w_i), 0\right) \tag{12}$$

The maximum similarity between $\boldsymbol{d}$ and $\boldsymbol{u}_k$ is denoted as $Sim_u(\boldsymbol{d})$ and represented as follows:

$$Sim_u(D) = \max\left(\cos(\boldsymbol{u_1}, \boldsymbol{d}_u), \cdots, \cos(\boldsymbol{u_n}, \boldsymbol{d}_u)\right). \tag{13}$$

When Sim_c is large and Sim_u is small, the relevance should become high. Thus, we ultimately define the relevance R of page D for the query as follows:

$$R(D) = Sim_c(D) \cdot (1 - Sim_u(D)) \tag{14}$$

4   Evaluation of the Proposed Methods

4.1   Test Sets

As described above, we utilize two methods of computing the page set vectors and three methods of computing the common part vector. Through combination

Table 1. The detail of the test sets

	Test Set 1	Test Set 2	Test Set 3	Test Set 4	Test Set 5
Whole pages	Science/ Astronomy (1481docs)	Arts/Performing Arts/Dance (2788docs)	Japanese/ Recreation (2630docs)	Japanese/ Recreation (2630docs)	Japanese/ Science (2630docs)
Relevant pages	Solar System (267docs)	Ballet (267docs)	gambling (71docs)	fortunetelling (43docs)	natural science/physics (91docs)
query	Mercury (9docs)	Don Quixote (4docs)	boat race (2docs)	tarot (4docs)	relativism (5docs) (5docs)
	Neptune (8docs)	The Nutcracker (5docs)	horse race (9docs)	four pillar astrology (3docs)	electromagnetics (5docs)
	Saturn (10docs)	Swan Lake (3docs)	bicycle race (5docs)	European astrology (10docs)	hydrodynamics (4docs)

of these methods, six overall methods are possible. Each is denoted according to the labels used in Formulas (1) and (2) and Formulas (4), (5), and (6). For example, the label (LM) means to use Formula (2) and Formula (4).

We compared and evaluated these six methods by using test sets, which consisted of Web pages from the Open Directory Project [3].

Table 1 is the detail of the test sets. In the case of the Test Set 1, first we collected Web pages under the directory **/Science/Astronomy/** in the ODP. Some of these pages have very little text content and consist mostly of images. As our approach is based on feature vectors, we cannot analyze such pages. Therefore, we removed pages containing very little text content (less than 2 KB) from the collected Web pages. As a result, the total number of pages in the test set was 1481 in this case. Next, we chose a query for the sibling page search. The directory **/Science/Astronomy/Solar_System/** contains 12 subdirectories. We chose three of them:

- /Science/Astronomy/Solar_System/Mercury/ ,
- /Science/Astronomy/Solar_System/Neptune/ ,
- /Science/Astronomy/Solar_System/Saturn/ .

8 to 10 pages are directly located in each of these directories, so each of these can be regarded as a page set. Hence, we obtained three page sets and used them as the query for Test Set 1.

Relevant pages for the query should be semantically sibling pages with respect to the query page sets. this means pages that are stored in the directory **/Science /Astronomy /Solar_System/** but not in the directories for the query – "Mercury", "Neptune", or "Saturn". For example, the pages in

- /Science/Astronomy/Solar_System/Earth/,
- /Science/Astronomy/Solar_System/Jupiter/, and
- /Science/Astronomy/Solar_System/Venus/

were included in the relevant pages for the query. The number of the relevant pages was 267.

In such way, we made 5 test sets from the ODP.

---

[3] http://dmoz.org/

Table 2. The page set vectors for "Mercury", "Neptune", and "Saturn"

Mercury	(N)	(L)	Neptune	(N)	(L)	Saturn	(N)	(L)
Mercury	1.000	1.000	Neptune	1.000	1.000	Saturn	1.000	1.000
planet	0.403	0.837	planet	0.616	0.911	ring	0.741	0.947
sun	0.273	0.767	orbit	0.276	0.766	image	0.285	0.778
image	0.261	0.759	Uranus	0.228	0.732	planet	0.248	0.754
Earth	0.233	0.739	spot	0.198	0.706	satellite	0.230	0.740
orbit	0.166	0.679	Earth	0.194	0.702	Cassini	0.223	0.735
km	0.150	0.662	image	0.194	0.702	voyage	0.204	0.720
surface	0.150	0.662	observe	0.190	0.698	moon	0.197	0.713
time	0.134	0.642	dark	0.185	0.694	system	0.153	0.670

Table 3. The common part vectors for "Mercury", "Neptune", and "Saturn"

	(NM)		(NA)		(NL)		(LM)		(LA)		(LL)
planet	0.395	planet	0.423	planet	0.248	planet	0.832	planet	0.834	planet	0.754
image	0.243	Saturn	0.369	image	0.194	image	0.746	image	0.747	image	0.702
orbit	0.178	Neptune	0.350	orbit	0.124	orbit	0.691	orbit	0.693	orbit	0.633
ring	0.176	Mercury	0.344	Earth	0.113	Earth	0.684	ring	0.691	Earth	0.617
Earth	0.172	ring	0.314	moon	0.107	ring	0.662	Earth	0.686	moon	0.602
moon	0.135	image	0.247	system	0.083	moon	0.640	moon	0.642	system	0.558
sun	0.126	orbit	0.189	observe	0.073	sun	0.624	Saturn	0.634	observe	0.542
Saturn	0.125	Earth	0.180	km	0.069	km	0.613	sun	0.632	km	0.533

4.2   Examples of Vectors in Each Method

We show examples of vectors in each method. Here, we use Test Set 1.

Table 2 shows the page set vectors. In these vectors, the terms describing each page set have high values. For example, in the vectors for the page set of the directory "Saturn", the two highest-valued terms are "Saturn" and "ring". There are several terms, however, that have high values in all page set vectors, such as "planet" and "image".

Table 3 shows the common part vector for each method. Here, terms such as "planet" and "image" have high values in all cases, because they are commonly related to the solar system.

Table 4 shows the unique part vectors for the directory "Saturn" for each method. The terms "image" and "planet" have the third and fourth highest values in the page set vector of "Saturn", but their values are relatively lower in the unique part vectors for each method.

4.3   Comparison of the Proposed Methods

For comparison, we calculated the relevance R of each page in the test set with each method. Then, we sorted the pages by assigning higher ranks to those with higher relevance. When $\theta(1 \leq \theta \leq$ the number of the whole pages) is given, the recall and the precision can be calculated, so a recall-precision graph can be drawn.

Figure 2 shows the recall-precision graphs for each of the proposed six methods for Test Set 2. When the graph for a certain method appears higher, that method is judged as better than those that appear below it. These graph shows the

Table 4. The unique part vectors for "Saturn"

(NM)		(NA)		(NL)	
Saturn	0.875	Saturn	0.631	Saturn	0.976
ring	0.565	ring	0.426	ring	0.693
Cassini	0.223	Cassini	0.148	Cassini	0.223
voyage	0.204	satellite	0.127	voyage	0.204
satellite	0.161	voyage	0.077	satellite	0.202
Titan	0.113	Titan	0.071	Titan	0.113
magnetosphere	0.088	moon	0.057	color	0.098
division	0.080	color	0.056	Jupiter	0.096
(LM)		(LA)		(LL)	
Cassini	0.735	Cassini	0.490	Cassini	0.735
voyage	0.720	division	0.372	voyage	0.720
Titan	0.617	Saturn	0.366	Saturn	0.649
magnetosphere	0.573	Saturnian	0.336	Titan	0.617
division	0.558	Gladman	0.329	magnetosphere	0.573
storm	0.524	Titan	0.328	division	0.558
plane	0.515	press	0.321	storm	0.524
Dione	0.504	magnetosphere	0.316	plane	0.515

Table 5. Average precision of the result for the test sets

	(NM)	(NA)	(NL)	(LM)	(LA)	(LL)
Top 5 pages	0.84	0.72	0.72	0.92	0.72	0.92
Top 10 pages	0.80	0.74	0.70	0.88	0.64	0.84
Top 20 pages	0.71	0.62	0.67	0.77	0.60	0.72
Top 50 pages	0.58	0.52	0.55	0.64	0.44	0.61

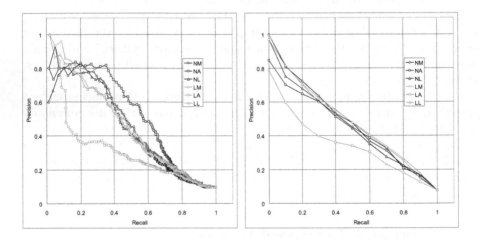

Fig. 2. Recall-precision graphs for Test Set 2

Fig. 3. Average recall-precision graphs for all test sets

method (LA) is not good and (NA) is a little better than others. However, this is just one case, so the average is more important. Figure 3 shows the average recall-precision graphs for all test sets. It shows that the methods (NM), (NL), (LM), (LA) are almost same and the best, that the method (NA) is worse in especially higher ranking, that the method (LA) is the worst. For Web search, in particular, users generally only see the top 10 or 20 pages of results, so the precision for the top 10 or 20 pages is quite important.

Table 5 shows the average precisions of the results for the test sets. By methods (NM), (LM) and (LL), more than 80% of the top 10 ranked pages are relevant, and more than 70% of the top 20 ranked pages are relevant. Even for the top 50 pages obtained by these three methods, about 60% are relevant pages. The average of the average precisions of the test sets is about 7.1% [4] , so we have concluded that about 60% is enough good.

As a result of these tests, we have shown that proposed methods (NM), (LM) and (LL) have the capability to find suitable pages for sibling page search.

5 Related Work

The SMART system [1] includes methods of representing a document as a feature vector, enabling us to search documents in the system by using the similarity. Our methods for generating vectors and calculating similarity are based on this work. The Okapi weighting proposed by Robertson et al. [2] is also a method for calculating relevance for content-based similarity search. It was developed in the TREC project. There are many search systems based on this method, but they can only search for pages similar to a query, rather than pages regarded semantically as "siblings" for the query. One way for a user to give more searching intention is a information filtering system using relevant feedback [3]. In relevant feedback systems, a user can indicate only either "relevant" or "irrelevant" [4]. However, in the sibling page search, user's holding documents contain both relevant part and irrelevant part, so it is very difficult to represent user's proper intention in relevant feedback systems.

Our method is a system which finds suitable documents by removing both irrelevant documents and ones relevant to user's query but not containing new information. Such ideas exist in the field of information filtering system. Zhang et al. [5] proposed a method to detect novelty and redundancy for the stream of documents. Their idea is that the feature appearing in old documents is redundant, but in the sibling page search, suitable documents need to contain such common feature.

Most Web search engines use keyword queries. Our system can be regarded as a search system based on query by page examples. Query by examples is commonly used in image or video retrieval. Recently, there have been reports on search systems based on query by examples for multimedia search. Example include MindReader by Ishikawa et al. [6] and the system developed by Westerveld et al. [7]. These systems, however, search for items similar to the query examples.

6 Conclusion

We have proposed a method for "sibling page search". When a user specifies some page sets as a query for a search, the relevant pages for the query should

---

[4] This average can be obtained from Table 1.

be similar in theme but have different content in each page set. Our approach, which includes six different methods, can evaluate whether a page is relevant for a query. It is implemented by computing the "common" part vector of the page sets and the "unique" part vector of each page set and then comparing those feature vectors and each retrieved page. We evaluated the proposed methods by applying them to test sets consisting of pages from the Open Directory Project (ODP). The results showed that proposed methods labeled by (NM), (LM) and (LL) work well for finding sibling pages with respect to a user's given sample pages. Our efforts in this paper is to calculate relevance of a document as a sibling page. Our future goal is to find sibling pages from the Web, so we will develop an efficient way to obtain candidate documents as sibling pages in future.

Acknowledgments

This work was supported in part by the Japanese Ministry of Education, Culture, Sports, Science and Technology (MEXT) project "Software Technologies for Search and Integration across Heterogeneous-Media Archives," by MEXT Grants-in-Aid for Scientific Research (Nos. 18049041 and 16700097), and by a 21st Century COE Program at Kyoto University called "Informatics Research Center for Development of Knowledge Society Infrastructure."

References

1. Gerard Salton and Michael McGill: Introduction to Modern Information Retrieval. McGraw-Hill (1983)
2. M. Beaulieu, M. Gatford, X. Huang, S. Robertson, S. Walker, and P. Williams: Okapi at TREC-5. Proceedings of TREC-5 (1997) 143–166
3. Meadow, C.T., Boyce, B.R., Kraft, D.H.: Text information retrieval systems. Second edn. Academic Press (2000)
4. Rocchio, J.: Relevance feedback in information retrieval, In The SMART Retrieval System : Experiments in Automatic Document Processing. Prentice-Hall (1971)
5. Zhang, Y., Callan, J., Minka, T.: Novelty and redundancy detection in adaptive filtering. Proceedings of the 25th Annual International ACM SIGIR Conference on Research and Development in Information Retrieval (SIGIR 2002) (2002) 81–88
6. Y. Ishikawa, R. Subramanya, and C. Faloutsos: MindReader: Querying databases through multiple examples. Proceedings 24th International Conference on Very Large Data Bases (1998) 218–227
7. T. Westerveld and A. de Vries: Multimedia retrieval using multiple examples. Proceedings of The Third International Conference on Image and Video Retrieval (CIVR 2004) (2004) 344–352

Contextualization of a RDF Knowledge Base in the VIKEF Project

Heiko Stoermer[1], Ignazio Palmisano[2], Domenico Redavid[2], Luigi Iannone[3],
Paolo Bouquet[1], and Giovanni Semeraro[2]

[1] University of Trento,
Dept. of Information and Communication Tech.,
Trento, Italy
{stoermer, bouquet}@dit.unitn.it
[2] Dipartimento di Informatica, Università degli Studi di Bari
Campus Universitario, Via Orabona 4, 70125 Bari, Italy
{palmisano, redavid, semeraro}@di.uniba.it
[3] Computer Science Department, Liverpool University
Ashton Building, Ashton Street, L69 BX Liverpool, UK
luigi@csc.liv.ac.uk

Abstract. Due to the simplicity of RDF data model and semantics, complex application scenarios in which RDF is used to represent the application data model raise important design issues. Modelling e.g. the temporary evolution, relevance, trust and provenance in Knowledge Bases require more than just a set of universally true statements, without any reference to a situation, a point in time, or generally a context. Our proposed solution is to use the notion of context to separate statements that refer to different contextual information, which could so far not explicitly be tied to the statements. In this paper we describe a practical solution to this problem, which has been implemented in the VIKEF project, which deals with making explicit and intelligently useable information contained in vast collections of documents, databases and metadata repositories.

1 Problem Description and Motivation

The VIKEF project[1] deals with creating large-scale information systems that base on Semantic Web technology. At the center of the envisioned systems there is an RDF (Resource Description Framework)[2] knowledge base (KB) that contains a large amount of information about documents and their contents. This information is gathered by information and knowledge extraction processes at the base level, then semantically enriched and related to ontological knowledge, and finally stored in a RDF triple store called RDFCore, which will be described

---

[1] European Commission 6th Framework Programme IST Integrated Project VIKEF - Virtual Information and Knowledge Environment Framework (Contract no. 507173, Priority 2.3.1.7 Semantic-based Knowledge Systems http://www.vikef.net)
[2] http://www.w3.org/TR/rdf-concepts/

S. Sugimoto et al. (Eds.): ICADL 2006, LNCS 4312, pp. 101–110, 2006.

in more detail in Sect. 3.1. On top of this KB, semantic-enabled services will be implemented to provide a next-generation information system.

Current RDF triple stores are built to represent a single bag of RDF triples, i.e. all statements are stored in the same information space together. However, from a Knowledge Representation point of view, RDF statements in general are context-free, and thus follow a notion of *universal truth*, while in our opinion knowledge in an information system is context-dependent. In effect, without a context-based system, it is possible (and probable) that semantically contradictory statements will be stored in the KB, such as for instance "Silvio Berlusconi is the Prime minister of Italy" and "Romano Prodi is the Prime minister of Italy" as the result of knowledge extracted from articles written in different years (supposing that being Prime Minister is possible only for a single person). These contradictions are however unwanted in a logical system because they would interfere with both simple queries over the data (e.g., the question "who is the Premier in Italy?" brings two answers instead of just one) and higher level reasoning that is to be performed to provide Semantic Web functionality, such as semantic browsing, search, visualization, etc. Additionally, we would like to be able to model other aspects such as relevance, credibility and validity of a statement, all of which require further qualification.

If we think about the Semantic Web as a whole, with a large number of un-coordinated information systems, the problem becomes even more evident. If every peer builds up a KB of unqualified RDF statements, the set of universally true facts in the Semantic Web becomes enormously large and impossible to handle from a semantic point of view; this is the case when, for example, tools for automatic extraction of metadata are used, as in [5] and [11]. In our opinion, such contradictions, contradictory beliefs and facts that become semantically incorrect in the absence of additional pragmatic or contextual information are likely to impose serious problems on the coordination and interoperation of information systems in the Semantic Web.

The remainder of the paper is organized as follows: after giving some definitions of *context* in Sect. 2, we present our architecture in Sect. 3. Some empirical evaluation results are presented in Sect. 4, and finally we draw some conclusions and future work directions in Sect. 5.

2   Context in RDF Knowledge Bases

We think that the mentioned issues can be approached by introducing the notion of *context* into RDF, to limit the scope of a RDF statement to the context in which it is relevant or valid, because in our opinion this is required for anything sensible to be expressed in the Semantic Web. We want to present a mechanism to qualify statements and thus to model that a statement is true *only under a certain set of conditions*, which will help us store information in the KB that would cause contradictions or inconsistencies in a plain RDF A-Box[3].

---

[3] In Description Logic, an A-Box is the set of assertions about instances (Assertional Box), while the T-Box is the portion of the KB containing the axioms, such as class and property definitions (Theoretical Box).

2.1   Context in KR - Multi Context Systems

The theoretical ideas presented in this paper base on the logical theory of *Multi Context Systems* and the principles of *Locality* and *Compatibility* presented e.g. in [8], with influences from [3,4]. Basically, this theory states that contexts can be seen in a peer-to-peer view, resembling more general aspects such as human beliefs, agent knowledge or distributed systems. The important aspect of this theory is that reasoning within a context follows standard mechanisms, as the non-elementary view on the large part of the axioms does not require to keep track of the context they are relevant for. Relations between contexts however, i.e. to reason across contexts, are to be expressed in so-called *compatibility relations* (CRs), that formalize exactly how under certain circumstances knowledge from other contexts becomes relevant. Regarding RDF in this case we claim that a RDF context can be thought of as a locally coherent set of axioms, each one with a set of parameters and values for these parameters, that specify the conditions under which the set of axioms is valid. We envision CRs to be modeled as a *semantic attachment* [12], as we will describe in more detail below.

2.2   Main Idea

The basic idea is to have all statements that belong to a context in a separate named RDF graph, and extend the RDF semantics in a way to enable contexts to appear as standard objects in RDF statements of other contexts. As we will illustrate in more detail in Sect. 3.2, for a reference implementation we will base on features of the SPARQL[4] query language.

Then, we want to model the mentioned CRs between contexts, to allow for reasoning across contexts. This aspect is probably the most important one, because from an application perspective it is crucial that sensible queries can be issued and *all* relevant information is taken into account - which requires reasoning across contexts and reasoning on the relations between contexts (i.e. on statements of the form $<c_x$ R $c_y>$ where c_x and c_y are RDF Contexts, or $<f$ R $c'>$ respectively $<c'$ R $f>$ with $f \in c$). We are only starting to explore in full depth the aspects of CRs that are relevant for the VIKEF project.

Several approaches can be thought of to model CRs in our architecture. First of all, one could think of allowing the implementer of an information system to provide their own vocabularies (ontologies) to describe relations between contexts. A similar option would be for us to provide such an ontology as part of the architecture. However, in our opinion the basic problem with these approaches is the fact that many interesting relations between architectures cannot be fully formalized with the help of a Semantic Web ontology, which is based on Description Logics.

As an example for this claim take a relation such as
$<c'$ EXTENDS $c>$
which expresses that c' represents an extension to c, e.g. for the reason that it is about the same object, but composed at a later point in time. The underlying

---

[4] http://www.w3.org/TR/rdf-sparql-query/

assumption of the *EXTENDS* relation is that the two contexts are compatible, i.e. they agree on the relevant context parameters. The semantics of this relation have to be expressed algorithmically:

```
if c and c' are compatible

then if no answer to a query q can be given in c

propagate query to c'
```

One of the questions that might arise is how these CRs are supposed to be modeled. At the moment, we see three approaches to do this, which, among other basic and preliminary results including some of the above ideas, have been presented in [1], which we recommend to the reader for more detailed information, references and a discussion of related work.

This work has led us to the conclusion that the approach to be chosen is to implement a CR as a *semantic attachment* [12], which can be thought of as a sort of plugin to the system, one attachment per CR. This has the positive effects that i) there is no restriction on how many and which kind of CRs are part of such a system and ii) implementation of the CRs is generally not restricted to any specific language or system.

2.3 Related Work

As mentioned before, [1] provides a discussion of relevant related work. The only related approach that has lead to actual results, up to our knowledge, is that of the W3C Named Graph Interest Group[5]. A substantial article has been published in 2005 [2], and implementational results are now part of the Named Graphs API for Jena (NG4J) [6]. The approach describes a way to represent a graph as an object in a RDF KB, and has mainly been driven by the need for developing a trust model in RDF, but it could also serve as an underlying implementation in order to provide a base for the CRs discussed above.

3   The Proposed Solution: System Architecture

Our practical solution to context issues is based on the following requirements:

- Easy and simple identification of contexts
- Separate and independent storage for each context
- Easy querying of one or more contexts
- Easy reasoning on context parameters values
- Ability to plug new CRs in the architecture
- Ability to use CRs of higher expressive level, i.e. higher than OWL and/or DL

---

[5] http://www.w3.org/2004/03/trix/
[6] http://www.wiwiss.fu-berlin.de/suhl/bizer/ng4j/

As sketched in Fig. 1, the two main parts of our implementation are what is "inside" RDFCore (i.e. the RDF storage level) and "outside" of it. In Sect. 3.1 and Sect. 3.2 we will discuss the details of the architecture.

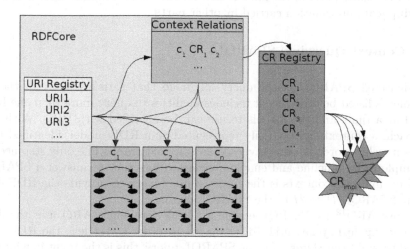

Fig. 1. Compatibility Relation Association Architecture

3.1 RDF Storage

As RDF storage, the VIKEF project chose to use RDFCore: presented in [7], it is a component used for storage and retrieval of RDF graphs, including multiuser support and extensible support for query languages.

In the VIKEF Project, RDFCore is the basic component for RDF metadata storage; being the VIKEF architecture based on the Web Services paradigm, its SOAP[7]-exposed services have been wrapped as a Web Service[8] for metadata storage, retrieval and querying.

RDFCore also has extensible support for different physical persistence solutions. At the time of writing, there are three implementations of *RDFEngineInterface* (the basic interface to be implemented by plugins), two based on the Jena Toolkit[9], one with MySQL RDBMS[10] as persistent storage, called *RDFEngineJENA*, and the other one using Microsoft SQL Server[11], called *RDFEngineMsSQL*. The third implementation is based on simple RDF/XML files, and is called *RDFEnginePlain*. All these implementations are based on the Jena API.

The component also offers multiuser support; users can choose whether some of the models they own should be private, publicly readable or writable, and can restrict access to single users or groups of users. This support is useful

---

[7] http://www.w3.org/2000/xp/Group/

[8] http://www.w3.org/2002/ws/

[9] http://jena.sourceforge.net

[10] http://dev.mysql.com/doc/mysql/en/index.html

[11] www.microsoft.com/sql/

when designing cooperative applications, thus enabling geographically dispersed teams to work together easily. RDFCore also can use a graph redundancy check algorithm (REDD)[6], which is useful in searching redundant portions of RDF graphs, i.e. those parts of the models that do not carry semantic information, or that duplicate information carried by other parts.

3.2 Context Querying: SPARQL

We identified SPARQL as the query language that satisfies many of the requirements listed before, since it includes facilities to query more than one RDF model at a time, and the models to use can be specified with URIs. With this approach, a context can be easily represented as a RDF model, identified by a URI – in other words, it can be viewed as a named graph. The only step needed to complete the pipeline and enable a generic repository to answer a SPARQL query on multiple contexts is the retrieval machinery to provide the RDF data for the SPARQL *Dataset* to the SPARQL engine.

We use ARQ[12] as SPARQL engine for RDFCore; since ARQ uses the Jena class com.hp.hpl.jena.util.FileManager in order to retrieve the RDF data needed to build the *Dataset* for the SPARQL query, this is the point in which we insert our mappings from graph names to URLs that the RDFCore component has to supply. Since RDFCore has multiuser support, however, it is necessary to implement a check on whether the user making the query has read access to the involved models; to do this, RDFCore extracts the graphs' URIs and checks that all the required models are accessible before pushing the SPARQL query to ARQ. Access to the data is done by ARQ through the use of a RDFCoreLocator, which implements the Locator interface defined in Jena. A small sketch of the process is depicted in Figure 2.

When the query is issued by an external application using the SPARQL protocol[13], the query can be executed only when all involved models are readable by any user (thus including any application that does not act on behalf of a user, and therefore has no explicit access to any model). At the moment, RDF-Core satisfies only the basic requirements for the SPARQL Protocol (HTTP and SOAP access), that is, RDFCore only accepts SPARQL queries with embedded dataset, where the dataset is composed of URIs that are registered as identifiers for RDF models publicly accessible in RDFCore. Accessing these models is realized through simple HTTP connection to a related RDFCore service, and it is automated in the query component through the implementation of the *Locator* interface in the Jena API, that is used as input to create the RDF dataset in the ARQ component. The use of the SPARQL protocol simplifies the design of those VIKEF components that only need read access to specific RDF models; in the case of distinct contexts, this is an easy way to ensure that no application can modify the information contained in a specific context.

---

[12] http://jena.sourceforge.net/ARQ/
[13] http://www.w3.org/TR/rdf-sparql-protocol/

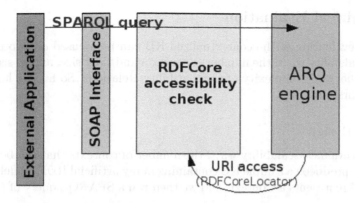

Fig. 2. SPARQL query processing

3.3 System Architecture

As sketched in Figure 1, the main parts of the architecture are:

- A *URI Registry*, used by applications to get the list of context URIs contained in a particular instance of RDFCore (including accessible and non accessible ones).
- A *Compatibility Relations model*, containing statements of the kind $<c'$ R $c>$, meaning that context c' is in relation R with context c (all three should be read as URIs for the contexts and the relation).
- A *Compatibility Relation Registry*, where each URI that identifies a CR is related to an implementation for that CR (*semantic attachment*).

The architecture presented so far is quite straightforward; however, the reasoning task on the *Compatibility Relations model* (i.e. the model containing the CR statements between contexts) cannot be carried out by a DL reasoner, since the complete semantics of the CRs we want to represent exceeds OWL expressiveness. In order to overcome this limitation of the architecture, we devised a plugin-oriented solution, where the URI of a CR identifies a plugin that implements the correct behavior to be carried out. As an example, consider a CR saying that:

"context *context* : *x* and context *context* : *y* are *context* : *compatible* if they have no contradictory statements" [14].

The relation named *context* : *compatible*, then, has to be inferred (or verified) through the use of some code that has to be associated with the relation, which in this case would do the job of taking the RDF models for the two contexts (i.e. the RDF models labeled *context* : *x* and *context* : *y*, available in RDFCore). A reasoner should then be used on the whole resulting RDF graph in order to evaluate consistency.

---

[14] Note that no specific reasoner level is set here: a real rule should also specify *how* to verify contradiction.

4   Empirical Evaluation

Empirical evaluation of the contextualized KB can be focused on two main aspects: i) scalability w.r.t. the number of contexts and their size, and ii) scalability w.r.t. number and complexity of Compatibility Relations. So far, we have evaluated the first aspect.

4.1   KB Design

In order to evaluate scalability w.r.t. the number of contexts that can be queried at once, we produced a sample KB containing many artificial RDF models, where each model represents a Context, and we then ran a SPARQL query of the kind:

```
CONSTRUCT \{?x ?y ?z\} FROM <urn:a1> FROM
<urn:a2> ... WHERE \{?x ?y ?z\}
```

where *urn:a1* represents the URI of a specific context and is used to retrieve the corresponding model from RDFCore. This query template simply retrieves all triples from the models named in the *FROM* clauses, and in our experiment we use queries that involve 10, 20 and 100 models respectively; in the first phase of testing, all the models have 100 statements in them, while in the second phase all the models have 1000 statements, so the total number of statements retrieved by a query scales from 1000 to 100000; the results are presented in Table 1. The last column of Table 1 shows the results obtained executing the same query on a single model containing the same number of triples of the union of the models, in order to verify the performance impact of partitioning a model into smaller contexts. As it emerges from the data, the performance overhead is small and tends to decrease when the total number of statements increase; the growth in the elapsed time has the same trend for both approaches, so we deduce that our architecture does not affect performances in a negative way, for such simple queries (however, note that any complex query is likely to retrieve a small number of statements w.r.t. the size of the model, so these very general queries are stressing the framework more than a very restrictive query that would only retrieve a single triple).

Table 1. Test Results

(artificial) graphs	stmt/graph	stmt retrieved	elapsed secs	elapsed secs on whole models
First Phase				
10	100	1000	~ 0.4	~ 0.1
20	100	2000	~ 0.6	~ 0.25
100	100	10000	~ 2.5	~ 1.5
Second Phase				
10	1000	10000	~ 2	~ 1.5
20	1000	20000	~ 4	~ 3.5
100	1000	100000	~ 20	~ 24

5 Conclusions and Future Work

We presented a possible solution to the issues related to uncontextualized knowledge, mostly arising from the notion of *universal truth* that RDF model semantics follows, and showed the architecture of our implementation for this solution. Future work we plan to do on this implementation consists of:

- A thorough stress test for the RDFCore component that acts like a "context" server in our architecture, to check for scalability issues w.r.t. CR number and complexity.
- Some implementations of CR "attachments", in order to provide the system with the needed expressive power to match VIKEF requirements.

Possible applications for this kind of KR are manifold, as partly described in [1,2,9,10]. Aspects such as beliefs, trust, incomplete knowledge and KB evolution in our opinion can all be tackled with a sensible context system as a base. We believe that in the long run, the vast amount of knowledge represented in the Semantic Web can only be handled properly if represented *in context*.

Additionally, we envision the outcomes of this work to go beyond local aspects and also become relevant from a distributed point of view. As the nature of the Semantic Web is inherently distributed, we think we can contribute to the semantic coordination of Semantic Web agents, firstly by offering the capabilities to make explicit that two knowledge bases belong to their respective agents and to enable the agents to establish semantic links to the KBs of other peers with the help of CRs.

Acknowledgments

This research was partially funded by the European Commission under the 6th Framework Programme IST Integrated Project VIKEF - Virtual Information and Knowledge Environment Framework (Contract no. 507173, Priority 2.3.1.7 Semantic-based Knowledge Systems; more information at http://www.vikef. net).

References

1. P. Bouquet, L. Serafini, and H. Stoermer. Introducing Context into RDF Knowledge Bases. In *Proceedings of SWAP 2005, the 2nd Italian Semantic Web Workshop, Trento, Italy, December 14-16, 2005. CEUR Workshop Proceedings, ISSN 1613-0073, online http://ceur-ws.org/Vol-166/70.pdf*, 2005.
2. J. Carroll, C. Bizer, P. Hayes, and P. Stickler. Named Graphs, Provenance and Trust. In *Proceedings of the Fourteenth International World Wide Web Conference (WWW2005), Chiba, Japan*, volume 14, pages 613–622, May 2005.
3. G. Criscuolo, F. Giunchiglia, and L. Serafini. A Foundation for Metareasoning, Part I: The proof theory. *Journal of Logic and Computation*, 12(1):167–208, 2002.

4. G. Criscuolo, F. Giunchiglia, and L. Serafini. A Foundation for Metareasoning, Part II: The model theory. *Journal of Logic and Computation*, 12(3):345–370, 2002.

5. F. Esposito, S. Ferilli, N. Di Mauro, T. M. A. Basile, L. Iannone, I. Palmisano, and G. Semeraro. Improving automatic labelling through rdf management. In Tengku M. T. Sembok, Halimah Badioze Zaman, Hsinchun Chen, Shalini R. Urs, and Sung-Hyon Myaeng, editors, *Digital Libraries: Technology and Management of Indigenous Knowledge for Global Access, 6th International Conference on Asian Digital Libraries, ICADL 2003, Kuala Lumpur, Malaysia, December 8-12, 2003, Proceedings*, volume 2911 of *Lecture Notes in Computer Science*, pages 578–589. Springer, 2003.

6. F. Esposito, L. Iannone, I. Palmisano, D. Redavid, and G. Semeraro. Redd: An algorithm for redundancy detection in rdf models. In Asunción Gómez-Pérez and Jérôme Euzenat, editors, *The Semantic Web: Research and Applications, Second European Semantic Web Conference, ESWC 2005, Heraklion, Crete, Greece, May 29 - June 1, 2005, Proceedings*, volume 3532 of *Lecture Notes in Computer Science*, pages 138–152. Springer, 2005.

7. F. Esposito, L. Iannone, I. Palmisano, and G. Semeraro. RDF Core: a Component for Effective Management of RDF Models. In Isabel F. Cruz, Vipul Kashyap, Stefan Decker, and Rainer Eckstein, editors, *Proceedings of SWDB'03, The first International Workshop on Semantic Web and Databases, Co-located with VLDB 2003, Humboldt-Universität, Berlin, Germany, September 7-8, 2003*, 2003.

8. C. Ghidini and F. Giunchiglia. Local models semantics, or contextual reasoning=locality+compatibility. *Artif. Intell.*, 127(2):221–259, 2001.

9. R. V. Guha, R. McCool, and R. Fikes. Contexts for the semantic web. In Sheila A. McIlraith, Dimitris Plexousakis, and Frank van Harmelen, editors, *International Semantic Web Conference*, volume 3298 of *Lecture Notes in Computer Science*, pages 32–46. Springer, 2004.

10. G. Klyne. *Contexts for RDF Information Modelling*. Content Technologies Ltd, October 2000. http://www.ninebynine.org/RDFNotes/RDFContexts.html.

11. G. Semeraro, F. Esposito, S. Ferilli, T. M.A. Basile, N. Di Mauro, L. Iannone, and I. Palmisano. Automatic management of annotations on cultural heritage material. In *International Conference on Digital Libraries, ICDL 2004, New Delhi, India, February 24-27, 2004, Proceedings*, pages 805–812, 2004.

12. R.W. Weyhrauch. Prolegomena to a Theory of Mechanized Formal Reasoning. *Artificial Intelligence*, 13(1):133–176, 1980.

Visualizing User Communities and Usage Trends of Digital Libraries Based on User Tracking Information

Seonho Kim, Subodh Lele, Sreeram Ramalingam, and Edward A. Fox

Department of Computer Science
Virginia Tech
Blacksburg, Virginia 24061 USA
{shk, subodhl, sreeram, fox}@vt.edu

Abstract. We describe VUDM, our Visual User-model Data Mining tool, and its application to data logged regarding interactions of 1,200 users of the Networked Digital Library of Theses and Dissertations (NDLTD). The goals of VUDM are to visualize social networks, patrons' distributions, and usage trends of NDLTD. The distinctive approach of this research is that we focus on analysis and visualization of users' implicit rating data, which was generated based on user tracking information, such as sending queries and browsing result sets – rather than focusing on explicit data obtained from a user survey, such as major, specialties, years of experience, and demographics. The VUDM interface uses spirals to portray virtual interest groups, positioned based on inter-group relationships. VUDM facilitates identifying trends related to changes in interest, as well as concept drift. A formative evaluation found that VUDM is perceived to be effective for five types of tasks. Future work will aim to improve the understandability and utility of VUDM.

1 Introduction

Digital libraries (DLs) support diverse users, but might do so even better if available data about those users could be employed to facilitate personalization. Work toward such a goal is in keeping with new trends to improve the WWW, such as the move toward "Web 2.0", where web applications become more flexible, and evolve with the collaboration of users. Fortunately, we may benefit from data mining and unsupervised learning techniques applied to the large volume of usage data from community-driven information systems like blogs [1], wikis, and other types of online journals. Thus, we can go beyond what is possible if only examining data from OLAP systems [2]. We begin to address challenging research questions about a DL such as:

- What are the current trends of information seeking for this DL?
- What kinds of people are using this DL? Who is a potential mentor for whom?
- How has the focus of retrieval changed for a particular user?
- What academic areas are emerging as popular attractions?
- How many people are interested in which topics? How many are experts?
- How many virtual groups, of users who share interests, exist in the DL?
- Which topics are related to which other topics?

S. Sugimoto et al. (Eds.): ICADL 2006, LNCS 4312, pp. 111–120, 2006.
© Springer-Verlag Berlin Heidelberg 2006

Fortunately, visualization supports direct involvement of users in exploration and data mining, so they can utilize their creativity, flexibility, and general knowledge [3].

There has been a great deal of prior work that relates to our research, so we only can touch on a small sample of papers touching on particular aspects of our approach.

Some of the broad areas of related work include: visualization of social networks, visualization of documents and topics, learning about users, and user modeling. For example, visualization of networks of criminals and criminal events can help unearth hidden patterns in crime data as well as detect terrorist threats [4]. Boyd, working with Social Network Fragments [5], visualized clusters of contacts derived from the *to* and *cc* lists in email archives. Heer, in Vizster, visualized relationships between members in an online date site Friendster [6], SPIRE Themescape [7] facilitates visualization of the topic distribution in a large document space. Probabilistic approaches to user modeling have made it possible to learn about user profiles, as well as to revise them based on additional data [8, 9]. Tang utilized users' browsing patterns for collaborative filtering [10]. Webb examined challenging user modeling approaches like data rating, concept drift, data sparseness, and computational complexity [11].

In Section 2 we describe the DL context and data preprocessing aspects of our study. Section 3 introduces VUDM and our approach to visualization. Section 4 gives details about the visualization and illustrates its use for key tasks. Section 5 summarizes our pilot user study, and identifies important areas for future work, while Section 6 presents conclusions.

2 Data Description and Preprocessing

The Networked Digital Library of Theses and Dissertations (NDLTD) union catalog [12] describes a collection of over 240,000 electronic theses or dissertations (ETDs) from more than 325 member institutions, such as universities and libraries. Our data set consists of 1,200 user models, describing those who registered to use our service between August 2005 and May 2006. During the registration process, new users explicitly provide data, called "explicit data", such as their specialty, major (area of interest), and number of years worked in each such area. Explicit data is easy to analyze with normal analysis tools. However, such data is insufficient when addressing the comprehensive questions listed in Section 1. Further, user interests and behavior change over time, so it is important to enhance user models with data from a user tracking system [13], i.e., "implicit (rating) data" (so-called because the data was not entered explicitly in answer to questions). Our implicit data consists of "queries" and two types of interest "topics" which have the form of noun phrases. The user tracking system runs on an NDLTD service that provides document clustering, and collects the cluster names that users traverse. It records positively rated, as well as ignored, hence negatively rated "topics" [14]. Our 1,200 user models contain both explicit data and implicit rating data that grow with use of NDLTD, but our focus is on visualizing such user models mainly using implicit rating data. The data allows us to characterize users, user groups, and broader user communities. At the same time, we can characterize topics and (scholarly) areas of interest. Combining the two types of information allows identification of areas of user expertise, mentoring relationships among users, and changes/trends related to the data and information considered. The next section explains our visualization interface (VUDM) that supports all this.

3 VUDM and Visualization Strategies

Our Visual User model Data Mining (VUDM) tool transforms available data into a set of windows as illustrated in Figure 1. The main window presents an overview of all users (shown as icons) and communities (i.e., groups, shown as spirals). The presentation is controlled by a slider, that specifies a user correlation threshold (θ, which will be explained later in this section), in order to determine if users should be in the same group. Another control determines whether an overview is shown, or if one should zoom into a region of particular interest. In addition, all user icons and group spirals can be dragged with the mouse, e.g., to examine a congested area.

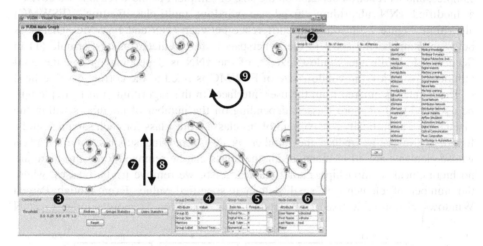

Fig. 1. The main window, 1, displays an overview of users, virtual interest groups, and their relationships. The statistics window, 2, presents detailed information, either about all users or about all groups in the system. The slide bar, 3, controls the correlation threshold (θ). The small tables at the bottom, 4, 5, and 6, show detailed information about groups, topics, and highlighted users, respectively. When using the right mouse button, dragging up and down, 7 and 8, and free dragging, 9, cause: zoom, un-zoom, and panning.

On demand, a small pop up window appears – see Figure 1 on the right (2). It provides detailed information about users or groups. It supports basic OLAP functions, such as sorting and listing. This and the main window are linked and synchronized. Thus, VUDM services combine strengths of graphical and text-oriented presentations.

The visualization of users and topic-based groups aims to summarize high dimensionality data, in order to support key tasks (see Section 4). Three degrees of freedom (three dimensions) are shown, since one can vary the position (x, y coordinates) of a spiral center, as well as the distance (of a user icon) from the center.

The positions of spirals (groups) are not controlled absolutely because the dimensionality of data is too high. It is only important to maintain relative distances among spirals (interest groups). For laying out the spirals, a "grid layout" method [15] is used. That is, the whole space is divided into equal-sized rectangles and the "groups of similar groups" are centered in each rectangle. Each "group of similar groups" consists of a representative (largest) group at the center and satellite similar groups around it at a distance based on the group similarity with the representative group.

Regarding classifying users into virtual interest groups and finding "groups of similar groups", we use the same algorithm. Because any statistical information about distribution and underlying densities of patrons, such as sample mean and standard deviation, are not known, nonparametric classification techniques, such as Parzen Windows and k-Nearest-Neighbor (kNN), should be used. But kNN is inappropriate since it assigns the test item into only one class, it needs well-classified training samples, and its function depends on the size of sample. For these reasons we devised a modified kNN algorithm: "fixed-size window multi-classification" (FSWMC) algorithm. Figure 2 illustrates the difference between kNN and FSWMC. Distances between samples (the spots in the hyperspace) are calculated using Formula (1) in Section 4.1. While the window size, r, of the kNN is dependent on 'n', the total number of samples, the window size of FSWMC is fixed to the correlation threshold θ. The θ value is entered from the user interface. In this algorithm, a test sample will be assigned to 0 or more classes, depending on the number of neighbors within the distance θ. Theoretically a maximum of 'n' classes, one class for each sample, can be found. However, we reduce the number by the "removing subclass rule": a class whose elements are all elements of another class can be removed to ensure there are no hierarchical relationships among classes. Also, we remove trivial classes, where the number of elements is smaller than a specified value. Even though Parzen Windows also uses a fixed-size window, our algorithm is more similar to kNN

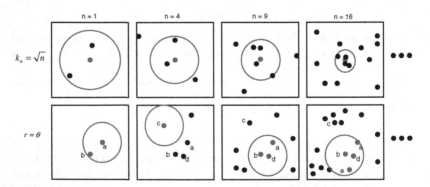

Fig. 2. Top Row: The kNN rule starts at the test point, red spot, among classified samples, and grows the surrounding circle until it contains 'k' samples. Then, it classifies the test point into the most dominant class in the circle. Bottom Row: The fixed-window multi-classification rule classifies all samples enclosed by the fixed sized, $r=\theta$, circle, surrounding the test point, into a new class. If this new class is a sub- or super-class of an already found class, remove the redundant sub-class. In this figure, two classes, {c} and {a,b,d,e}, are found up to stage n=16.

because *k*NN and FSWMC estimate directly the "a posterior" probabilities, P(class|feature), while the Parzen Windows estimates the density function p(feature|class). We also use our algorithm to find "groups of similar groups". However, in that case we assign the testing sample to the most dominant class among samples within the surrounding region, because a group should be assigned to only one "group of similar groups".

4 Support for Knowledge Finding Tasks

The goal of our visualization is to support understanding about users, user groups, and topics – and their interrelationships. We consider three categories of knowledge: user characteristics and relationships, virtual interest groups and relationships, and usage trends. These are discussed in detail in the following three subsections.

4.1 User Characteristics and Relations

User characteristics are the most important information for personalization. Many commercial online shopping malls, such as amazon.com and ebay.com, are already utilizing user characteristics for personalized services. VUDM visualizes each user's interest topics and expertise level by putting his icon on spirals in a 2D user space (see Figure 3 left). Each spiral represents a set of closely related topics shared by the users placed on the spiral. Because a user may be interested in multiple topics / scholarly areas, VUDM puts copies of his icon on all spirals that match his interests, linking copies together with connection lines when the user is highlighted (see Figure 1).

The amount of expertise on a topic for a user is used to determine the distance from the center of the spiral to that user's icon. The closer to the center of the spiral, the more expertise the person has about the topic. Expertise is computed as a function of the number of years the user has worked in the area, and of the length of usage history. High-ranked persons in a group are colored differently, and are classified as mentors; novice users may be encouraged to collaborate with them.

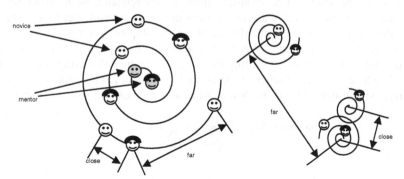

Fig. 3. Left: Each small face icon on the spiral is a user. A spiral represents a set of closely related topics and, thus, forms a virtual interest group with the users on the spiral who share the topics. The size of a spiral is proportional to the size of the group. Distance between user icons within a group reflects their similarity with regard to topics. Right: Distance between two spirals reflects the similarity between the two groups.

Decisions about the: formation of a virtual interest group, selection of users who make up a group, and location of each member icon's distance from the center of a spiral, are made by calculating correlations between users according to formulas (1) and (2). We used mainly implicit data rather than explicit data, because collecting implicit data is more practical than collecting explicit data, and it helps us avoid terminology issues (e.g., ambiguity) which are common in information systems [14].

$$correlation(a,b) = \frac{\sum_j (v_{a,j} - \bar{v}_a)(v_{b,j} - \bar{v}_b)}{\sqrt{\sum_j (v_{a,j} - \bar{v}_a)^2 \sum_j (v_{b,j} - \bar{v}_b)^2}} \tag{1}$$

$$\bar{v}_a = \frac{number\ of\ topics\ positively\ rated\ by\ 'a' + number\ of\ used\ queries\ by\ 'a'}{number\ of\ topics\ proposed\ to\ 'a' + number\ of\ used\ queries\ by\ 'a'} \tag{2}$$

(1) represents the correlation of users 'a' and 'b'. 'v_{aj}' is the rating value of item 'j' of user 'a' which means the number of positive ratings on 'j' made by 'a'. 'j' represents common topics or research interests which are rated by users 'a' and 'b'. '$\bar{v}_a$' is the average probability of positive rating of the user, as obtained by (2) [16].

4.2 Virtual Interest Group and Relations

Virtual Interest Groups are virtual clusters of DL users who share specific research interests and topics. Visualizing virtual interest groups helps us understand the characteristics of DL patrons, may help patrons identify potential collaborators, and may aid recommendation. From this visualization, it is possible to figure out distributions of users, preferences regarding research interests / topics, and potential interdisciplinary areas. The VUDM finds virtual interest groups by connecting user pairs with high correlation values (above a threshold). The higher the threshold, the more precise will be the virtual interest group.

VUDM arranges virtual interest groups in two dimensional user space according to their degree of relationship (similarity) with other groups. Relative distance between groups reflects the degree of relationship; more highly related groups are closer. We assume that in two highly related groups, users in one group will share interests with users in the other. We measure the degree of relationship between two groups either by calculating the vector similarity between the two group representatives (a union of the model data for all members), using Formula (3), or by calculating the Tanimoto Metric (4) which uses the number of members in common [17]. Compared to vector similarity, the Tanimoto Metric has lower computational cost but still is effective.

$$groupsim(A,B) = \sum_{i \in T} \frac{v_{A,i}}{\sqrt{\sum_{i \in T} v_{A,i}^2}} \frac{v_{B,i}}{\sqrt{\sum_{i \in T} v_{B,i}^2}} \tag{3}$$

$$D_{Tanimoto}(A,B) = \frac{n_A + n_B - 2n_{AB}}{n_A + n_B - n_{AB}} \tag{4}$$

(3) represents the group similarity between two virtual interest groups 'A' and 'B'. '$v_{A,j}$' is the sum of the frequencies of positive rating on topic 'i' made by all users in

group 'A'. 'T' is the set of all topics in the system that are rated positive at least once. (4) represents the similarity distance between two groups 'A' and 'B'. 'n_A' and 'n_B' are the number of users in A and B, respectively. 'n_{AB}' is the number of users in both groups A and B.

4.3 Usage Trends

In addition to characteristics and relationships among individual users and virtual interest groups, general usage trends also are of interest. Visualizing usage trends in VUDM is accomplished by providing overviews over time. Thus, Figure 4 shows VUDM results for three months. In June we see a cluster of small groups at the bottom. In July we see those are attracting more users and groups, and seem to be merging, while an old topic, the large spiral at the top, adds one more user. That large group shrinks in August, at the same time as there are further shifts among the small groups (now three) at the bottom. Thus, we see which areas emerge, are sustained, shrink, or grow. Further, we may extrapolate from series of changes to make predictions.

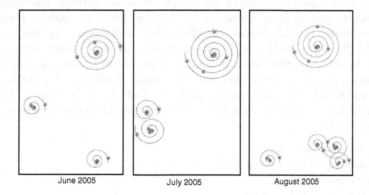

June 2005   July 2005   August 2005

Fig. 4. Visualizing user space at different times makes it possible to figure out and predict retrieval trends, emerging attractive topics, drifts of concepts, etc.

VUDM also can help digital librarians visualize *concept drift*, which is a well known problem in the machine learning area [11]. The real attributes of a user are likely to change over time [18]. In recommender systems, detecting the concept drift of a user allows making more timely recommendations (see Figure 5).

As a virtual interest group spiral represents a set of closely related topics and interests, it also can be regarded as a concept for each user who belongs in the spiral. If a concept of a user drifts to a new concept, a clone of his icon appears on the new spiral and a connection line links the new icon together with the previously existing icons to indicate that they are for a single person. Therefore, by tracing connection lines and spirals over time, it is possible to detect occurrences of concept drift.

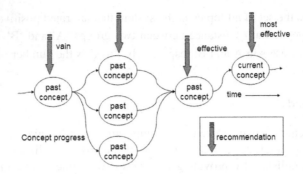

Fig. 5. Detecting drift of concepts makes it possible to provide timely recommendation

5 Evaluation and Future Work

It is difficult to evaluate a visualization tool objectively. Therefore, we conducted an analytic formative evaluation based on user interviews. Unlike a summative evaluation, whose goal is to prove the effectiveness of software statistically with many random participants, formative evaluation aims to collect professional suggestions from several domain-knowledgeable participants, as the system is developed [19]. Eight Ph.D students majoring in computer science were recruited, who have basic knowledge about Digital Library, Data Mining, and information visualization. Participants were given time to become familiar with VUDM and then were allowed to ask any questions that came to mind. After this process, they were asked to evaluate the effectiveness of VUDM with regard to providing each of five types of knowledge:

a. Information seeking trends?
b. Virtual interest group distributions?
c. User characteristics?
d. Trends in the near future?
e. Drift of concepts?

For each question, participants could answer either 'negative' or 'positive'. If they selected 'positive', they were asked to select the degree of agreement from 1 to 10. All participants answered positively for all questions, except two questions were answered negatively by one participant (see below). The average (non-negative) scores for each question were 89%, 85.5%, 86.2%, 75.8%, and 69%, respectively.

During the interview sessions, participants were asked to comment on problems with VUDM and to make suggestions. Most participants had difficulty understanding some of the features of the visualization. For example, some were confused about groups and their locations. Some didn't understand the reason that there are no labels for groups and users. The fact is that VUDM characterizes users and groups based on sets of topics (the user and group are involved with), and provides topic tables which consist of hundreds of topics ordered by frequencies, instead of labels.

One negative answer was about question 'c', using the topic tables. The participant commented that the topic tables don't work with visualization because they contain too much detail information. The other negative answer was about question 'd'. It is difficult for VUDM users to spot changes in usage trends since they must see multiple pictures about usage trends for the past several months to predict the next month. The participant commented that VUDM should provide better visualization for this task, such as animation or colored traces showing changes. Since our approach is new, it is not surprising that some users were confused about the novel features of VUDM.

Further testing, with more time allowed for users to become familiar with our approach, is needed. Another problem we identified is that our user model data is just cumulative. It is not easy to determine if and when a topic goes out of favor. If we worked with sliding windows covering different time periods, we might solve such problems. Also, because the NDLTD union catalog covers all scholarly fields, and we only had 1,200 registered users, finding virtual interest groups was hard. Adding more user data or applying VUDM to subject-specific DLs, like CITIDEL [20] or ETANA-DL [21], should solve this problem. Finally, privacy issues were identified. Devices and modifications were requested to secure sensitive information, such as user IDs.

6 Conclusions

We developed a visualization tool, VUDM, to support knowledge finding and decision making in personalization. VUDM visualizes user communities and usage trends. VUDM makes use of unsupervised learning methods for grouping, labeling, and arranging a presentation in a 2-dimensional space. For this, a modified kNN neighboring algorithm, fixed-size window multi-classification algorithm, was devised which is suitable for flexible classification of users and user groups. Also, we categorized the knowledge needs required for personalization into three subcategories: user characteristics and relationships, virtual interest group characteristics and relationships, and usage trends. We showed how each of these can be addressed. We applied VUDM to NDLTD, analyzing 1,200 user models which are largely based on implicit ratings collected by a user tracking system. Through a formative evaluation, we found that VUDM is positively viewed with regard to the three categories.

Acknowledgements

We thank the: people and organizations working on NDLTD, students participating in formative evaluation interviews, developers of the Piccolo and Jung Java libraries, and NDLTD users who answered our special survey. Thanks also go to NSF for support of grants DUE-0121679, DUE-0121741, IIS-0307867, and IIS-0325579.

References

1. Ravi Kumar, Jasmine Novak, Prabhakar Raghavan, Andrew Tomkins: Structure and Evolution of Blogspace. In Communications of the ACM, Vol. 47, No. 12 (2004) 35-39
2. Tom Soukup, Ian Davidson: Visual Data Mining: Techniques and Tools for Data Visualization and Mining. Wiley Computer Publishing, (2002)
3. Daniel A. Keim: Information Visualization and Visual Data Mining. IEEE Transaction on Visualization and Computer Graphics, Vol 8, No. 1 (2002) 1-8

4. Jennifer Xu, Hsinchun Chen: Criminal Network Analysis and Visualization. Communications of the ACM, Vol. 48, No. 6 (2005) 101-107
5. Danah Boyd, Jeffrey Potter: Social Network Fragments: An Interactive Tool for Exploring Digital Social Connections. In Proceedings of International Conference on Computer Graphics and Interactive Techniques (SIGGRAPH 2003) (2003) 1
6. Jeffrey Heer, Danah Boyd: Vizster: Visualizing Online Social Networks. In Proceeding of the 2005 IEEE Symposium on Information Visualization (INFOVIS'05) (2005) 5
7. James A. Wise, James J. Thomas, Kelly Pen-nock, David Lantrip, Marc Pottier, Anne Schur: Visualizing the non-visual: Spatial analysis and interaction with information from text documents. In Proc. of the Information Visualization Symposium, IEEE Computer Society Press, (1995) 51-58
8. Eren Manavoglu, Dmitry Pavlov, C. Lee Giles: Probabilistic User Behavior Models. In Proceedings of the Third IEEE International Conference on Data Mining (ICDM'03), (2003), 203-210
9. Michael Pazzani, Daniel Billsus: Learning and Revising User Profiles: The Identification of Interesting Web Sites. Machine Learning, Kluwer Academic Publishers, Vol 27 (1997) 313-331
10. Tiffany Ya Tang, Gordon McCalla: Mining Implicit Ratings for Focused Collaborative Filtering for Paper Recommendations. In Online Proceedings of Workshop on User and Group models for Web-based Adaptive Collaborative Environments (UM'03). Available at http://www.ia.uned.es/~elena/um03-ws/ (2006)
11. Geoffrey I. Webb, Michael J. Pazzani, Daniel Billsus: Machine Learning for User Modeling, User Modeling and User-Adapted Interaction. Kluwer Academic Publisher, Vol 11 (2001) 19-29
12. NDLTD, Networked Digital Library of Theses and Dissertations, available at http://www.ndltd.org (2006)
13. Uma Murthy, Sandi Vasile, Kapil Ahuja: Virginia Tech CS class project report. Available at http://collab. dlib.vt.edu/runwiki/wiki.pl?IsRproj_UserMod_Con (2006)
14. Seonho Kim, Uma Murthy, Kapil Ahuja, Sandi Vasile, Edward A. Fox: Effectiveness of Implicit Rating Data on Characterizing Users in Complex Information Systems. 9th European Conference on Research and Advanced Technology for Digital Libraries (ECDL'05), LNCS 3652, Springer-Verlag, Berlin Heidelberg New York (2005) 186-194
15. Ivan Herman, Guy Melançon, M. Scott Marshall: Graph Visualization and Navigation in Information Visualization: A Survey. IEEE Transactions on Visualization and Computer Graphics, Vol 6, Issue 1 (2000) 24-43
16. Seonho Kim, Edward A. Fox: Interest-based User Grouping Model for Collaborative Filtering in Digital Libraries. 7th International Conference of Asian Digital Libraries (ICADL'04), LNCS 3334, Springer-Verlag, Berlin Heidelberg New York (2004) 533-542
17. Richard O. Duda, Peter E. Hart, David G. Stork: Pattern Classification. A Wiley-Interscience Publication, (2000)
18. Gerhard Widmer, Miroslav Kubat: Learning in the Presence of Concept Drift and Hidden Contexts. Machine Learning. Kluwer Academic Publishers, Vol. 23 (1996) 69-101
19. Deborah Hix, H. Rex Hartson: Developing User Interfaces: Ensuring Usability Through Product & Process. Wiley Professional Computing, (1993)
20. CITIDEL, Computing and Information Technology Interactive Digital Educational Library. Available at http://www.citidel.org (2006)
21. ETANA-DL, Managing complex information applications: An archaeology digital library. Available at http://etana.dlib.vt.edu (2006)

Extracting Mnemonic Names of People from the Web

Tomoko Hokama[1] and Hiroyuki Kitagawa[1,2]

[1] Graduate School of Systems and Information Engineering, University of Tsukuba
[2] Center for Computational Sciences, University of Tsukuba
Tenno-dai 1-1-1 Tsukuba-shi, 305-8577 Japan
tomokoh@kde.cs.tsukuba.ac.jp, kitagawa@cs.tsukuba.ac.jp

Abstract. The web has gained much attention as new media reflecting real-time interest in the world. This attention is driven by the proliferation of tools like bulletin boards and weblogs. The web is a source from which we can collect and summarize information about a particular object (e.g., business organization, product, person, etc.) For example, the extraction of reputation information is a major research topic in information extraction and knowledge extraction from the web. The ability to collect web pages about a particular object is essential in obtaining such information and extracting knowledge from it. A big problem in the web page collection process is that the same objects are referred to in different ways in different web documents. For example, a person may be referred to by full name, first name, affiliation and title, or nicknames. This paper proposes a method for extracting these mnemonic names of people from the web and shows experimental results using real web data.

Keywords: knowledge extraction, object identification, web mining.

1 Introduction

The development of Internet technology affords us many ways to publish information without depending on mass media. For example, bulletin boards and weblogs are well known tools for disseminating personal opinions or comments to the world. The web has gained much attention as new media reflecting real-time interest in the world thanks to the proliferation of such tools.

Demand is great to extract useful information and knowledge from the web, and much work has been done in the area. For example, reputation information extraction is a major research topic in information extraction and knowledge extraction from the web [2]. In extracting reputation information, evaluative expressions about a particular object (e.g., business organization, product, person, etc.) are extracted from text surrounding the string that represents the object. The ability to collect web pages describing the target object is first needed to extract reputation information. Existing research extracts evaluative expressions from text surrounding the official name of the target object, such as the product name.

S. Sugimoto et al. (Eds.): ICADL 2006, LNCS 4312, pp. 121–130, 2006.

Specialized topic detection for a particular object will become important as well as reputation information extraction, which analyzes text around the object's name and extracts "local" information. With people, personal information sources exist, including; personal databases, public homepages, and Wikipedia. These are essentially static or official, so they cannot yield dynamic and unofficial information that includes recent popular topics about a particular person. Far larger web space that includes information sources such as bulletin boards and blogs must be covered to collect dynamic and unofficial information. Taking into account the nature of dynamic and unofficial sources, not only the topics are important, but we need to know how much attention these topics attract. Authors have proposed a method to detect people-related topics and estimate scales of detected topics [6].

A big problem in information extraction and knowledge extraction for a particular object is that the same objects are referred to in different ways in different web documents. For example, a person may be referred to by full name, first name, affiliation and title, or nicknames. In this paper, we use the term "mnemonic name" as a name other than the official name of the target object. In particular, people often use mnemonic names rather than an official name when they complain or evaluate an object unfavorably.

Objects include business organizations and products, but in this paper we focus on "people." We consider the full name of a person as the "official name." It is generally difficult to collect mnemonic names other than the first name or the last name. Our goal is to extract mnemonic names of people from the web. We use short strings adjacent to the full name of the target person to extract mnemonic names. The basic idea is inspired by information extraction techniques. In this paper, we consider only Japanese texts because we use a Japanese linguistic knowledge.

The following section reviews related work. Section 3 describes details of our proposed method for extracting mnemonic names of people from the web. We show experimental results using real web data in section 4. We conclude this work and mention future work in section 5.

2   Related Work

For data cleaning and integrating multiple databases, the merge/purge problem or duplicate detection techniques have been studied for decades [5,7]. Recently, object identification [9] is attracting attention to integrate information from multiple information sources on the web. Duplicate detection or object identification techniques need database schemas or HTML table tags to utilize attribute values.

[3] applies object identification to Personal Information Management (PIM). The authors analyze files on a user's PC and perform object identification using dependency relationships between multiple objects such as research papers, people, and conferences.

For Japanese plain text (web documents), several methods to classify web pages about people with the same name using profile information of people and document clustering techniques have been proposed [10,11]. There is no research, however, for collecting web pages that mention a person but do not include that person's name. Mnemonic name extraction is essentially needed to collect these pages.

There are lots of works on named entity recognition [4,1,8]. "PERSON", one of the types of named entity defined in MUC's named entity task, represents named person or family. Generally, named entity recognition aims to discover official names of entities. Our purpose is to extract "non-official" names of people. Therefore, our goal is different from that of named entity recognition.

3   Mnemonic Name Extraction of People

3.1   Basic Idea and Overview of the Proposed Method

This section gives the basic idea and an overview of our proposed method for extracting mnemonic names of people. The proposed method is based on the following two heuristics.

1. We usually say "*alias* こと *fullname*"[1] in Japanese to describe that a string *alias* is one of the mnemonic names of a person whose full name is *fullname*.[2]
2. The full name and mnemonic names often occur in similar contexts. Here, we call strings adjacent to the full name or mnemonic names "contexts." In other words, if strings "*prefix fullname*" or "*fullname suffix*" occur in some web documents, it is possible that strings "*prefix alias*" or "*alias suffix*" also occur in other web documents.

The proposed method is overviewed below.

1. Extract candidate mnemonic names of the target person from the web.
2. Extract strings adjacent to the full name of the target person (prefix patterns: strings that occur right before the full name, suffix patterns: strings that occur right after the full name) from the web, then calculate weights for all prefix and suffix patterns. Meaningful patterns are then selected as "adjacent patterns."
3. Evaluate candidate mnemonic names extracted in Step 1 using adjacent patterns extracted in Step 2. Then select top k candidates as "mnemonic names" of the target person.

Figure 1 shows the flow of the proposed method. The following sub-sections describe details of candidate mnemonic name extraction, adjacent pattern extraction, and candidate name evaluation.

---

[1] "こと" is a Japanese term pronounced "koto." The meaning of "こと" in English is "be called" in this context. "こと" is a very vague term, so it is not the decisive factor but a clue to discover mnemonic names.

[2] We describe the full name of a person as *fullname*.

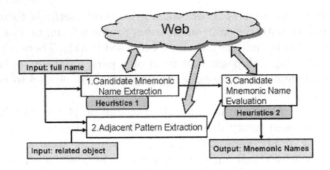

Fig. 1. Overview of the proposed method

3.2   Candidate Mnemonic Name Extraction

We usually say "*alias* こと *fullname*" in Japanese to describe the alias name or the nickname of a person. Therefore, the string that occurs right before "こと *fullname*" is potentially a mnemonic name of the person. If this string is commonly used as the mnemonic name of the person, it occurs in web documents repeatedly. Based on the above discussion, we extract candidate mnemonic names as follows:

1. Perform a query "こと *fullname*" on a web search engine, then get the URL list.
2. Get web pages in the URL list and analyze these pages, and then extract the string $<t_1 t_2 ... t_n>$ that occurs right before the string "こと *fullname*". (t_1, t_2, ... , t_n are morphemes.)
3. Extract sub-strings of $<t_1 t_2 ... t_n>$, $t_1 t_2 ... t_n$, $t_2 t_3 ... t_n$, $t_{n-1} t_n$, and t_n, and then select sub-strings whose first morpheme's POS tag is "general noun" as candidate mnemonic names. Then count the frequency of occurrences for each candidate.
4. Eliminate candidate mnemonic names that occur the only once in analyzed web pages.

Figure 2 shows an example of candidate mnemonic name extraction. A number of candidate mnemonic names of a Japanese MLB player "松井秀喜(Hideki Matsui)", who belongs to NY Yankees, is extracted in Figure 2.

3.3   Adjacent Pattern Extraction

Adjacent patterns are extracted from the web as well as candidate mnemonic names. Basically, we get web pages including the full name of the target person by performing a web search, and extract strings adjacent to the full name (prefix and suffix patterns.) Because there can be people with the same name, we add an object name that has great relevance to the target person (e.g., parent organization) to the search query. After extracting all prefix and suffix patterns, we calculate weights for all patterns by considering the co-occurrence relation between the full name and patterns.

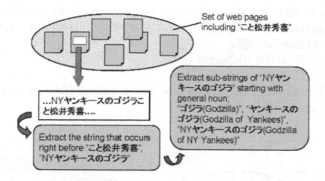

Fig. 2. Example of candidate mnemonic name extraction: "松井秀喜(Hideki Matsui)"

The weight of a prefix pattern *prefix* is calculated based on the following idea. Let the set of web pages including *prefix* be R, and let the set of web pages including "*prefix fullname*" be $R1$. $R1$ is a subset of R in theory, and it is considered that the more $R1$ accounts for R, the more frequently *fullname* and *prefix* co-occur (i.e., these two strings have a strong relationship) (Figure 3.) Therefore, we adopt the number of web pages including "*prefix fullname*" (the numbers of $R1$'s members) divided by the number of web pages including *prefix* (the number of R's members) as the weight of *prefix*. We calculate weights of suffix patterns in the same way.

The procedure for adjacent pattern extraction follows.

1. Let the object name that has great relevance to the target person be *rel_obj*. Perform the query "*fullname* AND *rel_obj*" on a web search engine, then get the URL list.
2. Analyze web pages in the URL list and extract strings adjacent to the full-name $<t_1 t_2 ... t_m>$. Extract sub-strings of $<t_1 t_2 ... t_m>$ in a similar fashion of candidate mnemonic name extraction (See section 3.2) and add these sub-strings to the list of prefix and suffix patterns. In this case, we do not consider POS tags because patterns may begin with any word tagged with any POS tags. Figure 4 shows an example of pattern extraction. Prefix and suffix patterns are extracted from text surrounding the full name "松井秀喜(Hideki Matsui)" in Figure 4. In Figure 4, the term "ヤンキース(Yankees)" is used as *rel_ojb*.
3. Calculate weights for all extracted prefix patterns as follows: The weight of a prefix pattern *prefix*, $w(prefix)$, is calculated by the following formulas.
   $r = searchResults(prefix)$[3]
   $r1 = searchResults("prefix fullname")$
   $w(prefix) = r1 \ / \ r$

---

[3] searchResults(*query*) is a function that returns the total number of web pages including *query*. In fact, it is impossible to know the total number of those web pages. We use Yahoo!API's totalResultsAvailable field for the estimated value.

4. Calculate weights for all extracted suffix patterns as follows: The weight of a suffix pattern *suffix*, $w(suffix)$, is calculated by following formulas.
   $r = searchResults(suffix)$
   $r1 = searchResults(\text{"fullname suffix"})$
   $w(suffix) = r1 \ / \ r$
5. Add prefix and suffix patterns whose weights exceed the given threshold to the "adjacent patterns" list.

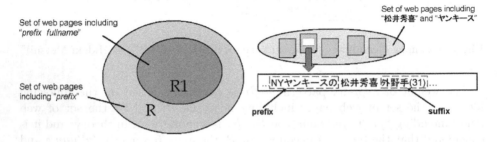

Fig. 3. Relationship between R and $R1$ **Fig. 4.** Example of pattern extraction: "松井秀喜(Hideki Matsui)", *rel_obj* is "ヤンキース(Yankees)"

3.4   Candidate Mnemonic Name Evaluation

In the final step, we evaluate candidate mnemonic names using adjacent patterns. We use the second heuristics in section 3.1. It is highly possible that a candidate mnemonic name *cand* is actually a mnemonic name of the target person if *cand* occurs just before or just after adjacent patterns. The evaluation procedure is shown below.

1. Set the initial score of *cand* to zero.
2. For all adjacent patterns, apply this procedure:
   (a) If the adjacent pattern is a prefix pattern, generate a string *"prefix cand"*. If the adjacent pattern is a suffix pattern, generate a string *"cand suffix"*.
   (b) Obtain the total number of web pages including the generated string *total* using a search engine. Add the product of *total* and the pattern's weight ($w(prefix)$ or $w(suffix)$) to the score. We adopt this calculation because it is highly possible that *cand* is the actual mnemonic name in those situations; there are many web pages including *"prefix cand"* or *"cand suffix"*, and the pattern's weight is big.

After calculating all scores of candidate mnemonic names, we select top k candidates as mnemonic names of the target person.

The pseudo code of candidate evaluation is as follows:

```
score(cand) = 0
for prefix in allAdjacentPrefixPatterns
  query = ''prefix cand''
  score(cand) += searchResults(query) * w(prefix)
end
for suffix in allAdjacentSuffixPatterns
  query = ''cand suffix''
  score(cand) += searchResults(query) * w(suffix)
end
```

4 Experimental Results

We conducted experiments to evaluate the effectiveness of our method using real web data. We used Yahoo!API to get the URL list and estimate the total number of search results in our experiments.

4.1 Parameter Settings

- Candidate mnemonic name Extraction
  - Number of web pages to analyze: 500
  - Max number of morphemes of candidate mnemonic name strings: 5
- Adjacent pattern extraction
  - Number of web pages to analyze: 500
  - Max number of morphemes of adjacent patterns: 3
  - Threshold of pattern's weight: 0.01
- Candidate mnemonic name evaluation
  - Max number of mnemonic names finally selected: 5

4.2 Experimental Results and Discussion

We extracted mnemonic names for 6 people using our proposed method. We consider only Japanese texts because the proposed method use a Japanese linguistic knowledge. Extracted candidate mnemonic names, adjacent patterns, and finally extracted mnemonic names are listed in Tables 1 to 6.

Table 1 is for "Jun-ichiro Koizumi", the Japanese prime minister. Table 2 is for "Hideki Matsui", a Japanese MLB player belonging to New York Yankees. Table 3 is for "Shizuka Arakawa", a Japanese figure skater who got the gold medal in Torino Olympic. Table 4 is for "Hidetoshi Nakata", a Japanese soccer player belonging to Bolton, a professional soccer team in Serie A (Italian soccer league.) Table 5 is for "Ryuichi Sakamoto", a Japanese musician known for his movie soundtracks. Table 6 is for "Takafumi Horie", the former president of a Japanese IT venture company, Livedoor.

As we see in the tables, extracted mnemonic names are generally appropriate. Because many inappropriate names are included in candidate mnemonic names, evaluation of candidates using adjacent patterns seems to work well. However, several inappropriate names were extracted (Tables 3, 6) and a few appropriate mnemonic names among candidates were missed. To improve precision and

Table 1. Target: "小泉純一郎(Jun-ichiro Koizumi)" (Related object: "自民(Liberal Democratic Party)")

candidates	純ちゃん(Jun-chan), ジュン様(Jun-sama), ライオンハート(Lion Heart),..., (9 candidates)
prefix adjacent pattern	由紀夫代表VS, 人びと放送人,松岡洋右と...
suffix adjacent pattern	の暴論青, 首相の汚い, 首相は二十二...
mnemonic names	ポチ(Pochi)[a], 純ちゃん(Jun-chan)[b], ジュン様(Jun-sama)[b], ライオンハート(Lion Heart)[c]

[a] "Pochi" is a tipycal pet dog's name in Japan.
[b] "chan" and "sama" make nicknames with a person's name (In this case, "Jun").
[c] Jun-ichiro Koizumi is often referred to by "Lion Heart" because of his hair style.

Table 2. Target: "松井秀喜(Hideki Matsui)" (Related object: "ヤンキース(Yankees)")

candidates	ゴジラ(Godzilla), ヤンキースのゴジラ(Godzilla of Yankees), 契約したゴジラ, 松井(Matsui), ... (44 candidates)
prefix adjacent pattern	庵ヤンキースの, がヤンキース無念, 善浩ヤンキースの,...
suffix adjacent pattern	応援記買い物, 手術成功追記, のチャンピョンリングゲットを,...
mnemonic names	松井(Matsui)[a], ゴジラ(Godzilla)[b], ゴジラ松井(Godzilla Matsui)[ab], マツイ(Matsui)[a]

[a] "Matsui" is his family name.
[b] "Godzilla" is the most popular nickname of Hideki Matsui.

Table 3. Target: "荒川静香(Shizuka Arakawa)" (Related object: "トリノ(Torino)")

candidates	ちゃん, 一ちゃん, イナバウアー(Ina Bauer), クールビューティー(Cool Beauty), ビューティー(Beauty),... (9 candidates)
prefix adjacent pattern	リアルタイムトリノ2,華麗に完勝, 最終日金,...
suffix adjacent pattern	選手24プリンスホテル, プロ初グラビア, 23プリンスホテル村主,...
mnemonic names	ちゃん[a], イナバウアー(Ina Bauer)[b], ビューティー(Beauty)[c], 一ちゃん[a], クールビューティー(Cool Beauty)[c]

[a] Inappropriate mnemonic name.
[b] "Ina Bauer" is one of her characteristic figure skating moves.
[c] Shizuka Arakawa is often called "Cool Beauty" because of her poker face.

coverage of the proposed method, more study on calculating adjacent pattern weights and candidate name's score is needed.

At this time, we only consider strings starting with a general noun in candidate extraction. It may be effective to consider strings starting with other part of speeches, such as adjectives. We also need to use extra-heuristics other than the Japanese term "こと" for collecting additional candidate mnemonic names.

Table 4. Target: "中田秀寿(Hidetoshi Nakata)" (Related object: "ボルトン(Bolton)")

candidates	ヒデ(Hide), ジーコジャパンの王様(The King of Zico Japan), 活躍するヒデ, キャプテンを務めるヒデ, ... (11 candidates)
prefix adjacent pattern	サングラスボルトン, セリエAフィオレンティーナMF, セルフブランディングの達人,...
suffix adjacent pattern	ヒデや日本, の伝説Hide, ヒデの記録,...
mnemonic names	ヒデ(Hide)[a], Hide[a]

---

[a] "Hide" is the sub-string of his first name, and the most popular nickname.

Table 5. Target: "坂本龍一(Ryuichi Sakamoto)" (Related object: "YMO(Yellow Magic Orchestra, a famous Japanese music group. Sakamoto was a member of it.)")

candidates	教授(The Professor), 世界のサカモト(Sakamoto of the World), アホマン2号, 音楽家教授, ...(33 candidates)
prefix adjacent pattern	音楽家教授こと, シールド写真集, オフィシャルスコアブック,...
suffix adjacent pattern	ウラBTTBピアノ, 高橋幸宏ウイリアム,...
mnemonic names	教授(The Professor)[a], 世界のサカモト(Sakamoto of the World), 龍一教授(The Professor Ryuichi)[b], キョージュ(The Professor)[a], 天才音楽家教授(The Genius Musicion Professor)[a]

---

[a] "The Professor" is the most popular nickname of Ryuichi Sakamoto. A member of YMO first called him "The Professor" because of Sakamoto's great musical knowledge.

Table 6. Target: "堀江貴文(Takafumi Horie)" (Related object: "Livedoor")

candidates	リエモン, ホリエモン(Horiemon), もん, ほりえもん(Horiemon), りえもん...(13 candidates)
prefix adjacent pattern	いる若きアントレプレナー, 思うヤツ集合, 容疑の要旨,...
suffix adjacent pattern	社長逮捕新, 社長郵政民営, 被告33ら,...
mnemonic names	ホリエモン(Horiemon)[a] ほりえもん(Horiemon)[a], 社長ホリエモン(The President Horiemon)[a], ホリえもん(Horiemon)[a], 事件ホリエモン[b]

---

[a] "Horiemon" is the most popular nickname of Takafumi Horie, originated in a Japanese famous cartoon film.

[b] Inappropriate mnemonic name.

We applied our proposed method to 6 people in this paper. To assess robustness of the proposed method, we intend to perform further experiments and examine the results for more cases. Application of the proposed method to "noncelebrity" people, of course, is one of important future issues.

5   Conclusion and Future Work

We proposed a new method for extracting mnemonic names of people from the web and evaluated the effectiveness of the method through experiments using real web data. Future work includes improving pattern's weight and candidate's score calculation, investigating generality and robustness of the method, and extending the method to other objects (e.g. organizations) and other languages.

Acknowledgement

This research has been supported in part by the Grant-in-Aid for Scientific Research from MEXT(#18049005.)

References

1. M.Collins and Y.Singer, Unsupervised Models for Named Entity Classification. In *Proceedings of 1999 Joint SIGDAT Conference on Empirical Methods in Natural Language Processing (EMNLP/VLC-99)*, June 1999.
2. K.Dave, S.Lawrence, and D.M.Pennock, Mining the Peanut Gallery: Opinion Extraction and Semantic Classification of Product Reviews. In *Proceedings of WWW 2003*, May 2003.
3. Xin Dong, A.Halevy, and J.Madhavan, Reference Reconciliation in Complex Information Spaces. In *Proceedings of ACM SIGMOD 2005*, June 2005.
4. R.Grishman and B.Sundheim, Message Understanding Conference - 6: A Brief History. In *Proceedings of The 16th International Conference on Computational Linguistics (COLING 1996)*, August 1996.
5. M.A.Hernandez and S.J.Stolfo, The Merge/Purge Problem for Large Databases. In *Proceedings of ACM SIGMOD 1995*, May 1995.
6. Tomoko Hokama and Hiroyuki Kitagawa, Detecting "Hot" Topics about a Person from Blogspace. In *Proceedings of the 16th European-Japanese Conference on Information Modeling and Knowledge Bases (EJC2006)*, pp. 290–294, May 2006.
7. S.Sarawagi and A.Bhamidipaty, Interactive Deduplication Using Active Learning. In *Proceedings of ACM SIGKDD 2002*, July 2002.
8. J.D.M.Rennie and T.Jaakkola, Using Term Informativeness for Named Entity Detection. In *Proceedings of ACM SIGIR 2005*, August 2005.
9. S.Tejada, C.A.Knoblock, and S.Minton, Learning Domain-Independent String Transformation Weights for High Accuracy Object Identification. In *Proceedings of SIGKDD 2002, Edmonton*, July 2002.
10. Rui Kimura, Hiroyuki Toda, and Katsumi Tanaka, Classifying Namesakes by Clustering Web Search Results (in Japanese.) In *Proceedings of the 17th Data Engineering Workshop*, March 2006.
11. Kenichi Shirasuna, Satoshi Oyama, Keishi Tajima, and Katsumi Tanaka, Object Identification using Web Structure Information and Profile Data Extraction (in Japanese.) In *Proceedings of the 17th Data Engineering Workshop*, March 2006.

Automatic Task Detection in the Web Logs and Analysis of Multitasking

Nikolai Buzikashvili

Institute of system analysis, Russian Academy of Science
9 prospect 60 Let Oktyabrya, 117312 Moscow, Russia
buzik@cs.isa.ru

Abstract. In this paper, we describe the conceptual basis and results of the Web search task detection study with emphasis on multitasking. The basis includes: logical structure of a search process, a space of physical realizations, mapping of a logical structure into the space of realizations. Questions on the users' manners of search realization are formulated, with emphasis on multiple tasks execution. An automatic analysis of the Web logs shows that multitasking is rare, usually it includes only two task sessions and is formed into a temporal inclusion of an interrupting task session into the interrupted one. Searchers follow the principle of least effort and select the cheapest tactics: sequential tasks execution as a rule or, in the rare case of multitasking, the least expensive form of it. Quantitative characteristics of search behavior in 3 classes of temporal sessions (1-task session, several tasks executed one-by-one, and multitasking session) were compared, and significant differences were revealed.

1 Introduction

Multitasking is actively investigated by cognitive science (e.g. [7], [8]). The conclusion is: multitasking is ineffective, expensive and risky manner. Since searching on the Web is an area of free choice of the manner of tasks execution the conclusion of the first study of multitasking search *"multitasking information searching is a common behavior"* [11] seems surprising. The work [11] started studying multitasking search on the Web. However, [9], [10], [11] consider any manner of execution of several tasks during some period as multitasking. Since such multitasking is mainly *successive* execution of several tasks one-by-one the revealed features are features of successive execution. A more interesting combination, which is just called multitasking, is a parallel search when a user executes different tasks, interrupting one and returning to the interrupted task. This manner is rare and it may not be representatively investigated in the procedures based on the manual task detection. The only way to study this multitasking search is an *automatic* detection of task sessions.

Since the classic information retrieval (IR) systems supported only successive realizations of a search process potential opportunities of parallel, branching and convergent searches were beyond the interests of the information search studies. Modern search environments directly support parallel and branching searches. This fact does not only prompt an investigation of multitasking by itself but also limelights the

S. Sugimoto et al. (Eds.): ICADL 2006, LNCS 4312, pp. 131–140, 2006.
© Springer-Verlag Berlin Heidelberg 2006

reconsideration of the concepts used to describe the searcher behavior. So we start from the re-schematization of the concepts, which allow us easily and suitably describe the search process. In particular, we draw a difference between the logical search process and its physical realizations. The concepts of the logical search structures, a space of physical realizations and mapping of the former on the latter are considered in Chapter 2. This is the convenient basis for description of search, in particular of parallel execution of independent tasks or different branches of the same task.

To study the multitasking search on the Web we use a 2-stage approach. The first stage includes an automatic detection of tasks and multitasking (Chapters 6, 7). To check the results of the first, automatic stage, we conduct the second stage, at which the samples of automatically detected multitasking are manually verified. The manual evaluation conducted on the samples from the sessions automatically detected as multitasking shows: while the automatic procedure nearly twice overestimates the number of these sessions, the correctly detected multitasking sessions demonstrate the same features of multitasking as all automatically detected. The results are: multitasking is a very uncommon behavior; it covers only two tasks; multitasking is usually realized in the "enveloped" form: a searcher interrupts one task, starts and completes the second task session and then returns to the unfinished task.

In the study, we classify any temporal session as: a 1-task session, or a session containing several tasks executed one-by-one, or a multitasking session. In fact, it would be a good point to compare separately 1) the characteristics of two manners of *several tasks* execution (multitasking and successive execution one-by-one), and 2) the characteristics of two classes of *successive* execution —1-task and sequentially executed several tasks rather than to combine all several tasks sessions or all successive sessions. Values of the metrics estimated for all 3 classes are different: not only multitasking differs from both classes of sequential execution but also 1-task temporal sessions differ from the sessions covering several tasks.

In Chapter 8, we study an effect of a temporal cut-off, the controllable variable used in the Web log studies on multitasking detection and on values of the metrics of each class of temporal sessions. This variable is used in the Web log analysis to segment client transaction into temporal sessions and it significantly influences the detected fractions of different classes and metrics.

2   Logical Structure of Search and Spaces of Physical Realization

Following [2] we distinguish a *logical structure* of the search process and a *physical realization* of this structure limited by the availability of the search instruments. A logical structure of the search process is relatively stable and independent of the object covering three types of search dependencies: *linear, branching and convergent*. Realizations of these structures may be supported, partly supported or not supported by the available search environment. For example, classic information retrieval (IR) systems supported only sequential execution. As a result, the opportunities of the parallel, branching and convergent search could not have been investigated.

Logical Structure of Search Process. We use the concept of the logical search structure as a cognitive construction, which describes a human search process and may have different physical realizations in the IR interactions. A logical search structure may be represented as a dependency graph, which contains 3 kinds of nodes (goals, queries, and retrieved results) and dependency edges.

Two classes of dependencies are used: 1) dependencies *"to be a result of"* applied to goals changed as a result of the retrieved results, to queries resulting from the goals, and to the retrieved results resulting from the queries, and 2) *composition dependencies* applied to a "compound" goal, which is initially decomposable into different subgoals such as each subgoal may be achieved independently after which an initial goal is achieved as a composition. "To be a result of" dependencies have a form of *linear* or *branching* (several outgoing edges, see also a tree of information needs introduced by I. Campbell [4]), composition dependencies are *convergent* (several entering edges). The structural primitives (linear, branching and convergent) used in the logical search schematization are invariant to physical realizations of a search.

Spaces of Physical Realization. Over the last two decades retrieval methods have changed insignificantly. However modern search differs immensely from 'traditional' search, and these changes are the changes of the *space of physical realizations*. A classic search was a successive search realized in the one-dimension space (*time*). A modern search is realized in the 3-dimension space (*browser window, search service,* and *time*): a single user may search simultaneously in different browser windows using several search engines. In particular, modern spaces support *multitasking*: either different branches of a single task or independent tasks may be performed *in parallel.*

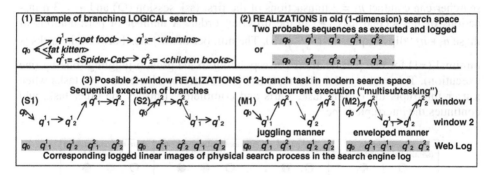

Fig. 1. Realizations of the branching logical search in the old and modern search spaces

A space of realizations is an available search environment, which includes all available search services (local IR systems, Web search engines) and available ways to use these services (successively or concurrently, in a single or in several windows). The same logical search structure may be differently mapped into different spaces of realizations and into the same if the structure contains branching task or several tasks.

3 Tasks Complexity, Resumption Costs and Human Limits

Thus, a modern searcher can perform simultaneously independent task sessions as well as different branches of the same branching or convergent task session. To what extent and in what manners the searchers use this opportunity?

Whereas our goal is to describe rather than to explain the mechanics of the parallel search, we keep in mind the likely cost model driving the search realization. Whatever form of a criterion a searcher may follow (minimization or acceptability of effort), the summary cost of the search at any moment consists of two components that vary during search process: (1) the *current* complexity of the executed task; (2) the *resumption cost* and the *risks of poor resumption* of the interrupted task. The resumption cost depends not only on the interrupted task complexity but also on the complexity of the interrupting task and on the duration of the interruption. A searcher pays for resumption rather than for any switching. Since a user cannot carefully estimate the duration of the interruption and the complexity of the interrupting task execution he runs the *risk* of poor restoring the interrupted task. Multitasking seems to be appropriate for a user if the summary complexity of multitasking is acceptable.

Parallel tasks execution has too little a common with a sequential one-by-one execution. While a juggle is a single task, the juggling is a striking metaphor for multiple tasks execution. When one flips a ball O several times and then flips second ball ● several times we don't speak about two balls juggling. This pseudo-juggle is a situation of a sequential execution (O...O ●...●) considered as multitasking in [9], [11]. Real juggle is described by other regularity: O●...O●, etc. Is it really a situation of parallel multitasking? In other words, how are ordered transactions of parallel tasks? Randomly, regularly, and if regularly, what laws describe regularities. How many parallel tasks does a searcher juggle? Fig. 2 shows the two tasks "juggling": a searcher can conduct $n_1 = 2$ transactions of the first task session (O) and $n_2 = 3$ transactions of the second task (●) in the different order. A number of permutations of these $n_1 + n_2$ "flips" equals to $\binom{n_1+n_2}{n_j} = 10$. The number of switches between the tasks is minimal (=1) for two permutations corresponding to the pseudo-juggling (one-by-one execution). The next in order of complexity is the enveloped execution of tasks when a user interrupts the current task, starts and completely finishes the other task, and continues the interrupted one.

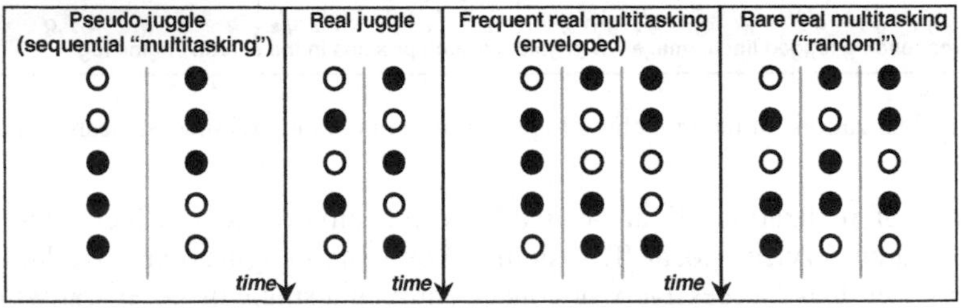

Pseudo-juggle (sequential "multitasking")		Real juggle		Frequent real multitasking (enveloped)			Rare real multitasking ("random")		
O	●	O	●	O	●	●	O	●	●
O	●	●	O	●	O	●	●	O	●
●	●	O	●	●	O	O	O	●	O
●	O	●	O	●	●	O	●	●	●
●	O	O	●	O	●	●	●	O	O

Fig. 2. Patterns of switching in "multitasking juggle"

The true source of the "multitasking troubles" is *resource sharing rather than multitasking by itself.* Following a computer metaphor we can say that when tasks do not share the same resource (body organs as "peripheral units" and brain regions as "specialized processors") they are successfully executed in parallel. For example, medieval laundresses laundered and sang. However cognominal tasks (e.g. search tasks) use the same processing chains, so multitasking search is inevitably sharing process.

4 Terms, Data and Preprocessing Technique

In this paper, we use the notions:

(1) a *temporal session* as a sequence of the single client's transactions with the search engine cut from previous and successive sessions by a certain time interval;

(2) a *task* as a search of the same or of similar objects;

(3) a *task session* as all transactions of a temporal session executed the same task;

(4) a temporal session may be either (*a*) *1-task session*, or (*b*) session consisting of *several tasks executed sequentially one-by-one* without the interruptions of unfinished tasks, or (*c*) *multitasking session* if it contains at least one resumption of the interrupted task.

(5) A maximum number of the unfinished tasks during a temporal session is called a *session width*. If the width of a temporal session is bigger than 1, this session is referred to as the *multitasking* or "*wide*" one.

To detect real-life multitasking search we use log samples of the two search engines: the Russian-language *Yandex* (a week sample, 2005, 175,000 users accepted cookies), and the *Excite*: 1999 log fragment (8 hours, 537,639 clients) and 2001 log sample (24 hours, 305,000 clients).

To reconstruct task sessions inside each temporal session of individual searchers we use the preprocessing stage (1) to exclude the clients, who are likely to be robots or local networks and (2) to segment a logged time series of transactions into temporal sessions. To exclude the clients who are not individual users we use the sliding temporal window technique [3]. In the study, we use different temporal cut-offs and the only client discriminator set to 5 unique queries per 1-hour sliding window.

5 Questions and Hypotheses

We suggest the following questions and hypotheses on multitasking search:

(*a*) How frequent is it? How are temporal sessions distributed over session width?

(*b*) Question on the *patterns of resumption*. How does an interrupted task session continue after the interruption — by a new query or by a continuation of viewing the results of the last query before the interruption? Does this manner differ from a manner of a "continuation" of an ordinal sequential session?

(*c*) How does a searcher juggle parallel task sessions? A hypothesis on the *patterns of switching*: for unfinished task sessions it is less likely that a transaction of one unfinished session be followed by a transaction of another session instead of continuing this one. In particular, for parallel task sessions the series of their transactions (currently remaining parts of these sessions) are not random permutations over time.

(*d*) Do quantitative characteristics of multitasking (a session length, duration, etc.) differ from the characteristics of several tasks executed one-by-one?

(*e*) It is interesting to compare quantitative characteristics of all three classes of temporal sessions: a 1-task session, several tasks executed one-by-one, and a multitasking session. A priori, if a searcher executes several tasks during a temporal session they are simple enough. On the other hand, executing several tasks concurrently is more expensive than executing one-by-one. The quantitative characteristics of the corresponding temporal sessions should reflect these features.

6 Method of Task Detection

We extract task sessions by pairwise similarity of queries ([5], [6] present other approaches to task detection). Namely, (1) we fill a matrix of pairwise similarity of all unique queries of the current temporal session; (2) than we make a transitive closure of this similarity relation and consider each connected component of the similarity graph as a single task session (Fig. 3).

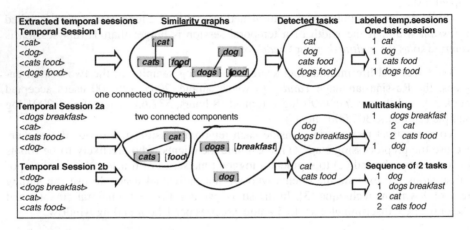

Fig. 3. Examples of tasks detection in three temporal sessions

We use a binary similarity measure and a direct (orthographical) detection of pairwise similarity. To avoid a problem of misprinting and of typing ambiguity we use the approximate string matching method (similar to the common subsequences approach [1]). The main idea of our approach is to take into account that the terms are natural language words and significance of auxiliary part of speech and words endings equals zero. We ignore contribution of auxiliary words and endings into similarity measure (in Russian, inflective ending may be up to 6 letters). There is no need to use vocabulary; however, we use a stop-dictionary to exclude auxiliary parts of speech such as conjunctions, articles, pronouns, etc. We convert a source queries into small letters, delete all delimiters (blanks and punctuations), i.e. "glue" all terms of a query into one low-case string, e.g. a source query <(*lazy fox*) & (*naive +dog*)> is transformed into *lazyfoxnaivedog* string, and check, are pair of such strings contain similar substrings. This procedure depends on the length of the source strings and takes into account the differences and inversions of the letters. If both substrings cover auxiliary parts of speech or endings (e.g. -*ing* or -*less*) in the *original* (with delimiters) *queries* we correspondingly diminish length of the substrings. If the resulting substrings are long enough, the original queries are considered as similar ones, otherwise we continue to check other high correlated substrings of these queries.

The advantage of the automatic task session extraction is: it effectively rejects 1-width sessions. While the temporal sessions detected as wide may frequently happen to be sequential ones, the temporal sessions detected as sequential are "hundred to one" detected correctly. This *systematic bias* saves us the trouble of manual checking the temporal sessions detected as 1-width (~98% of all). Furthermore, a manual check of the wide temporal sessions is much easily than a manual mark up used in the previous studies. On the other hand, the method does not extract the internal structure of the *task session*, i.e. it ignores branching of the same task. So it ignores switching inside the task. It is disadvantage since switching inside the same task does not differ from switching between different tasks.

7   Results of Automatic Analysis

The analysis of the automatically detected multitasking answers research questions. The searchers follow the principle of least effort and select the cheapest tactics:

(*a*) more than 98% of all temporal sessions elaborated under the commonly used cut-off values (15-30 min) are either sessions of the 1-task execution (about 85%, or sessions of sequential execution of several tasks (Table 1);

(*b*) during multitasking a searcher uses only two tasks and (*c*) he frequently executes them in an "enveloped manner": he interrupts one task session, starts and completes the second task session and returns to the unfinished task.

(*d, e*) Table 1 shows metrics for 3 classes of temporal sessions 1) sessions which include only one task; and two types of sessions containing more than 1 task and which, therefore, may be executed either 2) sequentially one-by-one or 3) in parallel. Values of the same metrics are surprisingly similar over different logs. Further, the metrics corresponding to 3 classes of temporal sessions (1-task, sequential tasks, parallel tasks) are very different: not only multitasking differs from both types of sequential execution but also execution of 1 task differs from sequential execution of several tasks.

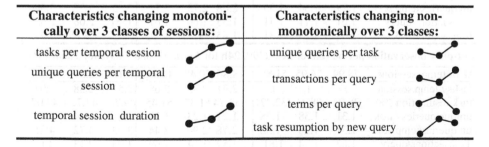

Characteristics changing monotoni-cally over 3 classes of sessions:	Characteristics changing non-monotonically over 3 classes:
tasks per temporal session	unique queries per task
unique queries per temporal session	transactions per query
temporal session duration	terms per query
	task resumption by new query

Fig. 4. Diagrams for metrics qualitative change over 3 types of temporal sessions (left circle – 1-task sessions; central – several tasks executed one-by-one; right circle – wide sessions)

Table 1. Metrics for 3 classes of temporal sessions under **temporal cut-off = 5 min**

Class of temporal sessions:	1-task			several tasks executed one-by-one			parallel tasks		
log and % of correspond. temp. sessions	Exc99 91.76	Exc01 91.21	Yand 91.90	Exc99 7.67	Exc01 8.18	Yand 7.63	Exc99 0.57	Exc01 0.61	Yand 0.47
tasks / temp.session	1	1	1	2.14	2.16	2.12	2.26	2.26	2.22
task resumption by new query (%) *	26.38	25.79	26.22	57.05	53.83	57.57	52.81	53.59	51.97
unique queries / task	1.19	1.22	1.20	1.14	1.15	1.14	1.44	1.47	1.46
Un.queries/temp.sess.	1.19	1.22	1.20	2.43	2.49	2.42	3.25	3.34	3.25
transactions/query	1.46	1.54	1.48	1.45	1.52	1.44	1.79	1.93	1.86
transactions/task	1.73	1.88	1.76	1.65	1.75	1.65	2.58	2.84	2.72
Duration (min) of:									
1-query temp.session	0.49	0.54	0.66						
2-query temp.session	2.28	2.37	2.65	2.64	2.62	2.94	4.86	5.14	6.08
3-query temp.session	3.98	4.05	4.38	4.36	4.22	4.77	5.32	5.79	6.54

* Task resumption by new query — % of temporal sessions of this class

temporal cut-off = 15 min

% of temp. sessions	87.56	86.87	86.40	11.32	11.94	12.53	1.12	1.19	1.07
tasks / temp.session	1	1	1	2.20	2.21	2.19	2.34	2.35	2.30
task resumption (%)	27.34	26.8	26.9	54.60	52.4	53.1	51.84	52.8	52.4
unique queries / task	1.24	1.3	1.3	1.17	1.2	1.2	1.45	1.5	1.5
un.queries/temp.sess.	1.24	1.3	1.3	2.56	2.6	2.6	3.40	3.5	3.4
Transactions/query	1.56	1.7	1.6	1.52	1.6	1.5	1.87	2.0	2.0
transactions/task	1.93	2.13	2.09	1.78	1.85	1.83	2.71	2.97	2.92
Duration (min) of:									
1-query temp.session	1.09	1.17	1.68						
2-query temp.session	4.37	4.45	5.60	5.84	5.72	6.89	10.62	11.52	13.55
3-query temp.session	7.35	7.36	8.97	9.27	8.87	11.04	11.16	11.79	14.30

temporal cut-off = 1 hour

% of temp. sessions	83.24	82.76	80.55	15.10	15.47	17.63	1.66	1.77	1.82
tasks / temp.session	1	1	1	2.26	2.27	2.25	2.43	2.43	2.43
task resumption (%)	28.28	27.58	27.81	53.85	51.93	51.37	51.37	51.24	51.58
unique queries / task	1.29	1.34	1.35	1.19	1.21	1.21	1.46	1.47	1.47
un.queries/temp.sess.	1.29	1.34	1.35	2.68	2.73	2.72	3.53	3.57	3.58
transactions/query	1.61	1.71	1.71	1.55	1.60	1.61	1.90	2.08	2.03
transactions/task	2.07	2.28	2.31	1.85	1.93	1.95	2.77	3.05	2.99

cut-off = observation period (8h for Ecxite'99, 24h for *Ecxite'01* and 7 days for *Yandex'05*)

% of temp. sessions	78.99	76.95	51.88	18.86	20.48	41.38	2.15	2.57	6.74
tasks / temp.session	1	1	1	2.31	2.35	2.68	2.52	2.58	3.07
task resumption (%)	28.93	28.41	32.77	53.74	51.37	51.45	49.75	47.72	44.07
unique queries / task	1.31	1.38	1.58	1.21	1.23	1.28	1.44	1.44	1.41
un.queries/temp.sess.	1.31	1.38	1.58	2.78	2.90	3.44	3.63	3.72	4.31
Transactions/query	1.63	1.74	1.81	1.57	1.64	1.69	1.93	2.13	2.17
transactions/task	2.13	2.39	2.85	1.89	2.02	2.17	2.79	3.07	3.05

The *queries/task*, *transactions/query* and *terms/query* metrics show an interesting non-monotonicity over different types of sessions (Fig. 4). Tasks of 1-task temporal sessions seem to be more (subjectively) complex than complexity of several tasks. Executing several tasks concurrently is more expensive than executing one-by-one.

8 Results-2: Effect of Temporal Segmentation of Logged Series

The fractions of different classes of temporal sessions depend on a temporal cut-off used to segment client transaction into temporal sessions. Usage of different values of this variable may lead to artifactual conclusions [3]. Indeed, the bigger a temporal cut-off, the longer temporal sessions are and as a result 1) the more tasks may be included into one temporal session, 2) the more probable multitasking detection since a user regularly returns to the same task or the same query. We study how method-dependent characteristics of 3 classes of temporal sessions behave depending on temporal cut-off. We change a temporal cut-off from 5 min value to the whole observation period. While cut-offs less than 15 min are not used to separate transactions into temporal sessions, the value of 5 min looks a good lower bound for the admitted region of cut-off values. In turn, when the whole observation period is assigned to a cut-off value, all user transactions are considered as belonging to the same temporal session, and we can speak about the "client" instead of the "temporal session". The observation period is long enough (7 days, the *Yandex* sample). So when a temporal cut-off equals the whole observation period we can expect that a majority of "temporal sessions" include several tasks and furthermore we expect dramatically big fraction of multitasking since users should regularly repeat the same tasks. Surprisingly, such task session characteristics as unique queries per task session don't increase.

A small fraction of temporal sessions, which contain more than one task and the smallest fraction of multitasking sessions do not come as a surprise when 5 min is assigned to a cut-off. The real surprise is that, under the *week* temporal cut off only 44% of "client sessions" include several tasks and only 6.7% are multitasking. In other words, only 6.7% of clients return to the same or similar queries during a week.

9 Conclusion

The procedure reveals great differences between each of the three classes of temporal sessions. However, are these differences real differences of real task sessions rather than procedural artifacts? Also, are automatically discovered multitasking properties real properties? The procedure doesn't always detect the queries similarity and doesn't detect compatibility. The number of the detected task sessions turns out to be bigger and the width of the temporal sessions is overestimated. However, we can use this systematic bias as an advantage: to check the results of the automatic multitasking extraction we should manually verify only those temporal sessions, which were detected as wide. 300 wide temporal sessions were manually verified. The results of manual evaluation are: 1) the automatic procedure nearly twice overestimates the number of tasks and wide sessions; 2) an automatic detection of sessions whose width is bigger than two is an artifact and may be explained by the active search: when a user searches actively he frequently reformulates queries of the same task in new terms (which are detected as new tasks) and returns to the previous queries (which results in multitasking detection); 3) in other respects manually approved multitasking shows the same dependencies as multitasking detected automatically.

The results of the multitasking study are:

* whilst [9], [11] speak about common multitasking behavior (11% of temporal sessions — cf. 11-12% of temporal session containing several one-by-one executed tasks detected under 15 min cut-off in Table 1), multitasking is very uncommon behavior (less than 1% of temporal sessions for reasonable cut-off values);
* multitasking covers only two tasks;
* multitasking usually realizes in the enveloped form: a searcher interrupts one task, starts and completes the second task session and returns to the unfinished task.

Thus, a searcher selects the least expensive manner (he avoids multitasking) but even in multitasking a searcher selects the least expensive manner (the nested execution of two tasks).

* Other results are the values of metrics corresponding to the different classes of temporal sessions containing 1-task, several sequential tasks, and parallel tasks. These values are different, and not only multitasking differs from both types of sequential execution but also characteristics of a 1-task temporal session significantly differs from the characteristics of a session covering several tasks.

Acknowledgements. The author feels obliged to thank Ian Ruthven, Pia Borlund, Katriina Byström and Sachi Arafat for valuable remarks. The author especially thanks Amanda Spink who pioneered the investigation of the Web multitasking search.

References

1. Apostolico, A.: String editing and longest common subsequences. *Handbook of Formal Languages*, vol, 2, Springer-Verlag, (1997), 361-398
2. Buzikashvili, N.: The Yandex Study. *Workshop on Evaluating user studies in information access*, Glasgow, 2005. Univ. of Strathclyde, BCS (2005) 48-55
3. Buzikashvili, N.: Comparing Web Logs: Sensitivity Analysis and Two Types of Cross-Analysis. *3rd Asian IR Symposium (AIRS)*, Singapore, 2006, LNCS 4182, Springer-Verlag, 508–513
4. Campbell I.: Supporting information needs by ostensive definition in an adaptive information space. *Workshop on Multimedia Inf. Retrieval (MIRO'95)*. Glasgow, BCS (1995).
5. Jung , J.J., Jo, G-S.: Semantic outlier analysis for sessionizing Web logs. *1st European Web Mining Forum*. (2004)
6. He, D., Goker, A., Harper, D.: Combining evidence for automatic Web session identification. *Information Processing & Management*, 38 (2002) 727-742
7. Monsell S.: Task switching. *Trends in Cognitive Sciences*, 7(3) (2003), 134-140
8. Rubinstein, J., Meyer, D., Evans, J.: Exucutive control of cognitive processes in task switching. *J. Exp. Psycol. Hum. Percept. Performance*, 27 (2001), 763-797
9. Spink, A., Jansen, B.J., Pedersen, J.: Multitasking Web search on Alta Vista. *ITCC'04* (Las-Vegas, 2004) IEEE CP. Vol. 2, 309-313
10. Spink, A., Jansen, B.J., Park M., Pedersen J.: Multitasking during Web search sessions. *Information Processing & Management*, 42(1) (2006) 264-275
11. Spink, A., Ozmutlu, H.C., Ozmutlu, S.: Multitasking information seeking and searching processes. *JASIST*, 53(8) (2002) 639-652

Extracting Structured Subject Information from Digital Document Archives

Jyi-Shane Liu[1,2] and Ching-Ying Lee[3]

[1] Department of Computer Science, National Chengchi University, Taiwan, R.O.C.
[2] University Library, National Chengchi University, Taiwan, R.O.C.
[3] Department of English, National Taiwan Normal University, Taiwan, R.O.C.
jsliu@cs.nccu.edu.tw

Abstract. Information extraction (IE) techniques are capable of decoding targeted subject information in documents, and reducing text data into a set of structured core information. The implication for digital libraries is that IE potentially serves as an enabling tool to extend the value of digital document archives. We present an approach, called sandwich extraction pattern, to address the closely coupled template relation tasks. The approach provides interactive capabilities for task specification, domain knowledge acquisition, and output evaluation. This allows users (e.g. librarians) to have direct control on the design of value-added content products and the performance of IE tools. We conducted empirical validation by implementing an IE system, called *SEP*, and field testing it in a practical document archive. Encouraged by successful test runs, NCCU library has formally initiated a project to develop a value-added content product of government personnel gazettes, including document images, electronic texts, and personnel changes database.

Keywords: information extraction, digital document archives, value-added services.

1 Introduction

Document is the primary form of recording many kinds of information and knowledge. Document digitization allows efficient preservation and duplication, as well as provides easy access over computer networks. Global digitization efforts, exemplified by Google Print and Open Content Alliance projects, have produced a tremendous amount of digitized documents of various types, such as books, articles, stories, papers, reports, memos, and gazettes. Usages of digital document archives are generally facilitated by indexing and full text searching. However, the time and efforts needed for a user to sift through the large quantities of retrieved documents have become unrealistically expensive. The fundamental problem is that current information retrieval tools produce coarse-grained information entities. User needed information is often buried somewhere in the large set of retrieved documents. In order to enable more effective use of digital document archives, we must develop tools that are capable of producing finer-grained information entities. To this end, a

S. Sugimoto et al. (Eds.): ICADL 2006, LNCS 4312, pp. 141–150, 2006.
© Springer-Verlag Berlin Heidelberg 2006

variety of information processing techniques, such as text categorization, text summarization, question answering, and text mining, are making encouraging progress.

Along the same line of retrieving finer-grained information entities, information extraction (IE) techniques are perhaps the most aggressive in pin-pointing needed information. IE seeks to find core semantic elements of designated subject within documents. In particular, IE techniques identify and give conceptual labels to a partial set of text strings in a document with regard to who did what to whom, when and where, and sometimes how [3]. Therefore, IE systems are useful in automatically scanning and decoding targeted subject information in a large quantity of documents, and reducing text data into a set of structured core information. The implication for digital libraries is that IE potentially serves as an enabling tool to extend the value of digital document archives. The transformation process from raw texts to information elements in structured subject databases allows precise and direct use of information elements, as well as their value-added aggregation. In this regard, digital document archives are source materials with which different content products can be designed and produced. This process involves librarians acting as knowledge workers to make judgment on what content products are useful and how IE (as well as other information processing) techniques are used for content production.

In general, the construction of IE systems can be classified into two paradigms [1]. The knowledge engineering paradigm involves human efforts with sufficient background knowledge in developing extraction rules for targeted subject domain. System performance largely depends on the accuracy and adequacy of domain-dependent extraction rules. The automatic training paradigm relies on annotated training corpus to derive necessary decision attributes and compiles into extraction rules with learning algorithms. The two paradigms contrast with each other in two primary issues of IE–performance and portability [7]. With domain dependent human efforts, hand-crafted, knowledge-based systems usually produce better results. On the other hand, automatic training and learning systems reduce the conversion cost between task domains. The tradeoff between performance and portability is mostly concerned with technical characteristics.

For a content product to be actually useful, reaching the highest level of quality should be the utmost goal. Instead of obliging to the technique-centered view, a better model is to put librarians in charge of the content product development process. With sufficient subject domain knowledge, librarians initiate the process by evaluating the condition of document archives, the potential value of a subject domain, and the overall applicability of IE tools. Once a decision is made to select a particular subject domain from a document archive, the librarians configure and manipulate IE tools such that the best possible result is achieved. In this model, a generic and fully automatic IE technique is not necessarily a better choice than a specialized and highly effective one with human assistance. After all, it is the data quality that ultimately determines the value of the content product. A good IE approach for the purpose of delivering highest possible data quality is to harness subject domain expertise and focus on subject specific coverage in extraction operations. This approach generally falls in the knowledge engineering paradigm. However, the librarian-centered model will be most effective if the IE approach provides the interactive feedback and modification capabilities. This allows the librarians to be really in control of how the

IE tool performs and what needs to be adjusted to obtain the best results. Unfortunately, most IE techniques are either too complex or too rigid to allow user manipulation. The lack of user input consideration has seemed to be an obstacle for the library community to embrace IE as a powerful value-adding tool and for the IE research to develop as many successful application domains as possible.

In this paper, we present an approach, called sandwich extraction pattern, to address the closely coupled template relation tasks (Section 2). The approach provides interactive capabilities for task specification, domain knowledge acquisition, and output evaluation (Section 3). We also present an exemplar application in a practical document archive to show that our approach has resulted in an actual content product (Section 4). Section 5 is a short conclusion.

2   IE Task Model

Template relation and named entity are IE tasks that seem to be of special interest to the purpose of deriving content products from digital document archives. For example, many documents contain information concerning to people, organization, location, date, and event. A possible content product designed by librarians may be to collect personal information and keep track of employment history of politicians, government officials, and enterprise executives. A database that contains information on who works where, when, and for what capacity may allow research issues such as top-tiered social networks and personal social links in bureaucratic systems, public and private sectors. Similar purposes of *entity profiling* are potentially fruitful avenues for adding values to digital document archives with suitable IE tools.

2.1   Identifying Closely Coupled Template Relations

We observed that the core information of entity profiling usually forms a closed coupling among a few named entities with a small set of template relations, such as the (de)association of person, organization, and job title. We categorize it as a sub-class of template relation and call it "closely coupled template relation" (CCTR) task. In written languages closely coupled template relations are mostly expressed as composition of semantic units with a limited set of patterns. A semantic unit is an conceptual element or an entity instantiated by a text string. Recognition of some semantic units in a template relation pattern may allow us to infer the existence and locations of the other semantic units based on the composition sequence. We propose the sandwich extraction pattern approach to address the CCTR task for extracting entity profiling information. The approach is centered on the notion of *semantic unit sandwich*. A semantic unit is recognizable if its instantiation in texts is limited to a set of collectable text strings. We considered some easily recognizable semantic units as providing invisible delimiters. When a semantic unit is sandwiched by two delimiters in a composition pattern, it can be isolated and inferred its conceptual label. *Semantic unit sandwich* refers to a pattern composed of one targeted semantic unit sandwiched by two recognizable semantic units. With pattern recognition and matching, the targeted semantic unit in the middle can be identified and the corresponding text strings can be correctly extracted.

The notion of semantic unit sandwich is substantially adequate for annotating more complicated representations of useful template relations as long as certain conditions are met. Consider a sentence appeared in a Chinese news report: "中國工業總會理事長林坤鐘任期屆滿，將由東和鋼鐵公司董事長侯貞雄接任。"(Chinese National Federation of Industries)(chairman)(LinKunChung)(term expired), (will be)(by)(Tung Ho Steel Enterprise Corp.)(chairman)(HoJenShyong)(take over). The template relation in the sentence that involves a management succession can be represented by the sandwich extraction pattern "*ON1-JT1-PN1-TC1-By-ON2-JT2-PN2-TC2*" (organization name1 + job title1 + person name1 + term condition1 + by + organization name2 + job title2 + person name2 + term condition2). The recognitions of *JT1*, *TC1*, *By*, *JT2*, and *TC2*, provide necessary delimiters for the formation of semantic unit sandwiches. Organization names and person names in the sentence can be isolated and extracted. Management succession relations among these entities can be recognized and marked.

2.2 Types of Semantic Units

For the purpose of CCTR tasks, semantic units in language expressions can be categorized based on feasibility of direct recognition. Some semantic units, such as job title and social title, are generally instantiated with a limited lexicon, which allows collection and automatic recognition. Other semantic units, such as person name and organization name, admit extremely large lexicon, and therefore, are considered as not suitable for direct recognition. A CCTR task may require the extraction of both types of semantic units. As long as the not-directly-recognizable semantic units are sandwiched by recognizable semantic units or delimiters, they can be successfully extracted.

We define three types of semantic units for the purpose of recognition and extraction in the IE process.

Extraction Only Unit (EOU). Semantic units of *EOU*-type are not-directly-recognizable IE task targets. They are either wide open for word creation or are error prone with direct recognition. The extraction of text strings corresponding to these semantic units must rely on their surrounding delimiters.

Recognition Only Unit (ROU). Semantic units of *ROU*-type are recognizable and potentially provide contextual information to IE tasks. Their word sets pertaining to the subject domain are limited in number and can be collected. The central effect of *ROU* is to serve as a preceding or succeeding delimiter for its adjacent semantic units and indicate types of template relations appeared.

Recognition Extraction Unit (REU). Semantic units of *REU*-type are recognizable and are required for extraction in IE tasks. Recognition of *REU* not only creates a delimiter that helps locate adjacent *EOUs* but also allows conceptual labeling.

The above definitions of three types of semantic units leave out the type that are neither directly recognizable nor IE task targets. It is not specifically defined due to its irrelevance in our approach.

2.3 Specification of Sandwich Extraction Pattern

Sandwich extraction patterns are the annotated expression and composition of targeted semantic units in a CCTR task. We considered only patterns that are strictly formed by compositions of *EOUs*, *ROUs*, and *REUs*. They usually map well to short or compact descriptions of template relations and reflect the closely coupled nature of the named entities involved. *ROUs* and *REUs* are used as invisible delimiters for the extraction of *EOUs*. We also consider symbols that mark sentence structure as usable delimiters. These symbols include period, comma, semicolon, and punctuation. In addition, the start of a sentence is also a usable delimiter.

The notion of sandwich extraction pattern provides a convenient way to annotate recognizable and extractable template relations. However, they must satisfy the following conditions in order to be admissible: (1) There are at least two semantic units in the pattern; (2) An *EOU* must be preceded by a delimiter or a *ROU* or a *REU*; (3) An *EOU* must be succeeded by a delimiter or a *ROU* or a *REU*. As long as these conditions are met, a sandwich extraction pattern can contain any number of *EOUs*, *ROUs*, and *REUs*. In the management succession relation pattern described previously, "*ON1-JT1-PN1-TC1-By-ON2-JT2-PN2-TC2*" is translated to its recognition and extraction types as "d_s-*EOU-REU-EOU-REU-ROU-EOU-REU-EOU-REU*", where d_s is the "start of sentence" delimiter. The pattern meets the admissible criteria.

3 An Interactive IE System Based on Sandwich Extraction Pattern

We developed an interactive IE system, called *SEP*, based on the approach of sandwich extraction pattern for CCTR task. *SEP* performs string-based pattern matching and extracts entity relation information based on sandwich extraction patterns. The system includes two sets of components: (1) pattern recognition and output generation mechanisms; (2) semantic unit lexicon and sandwich extraction pattern set. The first set of components is domain independent, which provides operation feedbacks and outputs for human evaluation. The second set is domain dependent, which allows users (e.g. librarians) to control and improve system performance by adding/modifying domain knowledge.

3.1 Finite State Transducers

We considered finite-state machines (FSMs) as *SEP*'s pattern matching mechanism based on its simplicity and robustness as both pattern-describer and pattern-recognizer. The sandwich extraction pattern approach implies a form of partial pattern recognition and contextual inference. For example, the sandwich extraction pattern of "*JT-PN-ST*" (job title + person name + social title) operates by recognizing the existence of job title and social title in an input strings and inferring the enclosed substrings as person name. We need a variation of straightforward FSMs that is capable of embedding sequential pattern recognition and outputting substrings as extracted pieces of information. Finite-state transducer (FST) is a special type of

FSMs with actions (or outputs) associated with state transition [4]. Each transition arc is labeled with a pair of symbols separated by a colon. The symbol in front of the colon is the input symbol that triggers the state transition. The symbol after the colon is the output produced by the state transition.

Fig. 1(a) shows an FST for the pattern form of *REU-EOU-ROU* (e.g., "*JT-PN-ST*"). The machine needs a lexicon for matching the two recognizable semantic units, *REU* (e.g., *JT*) and *ROU* (e.g., *ST*). When encountering a substring that matches with the lexicon of the *REU* (e.g., *JT*), the machine will leave state 1 and go to state 2. The state transition will also copy the substring as output with the conceptual label of the *REU* (e.g., *JT*). At state 2, only a substring that matches with the lexicon of the *ROU* (e.g., *ST*) will trigger the state transition to state 3. Any other substrings will follow the revisiting state transition that goes back to state 2 itself. The substring after *REU* (e.g., *JT*) and before *ROU* (e.g., *ST*) will be accumulated as output and marked with the conceptual label of the *EOU* (e.g., *PN*). State 3 is an accepting state, signaling the acceptance of the input string with respect to the pattern. State transition from state 2 to state 3 produces empty (ε) output. Fig. 1(b) shows an FST for the same pattern form but requires the input string to start with the specified *REU*. An input string starting with anything else will trigger a state transition to a sink state (state 0), signaling an immediate rejection of the input string.

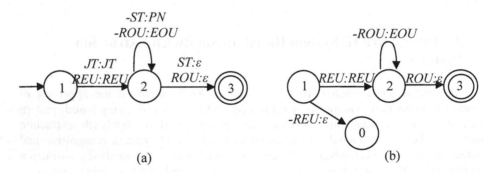

Fig. 1. FST for the pattern form *REU-EOU-ROU*

With standard FST generation algorithms, **SEP** can automatically generate an FST for each sandwich extraction pattern. The set of sandwich extraction patterns that are annotated for the targeted template relations can then be represented and operated by a set of FSTs. For an input string of a sentence, an FST is selected to receive the input string and run the process of state transition. The result is either an acceptance or a rejection. An acceptance means the sandwich extraction pattern described in the FST is recognized in the sentence and pieces of information are acquired from the FST's output substrings. **SEP** then continues IE tasks on the next input string. A rejection means the described pattern is not found in the sentence. In this case, another FST can be selected to receive the input string. The matching process between an input string and an FST is continued until an acceptance occurs or no FST is left unmatched in the FST table.

3.2 An Interactive IE System Architecture

Fig. 2 shows the system architecture of *SEP* that separates operation engines with domain knowledge to enable task performance interactivity. Users provide CCTR task definition and subject domain knowledge via user interface module. These include specifications of template relation and sandwich extraction patterns, as well as lexicons of *ROU* and *REU*-typed semantic units. *SEP* stores user inputs in the form of a lexicon table and an FST table. Text documents are processed for pattern matching and contextual inference in the unit of a sentence. Each sentence is matched with an FST sequentially selected from the sorted FST table. The matching process is executed by the selected FST as described above. Successful matches produce information instances of template relations in designated output format. Rejected sentences are no match to all FSTs stored in *SEP*. This indicates that either these sentences need to be processed with new domain knowledge (e.g. sandwich extraction patterns and lexicons) or they contain no relevant information. All these outputs are accessible via user interface for evaluation and subsequent addition/modification of domain knowledge.

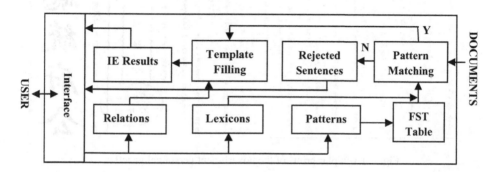

Fig. 2. *SEP*'s system architecture

By establishing an interactive loop of execution and feedback, *SEP* provides user with direct controllability of task performance. Therefore, *SEP* can be used as a self-contained tool for a user (e.g. librarian) to engage in an information extraction task. This typically involves a two-staged process. At the training stage, users can test-run *SEP* on the targeted document archive and incrementally buildup system databases of subject domain knowledge. When *SEP*'s outputs are evaluated by users as satisfactory, the process will enter the full production stage where *SEP* automatically performs specified IE task on large quantities of documents. The final output is a structured subject database filled with entries extracted from the selected document archive.

4 Empirical Validation and Application Results

We conducted empirical validation by field testing *SEP* in a practical document archive. The development process was carried out by librarians in NCCU library and was intended to serve three purposes: (1) to evaluate ***SEP***'s capability for CCTR tasks; (2) to demonstrate ***SEP*** as an interactive tool for value-added processing on documents; (3) to develop an actual content product that is of practical values.

4.1 Subject Domain

Government gazettes are official publications recording authoritative information of public affairs and are collected as document archives by major libraries. Among the many subjects, personnel gazette is selected based on its applicability as CCTR task and its content value. The documents record personnel changes of all government units in the form of presidential order. Examples of the government personnel gazettes are shown in Fig. 3 with original texts in Chinese, and in Fig. 4 with English translation on partial contents. Note that the translation is broken down into sequences of semantic units in order to reveal original content characteristics.

總統令 中華民國九十一年五月二十四日

任命鄒擅銘為國史館臺灣文獻館簡任第十職等組長。

任命楊合進為法務部簡任第十一職等權理簡任第十二職等司長。

任命吳文慎為交通部臺灣區國道新建工程局人事室簡任第十職等主任，林渭鵬為經濟部水利處人事室簡任第十職等主任。

任命曾沼良為行政院公共工程委員會簡任第十職等技正。

任命鍾萬梅為行政院客家委員會簡任第十二職等處長，黃崇烈為簡任第十一職等副處長。

任命戴正道為薦任公務人員。

任命葉玉芳、陳為成、何大雄、杜慶鳴、陳財益、滕忠信為薦任公務人員。

任命林宗輝為薦任公務人員。

任命王美玉、李殷豐、潘健發、洪建銘、郭肇喜、陳昌灝為薦任公務人員。

任命陳建志、黃姿華、張明慎、高露玉、賴炯明、蔡逸發為薦任公務人員。

任命范惠玫、賴淑華、施訓玉、張文靜為薦任公務人員。

總統府公報 第六四六六號

中華郵政台字第一三七二號執照登記為新聞紙交寄

總統府公

中華民國八十五年六月十九日（星期

總統令

政府出版品室 不外借

總統令 中華民國八十五年六月十三日

經濟部政務次長楊世緘，交通部政務次長蔡兆陽另有任用；財政部政務次長王政一、僑務委員會副委員長王能章、張植珊辭職已准；均應予免職。

行政院大陸委員會副主任委員葉金鳳、蘇 起，行政院經濟

總統府公報 第六〇九九號

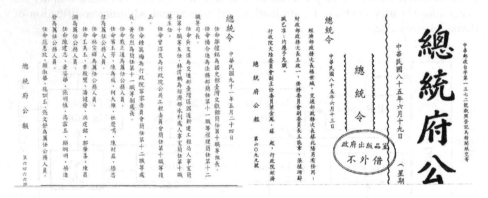

Fig. 3. Exemplar prints of the government personnel gazettes

(Ministry of Economic Affairs)(deputy minister)(YangShihJhen), (Ministry of Transportation and Communications)(deputy minister)(TsaiJhaoYang)(appointed to other assignments), (Ministry of Finance)(vice minister)(WangJhengYi), (Overseas Chinese Affairs Commission) (vice minister)(WangNengJang), (JangJhihShan)(resignation granted);(all shall be dismissed).

(Appoint)(ZouShanMing)(as)(Academia Historica)(Taiwan Historica)(management rank level ten)(section chief).
(Appoint)(JhongWanMei)(as)(Executive Yuan)(Counsel for Hakka Affairs)(management rank level twelve)(division chief), (HuangChongLie)(as)(management rank level eleven) (division deputy chief).

Fig. 4. English translation on partial contents

4.2 Product Development

The product development process was started by the librarians surveying the personnel gazettes and consulting faculty of public administration department to establish necessary domain knowledge. At first, CCTR task was specified by a set of relation slots that include person name, organization name, rank, job title, type of changes, and date. An initial set of semantic units, lexicons, and extraction patterns, were also added to *SEP*. Then, the librarians began the interactive loop of activating *SEP*'s task execution, examining task outputs, and adding new domain knowledge. After 60 man-hours of training, *SEP*'s performance reached upper 90 percents in precision and recall with approximately 30 extraction patterns and 670 lexicons.

Encouraged by the successful test runs, NCCU library has formally initiated a project to develop a content product of government personnel gazettes, including document images, electronic texts, and personnel changes database. Currently, the database covers the time period from 1981 to 2005 and contains approximately 300,000 entries, 165,000 individuals, 11,000 government units, 650 job titles, and 2840 image files. Besides from the structured information, each retrieved entry is linked to a document image that contains the original personnel order in texts. The product is expected to expand retrospectively to year 1934 in order to provide a complete coverage in time. Fig. 5 shows screen shots of the web-based government personnel changes database. The database supports search options of logical combination on multiple fields (Fig. 5(a)). A typical use of the database is to view a person's career path in the government (Fig. 5(b)).

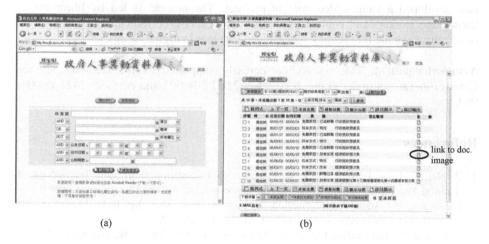

(a)   (b)

Fig. 5. Web interfaces of NCCU library's government personnel changes database

4.3 Extensions and Implications

Our research differs from most IE approaches [2][6] in providing a systematic way of transforming domain knowledge into effective operations and enabling user controllability on task execution. These characteristics are essential for librarians to explore the potential of value added services [5] on digital document archives. For example, we may want to develop a database that collects personal information of politicians, enterprise executives, and civil leaders, such as name, birth place, birth date, school attended/graduated, job affiliation, etc., Exemplar expressions in Table 1, which are abundant in general texts, provide partial and conceptual evidences for the commonality of the CCTR tasks and the utility of our approach. The derived products that support structured query will be able to provide further value-added services in many aspects, such as statistics, comparison, analysis, data mining, and even language resources.

Table 1. Exemplar semantic expressions of CCTR characteristics

(person name) + born at + (location name) + (date)
(person name) + graduated from + (school name)
(organization name) + announced the promotion of + (person name) + to + (job title)
(organization name) + reappointed + (person name) + to + (job title)
(person name1) + replaced + (person name2) + as + (job title)

5 Conclusion

Our research contribution is to propose a framework that provides a systematic way of capturing the unique characteristics of a particular sub-class of IE tasks, transforming domain knowledge into effective recognition and extraction, and enabling interactive control of the process. We demonstrated the approach in a practical document archive and developed a value-added content product. The process is led by librarians as knowledge workers and content producers. Our experience indicates that this might be a fruitful avenue for creating value added services in digital libraries.

Acknowledgement. This research is partially supported by the National Science Counsel in Taiwan under grants NSC-94-2422-H-004-002 and NSC-95-2422-H-004-003.

References

1. Applet, D. E. and Israel, D. J.: Introduction to Information Extraction Technology. A Tutorial, Proceedings of the 16th Int'l Joint Conference on Artificial Intelligence (1999).
2. Ciravegna, F. Adaptive Information Extraction from Text by Rule Induction and Generalisation. Proceedings of the 17th IJCAI (2001), 1251-1256.
3. Grishman, R.: Information Extraction: Techniques and Challenges. In: Pazienza, M. (ed.): Proceedings of SCIE. Springer-Verlag (1997) 10-27.
4. Mohri, M.: Finite-State Transducers in Language and Speech Processing. Computational Linguistics 23:2 (1997) 269-311.
5. Saracevic, T. and Kantor, P. B.: Studying the Value of Library and Information Services, Part I: Establishing a Theoretical Framework. Journal of the American Society for Information Science 48:6 (1997) 527-542.
6. Soderland, S.: Learning Information Extraction Rules for Semi-Structured and Free Text. Machine Learning 34:1-3 (1999) 233-272.
7. Wilks, Y. and Catizone, R.: Can We Make Information Extraction More Adaptive? In: Pazienza, M. (ed.): Proceedings of SCIE. Springer-Verlag (1999).

Topic Structure Mining Using PageRank Without Hyperlinks

Hiroyuki Toda[1,2], Ko Fujimura[1], Ryoji Kataoka[1], and Hiroyuki Kitagawa[2,3]

[1] NTT Cyber Solutions Laboratories, NTT Corporation,
1-1 Hikarinooka Yokosuka-shi, Kanagawa 239-0847, Japan
[2] Graduate School of Systems and Information Engineering,
[3] Center for Computational Sciences,
University of Tsukuba, Tennoudai, Tsukuba-shi, Ibaraki 305-8573, Japan
toda.hiroyuki@lab.ntt.co.jp

Abstract. This paper proposes a novel text mining method for any given document set. It is based on PageRank-based centrality scores within the graph structure generated from the similarity of all document pairs. Evaluations using a newspaper collection show that the proposed approach yields much better performance in terms of main topic identification and topical clustering than the baseline method. Furthermore, we show an example of document set visualization that offers novel document browsing through the topic structure. Experiments show that our topic structure mining method is useful for user-oriented document selection.

1 Introduction

Users have always wanted to be able to find the desired documents and information quickly and easily from a set of documents such as search engine results and the latest articles in RSS feeds. We consider that the user has two main goals.

- get an outline of the document set
- access the documents of specified topics present in the document set

A simple assessment shows that the first goal is equivalent to browsing and summarizing with the user receiving a list of the main topics in the document set. The second goal is set by the user who has clear information needs; for this we must collect the documents related to each topic.

One way to achieve this goal is to apply clustering algorithms [4][3][12][13][10]. They are intended to output document clusters that assist the user in understanding the outline of the document set. However, if we consider the situation in which the user wants to select a document from the document set or get some information from the document set, we find that we can select documents and get information, more accurately and more easily, if we can know not only "main topic list" and "cluster assignment of each document" but also "the relationship between topics" and/or "the type of each document in each cluster",

S. Sugimoto et al. (Eds.): ICADL 2006, LNCS 4312, pp. 151–162, 2006.

Here, "the type of each document in each cluster" is, for example, "the documents that represent core topics" and "the documents that are certainly related to core topics but also contain unexpected or new information". This allows us to select the former type of document when we want to access only the main topics, and the latter type of document when we already know the main topics and want to discover surrounding or novel topics.

Therefore, this paper proposes topic structure mining (TSM) which yields not only "main topic list" and "cluster assignment of each document" but also "the relationship between topics" and/or "the types of documents in each cluster". This is a graph-based method that uses the level of similarity between documents to identify core documents, those that have the highest level of connection density (centrality score). Each core document is taken to represent a different topic. The centrality scores of the documents are, together with the graph structure, used to segregate the documents so that we form sets of documents; one set equals one topic. Documents that are only weakly associated with the grouped documents are treated as outliers. Next, for each topic, the documents other than the core document are ranked as either supplemental documents, those that are strongly associated with the core document, and subtopic documents, those that are slightly associated with either of the other two types.

Experiments confirm the ability of our proposal to realize main topic identification and topical clustering as basic properties. Moreover, we show the meaning of TSM. Our visualization and evaluation show that our method can mine topic structure, for example, "the relationship between clusters (topics)" and/or "the type of each document in each cluster" and so realize effective document browsing and user-oriented document selection.

In this paper, one "document" corresponds to one "node". When we discuss the graph structure, we will mainly use the word "node".

The paper is organized as follows. The next section introduces related works. In Section 3, we detail the proposed method. Section 4 evaluates the basic properties of the proposed method. Section 5 shows a verification of the meaning of TSM. Finally we conclude the paper in Section 6.

2   Related Works

Graph-based NLP methods are being used more often to extract the implicit relationships between documents or other linguistic items. Mihalcea et al. [9] experimentally proved that PageRank [1] is effective for achieving these goals if the edges of the graph have weight or do not have direction. They also report that the method is useful for the tasks of text summarization and keyword extraction. Erkan [2] also proposed a graph-based method for text summarization and reported that the method yields much higher precision than any other method. Furthermore, Kurland et al. [7][8] proposed a graph based on a language model for calculating PageRank or HITS [6] and used it to rerank search results. Our method also uses the centrality score of graphs generated by the implicit relationships between documents. Though ordinary methods simply use the centrality score for ranking items or selecting top ranked items, we use both the centrality scores and graph structure for segregating items into topics.

3   Proposed Method

The method proposed in this paper first identifies the graph structure based on similarity links within the document set, and then determines core documents, those that have the highest level of centrality. Each core document represents a different topic. Next, the centrality scores are used together with the graph structure to identify those documents that are strongly associated with the core documents. Section 3.1 describes how the graph structure is generated. Section 3.2 explains the calculation of the centrality score of each node in the graph structure. The meaning of the centrality score is elucidated in Section 3.3, along with information extraction based on node meaning.

3.1   Generation of Graph Structure

We construct a graph structure, where each node represents one document and each edge represents the relationship between a pair of documents. This graph structure is based on the "Interested Reader model" proposed by Kamvar [5]. This model is similar to the "Random Surfer model" of PageRank [1]. It assumes that the document collection consists of documents covering several topics, and that the reader starts to read some document in the collection and then go on to read other documents. The reader's next choice is strongly related to his current document. These transition probabilities define a Markov chain among the documents in the collection. If many documents are strongly related, the transition probability among the documents is high while the transition probability to other documents is low. Furthermore, this model assumes the following. The self transition probability is high, when all documents are dissimilar. On the other hand, when there are many similar documents, the self transition probability is low. According to this assumption, the matrix is calculated by the following equation.

$$N = (A + d_{max}E - D)/d_{max} \qquad (1)$$

Here, N is the matrix based on the "interested reader model". E is a unit matrix. D is a diagonal matrix whose elements $D_{ii} = \sum_j A_{ij}$, where d_{max} is the largest element of D. The term "$d_{max}E - D$" represents a degree of self transition in each node. A is an adjacent matrix that indicates the similarity between nodes; it is defined in this paper as follows.

$$A_{i,j} = \begin{cases} sim(i,j) & if \ \ j \in TopSim_p(i) \\ 0 & otherwise \end{cases} \qquad (2)$$

Here, $TopSim_p(i)$ means the set of documents that have top p ranking with regard to their similarity to document i. Our reason for using only documents with highest similarity to generate the outlinks, is that accuracy is degraded

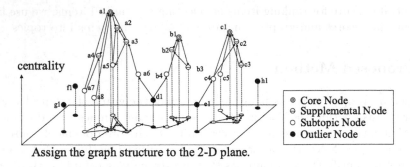

Assign the graph structure to the 2-D plane.

Fig. 1. Document set structure using graph structure and centrality score

when all similarity values are used [5][7]. $sim(i,j)$ is calculated by the cosine measure of log tf-idf weighted document vectors.

We note that the number of outlinks from all nodes is the same in the graphs generated by the above method. This situation is strange, because a node that has many similar nodes should have more links than a node that has few similar nodes. Moreover, some nodes have very small link weights. Our approach is to remove the surplus links, those that have very small weights. This operation is described by the following equation.

$$N'_{i,j} = \begin{cases} N_{i,j}/l_{i,q} & if \quad j \in TopLink_q(i) \\ 0 & otherwise \end{cases} \quad (3)$$

Here, $l_{i,q}$ is the sum of transitional probability, where we order the outlinks of node i by their transitional probability (descending order) and sum the probabilities until the sum exceeds threshold q. $TopLink_q(i)$ means the group of nodes that are the destinations of the above outlinks of node i. In this equation, we normalise each element with $l_{i,q}$ to surppress the influence of surplus links.

3.2 Calculating Centrality of the Graph

We consider here PageRank [1] since it is one of the most representative methods of calculating centrality.

One characteristic of PageRank is that it considers random jumping. Random jumping helps the random walker move from periodic node or unconnected nodes to any node in the graph. In our method, we use PageRank to calculate the centrality and we also use random jumping. We differ from PageRank with regard to edge weighting; we use the following equation to calculate node centrality.

$$S(i) = (1 - d) \times \sum_{\forall j} (N'_{j,i} \times S(j)) + d \quad (4)$$

Here, $S(i)$ is the centrality score of node i. d is a damping factor that represents the probability of random jumping.

3.3   Data Mining Using Centrality Scores and the Graph Structure

Our proposal is to assign the graph structure to a plane and plot the node centrality scores in the 3rd dimension. A typical image is shown in Fig 1. The nodes named "ax" ("bx"..) indicate the documents related to topic "a" ("b"..).

The method of [7] simply uses the centrality scores to rank the documents. However, our purpose is to segregate items by extracting topics. We cannot extract items separately if only the centrality score is used. Namely, if we order the nodes in Fig. 1 according to their centrality score, we get the order "a1,a2,c1,b1,a3,c2,b2,..." so topics are mixed together.

To realize segregation, we use the mountain-like structure generated by the graph structure and centrality scores to uncover the topics and permit information extraction based on node meaning.

First, we consider the relationship between graph structure and centrality score. According to the definition of the centrality score, areas that have many edges have high scores. Such an area also has high transition probability between the nodes in the area and the similarity between each node in this area is high. That is to say, the documents in this area cover the same topic. Accordingly, each mountain-like area in Fig.1 is considered to correspond to a different topic. Next, we assign each node to one of 4 types.

The 1st type are the top nodes (a1, b1, and c1 in Fig.1) of the area peaks (one top node per area). This kind of node has the highest transition probability from surrounding nodes and is the most representative of the topic. That is to say, the document of a top node specifies the main topic in the area. We call this the core document (node).

The 2nd type are neighbor nodes (a2, a3, a4, b2, b3, c2, and c3 in Fig.1). These nodes are reached from the top node only via two-way links either directly with the top node or via another neighbor node. A two-way link is bidirectional and has high connectivity. These nodes have high transition probability with the top node and their contents are similar to that of the top node. If the top node is quite close to one or more neighbors nodes, the topic may need to be identified from several nodes; this situation must be considered in subsequent research. We call these supplemental documents (nodes).

The 3rd type covers nodes that are linked to the top node or neighbor nodes; examples are a5, a6, a7, a8, b4, c4, and c5 in Fig. 1. This type of node, which has higher transition probability to the top or top neighbor node than to outside nodes or self-transition, are documents that are strongly related to the topic. This kind of document provides somewhat unexpected information. We call these subtopic documents (nodes).

The last type covers nodes that are not strongly associated with any topic. d1, e1, f1, g1, and h1 of Fig.1 is examples of this type. This node does not have any other similar node and its self-transition probability is high. We call these outlier documents (nodes).

The 4 node types are shown in Fig.1. The node set related to a topic is hierarchically sited around the top node.

To use this structure, the user can access the documents related to a particular topic. Furthermore, the user can select documents within one topic; for example, the document that is most representative of the topic or a document that may provide unexpected information. Furthermore, the relationship of two topics can be discerned through their sharing of supplemental and subtopic nodes.

Section 4.2 shows the result of topic identification by selecting the core nodes. Section 4.3 shows the effectiveness of collecting documents according to their topic. In Section 5, we verify the meaning of TSM using an example of visualization and experimental results.

4   Evaluation

4.1   Evaluation Resource

In this evaluation, we used search results of a Japanese newspaper collection. The collection covers 2 years (1994 and 1995) and holds about 200,000 articles. Two corpora were created by submitting the queries "scandal or bribery or corruption" and "murder", and recording the top 200 search results. We called these corpora "scandal" and "murder", respectively. The documents in the corpora were manually labeled after being read. Each label reflects the dominant topic in the document and each document is labeled by a label. We created main topic lists by selecting the topics with at least 2 documents. The documents were grouped according the main topic lists. Details are shown in Table 1. The main difference between the two corpus is the average cluster size. In the evaluations that used these corpora, the baseline method used the "K-Means" and "Agglomerative method using centroid".

4.2   Main Topic Identification

Here, we show the performance of topic identification using the core document.

As a baseline system, we used two methods based on clustering. First, these methods cluster each corpus with ideal cluster number [1] and select, for each cluster, the document that is most similar to the cluster's centroid. We estimated recall, precision, and F-Measure to evaluate the performance of topic identification. The equations of recall and precision are shown here.

$$\text{Recall} = \frac{\#\text{ of identified relevant topics}}{\#\text{ of relevant topics}} \tag{5}$$

$$\text{Precision} = \frac{\#\text{ of identified relevant topics}}{\#\text{ of identified topics}} \tag{6}$$

In this evaluation, we used $p = 3, 5$ (p is the permissible number of outlinks in each node) and $q \in [0.5, \dots, 1]$ is the threshold for surplus link elimination). The evaluation results are shown in Table 2.

---

[1] The cluster number is sum of "# of topic in topic list" and "# of documents not related to main topics" in each newspaper corpus. $k = 128$ (murder),$k = 52$ (scandal).

Table 1. Specification of the corpora for evaluation

name of corpus	scandal	murder
# of docs.	200	200
# of labels (main topics)	22	26
# of labeled docs. (docs related to a topic in main topic list)	170	98
average cluster size	7.7	3.8

Table 2. Evaluation result of topic identification

Condition	murder			scandal		
	Recall	Precision	F-measure	Recall	Precision	F-measure
TSM ($p = 3, q = 1$)	0.4615	**0.8**	0.5854	0.7727	0.8095	0.7907
TSM ($p = 3, q = 0.9$)	0.5385	0.7	0.6087	0.7727	0.7727	0.7727
TSM ($p = 3, q = 0.8$)	0.8077	0.6	0.6885	0.9091	0.7727	0.7843
TSM ($p = 3, q = 0.7$)	**0.8462**	0.6471	**0.7333**	0.9091	0.6897	0.7843
TSM ($p = 3, q = 0.6$)	0.7692	0.6451	0.7018	0.9091	0.5128	0.6557
TSM ($p = 3, q = 0.5$)	0.5769	0.6522	0.6122	0.8636	0.5588	0.6786
TSM ($p = 5, q = 1$))	0.1538	0.6667	0.25	0.4545	1	0.625
TSM ($p = 5, q = 0.9$)	0.3846	0.7692	0.5128	0.5	0.9167	0.6471
TSM ($p = 5, q = 0.8$)	0.5769	0.625	0.6	0.7727	0.7391	0.7556
TSM ($p = 5, q = 0.7$)	0.7308	0.6552	0.6909	**0.9546**	0.6774	**0.7925**
TSM ($p = 5, q = 0.6$)	0.7308	0.6552	0.6909	0.9091	0.5405	0.678
TSM ($p = 5, q = 0.5$)	0.4615	0.5714	0.5106	0.8636	0.5588	0.6786
K-Means	0.6154	0.4706	0.5333	0.7273	0.5926	0.6531
Agglomerative (centroid)	0.6538	0.7319	0.6939	0.6364	0.7	0.6667

When $q = 1$, precision tends to be high (more than 0.8 in three of four conditions) but recall is low (less than 0.5 in three of four conditions). The reason for this is that the document that should be a core document was not selected as a core document because of surplus links, when the number of documents related to each topic was small (for example 2 or 3). This is also the cause of "Recall of $p = 5$ is lower than that of $p = 3$" and "Recall of "murder" corpus, which have small average cluster size, is low". In this case, this document is subordinated by another core document which is connected by surpus link to this document.

When q falls under 1, recall first increases ($q = 0.9, 0.8$), reaches a peak score ($q = 0.8, 0.7$), and then decreases ($q = 0.6, 0.5$). This tendency is observed in both corpora and with all p values; the maximum degree of rise is about 40 points. The reason for the fall in recall is that links are strongly filtered so the graph structure is extremely sparse. On the other hand, the precision falls when we decrease q. The range of change, however, is small, so F-measure is basically higher than the scores of $q = 1$.

For almost all conditions in which $q < 1$, the proposed method offers a better score than the baseline method. It can said that the proposed method offers high accuracy, because the baseline method is given the ideal cluster size, this is not possible in actual applications.

Table 3. Evaluation result of topical clustering

Condition	murder	scandal
TSM ($p = 3, q = 1$)	0.6127	0.7855
TSM ($p = 3, q = 0.9$)	0.6656	0.7855
TSM ($p = 3, q = 0.8$)	**0.8081**	**0.7984**
TSM ($p = 3, q = 0.7$)	0.7232	0.7818
TSM ($p = 3, q = 0.6$)	0.6337	0.7592
TSM ($p = 3, q = 0.5$)	0.5795	0.7381
K-Means	0.3741	0.5279
Agglomerative (centroid)	0.6821	0.6343

4.3   Topical Clustering

We also evaluated the accuracy of topical document clustering according to their topic and document segregation from core node. This clustering involves only "core document", "supplementary documents", and "subtopic documents".

We used F-score to evaluate the selected document set. F-score is an evaluation method of clustering. F-score represents the weighted average of accuracy of the clusters that are most similar to the clusters in the correct cluster data. F-Score details are shown in [14]. For this evaluation, we used the main topic list and assigned documents. As the baseline system, we used the same two methods used in the main topic identification task.

In this evaluation, we set $p = 3$ because this yields better accuracy in topic identification and the accuracy of clustering seems to be impacted by the accuracy. According to a preliminary experiment on collecting subtopic nodes, some node are related to the topic even if the transition probability to the top or neighbor nodes (t) is slightly under 0.5 (This value comes from subtopic node definition given in Section 3.3). Accordingly, we set $t = 0.3$ in this experiment.

Results are shown in Table 3. The general tendency is that clustering accuracy is related to the F-measure of main topic identification. That is, the condition that yields high F-measure in the topic identification task, yields high clustering accuracy. Furthermore, clustering accuracy is not related to the precision of the topic identification task but is related to recall. This tendency seems to represent the characteristics of our methods, which segregate the cluster members (documents) using the links from the core nodes.

For "scandal", the proposed system was significantly better than the baseline system in all conditions. For "murder", it was superior to the baseline system only for a few conditions. The difference between "scandal" and "murder" is the size of topics. The "murder" corpus includes small clusters; average cluster size is small (see Table 1).

Because the proposed method uses centrality to detect the core documents, it exhibits some weakness when the topics are small, that is, the increase in centrality is not so large and the parameter selection becomes more difficult.

5   Verification of Meaning of Topic Structure Mining

We verify whether the proposed TSM method is useful for document set utilization. In Section 5.1, we show examples of visualization and of novel browsing. In Section 5.2, we show the result of simulation evaluations that verified whether the TSM is useful for effective document selecting adapt to user needs.

5.1   Visualization

Fig.2 shows a visualization of the "murder" set; the graph structure generated by proposed method ($p = 3, q = 0.8$) is assigned to 2-D plane by Yamada's method [11] and the centrality scores are plotted on the 3rd dimension. The white spheres are nodes (documents) and the lines between them are links. The direction of the link is represented by the gradation: the "from" side is light and the "to" side is dark. Two way links are white. Though we show the label and document id of each node (the light colored character), we could display the document titles instead of the labels.

In Fig.2, there are two mountains, each mountain represents one topic ("AUM-Lynch" and "AUM-Matsumoto Sarin") and the top node is the "core node". The positioning of the supplementary and subtopic documents makes it easy to find documents related to particular topics as well as understanding the relationships between topics. Fig.2 also shows that two mountains are shared a high level node (supplemental node). This suggests that the two topics are strongly related. In fact, these topics involve murder by the same religious community.

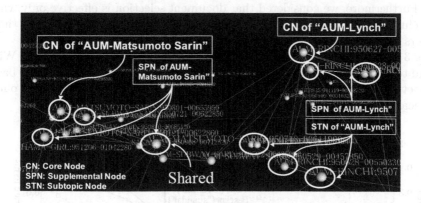

Fig. 2. Visualization example of corpus "murder"

It is clear that this visualization will trigger new browsing methods and enhance the knowledge discovery process. The results confirm the method's usefulness for browsing and analyzing document sets.

5.2   Verification of Usefullness of TSM for Document Selection

TSM enables the documents that meet the user's needs to be effectively identified from documents related to particular topics. Here, we verify whether our method is useful in achieving the following two goals.

- Get document(s) that represent main topics.
- Get document(s) that are related to main topics but include unexpected or novel information.

For this verification, we used the newspaper corpora used in Section 4, First, we made document clusters using the proposed method ($p = 3, q = 0.8$). The documents in each cluster were tagged as "Core Node", "Supplemental Node", or "Subtopic Node". Documents of the same type (Supplemental and Subtopic) were ranked by PageRank in descending order. As the baseline method, the documents in each cluster were ordered against the centroid of each cluster. We assumed that for the proposed method, goal one (two) is satisfied by selecting documents in the order (reverse order) of Core, Supplemental, Subtopic. For the baseline method, goal one (two) is satisfied by selecting documents in descending (ascending) degree of similarity to the centroid.

The performance metrics were the following criteria.

- coverage of frequent terms in the cluster
- coverage of rare terms in the cluster

We estimated the coverage rates for 1 to 5 documents. Higher performance is indicated by a higher coverage rate. In this evaluation, we removed frequent terms (document frequency threshold was set at 5000) in the newspaper collection. Furthermore, we considered that document selection is effective only when each cluster contains several documents. The above evaluation used only those clusters that had more than five documents.

Fig.3 shows the results. Each plot is the average value of all clusters. With regard to goal one, the proposed method provides better coverage than the baseline method with just a few documents. For goal two, the proposed method offers significantly better coverage than the baseline method.

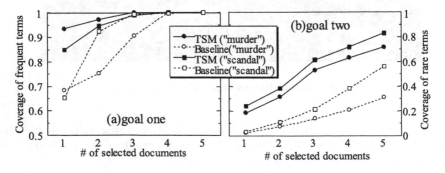

Fig. 3. Verification Results

The centroid method allows documents with high idf words to lie close to the centroid. These high idf words, however, tend to be very specific and documents with a lot of these words are not representative of the main topic. Erkan et al. [2] reported the same tendency. On the other hand, document clustering is related to the density of document linkage as determined by the graph structure. The resultant document order is extremely useful in clearly elucidating the main topic. The same argument is true with regard to the poor performance of the baseline method in achieving goal two.

6   Conclusion

This paper proposed a novel text mining method for document sets and also proposed a novel document browsing and selection method based on the first proposal. The proposed method uses a similarity-based graph structure and the centrality socres of nodes in the graph structure. The proposed method has three main benefits.

- Main topic identification and topical clustering with high accuracy.
- Novel document browsing and mining using visualization of topic structure.
- Novel user-oriented document selecting using document type.

Our future works include a comparison using large corpora and some refinement of the proposed method.

References

1. Brin, S. and Page, L.: "The anatomy of a large-scale hypertextual web search engine." *Proceedings of WWW7, pp.107-117,* 1998.
2. Erkan, G. and Radev, D. R.: "LexRank: Graph-based Lexical Centrality as Salience in Text Summarization." *Journal of Artificial Intelligence Research, Vo. 22, pp.457-479,* 2004.
3. He, X., Ding, C. H. Q., Zha, H. and Simon, H. D.: "Automatic Topic Identification Using Webpage Clustering." *Proc. of ICDM'01, pp.195-202,* 2001.
4. Hearst, M., and Pedersen, J.: "Reexamining the cluster hypothesis: scatter/gather on retrieval results." *Proc. of SIGIR'96, pp.76-84,* 1996.
5. Kamvar, S. D., Klein, D. and Manning, C. D.: "Spectral Learning." *Proc. of IJ-CAI'03, pp.561-566,* 2003.
6. Kleinberg, J.: "Authoritative source in a hyperlinked environment." *Journal of the ACM, Vol. 46, pp.604-632,* 1999.
7. Kurland, O. and Lee, L.: "PageRank without hyperlinks: Structural re-ranking using links induced by language models." *Proc. of SIGIR'05, pp.306-313,* 2005.
8. Kurland, O. and Lee, L.: Respect My Authority! HITS Without Hyperlinks, Utilizing Cluster-Based Language Models." *Proc. of SIGIR'06, pp.83-90,* 2006.
9. Mihalcea, R. and Tarau, P.: "TextRank: Bringing Order into Texts." *Proc. of EMNLP'04, pp.404-411,* 2004.
10. Toda, H. and Kataoka, R.: "A search result clustering method using informatively named entities." *Proc. of WIDM'05, pp.81-86,* 2005.

11. Yamada, T., Saito, K. and Ueda, N.: "Cross-Entropy Directed Embedding of Network Data." *Proc. of ICML'03, pp.832-839,* 2003.
12. Zamir, O., and Etzioni, O.: "Grouper: A Dynamic Clustering Interface to Web Search Results." *Proc. of WWW8, pp.1361-1374,* 1999.
13. Zeng, H. J., He, Q. C., Chen, Z., Ma, W. Y. and Ma, J.: "Learning to Cluster Web Search Results." *Proc. of SIGIR'04, pp.210-217,* 2004.
14. Zhao, Y. and Karypis, G.: "Evaluation of Hierarchical Clustering Algorithms for Document Datasets" *Proc. of CIKM'02, pp.515-524,* 2002.

Personalized Information Delivering Service in Blog-Like Digital Libraries

Jason J. Jung[1,2]

[1] Department of Computer & Information Eng., Inha University
253 Yonghyun-Dong, Nam-Gu, Incheon, Korea 402-751
[2] INRIA Rhône-Alpes
ZIRST 655 avenue de l'Europe, Montbonnot
38334 Saint Ismier cedex, France
j2jung@intelligent.pe.kr

Abstract. With increasing concerns about the personalized digital libraries (e.g., blogs), people need to share relevant information and knowledge with other like-minded users. In this paper, we aim at building a grid environment for information recommendation, in order to support users' information searching tasks. By thoroughly analyzing the social linkage and social interaction patterns, we want to extract the meaningful relationships between the unknown users by co-occurrence analysis. Therefore, social grid environment can be constructed by aggregating a set of virtual hubs discovered from the hidden connections. For implementation and evaluation, we exploit the proposed method to blogosphere. The BlogGrid framework is proposed to provide efficient information pushing service to bloggers without requesting any user intervention.

1 Introduction

Since personalized information spaces (e.g. blogs[1]) were introduced, the usage has been spread to many fields [1,2]. More importantly, each blogger can make explicit connections with other acquaintances (e.g., family members and friends), and take social activities such as information (or knowledge) sharing, responding to answers, and referring to further information [3]. Thus, they can organize communities in a form of socialized information space. On blogosphere, however, we have been facing on two problems. Firstly, a large amount of *information overwhelming to users* means that users are getting much more overloaded to search for relevant information related to a certain topic and, more specifically, the like-minded users. Next problem is *network isolation phenomenon*. Communities tend to be initially organized from the private relations among users. But, the number of members in this community may keeps constant over time, because social interactions between different community members are rarely occurred. We find out the limitation of information flows caused by not only the community policy for protecting the privacy of members but also the topological isolation of social structure.

---

[1] This is the shorten expression of "weblogs," and this paper uses only "blog".

S. Sugimoto et al. (Eds.): ICADL 2006, LNCS 4312, pp. 163–172, 2006.

In order to solve these problems, we exploit the grid computing paradigm [4] to personal information spaces and users, supporting an efficient framework of information and knowledge sharing between heterogeneous sources. Thereby, each user's behaviors should be captured and analyzed to extract meaningful context (e.g., what topics he is (or they are) interested in and, more exactly, what he has been trying to search for). In particular, we implement a grid environment (called BlogGrid [5]), in order to provide information pushing service on blogosphere. The goal of this service is efficient information diffusion on blogosphere. It means that a certain information should be delivered to the bloggers who have been looking for the information as quickly as possible, regardless of the social distances and topologies.

We exploit co-occurrence analysis between user activities to predict the relationships between the corresponding bloggers. Virtual hubs built by shortest paths are applied to adapting the strength of hub centrality of personal information space.

The outline of this paper is as follows: Section 2 describes modeling user behaviors on blogosphere and analyzing social interactions. In section 3, we explain the main steps of BlogGrid framework. Section 4 addresses implementation with experimental results and some important issues. Finally, in section 5, we draw some conclusions and explain future work.

2   Analyzing Social Interactions Between Users

In order to recognize the relationships between users, we want to model each user's behaviors and measure the distance between them. We can fomulate the behavior of users on social network $\mathcal{SN} = \{U_1, U_2, \ldots, U_N\}$ where N is the total number of users participating in this social network.

2.1   Modeling Behaviors on Blogspace

We assume that each action taken by users have implicit meaning and be able to be applied to extract useful information about their preferences. Also, this information should be used to recognize the relationships between users. We classify the behaviors $\mathcal{B} = \{\mathcal{A}, \mathcal{L}, \mathcal{N}, \mathcal{R}, \mathcal{C}\}$;

1. *Posting articles $\mathcal{A}$.* Users input various information and enrich their own spaces. This action explicitly represents the corresponding user's preferences. A set of articles of U_i is denoted as $\mathcal{A}_i = \{a_1, a_2, \ldots, a_K\}$.
2. *Linking with other blogspaces $\mathcal{L}$.* It is for explicit construction of a social network. More importantly, in order to share information about a particular topic, people can organize a community and actively participate it. We assume this link to be directional. Thus, the neighbors of U_i is represented as $\mathcal{L}_i$ combining two links $\mathcal{L}^{\mathcal{O}}$ (pointing to others) and $\mathcal{L}^{\mathcal{I}}$ (pointed by others).

$$\mathcal{L}_i = \mathcal{L}_i^{\mathcal{O}} + \mathcal{L}_i^{\mathcal{I}} = \{U_p\}_i^{\mathcal{O}} + \{U_q\}_i^{\mathcal{I}} \tag{1}$$

Reversely, Equ. 1 can also be represented as $\{U_m | U_i \in \mathcal{L}_m^{\mathcal{I}}\} + \{U_n | U_i \in \mathcal{L}_n^{\mathcal{O}}\}$.

3. *Navigating $\mathcal{N}$*. In order to get relevant information within personal information spaces, people should visit other spaces, by the following two methods;
   - **Random browsing**. A blogger randomly jump into other blogspaces.
   - **Accessing to neighbors on social network**. By referring to the list
     of neighbors, a blogger easily moves into the blogs of his neighbors. In
     the same way, he can access to the blogs of his neighbors' neighbors.
4. *Responding $\mathcal{R}$*. A user can respond to a certain information by two ways;
   i) *comment* and *ii*) *trackback*[2]. Moreover, not only a free-text sentence but
   also numeric rating format (e.g., from 0 to 5) and voting format (e.g., "Yes"
   or "No") can be applied to reflect the degree of the corresponding user's
   interests and opinions. Another feature is that the responding can be nested.
   It means that bloggers can respond to a certain comment already attached
   to articles. Thus, the responses by user U_i is given as $\mathcal{R}_i = \{r_i^{a_\alpha}, r_i^{r_\beta} | a_\alpha \in
   \mathcal{A}_j, r_\beta \in \mathcal{R}_k\}$ where $\mathcal{A}_j$ and $\mathcal{R}_k$ mean a set of articles by user u_j and a set
   of responds by user u_k, respectively.
5. *Categorizing blogspaces $\mathcal{C}$*. Each blog can be labeled with topics, which is
   represented as hierarchical path on taxonomies. It is represented as $\mathcal{C}_i =
   \{c_i | c_i \in \mathcal{O}\}$ where $\mathcal{O}$ is a hierarchical taxonomy (e.g., ODP and TopicMap).

2.2   Virtual Hub Generation by Co-occurrence Analysis

Co-occurrence analysis between their behaviors can generate a set of virtual hubs
($\mathcal{VH}$). It is play a role of alternative channels to communicate among potential
users. In our previous work [6], we found out that responding behaviors $\mathcal{R}$ has
shown more significant effects rather than other ones. For the moment, this
paper is considering only responding behaviors $\mathcal{R}$ to measuring co-occurrence
between two users. (Of cause, the others' co-occurrence patterns can be easily
discovered, as extending according to $\mathcal{B} = \{\mathcal{A}, \mathcal{L}, \mathcal{N}, \mathcal{R}, \mathcal{C}\}$.) Two arbitrary users
who commonly respond to a certain article a_β ($\in \mathcal{A}_\alpha$) of personal space of user
U_α are regarded as like-minded users. For example, let two users U_A and U_B
respond to a certain article in U_C's blog. Even though they are geometrically far
away on social network, their preferences are probably similar with each other.
In order to make them closer, we formulate some measurements. Simply the
(geodesic) distance $\mathcal{D}$ between two users can be measured by

$$\mathcal{D}(U_i, U_j) = shortest\_path(U_i, U_j)$$
$$= \min(path(U_i, U_j)). \tag{2}$$

It is the length of linked path between U_i and U_j, and it is computed by counting
all the edges on the shortest path.

Next, we need to recognize the "power" from social linkage patterns in $\mathcal{SN}$,
we deploy the hub ($\mathcal{HUB}$) and authority ($\mathcal{AUTH}$) weighting scheme [7] to measure the centralities of every users. Similar to the betweenness [8], hub weight
indicates the structural position of the corresponding user. It is a measure of

---

[2] Movable Type. http://www.sixapart.com/movabletype/.

the influence that people has over the spread of information through the network. On the other hand, authoritative weight is a measure of the information quantity that people occupies. These weights can be iteratively computed by $\mathcal{HUB}_{t-1}^{\langle U_i \rangle} \leftarrow \sum_{U_j : \in \mathcal{L}_i^O} \mathcal{AUTH}_{t-1}^{\langle U_j \rangle}$ and $\mathcal{AUTH}_t^{\langle u_i \rangle} \leftarrow \sum_{U_j \in \mathcal{L}_i^I} \mathcal{HUB}_{t-1}^{\langle U_j \rangle}$ where $\mathcal{AUTH}_0$ is initialized with 1. Additionally, for the "equilibrium" values of the weights, iteration process should be conducted.

Now, we propose a novel similarity (or distance) measurement based on the "hub" weights of neighbors. By using the response $r^{a\beta}$ co-occurred by a group of users U_{CO}, the hub similarities $\mathcal{S}_{\mathcal{HUB}}$ is represented as a square matrix of which size is $|U_{CO}| \times |U_{CO}|$, and each element is given by

$$\mathcal{S}_{\mathcal{HUB}}(i,j) = \frac{\mathcal{D}(U_i, U_j)}{\sum_{U_k} \mathcal{HUB}^{\langle U_k \rangle}} \times \frac{1}{\exp(|U_{CO}|)} \tag{3}$$

where $U_k \in shortest\_path(U_i, U_j)$ and $U_i, U_j \in U_{CO}$. If $\mathcal{D}(U_i, U_j)$ is less than two (e.g., the diagonal elements), $\mathcal{S}_{\mathcal{HUB}}(i,i)$ is zero. We assume that the longer distance and the lower hub weights between two users indicate the higher similarity. In the second term, we express that the higher number of co-occurring users exponentially decays the hub similarity among them. The $\mathcal{VH}$ among the corresponding users, therefore, is generated, as shown in Fig. 1. Then, as

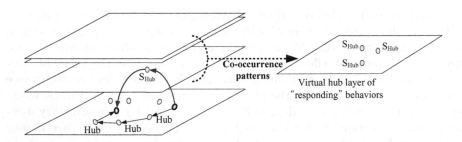

Fig. 1. Measuring hub similarities with common responses and aggregating with others

accumulating the $\mathcal{VH}$'s generated by all co-occurred response patterns, we can construct the $\mathcal{VH}$ layer ($\mathcal{VHL}$). In case of this paper considering only patterns from "response" behaviors, it can be denoted as $\mathcal{VHL}_{\mathcal{R}}$. This is simply based on matrix concatenation tasks, but we have to focus on the duplications. Here, for adaptability, $\mathcal{S}_{\mathcal{HUB}}$ between the repeated pairs of users U_i and U_j have to be reinforced twice by

$$\mathcal{S}_{\mathcal{HUB}}(i,k)' = \mathcal{S}_{\mathcal{HUB}}(i,k) \tag{4}$$

$$\times \left\{ \begin{array}{ll} 1 + \Delta & \text{if } k = j; \\ 1 - \frac{\Delta \times \mathcal{S}_{\mathcal{HUB}}(i,k)}{|U_{CO}| - 1} & \text{otherwise;} \end{array} \right.$$

and $\mathcal{S}_{\mathcal{HUB}}(k,j)'$, which can be obtained by exactly opposite way to Equ. 5. Δ is the coefficient of learning rate in $(0, 1]$, and $U_{CO} = U_{CO_1} \cup \ldots \cup U_{CO_N}$. Of cause, instead of the adaptation scheme based on *Hebbian* learning that we apply for simplicity, the other various learning methods are exploitable.

3   Information Delivering on BlogGrid

Each information should be pushed (more exactly, notified) to the users who are interested in and searching for it. A facilitator agent has to conduct this service, and it is simply composed of two main processes; i) ranking-based organization of user group, and ii) propagation of relevant information. Thereby, when a response behavior $\mathcal{B}_i$ (e.g., in this paper, $r_i \in \mathcal{R}_i$) by user U_i is detected, this facilitator should predict the candidate users U_x who is potentially close to U_i by ranking $\mathcal{S}_{\mathcal{HUB}}(i, x)$ from the $\mathcal{VHL}$. As measuring the hub similarity between two users by the given response patterns, we can infer their relationship and make a decision whether they should be participated in a same article together or not. Especially, this task should be transparently done, which means it has to be performed without user's intervention and realization.

Along with the established $\mathcal{VHL}$, the relevant pieces of information should be pushed actively. Information pushing service proposed in this paper is remote and synchronous because this is based on web-based blogging system and information is promptly propagated according to the participant's interests extracted from his own behaviors. Figure 2 shows the whole system architecture.

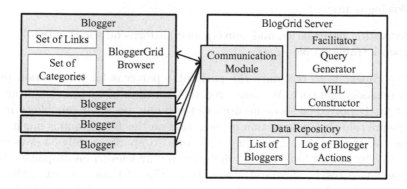

Fig. 2. System architecture of BlogGrid

It consists of two main parts, which are a facilitator located between the users and the client-side blogspace browser that communicates with the facilitator. We embed autonomous and proactive agent module into this system. Every communication between agents is conducted, regardless of user's interventions. Also, while browsing blogspaces to search information, users can be "implicitly" recommended from the facilitator in the following two ways:

- *By querying specific information for the facilitator.* After the information about a particular topic is requested, the facilitator can determine who has the maximum weight value of that topic by scanning his yellow pages.
- *By broadcasting new information of like-minded bloggers from the facilitator.* Every time a user responds a new comment, this fact, after normalization, is sent to the facilitator. Users thereby can obtain information related to the common concepts in their own preferences from neighbors.

Each blogger needs personal agent module. This agent initializes and manages the preference of the corresponding blogger based on blogspace repository. Through personal agents' reporting responding activities of bloggers, the facilitator agent can automatically generate queries and recommendations.

4   Experimental Results

For evaluating the performance of adaptive socialization on BlogGrid, we randomly divided the students into two groups, named *Alpha* (75 students) and *Beta* (75 students). Only students in a group Beta could use BlogGrid browser. The students within the same group were able to make linkages with their acquaintances for constructing social networks, access to the other blogspaces, and share information with each other for ten weeks (from 14 February, 2005 to 23 April, 2005). We monitored all bloggers' activities in these two groups with respect to the following issues;

- Information propagation and convergence patterns on social network
- Network traffic on blogspaces

First experiment is to recognize the particular patterns for information propagation on social network. We measured the duration of each article from the moment firstly posted on social network to the finally posted in any blogs. In figure 3, we are told that information propagation on the *Beta* group is much more dynamic rather than the *Alpha*. The *Alpha* needed approximately 54 days to be settled. In contrast, it took only 34 days for any articles to be propagated and converged. As a result, BlogGrid made about 37% of time cost saved through efficient recommendation. Next test is measuring the network traffic of bloggers (*Alpha* and *Beta*) during ten weeks. It proves the performance of BlogGrid's information pushing service. To do so, we counted the total number of HTTP requests related to URL's of our testing bed. As shown in Fig. 4, after 21 days, the network traffic of *Beta* group was kept to be lower than that of *Alpha*. Specially, after 34 days, we have seen that the number of HTTP requests in *Beta* was only 61% of *Alpha*'s.

Another evaluation is the degree of user satisfaction about BlogGrid's recommendation in group *Beta*. It is a measurement for how accurately BlogGrid recommended information to each blogger. We measured the ratio of the number of posts by BlogGrid's recommendation to the total number of posts. With human evaluation by interviewing with bloggers, we verified that

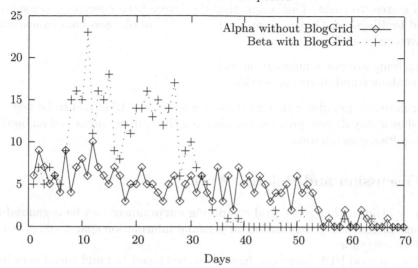

Fig. 3. Experimental results of the durations of each article posted on blogspace

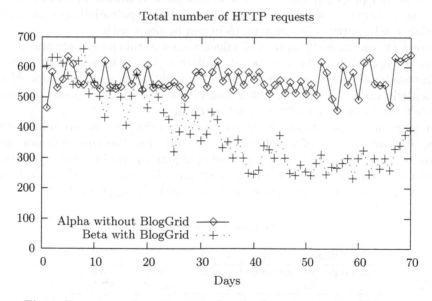

Fig. 4. Experimental results of the length of traversal paths of bloggers

- 47 bloggers, who is 62.67% of total bloggers in *Beta*, were fully satisfied,
- 16 bloggers, who is 21.3%, were partially satisfied,
- 8 blogger, who is 10.67%, was partially unsatisfied, and
- 4 blogger, who is 5.33%, were fully unsatisfied

with BlogGrid's recommendations. About 84% of bloggers rated BlogGrid as a useful system to them. This means that they were been effectively helped and guided by BlogGrid. On the other hand, only 16% of bloggers complained some inconveniences such as

- receiving irrelevant information and
- installing stand-alone application.

Particularly, we found out that most users who judged BlogGrid to be negative have shown very diverse preferences. Also, relatively many users had an opinion about software installation.

5 Discussion and Related Work

We have claimed that social grid computing environment can be organized for efficient information dissemination on personal information space, and it can be adaptive over time.

So far, several RDF languages have been developed to build social networks. Such languages are FOAF (Friend Of A Friend)[3] and SIOC (Semantically-Interlinked Online Communities) [9]. While these are based on user's explicit assertions, our proposed system is based on implicit relations. From this difference, our system can detect the relationships between potentially similar users. In other words, network isolation problem can be dealt with.

In order to maximize the spread of influence on a certain social network, game-theoretical approach has been proposed. Similar to [10], we have been attempting on discovering the more influential person (or node) from social network. More particularly, on our system, the influential weight, meaning the power on social network, can be incrementally updated over time.

In addition, we have to discuss the scalability of this system. We have tested three different number of members (25, 50, and 75). The time duration was measured as shown in Table 1. As the number of participants increases, delivering a certain information shows better performance. It proves that BlogGrid was well-organized user communities, even the number of people was larger.

Table 1. Scalability testing

Number of users	25	50	75
Average duration (days)	62.3	56.2	54.3
Ratio	-	90.21%	87.16%

Finally, we want to mention privacy issues while propagating information on distributed environment. A variety of work has been introduced to measure the reputation (or trust) weight on users [11]. In our case, we also adopt this kind approach on each hub node on social network.

---

[3] http://www.foaf-project.org/

6 Concluding Remarks and Future Work

As many information systems have been concerning about the paradigm of personal information space, efficient information delivering function is desperately necessary to them. We were motivated to enhance this primitive blogspace with cooperative computing methodologies. This paper proposes BlogGrid system to help bloggers and optimize efficiency of information diffusion, by analyzing and recognizing user activity and interests on social space. Most importantly, we propose an adaptive socialization method by adjusting "Hub" weighting. Therefore, bloggers were able to get information pushing service with BlogGrid's recommendation, which consists of mainly two steps; i) organization of virtual communities and ii) information pushing by facilitator. This system can conduct users overcoming the local minima by putting the effect of simulated annealing into the social network.

We developed BlogGrid system by using Blojsom[4] libraries and Borland Delphi software[5]. BlogGrid browser's graphic user interface can visualize the communications and relationships between bloggers. More importantly, the facilitator of BlogGrid is capable of

1. investigating the factors which influence relationships,
2. drawing out implications of the relational data, and
3. making recommendations to improve communications between people.

Through two main experimentations and one human evaluation, we have shown that a relatively large part of bloggers were satisfied with this service.

For short discussion and future work, we have used quite a poor size of testing bed for experimentation, so we will invite more bloggers and exploit virtual user models. Also, we are considering the topological features of social networks mentioned in [7], for recognizing more accurate relationships between bloggers. Moreover, we are considering to applying natural language processing methods to free-text articles posted on blogspaces. Similar to [12] and [13], we also plan to apply semantic information like ontologies. We are expecting it will be very powerful to interoperate between heterogeneous blogspaces. Moreover, we have to select the most appropriate domain to which BlogGrid should be applied. Various personalized or e-bussiness applications such as e-learning domain are possibly potential. Practically, BlogGrid framework will be embodied with RDF site summary (RSS)[6] service for the usability of users.

Acknowledgement. This work was supported by the Korea Research Foundation Grant funded by the Korean Government (MOEHRD). (KRF-2005-214-D00347).

References

1. Dekker, A.: A category-theoretic approach to social network analysis. Electronic Notes in Theoretical Computer Science **61** (2002) 21–33
2. Rosenbloom, A.: The blogosphere. Communications of ACM **47**(12) (2004) 31–33

---

[4] http://wiki.blojsom.com/wiki/display/blojsom/About+blojsom.
[5] http://www.borland.com/us/products/delphi/index.html.
[6] RDF site summary (RSS). http://web.resource.org/rss/1.0/.

3. Nardi, B., Schiano, D., Gumbrecht, M., Swartz, L.: Why we blog. Communications of ACM **47**(12) (2004) 41–46
4. Zhuge, H.: Semantics, resource and grid. Future Generation Computer Systems **21**(1) (2004) 1–5
5. Jung, J.J., Ha, I., Jo, G.: BlogGrid: Towards and efficient information pushing service on blogspace. In Zhung, H., Fox, G., eds.: Proceedings of the International Conference on Grid and Cooperative Computing (GCC 2005). Volume 3795 of Lecture Notes in Computer Science., Springer-Verlag (2005) 178–183
6. Jung, J.J.: Constructing virtual communities with social interactions on blogspaces. Computing and Informatics **submitted**(x) (xxxx) xxx–xxx
7. Kleinberg, J.M.: Authoritative sources in a hyperlinked environment. Journal of the ACM **46**(5) (1999) 604–632
8. Freeman, L.: Centrality in social networks: Conceptual clarification. Social Networks **1** (1979) 215–239
9. Breslin, J.G., Harth, A., Bojars, U., Decker, S.: Towards semantically-interlinked online communities. In Gómez-Pérez, A., Euzenat, J., eds.: Proceedings of the 3th European Semantic Web Conference. Volume 3532 of Lecture Notes in Computer Science., Springer-Verlag (2005) 500–514
10. Kempe, D., Kleinberg, J., Éva Tardos: Maximizing the spread of influence through a social network. In: Proceedings of the ACM SIGKDD. (2003)
11. Wang, Y., Vassileva, J.: Trust-based community formation in peer-to-peer file sharing networks. In: Proceedings of the 2004 IEEE/WIC/ACM International Conference on Web Intelligence (WI 2004), 20-24 September 2004, IEEE Computer Society (2004) 341–348
12. Cayzer, S.: Semantic blogging and distributed knowledge management. Communications of ACM **47**(12) (2004) 47–52
13. Jung, J.J.: An application of collaborative web browsing based on ontology learning from user activities on the web. Computing and Informatics **23**(4) (2004) 337–353

A Personal Ontology Model for Library Recommendation System

I-En Liao[1], Shu-Chuan Liao[2], Kuo-Fong Kao[1,3], and Ine-Fei Harn[1]

[1] Dept. of Computer Science, National Chung Hsing University, Taichung, Taiwan
[2] Dept. of Social Work, Asia University, Taichung, Taiwan
[3] Dept. of Information Networking Technology, Hsiuping Institute of Technology,
Taichung, Taiwan
ieliao@cs.nchu.edu.tw

Abstract. With the advent of information technology, library services are facing tremendous changes in the form of digitalization. In addition to the digitalization of library resources, personalized systems and recommendation systems are two of highly desirable services among library patrons. This study proposes a novel recommendation system based on analysis of loan records. In our system, we use the traditional cataloging scheme, such as the Library of Congress Classification (LCC), as the reference ontology and build personal ontology by mining interested subjects and relationships among subjects from patron's borrowing records. The proposed scheme can meet diversified demands of individual patron and provide patrons with a user-friendly interface to help them access needed information.

Keywords: personalized service, personal ontology, information filtering, recommendation system.

1 Introduction

As the libraries are evolving toward digital libraries, several university libraries have built customizable, user-centric tools for providing personalized services to patrons[1,2,3,4,5,6]. These systems usually take the user profiling approach by allowing a user to select his interested subjects[4] or to input interested keywords[1]. The problem of this approach is that the interests of users vary over time. Users thus should update the profiles constantly in order to make sure that they obtain the recommendation they need. However, in practice few users regularly do this.

Because the books which a user borrowed always represent user's interests, this study develops a novel recommendation system based on the personal ontology built from mining personal loan records. Even changes in user's interests will be clearly shown in his loan records. This system thus does not need user to set his own interests. User interests are mined automatically from loan records. To increase the accuracy of mining user interests, the proposed method uses the library ontology information, and the interested topics of the user are reorganized as the personal ontology. The keywords and books in each topic are measured

S. Sugimoto et al. (Eds.): ICADL 2006, LNCS 4312, pp. 173–182, 2006.

using a favorite score, and those of which receive high scores are recommended to the user. This study only presents the system model and ignores the implementation details owing to limitations of space. Implementation issues are discussed in Harn[7,8] which described a prototype system using Chinese book data and loan records from the library at National Chung Hsing University in Taiwan.

The rest of this paper is organized as follows. Section 2 summarizes the system architecture and data structures used. Section 3 then presents the algorithm for mining the personal ontology. Section 4 presents the method for mining the favorite keywords in a category. Subsequently, Section 5 describes the method used to list the recommended books. Section 6 then discusses the related work. Finally, conclusions and future research directions are presented in Section 7.

2   System Architecture and Data Structures

The recommendation system is designed as a web based application. Once a user logs in from the home page of the library, the system then analyzes the personal data in the database and mines the recommended user information. The system first identifies favorite topics of the user and then searches for the interested keywords related to the favorite topics of the user. These favorite topics of individual user are assembled into a personal ontology. Additionally, the books related to the interested keywords for favorite topics are recommended to the user. The books are also measured using preference scores. Once the user clicks a topic in the personal ontology, the books related to the topic and which have high preference scores are recommended to the user. The architecture of the proposed system is shown in Fig. 1:

The data sources for mining include book information, user loan records and hierarchy information from the library catalogue. The book information includes book id, authors, book category, book title, publisher, year of publication, and so on. These book publication data are then transformed into two tables: Keyword table and Distinctness table.

The Keyword table contains three attributes: Category, ISBN, and Keyword. The Keyword attribute represents the keywords of the books which may be specified by the librarian or may be extracted from the book title. For example, as shown in the left hand side table of Fig. 2, the book "Applied statistics and the SAS programming language" with ISBN of 0444011927 is in category 519.5 and has the keywords: statistics, SAS, programming, language and programming language. Another book "Introduction to Java Programming" of ISBN 0131430491 belongs to the same category and contains the keywords java and programming.

If the keywords of a book are not given, then they can be extracted from the book title. In our previous research[7,8], the Chinese Word Segmentation System (CKIP)[9] developed by Academia Sinica in Taiwan was used to extract keywords. The keyword extraction technique is another important research issue, but it is not discussed further in this paper.

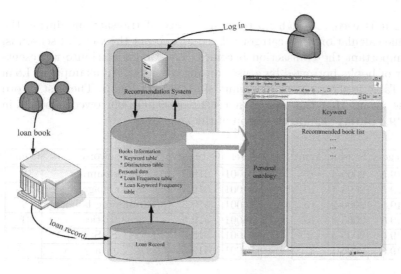

Fig. 1. System Architecture

Category	ISBN	Keyword
519.5	0444011927	statistics
519.5	0444011927	SAS
519.5	0444011927	programming
519.5	0444011927	language
519.5	0444011927	programming language
519.5	0131430491	java
519.5	0131430491	programming

Category	Keyword	Distinctness
519.5	program	0.9
519.5	statistics	0.6
519.5	SAS	0.8
519.5	language	0.7
519.6	program	0.6
⋮	⋮	⋮

Fig. 2. Example of Keyword Table and Distinctness Table

The Distinctness table contains three attributes: Category, Keyword and Distinctness. The Distinctness attribute stores the degree of distinctness of the keyword within the category. The meaning of a keyword differs between subjects, and keywords should be assigned different weights to show their distinctness in each category. Thus one keyword has a unique distinctness value in a category, and the distinctness values of the same keyword always differ between categories. For example, the word "program" may be an important keyword with distinctness value of 0.9 in category 519.5. Moreover the keyword "program" may be a less important keyword with distinctness value of 0.6 in 519.6 category, and it might not be a keyword at all in other categories. An example of the Distinctness table is shown in the right hand side table of Fig. 2.

The loan records contain the user ID, cataloging category, book title, ISBN, loan date, etc. These records are aggregated into two tables: the Loan Frequency table and Loan Keyword Frequency table. The Loan Frequency table contains four attributes: UserID, Category, Season, and Count. The Season attribute represents the season of a year during which a user has transactions with the

library, and it is used to weigh up the importance of transactions during the
favorite value calculation for a category. The more recent the value of season is,
the more important the transaction becomes. The Count attribute represents
the number of books borrowed by a user during a season. An example of Loan
Frequency Table is shown in the left hand side table of Fig. 3. The first record
of the table means that the user with userId of s94001 borrowed 6 books in
category 519.5 during the fourth season of the year 2005.

UserID	Category	Season	Count
s94001	519.5	2005-4	6
s94001	519.5	2006-1	10
s94001	519.5	2006-2	10
s94001	519.6	2005-3	10
s94001	519.6	2005-4	2
s94001	519.6	2006-1	2

User	Category	Keyword	Count
s94001	519.5	programming	2
s94001	519.5	language	1
s94001	519.5	programming language	1
s94001	519.5	statistics	1
s94001	519.5	SAS	1
s94001	519.5	java	1

Fig. 3. Example of Loan Frequency Table and Loan Keyword Frequency Table

The Loan Keyword Frequency table records the keyword frequency among
the books borrowed by a user in a category. It contains four attributes: UserID,
Category, Keyword, and Count. The Count attribute represents the number of
appearances of the keyword in the books borrowed by a user in a category. The
keywords of books are stored in the Keyword table. Once a book is borrowed, the
proposed system queries the Keyword table about the keywords of that book, and
adds one to the corresponding Count attributes to the Loan Keyword Frequency
table. For example, assume that the user with UserId s94001 loaned two books
with ISBN of 0444011927 and 0131430491, respectively. Then according to Fig.
2., it will generate a Loan Keyword Frequency table as shown in the right hand
side table of Fig. 3.

3   Personal Ontology Model

In this section, we will derive formulas for creating personal ontology model based
on the reference ontology such as Library of Congress Classification (LCC)[10]
or Classification for Chinese Libraries (CCL)[11]. Assume that there are n categories in the reference ontology and that the maximum number of seasons in
the loan record database is m. We then map the values in the Season attribute
of Loan Frequency table to the set of $\{1,2,..., m\}$ with 1 as the current season,
2 as the season before the current one, and so on. As we mentioned before,
the smaller the value of season is, the more important the transaction becomes.
Therefore, we define the impact factor of a record in the Loan Frequency table
as a decreasing function of season.

Let F_i, $1 \leq i \leq n$, denote the favorite value of category i. The count of loaned
books of category i during season j, $1 \leq j \leq m$, is denoted as a_{ij}. Then the favorite
value of category i for a particular user can be formulated as Equation (1).

$$F_i = \sum_{j=1}^{m} (a_{ij} * (\frac{1}{2})^{(j-1)}), \; for \; 1 \leq i \leq n \; and \; 1 \leq j \leq m \qquad (1)$$

After the calculation of favorite value of each category using Equation (1), the categories with favorite values exceeding a specified threshold can be considered as the favorite categories of a user. However, this method is naive and does not consider relationships between categories. For example, assume that the favorite value of a category is slightly below the threshold, and thus the category is judged not to be the favorite. However the descendant categories of this category may all have very high favorite values. In the ontology hierarchy, the domain of the ancestor category includes the domains of descendant categories. It is unreasonable to only be interested in these descendant categories but not in the ancestor category. Therefore, classifying this ancestor category as the favorite category may be more satisfactory.

Ontology is the systematic explanation for the entities that exists in the world. Moreover, domain ontology is the systematic explanation focused on a specific domain. Domain ontology resembles the special knowledge of experts, which includes knowledge terms and their interrelationships. This knowledge is helpful for exactly locating topics of interest to users. Library cataloging, such as the Library of Congress Classification (LCC)[10] or Classification for Chinese Libraries (CCL)[11], are typical domain ontologies. All books are classified in an orderly manner within the tree structure ontology, and this structure is a good guide for producing more precise estimates of user interests. The proposed recommendation algorithm calculates the favorite value of a category by considering the factors of descendant, ancestor, and sibling categories. Therefore, the Equation (1) is modified as Equation (2) with LCC or CCL as reference ontology.

$$F_i' = F_i * (1 + O_i), \; for \; 1 \leq i \leq n \qquad (2)$$

$$O_i = \beta_1 \frac{\sum_{k=1}^{C_i} Child(i,k)}{C_i} + \beta_2 Parent(i) + \beta_3 \frac{\sum_{k=1}^{S_i} Sibling(i,k)}{S_i} \qquad (3)$$

The O_i denotes the impact factor inferred from the reference ontology. Moreover, O_i contains three component: child, parent, and sibling, and $\beta_1, \beta_2, \beta_3$ are used to weight the impact level of these three components. The C_i denotes the number of children of category i, and S_i is the number of sibling of category i. The function $Child(i,k)$ returns the Eqn. (1) favorite value of the k th child of category i, and the function $Sibling(i,k)$ returns the Eqn (1) favorite value of the k th sibling of category i. Every category has only one parent except the root. Thus the function $Parent(i)$ returns the Eqn. (1) favorite value of the parent of category i.

The left hand side of Fig. 4 shows a partial sample of reference ontology. At each node, the number on the top represents the classification number of a category in the reference ontology , while the value in the parentheses is the favorite value according to equation (2). The categories with F_i' value exceeding a specific threshold will be the favorite categories of a particular user. As a result, we reorganize these favorite categories into the personal ontology for the user.

First the categories whose favorite values are below the threshold are filtered out. The remaining categories are then reorganized into the personal ontology of the user in question. The display of personal ontology can be set according to the favorite values. For example, the category with higher favorite value is shown as a large circle and thick link, while the category with lower favorite value is shown as a small circle and thin link. The example is drawn on the right hand side of Fig. 4. The structure of the personal ontology is more friendly than that of the original complete ontology structure and can provide a more useful guide to users seeking information.

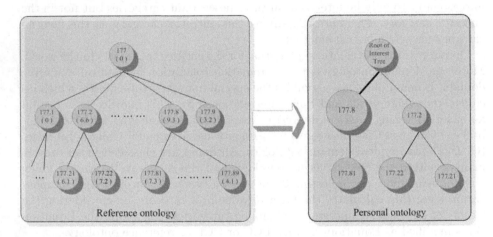

Fig. 4. Transformation from Reference Ontology to Personal Ontology

4   Interested Keywords in the Category

After identifying the favorite categories, the next job is to find the interested keywords in each category. One intuitive way is to count the number of times the keywords appear in the borrowed books of each user. The frequency provides a rough indicator of user interest in this keyword. The higher the frequency, the greater the interest of users in this keyword. In this rough measure, all keywords have the same weight. However, this approach is unreasonable, and we think that each keyword should have a different weighting determined by the distinctness level described in Section 2.

Assume there are p users and q keywords in a specific category. Let I_{ij}, $1 \leq i \leq p$ and $1 \leq j \leq q$, denote the level of interest of user i in keyword j. The frequency with which keyword j appears in the loan books of user i is denoted as bf_{ij}, and the distinctness level of this keyword is denoted as d_j. I_{ij} can then be formulated as follows:

$$I_{ij} = bf_{ij} * d_j, \text{ for } 1 \leq i \leq p \text{ and } 1 \leq j \leq q. \tag{4}$$

The distinctness level of a keyword is decided based on the appearance frequency of the keyword in both its category and that of its sibling. If the word frequently appears in one category and rarely appears in other categories, then this word is unique and has high distinctness level in the category in question. Meanwhile, even if the word frequently appears in a given category but also appears equally frequently in other categories, then the word is not sufficiently unique and has low distinctness level in this category . Based on the above discussion, d_j can be formulated as follows:

$$d_j = kf_j * log^{(\frac{N}{cf_j} * w_j)}, \text{ for } 1 \leq j \leq q. \tag{5}$$

Keyword frequency, kf_j, represents the number of books which contain keyword j in this category. Moreover, category frequency, cf_j, represents the number of sibling categories containing books with keyword j. N represents the total number of sibling categories of the category under consideration, and w_j represents the number of words in keyword j. Multiple-word terms are assigned heavier weights than single-word terms because multiple-word terms usually convey more precise semantic meanings than single word terms.

5   Recommended Book List

In our system, we provide three modes to the user for listing the recommended books. The first is recommendation by the keywords, and the second is recommendation by book preference value of a specific category, and the third is recommendation by book preference value of a subtree below a specific category.

In the first mode, the interested keywords in a category on the user's personal ontology are sorted in the order of the interested values, and users can then click on individual keyword. The system displays recommended books related to the clicked keyword.

In the second mode, a user can request recommended books from a category without considering the descendants of that category. Book preference value is calculated based on interested values of keywords. Each book can have multiple keywords, and the highest value among all of the interested keyword values serves as the preference value of that book. Then the books with preference value greater than a specific threshold will be recommended.

In the third mode, a user can request recommended books from a category with its descendants under consideration. Assume there are r categories in the subtree below the requested category, and bn_i denotes the number of books in category i, $1 \leq i \leq r$. Let $P_{ij}, 1 \leq j \leq bn_i$ be the preference value of book j in category i based on the second mode. Then the preference value P'_{ij} of book j in category i for the third mode is defined as follows:

$$P'_{ij} \equiv P_{ij} * F'_i, \text{ for } 1 \leq i \leq r \text{ and } 1 \leq j \leq bn_i. \tag{6}$$

Assume the threshold value of preference score is set to t, then those books with P' value exceeding t are recommended.

6   Related Work

The rapid growth in information on digital libraries and the ubiquity of the WWW have led to the concept of personal libraries[12,13]. MyLibrary@ NCState[4] is one of the most well-known systems of the early personal library system, and some universities have used it to develop their own personal systems[14]. Recently, other follow-up personalization systems have been developed[1,2,3,5,6,15,16]. Most systems provide the static recommendation function. Section 1 described the weaknesses of this method.

Moreover, data mining techniques were used to create an advanced recommendation system based on analysis of loan records. These techniques are generally used in online book stores. Two of the most widely used mining techniques are collaborative filtering and association rule mining[1,5,17]. These two approaches assume that the tastes of a given user are the same as those of other system users. Once systems find the frequent loan patterns, they make recommendations to users based on these patterns. These approaches have been successfully applied to many retail businesses[18], but is not suitable for library. In retail business the amount of a specific selling object is always large enough to support user demands. However in library the amount of a specific book is limited to a few. Hence the confidence of the mined rules by collaborative approach is always very low which makes those rules uninteresting. Besides, most books are utilized by very few patrons, but the nature of collaborative approaches is to find the popular rules. This conflict results in this approach failing to find different rules for different individuals.

Another approach is the content-based recommendation [7,8,19] or hybrid system[20]. This approach allows the system to uniquely characterize individual patron without matching their interests to those of others. Books are recommended based on unique user information rather than on the preferences of other users. The proposed algorithm belongs to this approach, and enhances the recommendation accuracy using the knowledge in ontology[21].

7   Conclusions and Future Work

This study brings up the personal ontology model for a library recommendation system. The design of proposed algorithms and underlying storage structures are described in detail. The whole system is now under development for the library of National Chung Hsing University in Taiwan. The system can provide better personalized service by creating personal ontology based on the reference ontology such as LCC or CLL and mining on patron's loan records. In the future, the semantic index technique[22,23] can be applied to reduce restrictions on exact keyword matching.

References

1. Dai, Y.M.: A data mining system for mining library borrowing history records. Master Thesis of National Chiao-Tung University (2002)
2. Fernández, L., Sánchez, J.A., García, A.: Mibiblio: personal spaces in a digital library universe. In: DL '00: Proceedings of the fifth ACM conference on Digital libraries, New York, NY, USA, ACM Press (2000) 232–233
3. He, W., Shen, D.: MyPDL: a web-based personal digital library. In: JCDL '05: Proceedings of the 5th ACM/IEEE-CS joint conference on Digital libraries, New York, NY, USA, ACM Press (2005) 380–380
4. Milosavljevic, M., Paradis, F., Paris, C., Wilkinson, R.: Customised information delivery: a sigir 99 workshop. SIGIR Forum **33**(1) (1999) 28–31
5. Sun, K.H.: A Data Mining Methodology for Library New Book Recommendation. Master Thesis of National Sun Yat-sen University (1999)
6. Tsao, J.H.: Apply Data Mining Techniques to Enable Personalized Services and Management on Digital Library. Master Thesis of Nanhua University (2003)
7. Harn, I.F.: A Personalized Recommendation System for Library Services. Master Thesis of National Chung Hsing University (2005)
8. Harn, I.F., Kao, K.F., Liao, I.E.: A Study on Personalized Recommendation System for Library Web Site. In: Proceedings of TANET. (2005)
9. Ma, W.Y., Chen, K.J.: Introduction to CKIP Chinese Word Segmentation System for the First International Chinese Word Segmentation Bakeoff. In: Proceedings of ACL, Second SIGHAN Workshop on Chinese Language Processing. (2003) 168–171
10. : Library of Congress Classification. (http://www.loc.gov/catdir/cpso/lcco/lcco.html)
11. ZHANG, W.: Classification for Chinese Libraries (CCL): Histories, Accomplishments, Problems and Its Comparisons. Journal of Educational Media and Library Sciences **41**(1) (2003)
12. Hafner, W., III, J.J.K., Lin, Z.Y.: One-to-one customization of library patron relationships using web-based networks and information technologies on the college or university campus. Journal of Library and Information Science **26**(2) (2000) 19–29
13. Kikuchi, H., Mishina, Y., Ashizawa, M., Yamazaki, N., Fujisawa, H.: User interface for a digital library to support construction of a virtual personal library. In: Proceedings of the Third IEEE International Conference on Multimedia Computing and Systems. (1996) 429–432
14. : Development Site of MyLibrary. (http://dewey.library.nd.edu/mylibrary/)
15. Janssen, W.C., Popat, K.: UpLib: a universal personal digital library system. In: DocEng '03: Proceedings of the 2003 ACM symposium on Document engineering, New York, NY, USA, ACM Press (2003) 234–242
16. Yucha, J.B.: Convenience: are you providing it? In: SIGUCCS '04: Proceedings of the 32nd annual ACM SIGUCCS conference on User services, New York, NY, USA, ACM Press (2004) 44–46
17. Michail, A.: Data mining library reuse patterns using generalized association rules. In: ICSE '00: Proceedings of the 22nd international conference on Software engineering, New York, NY, USA, ACM Press (2000) 167–176
18. Schafer, J.B., Konstan, J.A., Riedl, J.: E-commerce recommendation applications. Data Min. Knowl. Discov. **5**(1-2) (2001) 115–153
19. Mooney, R.J., Roy, L.: Content-based book recommending using learning for text categorization. In: DL '00: Proceedings of the fifth ACM conference on Digital libraries, New York, NY, USA, ACM Press (2000) 195–204

20. Huang, Z., Chung, W., Ong, T.H., Chen, H.: A graph-based recommender system for digital library. In: JCDL '02: Proceedings of the 2nd ACM/IEEE-CS joint conference on Digital libraries, New York, NY, USA, ACM Press (2002) 65 73

21. Gruber, T.R.: Toward principles for the design of ontologies used for knowledge sharing. Int. J. Hum.-Comput. Stud. **43**(5-6) (1995) 907–928

22. Chen, H., Schatz, B., Ng, T., Martinez, J., Kirchhoff, A., Lin, C.: A parallel computing approach to creating engineering concept spaces for semantic retrieval: The illinois digital library initiative project. IEEE Trans. Pattern Anal. Mach. Intell. **18**(8) (1996) 771–782

23. Chung, Y.M., He, Q., Powell, K., Schatz, B.: Semantic indexing for a complete subject discipline. In: DL '99: Proceedings of the fourth ACM conference on Digital libraries, New York, NY, USA, ACM Press (1999) 39–48

Research and Implementation of a Personalized Recommendation System

Li Dong[1,2], Yu Nie[3], Chunxiao Xing[4], and Kehong Wang[1]

[1] Department of Computer Science and Technology, Tsinghua University,
100084 Beijing, P.R. China
dongli91@tsinghua.org.cn, wkh-dcs@tsinghua.edu.cn
[2] System Division of Library, Tsinghua University, 100084 Beijing, P.R. China
dongli@lib.tsinghua.edu.cn
[3] SINA Corporation, 100084 Beijing, P.R. China
nieyu@sina.com
[4] Research Institute of Information Technology, Tsinghua University,
100084 Beijing, P.R. China
xingcx@tsinghua.edu.cn

Abstract. Personalized Recommendation System is a necessary part of Personalized Information Service System. In this paper, a personalized recommendation system is implemented and tested with actual website access data. According to the test result analysis, we present some new methods to improve the recommendation effectiveness.

Keywords: Personalized recommendation, Algorithm evaluation.

1 Introduction

Personalized Recommendation System is a necessary part of Personalized Information Service System. There are different types of Website information recommendation methods: (1) Semi-automatic personalization based on interest model, such as WebWatcher[1], AVANTI[2], which needs many user interactions; (2) Automatic user behavior analysis, which can also be divided into two sub-types, one is based on user browsing path analysis, the other is based on Web pages relative analysis; typical example of the former type is Footprints[3], YANG's Web user's view[4], and the representative of the latter is PageGather[5]; (3) Collaborative filtering, such as Ringo[6], GroupLens[7], which also needs many user interactions; (4) Optimizing with the structure of Website, such as STRUDEL[8], which needs to reconstruct the structure of the Website, and is difficult to migrate; (5) Client-side personalization, typical system is Letizia[9], PINS[10] etc, this type of personalization can be combined with server-side personalized system. Among those methods, after comparing their autoimmunization, technical feasibilities and result quantities, we find that type (2) is a more competitive method. In our system, we choose PageGather[5] as a base algorithm to use cluster mining to find collections of related pages at a web site, and test our recommendation algorithm with actual website access

S. Sugimoto et al. (Eds.): ICADL 2006, LNCS 4312, pp. 183–191, 2006.
© Springer-Verlag Berlin Heidelberg 2006

data. In this paper, we'll introduce the recommendation algorithm of our system and give the result analysis to improve the recommendation effectiveness.

2 Recommendation System

2.1 Personalized Information Service System

Figure 1 describes the main structure of our personalized information service system.

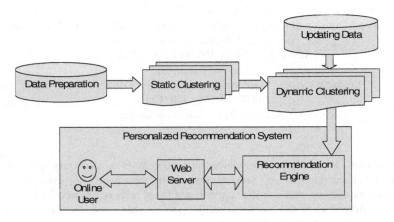

Fig. 1. Personalized Information Service System

Data Preparation: This module processes the original website data and produces certain format data for later clustering.

Static Clustering: Analyzing the processed history data and clustering the formatted data into collections of relative pages, which are the basis for personalized recommendation. In theory, this process only needs to execute once.

Dynamic Clustering: As the pages of a website increases, the clustering result should be updated dynamically, adding relative new pages into result clusters and removing outdated pages out of clusters. In practical, this process can be executed periodically.

Recommendation Engine: This module analyzes online users' behaviors and matches them with clustering result, then recommends relative pages to users.

2.2 Clustering Algorithm

From Section 2.1, we know that clustering and recommendation engine are two main modules of a personalized information service system. In our system, we present two improved PageGather algorithm, we call PG+ and PG++ to fulfill user behavior analysis and clustering.

M. Perkowitz and O. Etzioni [5] presented original PageGather algorithm, which analyzes the website's access log, finds the visitors access pattern, and automatically synthesizes web pages. The main idea of PageGather is that it is not necessary to analyze the content of pages, but it gains the similarity of pages from visitors' access pattern (website log). The pages in a cluster are highly possible to be visited again by users within a session. Subsequently, when a user browses a web page in a cluster, we can recommend the other pages in the same cluster, which will make the users' visit more conveniently.

The original PageGather algorithm is static, which needs too much data input and too much computing time. In our system, incremental learning and distributed computation mechanisms are introduced into PageGather, as we call the two improved algorithms PG+ and PG++. The two algorithms significantly reduced the size of data input and the time complexity of PageGather, so that they are applicable in large web sites. Those two improved algorithms are discussed detailed in WANG Qixin's paper[11], we'll mainly discuss the recommendation algorithm in this paper.

2.3 Recommendation Engine Implementation and Test

2.3.1 Factors of Recommendation
There are several factors to consider when we calculate the recommendation pages.

(1) The match evaluation score of online users' behavior comparing with the clustering result produced in Section 2.2, we'll give a formula of it later.

(2) The size of a user's visit pages window for matching with result clusters. For a whole user's visit, he may want to browse different types of pages; we use a 'session window' to describe those phrases for matching. For example, if the size of a session window is 3, when a user visited URL1, URL2, URL3 continuously, current session window is represented as <URL1, URL2, URL3>; afterwards, he visited URL4, then the session window is represented as <URL2, URL3, URL4>, only pages in current session window affect the matching score.

(3) Whether the candidate pages have been visited in a session. If a page have been visited in a session, it's no need to recommend it once more.

(4) The distance of an online user's visiting position with candidate pages' linking position. In order to calculate the distance factor, we define following definitions:

G(V, E): represent a website's topology, V is a point set which represent all URL, E is a relation set of all URL.

d(u, s, G): represent the minimal distance of u with all points in s, u is a candidate page, s is a point set of a session window.

The distance factor is defined as:

$$ldf(u,s) = \begin{cases} 0 & u \in s \\ \log(d(u,s,G))+1 & u \notin s \end{cases} \tag{1}$$

2.3.2 Recommendation Algorithm
The result clusters can be represented as:

$$C = \langle c_1, c_2, \ldots, c_m \rangle \tag{2}$$

For every $c_k \in C$, we can use a vector to describe it:

$$\vec{c} = \langle u_1^c, u_2^c, \ldots, u_n^c \rangle \qquad u_i^c = \begin{cases} 0 & url_i \notin C \\ 1 & url_i \in C \end{cases} \tag{3}$$

For a user's active session, we also use a vector to describe it:

$$\vec{s} = \langle s_1, s_2, \ldots, s_n \rangle$$

$$S_i = \begin{cases} 0 & url_i \notin current\ slipping\ window \\ 1 & url_i \in current\ slipping\ window \end{cases} \tag{4}$$

'n' is the number of all visiting pages.

For a user's active session 's', we can define the matching score of 's' with a cluster 'c':

$$match(s,c) = \frac{\sum_k u_k^c \cdot s_k}{\sqrt{\sum_k s_k^2} \cdot \sqrt{\sum_k (u_k^c)^2}} \tag{5}$$

According to the matching score, we can calculate the recommendation score of each URL page 'u' with a session 's':

$$Rec(u,s) = \begin{cases} 0 & u \notin c \\ \sqrt{match(s,c) \cdot weight(c,u)} \cdot ldf(u,s) & u \in c \end{cases} \tag{6}$$

weight(c, u) represents the tightness of page 'u' with cluster 'c', for example, we can use the average similarity score of page 'u' with other pages in cluster 'c' as weight(c, u).

Then we can get a recommendation pages set as:

$$recommendation(s) = \left\{ u_i^c \middle| c \in C, Rec(s, u_i^c) \geq \rho \right\} \tag{7}$$

'ρ' is the threshold for recommendation score.

2.3.3 Recommendation Evaluation

For a given cluster 'c' and a fixed session window size 'n', we define a simulation session window:

$$s = < u_1, u_2, \ldots, u_n >, u_j \in c \in C \tag{8}$$

With former recommendation algorithm, we get a recommendation pages set:

$$recommendation(s) = \{u_1, u_2, \ldots, u_m\} \tag{9}$$

Then we get a evaluation score for cluster 'c':

$$Per(c,n) = \frac{|\{u | u \in recommendatin(s), u \in c\}|}{|c|} \tag{10}$$

Select |c| - n + 1 times 's' randomly, and calculate the average, then we get the recommendation accuracy of some cluster 'c' in condition of fixed session window size 'n':

$$\overline{Per(c,n)} \tag{11}$$

For each c ∈ C, calculate it's recommendation accuracy, then we get the recommendation accuracy of result clusters' set 'C' in condition of fixed session window size 'n':

$$Acc(C,n) = \sum_{c \in C} \frac{\overline{Per(c,n)}}{|C|} \Big/ \sum_{s \in S} \frac{|recommendation(s)|}{|S|} \tag{12}$$

The recommendation accuracy factor can be used to test the recommendation algorithm's stability, if the factor can keep a rather stable result under different clustering algorithm, we can conclude that the recommendation algorithm has a better stability.

2.3.4 Recommendation Test

We use the clustering result of our system as the recommendation test data, and do two experiments.

2.3.4.1 Recommendation Accuracy Under Different Matching Threshold

Table 1. The result of recommendation accuracy with session window size=3

Recommendation Threshold	Accuracy	Mean size of Recommendation_set	Average accuracy
0.1	0.590	11.289	0.0522
0.2	0.610	11.341	0.0537
0.3	1.0	1.681	0.594
0.4	1.0	1.681	0.594
0.5	1.0	1.681	0.594
0.6	1.0	1.373	0.728
0.7	1.0	1.303	0.767
0.8	1.0	0.626	1.595
0.9	1.0	0.0	Infinity

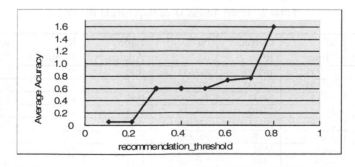

Fig. 2. Result of recommendation accuracy (window size = 3)

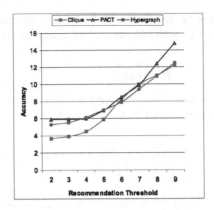

Fig. 3. Recommendation accuracy under three different clustering algorithm (window size =3)

2.3.4.2   Test with Actual Website Access Data. In this experiment, we use a real large-scale commercial synthetically website in China. We analyzed 13,242 news web pages of the website and trained more than 468,692 logs (that is 468,692 hits) for two days, then use the 3rd day's access data to simulate recommendation and evaluate the result.

In order to describe the result, we make some definitions as following:

(1) *correct_recommendation_times*, if the recommendation pages set include pages which are going to be visited in reality, then add one to this score.

(2) *recommendation_times*, represent the total number of recommendation for users.

(3) *no_recommendation_times*, represent the number of null recommendation.

(4)   *recommendation_accuracy*   =   *correct_recommendation_times   / recommendation_times*.

(5) *page_accuracy* = page number of successful recommendation / total number of recommendation pages.

(6) *recommendation_percent* = *recommendation_times* / （*recommendation_times* + *no_recommendation_times*）.

The result of this experiment is described as Table 2.

Table 2. Actual Access Data Experiment Result

RC Threshold	RC Times	Correct RC	No RC	Page Accuracy	RC Accuracy	RC Percent
0.1	103771	103771	291652	0.49	1.0	0.26
0.2	103194	103194	292229	0.49	1.0	0.26
0.3	34513	34513	360910	0.59	1.0	0.09
0.4	27105	27105	368318	0.65	1.0	0.07
0.5	20316	20316	375107	0.69	1.0	0.05
0.6	3568	3568	391855	0.75	1.0	0.01
0.7	3561	3561	391862	0.75	1.0	0.01
0.8	1859	1859	393564	0.81	1.0	0.01
0.9	0	0	395423	NaN	NaN	

The graph representation is Figure 4.

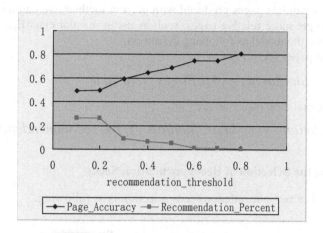

Fig. 4. Actual Access Data Experiment Result

3   Analysis of Recommendation Algorithm

From the experiment result in Section 2.3.4.2, we can find that the result has some regulations:

(1) The *recommendation_percent* decreases quickly as the recommendation threshold increases;

(2) As the threshold increases, the *page_accuracy* increases stably;

(3) No matter what the threshold is, the *recommendation_accuracy* is always 1.

These results indicate that our recommendation algorithm and evaluation method have some limitations:

(1) The area of candidate recommendation pages is too small. In current algorithm, those candidate pages can only be got from the clustering result, which are often in a small number and can not fulfill the real requirement.

(2) The session window only reflects the latest visiting status, can not represent a whole visit's all-sided aims. Besides, this choice of recommendation seeds often select pages in a same website directory, this is not the ideal purpose of recommendation; ideally, we want to get cross-directory recommendation.

(3) Recommendation accuracy is not suitable to evaluate the recommendation results; high accuracy with low recommendation rate is of little use in reality.

4   Some Improvements of Recommendation Algorithm

According to the result analysis, we can try some improvements on those limitations.

4.1 Enlarging the Recommendation Pages Set

Besides those candidate pages produced with current method, we can use some other information to get more relative pages, such as using manual classified information. We can describe the model as following definition:

The relative pages set of page 'u' is:

$$Similar(u) = \{All\ Pages\ Near\ to\ u\} \tag{13}$$

The recommendation pages set are:

$$recommendation^{++}(s) = \{u|u \in Similar(p), p \in recommendation(s)\} \tag{14}$$

4.2 Updating the Selection of Recommendation Seeds

Current method of recommendation seeds selection is as following:

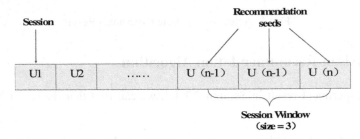

Fig. 5. Current Method of Selecting Recommendation Seeds

In order to get a better representation of the whole visit session, we present a new method of selecting the Recommendation Seeds, which is described as Figure 6.

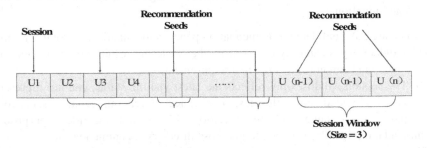

Fig. 6. New method of Selecting Recommendation Seeds

The new method can be described in 3 steps:

− Step1: Give a window size 'm', take the latest browsing page as the starting point, go backwards and divide the whole visit session into segments with size 'm', continue the process until the left pages are less than 'm';

- Step2: Pages in the latest window add to the recommendation seeds set;
- Step3: Select one page from each window and add them into the recommendation seeds set.

5 Conclusions and Future Work

In this paper, we have implemented a website personalized recommendation engine, and test the recommendation result with some experiments. According to result analysis, we find some limitations of current recommendation algorithm and present some improvements. In the future, we need to do more experiments to test the improvements.

Acknowledgements. This work is supported by the National Natural Science Foundation of China under Grant No. 60473078. We should also thank to Tsinghua University Library for her encourages and supports.

References

1. Joachims, T., Freitag, D., Mitchell, T. WebWatcher: a tour guide for the World Wide Web. In: Proceedings of the 15th International Joint Conference on Artificial Intelligence. San Francisco, CA: Morgan Kaufmann Publishers, 1997. 770~775.
2. Fink, J., Kobsa, A., Nill, A. User oriented adaptivity and adaptability in AVANTI project. In: Proceedings of the Software-Ergonomie'97. Stuttgart: B.G. Teubner, 1997. 135~144.
3. Wexelblat, A., Maes, P. Footprints: history-rich Web browsing. In: Proceedings of the Conference Computer-Assisted Information Retrieval. 1997. 75~84.
4. Yang, Xiao-hua, Zhou, Long-xiang. View of Web users. Journal of Software, 1999,7:690~693 (in Chinese).
5. Perkowitz, M., Etzioni, O. Adaptive Web sites: automatically synthesizing Web pages. In: Proceedings of the 15th National Conference on Artificial Intelligence (AAAI-98). Menlo Park, CA: AAAI Press/MIT Press, 1998. 727~732.
6. Shardanand, U., Maes, P. Social information filtering: algorithms for automating "Word of Mouth". In: Proceedings of the Conference in Human Factors in Computing Systems. Denver, Colorado: ACM Press, 1995. 210~217.
7. Resnick, P., Iacovou, N., Suchak, M., et al. GroupLens: an open architecture for collaborative filtering of netnews. In: Proceedings of the Conference on Computer Supported Cooperative Work CSCW'94. New York, NY: ACM Press, 1994. 175~186.
8. Fernandez, M., Florescu, D., Kang, J., et al. System demonstration-strudel: a Web-site management system. In: Proceedings of the ACM SIGMOD Conference on Management of Data. 1997. 549~552.
9. Lieberman, H. Letizia: an agent that assists Web browsing. FS-95-03, Menlo Park, CA: AAAI Press, 1995. 97~102.
10. Dong, Li, Li, Jing-hua, Wang, Ke-hong. A personalized intelligent navigation system-PINS based on CORBA and Java technologies. In: Proceedings of the 4th International Conference/Exhibition on High Performance Computing in the Asia-Pacific Region. Los Alamitos, CA: IEEE Computer Socity, 2000. 518~521.
11. WANG Qixin, LI Yi, DONG Li, NIE Yu, WANG Kehong. Incremental and Distributed Web Page Clustering Algorithms PG+ and PG++. Journal of Software, 2002,8:1500~1507(In Chinese).

An Application Framework for Distributed Information Retrieval

Fabio Simeoni, Leif Azzopardi, and Fabio Crestani

Dept. of Computing and Information Sciences,
University of Strathclyde, Glasgow, UK
{fabios, leif, fabioc}@cis.strath.ac.uk

Abstract. To date, the adoption of content-based Distributed Information Retrieval (DIR) solutions within the domain of Digital Libraries
(DL) remains rather limited. We contend that the lack of open application frameworks is a major obstacle. Not only to the rapid development
and reuse of state-of-the art DIR functionality, but also to the holistic
evaluation of competing DIR approaches. In this paper, we present the
design and implementation of one such framework; as well as its use
within the context of the DILIGENT infrastructure: a testbed of dedicated hardware, middleware and application services built explicitly for
the DL domain upon the lower-level facilities of the first European GRID
platform (EGEE). We conclude with a summary of future plans for its
large scale deployment, testing and evaluation within this context.

1 Introduction

For over ten years, research in Distributed Information Retrieval (DIR) has
sought efficient and effective ways of retrieving intellectual content which is distributed across internetworked but operationally autonomous sources (*content-
based*[1] or *document retrieval*) [3,5]. The *description* of sources, their *selection* for
query distribution, and the *fusion* of the result sets they produce have been identified as the key activities of a *search broker* which mediates between user queries
and distributed content within a standard client/server architecture (cf. Fig.1).

To date, however, there is little evidence of the uptake of DIR solutions in the
practice of Digital Library (DL) services. While content-based retrieval engines
are commonplace in centralized DLs, search brokers are rarely part of the widely
distributed architectures which characterize modern DL developments worldwide
(e.g. [9,1,15,8]). State-of-the-art DIR prototypes have been recently announced
(cf. the FedStats portal [2]), but real-world applications seem to be confined to

---

[1] With the term 'content-based', we characterize retrieval processes defined over indices of essentially unstructured content. Content-based retrieval lies at one end of a
spectrum which is otherwise bound by *structure-based* retrieval (also known as *data
retrieval*), where indices are extracted instead from rigidly structured data. Full-text
retrieval and retrieval of relational data are by far the most common examples of
content-based and structured retrieval, respectively.

S. Sugimoto et al. (Eds.): ICADL 2006, LNCS 4312, pp. 192–201, 2006.

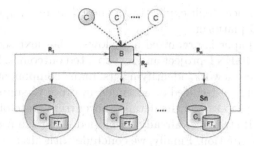

Fig. 1. Data flow in basic client/server retrieval. A search broker B interfaces clients C and dispatches their queries Q to content sources $S_1, S_2, , S_n$, each of which executes it against an index FT_i of some collection C_i before returning results R_i back to B which merges them and relays them to C.

Web metasearchers (cf. [11]) and appear to make little use of the rich array of techniques reported in the literature.

This state of affairs is in stark contrast with the penetration of structure-based distributed retrieval within the DL domain. In particular the role that the harvesting protocol of the OAI Initiative is having on the shaping of large-scale DL efforts, and the long-standing tradition of Z39.50-based DL federations [16]. Many reasons may account for this imbalance, including the inherent complexity/cost of DIR solutions and the latencies/failures associated with real-time usage of wide-area networks. We believe, however, that a major obstacle to the adoption of DIR solutions is the lack of a development and deployment infrastructure built around *open application frameworks* and *standard formats, languages, and protocols*. Without the latter, the costs of interoperability fall entirely onto the search broker and thus limit the scalability of its service (cf. well-known problems of 'source wrapping' [2,5]). Similarly, without dedicated application frameworks, development faces the full costs of end-to-end implementations and cannot reuse high-quality system-level and application-level functionality (e.g. transparent mechanisms for resultset streaming as well as state-of-the-art fusion algorithms built upon those mechanisms). Early attempts to gather consensus around protocol and formats for DIR proved unsuccessful [7], but DL developments outside the DIR field have rallied some interest around modern incarnations of the Z39.50 protocol (e.g.[13]) . To the best of our knowledge, true application frameworks for DIR are instead still unavailable, and DL practitioners are left with the unappealing alternative of entirely home-growing solutions or else re-purposing simulation code intended for ad-hoc research evaluations (e.g. The distributed modules with the Lemur Toolkit[2]).

In this paper, we report on the design and implementation of the first open application framework for DIR. The *DILIGENT DIR framework* takes its name from the ongoing EU project which funds its development and defines its initial operational context: namely, a fully distributed infrastructure of middleware and

---

[2] http://www.lemurproject.org

application-level services built explicitly for the DL domain upon the lower-level facilities of a GRID platform.

The rest of the paper is organized as follows. The next section provides an overview of the DILIGENT project and its expected outcomes. Section 3 outlines the design of the framework, identifying its main components and workflows and how they may be customized or extended in order to support different DIR strategies. Section 4 reports on the details and current state of implementation, particularly the DIR strategies already developed using the framework and now embedded in its distribution. Finally, we conclude with directions of future work in Section 5.

2   The DILIGENT Project

The DILIGENT project[10][3] is an attempt at systematically 'lifting' into the DL domain, the low-level computational services of a European GRID platform (see the *EGEE* project[4]). The expected outcome is a rich infrastructure of internet-worked machines, middleware services, and application-level services intended to serve as an advanced test-bed for secure, dynamic, and cost-effective collaboration among distributed e-Science communities. Collaboration on the testbed relies on Virtual Digital Libraries (VDLs) which are:

1. built *declaratively* from community-provided datasets and available application services, and then
2. deployed *on demand* by middleware services across machines, according to availability, performance, and functional constraints. With its dynamic deployment of services – and re-deployment, as constraints change over time – DILIGENT's goal is to bring the GRID philosophy of dynamic and coordinated resource sharing to the DL domain. This is ambitious, for it raises the state-of-the-art in GRID technologies (GRIDs themselves are currently statically deployed), and because it may invalidate assessments of DL technologies based on their cost of adoption within standard deployment scenarios (technologies with high adoption costs may be "outsourced" to the DILIGENT infrastructure, see subsection 2.1).
3. finally, the *Application-Specific Layer* (ASL) contains services which mediate the interaction between VDL users and the underlying machine-to-machine services.

2.1   Infrastructure

The DILIGENT infrastructure is framed by the Open Grid Services Architecture Framework (OGSA)[6] and thus relies on Service Oriented Architecture (SOA) principles and second-generation Web Service standards. Most notably those defined by the Web Service Resource Framework (WSRF) [12] to regulate stateful

---

[3] http://www.diligentproject.org
[4] http://public.eu-egee.org/

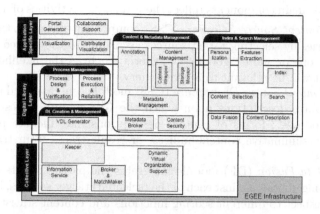

Fig. 2. The DILIGENT Architecture

service interactions. As shown in Fig. 2, the DILIGENT SOA is functionally layered. The *Collective Layer* (CL) groups the services which support the definition, deployment, and secure operation of VDLs; for example, the Information Service allows services to dynamically and anonymously discover each other regardless of the current location in the hardware infrastructure. The *Digital Library Layer* (DLL) aggregates services which implement VDL functionality, including those that provide persistence, metadata management, process orchestration, indexing, feature extraction, personalization, and search; extending the facilities of the underlying GRID platform. For example, Content Management services provide a transparent interface to distributed and replicated storage.

Our framework supports the definition of DIR services in the DLL of the DILIGENT architecture through interaction with Search and Indexing services to support content-based query execution. However, our framework also supports the definition of DIR services outwith the DILIGENT architecture, thus providing an open application framework for DIR.

3   Framework

The DILIGENT architecture defines the primary application domain for the DIR framework, or its *reference embedding*. The framework, however, is independent from particular embeddings and can be used even in the lack of an infrastructure. Its main components may be fully distributed across the network and interfaced as the Web Services of a service-oriented infrastructure; or else they may interact within a single process space as the internal modules of an ad-hoc search broker. Similarly, its workflows may be customized to accommodate or else entirely bypass interaction with external middleware services, including discovery, persistence, metadata, external indexing, and external search services.

The three main components reflect the primary of activities of a search broker:

- The *Content Source Selection* (CSS) component optimizes the distribution of queries by selecting target sources according to the degree to which they satisfy one or more "goodness" criteria, such as the likelihood that their content will be relevant to a given query.
- The *Content Source Description* (CSS) module generates and maintains content source descriptions upon which the CSS module bases its estimation of "goodness"; forms of content descriptions may include partial content indices, summative content indices, or result traces from training or past queries.
- The *Data Fusion* (DF) module integrates the partial results obtained from executing queries against each of the (selected) target sources, by normalizing with respect to different scoring functions and content statistics.

Independently from deployment scenarios, the design of the framework has been informed by the following requirements: (i) *flexibility*: it should support the implementation and configuration of the wide range of cooperative and uncooperative strategies which characterize the current scope of the DIR field, (ii) *efficiency*: it should optimize the consumption of computational resources, including computing cycles, storage, and bandwidth, (iii) *responsiveness*: it should minimize the latencies and interruptions of service typically associated with DIR processes which make real-time use of the network, and (iv) *open-ness*: it should adopt open and portable technology standards, from data formats and application protocols to language and system platforms.

For example a concrete CSD service may describe textual sources with term histograms derived from full-text indices of source content, another may do so with partial full-text indices derived directly from the content through query-based-sampling techniques[3], and yet another with a combination of manually gathered content. Similarly, a concrete DF service may rely on a round robin algorithm to merge results which emanate from different sources, another may be biased by the output of the CSS service, and yet another may employ non-heuristic techniques and leverage the output of some CSD service towards forms of "consistent" fusion.

4   Reference Services

We have tested the design framework of the CSD, CSS, and DF services by instantiating it into a set of concrete services for the DILIGENT testbed (*the reference services*). Common to all the reference services is their focus on effectiveness, which we could obtain by leveraging the degrees of cooperation available within the project. This does not preclude the interaction with uncooperative services, but these will be implemented at a later phase in the project.

4.1   CSD Service

The reference CSD service generates and maintains *term histograms* of textual sources, a coarse-grained form of index where containment relationships between terms and documents is intentionally abstracted over. The service interacts with the Index Management service to derive term histograms from full-text indices of collections and also to subscribe for point-to-point notifications of changes to such indices. Term histograms are exposed to consuming services via synchronous calls suitable for fine-grained access and via asynchronous, file-based exchange suitable for coarse-grained access. Term histograms are regenerated with respect to policies based on a combination of time and space criteria (i.e. every so often or whenever the content has changed by an agreed proportion).

4.2   CSS Service

Two reference CSS services have been implemented that select among textual sources on the basis of terms histograms for those sources. One is based on the CORI[4,3] selection algorithm (the standard collection selection mechanism), the other is based on Language Modeling techniques[14]. Both rank according to estimates of the relevance of source content to the information needs which underlie queries. Invoked by the Search service during query execution, the service selects "good" sources in accordance to configurable criteria and, for each such source, returns the goodness score which motivated its selection; such scores may then drive the selection of results which emanate from each selected source. The service stages term histograms from the reference CSD service prior to query execution, subscribes with that service for changes to the staged histograms, and updates the histograms upon receiving notification of such changes.

4.3   Reference DF Service

Finally, two reference DF services have also been implemented. The first is based on the notion of providing a consistent ranking of results, the other is an implementation of round robin. Both achieve the goal of data fusion, but have different advantages and disadvantages. The first guarantees a consistent merging of the results sets which emanate from a given number of text collections in response to a given query. In particular, the service recomputes the relevance estimates of the documents identified in the result sets from (i) term histograms for the collections obtained by the reference CSD service, and (ii) per-result term occurrence statistics provided by the Search service and emanating from the Index Management service. Hence, it requires more information from the content sources (and thus only applicable when cooperation is available) and requires additional computational time (as the full set of results from each source is required to compute the final ranking of results). On the other hand, the round robin approach makes no such guarantees about the quality of results presents and treats each source, and document, equally. The final result set is produced by taking the top document from each source and adding it to the final result set (the process is then repeated), thus the name round robin. Whilst this can not assure the results are ranked in some consistent fashion, there is no need to wait for all results to be streamed (only the top results), nor does any re-computation

of scores need to be performed, thus minimizing the amount of cooperation required from the Index Management service. The two reference services provide
two different approaches to fusion and demonstrates how the framework can be
used to compare and contrast different strategies within DIR.

4.4   Interaction and Relationship to Other Services

The search broker is responsible for the DIR search setup and coordinating the
search workflow process.

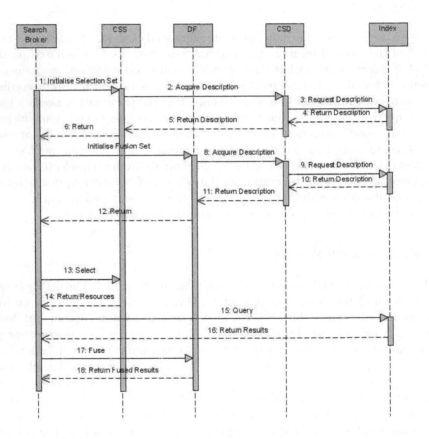

Fig. 3. Sequence Diagram of the Interaction between Search Broker and Services. Steps
(1)-(12) denote the warm up sequence and steps (13)-(18) denote the querying sequence.

Assuming that the services have been configured with the desired setup then
the sequence of interactions is shown in Figure 3. For instance, a possible configuration is: (i) CSS with the CORI reference algorithm, which requires CSD with
term histogram, (ii) DF with the consistent fusion reference implementation,
and (iii) cooperative Indexes.

The first stage of the process is the warm up sequences denoted in the figure as steps (1)-(12). In step (1), the CSS is contacted by the search broker to initialize the service to select over a set of indexes. (2) The CSS contacts the CSD to acquire a description of each index. (3) The CSD request the description from the index. Note that this in a cooperative environment the index provides the collection statistics in a pre-defined format to the CSD and is returned in step (4). However, in an uncooperative environment a different implementation of the CSD would be required (and would perform Query Based Sampling[3] for example). The CSD returns the description to the CSS in step (5). Steps (2)-(5) are repeated for each index, until the all indexes are described, and the warm up of the CSS is complete at step (6). A similar procedure is performed to warm up the DF in steps (7)-(12). However, if the DF service did not require any collection statistics, as is the case for the round robin reference implementation of DF, then steps (8)-(11) would be bypassed.

Once the warm up of CSS and DF is complete, querying is now possible. When a query is submitted, the search broker performs the following steps: (13) The query is sent to the CSS for selection of the set of indexes. The CSS returns a ranked list of indexes in step (14). This may be the top n indexes which are most likely to satisfy the query, or all those indexes above a certain threshold. These criteria can be defined when performing the selection. The selected indexes are then contacted directly in step (15) and queried. This process is performed concurrently for efficiency (via threading). In step (16) a reference to the result sets produced by each index is returned to the search broker, who then passes these references to the DF service in step (17) to perform fusion. Once the DF has merged the results, the final result set is passed back to the search broker. Note, that the entire result set need not be constructed, before a reference to the result set is available as the results are streamed into the result set. This is advantageous in the case of the round robin reference implementation of DF, which only requires a handful of results to be available before merging can begin. However, in the case of consistent fusion reference implementation, the complete result sets are required. This is because results which have a low ranking according to the index that provides them, may have a high ranking globally.

Whilst we have described the interaction of services under the standard approach to Distributed Information Retrieval, this does not preclude other possible configurations. For instance, Data fusion may not be require if after selection only the best index is queried.

4.5 Evaluation

Several test case scenarios have been constructed and are currently being setup and evaluated. Our pilot testing of the above scenario has been performed using several small collections to ensure that the algorithms are being computed correctly and that above interactions are achieved (i.e. unit testing). However, the next stage in the evaluation cycle is full scale simulation of the the above interactions using a DIR testbed extracted from the TREC Aquaint data collection.

This testbed contains 86 sub-collections to select over, which will be indexed, and 50 queries for the search broker to execute. In this simulated environment we will perform load testing and capture individual and aggregated response times under various configurations of the services; this will include testing on local machines, networked machines and grid machines. The goal will be to ensure that reasonable performance (in terms of efficiency) can be attained, and to identify where improvements can be made. Once completed, then the services will be deployed within DILIGENT to support two user communities where live user testing will be conducted. At the end of each cycle of evaluation, we shall refine the services and interactions as required to support real time usage. We believe that this may entail the design of algorithms which specifically cater to the inefficiencies of the distributed environment, but maintain a reasonably good quality of service (in terms of retrieval effectiveness). These are issues that remain largely unexplored.

5   Discussion and Conclusions

The reference services have been deployed, and testing and evaluation is currently being undertaken within a simulated environment to determine the projects viability in terms of retrieval effectiveness and retrieval efficiency. The main aims of the evaluation are focused on (i) identifying activities within the search workflow that impede efficient retrieval, and (ii) whether algorithms can be developed such that an efficient service can be delivered in a distributed environment, without compromising the effectiveness of the retrieval system. For instance, whilst state-of-the-art algorithms have been shown to provide excellent retrieval performance, the cost in terms of retrieval efficiency is not known. Given that the distributed environment creates overheads not incurred in a centralized system, this does not mean that solutions can not be developed to overcome these problems. Instead, future research needs to be directed towards designing algorithms that ensure efficient run time operation, given these constraints. If this can be successfully achieved, further work will be conducted in real world environments within two different user communities.

In this paper, we have presented an outline of a service oriented architecture for the development of DIR applications along with details of the framework. As we have argued, the lack of an application framework has been key factor restricting the uptake of such solutions, and we believe that we have taken steps to address this issue. Now that an architecture is in place the focus of future work will be on analyzing its utility and viability in distributed search environments.

References

1. H. Anan, X. Liu, K. Maly, M. Nelson, M. Zubair, J. C. French, E. Fox, and P. Shivakumar. Preservation and transition of ncstrl using an oai-based architecture. In *JCDL '02: Proceedings of the 2nd ACM/IEEE-CS joint conference on Digital libraries*, pages 181–182, New York, NY, USA, 2002. ACM Press.

2. Thi Truong Avrahami, Lawrence Yau, Luo Si, and Jamie Callan. The fedlemur project: Federated search in the real world. *J. Am. Soc. Inf. Sci. Technol.*, 57(3):347–358, 2006.
3. James Callan. *Advances in Information Retrieval*, chapter Distributed Information Retrieval, pages 127–150. Kluwer Academic Publishers, 2000.
4. James P. Callan, Zhihong Lu, and W. Bruce Croft. Searching distributed collections with inference networks. In *SIGIR '95: Proceedings of the 18th annual international ACM SIGIR conference on Research and development in information retrieval*, pages 21–28, 1995.
5. Nicholas Eric Craswell. *Methods for Distributed Information Retrieval*. PhD thesis, Australian National University, May 2000.
6. I. Foster, C. Kesselman, J. M. Nick, and S. Tuecke. Grid services for distributed system integration. *Computer*, 35:37–46, 2002.
7. Luis Gravano, Chen-Chuan K. Chang, Hector Garcia-Molina, and Andreas Paepcke. Starts: Stanford proposal for internet meta-searching. In *SIGMOD '97: Proceedings of the 1997 ACM SIGMOD international conference on Management of data*, pages 207–218, New York, NY, USA, 1997. ACM Press.
8. Joint Information Systems Committee. Information environment: Development strategy 2001-2005. Public Draft, August 2001.
9. Carl Lagoze, William Arms, Stoney Gan, Diane Hillmann, Christopher Ingram, Dean Krafft, Richard Marisa, Jon Phipps, John Saylor, Carol Terrizzi, Walter Hoehn, David Millman, James Allan, Sergio Guzman-Lara, and Tom Kalt. Core services in the architecture of the national science digital library (nsdl). In *JCDL '02: Proceedings of the 2nd ACM/IEEE-CS joint conference on Digital libraries*, pages 201–209, New York, NY, USA, 2002. ACM Press.
10. Pasquale Pagano Heiko Schuldt Manuele Simi Laura Voicu Leonardo Candela, Donatella Castelli Christoph Langguth. On-demand service deployment and process support in e-science dls: the diligent experience. In *To Appear in the Proceedings of the European Conference on Digital Libraries Workshop - Digital Library Goes e-Science: Perspectives and Challenges*, 2006.
11. Weiyi Meng, Clement Yu, and King-Lup Liu. Building efficient and effective metasearch engines. *ACM Comput. Surv.*, 34(1):48–89, 2002.
12. OASIS. Web service resource framework. Technical report, W3C, 2004.
13. Rob Sanderson. Srw: Search/retrieve webservice. Public Draft, 2003.
14. Luo Si, Rong Jin, Jamie Callan, and Paul Ogilvie. A language modeling framework for resource selection and results merging. In *CIKM '02: Proceedings of the eleventh international conference on Information and knowledge management*, pages 391–397, 2002.
15. Annemiek van der Kuil and Martin Feijen. The dawning of the dutch network of digital academic repositories (dare): A shared experience. *Ariadne Magazine*, (41), October 2004.
16. Z39.50 Maintenance Agency. Information retrieval (z39.50): Application service definition and protocol specification, 2003.

A Plugin Architecture Enabling Federated Search for Digital Libraries

Sergey Chernov, Christian Kohlschütter, and Wolfgang Nejdl

L3S Research Center, University of Hannover, Expo Plaza 1, 30539 Hannover, Germany
{chernov, kohlschuetter, nejdl}@l3s.de

Abstract. Today, users expect a variety of digital libraries to be searchable from a single Web page. The German Vascoda project provides this service for dozens of information sources. Its ultimate goal is to provide search quality close to the ranking of a central database containing documents from all participating libraries. Currently, however, the Vascoda portal is based on a non-cooperative metasearch approach, where results from sources are merged randomly and ranking quality is sub-optimal. In this paper, we describe a Lucene-based plugin which replaces this method by a truly federated search across different search engines, where the exchange of document statistics improves document ranking. Preliminary evaluation results show ranking results equal to a centralized setup.

1 Introduction

Information integration over distributed sources is an urgent problem to be solved for providing access to a variety of Digital Libraries through a common search interface and portal. The German Vascoda project [15] tries to accomplish this ambitious task, integrating distributed scientific information resources from all over Germany. Its Web portal is the major German Website for providing unified access to interdisciplinary scientific and scholarly information. It comprises the Internet services from more than 40 academic libraries and institutions, and enables unified access to electronic full-text documents, document delivery services and pay-per-view options. The architecture is designed for expansion and new libraries can easily join Vascoda, thus positioning Vascoda as the main information source for the scholarly and research community in Germany as well as in Europe.

Currently, the Vascoda Information Portal provides a non-cooperative metasearch environment only[1]. Metasearch has inherent limitations for merging documents from heterogeneous sources into one consistent document ranking. As different search engines execute queries on different collections, document relevance is computed using diverse statistics, making results incomparable. It is thus virtually impossible to merge results into a single, consistent ranking without additional statistics about these collections.

Unfortunately, simply indexing all documents in a single search engine installation is not a useful option. While such a central approach would be technically feasible, taking content and collection restrictions for all participating libraries into account is

---

[1] From now on, by *metasearch* we refer to non-cooperative distributed search.

S. Sugimoto et al. (Eds.): ICADL 2006, LNCS 4312, pp. 202–211, 2006.

not an easy task, and sometimes plain impossible as some license contracts do not allow sharing data beyond the original library.

We therefore investigated a *federated* search infrastructure, where all partners can run their own (existing) search systems in a decentralized manner, but are still able to provide homogeneous search and ranking over all available collections. To achieve this, we provide a Lucene-based plugin for decentralized search engines, which is responsible for providing search across all collections and for exchanging document statistics between the connected sites.

In our project, we have explored this setup between two libraries with different search infrastructures, the German National Library of Science and Technology (TIB), and the Bielefeld University Library. TIB runs a search engine based on the open-source search engine library Apache Lucene [6,8], Bielefeld uses an installation of FAST Data Search[2]). While both members want to integrate their systems in a federated search architecture within Vascoda, they need to keep their existing systems - completely replacing their search infrastructure is not an option. Besides designing and implementing a federated architecture for this setup, we ran experiments on the HU-Berlin EDOC, ArXiv and Citeseer document collections, split across the two participants, with promising results.

The paper is structured as follows: Section 2 introduces general issues of distributed information retrieval, relevant components for the federated search and the Lucene and FAST search engines. In Section 3 we discuss our Lucene-based plugin in more detail, and provide evaluation details in Section 4. Finally, we summarize and outline future work in Section 5.

2   Relevant Background

2.1   Distributed Information Retrieval

Good surveys on distributed information retrieval problems and solutions can be found in [2,4,5,13,16]. Here we only briefly review the underlying data model and main problems in distributed search.

Vector Space Model. For our federated search infrastructure we used the Vector Space Model [17]. It is effective, simple and well-known in the DL community. In this model, a document D is represented by the vector $d = (w_1, w_2, \ldots, w_m)$ where m is the number of distinct terms and w_i is the weight indicating the "importance" of term t_i. The weight is combined from the Term Frequency (TF_i) (the number of the term's occurrences in the document[3]) and Inverse Document Frequency (IDF_i) (the logarithm of the ratio N/DF_i, where DF_i is the number of documents containing the term t_i, and N is the overall number of documents in the collection). A common standard for term weighting is the $TFxIDF$ product and its variants.

Metasearch vs. Federated Search. In general, we can divide distributed search environments into two categories: uncooperative, isolated environments (metasearch) and

---

[2] http://www.base-search.net/

[3] In information retrieval terminology, the term "frequency" is used as a synonym for "count".

cooperative, integrated environments (federated search). Metasearch participants have no other access to the individual databases than a ranked list of document descriptions in the response to a query, while federated search participants have access to collection-wide statistics like DF and N. As a consequence, the result rankings produced by metasearch are less homogeneous than using federated search.

Search Broker. The unifying unit in distributed information retrieval is a search broker, which provides access to several search engines. Figure 1 visualizes this unit in the distributed setup between TIB and Bielefeld University. Distributed search has much in common with search on a single source, but entails additional tasks (listed in [5][4]):

Resource Description. A full-text database provides information about its contents through a set of statistics, which is called *resource description*. Initially, the broker obtains and stores resource descriptions for every search engine. Every description is divided into *content summary*, *metadata summary* and *search engine configuration* [10]. The content summary is a limited set of statistics about each database/search engine. The metadata summary characterizes the metadata schema of resources and fields available for search. The search engine configuration finally represents the current state of customizable, search engine-wide parameters such as text pre-processing rules.

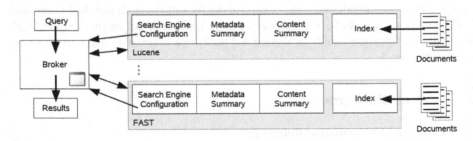

Fig. 1. Federated Search with Lucene and FAST Search Engines

Database Selection. The collected resource descriptions are used for database selection and query routing tasks. We want to select only those databases that are relevant to our query, according to their resource descriptions. The most natural way to do this is to ask the user to manually pick the set of interesting information sources. A better option is to automatically calculate a query-dependent "usefulness measure" of each database, based on the vector space model or language modeling approach [18].

Query Mapping. An important and difficult task is the handling of different document schemata and query languages. Some databases cover basic reference data only, while other contain enriched information with subject or classification information, abstract or additional description parts. The resource descriptions are helpful for a proper query mapping.

Result Merging. When a query is performed over several selected databases, one single ranking should be created integrating these results. Due to differences in search

---

[4] We enlarged this list by the "Query mapping task".

engine implementations and DL schemata, this is not an easy task. Document simi-larity/importance scores are not directly comparable among different collections and require a global normalization using collection-wide statistics. This requires a coopera-tive search environment, distributed search over non-cooperative DLs results in loss of search quality [1].

Difficulties in Distributed Ranking. Even in a cooperative environment, where all search engines provide all necessary statistics, it is hard to guarantee exactly the same ranking as that of the centralized database. The following factors may reduce search quality (we enlarged the list from [9]):

- Relevant documents are missed after the database selection step;
- Different stemmers and stopword lists influence both TF and DF values;
- Overlap affects globally computed DF values;
- Query syntax may be incompatible;
- Unknown features of proprietary algorithms cannot be disabled;
- Document schemata (e.g., field names) on resources do not match.

2.2 Distributed Search in Digital Libraries

Related Projects. Several projects have attempted to improve distributed search in dig-ital libraries. A recent effort is the DAFFODIL project [7], a system to support infor-mation search in distributed digital libraries. The project employs an advanced user interface for supporting search stratagems. While it also addresses the quality of rank-ing, it focuses on extended search functionality rather than the problems of distributed indexing and result merging. Another approach, pursued in the DILIGENT project [3], is to combine digital libraries using Grid technology. The project goal is to create a pro-totype Grid infrastructure for digital libraries. The project does not focus on the objec-tives of federated search. Commercial distributed search systems like Scirus[5] or Google Scholar[6] are interesting, but their implementation details are not publicly available.

Protocols for DLs Interoperability. In federated search, brokers and search engines cooperate in order to deliver a common, consistent ranking, just as if search were per-formed by a single search engine. Factors like stemming algorithms, stop word lists, local collection statistics, ranking formulae etc. have to be unified across the federation. Combining information from many digital libraries thus requires a common standard interface for query and result exchange. Among the protocols like *Z39.50* [14], *OAI-PMH* [11,12] and *SDARTS* [10], SDARTS is the most suitable one. It provides most of the Z39.50 functionality, but is much easier to support. The protocol keeps the com-mon requirements for implementers to a minimum, while still supporting sophisticated features of advanced search engines.

FAST and Lucene Search Engines. The *FAST Data Search* engine is a commercial system by Fast Search & Transfer ASA (FAST). Its core consists of a full-text engine based on the Vector Space Model, extending it with additional features. The user can

---

[5] http://www.scirus.com/srsapp/
[6] http://scholar.google.com/

configure just a subset of all parameters. FAST plays an important role in the Vascoda project, since several members already use it for their local search service. *Lucene* [8] is also used as the basis for several search engines of VASCODA members. By itself, it is not a complete search engine, but rather a programming library which allows the easy creation of search engines with the desired properties and functionality. Lucene has been implemented in several programming languages, in this project we build upon its original (and main-line) implementation in Java.

3   Plugin Architecture

3.1   Integrating FAST Data Search and Lucene Search

While being very similar at some points, the two engines are incompatible on several levels, including index structures, API and ranking. Since FAST is a commercial, closed-source product, neither are all technical internals of FAST available nor are they exposed through the FAST API.

It is however possible to use intermediate results of the FAST pipeline for further computation, such that the FAST pipeline handles all crawling and text extraction tasks, while indexing and query evaluation for distributed search is handled by Lucene (local search is of course still handled by FAST in the FAST environment). Specifically, we take pre-processed plain-text documents, including metadata from both FAST and Lucene pipelines, and (re-)index them in a homogeneous manner, using a common lemmatization/stemming schema. This wrapper / *plugin* approach encapsulates the original search engine system and provides a common interface to the federation. Search is then performed over these plugins instead of the original vendor's system. Since Lucene is open-source and already provides distributed search facilities, we decided to implemented a Lucene-based plugin.

Given the modular nature of the FAST pipeline, (re-)indexing in the FAST context is easy. FAST Data Search provides a textual, XML-structured representation of indexed documents in its so-called FIXML format. Documents are described as field-structured plain text, which makes the transition to the Lucene indexing module quite easy. This plugin concept is extensible to other search engine products as well, as long as their processing pipelines are modular enough to provide the required intermediate results.

Figure 2 shows the resulting plugin-enriched federated search infrastructure. Before query time, all necessary statistics information (number of documents N and document frequencies DF_t) is being collected on a regular basis and cached by the searcher (for each term t, all the plugins' DF_t values are accumulated to one global DF_t). The search itself then proceeds as follows: the searcher parses the user's query into a Lucene-specific representation and transmits that to all (or a to a selected subset of the) available plugins. At query time, the plugins receive global DF_t and N statistics information from the searcher in order to rank their results accordingly. When the rank score has been determined, they call the searcher to *consume* the *hit*, i.e. Lucene-specific document ID plus rank score. This ID can then later be used to access document information, e.g. for the summaries on the results page.

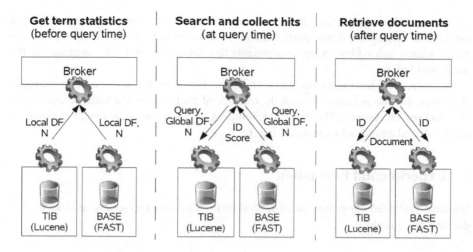

Fig. 2. Federated Search Infrastructure using the Lucene-based Plugin

Participating institutions may provide custom plugins for their own search engines. They can also connect their own user interfaces, with different layouts and functionality, to the federation.

3.2 Index and Search Capabilities

Our approach provides the advantages of centralized search (homogeneous index structure and ranking), while offering distributed search using standard Lucene features. In order to support this, the original document collection has only to be re-indexed by our Lucene-based plugin. This can be done automatically and incrementally by Lucene, so only added, deleted or changed documents are affected.

It is clear that the federation can only provide a common subset of all possible search features. While this set is actually quite large, our approach keeps the DLs' existing search engines untouched, so search outside the federation remains available.

The following capabilities are explicitly supported by our implementation:

– **Homogeneous Ranking**, based on the TF/IDF weighted vector-space model. Since the mapping from words to terms is homogeneous, the TF/IDF statistics can safely be used.
– **De-Duplication.** Since true duplicates yield the same rank score, they can easily be filtered out when creating the results page.
– **Database selection.** Query term-based database selection is easily performed by checking all plugin DF statistics before submitting the query.

3.3 Costs for Joining the Federation

An obvious question is what a digital library has to do when it wants to join the federation and how much it has to invest. In general, it only has to provide a fast Internet connection (since the majority of queries may be routed to all participants) and additional computational power. Clearly, these resources would be necessary for participating in any kind of federation. A new participant also has to provide storage space for the federated search index files: in our experiments this meant about a 30% increase for the additional index.

Compared to a homogeneous search engine architecture, the asset costs are manageable since they do not increase with the number of participants but with the number of different search systems. The costs of developing a plugin for a new search engine type can be shared among all members using it.

4   Experimental Evaluation

We have evaluated our prototype on several test collections and setups, as described in the next paragraphs.

4.1   Federation Setup

Data. Regarding collections, we used a document corpus based on the HU-Berlin EDOC document set and the ArXiv collection (metadata and full-text), together with the Citeseer OAI collection (metadata only). EDOC[7] is the institutional repository of Humboldt University, it encompasses about 2,500 annotated full-text documents of theses, dissertations, scientific publications and public readings. CiteSeer[8] is a system at Penn State University, USA, with the focus on literature in computer and information sciences. At the moment, the system contains more than 700,000 documents. The ArXiv pre-print server[9] is located at Cornell University Libraries and provides access to more than 350,000 electronic documents in Physics, Mathematics, Computer Science and Quantitative Biology.

Servers. For the experiments, we have set up a small federation of two search engines, one in Bielefeld and one in Hannover. The servers communicate via a regular Internet connection. On each server, we have installed our plugin prototype and the corresponding Web front-end. The front-end only communicates to the local plugin, which then accesses local, disk-based Lucene document collections, or external, network-connected plugins, depending on the exact evaluation task. The server in Hannover was a Dual Intel Xeon 2.8 GHz machine, the server in Bielefeld was powered by a Dual AMD Opteron 250. On the Bielefeld server, a Lucene-plugin based version of the BASE (Bielefeld Academic Search Engine) Web user interface has been deployed, on the Hannover server, a fictitious "HASE" (Hannover Academic Search Engine) front-end also runs based on a Lucene-based search engine. Both GUIs, HASE and BASE are only connected to their local search plugins. The plugins then connect to the local collections (ArXiv and CiteSeer in Bielefeld and EDOC in Hannover) and to the plugin at the other site. This setup is depicted in Figure 3.

---

[7] http://edoc.hu-berlin.de
[8] http://citeseer.ist.psu.edu/
[9] http://arxiv.org/

4.2 Hypotheses

Due to the underlying algorithms, we expected no difference in the result set (both item presence and position in the result list) between a centralized, combined index covering all collections and the distributed scenario proposed using Lucene-based Federated Search. Also, we expected almost no difference in search performance, since the collection statistics information is not exchanged at query time, but only at startup time and whenever updates in any of the included collections have occurred. Since the result display only lists a fixed number of results per page (usually 10 short descriptions, all of about the same length), the time necessary for retrieving the results lists from the contributing plugins is constant, i.e. not dependent on the number of found entries, but just on the servers' overall performance (CPU + network I/O).

4.3 Results

Re-indexing. Our current prototype re-indexed the metadata-only ArXiv collection (350,000 entries) in about 2 hours; the EDOC full-text document set (2,500 documents) was imported in 19 minutes. We expect that re-indexing will be even faster with a production–level implementation. The resulting index structure was about 20-40% of the size of the uncompressed FIXML data (depending on collection input) and also, interestingly, only about a third of the size of the original FAST index data. This is possibly due to extra data structures for the FAST engine, which are not necessary for our Lucene-based Federated Search. Based on these numbers, no significant overhead is induced by the necessary re-indexing step compared to a centralized index based on FAST Data Search.

Search. We performed several searches (one-word-, multi-word- and phrase queries) on our federation as well as on a local index, both using Lucene. We measured average query time and compared the rankings for one word, multi-word and phrase queries. Query times of a distributed setup were almost equal to the local setup, about 0.05-0.15 seconds per query, with an overhead of about 0.4 seconds for the distributed setup. The resulting ranking is equal to the one of a centralized setup.

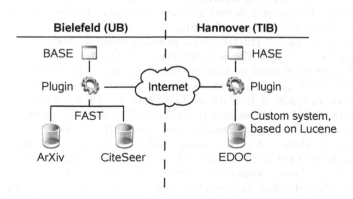

Fig. 3. Test Scenario for Federated Search

5 Conclusions

This paper describes ongoing work on the federated search infrastructure for digital libraries in the context of the Vascoda project, and discussed a Lucene-plugin based solutions for federated search, which provides high search quality even for decentralized collections and engines, easy integration of new members and preservation of existing systems and workflows.

A prototype based on the Lucene-plugin described in this paper integrates two search engine installations, one based on FAST Data Search at Bielefeld University Library and another Lucene-based search system at the German National Library of Science and Technology TIB. The federated system provides a final result ranking equal to search on a centralized database, while overall computational and maintenance costs remain reasonably low. The next major step will be to implement a stable version of the plugin for all collections of the current participants, and to make it publicly accessible.

References

1. Wolf-Tilo Balke, Wolfgang Nejdl, Wolf Siberski, and Uwe Thaden. DL meets P2P – Distributed Document Retrieval based on Classification and Content. In *ECDL '05: Proceedings of the 9th European Conference on Research and Advanced Technology for Digital Libraries*, pages 379–390, 2005.
2. Jamie Callan. *Advances in information retrieval, W.B. Croft, editor*, chapter Distributed Information Retrieval, pages 127–150. 2000.
3. Donatella Castelli. DILIGENT: A Digital Library Infrastructure on Grid Enabled Technology. http://www.ercim.org/publication/ercim_news/enw59/castelli.html. *ERCIM News*, 59, 2004.
4. Nicholas Eric Craswell. *Methods for Distributed Information Retrieval. http://eprints. anu.edu.au/archive/00000503/*. PhD thesis, ANU, January 01 2001.
5. W. Bruce Croft. Combining Approaches to IR. In *DELOS Workshop: Information Seeking, Searching and Querying in Digital Libraries*, 2000.
6. Doug Cutting et al. Lucene. http://lucene.apache.org.
7. Norbert Fuhr, Claus-Peter Klas, Andre Schaefer, and Peter Mutschke. Daffodil: An Integrated Desktop for Supporting High-Level Search Activities in Federated Digital Libraries. In *ECDL '02: Proceedings of the 6th European Conference on Research and Advanced Technology for Digital Libraries*, pages 597–612, 2002.
8. Otis Gospodnetic and Erik Hatcher. *Lucene in Action*. Manning, 2005.
9. Luis Gravano, Kevin Chen-Chuan Chang, Hector Garcia-Molina, and Andreas Paepcke. STARTS: Stanford Proposal for Internet Meta-Searching. In *SIGMOD '97: Proceedings of the 1997 ACM International Conference on Management of Data*, pages 207–218, 1997.
10. Noah Green, Panagiotis G. Ipeirotis, and Luis Gravano. SDLIP + STARTS = SDARTS a Protocol and Toolkit for Metasearching. In *JCDL '01: Proceedings of the The First ACM and IEEE Joint Conference on Digital Libraries*, pages 207–214, 2001.
11. Carl Lagoze, Herbert Van de Sompel, Michael Nelson, and Simeon Warner. The Open Archives Initiative Protocol for Metadata Harvesting Protocol Version 2.0 of 2002-06-14. http://www.openarchives.org/oai/openarchivesprotocol.html.
12. X. Liu, K. Maly, M. Zubair, Q. Hong, M.L. Nelson, F. Knudson, and Holtkamp. Federated Searching Interface Techniques for Heterogeneous OAI Repositories. *Journal of Digital Information*, 4(2), 2002.

13. Weiyi Meng, Clement T. Yu, and King-Lup Liu. Building Efficient and Effective Meta-search Engines. http://doi.acm.org/10.1145/505282.505284. *ACM Comput. Surv.*, 34(1):48–89, 2002.
14. National Information Standards Organization. Z39.50: Application Service Definition and Protocol Specification, 2003.
15. Heike Neuroth and Tamara Pianos. VASCODA: A German Scientific Portal for Cross-Searching Distributed Digital Resource Collections. In *ECDL '03: Proceedings of the 7th European Conference on Research and Advanced Technology for Digital Libraries*, pages 257–262, 2003.
16. Tamar Sadeh. Google Scholar Versus Metasearch Systems. *High Energy Physics Libraries Webzine*, 12, 2006.
17. Gerard Salton, A. Wong, and C. S. Yang. A Vector Space Model for Automatic Indexing. *Commun. ACM*, 18(11):613–620, 1975.
18. Luo Si, Rong Jin, James P. Callan, and Paul Ogilvie. A Language Modeling Framework for Resource Selection and Results Merging. http://doi.acm.org/10.1145/584792.584856. In *CIKM '02: Proceedings of the ACM 11th Conference on Information and Knowledge Management*, pages 391–397, 2002.

A User Study on Features Supporting Subjective Relevance for Information Retrieval Interfaces

Shu-Shing Lee, Yin-Leng Theng,
Dion Hoe-Lian Goh, and Schubert Shou-Boon Foo

Division of Information Studies
School of Communication and Information
Nanyang Technological University
Singapore 637718
{ps7918592b, tyltheng, ashlgoh, assfoo}@ntu.edu.sg

Abstract. Objective relevance regards retrieved documents as relevant without considering users' tasks. Subjective relevance, in contrast, focuses on usefulness of documents for users' contexts. This paper aims to enhance objective relevance and address its limitations by designing a mock-up interface based on ACM Digital Library so as to enhance its support for users' evaluating the subjective relevance of documents. Important features elicited using a factor analytic approach from an earlier study were used to inform the design of the search, results list and document record pages in the mock-up. A pilot study was conducted to gather users' feedback about usefulness of designed features. Findings indicated that majority of important features designed were useful. However, subjects suggested that the design of some features could be further improved to facilitate their support for SR. The paper concludes by discussing recommendations for improving the mock-up.

1 Introduction

Information retrieval (IR) systems are traditionally developed using the "best match" principle assuming that users can specify their needs in queries [2]. This principle retrieves documents by matching query terms to terms in documents, and regards retrieved documents as relevant. Here, relevance is computed objectively without considering users' needs and tasks [11].

This paper enhances objective relevance and addresses its limitations by using the subjective relevance approach to design a mock-up IR interface supporting users' evaluations of subjective relevance of documents. The SR concept provides suitable theoretical underpinnings as it focuses on document's relevance for users' needs [6]. Our paper builds on an earlier quantitative study [7] where users' perceptions of importance of SR features were investigated using a factor-analytic approach. Here, we highlight how important features elicited from the earlier study are designed in a mock-up IR interface based on ACM Digital Library (ACMDL) so as to enhance its support for SR. A pilot study was conducted to gather users' feedback on usefulness of designed features and how its design could be improved. The paper concludes with recommendations to enhance the mock-up interface's support for SR.

S. Sugimoto et al. (Eds.): ICADL 2006, LNCS 4312, pp. 212–222, 2006.

2   Related Work

Different approaches have been used to develop user-centered IR systems aimed at enhancing objective relevance. In the digital library domain, researchers have designed user-centered systems that guide users retrieve relevant documents. For example, the *Digital Work Environment* [8] points users to documents based on user categories and tasks. Another example uses participatory design techniques to develop a user-centered children's digital library called *SearchKids* [5].

A different research area aims to enhance objective relevance by looking at user-centered criteria and dimensions affecting relevance judgments. Examples of such works are [1] and [9]. These works allow designers provide appropriate information in IR systems to help users find relevant documents for tasks.

3   Our Previous Work

Here, we briefly describe an earlier quantitative study [7] to provide background for this paper. SR types [4] and exploratory factor analysis were used to provide rationale for the quantitative study. In that study, users rated their perceived importance of SR features. The SR concept was defined as usefulness of an information object for users' needs [3]. SR also referred to different intellectual interpretations that users engaged to interpret if an information object was useful [3]. The SR types were [4]:

- Topical relevance: This relevance is achieved if the topic covered by the assessed information object corresponds to the topic in user's information need.
- Pertinence relevance: This relevance is measured based on a relation between user's knowledge state and retrieved information objects as interpreted by the user.
- Situational relevance: This relevance is determined based on whether the user can use retrieved information objects to address a particular task.
- Motivational relevance: This relevance is assessed based on whether the user can use retrieved information objects in ways that are accepted by the community.

In that study, SR features were organized into three IR interaction stages: 1) the search page; 2) results list page; and 3) document record page. Data gathered was analyzed using exploratory factor analysis to identify groups of important SR features for each stage. Findings indicated different groups of important SR features for the search page, results list page and document record page. These groupings highlighted an order of importance amongst groups of features for each stage. Hence, findings were implied that different clusters of features could be combined to provide rationale for designing different levels of SR support in the search page, results list page, and document record page. Details for this study are found in [7].

4   Using Factor Analysis to Inform Interface Design

The mock-up IR interface was designed using findings elicited through a factor analytic approach in our earlier study. The mock-up was designed to enhance ACMDL's support for SR by implementing new features and different levels of SR support so that users' evaluations of subjective relevance of documents were facilitated. Reason for enhancing ACMDL's interface was because its features were in line with important features highlighted in the earlier study. Thus, it was inferred that ACMDL's interface had the potential to provide better SR support if findings from our earlier study were incorporated.

Groups of SR features elicited from our earlier study were implied as different clusters of important features that could be designed to provide different levels of SR support for the search page, results list page and document record page. These levels of SR support were conceptualized in the mock-up as basic/advanced search pages; results list page in brief/extended format; and document record page in brief/extended format. Although findings from the earlier study provided important SR features to incorporate in the mock-up, it did not indicate the general look and feel of the interface. Hence, Shneiderman's [10] design heuristics were used to inform the design of the mockup. Detailed design of each page for the mock-up is described below.

Design of Basic and Advanced Search Pages

Three groups of important SR features were elicited from the earlier study [7]. These groups focused on three aspects of the search page: 1) providing search options; 2) providing additional features in basic and advanced search pages; and 3) providing default search features. These groups were interpreted as follows: 1) for features in groups that did not specify if it should be designed in the basic or advanced search pages, such features were implemented in both search pages and 2) in instances where the feature was only applicable to either of the search page, it was designed for the specific page. In addition, one feature in the third group specified that the method of entering queries should be similar to those in search engines. Thus, it was inferred that the basic search page should have one query box while the advanced search page should have multiple query boxes for users to construct complex queries.

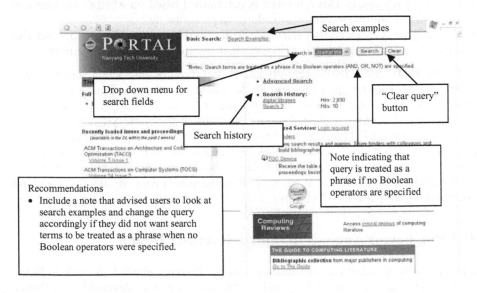

Fig. 1. Features and Recommendations for Basic Search Page

The basic search page was designed with the simplistic design of search engines in mind. This page consisted of a query box and a drop down menu of search fields. Search examples, "clear query" button, and search history were included to support query formulation and re-formulation. A note was designed to indicate that queries were treated as a phrase search if no Boolean operators were specified. These features designed were new as the original ACMDL interface only included a query box and a "search" button. Design of basic search page is presented in Figure 1.

Design of advanced search page was based on the advanced search page in ACMDL. Query boxes from ACMDL were maintained and changes were made to the drop down menu of search fields. The advanced search page included features, such as, "clear query" button, search examples and search history to facilitate query formulation. Our design streamlined the original advanced search page in ACMDL by only providing multiple query boxes with different search options so users could build complex queries. Moreover, our design also incorporated new features, like, search history and "clear query" button. Figure 2 shows the designed advanced search page.

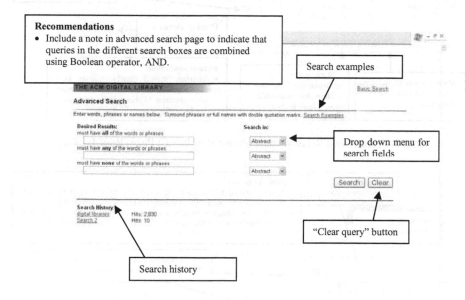

Fig. 2. Features and Recommendations for Advanced Search Page

Design of Results List Page in Brief and Extended Format

Exploratory factor analysis conducted in our earlier study highlighted five groups of important SR features [7]. The groups focused on different parts of the results list page, like: 1) pointing users to other documents; 2) providing features that supported evaluation of contents and document type for tasks; 3) providing alternate ways of presenting results list; 4) provide additional information to support evaluation; and 5) provide common features available in results list. These groups were implied as having a decreasing order of importance.

To provide different levels of SR support for the results list page, features in groups 1 and 5 were combined to design a brief format results list page. Reason being group 5 focused on common features, like, ordering documents by relevance, showing relevance percentage and searching within results list, while group 1 focused on pointing users to other documents, thus, features in group 1 could not stand on its own to form a results list page. Figure 3 shows the results list page in brief format.

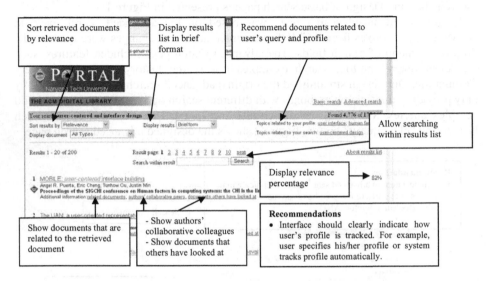

Fig. 3. Features and Recommendations for Results List Page (Brief Format)

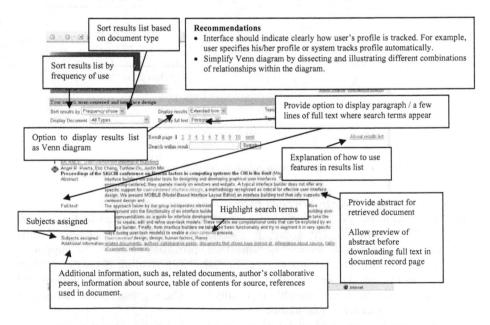

Fig. 4. Features and Recommendations for Result List Page (Extended Format)

The extended format results list page included all groups of important features elicited in the earlier study [7]. This page provided features that helped users evaluated appropriate contents and document type for tasks. Examples of features were: 1) provided abstract for each document; 2) displayed paragraph/few lines of full text where search terms appeared; and 3) categorized documents by document type. Different ways of presenting retrieved documents were also designed. This included: 1) sorted documents retrieved by frequency of use and 2) presented results list in Venn diagram format based on query issued. Due to the different ways of presenting results list, an "about results list" feature was designed to provide explanation of how to use features in this page. This page also included additional information to support document evaluation, such as: 1) provided general information about document source; 2) provided document source's table of contents; and 3) provided subject categories. The designed extended format results list page is shown in Figure 4.

Our design enhanced ACMDL by providing two levels of SR support through the results list page in brief and extended formats. New features implemented were: 1) providing different ways of pointing users to other documents; 2) providing various ways of presenting results list; 3) providing additional information about the document to support evaluation; and 4) providing different ways of showing contents either through an abstract or paragraph of full text where query terms appeared.

Design of Document Record Page in Brief and Extended Format
Our earlier study elicited three groups of SR features for the document record page [7]. These groups focused on: 1) allowing users to seek others' help in evaluating documents; 2) providing features that supported access and management of full text; and 3) highlighting portions in full text plus pointing users to other documents. When designing the page, these groups were considered in decreasing order of importance.

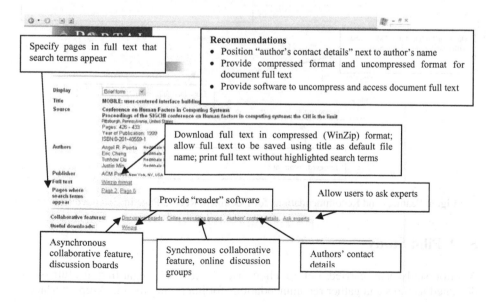

Fig. 5. Features and Recommendations for Document Record Page in Brief Format

Users in the earlier study rated importance of features based on an understanding that this page included detailed information about the document, thus, the document record page in brief format incorporated features from groups 1 and 2 plus details about documents, such as, title, author, publisher, source, etc.. Figure 5 shows the mockup of document record page in brief format.

The document record page in extended format was designed by implementing all groups of features elicited for document record page in our earlier study [7]. This page had all features designed in the brief format plus three extra features. These features were: 1) highlighted search terms in html format full text; 2) provided links to full text of documents referenced in the current document; 3) provided full text in PDF format. The document record page (extended format) is shown in Figure 6.

The improvement done to ACMDL was to provide two versions of the document record page depending on the amount of information users needed to support their subjective evaluations of documents. Our design of the document record page valued-added ACMDL by: 1) providing different kinds of collaborative features for users to contact others and authors; 2) facilitating access by providing full text in compressed / uncompressed format; 3) providing "reader" software to decompress files; and 4) linking users to pages in full text where search terms appeared. Moreover, the document record page (extended format) included a feature that highlighted search terms in full text. This feature was unavailable in the original ACMDL's interface.

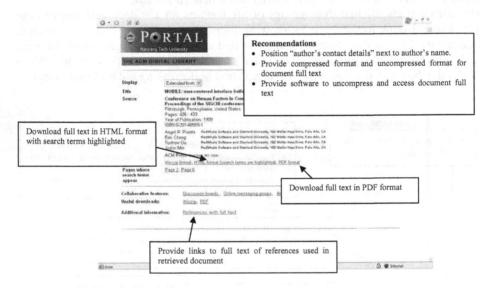

Fig. 6. Features and Recommendations for Document Record Page in Extended Format

5 A Pilot Study

A pilot study was carried out to elicit users' feedback regarding usefulness of designed features and gather recommendations for improving the mock-up interface.

Selected Groups: Profiles of Subjects
Two experts and novices were respectively selected to participate in the study. All
four subjects were postgraduate students. Subjects were considered experts based on
whether they were doing research on interface design.

Methodology
The study consisted of two parts. In the first part, subjects completed three tasks using
the mock-up IR interface. The three tasks were: 1) finding a particular document in
the results list page; 2) finding an expert for a particular document and 3)
downloading the full text of a particular document. This was done to expose subjects
to how the interface worked. In the second part, a demonstration of each feature was
shown. Next, subjects indicated in a handout the extent of usefulness for each feature
using a five point scale (very useful, useful, neutral, not useful, and not useful at all).
Subjects also came together to discuss comments on how features could be improved.

6 Findings

Here, we discuss how subjects rated the usefulness of features designed in the search
page, results list page and document record page in comparison with important features
elicited in the earlier study. We will also highlight subjects' recommendations for
improving the interface. To facilitate discussion, expert subjects are referred as subjects
1 and 2 while novice subjects are labeled as subjects 3 and 4.

6.1 Findings for Basic and Advanced Search Pages

Subjects indicated that majority of features designed were very useful or useful.
Thus, findings elicited here were in line with important features highlighted in our
earlier study. Subjects also provided feedback on how the design of some SR features
could be improved. For example, subject 2 felt that the "clear query" button might not
facilitate query formulation in the basic and advanced search pages. This was because
users might not want to clear the entire query or they could easily "clear" a query by
using the "backspace" key on the keyboard. However, this feedback was not used to
refine the mock-up as the other subjects did not mention this problem.

Subjects commented that although it was useful to treat queries as a phrase if no
Boolean operators were specified, this feature might be problematic when users
specified two query keywords that were not meaningful when combined as a phrase.
Thus, no documents might be retrieved. This feature could also be tricky when users
specified two query phrases. The interface then had to consider if it should combine
the phrases using Boolean operator, AND, or treat the phrases as one phrase. Hence,
to reduce the negative aspects of this feature, the recommendation was for the basic
search page to include a note which advised users to look at search examples and
change the query accordingly if they did not want search terms to be treated as a
phrase when no Boolean operators were specified.

Subject 2 also commented that it would be good to indicate how users' queries in
the different search boxes might be combined when they executed queries in the
advanced search page. The recommendation here was to include a note in the
advanced search page to indicate that queries in the different search boxes would be
combined using Boolean operator, AND. Respective recommendations for basic and
advanced search pages are shown in Figures 1 and 2.

6.2   Findings for Results List Page in Brief and Extended Format

Similarly, subjects' feedback on usefulness of designed features was in line with important features elicited in the earlier study.

Although recommendations of documents based on users' profiles was indicated as an important feature in our earlier study, subject 2 indicated limitations regarding the design of this feature in the mock-up. Specifically, subject 2 highlighted that this feature designed in the results list page for both formats had to clearly state how it tracked users' profiles to make document recommendations. For example, system could track users' profiles automatically or recommendations could be based on a user specified profile.

Subject 2 indicated that the features designed for results list page (extended format) such as: 1) sorting retrieved documents by frequency of use and 2) showing a paragraph in which search terms appeared could be enhanced. This was because it was difficult to measure frequency of use as frequency of documents being accessed might not imply relevance. However, since subject 2 was the only person who bought up this point, no further recommendations were suggested. Moreover, subject 2 also mentioned that showing all paragraphs of full text where search terms appeared could be more useful than showing just one paragraph. However, this recommendation might not be appropriate as it could cause the interface to be cluttered.

All subjects mentioned that the attempt to represent results list in a Venn diagram was interesting. However, they commented that this representation might be confusing when there were more than three query terms. Hence, the recommendation for results list page in extended format was to simplify the Venn diagram into individual parts and show the different combinations of relationships within the diagram. Recommendations for results list page in brief and extended format are shown in Figures 4 and 5 respectively.

6.3   Findings for Document Record Page in Brief and Extended Format

Subjects indicated that important features elicited from our earlier study that were implemented in the document record page for brief and extended formats were useful. However, there was room for improvement based on subjects' remarks for refining the design of some features.

All subjects suggested that the feature, "authors' contact details" should be placed next to the each authors' name rather than at the bottom of the page so that the overall design becomes more integrated. Subjects 1 and 3 indicated that the document record pages should not only specify the full text's compressed format but it should also indicate the document format when the file had been uncompressed. Moreover, "reader" software for uncompressing and accessing full text should be available.

7   Discussion

Our mock-up interface was designed based on groups of important features elicited from an earlier, quantitative study. Hence, it was expected that all features designed should be useful to subjects in our current study. However, subjects indicated that majority of features designed were useful but some features needed further improvement. This could be due to two reasons: 1) users in the earlier quantitative study rated importance of SR features based on their perceptions without actually looking at how features were designed; and 2) features in the mock-up were useful but due to the way it was designed, the feature could not reach its maximum potential. Hence, based on subjects' comments and eliciting feedback from more subjects, the mock-up could be refined so all features implemented were useful for SR.

Our methodology asked subjects to discuss and agree on different recommend-dations to improve the design of SR features. However, it was noted that novice subjects were concerned with the functionality and how they could use SR features effectively to help them evaluate relevant documents. Expert subjects, in contrast, were concerned with how features were designed so that users could easily understand its functionality and use it for their needs.

Although our work described here employed user-centered methods to guide the design of a mock-up interface, techniques used were different from those in [5; 8]. In our context, a factor analytic approach was employed to understand users' perceptions of importance of SR features. Next, important features elicited were designed to enhance ACMDL's support for SR. Then a pilot study was conducted to gather users' feedback on usefulness of designed features and comments to improve the interface.

Our work also differed from those investigating user-centered criteria for relevance judgments, such as, [1] and [9]. Our approach here focused on usefulness of features in helping users evaluate the subjective relevance of documents rather than investigate the criteria used to make relevance judgments of documents.

8 Conclusion and On-Going Work

In this paper, we have shown how important SR features elicited using a factor analytic approach in an earlier study was designed in an IR interface. These important features were designed in a mock-up based on ACMDL's interface so as to enhance ACMDL's support for SR. A pilot study was conducted to understand usefulness of designed features and comments were elicited to improve the interface.

Our approach described here has contributions to research. Our work has shown how important features elicited using factor analysis could inform the design of an IR interface supporting SR. Moreover, to ensure that important features designed were useful in helping users evaluate the subjective relevance of documents, a pilot study was conducted. The study gathered feedback to refine the interface's support for SR.

Findings presented here are preliminary and part of on-going research. Future work could focus on conducting evaluations with more users to elicit comprehensive feedback about features designed in the interface. Moreover, elicited feedback could be implemented to further enhance the interface's support for SR.

References

1. Barry, C. L. (1994). User-defined relevance criteria: an exploratory study. *Journal of the American Society for Information Science, 45* (3), 149-159.
2. Belkin, N. J., Oddy, R. N., and Brooks, H.(1982). ASK for information retrieval: Part I. background and theory. *The Journal of Documentation, 38* (2), 61-71.
3. Cosijin, E., and Ingwersen, P. (2000). Dimensions of relevance. *Information Processing and Management 63,*533-550.

4. Borlund, P. and Ingwersen, P. (1998). Measures for relative relevance and ranked half-life: Performance indicators for interactive IR. *Proceedings of the 21st Annual International ACM SIGIR Conference on Research and Development in Information Retrieval,* ACM Press, 324-331.
5. Druin, A. et al. (2001). Designing a digital library for young children: An intergenerational partnership. *Proceedings of the 1st ACM/IEEE-CS Joint Conference on Digital Libraries,* ACM Press, 398-401.
6. Ingwersen, P. and Borlund, P. (1996). Information transfer viewed as interactive cognitive processes. In Ingwersen, P. and Pors, N. O. (Eds.). *Information Science: Integration in Perspective.* Royal School of Librarianship, Denmark, 219-232.
7. Lee, S. -S., Theng, Y.-L., Goh, H.-L. D., and Foo, S. -B. S. (2006). An exploratory factor analytic approach to understand design features for academic learning environments. *Accepted for publication in ECDL 2006.*
8. Meyyapan, N., Chowdhury, G. G. and Foo, S. (2001). Use of a digital work environment prototype to create a user-centered university library. *Journal of Information Science, 27* (4), 249-264.
9. Mizzaro, S. (1998). How many relevances in information retrieval?. *Interacting with Computers, 10,* 303-320.
10. Shneiderman, B. (1998). *Designing the user interface: Strategies for effective human-computer interaction.* USA: Addison Wesley Longman, Inc..
11. Tang, R. and Soloman, P. (1998). Toward an understanding of the dynamics of relevance judgment: An analysis of one person's search behavior. *Information Process and Management 34,* 237-256.

The Effect of Lexical Relationships on the Quality of Query Clusters

Chandrani Sinha Ray, Dion Hoe-Lian Goh, and Schubert Foo

Division of Information Studies, School of Communication and Information
Nanyang Technological University, Singapore 637718
{rayc0001, ashlgoh, assfoo}@ntu.edu.sg

Abstract. Query clustering helps users frame an optimum query to obtain relevant documents. The content-based approach to query clustering has been criticized since queries are usually very short and consist of a wide variety of keywords, making this method ineffective in finding clusters. Clustering based on similar search results URLs has also performed inadequately due to the large number of distinct URLs. Our previous work has demonstrated that a hybrid approach combining the two is effective in generating good clusters. This study aims to extend our work by using lexical knowledge from WordNet to examine the effect on the quality of query clusters. Our results show that surprisingly, the use of lexical knowledge does not produce any significant improvement in quality, thus demonstrating the robustness of the hybrid clustering approach.

Keywords: Query Clustering, WordNet, Collaborative Querying.

1 Introduction

Collaborative querying is a tool for increasing the relevance of search results. It borrows from research in information seeking behavior, demonstrating that interaction and collaboration with others is an important part of the information seeking process [10]. The technique typically uses a history of past search experiences to enhance the current search [5]. Query clustering is often employed (e.g. [5], [16]) in collaborative querying, which mines the information contained in query logs to discover queries that are similar to other queries based on various criteria.

Query clustering is different from document clustering where a document is represented by a relatively large number of terms. In contrast, queries are usually short and ambiguous [1]. Previous work has revealed that the average length of queries submitted to Web search engines is usually 2 to 3 words [9]. Hence, it is often difficult to judge the specific information need or semantics of the query terms. For example, a user who types in "amazon" as a query may be looking for Amazon.com, the online bookstore or for information on the Amazon River. Further, people use a great variety of words to refer to the same thing [7].

Methods used for clustering queries can be categorized into content-based, feedback-based and results-based approaches [5]. The feedback-based approach assumes that if users clicked on the same documents for different queries, these

S. Sugimoto et al. (Eds.): ICADL 2006, LNCS 4312, pp. 223–233, 2006.

queries are similar [13]. The results-based approach is based on the principle that if two queries return the same result URLs, they are similar [2, 16]. These two approaches make use of only the results URLs returned by the user's query and have the drawback that they ignore the information contained in the query terms. Moreover, the number of distinct result URLs is very large in a Web search engine which may lead to many similar queries not being grouped due to the lack of common URLs [2]. The content-based approach is based on the principle that if queries share a certain number of common keywords, they can be considered as similar. Its success in document clustering can be attributed to the fact that documents contain larger number of terms and hence, it is easier to find related documents. On the other hand, this approach performs poorly in the case of queries primarily because of short query lengths. This limits its capacity to find similar queries which may express the same information need but have been framed differently using different keywords.

A method for improved text classification that incorporates linguistic knowledge into the content-based approach using hypernyms from WordNet was proposed in [11]. The authors use synsets (groups of synonymous words interchangeable in some context like {mode, style, fashion}) from WordNet to replace nouns and verbs in documents. They were able to achieve a 47% drop in the number of errors as compared to the bag-of-words approach. The best performance was observed for cases where documents were authored by multiple authors employing very different terminologies like Digitrad, a public domain collection of folk song lyrics.

A similarity may be drawn between queries and Digitrad in that users use very different sets of keywords while searching [7]. Hence, it may be hypothesized that incorporating linguistic knowledge into query clustering can improve the quality of query clusters as compared to the content-based approach. This paper thus uses lexical information from WordNet to generate query clusters, and compares its performance against our previous query clustering approaches [5]. The synonymy relations from WordNet are used to replace the query terms with appropriate synsets. A new representation of query vectors in terms of the synsets is used to calculate the similarity between query vectors. These similarity measures are then used to generate query clusters. Finally, the quality of the generated clusters is measured using performance measures such as average cluster size, coverage, precision and recall. These results are then compared against those obtained from other approaches.

2   Related Work

The mining of query logs for the purposes of query reformulation has often been used in research on collaborative querying [3, 6]. The information contained have then been used either for query expansion [3] for suggesting terms related to users' queries to help in query reformulation [8] or for suggesting alternate queries to the user [6].

Using text mining techniques, these logs are processed to discover useful and interesting patterns in queries. For example, [16] used the content-based and the feedback-based approach for clustering queries from the Encarta encyclopedia and found that a combination of the two approaches performed better than the individual approaches at low thresholds of similarity. [5] presented a comparison of the content-based and the results-based approaches, and a hybrid approach combining the two.

They concluded that the hybrid approach performed better than the two individual approaches. Besides clustering, [4] used association rule mining to discover similar queries within a query session of a particular user. A problem faced in this approach is the difficulty in determining queries that form part of the same search session. Cui et al. [3] proposed yet another method based on probabilistic correlations for isolating similar queries. The algorithm established correlations between the query terms and the clicked documents. Highly correlated terms were then used for query expansion.

The use of lexical and semantic information to improve retrieval has been researched extensively. In particular, [11] replaced text with hypernym synsets from WordNet for text classification. Their work concluded that this approach shows significant improvement in accuracy where documents were authored by multiple authors employing a wide range of terminologies. Besides text classification, linguistic knowledge has also been applied to query expansion. Voorhees [15] manually selected relevant synsets from WordNet for query expansion. It was found that this technique improved retrieval effectiveness for queries that were short and incompletely formulated but not as effective for well-framed long queries. A different approach for query expansion, using knowledge of the *semantic domain* of the query terms, rather than synonymy and hypernymy relations, was used by [14]. They draw on knowledge about word co-occurrence from the word sense definitions in Wordnet.

Although there is a fair amount of research on the use of semantic knowledge to improve document organization, its application to query clustering is limited. Our study presents an automated method for extracting and applying synsets to cluster queries. Since the query terms themselves are used to pick synsets, this approach also makes use of the important information conveyed by the content of the query.

3 Query Clustering Mechanism

Six months of query logs obtained from the Nanyang Technological University (NTU, Singapore) digital library was used in this work. The queries cover a wide variety of subject areas such as various engineering disciplines, business, arts, etc. The query logs were preprocessed similar to [5] for purposes of comparison. A random sample of 35,000 queries was selected. Query terms were extracted leaving out additional information such as advanced options. Repeated queries and queries containing misspelled terms were discarded. Stop words were also removed.

After preprocessing, approximately 16,000 distinct queries were obtained. Before passing these queries to WordNet, numbers and special characters were eliminated as they would not be mapped to any synsets in WordNet. In addition, proper nouns such as names of countries and authors were themselves treated as WordNet synsets (eg. the query term "japan" was converted to the synset {Japan}). This was necessary as it was observed that proper nouns were either converted into higher level synsets such as {Asian country, Asian nation} for "japan" or they would not be recognized and be eliminated. Proper nouns were detected with the help of WordNet as indicated by the capitalization of the first letter of the word, for example {Asia}. Part-of-speech taggers could not be applied to our queries since they identify proper nouns by the case of the first letter while searchers typically do not pay attention to the case of letters when they type in their queries. Table 1 shows some sample queries.

3.1 Extracting Synonyms from Wordnet

Figure 1 shows an example of an entry in WordNet. The first line of the entry gives the *sense number,* representing the different meanings of a word form. In the next line, the 8-digit number is the unique identifier or *synset offset* of the *synset* {absent, remove}, henceforth referred to as synsetID. The part of the record following the "__" symbol is a *gloss* or definition of the synset followed by some examples of usage.

Sense 1
{00409402} absent, remove -- (go away or leave; "He absented himself")

Fig. 1. An example of an entry in WordNet

Table 1. Algorithm for extracting synsets from Wordnet

```
1.    read q_t;
2.    for each q_t ∈ Q
3.        word = dictionary.lookupIndexWord(POS.NOUN,q_t);
4.        if (word != null)
5.            getSynset(q_t);
6.        word = dictionary.lookupIndexWord(POS.VERB,q_t);
7.        if (word != null)
8.            getSynset(q_t);
9.        word = dictionary.lookupIndexWord(POS.ADJECTIVE,
          q_t);
10.           if (word != null)
11.               while (satellite synsets exist)
12.                   write synID, s;
13.    function getSynset(q_t)
14.        get n;
15.        for (i=1; i<= n ; i++)
16.            getHypernymTree for sense i up to level 1;
17.        write synID, s;

Key: Q = query; q_t = query term; synID = synsetID; s =
synset; n = no. of senses
```

The JWNL API to WordNet (http://sourceforge.net/projects/jwordnet) was implemented in a Java program to look up each query term and prepare a list of all its synonym synsets along with the corresponding synsetID. The algorithm in Table 2 shows our approach. Firstly, query terms are read from a file. For each query term, we first check WordNet to see if a noun form of the word exists (step 3). The lookupIndexWord method searches for string q_t in file POS.NOUN (the part-of-speech noun word list of the dictionary). If the noun form exists, we call the function getSynset() which does the rest of the processing. The same procedure is repeated for the verb form (steps 6-8). For the adjective form (steps 9-12), we look for the satellite synsets of the word, since an adjective does not have a hypernym tree as in the case of nouns and verbs. If satellite synsets exist, the corresponding synsets and synsetIDs are written to the query database.

Within getSynset() in step 13, we first find the number of senses in which the term is defined (step 14) since we need to collect synsets from each. We then iterate over all the senses to extract the first child of the hypernym tree (in the getHypernymTree method) which defines the synonyms of the word and retrieve the corresponding synset and synsetID in steps 15-17. These are written to the query database.

Following this phase, query terms are replaced by synsets, identified by their respective synsetIDs. Thus, while in the original content-based approach, queries themselves form the feature set, in the new representation, each query is represented as a feature vector in terms of a set of synsetIDs. Thus, if we define the set of queries as $Q = \{Q_1, Q_2...Q_i, Q_j.... Q_n\}$, then each query Q_j can be represented as:

$$Q_j = \{<s_1, w_{s1}>, <s_2, w_{s2}>, ...<s_i, w_{Sj}>\} \tag{1}$$

where s_i is a synset in Q_j, and w_{Sj} is the weight of the s_jth synset.

3.2 Weighting of Synsets and Similarity Computation

In our approach, two or more query terms may be mapped onto the same synset. This repetition enforces the context of a term's usage in a query. Consequently, an appropriate weighting scheme can be used to assign greater importance to these repeating synsets over others. Here, the traditional TF-IDF scheme was used for weighting the synsets. TF is the frequency of occurrence of a synset within a query, n is the total number of queries and qf_i is the query frequency.

$$tf_{iQi}' = 1 + \log(tf_{iQi}) \qquad\qquad iqf_i = \log\left(\frac{n}{qf_i}\right) \tag{2}$$

Finally, the synset weight is calculated as:

$$w_{si} = [1 + \log(tf_{iQi}')] * iqf_i \tag{3}$$

It should be noted that no distinction is made between parts of speech and word senses when picking synsets. This is due to the fact that, as mentioned earlier, it is difficult to discern the context of term usage. This is not a matter of concern in for long queries, where many query terms map onto the same synset and increase the weight of the relevant synset. As for short queries, the approach may cause some less relevant queries to be clustered. However, since very short queries are typically ambiguous and may not return a good set of results, it would be good to present the user with a range of query suggestions to help in query reformulation.

Similar to [5], the cosine similarity measure is adopted for measuring similarity. The numerator takes into account the synset vector containing common synsets between two queries Q_i and Q_j. The cosine measure may thus be expressed as follows:

$$Sim\_cosine(Q_i, Q_j) = \frac{\sum_{i=1}^{k} cw_{iQi} \times cw_{iQj}}{\sqrt{\sum_{i=1}^{k} cw_{iQ_i}^2} * \sqrt{\sum_{i=1}^{k} cw_{iQ_j}^2}} \tag{4}$$

where cw_{iQi} refers to the weight of ith common synset of C_{ij} in query Qi and w_{iQi} is the weight of the ith synset in query Qi.

3.3 Formation of Query Clusters and Their Evaluation

The clustering algorithm clusters two queries whenever their similarity value exceeds a certain threshold. A cluster G is thus constructed for each query in the query set Q using the definition in Table 3 [12] where $1 < i < n$, n being the total number of queries. Sim_cosine is the similarity value calculated for a pair of queries (equation 4). Threshold is the minimum value of sim_cosine which determines whether two queries should be clustered. Thus, different thresholds will result in different clusters. We defined four similarity thresholds of 0.25, 0.50, 0.75 and 0.90 to measure the quality of clusters, to facilitate comparison with [5]. The quality of the clusters at these four thresholds is subsequently measured.

Table 2. Clustering Algorithm

for each $Q_i (1 \leq i \leq n)$
    for each $Q_j (1 \leq j \leq n)$
        if *sim_cosine* $(Q_i, Q_j) \geq$ *threshold* then $(Q_i, Q_j) \ \varepsilon \ G(Q_i)$;

Our quality indices measure how close the clusters obtained by the clustering algorithm are to those produced by human clustering. These measures include average cluster size, coverage, precision and recall. The average cluster size measures the ability of the clustering algorithm to provide recommended queries on a given query. It thus quantifies the variety of queries recommended to a user. Coverage is defined as the percentage of queries for which the clustering algorithm is able to provide a cluster. Precision is defined as the ratio of number of similar queries to the total number of queries in a cluster. Recall was difficult to compute as no standard clusters were available in the data set. Hence, we used an alternative measure known as *normalized recall* [16], defined as the ratio of the number of queries judged as correctly clustered in the 100 sample clusters for a particular threshold, to the maximum number of queries judged as correctly clustered in the 100 sample clusters across all thresholds. In order to compute precision and recall, a sample of 100 clusters were manually evaluated by two evaluators. Analysis of variance tests (ANOVA) were also conducted to reveal whether there were significant differences in average cluster size, precision and recall across thresholds. The chi-square test was used to measure the effect of thresholds on coverage, as the values were categorical.

4   Experimental Findings

By varying the similarity thresholds from 0.25 to 0.90, average cluster size decreases from 93.09 to 10.42 (Table 4). A one-way ANOVA yielded a statistically significant variability in average cluster size across the thresholds, $F(3) = 29.03$, $p < .001$. At lower thresholds the clustering algorithm is able to provide a wider variety of queries for a given query. As stated earlier, users tend to use a variety of words to express the same information need. Clustering with content words alone is unable to find queries that use synonyms of the same word, and hence the size of generated clusters is small as in [5]. The larger cluster sizes in our present work can be attributed to enriching the queries with semantic information. In terms of coverage, even at a threshold of 0.90, the algorithm is able to provide clusters for a majority of queries (86.25%). At a threshold of 0.25, nearly all queries (99.56%) belong to one or more clusters, and hence, the probability of a user getting a recommendation for his query is high. A chi-square test for differences in coverage was statistically significant, X^2 (3, N=48 000) = 4810, p < .001. The high coverage indicates that this approach is good at finding related queries for a given query.

The values for precision indicate an increase from 65.40% at a threshold of 0.25 to 93.21% at 0.90, indicating that at this threshold, a good percentage of queries have been correctly clustered. A one-way ANOVA yielded a statistically significant variability in precision across the four thresholds, F (3) = 20.88, p < .001. An examination of our clusters revealed an interesting observation which would also be applicable to the content-based approach. Most queries were very short and contained common and ambiguous words like "basic", "process" and "design". At higher thresholds of similarity, their effect is minimized by the more important concepts in the query like "malay" in the query "basic malay". On the other hand, at lower thresholds, these words act as stopwords and tend to attract many irrelevant queries to the cluster. Figure 2 illustrates this phenomenon where the broad keyword "process" attracts queries which are not appropriate in the light of the core concept of the query, i.e. desalination. This affects the precision at lower thresholds to some extent. However, at the threshold of 0.50, this issue is mitigated as precision is good at 80%, which means that the chances of a user getting a good recommendation are high.

Table 3. Performance Results

Performance Measure	Threshold			
	0.25	0.50	0.75	0.90
Average Cluster Size	93.09	39.67	16.87	10.42
Coverage	0.99	0.98	0.93	0.86
Precision	0.65	0.80	0.86	0.93
Recall	1.00	0.52	0.24	0.16

desalination process	construction process and model
desalination process	thin film process
desalination process	Managing product and process development
desalination process	video process
desalination process	business process analysis

Fig. 2. Incorrectly clustered queries at threshold 0.25

For the *normalized recall* computation [8], the maximum number of correctly clustered queries resulted for threshold 0.25. Hence, recall at this threshold was 100% [5], indicating that all the similar queries had been clustered. As can be seen from the table, there is a sharp drop in recall in the threshold range [0.25, 0.75]. A one-way ANOVA yielded a statistically significant variability in recall across the thresholds, F (3) = 15.80, p < .001. Although the normalized recall is only an approximate measure of recall, it is able to give a fairly good indication of recall. Similar to the traditional recall measure, the normalized recall also varies inversely as precision and gives an estimate of the percentage of similar queries that have been clustered. Recall is good in the threshold range [0.25, 0.50] but suffers at higher thresholds as compared to [5]. The low recall at higher thresholds can be attributed to two reasons:

1. The clustering algorithm was not able to relate acronyms with their corresponding expanded forms (eg "OOP" and "object-oriented programming"). Hence, though queries containing these terms should have been clustered, they were treated as different. Some form of acronym resolution would be required to resolve this.
2. A number of queries contained technical terms which do not occur in the WordNet database (eg. "likert scale", "OCR recognition"). Hence such terms were not provided with synsets, which resulted in inappropriate weighting of such queries. In the query "fabrication of CMOS" for instance, the term CMOS, which is the main subject matter of the query, is eliminated since it is not found in WordNet. Thus, queries such as "CMOS VLSI", and "analogue circuit design cmos" are not clustered. These would otherwise have been clustered using the simple content-based approach. This problem could be resolved by using an appropriate thesaurus.

4.1 Comparison of Results with Other Approaches

The results of our present work and those obtained by [5] are compared in Figure 3. Four clustering approaches have been plotted: Sim_syn (our synonym-based approach); Sim_cos (simple content-based approach); Sim_res (results-based approach); Sim_hyb (hybrid approach combining sim_cos and sim_res) [5].

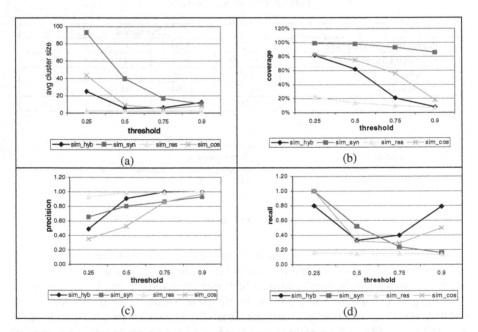

Fig. 3. Comparison of results with [5], (a) avg cluster size, (b) coverage, (c) precision, (d) recall

As can be seen from the figure, average cluster sizes are highest for sim_syn at most thresholds. At thresholds of 0.5 and above, the cluster sizes produced by this algorithm are the best, but at 0.25, the cluster sizes are too large to be of much value.

In terms of coverage, sim_syn performs better with respect to the other approaches consistently, having clustered nearly all queries at the 0.25 threshold. This indicates that sim_syn has a better ability to provide recommendations for a given query. In terms of precision, sim_res gives the best set of results (nearly 100% in the threshold range [0.50, 0.90]). Sim_syn performs only slightly better than sim_cos at the lower thresholds. Sim_hyb performs best with respect to recall at the higher thresholds, where nearly 80% of similar queries have been clustered at threshold 0.90. At the lower thresholds, sim_syn performs best for recall.

Our results indicate that the use of lexical information yields only slight improvement in the quality of query clusters as compared to the content-based approach. Since it uses the content of the query terms to add lexical information, it is affected by many of the inherent weaknesses of the content-based approach. Even though in many cases the synonym based approach is able to find queries which would not otherwise have been clustered by the content-based approach, as shown in Table 5, the ambiguity of query terms also helps to attract irrelevant queries to the cluster. This greatly compromises on the precision of query clusters.

Table 4. Examples of clustered queries

Query	Related Query
the econometrics of financial returns	Macroeconomics Blanchard
welding of ultra high strength steel	Soldering
procurement process	Internet purchase

Recall suffers mainly on account of the large number of technical terms in our queries which were not adequately handled by WordNet. This synonym-based approach might be more useful in the case of longer queries, or where the context of the query is better understood through other means such as by examining results documents. This way, query terms can be properly weighted to reflect their relative importance. This will in turn help to select appropriate synonyms in order to increase the precision. Each of the approaches discussed above perform well with respect to some quality measure, so by combining them in a suitable way, more balanced sets of results can be achieved. This is demonstrated by sim_hybrid, which combines the content-based approach and the results-based approach. It discounts the limitations of each of the approaches while also combining their strengths. Hence, the hybrid approach for query clustering is more robust as it can provide the best quality recommendations for a given query as compared to any other approach.

5 Conclusion

Our results show that by integrating lexical knowledge (using WordNet) in query clustering, coverage increases but precision and recall of clusters is low. While the technique is able to find many queries that are related but are not identified by the content-based approach (e.g. [5]), it does not perform as well as the hybrid approach, combining the content-based and results-based approaches. Thus, the short length of queries may pose a problem to forming good quality query clusters even when lexical information is added. Techniques for better understanding the content of queries are therefore required before lexical information can be applied accurately to queries.

Given our findings, we propose to extend our work, firstly, by applying word sense disambiguation or part-of-speech resolution on the query terms to enhance the precision of query clusters. Statistically determining word co-occurrence information from a large corpus is one possible way of doing so (e.g. [13]). Such co-occurrence patterns in queries can be used to pick out only relevant synsets instead of the complete list. It may also be possible to categorize queries according to genre or subject domain using available taxonomies such as Google Directory. This approach will allow users to choose optimally from their area of interest without forcing them to consider all forms of alternate queries.

Acknowledgments. This project is partially supported by NTU research grant number RG25/05.

References

1. Chien, S. & Immorlica, N. Semantic similarity between search engine queries using temporal correlation. *WWW 2005*, (2005) 2-11.
2. Chuang, S.L. & Chien, L.F. Towards automatic generation of query taxonomy: a hierarchical query clustering approach. *Proceedings of IEEE 2002 International Conference on Data Mining*, (2002).75-82.
3. Cui, H., Wen, J.R., Nie, J.Y. & Ma, W.Y. Probabilistic query expansion using query logs. *Proceedings of the eleventh international conference on World Wide Web*, (2002) 325 – 332.
4. Fonseca, B.M., Golgher, P.B., De Moura, E.S. & Ziviani, N. Using association rules to discover search engines related queries. *First Latin American Web Congress (LA-WEB'03)*, (2003) 66-71.
5. Fu, L., Goh, D.H., Foo, S. & Na, J.C. Collaborative querying through a hybrid query clustering approach. *Digital libraries: Technology and management of indigenous knowledge for global access, ICADL 2003*, (2003) 111-122.
6. Fu, L., Goh, D.H., Foo, S. & Supangat, Y. Collaborative querying for enhanced information retrieval. *European conference on research and advanced technology for digital libraries (ECDL 2004)*, (2004) 378-388.
7. Furnas, G.W., Landauer, T.K. , Gomez, L.M. & Dumais, S.T. The vocabulary problem in human-system communication. *Communications of the ACM, 30*(11), (1987) 964-971.
8. Huang, C.K., Oyang, Y.J. & Chien, L.F. A contextual term suggestion mechanism for interactive search. *Proceedings of 2001 Web Intelligence Conference (WI'2001)*, (2001) pp. 272-281.
9. Jansen, B. J., Spink, A. & Saracevic, T. Real life, real users and real needs: A study and analysis of users queries on the Web. *Information Processing and Management, 36*(2), (2000) 207-227.
10. Lokman, I.M. & Stephanie, W.H. Information–seeking behavior and use of social science faculty studying stateless nations: A case study. *Journal of library and Information Science Research, 23*(1), (2001) 5-25.

11. Matwin, S. & Scott, S. Text classification using wordnet hypernyms. *Proceedings of the COLING/ACL Workshop on Usage of WordNet in Natural Language Processing Systems, COLING-ACL'98*, (1998) 45-52.
12. Raghavan, V.V. & Sever, H. On the reuse of past optimal queries. Proceedings of the Eighteenth International ACM SIGIR Conference on Research and Development in Information Retrieval, (1995) 344-350.
13. Turney, P.D. Word sense disambiguation by web mining for word co-occurrence probabilities. *Proceedings Third International Workshop on the Evaluation of Systems for the Semantic Analysis of Text (SENSEVAL-3)*, (2004) 239-242.
14. Velardi, P. & Navigli, R. An analysis of ontology-based query expansion strategies. *Workshop on Adaptive Text Extraction and Mining at the 14th European Conference on Machine Learning, ECML 2003*, (2003) 210-221.
15. Voorhees, E. Using wordnet to disambiguate word senses for text retrieval. *Proceedings of the 16th annual international ACM SIGIR conference on Research and development in information retrieval*, (1993) 171-180.
16. Wen, J.R., Nie, J.Y. & Zhang, H.J. Query clustering using user logs. *ACM Transactions on Information Systems, 20* (1), (2002) 59-81.

Query Generation Using Semantic Features

Seung-Eun Shin[1] and Young-Hoon Seo[2]

[1] Chungbuk National University BK21 Chungbuk Information Tecnology Center
seshin@nlp.chungbuk.ac.kr
[2] School of Electrical & Computer Engineering, Chungbuk National University,
Cheongju, Chungbuk, 361-763, Korea
yhseo@chungbuk.ac.kr

Abstract. This paper describes a query generation using semantic features to represent the information demand of users for question answering and information retrieval. One of fundamental reasons why unwanted results are included in responses of all information retrieval systems is because queries do not exactly represent the information demand of users. To solve this problem, a query generaton using the semantic feature is intended to extract semantic features which appear commonly in natural language questions of similar type and utilize them for question answering and information retrieval. We extract semantic features from natural language questions using a grammar and generate queries which represent enough information demands of users using semantic features and syntactic structures. For performance improvement of question answering and information retrieval, we introduce a query-document similarity used to rank documents which include generated queries in the high position. We evaluated our mechanism using 100 queries about a person in the web. There was a notable improvement in the precision at N documents when our approach is applied. Especially, we found that an efficient document retrieval is possible by a question analysis based on semantic features on natural language questions which are comparatively short but fully expressing the information demand of users.

Keywords: Question Analysis, Query Generation, Semantic Feature, Question Answering, Information Retrieval.

1 Introduction

IR(Information Retrieval) techniques used to find information fast and exactly from tremendous documents in the web have been rapidly developed with the growth and commercial application of the Internet. However, we can often find that high ranked documents retrieved from a general web search engine may be far from a user intension. Therefore, effective retrieval and rank techniques are needed to provide more relevant documents to users and question answering systems are demanded for user's convenience.

The task of a QA(Question Answering) system is to provide direct, succinct responses to natural language questions posed by a user. Functionally, most question answering systems today can be decomposed into four major components: question

S. Sugimoto et al. (Eds.): ICADL 2006, LNCS 4312, pp. 234–243, 2006.
© Springer-Verlag Berlin Heidelberg 2006

analysis, document retrieval, passage retrieval, and answer extraction [1]. The question analysis component classifies user questions by expected semantic types of answers, e.g., the expected answer type of "Who wrote Hamlet?" is a person. That is only the difference of the question analysis component between QA system and IR system.

Current research trends tend to focus on applying an NLP(Natural Language Processing) technique for an efficient IR [2], [3], [4], [5]. However, such approaches cannot effectively reflect the meaning of sentences by using only index terms because NLP techniques used in almost commercial IR systems index questions and documents by using the morpheme analysis or n-gram method. Retrieval results of all IR systems include non-relevant documents because the index cannot naturally reflect the contents of documents and queries used in IR systems cannot represent enough information demands of users [6]. Most of IR systems extract index terms from the user's question and generate queries by the query expansion for index terms [7], [8], [9]. But the statistical IR model cannot understand a user's intention because it does not consider semantics of index terms. That is an essential reason of the inaccurate IR. Although query expansion can increase recall, it is operationally impractical because the precision of top ranked documents can be lower than IR systems without query expansion [10], [11], [12], [13].

There was research about the generation of lexical paraphrases of queries posed to Internet resource [14]. Such paraphrases are generated using WordNet and part-of-speech information to propose synonyms for the content words in the queries. Statistical information, obtained from a corpus, is then used to rank the paraphrases. However, this approach generates only lexical paraphrases that do not consider the semantics of queries. This is similar to the approach that uses only synonyms for query expansion.

In this paper, we propose a query generation using semantic features which reflect a user's intention in queries. To improve the precision of top ranked documents, we analyze the user's intention from natural language questions and utilize it for the IR. General IR systems cannot rank documents retrieved by the expanded query in high position because they give a lower weight to the expanded query than to the index term of the user's question. It means that the query expansion does not have an influence on information retrieval results. Therefore, we analyze the user's question semantically and extract semantic features from it. And then we generate queries which represent enough information demands of users and suggest the query-document similarity used to rank documents which include generated queries in high position.

2 Query Generation Using Semantic Features

Query generation using semantic features applies NLP techniques on a user's natural language questions and analyzes them semantically to generate queries for an efficient IR. We extract semantic features from a user's natural language questions and generate queries using them. Let's consider following questions, where an answer type is either an author or time.

(Author 1) <u>Who</u> <u>wrote</u> <u>Hamlet</u>?
(Author 2) <u>Who</u> is the <u>author</u> of the <u>book</u>, "<u>The Iron Lady: A Biography of</u>
         <u>Margaret Thatcher</u>"?
(Author 3) <u>Writer</u> of "<u>Romeo and Juliet</u>"?

(Time 1) <u>When</u> was the <u>American Legion</u> <u>founded</u>?
(Time 2) <u>When</u> was the <u>Louvre</u> <u>transformed</u> into a <u>museum</u>?
(Time 3) <u>When</u> was <u>Hong Kong</u> <u>returned</u> to <u>Chinese</u> <u>sovereignty</u>?

Semantic features are common concepts occurred in a similar type of questions such as the title of a book, an interrogative pronoun in case of questions for authors of a book. We can see semantic features to be used commonly to represent the information demand of users in questions (Author 1-3) whose answer type is an author. They are titles of books ("The Iron Lady: A Biography of Margaret Thatcher", "Hamlet", "Romeo and Juliet"), an interrogative pronoun (who), nouns to express the author (author, writer), verbs to express the author (write), and nouns to express the genre (book). Semantic features to be used commonly in questions (Time 1-3) whose answer type is time are objects of an event (American Legion, Louvre, Hong Kong), verbs to represent an event (found, transform, return), an interrogative pronoun (when), and nouns to be related with an event (museum, Chinese, sovereignty).

The statistical IR model extracts index terms (Who, write, Hamlet) from Author 1 and index terms (When, American Legion, found) from Time 1. Then it generates queries using index terms and retrieves relevant documents by the query-document similarity. Therefore, it will retrieve a document which includes simply many index terms than a document which includes sentences such as "Shakespeare is the author of Hamlet" as a more relevant document. Besides, users consider the precision at top documents more important than the total precision because most IR systems offer results over the hundreds of thousands of documents. To solve this problem and improve the users' retrieval satisfaction, we extract semantic features from a user's natural language questions and generate queries by using them for an efficient IR.

< Results of Query Generation using Semantic Features >

(Author 1) Who wrote Hamlet?
  • Answer type : Person
  • Subtype of the answer : Author
  • The title of a book : Hamlet
  • Generated queries :
        write|wrote|to write|… Hamlet
        compose|composed|to compose|… Hamlet
        writer|author of Hamlet

        ……

(Time 1) When was the American Legion founded?
  • Answer type : Time
  • Subtype of the answer : Date of Foundation

- Object of a event : American Legion
- Generated queries :
  American Legion founded|organized|established|... (in)
  American Legion was founded|organized|established|... (in)
  American Legion, which was founded|organized|established|... (in)
  ......

As shown above, we determine answer types and subtypes of answers and extract semantic features from user's questions. Then we generate queries using them and utilize queries for an IR. We can rank a document which include generated queries in the high position and improve the precision of top documents. Other approaches that do not analyze the user's question semantically cannot obtain queries whose syntactic structure is different from the user's question, but our approach can generate queries using the subtype of the answer and semantic features as <Results of Query Generation using Semantic Features>.

2.1 Semantic Feature Extraction

Semantic features are common concepts occurred in similar types of questions such as the title of a book, nationality of an author in case of question for the author of a book. A semantic feature is not simple meaning of a word but the super ordinate concept of a word to be used in sentences and is used to represent the user's intention. We defined subtypes of the answer and semantic features from 643 questions about a person in TREC-8/TREC-9 corpus and Web, and we constructed a semantic feature dictionary of nouns and verbs by tagging semantic features on those questions and expanded it using a synonym dictionary.

Table 1 shows a sample of subtypes of the answer and semantic features. The subtype of the answer is classified by 24 categories such as author, family, prizewinner, politician, developer, inventor, scholar, entertainer, player etc. The subtype "Common" includes semantic features commonly used in all subtypes. The total number of semantic features is 125. The semantic feature dictionary consists of 1761 nouns and 278 verbs.

Table 1. The sample of subtypes of the answer and semantic features

Subtype of the answer	Semantic Features
Common	Nationality, Time, Sex, Person, ...
Author	Title, Pen_Name, Author_Noun, Author_Verb, ...
Family	Relationship, Standard_Person, Relationship_Info, ...
Prizewinner	Prize, Prize_Noun, Prize_Verb, Ceremony/Place, ...
Politician	Position, Event, Organization, Election_Noun, ...

We designed a grammar for semantic feature extraction in order to determine the subtype of answers and extract semantic features from a user's questions. Such a grammar is represented as semantic features and grammatical morphemes in order to consider semantic and syntactic structure of the user's questions. Fig. 1 shows the BNF notation of the semantic feature extraction grammar and characteristics of

Korean considered in our discussion. The semantic feature extraction grammar consists of lists of <word information> and <word information> consists of semantic features and grammatical morphemes according to the subtype of the answer.

<Subtype of the Answer> ::= <Word List>
<Word List> ::= <Word Information> | <Word List><Word Information>
<Word Information> ::= '(' <Semantic Feature> ')' |
                              '(' <Semantic Feature> <Grammatical Morpheme> ')'
<Semantic Feature> ::= '@Who'|'@Person'|'@Author_N'|'@Author_V'|'@Genre'|
                              '@Family'|'#Standard_Person'|'#Book'|...
<Grammatical Morpheme> ::= 'jc'|'jx'|'jm'|'etm'|'co'|'ef'|'oj'|'co+etm'

jc : case particle	co : copula
jx : auxiliary particle	etm : adnominal transition ending
jm : adnominal case particle	ef : sentence ending
oj : objective case particle	

'@' is a property symbol whose semantic feature is found in semantic feature dictionary.
'#' is a property symbol whose semantic feature is extracted from the user's question.

Fig. 1. BNF notation for the semantic feature extraction grammar

- Example of the semantic feature extraction grammar for the author
  ......
  4. (#Book jc) (@Author_V etm) (@Person|@Author_N jx?) (@Who)?
  5. (#Book jm) (@Author_N jx?) (@Who)?
  ......

The above example is a semantic feature extraction grammar for 'author' that is represented as an extended BNF. The following example shows results of the semantic feature extraction using the grammar.

< Results of the semantic feature extraction >

(Question 1) Hamlet-eul jeo-sul-han sa-ram-eun nu-gu-in-ga? (Korean)
              (Who wrote Hamlet?)
- Applied grammar :
    (#Book jc) (@Author_V etm) (@Person|@Author_N jx?) (@Who)?
- Answer type : Person
- Subtype of the answer : Author
- The title of a book : Hamlet

(Question 2) Hamlet-ui jeo-ja-neun? (Korean)
              (Author of Hamlet?)
- Applied grammar : (#Book jm) (@Author_N jx?) (@Who)?
- Answer type : Person
- Subtype of the answer : Author
- The title of a book : Hamlet

As noted, we can determine subtypes of answers and extract semantic features from the user's question. They are used to generate queries for an efficient IR. Our approach can analyze user's questions equally whose syntactic structure is different as Question 1 and Question 2 and we can determine the subtype of the answer("Author") and extract semantic feature(Title: "Hamlet") from them.

If there is not the semantic feature extraction grammar to be applied to a user's questions, we extract semantic features from the user's questions by the syntactic structure. We classified questions whose answer type is a person into the question which includes a verb and the question which doesn't include a verb. The question which includes a verb consists of Event_V (verb to represent an event), Person (noun to represent a person), Property_N (noun to represent the property of a person such as doctor, author, and so on), and Who (interrogative). The question which does not include a verb consists of Property_N, NP (noun phrase), and Who. Therefore, we designed the semantic feature extraction grammar according to the syntactic structure of Korean natural language questions as follow.

- Semantic Feature Extraction Grammar for the question which includes a verb
    1. (NP jc) (#Event_V etm) (@Person|@Property_N) (@Who)?
    2. (NP jx) (@Who) (#Event_V ef)
    3. (@Who) (NP jc) (#Event_V ef)

- Semantic Feature Extraction Grammar for the question which does not include a verb
    1. (NP jm) (@Property_N) (@Who)?
    2. (NP jc) (@Property_N) (@Who)?
    3. (@Property_N) (@Who)?

Although we cannot determine the subtype of the answer, we can extract semantic features from a user's question which has not the semantic feature extraction grammar to be applied as below.

< Results of the semantic feature extraction >

(Question 3) Nam-keuk-e do-chak-han choi-cho-ui sa-ram-eun? (Korean)
             (Who arrived first at the South Pole?)
- Applied grammar :
    (NP jc) (#Event_V etm) (@Person|@Property_N) (@Who)?
- Answer type : Person
- Clue adverb : choi-cho(first)
- Event_V : do-chak-ha(arrive)
- NP : Nam-keuk(the South Pole)

2.2 Query Generation

We designed query generation rules in order to generate queries for an efficient IR, and it is made of semantic features and grammatical morphemes. The query generation rules have syntactic structures used to represent an answer. We can generate queries using the query generation rules, semantic features, semantic feature dictionary, and synonym dictionary. The rule, <Query generation rules for an author>, is an example of query generation rules for an author.

< Query generation rules for an author >

1. (Book oj) (Author_V)
2. (Book jm) (Author_N)
3. (Book_Info jc) (About) (Genre oj) (Author_V)
4. (Book co+etm) (Genre oj) (Author_V)
5. (Book co+etm) (Genre jm) (Author_N)

We can generate queries using query generation rules and results of the semantic feature extraction of (Question 1) and (Question 2) as below.

< Results of the query generation >

- Query generation rule 1 : (Book oj) (Author_V)
  - Book(The title of a book) : Hamlet
  - Author_V : jeo-sul-ha, jeo-jak-ha, ..., sseu
  - Generated queries :
    Hamlet-eul jeo-sul-haljeo-jak-hal......lsseu
    (writelwrotel......lto compose Hamlet)

- Query generation rule 2 : (Book jm) (Author_N)
  - Book(The title of a book) : Hamlet
  - Author_N : jeo-ja, jak-ga, ..., geul-sseun-i
  - Generated queries :
    Hamlet-ui jeo-jaljak-gal......lgeul-sseun-i
    (writerlauthor of Hamlet)

Our approach can generate same queries from questions (Question 1 and Question 2) whose syntactic structures are different. We can generate queries such as 'write Hamlet', 'wrote Hamlet', 'to write Hamlet', 'author of Hamlet', 'writer of Hamlet' from the subtype of the answer 'Author' and the title of a book 'Hamlet' in the query generation. We use generated queries to improve the precision of top documents at IR systems. We calculate the query-document similarity by using formula (1) to rank a document which includes generated queries in the high position.

$$\text{if } \vec{d_i} \cdot \vec{q}_{ge} \neq 0 \text{ then } sim(d_i, q_u) = \vec{d_i} \cdot \vec{q}_{ge}$$

$$\text{else } sim(d_i, q_u) = \frac{\vec{d_i} \cdot \vec{q}_u}{|\vec{d_i}| \, \|\vec{q}_u|}$$

(1)

d_i : document, q_u : user's question, $\vec{d_i}$: document vector

$\vec{q}_{ge}$: generated query vector, $\vec{q}_u$: query vector by query expansion

Formula (1) is a transformation of the cosine coefficient to determine query-document similarity in the vector model. We can rank documents by formula (1) because queries are generated by semantic features and syntactic structures which are used to represent an answer. We can increase the precision at N documents by ranking documents which include an expanded query in the high position.

3 Experimental Results

We randomly selected 100 questions as a test set from natural language questions whose answer type is a person. They were questions which were used actually for IR in the Web. We measured the precision at N documents. In our experiments, we used Google and Yahoo as the IR systems and used only top 30 results of such systems for the precision at N documents.

Table 2 shows the IR result of Google and Yahoo for the test set and Table 3 shows the precision at N documents.

Table 2. The result of Google and Yahoo for the test set

	Number of Questions	Number of Retrieved Documents	Number of Relevant Documents	Macro Averaging Precision	Micro Averaging Precision
Google	100	1,896	904	0.5023	0.4768
Yahoo	100	2,281	1067	0.4604	0.4678

Table 3. Precision at N documents

	Micro Averaging Precision			
N	Google	Google+ Our approach	Yahoo	Yahoo+ Our approach
At 3 docs	0.5839	0.8029(+0.2190)	0.5804	0.8042(+0.2238)
At 5 docs	0.5853	0.7696(+0.1843)	0.5570	0.7426(+0.1856)
At 10 docs	0.5479	0.6462(+0.0983)	0.5106	0.6038(+0.0932)
At 15 docs	0.5229	0.5908(+0.0679)	0.4776	0.5412(+0.0636)
At 20 docs	0.4881	0.5410(+0.0529)	0.4576	0.5061(+0.0485)

Precision at N documents: The percentage of documents retrieved in the top N that is relevant. If the number of documents retrieved is fewer than N, then all missing documents are assumed to be non-relevant. Precision considers each retrieved relevant document to be equally important, no matter what is retrieved for a query with 500 relevant documents or a query with two relevant documents.

In case that the suggested query generation is applied to Google and Yahoo, the test of precision at N documents was improved by +0.2214(N=3), +0.1850(N=5) and +0.0958 (N=10). If our approach is applied to more documents, the precision at N documents can be improved more than that of table 3. Especially, the improvement of precision at N documents means that performance of information retrieval systems and users' retrieval satisfaction level can be highly improved. In addition, we found that it is possible to make information retrieval more efficient by analyzing questions based on semantic features of natural language questions which are comparatively short but fully expressing a user's intentions.

4   Conclusion and Future Work

In this paper, we proposed query generation using semantic features for an efficient IR. Semantic features are common concepts occurred in questions whose answer type is same. We defined subtypes of answers and semantic features from questions whose answer type is a person, and we constructed the semantic feature dictionary for nouns and verbs using those questions and synonym dictionary. We analyzed the user's questions semantically, determined the subtype of the answer, and extracted semantic features. And then we generated queries which represent enough the information demands of users using them and ranked documents by our query-document similarity. We could increase the precision at N documents by ranking documents which include generated queries in the high position.

In case the suggested approach is applied to Google and Yahoo, our experiments showed that our approach results in a notable improvement (+0.2214, N=3) in the precision at N documents. It means that our approach can be used for an efficient IR. Especially, the improvement of precision at N documents means that performance of information retrieval systems and users' retrieval satisfaction level can be highly improved.

Our approach is language independent except for semantic feature extraction grammars and query generation rules. They include characteristics of the language such as syntactic structures and grammatical morphemes.

As our future work, we consider to expand the semantic feature extraction grammar and the query generation rules for various users' questions. Also, we have a plan to apply our approach to other questions besides questions whose answer type is a person. We can expect a performance improvement though only the semantic feature extraction grammar and the query generation rules for question types which are used often are expanded.

Acknowledgments. This research was supported by the MIC(Ministry of Information and Communication), Korea, under the ITRC(Information Technology Research Center) support program supervised by the IITA(Institute of Information Technology Assessment).

References

1. Matthew W. Bilotti, Boris Katz, and Jimmy Lin: What Works Better for Question Answering: Stemming or Morphological Query Expansion? IR4QA: Information Retrieval for Question Answering, A SIGIR 2004 Workshop, (2004)
2. A.T. Arampatzis, T. Tsoris, C.H.A. Koster and Th.P. van der Weide: Phrase-based Information Retrieval. Journal of Information Processing & Management, 34(6), (1998) 693–707
3. Boris V. Dobrow, N.V. Loukachevitch and T.N. Yudina: Conceptual Indexing Using thematic Representation of Texts. TREC-6, (1997)
4. Jose Perez-Carballo and Tomek Strzalkowski: Natural language information retrieval: progress report. Journal of Information Processing & Management, 36(1), (2000) 155–178
5. C. Zhai: Fast Statistical Parsing of Noun Phrases for Document Indexing. In Proceedings of the Fifth Conference of Applied Natural Language Processing, (1997)
6. S. H. Myaeng: Current Status and New Directions of Information Retrieval Technique. Communications of the Korea Information Science Society, 24(4), (2004) 6–14
7. Salton, G., E. Fox, and H. Wu: Extended boolean information retrieval. Communication of the ACM, 26(11), (1983) 1022–1036
8. Salton, G.: Automatic Text Processing. Addison-Wesley, (1989)
9. Maron, M. E. and J. L. Kuhns: On relevance, probabilistic indexing and information retrieval. Journal of the ACM, (1960) 216–244
10. Voorhees, E.: Query Expansion using Lexical Semantic Relation. In Proceedings of the 17th ACM-SIGIR Conference, (1994) 61–69
11. Larry Fitzpatrick and Mei Dent: Automatic Feedback Using Past Queries: Social Searching?. In Proc. 20'th ACM SIGIR International Conference on Research and Development in Information Retrieval, (1997) 306–313
12. Mandela, R., T. Tokunage and H. Tanaka: Combining Multiple Evidence from Different Types of Thesaurus for Query Expansion. In Proceedings of the 22nd Annual International ACM SIGIR Conference, (1999) 15–19
13. Moldovan, D. and R. Mihalcea: Using WordNet and Lexical Operators to Improve Internet Searches. In Proceedings of IEEE Internet Computing, (2000) 34–43
14. Ingrid Zukerman and Bhavani Raskutti: Lexical Query Paraphrasing for Document Retrieval. The 17th International Conference on Computational Linguistics, COLING 2002 (2002)

Page Sets as Web Search Answers

Takayuki Yumoto and Katsumi Tanaka

Dept. of Social Informatics, Graduate School of Informatics, Kyoto University,
Yoshida Honmachi Sakyo-ku Kyoto 606-8501, Japan
{yumoto, tanaka}@dl.kuis.kyoto-u.ac.jp

Abstract. Conventional Web search engines rank their searched results page by page. That is, conventionally, the information unit for both searching and ranking is a single Web page. There are, however, cases where a set of searched pages shows a better similarity (relevance) to a given (keyword) query than each individually searched page. This is because the information a user wishes to have is sometimes distributed on multiple Web pages. In such cases, the information unit used for ranking should be a set of pages rather than a single page. In this paper, we propose the notion of a "page set ranking", which is to rank each pertinent set of searched Web pages. We describe our new algorithm of the page set ranking to efficiently construct and rank page sets. We present some experimental results and the effectiveness of our approach.

1 Introduction

Conventional search engines can mostly find pertinent search results. However, when the information, that a user wishes to have, is sometimes distributed on multiple pages, no single Web page satisfy the users' demands, and so they can't find pertinent search results.

First example is the case where users wish to have the overview about "Edinburgh". In this case, the users need the page sets that describe as many aspects of Edinburgh such as its history, culture, industry, gourmet, sightseeing, and so on as possible. (We call this type of query "overview query".)

Second example is the case where users wish to know the relationships between "wind power generation" and "nuclear power generation". Some pages may be described from the viewpoint of wind power generation and others from the viewpoint of nuclear power generation. A single page with one viewpoint will not provide enough answers. In this case, the users need page sets consisting of the pages described from different viewpoints. (We call this type of query "comparison query".)

In this paper, we propose a new ranking algorithm, called the "page set ranking", which ranks the sets of the searched Web pages in stead of individual Web pages. We take a vector-space model based approach for the page set ranking. In page set ranking, we can efficiently compute the ranking by using "valuable" page sets. Here, a valuable page set intuitively means a page set whose similarity degree to a query is greater than the similarity degree of any subsets of itself to the query. We show our evaluation results and the effectiveness of our approach.

S. Sugimoto et al. (Eds.): ICADL 2006, LNCS 4312, pp. 244–253, 2006.

2   Related Work

Cutting *et al.* proposed document clustering for efficient browsing [1], and some search engines take this approach. They prepare clusters from search results and display each page[2]. In this approach, the users know which results are similar but do not know how to choose the results when more information is needed.

Conventional Web search engines compute ranking scores for searched pages by the content-analysis approach (computation of page similarity to a query) or the link-analysis approach (such as Google's PageRank[3]). We also use the content-analysis approach like classic information retrieval. We proposed a page pair ranking[4] and now are expanding it to arbitrary page sets. Sun *et al.* also proposed CWS[5] to search two comparative pages described two given keywords respectively and make page pairs from them. In CWS, users should compare two pages to know the differences about two keywords. However, page pair ranking is to search pages in which two given keywords are compared and make page pairs from Web pages described from different viewpoints. Therefore, in page pair ranking, the authors of pages have already compared about two keywords and provided their viewpoint to users, and it is easy to understand the differences for users.

The major differences between these work and other work is that the information unit for ranking is not a single page, but a page set. Extensions of our approach to the link-analysis method remain as future work. Figure 1 shows the relationship between our approach and other research.

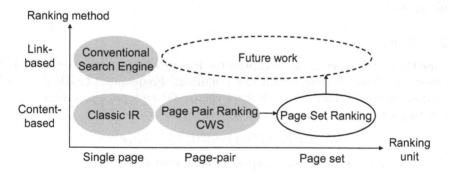

Fig. 1. Relationship between our approach and other research

3   Page Set Ranking

3.1   Basic Concept

The "page set ranking" is a method to construct page sets from individual Web pages, evaluating and ranking them as ranking units instead of page-by-page ranking. Figure 2 shows our concept of page set ranking.

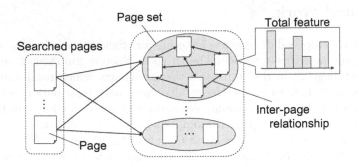

Fig. 2. Image of page set ranking

The page set ranking uses mainly two aspects. They are "total feature" and "inter-page relationship" of the page sets. The total feature aspect corresponds to the information found in a page set. The inter-page relationship aspect corresponds to what pages compose the set. With the page set ranking, different ranking functions and the constraints which a desirable page set should satisfy are implemented for each purpose. They are related to the total feature and inter-page relationship.

The purpose of page set ranking is to find the page sets that have high scores of functions and satisfy the constraints. In general case, we must examine all of the possible page sets, and the time complexity is $O(2^n)$. However, by using the characteristics of the ranking function and constraints, we can reduce the ranking costs.

3.2 Model

We use the vector-space model to express the feature of Web pages, page sets, and queries. The Term Frequency/Inverse Document Frequency (TFIDF)[6] word weighting method is used for the feature-vector. Given a page p, a term t and a set of pages P, we define the term weight of term t by:

$$w(t, p, P) = tf'(t, p) \cdot idf(t, P) \cdot wq(t, q) \tag{1}$$

tf is the number of times words appear in each document,

$$tf'(t, p) = \begin{cases} \log(tf(t, p)) + 1 & \text{(if } tf(t, p) \neq 0) \\ 0 & \text{(if otherwise.)} \end{cases} \tag{2}$$

IDF of keyword t is calculated as follows:

$$idf(t, P) = \begin{cases} \log \dfrac{|P|}{df(t, P)} + 1 & \text{(if } df(t, P) \neq 0) \\ 0 & \text{(if otherwise.)} \end{cases} \tag{3}$$

$|P|$ is the number of pages in P, and $df(t, P)$ is the number of pages including term t. $wq(t, q)$ is the weight for the term in the query. Its value is 2 when the query q or its detailing keywords[7] include term t. Otherwise, it is 1.

$s = \{p_1, \cdots, p_n\}$ denotes that page set s consists of pages $p_1, \cdots, p_n$. $p_i \in s$ denotes page p_i is one of the pages which compose page set s. $\{p\}$ is a page set which consists of page p only, and $s \cup \{p\} = \{p_1, \cdots, p_n, p\}$. $s' \subset s$ denotes $p \in s' \Rightarrow p \in s$, where $s \neq s'$.

In the feature-vector of a page set, the TF values are the summation of the TF values of each member of the page set, and the IDF values are calculated from all of the possible page sets. We define the term weight of a page set as follows:

$$w'(t, s, P) = tf'(t, c) \cdot idf(t, 2^P) \cdot wq(t, q) \tag{4}$$

$$tf'(t, s) = \begin{cases} \log(tf(t, s)) + 1 & \text{(if } tf(t, s) \neq 0) \\ 0 & \text{(if otherwise.)} \end{cases}$$

$$tf(t, s) = \sum_{p \in s} tf(t, p),$$

where 2^P is the power set of P.

$$df(t, 2^P) = (2^{|P|} - 1) - (2^{|P| - df(t,P)} - 1) = 2^{|P| - df(t,P)}(2^{df(t,P)} - 1) \tag{5}$$

From equation (5), IDF is calculated and approximated as follows:

$$idf(t, 2^P) = \log \frac{(2^{|P|} - 1)}{2^{|P| - df(t,P)}(2^{df(t,P)} - 1)} + 1$$

$$= \log(1 - 2^{-|P|}) - \log(1 - 2^{-df(t,P)}) + 1 \tag{6}$$

$$\approx 1 - \log(1 - 2^{-df(t,P)}) \tag{7}$$

When $|P|$ is large, we can approximate equation (6) to equation (7).

$|s|$ is the number of pages that compose page set s. The evaluation vector v_q is computed from query q and depends on the purpose of the ranking.

3.3   Evaluation Function

In order to evaluate a given page set s, we prepared the following three evaluation functions:

- *query-set similarity*: $sim(s, q) = \cos(v_s, v_q)$.
- *inter-page similarity*: $ips(s) = \max_{p_i, p_j \in s} (sim(v_{p_i}, v_{p_j}))$
- *inter-page un-similarity*:

$$ipu(s) = \sqrt[m]{\prod_{p_i, p_j \in s} (1 - \cos(v_{p_i}, v_{p_j}))} \quad (m = |s|(|s| - 1)/2)$$

v_s is the feature vector of page set s and v_p is the feature vector of a page p. We adopt a cosine correlation value for the similarity. That is, the similarity for feature vectors v_1 and v_2 is calculated as $\cos(v_1, v_2) = (v_1 \cdot v_2)/(|v_1||v_2|)$.

Query-set similarity indicates how pertinent a page set is for a given query. This corresponds to the total feature previously mentioned. Page sets with higher values are the better page sets. Inter-page similarity indicates how much duplication there is between pages in a page set. This corresponds to the inter-page relationship. Inter-page un-similarity indicates how many differences there are between pages in a page set. This also corresponds to the inter-page relationship.

3.4   Valuable Page Set and Page

A "valuable" page set s is defined as a page set that satisfies the following:

$$\forall s' \subset s, sim(s, q) - sim(s', q) > \theta_{diff} \tag{8}$$

Here, q and θ_{diff} denote a given query and a predefined threshold value, respectively. It is possible that there is a valuable page set that includes another valuable page set s. Valuable page set is pertinent as a ranking target.

We also define a "valuable page" p for a page set s, if p satisfies the following:

$$sim(s \cup \{p\}, q) - max(sim(s, q), sim(\{p\}, q)) > \theta_{diff} \quad (p \notin s) \tag{9}$$

4   Ranking Algorithm

4.1   Basic Algorithm

By being given searched Web pages by a search engine, we gather the set of Web pages and construct and rank page sets made from them. In order to gather a set of Web pages, we use a conventional search engine. The conventional search engine can find the pertinent individual pages. When we construct and rank the page sets, we use the ranking scores under the constraints for the pertinence. A ranking score is used to decide the ranking of page sets. A constraint for pertinence is the constraint which the pertinent page sets should satisfy. The ranking score and constraints for pertinence are different for each purpose. The constraints for pertinence reduce the number of page sets to be constructed. However, the number is still too large to calculate all the ranking scores.

In order to solve this problem, we introduce constraints for the approximation, and we adopt maximal and valuable page set as our ranking target.

A constraint for approximation is the constraint which most of the pertinent page sets satisfy. When the constraints for approximation are used, we can't find some of pertinent page sets but the number of page sets to be constructed is reduced. The constraints for approximation are also different for each purpose.

We define a maximal page set s as a page set that satisfies following condition: $\nexists p \in P$ s.t. $p \notin s$, $s' = s \cup \{p\}$, s' satisfies the constraints for pertinence and the constraints for approximation. (P is a set of searched pages.) When we add the pages to the page sets one by one, maximal page sets can be found by a width-first search. It also reduces the number of the page sets to be constructed.

Our basic algorithm for page set ranking is as follows:

1. Gather $P = \{p_1, p_2, \cdots, p_n\}$ with the search engine using search keywords
2. Compute an evaluation vector v_q from query q
3. $S_1 = \{\{p_1\}, \cdots, \{p_n\}\}, i \leftarrow 1, L \leftarrow \phi$
4. $S_{i+1} \leftarrow \phi$
5. For $s \in S_i$ compute $s' = s \cup \{p\}$ $(p \in P, p \notin s)$
   (a) For all s',
       if s' satisfies the constraints for pertinence and approximation
       then $S_{i+1} \leftarrow S_{i+1} \cup \{s'\}$
   (b) If s is a maximal page set then $L \leftarrow L \cup \{s\}$
6. If $S_{i+1} \neq \phi$ then $i \leftarrow i + 1$, goto 4
   else sort $s \in L$ by the ranking score

S_i is a set of page sets whose number of pages are i. L is a set of candidate page sets.

4.2 Algorithm for Overview Query

Overview query is to get the overview about given keywords. In overview queries, total feature is more important than inter-page relationship. Therefore, we use total feature to calculate ranking score and inter-page relationship to express constraints for pertinence. We adopt query-set similarity as ranking score and make evaluation vector from detailing keywords[7] of a given query. However, if we use the search keywords to calculate the query-set similarity, its term weight is so large that other detailing keywords make very little effect on the query-set similarity. Therefore, we use search keywords only when we gather the web pages, and we use detailing keywords only when we calculate the evaluation vector. In other words, we use the following vector v' instead of the vector $v = (v^{(1)}, v^{(2)}, \cdots, v^{(n)})$.

$$v' = (v'^{(1)}, v'^{(2)}, \cdots, v'^{(n)}) \tag{10}$$

$$v'^{(i)} = \begin{cases} 0 & \text{(if term } t_i \text{ is in the query)} \\ v^{(i)} & \text{(if otherwise.)} \end{cases}$$

Evaluation vector v_q is

$$v_q = (v_q^{(1)}, v_q^{(2)}, \cdots, v_q^{(n)}) \tag{11}$$

$$v_q^{(i)} = \begin{cases} 1 & \text{(if term } t_i \text{ in the detailing keywords of query)} \\ 0 & \text{(if otherwise.)} \end{cases}$$

We adopt the constraint that the inter-page similarity should be lower than threshold θ_{ips} as a constraint for pertinence. Inter-page similarities satisfy the following equation.

$$ips(s) > \theta_{ips} \Rightarrow \forall p, ips(s \cup \{p\}) > \theta_{ips} \tag{12}$$

Therefore, we can reduce the number of page sets to be constructed. We also adopt the constraint that only the valuable pages can be added to page sets as a constraint for approximation.

Thus, we use the following conditions in overview queries:

- ranking score: $\cos(v'_s, v_q)$
- constraint for pertinence: $ips(s) < \theta_{ips}$
- constraint for approximation: all the candidates page sets are calculated to add the valuable page to other candidates under the parameter θ_{diff}

4.3 Algorithm for Comparison Query

Comparison query is to gather Web pages comparing about given keywords from different viewpoints. In comparison queries, users wish to have Web pages that are described from different viewpoints, and inter-page un-similarity is more important than total feature. Therefore, we use inter-page un-similarity to calculate ranking score. However, according to the following equation, inter-page un-similarity of page set s is the maximum where $|s| = 2$.

$$ipu(s) = \sqrt[m]{\prod_{p_i,p_j \in s} (1 - \cos(v_{p_i}, v_{p_j}))} \leq \sqrt[m]{\left(\max_{p_i,p_j \in s} (1 - \cos(v_{p_i}, v_{p_j})) \right)^m}$$

$$= \max_{p_i,p_j \in s} (1 - \cos(v_{p_i}, v_{p_j})) = \max_{p_i,p_j \in s} ipu(\{p_i, p_j\}), \tag{13}$$

where $i < j$. It is not suitable for the purpose of comparison queries. Therefore, we use $(\log |s| + 1)ipu(s)$ as ranking score instead of $ipu(s)$.

We use query-set similarity to express a constraint for pertinence. We adopt the constraint that the query-set similarity should be higher than threshold θ_{qs} as a constraint for pertinence. In the evaluation vector v_q for comparison query, we define the elements corresponding to term t_i in query are 1 and other elements are 0.

Page sets, whose inter-page un-similarities are low, have the low ranking score. Therefore, we add the constraints that inter-page un-similarity should be higher than threshold θ_{ipu} as a constraint for approximation.

Thus, we use the following conditions in overview queries:

- ranking score: $(\log |s| + 1)ipu(s)$
- constraint for pertinence: $sim(s, q) > \theta_{qs}$
- constraint for approximation: $ipu(s) > \theta_{ipu}$

5   Experiments and Discussions

5.1   Environment

In our experiments, we used Google[3] and obtained 50 Web pages for each query. We constructed page sets from them. All the original query terms were in Japanese.

Table 1. Search keywords and detailing keywords

Search keywords	Evaluation keywords
Edinburgh	Scotland, London, castle, Britain, University, Festival, Pub, Bagpipe, ...
dioxin	survey, concentration, pollution, criterion, measurement, soil, poison, ...
avian flu	infection, pathogenicity, case, virus, chicken, wild bird, disinfect, egg, ...

Table 2. Example of overview query

S	P	Page title
1	1	About Edinburgh
	4	Edinburgh City 1
	5	Scotland and Edinburgh
	8	From the site of a Japanese education in the world
2	1	About Edinburgh
	4	Edinburgh City 1
	5	Scotland and Edinburgh
	9	EDINBURGH & KYOTO ART EXCHANGE
3	1	About Edinburgh
	4	Edinburgh City 1
	5	Scotland and Edinburgh
	15	Alumni of Management School of Edinburgh University

S: Ranking of page sets, P: Ranking of pages

5.2 Overview Query

We got the detailing terms using Oyama's algorithm[7], and used them for the evaluation vector. We used the queries and their detailing keywords in Table 1.

Table 2 shows the example of the overview query in the case that query keyword is "Edinburgh".

To evaluate the page sets, we defined the coverage degree as:

$$coverage(s, q) = |kw(s, q)|/|kw(q)| \qquad (14)$$

$|kw(s,q)|$ is the number of keywords that appeared in page set s and detailing keywords of query q. $|kw(q)|$ is the number of detailing keywords of query q. This satisfies $0 \leq coverage(s, q) \leq 1$. Higher coverage is the best.

We used the following parameters, $|s| < 5$, $\theta_{diff} = 0.01$, and $\theta_{ips} = 0.5$.

In order to evaluate our ranking algorithm, we compared (1) the page sets in the top 50 of the ranking calculated by our algorithm, (2) the single pages, and (3) the page sets in the top 50 calculated using the query keywords about (a) the maximum of query-set similarities, (b) the average of coverage, and (c) the average of $|s|$ in the top 50 page sets. We show the results in Table 3. From this table, we can see that the page sets calculated by our algorithm have higher query-set similarities and higher coverage scores than what the single pages have.

This means that the page sets are more pertinent than single pages as search results. We can also find that the page sets calculated by our algorithm have higher coverage scores than scores of the page sets calculated using the query keywords. This means that the query keywords have such a strong effect that the query-set similarities are decided almost by the number of query keywords in the page sets when we use the query keywords in the evaluation vector. Therefore, our algorithm, in which we don't use the query keywords, can find more pertinent page sets.

Table 3. Evaluation of page sets and single pages as search results

Search keyword	Sets (our algorithm)			Pages		Sets (using query keyword)		
	(a)	(b)	(c)	(a)	(b)	(a)	(b)	(c)
Edinburgh	0.406	0.876	3.900	0.387	0.145	0.409	0.275	3.940
dioxin	0.389	0.876	3.975	0.341	0.255	0.393	0.656	2.620
avian flu	0.593	0.869	3.960	0.490	0.250	0.576	0.666	2.820

(a) max of query-set similarity, (b) average of coverage, (c) average of $|s|$

5.3 Comparison Query

We made the comparison queries consisting of two keywords. We used the following parameters, $|s| < 5$, $\theta_{ipu} = 0.5$, and $\theta_{qs} = 0.3$. Table 4 shows the example of comparison query when query keywords are "wind power generation" and "nuclear power generation".

We examined whether the top 50 page sets included both pages, describing from the viewpoint of each keyword. Table 5 shows the precision of the comparison queries in the pages and the page sets. In Table 5, "Pages" and "Sets" labels mean the precision in the case when ranking unit is a single Web page and a page set respectively. (We also regarded the pages which fairly describe about both keywords as correct answers.) "$|s|$" label means the average of the number of pages which the page sets in the top 50 have. In all the cases, the precision of page sets are higher than the precision of pages.

Table 4. Example of comparison query

S	P	Page title
	11	Learning Experience in Ishikawa
1	1	Can nuclear be replaced by new energy?
	16	Energy trend
	35	Mail Magazine (Energy in China)
2	1	Can nuclear be replaced by new energy?
	16	Energy trend
	36	Energy in China
3	1	Can nuclear be replaced by new energy?
	16	Energy trend

S: Ranking of page sets, P: Ranking of pages

Table 5. Evaluation of comparison queries

Query	Pages	Sets	$\|s\|$
wind power generation, nuclear power generation	22%	44%	3.00
sony, apple	50%	88%	3.88
the Republican Party, the Democratic Party	26%	30%	3.10

6 Conclusions

In this paper, we proposed the notion of "page set ranking", which is to rank page sets that consist of searched Web pages as ranking units. We focused on overview query and comparison query. We presented the algorithm for efficiently constructing and ranking the page set, and evaluated our ranking algorithm. We confirmed that there were the page sets that were more pertinent as search results than single Web pages and our algorithm could efficiently find them.

The future works are the development of an effective presentation method for the page set, and extensions of our approach to the link-analysis method.

Acknowledgments

This work was supported in part by MEXT The 21st Century COE (Center of Excellence) Program "Informatics Research Center for Development of Knowledge Society Infrastructure" (Leader: Katsumi Tanaka, 2002-2006), and MEXT Grant for "Development of Fundamental Software Technologies for Digital Archives", Software Technologies for Search and Integration across Heterogeneous-Media Archives (Project Leader: Katsumi Tanaka).

References

1. Cutting, D.R., Pedersen, J.O., Karger, D., Tukey, J.W.: Scatter/gather: A cluster-based approach to browsing large document collections. In: Proceedings of the Fifteenth Annual International ACM SIGIR Conference on Research and Development in Information Retrieval. (1992) 318–329
2. clusty.com. (http://clusty.com/)
3. Google. (http://www.google.com/)
4. Yumoto, T., Tanaka, K.: Finding pertinent page-pairs from web search results. In: Proceedings of The 8th International Conference on Asian Digital Libraries (ICADL2005). (2005) 301–310
5. Sun, J.T., Wang, X., Shen, D., Zeng, H.J., Chen, Z.: CWS: a comparative web search system. In: WWW '06: Proceedings of the 15th international conference on World Wide Web, New York, NY, USA, ACM Press (2006) 467–476
6. Salton, G.: Developments in automatic text retrieval. Science **253** (1991) 974–979
7. Oyama, S., Tanaka, K.: Query modification by discovering topics from web page structures. In: Proceedings of the Sixth Asia Pacific Web Conference (APWEB'04). Volume 3007 of Lecture Notes in Computer Science. (2004) 553–564

Applying FRBR Model as a Conceptual Model in Development of Metadata for Digitized Thai Palm Leaf Manuscripts

Nisachol Chamnongsri[1], Lampang Manmart[1], Vilas Wuwongse[2], and Elin K. Jacob[3]

[1] Information Studies Program, Faculty of Humanities and Information Science,
Khon Kaen University, Thailand
[2] School of Engineering and Technology, Asian Institute of Technology, Thailand
[3] School of Library and Information Science, Indiana University, USA
nisachol@sut.ac.th, lamman@kku.ac.th, vilasw@ait.ac.th,
jacob@indiana.edu

Abstract. This paper outlines the adaptation of IFLA's Functional Requirements for Bibliographic Records (FRBR) for development of a metadata scheme to represent palm leaf manuscripts (PLMs) and facilitate their retrieval in digital collections. The FRBR model uses a structured, four-level hierarchy to represent an intellectual work with multiple titles, editions or formats. Because FRBR focuses on representation of the conceptual work rather than the physical entity, it must be modified for representation of PLMs. In this modified model, the level of *work* applies to the physical PLM rather than its conceptual content; *expression* applies to the languages in which the PLM occurs; *manifestation* applies to the formats in which each expression is available; and *item* applies to individual copies of a single format. The modified model has been used to devise a metadata scheme where each level has its own set of elements.

Keywords: Metadata, FRBR Model, Palm Leaf Manuscript, Digital Collection.

1 Introduction

In the new, knowledge-based world economic system, the production, dissemination and use of knowledge are crucial factors for enhancing economic growth, job creation, competitiveness and welfare [1]. In Thailand, the 9th National Economic and Social Development Plan, 2002-2006, proposes that Thailand will become more competitive through development of innovation by integrating modern science and technology and "local wisdom". This approach will lay the foundation of Thai's intellectual capital that can be used to develop competency and strengthen economic and social foundations for long-term, sustainable growth [2]. For example, the One Tambol One Product (OTOP) projects encourage villagers in each district to create their original products by applying local wisdom or resources and modern technology, thereby giving the old products added value and new marketplace appeal [3].

"Local wisdom", which is being promoted as one of the country's strengths, is a holistic, knowledge-based approach rooted in local circumstances such as the

S. Sugimoto et al. (Eds.): ICADL 2006, LNCS 4312, pp. 254–263, 2006.

experiences and problem-solving skills of Thai ancestors [4] that are recorded in ancient documents. Palm Leaf Manuscripts (PLMs) is an ancient document form that comprises a significant documentary heritage of the Isan people of Northeastern Thailand. These manuscripts contain a vast amount of knowledge that can be classified in eight categories: Buddhism (or Religion), Tradition and Beliefs, Customary Law, Economics, Traditional Medicine, Science, Liberal Arts, and History. 70% of the content recorded in PLMs consists of Buddhist stories and doctrine and 30% records local wisdom in the form of folktales, diaries, poetries, ethics, customary law, rites and rituals [5], [6].

However, the local wisdom recorded in these manuscripts is often difficult to access and use. There are several obstacles to access: PLMs are scattered in many places, such as temples and households in rural areas, making them difficult to collect [7]; they are regarded as holy objects and their owners may not allow access to them; some of the original manuscripts have disappeared or been destroyed [8]; manuscripts that have survived are very fragile and easily damaged [9]; and, perhaps most importantly, the languages in which they are written are either archaic or undergoing shift. Additionally, access to the content of the original manuscripts is problematic because they are written in three archaic orthographies [10], requiring expert translation.

Creation of digital collections of PLMs promises the possibility of dissemination and access to these manuscripts; furthermore, it is another way to preserve the original document. In order to gain more efficiency in using digitized palm leaf manuscript collections, metadata is required. This paper outlines the adaptation of IFLA's Functional Requirements for Bibliographic Records (FRBR) for development of a metadata scheme to provide effective and efficient access to PLMs in digital collections.

2 Information Representation in Digital Libraries

Because it is recognized that knowledge recorded in PLMs can be used to strengthen Thai economic and social foundations, several research and preservation projects are attempting to collect and register PLMs. In order to preserve the original manuscripts, PLMs are microfilmed, transcribed and digitized to make them easier to use. However, access to the knowledge contained in these manuscripts is limited because of the lack of a plan for systematic management that would establish and maintain effective services for users. Additionally, because individual PLMs may be available in both archaic and modern languages as well as in several different formats, an effective system of information representation is important in order to provide for efficient access to and use of PLMs. Such a system would allow users to identify the desired PLM in the most appropriate format. At the same time, a well-structured system of representation would also be helpful in collection management, record updating and maintenance.

In the digital environment, different versions of a single intellectual work can be accessed under different titles and in various formats. To support users in searching for and accessing the content of PLMs and to reduce the cost and time involved in maintaining a digital collection, information retrieval systems need a more effective approach to representation than the traditional flat cataloging system. This new approach to cataloging would support a hierarchical catalog where each level in the hierarchy would inherit information from the preceding level, allowing various versions and formats of the same work to be cataloged more quickly and permitting catalog records to be stored and updated more efficiently [11].

To support this approach to cataloging, the description of each version or format of a work requires an explicit statement of the structural relationships between hierarchical levels as well as clear definition of how each data element in the scheme is linked to the description of a particular work and its available version or formats. Otherwise, digital materials may be unusable because they are not linked correctly to their related bibliographic records [12].

In addition, a digital format may be composed of several components (text, pictures, and etc.) captured in various formats and stored in different places. In order to display information about a PLM (work) on screen in a logical way, structural metadata is required to model the object [13]. Moreover, a representation can be created for any format (item) that someone determines needs metadata access [14]. This addresses a discussion of granularity or the level at which an item is described [12], which is the conceptual key for understanding representation of information about digital objects. Thus, creating successful document representations (metadata) for a digital library requires a useful model to help clarify what the digital library project is trying to do with metadata, what functions are required, how the metadata record should be structured, and what data elements it should contain [15].

3 The FRBR Model

The Functional Requirements for Bibliographic Records (FRBR) model was proposed by the International Federation of Library Associations and Institutions (IFLA) in 1998. FRBR is a conceptual model that defines a structured framework and the relationships between metadata records by focusing on the kinds of resources that a data record describes. In order to solve the problem of searching for intellectual works in a digital library, where one work may have variation in titles, versions and/or formats, FRBR uses a hierarchical structure that establishes relationships between four levels of representation: a work, its expression(s), an expression's manifestation(s), and the individual item(s). This approach ensures that the user will be able to select the most appropriate version or format of the desired work.

The hierarchical model of FRBR was inspired by the entity relationship model for relational databases and by the concept of inheritance, which ensures that the properties (or data elements) described at superordinate levels of representation are inherited by all the subordinate levels nested under them [15]. FRBR lays the foundation for hierarchical catalog records by recognizing the difference between a particular work, several expressions of work, various formats in which an expression exists, and the particular item [11]:

- *Work* represents an intellectual concept of works, identified by titles and realized through its relationship with expression;
- *Expression* represents the various versions or revisions of a work established in its relationship with one or more manifestations;
- *Manifestation* represents the physical embodiment of an expression; and
- *Item* represents the individual unit of a manifestation

The FRBR model uses an entity analysis technique to identify entities and relationships. Analysis begins by isolating key entities to be represented. The attributes associated with each entity are then identified with the emphasis on attributes important in formulating bibliographic searches, interpreting responses to those searches, and navigating the universe of entities described in bibliographic records [16].

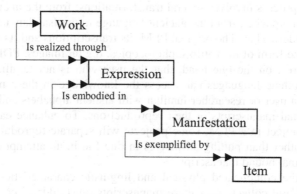

Fig. 1. FRBR model: primary entities and relationships [16]

The FRBR model assists in identifying and defining relationships between key entities, especially for complicated documents such as film, music or museum material, which may have a range of expressions and formats. It is widely accepted and frequently used in digital library projects as a model for analysis of metadata requirements and the development of metadata schemas [17], [18].

4 The Characteristics of Isan Palm Leaf Manuscripts

Isan PLMs vary in size. A standard palm leaf manuscript is generally 5-6 cm. in width and 50-60 cm. in length with 48 pages (24 leaves written on both sides). PLMs can be as short as 15 cm. or as long as 80 cm. and can vary as to the number of pages (i.e., leaves). The Isan people use the different sizes in different ways: the longer PLM is used as a textbook to recorded Buddhist stories and doctrine [19], while the shorter one is used as a notebook to record local wisdom related to daily life [10]. The languages in which PLMs are written are either local or undergoing shift (Pali, Isan, and Khmer) [8]; and the manuscripts are written in three archaic orthographies (Tham-Isan, Thai Noi, and Khmer) [10], requiring expert translation. Because the length of a PLM is determined by it physical dimensions rather than its content, a single manuscript may record many stories or a single story may require more than one manuscript [20]. Finally, a PLM may have pictures in addition to text.

The only access point to the bound manuscript is its title; but this presents a problem for the user who is not already familiar with both the content of a specific PLM and the archaic language in which it is written. Furthermore, access to individual stories is difficult when many stories are recorded in one bound manuscript or when a particular story has different titles in different PLMs. However, because users generally access manuscripts using title or subject, the title (or story) is obviously the most important access point to the knowledge contained in PLMs.

To preserve the knowledge recorded in palm leaf manuscripts and make it accessible to modern users, preservation projects transcribe a PLM in modern Thai alphabet and language and then reproduce the transcription in a variety of formats. The translation process involves several transformations: from the ancient alphabet to the modern Thai alphabet, from the ancient language to the Isan language, and finally from Isan to modern Thai. The original PLM, its transcriptions and its translations are reproduced in the form of microfilms, photocopies, digital images, PDF files, and text files. This ensures, on the one hand, that the user who is not familiar with ancient salphabets or archaic languages can access the knowledge in these manuscripts; on the other hand, a user or researcher familiar with ancient alphabets and languages can access the original manuscripts or their reproductions. To enhance ease of access to each story or subject in a PLM, some projects will separate reproductions or image files by story rather than putting all images in one file in an attempt to maintain the look of the original bound manuscript.

Because of the complicated physical and linguistic characteristics of PLMs, the creation of a digital collection of these manuscripts must address complex issues of description, representation, organization, and use of the knowledge in PLMs. A hierarchical relationship model such as FRBR can help to develop a conceptual framework for metadata that will support access to one work in its various versions and formats; maintain the link between creators or owners; and help to manage the relationship between an original manuscript and the stories it contains.

5 Adapting FRBR to PLMs Metadata Model

When searching for PLMs, users will have many questions: Which PLM recorded the desire knowledge? What is the title of that PLM? Where was it created? Who was the patron who paid for inscription of the PLM? Who currently owns the PLM? Where is it stored? Where was it found? Who is the owner of each version? Is it available only as an original manuscript? Is it available in translation? Who is the translator? Is there a digital format available? How is the digital version accessed?

The hierarchical relationship established by the FRBR model holds potential for development of a metadata scheme that will enable the user to discover, select, locate, and access PLMs in the most appropriate versions and formats. Moreover, this model can be used to develop metadata that will support the collection management, manuscript preservation and use restrictions. However, the concept of work as the top level in the FRBR model is not suitable for representation of PLMs since FRBR focuses on work as a conceptual entity. Because a PLM exists as a physical rather than a conceptual entity, an effective metadata scheme must consider orthographies and languages, the physical and digital formats in which those expressions are available, and the individual copies of a given manifestation.

Accordingly, the revised FRBR model applies the concept of *work* to the physical manuscript, which may contain one or more stories or only a part of a story. The *expression* applies to the alphabets and languages in which PLMs occur: the Khmer language, Pali language, or Isan language in its original archaic alphabet (Khmer, Tham-Isan, or Thai-Noi); the modern Thai alphabet transcription of the PLM's archaic alphabet for users familiar with the original language who can not read the archaic alphabet; and the modern Thai language, using the Thai alphabet, for users who are not familiar with the archaic languages. The *manifestation* addresses the various formats in which each expression is available: the original bound manuscript, microfilm, photocopy, digital image (formatted for archiving and distribution), and text files in both modern Thai and archaic alphabets. The *item* applies to individual copies of a single format.

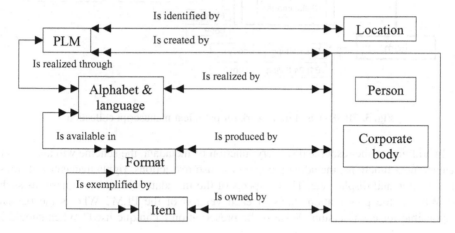

Fig. 2. The Model of relationships between key entities in PLM metadata

In the entity analysis of PLMs, the element *location* was added to the model, because the intellectual concept—that is, the stories recorded in a PLM—may show little variation across PLMs. What does vary, however, is the treatment of the story, which will reflect local wisdom: because the writing style of the PLM's author will reflect the tradition and belief of their communities, each story and therefore each manuscript will be unique even if it shares the same content with other PLMs. Thus, *location* is a key characteristic of the uniqueness of a PLM because it is location that shapes intellectual content.

Each entity (or hierarchical level) in the model was then identified by those characteristics or attributes associated with it which would be important for users in searching, identifying, selecting, accessing, and using PLMs. The establishing of metadata elements is based on the results of analyses of (1) the physical structure and content of palm leaf manuscripts, (2) the user needs and expectations with respect to these manuscripts, and (3) the requirements for managing collections of palm leaf manuscripts. In order to specify the semantic interpretation for each of these attributes, the metadata elements and their possible values across different collections and uses will be defined in an ontology. This will ensure consistent application of the metadata scheme and provide for interoperability across different collections and different retrieval systems.

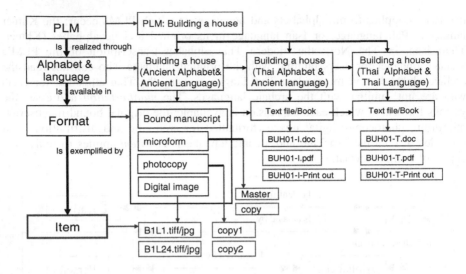

Fig. 3. FRBR- based framework for palm leaf manuscript collection

In addition to the resource discovery function of metadata, the scheme will also cover management functions, including preservation, use restrictions, rights management, files organization and display, etc. These aspects of the metadata will address questions such as: What is the preservation status of each version of the PLM? Who is the person responsible for each version? What is the preservation technique used? When should a

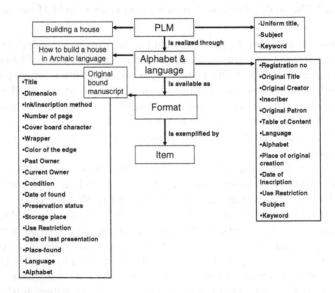

Fig. 4. Attributes of the entity: example

digital version be migrated? Who is allowed to use the PLM and in which version? Who hold the copyright for each version of PLM? How should the digital version be displayed?

The process of designing administrative and structural metadata will require identification of the various functions involved in collection management and use. The FRBR model can be help in analyzing at which level each function applies and the relationship between functions since some functions will not apply at all levels. For example, in the level of expression, the original manuscript will not require structural metadata intended to support digital functions. Thus, the model indicates that structural metadata at each level can be linked across different functions by using the identification number assigned to the unique record.

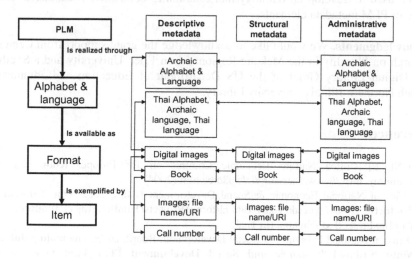

Fig. 5. Functional structure for PLM metadata example

6   Conclusion and Future Work

Development of a metadata scheme for management of palm leaf manuscript collections will not only increase efficiency in discovering, accessing, and using these manuscripts, but will also support preservation of the original manuscripts and the administration of digital versions. The FRBR model offers a conceptual framework for development of a metadata scheme that will support the main functions of PLM management: resource discovery, access and use; record maintenance; digital preservation; and rights management. FRBR's four-level hierarchical model allows the metadata record at each level to represent the data applicable to the various expressions and different formats as well as individual items. Moreover, the FRBR model will be of assistance in defining those metadata elements which are required for each function of the digital collection. The fact that PLMs are physical objects is seemingly at odds with FRBR's notion of *work* as a conceptual entity. However, by reconceptualizing *work* as a representation of the original palm leaf manuscript,

FRBR's hierarchical structure provides an effective framework for the design of a metadata scheme that can support the various functions required for access to and management of resources in PLM collections.

This revised FRBR model is based on a preliminary study of user needs that was conducted in 2005 and included literature review, observation and unstructured interviews with the staff of four palm leaf manuscript preservation projects at four different institutes as well as unstructured interviews with four researchers (anthropologist, linguist, sociologist, local scholar). Following actual data collection with users and administrators of PLM collections, the current model will be revised to reflect specific needs; and to resolve problems of semantics and to support access to PLM collections via the Semantic Web, RDF (Resource Description Framework) will then be used to develop an ontology that establishes controlled vocabularies for the values of PLM metadata elements.

Acknowledgments. We would like to acknowledge the grant support from Center for Research on Plurality in the Mekong Region, Khon Kaen University and a Southeast Asia Digital Library Grant of the US Department of Education and administered through Northern Illinois University Library.

References

1. [UNECE] United Nations Economic Commission for Europe. **Knowledge-Based Economy**. http://www.unece.org/ie/wp8/kbe.htm (2004).
2. Office of National Economic & Social Development Board. 2002. **One Tambon One Product**. http://ie.nesdb.go.th/gd/html/forms/Projects/TumBonProject/TumBonExPlain/TumBonProjectExPlain.htm. (In Thai)
3. Office of National Economic & Social Development Board. 2003. **The main point of the Ninth National Economic and Social Development Plan**. http://www.nesd.go.th/interesting_ menu/progress_plan/plan9_data. (In Thai)
4. Office of the National Education Commission. 1999. **The promoting policy of Thailand's Knowledge on education**. in the conference on management of local information. Mahasarakham: Central Library, Mahasarakham University. (In Thai)
5. Suphon Somchitsripanya. 2001. **Perspective from palm leaf manuscript: language and literature**. The conference on Study of Knowledge Recorded in Palm Leaf Manuscript in Northeastern Thailand.
6. Phanphen Khlue-Thai. 2003. **The studies of inscription and ancient document by Social Research Institute Chaingmai University**. In Language and Inscription Volume 9. Nakhon Prathom: Department of Eastern Language, Faculty of Archeology, Sillapakhon University. p. 32-59. (In Thai)
7. Suriya Samutkhup and Pattana Kittiarsa. 2003. Why was a female lower garment used as a wrapper of palm-leaf manuscripts in Northeast Thailand? An anthropology approach to Isan-palm-leaf manuscripts. **Art & Culture Magazine.** 24(6): 82-95. (In Thai)
8. Northeastern Thai Palm Leaf Manuscript Preservation Project, Mahasarakham University. 2004. http://www.msu.ac.th/BL/bailan/PAG2.ASP. (In Thai)
9. Sineenart Somboon-a-nake. 1998. Palm leaf manuscript: cultural heritage of Lanna people. **Library Association Bulletin** 42(2): 25-36. (In Thai)
10. Ekawit na Thalang. 2001. Isan's knowledge. Bangkok: Ammarin. (In Thai)

11. Mimno, David; Crane, Gregory; Jones, Alison. Hierarchical Catalog Records implementing a FRBR Catalog. **D-Lib Magazine** 11(10) (2005). http://dlib.anu.edu.au/dlib/ october05/crane/10crane.html.
12. Devis-Brown, Beth. 1999. Information organization: old concepts, new challenges. In **WTEC Panel report on Digital information organization in Japan**. International Technology Research Institute, World Technology (WTEC) Division. http://www.wtec.org/loyola/digilibs/toc.htm
13. Proffitt, Merrilee. 2004. Pulling it all together: use of METS in RLG cultural materials service. **Library Hi Tech** 22(1): 65-68.
14. Taylor, Arlene G. 1999. **The organization of information**. Englewood, Colorado: Library Association.
15. Coyle, Karen. 2004. Future considerations: the functional library system record. **Library Hi Tech** 22(2): 166-174.
16. [IFLA] IFLA Study Group on the Functional Requirements for Bibliographic Records. 1998. **Functional Requirements for Bibliographic Records: Final Report.** UBCIM Publications-New Series. Vol. 19, Munchen: K.G.Saur, (1998). http://www.ifla.org/VII/s13/frbr/frbr.htm.
17. Lin, Simon C. and et al. 2001. A Metadata case study for the FRBR model based on Chinese painting and calligraphy at the National Palace Museum in Taipei. In **DC-2001 Proceedings of the international conference on Dublin Core and metadata applications 2001**. (2001) (pp. 51-59). Tokyo: NII.
18. Caplan, Priscilla. 2003. **Metadata fundamentals for all librarians**. Chicago: American Library Association.
19. Surajit Chantharasakha. 2001. **Isan palm leaf manuscript**. The conference on Study of Knowledge Recorded in Palm Leaf Manuscript in Northeastern Thailand.
20. Wirat Unnatwaranggul. Palm leaf manuscript. In **The Royal edition of palm leaf manuscript in Rattanakosin Era**. Bangkok: National Library, (1984): p 1-11. (In Thai)

Management of Metadata Standards: The Case of UNIMARC

Hugo Manguinhas, Nuno Freire, and José Borbinha

INESC-ID, Rua Alves Redol, 9, Apartado 13069, 1000-029 Lisboa, Portugal
mangas@bn.pt
National Library of Portugal, Campo Grande, 83, 1741-081 Lisboa, Portugal
nuno.freire@bn.pt
INESC-ID, Rua Alves Redol, 9, Apartado 13069, 1000-029 Lisboa, Portugal
jlb@ist.utl.pt

Abstract. UNIMARC is a family of bibliographic metadata schemas with formats for descriptive information, classification, authorities and holdings. This paper describes the problem of maintenance and management of these schemas, with their online publishing for human and machine readable. This is accomplished by a Model View Controller (MVC) architecture managing the format schemas and schema descriptions in XML, as model representations, and XSLT transformations for the publishing in HTML, PDF, and other possible option. This work is an activity of a larger project toward the development of the international UNIMARC Metadata Registry, in the scope of the IFLA-CDNL Alliance for Bibliographic Standards activities.

1 Introduction

UNIMARC is a family of bibliographic metadata schemas with formats for descriptive information, classification, authorities and holdings. It was maintained traditionally by the UBCIM (IFLA[1] Universal Bibliographic Control and International MARC Core Activity) programme, replaced recently by the ICABS (IFLA-CDNL Alliance for Bibliographic Standards) activities. The textual descriptions of the formats have been published traditionally in printed paper. The reference language has been English, but translations to other languages exist in some cases. The most recent reference version of at least the bibliographic format has been accessible online, in HTML [1].

The MARC standards represent a family of very rich metadata standards traditionally used in libraries. They cover a wide range of metadata requirements, but they have bee used especially for very rich descriptive metadata. Those formats have been seen as too complex and expensive for most of the digital libraries scenarios, which motivated the development of more pragmatic alternatives, such as Dublin Core. However, the high value of the millions of records already created worldwide based on these formats can not be ignored. They represent a huge investment of a large

---

[1] IFLA – Internacional Federation of Library Associations and Institutions (http://www.ifla.org).

S. Sugimoto et al. (Eds.): ICADL 2006, LNCS 4312, pp. 264–273, 2006.
© Springer-Verlag Berlin Heidelberg 2006

community of very high skilled professionals, and in fact they've been already used as the foundation of new digital libraries services. Those are for example the cases of the TEL[2] and Google Scholar[3] services, to which the National Library of Portugal (BN) provides, respectively, its full UNIMARC records trough OAI-PMH and partial UNIMARC based metadata trough a proprietary interface),

To promote the approach between these two worlds, BN has been promoting an activity in the scope of the ICABS to develop formal representations of the structure and descriptions of the UNIMARC formats. The purpose is to use them for a more formal maintenance and more flexible publishing in different languages, format and media. This has been all done in the scope of a wider activity towards the development of an UNIMARC Metadata Registry, which might become a reference point for the professionals, organisations and information systems requiring it. This paper focus only in the results already reached for the description of the schemas in XML and their publishing. The details of the registry are out of the scope of this paper.

The paper follows with a generic description of the UNIMARC format, followed by the core part of the work here reported, which is the detailed description of the publishing process. Than we provide a short description of the UNIMARC Metadata Registry, and finally we present the conclusions and describe the work in progress.

2 UNIMARC

The primary purpose of UNIMARC is to facilitate the international exchange of bibliographic data in machine-readable form between library management systems, especially between national bibliographic agencies. UNIMARC belongs to a family of other MARC formats, like MARC21 [3]. These formats are intended to be carrier formats for exchange purposes. They do not stipulate the form, content, or record structure of the data within individual information systems. They provide recommendations only on the form and content of data for when it is to be exchanged.

Like other MARC formats, UNIMARC is a specific implementation of ISO 2709, an international standard that specifies the structure of records containing bibliographic data. Every record must consist of a record label (a 24 character data element), followed by an undefined number of fields. A field is identified by a tag, which is a numeric code of three characters, and can be classified as a control or data field. Control fields contain a well defined set of character data. Data fields may optionally contain one or two indicators, in the form of alphanumeric character, adding information about field content, relationships between fields, or about necessary data manipulation procedures. Data field can be also subdivided into subfields. A subfield is identified by one alphanumeric character and can contain data.

Figure 1 shows a data model (class diagram) for a generic UNIMARC format. The scope of UNIMARC is to specify the content designators (tags, indicators and subfield codes) to be assigned to bibliographic records and to specify the logical and physical format of the records. Those records can cover monographs, serials, carto-

---

[2] TEL – The European Library (http://www.theeuropeanlibrary.org/portal/index.html).
[3] Google Scholar (http://scholar.google.com/).

graphic materials, music, sound recordings, graphics, projected and video materials, rare books, electronic resources, etc. The UNIMARC format was first published in 1977 under the title "UNIMARC - Universal MARC Format". In 1985 UNIMARC was definitively adopted by IFLA as the international format for record exchange between national bibliographic agencies and recommended as a model for further national MARC based formats in countries lacking an official format.

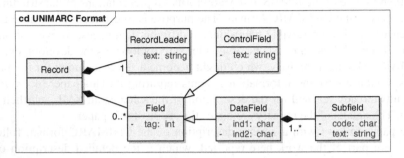

Fig. 1. A generic data model for the UNIMARC format

Initially it contained specifications for book and printed serial material and provisional fields for various non-book materials such as music, motion pictures, etc. Like most of the standards, UNIMARC evolved to accommodate new requirements, such as cataloguing practices related to existing or new bibliographic materials. Following editions updated several fields, and added data fields for cartographic materials, sound recordings, visual projections, video recordings, motion pictures, graphics, printed music and microforms. These changes defined additional fields, indicators, subfields and new coded values.

Meanwhile, it was developed a XML schema, named MARCXML, to replace ISO 2709 as a solution to transport MARC records [2]. This was intended initially for the MARC21, but it has been also used naturally for UNIMARC. Finally, the challenge to define a XML so that any existing format based on ISO 2709 could be represented was taken by the MarcXchange schema [3]. The usefulness of the basic structure from MARCXML was recognized, so it was copied to MarcXchange (making it possible to consider MARCXML files compatible).

3 Publishing UNIMARC

In this paper we are describing the solution to manage the processes of maintenance and publishing of the descriptions of the UNIMARC formats. That must provide interfaces for humans and machine), which is assured by a Model-View-Controller[4] (MVC) architecture, with the workflow show in the figure 2.

The Model part of this MVC architecture consists in fact of two complementary models, actually both expressed in XML: a **format schema** for each UNIMARC

---

[4] http://en.wikipedia.org/wiki/Model_view_controller

format, comprising a grammar with all the rules and relations; a **schema description**, containing the corresponding textual descriptions for the elements of the format as defined in the schema.

Both these models use URN [4] identifiers for reference and linkage. Their source is a Metadata Registry, which is also a very important part of our work (a short description for it is provided in the end). The Controller applies the transformations and appends for the two source models (extra texts, not structured, and complementary to the formal description), using DocBook[5] as an intermediate format. With this architecture we can generate any publishing format views as output, either for human (HTML, RTF, PDF, etc.) or for machine processing (XML).

In this moment we publish also each format in two main options: A **concise format**, containing only the labels for the elements, removing extended descriptions, notes, examples, relationships and appendices. This is a very practical format, for fast consulting. The **complete format** containing all the detailed descriptions and also other information elements, including examples.

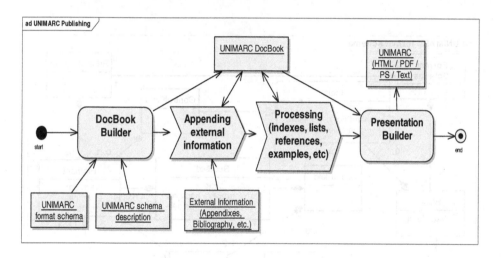

Fig. 2. Activity diagram for the publication of a UNIMARC format

3.1 The UNIMARC Schema

UNIMARC is a format with a very complex structure. Besides the common syntactic rules for elements, attributes and values, it also defines semantic relations between them. These relations may even define the interpretation made for a given element or attribute. UNIMARC also requires grouping information in subsets of rules (aggregation) that are required to represent blocks of fields. This requirement is not essential for the validation of the records, but is important to define element semantic coupling.

---

[5] DocBook (http://www.docbook.org).

```
<uri>        ::= "urn:" <body> "://" <path>
<body>       ::= <format> ":" <subformat> ":" <version>
<format>     ::= "unimarc"
<subformat>  ::= "bibliographic" | "authority" | "item" | "classification"
<version>    ::= <edition> | <edition> "." <revision>
<edition>    ::= <integer>
<revision>   ::= <integer>
<path>       ::= <leader> | <block> | <field> | <unit>
<leader>     ::= "leader" | "leader" "/" <element>
<block>      ::= <digit> ( <digit> "-" | "-" "-")
<field>      ::= 3*<digit> ( | "." <subfield> | "/" <indicator> | "/" <element>)
<indicator>  ::= "i" ("1" | "2")
<subfield>   ::= <character> | <character> "/" <element>
<element>    ::= <integer> | <integer> "." <element>
<unit>       ::= <string> | <string> "." <character>
```

Fig. 3. URN identifiers syntax for the UNIMARC format coded in BNF notation

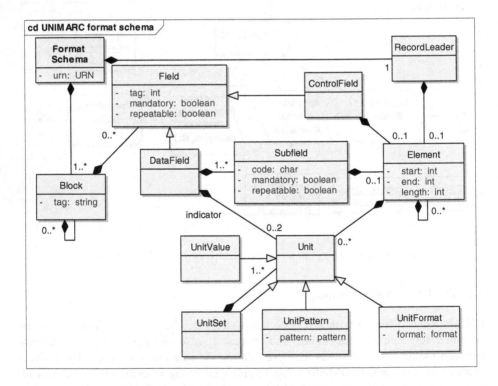

Fig. 4. The UNIMARC format schema Class Diagram

Currently schema languages, like XMLSchema[6] and RELAX-NG[7], allow the definition of syntactic rules based on elements, attributes and values, but they lack semantic rules for defining relations between them. Schematron[8] is the only language that allows defining these semantic relations. On the other hand, existing format schemas tend to evolve in time or be forgotten, while we need a stable format. We also required a schema that was close to the concepts involved even if it required, for validation purposes, the conversion to another schema format (if possible).

We decided not to use any of the existing schema languages, but to develop our own for describing the UNIMARC formats, gathering all syntactic and semantic rules, each uniquely identified by an URN. Figure 3 shows the URN identifiers syntax for the UNIMARC format ("urn:unimarc:bibliographic:1:/100.a" is an example for the field 100, subfield $a of the first edition of UNIMARC bibliographic format). As shown in Figure 4, this format schema is an extension of the generic MARC schema (remember Figure 1), where we added aggregation information (Blocks of Fields) and structural content value for elements like Controlfields, Subfields and RecordLeader.

Each UNIMARC format schema (Bibliographic, Authority, Holdings and Classification), as also the respective versions, has its own format schema file with the corresponding format rules. The most recent version of the bibliographic format, for example, is actually an XML file with 3700 lines. Any format schema file can inherit the structural information of another format schema file, making it possible to represent the evolution of a format by simply adding and replacing (overloading) rules in the new versions.

3.2 The UNIMARC Schema Description

Each UNIMARC format schema has also a complementary schema description of the terms. This schema contains therefore the relations between the URN identifiers of the elements and their corresponding textual descriptions. Each definition of an element of a format schema comprises: a **label**, a limited length character data, to define the name given to the element; a **definition**, a unlimited length structured data that describes the element; **notes**, as unlimited length structured data which adds information about the use and purpose of the element; **examples**, a unlimited structured data that provide information about possible uses of the element; **relationships**, an unlimited structured data that pinpoints relations with other elements of the given format.

New descriptions of the schema can be declared at any time to satisfy new requirements. Figure 5 shows a class diagram for a UNIMARC schema description with all the currently defined elements and attributes. Current schema description formats involve declarations in RDF[9] and other ontology schema description formats. We don't need a complex schema description, so we decided to take advantage of the XML namespace functionality and build an extension of an XML properties schema to contain both text and structured information. This description can be multilingual

---

[6] XML Schema (http://www.w3.org/XML/Schema).
[7] RELAX-NG (http://relaxng.org).
[8] Schematron (http://www.schematron.com).
[9] RDF - Resource Description Framework (http://www.w3.org/RDF/).

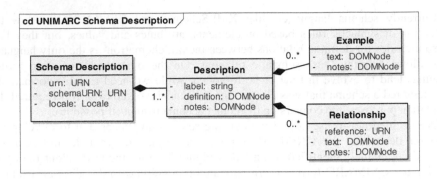

Fig. 5. A data model for the UNIMARC schema description

and multi-version, where each case is represented by a specific XML file. The URN identifiers to the UNIMARC format description are built by adding locale information to the element's URN (<body> ::= <body> ":" <locale>).

3.3   Controller

For the Controller part we decided to use XSLT technology [5]. This provides a great flexibility and makes it possible an easy access and usage by third party applications. To support this framework, we use an intermediate representation of the formats expressed in the DocBook schema. DocBook is a collection of widely accepted standards and tools for technical publishing.

This solution enables the execution of a number of tasks needed before the generation of the final publishing view. The controller starts by merging the two model representations, using the format schema as source for document tree building and using the schema description for content. This is done by fetching the description of each document tree node in the description model, which is done using the document node URN as search key, and applying to the current document node. As a result, the first DocBook/XML representation of the document is built.

Among the executed tasks are the adding of extra information, such as bibliographic information (like title, authority, etc.), preface, introduction, appendices and annexes, as well as the generation of all kinds of indexes (tables of contents and annexes indexes), references, lists and glossaries of terms. When transforming from the Model to View, all URN references to terms are translated to real links (in a HTML document, those will be URL links).

Some tasks can be ignored or made differently, according to the type of publication that is desired. For example, the concise publication needs less work from the controller part than the complete publication.

3.4   View

After all the Controller workflow is done, it takes place the final publishing View. This is built using an appropriate XSLT or XSLT-FO transformation for the intended

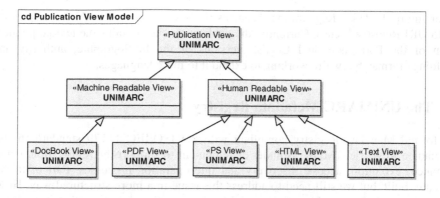

Fig. 6. Publication View Model Class Diagram

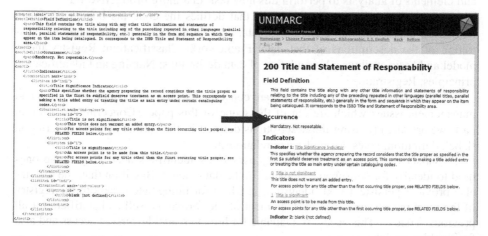

Fig. 7. The publication of the UNIMARC bibliographic description (the DocBook/XML description is converted in HTML)

publishing format. At the moment we are publishing in all currently available human readable formats for DocBook (HTML, PS, PDF, etc.). Figure 6 shows all publication views currently available. Figure 7 shows an example of the HTML version of the description of one part of the bibliographic format, as the resulting of this process. Nevertheless other human readable formats (RTF and Doc formats) can be built using some of the already available publications. We are also using DocBook/XML for the publication of the machine readable version.

All the produced publications are actually accessible online at http://www. unimarc.info. This is only to access the UNIMARC publication views. The site uses a simple syntax for the construction of the URLs, based on the conceptual tree structure of the description. This provides to external services immediate and permanent access to the available format publications. Third party services only need to understand the URN syntax to link to this publishing service. This service will be registered in the near future the URN Registration Agencies (IANA Registry of URN Namespaces[10], Info URI Registry[11], etc.). Currently, the publication site contains the textual publication of the Portuguese and English versions of the bibliographic, authority and holdings format, but we're working to extend it to more languages.

4 The UNIMARC Metadata Registry

A formal Metadata Registry compliant with the ISO/IEC 11179 standard [6] for Metadata Registries (MDR) is under development to support the registration, maintenance, evolution, access, discovery and interoperation processes. Part of it was already built, but we still need to address this issue in a more structured way. However, the work done so far was essential because on the same time that it produced already the results that we've described above, it gave us the necessary experience and elements of analysis to perform this new task in a more productive way.

ISO/IEC 11179 is a six part standard that defines the concepts behind Metadata Registries, addressing the semantics of data, the representation of data, and the registration of the descriptions of that data: Framework; Classification; Registry metamodel and basic attributes; Formulation of data definitions; Naming and identification principles; Registration.

The first three parts of the standard are concerned with design, implementation and management issues which are out of the scope of this paper. Concerning the fourth part, we are already using the descriptions defined in the format schema description (label, definition, notes, examples and relationships).

To satisfy the fifth part, the registry uses URN identifiers according to the ones used to identify format schema elements in the data model. Based on that, the registry also provides persistent URL identifiers (PURL) for immediate access to the registry of the most recent version of each element of the format as well as identifiers for all previous versions. This access is available for human readable version access and also for machine readable access.

Registration, the sixth part, is made according to levels of administration. Professionals responsible for the edition and revision of the format can access this register online and edit changes in the format descriptions. These changes are registered directly in the description XML file with the descriptions. Usually, there is one professional responsible for a given language and format, in all its versions. On the other hand professionals responsible for managing the evolution of the format can also edit online the schema of that format. These changes are registered directly in the XML file of the format schema. Usually, there is a group of professionals responsible for all the format versions, involved in a higher level network of responsibilities and tasks, different from the editors and reviewers.

This Metadata Registry also serves as the primary source for format discovery and provides access to all the available information and services concerning the format.

Concerning the publication, this registry acts primarily as the source for the necessary models required for the publication process, and secondly as the source for

---

[10] http://www.iana.org/assignments/urn-namespaces
[11] http://info-uri.info/

discovery by providing links to all available published formats' views (including the formats' versions).

Changes made to the format, whether concerning the structure or the description, can be immediately available to the online publication site in all provided views.

The Registry shares also another important feature, enabling the comparison between different versions of the same format. With this we can profile the evolution of the formats and track changes between them. All this information can also be published along with the publication of the formats.

5 Conclusions and Work in Progress

To publish the UNIMARC formats in all languages which countries have adopted them involves collecting the existing textual descriptions, usually used for printing, and represent them in format descriptions according to our model. This is an activity in progress, which will be followed by the generation of the corresponding format schema and schema description files.

In another front, we need to review the requirements for the conversion between our schema language and other existing schema languages, as also the viability of defining format schema descriptions with an ontology schema description language like RDF (this has been a target since the first moment, but in a first moment we hade to stick with pure XML in order to assure back compatibility with tools and other systems already in use at BN).

We are also developing a large number of controllers for the schema publication views, making use of the already available publishing formats. Among others, we want to assure that we can provide reliable publication views in the most common formats, such as HTML, RTF, Microsoft Word, PDF, etc.

In a broader perspective, the functional development of the UNIMARC Metadata Registry is in progress, The infrastructure used to produce the results reported in this paper was designed to be already compatible with that, but we need to review it more carefully according to the requirements of the ISO/IEC 11179 standard.

References

1. IFLA - UNIMARC Manual: Bibliographic Format, 1994 (http://www.ifla.org/VI/3/p1996-1/sec-uni.htm).
2. LoC - MARC Standards, MARC in XML, September 2004 (http://www.loc.gov/marc/marcxml.html).
3. ISO. ISO/DIS 25577: Information and documentation – MarcXchange 30 November 2005. (http://www.niso.org/international/SC4/n577.pdf)
4. Moats, R URN Syntax, RFC 2141, May 1997.
5. Clark, James. XSL Transformations (XSLT) Version 1.0, November 1999 (http://www.w3.org/TR/xslt).
6. ISO/IEC 11179, Information Technology - Metadata Registries (MDR) (http://metadata-standards.org/11179).

Taxonomy Alignment for Interoperability Between Heterogeneous Digital Libraries

Jason J. Jung[1,2]

[1] Department of Computer & Information Eng., Inha University
253 Yonghyun-Dong, Nam-Gu, Incheon, Korea 402-751
[2] INRIA Rhône-Alpes
ZIRST 655 avenue de l'Europe, Montbonnot
38334 Saint Ismier cedex, France
j2jung@intelligent.pe.kr

Abstract. Resources located in digital libraries are labeled (or classified) based on taxonomies. On multiple digital libraries, however, heterogeneity between taxonomies is a serious problem for efficient interoperation processes (e.g., information sharing and query transformation). In order to overcome this problem, we propose a novel framework based on aligning taxonomies of digital libraries. Thereby, the best mapping between concepts has to be discovered to maximize the summation of a set of partial similarities. For experimentation, three digital libraries were built based on different taxonomies. Taxonomy alignment-based resource retrieval was evaluated by human experts, and we measured recall and precision measures retrieved by concept replacement strategy.

1 Introduction

Digital library (DL) has been regarded as one of the richest online information space. Many studies have been proposed to efficiently retrieve relevance resources from a DL source. However, recently, we are able to realize that people are accessing to a variety of DLs and suffering from searching for relevant information efficiently. We can intuitively find out that this problem results from a large number of DLs on the network. Simply, with respect to the scale of DLs, there are not only a few major digital libraries but also more domain-specialized DLs (e.g., in computer science, ACM Portal[1], IEEE Xplore[2], and Elsevier ScienceDirect[3]). Moreover, even personal DLs have been jumbled up on the web.

More seriously, another problem is semantic heterogeneity between DLs. Each DL basically has applied classification system to manage the resources (e.g., digital documents, multimedia information, and etc.) in repositories. One of the popular approaches for classifying resources is a taxonomy. It is represented as a hierarchical structure between topics (or classes). For instance, some resources

---

[1] http://portal.acm.org/
[2] http://ieeexplore.ieee.org/
[3] http://www.sciencedirect.com/

S. Sugimoto et al. (Eds.): ICADL 2006, LNCS 4312, pp. 274–282, 2006.

about "digital library" can be annotated with *"Information Systems> Information Storage and Retrieval> Library Automation."* However, the keywords expressing the classes and the hierarchical structure between classes of a taxonomy might be different from that of other DLs. The users need take some time to be aware of (or adjusted to) the new DL environment.

In this paper, we are focusing on supporting end-users through aligning the taxonomies applied to annotate (or classify) the resources on DLs. It means the local end-users in a certain DL can access to the other DLs which are unfamiliar with him. Unlike a centralized portal systems (e.g., meta search engines), the end-users in a DL can be provided a set of topic correspondences from aligning other DLs directly, so that they can deploy meaningful translation services (e.g., query expansion [1] and transformation).

In the following Sect. 2, we describe the problem of semantic heterogeneity between DLs. Sect. 3 and Sect. 4 propose a novel similarity measurement between taxonomies and alignment approach by using these similarity measurement. In Sect. 5, experimental results will be shown to evaluate our approach. Sect. 6 discusses some significant issues and compares our contributions with the previous studies. Finally, Sect. 7 draws our conclusions of this work.

2   Heterogeneous Taxonomies

A hierarchical taxonomy is a tree structure of classifications for a given set of objects. At the top of this structure is a single classification, the root node, that applies to all objects. Nodes below this root are more specific classifications that apply to subsets of the total set of classified objects.

Definition 1 (Taxonomy). *A taxonomy T is defined as a set of assertions*

$$T = \{c_{root}, \langle c_i, c_j \rangle | c_j = subClass(c_i)\} \tag{1}$$

where c_i means a superclass of c_j. Each instance is annotated with a set of classes related to its topic.

Generally, users have some difficulties on information seeking in hyperspace (e.g., www). It is caused by lack of knowledge about internal structure of the hyperspace. We are motivated by the similar problem in the conventional DLs of which taxonomies are built by the domain expert's heuristics and knowledge. We refer it as "Lost in digital libraries." Thus, we note the semantic heterogeneity between taxonomies in DLs.

- lexical heterogeneities resulting from *i*) multi-lingual problem and *ii*) synonyms (or antonyms) [2]
- structural conflicts, e.g., class duplications between identical categories and the subordination between dependent categories [3]

For example, in Fig. 1, not only the languages (e.g, squares and circles) representing classes but also the structural patterns (e.g., number of branches and depth) of taxonomies T_1 and T_2 are different from each other.

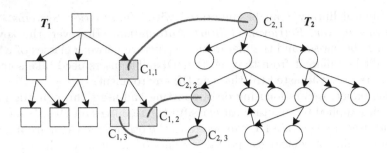

Fig. 1. Mapping heterogeneous taxonomies. Red lines indicate the pairs of aligned classes from both taxonomies.

In order to solve these drawbacks, a set of given taxonomies have to be matched as finding out the best configuration of alignments between classes (e.g., red lines shown in Fig. 1). We assume that the best configuration should be maximizing the summation of class similarities (It will be explained in next section). As shown in Fig. 1, three pairs of classes can be matched, when $Sim_C(c_{1,1}, c_{2,1}) + Sim_C(c_{1,2}, c_{2,2}) + Sim_C(c_{1,3}, c_{2,3})$ is the best combination.

3   Taxonomy Alignment with Class Similarities

In order to find optimal alignment between two taxonomies, we have to measure the similarity between classes consisting of the taxonomies.

Definition 2 (Class similarity). *Given a pair of classes from two different taxonomies, the similarity (Sim_C) between c and c' is defined as*

$$Sim_C(c, c') = \sum_{E \in \mathcal{N}(C)} \pi_E^C MSim_Y(E(c), E(c')) \tag{2}$$

where $\mathcal{N}(C) \subseteq \{E^1 \dots E^n\}$ is the set of all relationships in which classes participate (for instance, subclass, instances, or attributes). The weights π_E^C are normalized (i.e., $\sum_{E \in \mathcal{N}(C)} \pi_E^C = 1$). Class similarity measure Sim_C is assigned in $[0, 1]$.

In case of hierarchical taxonomies, we consider class labels (L) and two relationships in $\mathcal{N}(C)$, which are the superclass (E^{sup}) and the subclass (E^{sub}), Eq. 2 is rewritten as:

$$\begin{aligned}
Sim_C(c, c') = {} & \pi_L^C sim_L(L(A_i), LF(B_j)) \\
& + \pi_{sup}^C MSim_C(E^{sup}(c), E^{sup}(c')) \\
& + \pi_{sub}^C MSim_C(E^{sub}(c), E^{sub}(c')).
\end{aligned} \tag{3}$$

where the set functions $MSim_C$ compute the similarity of two entity collections.

As a matter of fact, a distance between two set of classes can be established by finding a maximal matching maximizing the summed similarity between the classes:

$$MSim_C(S, S') = \frac{\max(\sum_{\langle c,c' \rangle \in Pairing(S,S')} (Sim_C(c, c')))}{\max(|S|, |S'|)}, \tag{4}$$

in which $Pairing$ provides a matching of the two set of classes. Methods like the Hungarian method allow to find directly the pairing which maximizes similarity. The algorithm is an iterative algorithm that compute this similarity [4]. This measure is normalized because if Sim_C is normalized, the divisor is always greater or equal to the dividend.

Hence, the alignment between heterogeneous taxonomies can be represented as a set of pairs of concepts from each taxonomy. We refer this concept pair to correspondence (e.g., equivalence or subsumption).

Definition 3 (Alignment). *Given two taxonomies $\mathcal{T}_i$ and $\mathcal{T}_j$, an alignment between two taxonomies are represented as a set of correspondences $CRSP_{ij} = \{\langle c, c', r \rangle | c \in \mathcal{T}_i, c' \in \mathcal{T}_j\}$ where r means the relationship between c and c', by maximizing the summation of class similarities $\sum_{(c,c')} Sim_{C(c,c')}$.*

We want to show a simple example. In Fig. 2, an alignment between two taxonomies is occurred as showing the best mappings between them. All relations mean only subclass relations, and the weights are assumed as $\pi_L^C = 0.8$, $\pi_{sub}^C = 0.2$. In the alignment between taxonomy T1 and T2, label similarity based on

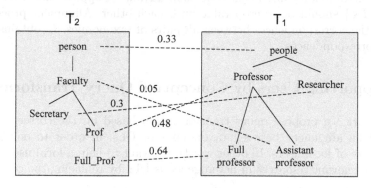

Fig. 2. Example of similarity-based alignment

edit (or Levenshtein) distance [5] is measured by $sim_L(c_i, c_j) = 1 - \frac{Dist(c_i, c_j)}{\max(|c_i|, |c_j|)}$. The maximal label similarity of each pair of features is shown as follows.

$$sim_L(\text{person, Professor}) = 0.44 \tag{5}$$
$$sim_L(\text{Faculty, people}) = 0.14$$
$$sim_L(\text{Secretary, Researcher}) = 0.30$$

$$sim_L(\text{Prof, Professor}) = 0.44 \tag{6}$$
$$sim_L(\text{Full\_Prof, Full\_professor}) = 0.64, \tag{7}$$

Then, the most similar pair of features can be found out 'Full_Prof' of T_1 and 'Full_rofessor' of T_2 in Equ. 7. As shown in Equ. 5 and 6, features 'person' and 'Prof' in T_1 have shown the same label similarities with 'Professor' in T_2. We have to pay attention to the subclasses. Thus, the summation of similarities are calculated by

$$Sim_C(\text{person, Professor}) = 0.352 + 0.2 \times \max(0.07, 0.05) = 0.366 \tag{8}$$

where $Sim_C(\text{Faculty, Full\_professor})$ and $Sim_C(\text{Faculty, Assistant\_professor})$ are assigned into 0.07 are 0.05, respectively. Similarly, we can calculate

$$Sim_C(\text{Prof, Professor}) = 0.352 + 0.2 \times \max(0.64, 0.26) = 0.48, \tag{9}$$

where $Sim_C(\text{Full\_Prof, Full\_professor})$ and $Sim_C(\text{Full\_Prof, Assistant\_professor})$ are 0.64 and 0.26, respectively. This ca means that 'Prof' in T_2 has to be aligned to 'Professor' in T_1. Additionally, for measuring the distance between labels, we can employ various methods (e.g., substring distance [6]). Moreover, we employ a threshold τ_C to filter out some correspondences of which class similarities are less than the threshold.

Alignment process makes heterogeneous DLs interoperable (even partially). The local users in a DL can easily access to the other DLs. To do so, DLs have to conduct the taxonomy alignment process in advance. Suppose that a set of DLs $\{L_1, \ldots, L_N\}$ should be interoperable with each other. Alignment process can find out the correspondences between all pairs of taxonomies. L_i obtains $N - 1$ sets of correspondences.

4   Supporting Users by Conceptual Query Transformation

In this work we propose query transformation based on the correspondences obtained by alignment between taxonomies of DLs, in order to enhance the accessibility of local users. In other words, we want to help a local user in L_i to search for relevant resources in heterogeneous DLs by replacing the concepts in queries.

Basically, a query by a user u_i is represented as a set of keywords attached with a set of operators (e.g., $\cup$, $\cap$, and 'not'). For conceptual query transformation from DL_i to DL_j, we exploit simple class replacement strategy using the aligned correspondences between T_i and T_j. As an example, in DL_i, a query "Media $\cap$ Art" expresses the intersection between two sets of resources annotated with classes "Media" and "Art," respectively. If there is a correspondence $\langle$Media, Video, SubClass$\rangle$ between T_i and T_j, the query can be modified to "Video $\cap$ Art" in DL_j.

Definition 4 (Query transformation). *Let a query* $q_i = \{c^+, c^- | c^+, c^- \in T_i\}$ *be operable in* DL_i, *by a set of correspondences* $CRSP_{ij} = \{\langle c^+, c', r \rangle | c^+ \in T_i, c' \in T_j\}$ *between two taxonomies of* DL_i *and* DL_j. *A class* c *in* q_i *can be replaced to the classes* c' *in* T_j, *if and if only*

- c' *is equivalent with* c, *or*
- c' *is a subclass of* c.

Hence, a query q_j *is represented as* $\{c^-, c' | c^- \in T_i, c' \in T_j\}$ *and becomes partially operable in* DL_j.

In case of replacement with subclasses, the transformed query may express more specified concepts. It makes the precision of the retrieved information improved, while the coverage rate is reduced.

5   Experimental Results

To evaluate our contribution, we built testing bed consisting of three DLs by using three different taxonomies.

- (T_1): ACM Computing Classification[4]
- (T_2): On-line Medical Dictionary (OMD)[5]
- (T_3): Open Directory Project (ODP)[6]

Table 1 shows the specifications of our testing bed. With respect to density ($\frac{\text{Number of resources}}{\text{Number of classes}}$), DL_1 has included the largest number of resource annotated with a class. Especially, for T_3, we extracted the classes from 'Computer' and 'Medicine' together.

Table 1. Specifications of testing bed

	Number of classes	Number of resources	Density
DL_1	37	422	11.41
DL_2	40	318	7.95
DL_3	67	207	3.09

As the first issue, we performed alignment process between three possible combinations. We set the threshold $\tau_C = 0.2$, and we collected the semantic correspondences. As shown in Table 2, three human experts (E_1, E_2, and E_3) were asked to find the mismatched correspondences from the results. We found out our alignment process has shown approximately 35.5% error rate (i.e., the mismatched correspondences). In the worst case (alignment between T_1 and T_2), we realized that mainly the diffences between domain-specific terminologies have

---

[4] http://www.acm.org/class/1998/
[5] http://cancerweb.ncl.ac.uk/omd/
[6] http://dmoz.org/

Table 2. Results of correspondences

Alignment	T_1 - T_2	T_2 - T_3	T_3 - T_1
Correspondences	7	23	18
Mismatched	3 (42.9%)	7 (30.4%)	6 (33.3%)

Table 3. Precision and recall by query transformation

	Recall			Precision		
	DL_1	DL_2	DL_3	DL_1	DL_2	DL_3
DL_1	-	36.6%	67.3%	-	72.5%	82.3%
DL_2	41.0%	-	52.7%	80.5%	-	76.8%
DL_3	62.3%	63.2%	-	83.5%	81.7%	-

influenced string matching-based alignments (in our case, we measured the edit distance between labels).

As second issue, by using these correspondences (including the mismatched ones), the queries by end users were transformed into two different DLs. Table 3 shows two measurement (recall and precision) computed by human experts. We are considering the direction of query transformation, so that lower diagonal element values mean the result by transformation from columns to rows (vice versa). For example, recall of the transformation from DL_1 to DL_2 is 36.6% (the inverse transformation's recall is 41.0%).

With respect to recall, the queries from DL_3 has well transformed by about 17% and 25%, compared with DL_1 and DL_2, respectively. While recall has shown only around 54% performance, the precision obtained relatively high result (about 79.6%).

Overall, precision measures have shown better results rather than recall measure. We consider that our concept replacement strategy is only based on "equivalence" and "subclass" relationships.

6   Discussion and Related Work

Fig. 3 shows the difference between two main approaches to access to multiple information sources, in terms of end-users' accessing strategies. While portal systems (e.g., meta search engines) provide a centralized integration service from these information sources, distributed approaches like our system can consider more domain-specific features. Moreover, they can expect some personalization techniques to their local users.

We consider the taxonomies are a part of ontologies in semantically heterogeneous environment. While the main relationship between classes in taxonomies is SubClass, ontologies are containing a variety of relationships between classes such as SubClass, SuperClass, Property, SubProperty, Domain, Range, and so on. However, in [7], the taxonomic patterns are capable of ontological relationships. Also, many work has been proposed to match, align and merge taxonomies like similarity flooding [8].

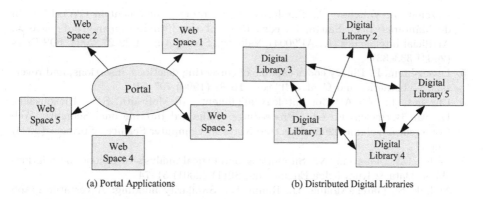

(a) Portal Applications   (b) Distributed Digital Libraries

Fig. 3. Comparison of integration schemes between a) centralized portal applications and b) alignment-based systems

In context of query transformation, since concept-based query transformation scheme was introduced in [1], several approaches have been investigated. Examples of such approaches are probabilistic query expansion based on concept similarity [9], logical inference [10], and background knowledge-based systems [11, 12].

7 Concluding Remarks and Future Work

As a conclusion, we proposed alignment-based query transformation scheme on heterogeneous DLs. Each pair of taxonomies were aligned by measuring the similarities between classes. We assume that the maximal summation of these class similarities be the best alignment between the corresponding taxonomies. Based on this alignment, we supported the local users to access to the other heterogeneous DLs.

In the future, we have to evaluate the scalability of our alignment-based distributed DLs, as increasing the number of testing beds. More importantly, we are planning to evaluate our alignment method by evaluation methods of taxonomy mapping algorithms proposed in [13].

References

1. Qiu, Y., Frei, H.P.: Concept based query expansion. In: Proceedings of the 16th annual international ACM SIGIR conference on Research and development in information retrieval (SIGIR '93), New York, NY, USA, ACM Press (1993) 160–169
2. Menczer, F.: Lexical and semantic clustering by web links. Journal of the American Society for Information Science and Technology **55**(14) (2004) 1261–1269
3. Jung, J.J.: Collaborative web browsing based on semantic extraction of user interests with bookmarks. Journal of Universal Computer Science **11**(2) (2005) 213–228

4. Euzenat, J., Valtchev, P.: Similarity-based ontology alignment in OWL-Lite. In de Mántaras, R.L., Saitta, L., eds.: Proc. of the 16th European Conference on Artificial Intelligence (ECAI'2004), Valencia, Spain, August 22-27, 2004, IOS Press (2004) 333–337

5. Levenshtein, I.: Binary codes capable of correcting deletions, insertions, and reversals. Cybernetics and Control Theory **10**(8) (1996) 707–710

6. Euzenat, J.: An API for ontology alignment. In McIlraith, S.A., Plexousakis, D., van Harmelen, F., eds.: Proceedings of the 3rd International Semantic Web Conference. Volume 3298 of Lecture Notes in Computer Science., Springer (2004) 698–712

7. Welty, C.A., Guarino, N.: Supporting ontological analysis of taxonomic relationships. Data & Knowledge Engineering **39**(1) (2001) 51–74

8. Melnik, S., Garcia-Molina, H., Rahm, E.: Similarity flooding: A versatile graph matching algorithm and its application to schema matching. In: Proceedings of the 18th International Conference on Data Engineering (ICDE), IEEE Computer Society (2002) 117–128

9. Cui, H., Wen, J.R., Nie, J.Y., Ma, W.Y.: Probabilistic query expansion using query logs. In: Proceedings of the 11th international conference on World Wide Web, New York, NY, USA, ACM Press (2002) 325–332

10. Nie, J.Y.: Query expansion and query translation as logical inference. Journal of the American Society for Information Science and Technology **54**(4) (2003) 335–346

11. Liu, Z., Chu, W.W.: Knowledge-based query expansion to support scenario-specific retrieval of medical free text. In: Proceedings of the 2005 ACM symposium on Applied computing (SAC '05), New York, NY, USA, ACM Press (2005) 1076–1083

12. Ángel F. Zazo, Figuerola, C.G., Berrocal, J.L.A., Rodríguez, E.: Reformulation of queries using similarity thesauri. Information Processing and Management: an International Journal **41**(5) (2005) 1163–1173

13. Avesani, P., Giunchiglia, F., Yatskevich, M.: A large scale taxonomy mapping evaluation. In Gil, Y., Motta, E., Benjamins, V.R., Musen, M.A., eds.: International Semantic Web Conference. Volume 3729 of Lecture Notes in Computer Science., Springer (2005) 67–81

A Process and Tool for the Conversion of MARC Records to a Normalized FRBR Implementation

Trond Aalberg

Norwegian University of Science and Technology,
Department of Computer and Information Science

Abstract. This paper presents a generic process and a tool for the conversion of MARC-based bibliographic records to the ER-based model of the Function Requirements for Bibliographic Records. The interpretation of a record, the construction of a new set of records and the final normalization needed, is decomposed into a series of steps that is implemented in the tool using XSL transformations. The purpose of the tool is to support researchers and developers who want to explore FRBR or develop solutions for using FRBR with existing MARC-based bibliographic catalogues.

1 Introduction

The *Functional Requirement for Bibliographic Records* (FRBR) that was published by the *International Foundation for Library Associations and Institutions* in 1998 [8], is a major contribution to the next generation of bibliographic catalogues and may significantly change the way bibliographic agencies create, maintain and exchange information in the future.

Existing library catalogues are to a large extend based on the use of the MARC format and naturally many libraries would like to implement support for FRBR in existing bibliographic information system. Although many projects have explored the use of FRBR in different contexts and some tools exist, there is little support for the systematic processing of information in MARC records into a proper representation that directly reflects the entities, attributes and relationships of the FRBR model. Researchers and developers beginning work in this area typically need to reinvent the conversion process and write their own interpretation system due to the lack of reusable solutions.

This paper presents an approach for the processing of MARC records into a normalized set or FRBR records. The different steps needed in the conversion process are identified and a tool that implements this process is presented. The conversion tool is based on the use of XML and XSL transformations and supports reuse across catalogues by separating the rules and conditions that govern the conversion from the general control structures that can be applied to any MARC-based catalogues.

S. Sugimoto et al. (Eds.): ICADL 2006, LNCS 4312, pp. 283–292, 2006.

2 MARC and FRBR

Most of todays bibliographic information is based on a common framework of rules and formats such as the International Standard Bibliographic Description (ISBD), the Anglo American Cataloguing Rules (AACR2), and the MARC format. The main components of a MARC record are the leader field, the control fields and the data fields. The leader and the control fields contain fixed length data elements identified by relative character position, whereas the data fields may contain variable length data elements identified by subfield codes. The data fields of a MARC record typically represents a logical grouping of the data, and the subfields represent the various attributes describing the logical unit. Data fields may additionally have indicators at the beginning of the field that supplement the data or are used to interpret the data found in the field.

There are actually a number of MARC-formats in use, but different formats are often inspired by each other or are extensions or subsets of other MARC formats. Many catalogues are based on the use of either MARC 21 or UNIMARC, but there are still many national or vendor-specific versions of the MARC format in use. Additionally we often find that libraries use the same format in different ways and/or use national or local adaptations of the cataloguing rules, and for these reason even libraries that officially share the same format may need different rules in a conversion of the catalogue.

The aim of FRBR is to establish a precisely stated and commonly shared understanding of what it is that the bibliographic record aims to provide information about. This is defined by the use of an entity-relationship model (ER-model) that defines the key entities that are of interest to users of bibliographic data. The entities *work, expression, manifestation* and *item* are the core of the model and reflects the products of intellectual and artistic endeavor at different levels of abstraction. The entities *person* and *corporate body* represents the various actors of concern in bibliographic descriptions. The model additionally defines the attributes for describing these entities and the relationships that may exist between entities.

The process of applying FRBR as an implementation model for existing catalogues is often referred to as "FRBRization", and studies and experimental applications are reported by many. The identification of FRBR entities in catalogues have been explored e.g. in [1,2,3,5,9]. A few tools for experimenting with the FRBR model are available such as the FRBR display tool made available by The Library of Congress Network Development and MARC Standards Office [10], and the workset algorithm developed by OCLC [7]. Most experiments and tools are quite incomplete and only partially show the application of FRBR in library catalogues, but a few more extensive implementations of FRBR are available such as OCLC's FictionFinder [6] and VTLS' library system Virtua [12]. Except for the mapping between MARC 21 and FRBR produced for The Library of Congress Network Development and MARC Standards Office [11], no attempts have so far been made to formalize the process of conversion between MARC and FRBR and the work reported in this paper contributes towards this.

3   Interpreting MARC Records

The transformation from MARC to FRBR is a complex task that in many ways is different from a simple sequential transformation of records in one format into equivalent records in a different format. The process described in this paper aims to produce a normalized set of FRBR records and by this we mean that each entity instance finally should be described in only one record with a proper set of relationship to other entities.

In the context of FRBR, each MARC-record may be seen as a self contained universe of entities, attributes and relationships. At the most generic level the process of interpreting a MARC record consists of (1) identifying the various entities described in the record, (2) selecting the fields that describe each entity and (3) finding the relationships between entities. This approach can be used to decompose each record into a corresponding set of interrelated entities, but because many records may contain descriptions of the same entity (e.g. an author with multiple publications will be described in many records) a conversion process additionally needs to (4) support normalization by finding and merging equivalent records.

3.1   Identifying Entities

Identifying entities is a process that includes inspecting a MARC record to determine what entities that are described in the record and what role this entity has in its relationship to other entities. This is not a trivial process, but due to the logical grouping of data in a MARC record certain fields will reflect specific FRBR entities and the role of these entities. A record may e.g. include person entries in both the 100- and 600-fields. These tags represent the same kind of entity but the entities have different roles. The former is the author of a work and the latter is the subject of a work.

Persons, corporate bodies and works are typically identified by the presence of specific fields such as main entry fields (1XX), title fields (24X) or added entry fields (7XX). Additional persons, corporate bodies and works can be identified in some of the subject access fields (6XX-fields) and series added entry fields (8XX). Expression entities are often considered to be more vaguely defined in a MARC record due to the lack of specific fields for expression titles, but can on the other hand be derived from work entities already identified. If a work is identified by the presence of a 240-entry, an expression can be identified based on the same field as well. Finally, the fact that each record corresponds to a manifestation can be used to identify manifestation entities although there may be a need to consider special cases based on the rules for cataloguing multivolumed manifestations etc. Items are typically listed using holdings information fields and each item can usually be identified for each entry.

The identification of entities can be formalized using a set of conditions for testing whether an entity is present in the record or not. Due to the many different occurrences of entities this is most conveniently solved by defining a condition for each of the possible entity occurrences.

3.2 Assigning Attributes

FRBR defines a comprehensive set of attributes for the entities that is based on what typically is reflected in bibliographic records. On the other hand, the model does not define the various possible data elements of an attribute in the same way as in a MARC format. A possible solution for this discrepancy is to maintain the subfield structure from the MARC record but additionally associate FRBR attribute names with the subfields.

Many subfields can only be assigned to a single entity occurring in the record. If a work is identified by the presence of a 130-field, the mapping for this entity will include the 130-subfields and possible other fields that are interpreted as describing the work identified in the 130-field. In some cases subfields can be assigned to several entity occurences such the language code that describes the language of all expressions identified in a record (e.g. analytical entries). Sometimes the assignment even have to be based on the actual data found in a subfield e.g. if a subfield contains information that in some cases belongs to an expression and in other cases belongs to the manifestation.

The selection of what attributes that is associated to what entity can basically be defined in a mapping table that describes what datafields/subfields that belongs to what entity occurrence and additional conditions for determining if an assignment should be made or not.

3.3 Establishing Relationships

The interpretation of relationships between entities can either be based on the implicit roles of the entities occurring in a record or it can be based on explicit information about roles and relationships found in indicators, relator codes or field linking subfields. Essentially this is a process that must be based on a definition of what kinds of relationships that may exist between entities. For each kind of relationship it is necessary to know the conditions for when a relationship can be identified as well as the condition for determining what target entity the relationship points to.

3.4 Normalizing the Result

The process outlined so far is only concerned with the conversion of a single MARC record into a corresponding set of interrelated entities without considering other records in the collection. To achieve a final set of interrelated entities with a consistent set of relationships between all entities in the whole collection, the output from the previous interpretation must be normalized. By this we imply that equivalent entities need to be merged to avoid redundant information and a fragmented network of relationships.

This process is mainly a question about equivalence between records. In some cases already existing identifiers may be used. If two records have the same identifier they describe the same entity instance and can be merged. Most entities, however, do not have proper identifiers and in this case records must be compared in a way that can be used to determine whether the records describe e.g. the same work. If two equivalent records are found, the merging process must create a new record that maintains the relationships found in both records and additionally create a new description that includes the union of distinct data fields and values found in both records.

4   The Frbrization Tool

The conversion process described in the previous section is implemented as a conversion tool that is based on the use of XML and XSL transformations. The interpretation and creation of FRBR records is performed by the use of XSLT, but other parts of the conversion are solved by the use of a program written in Java. The conversion tool accepts records in the MarcXchange [4] format and the output is a set of records in a format that uses the same field and subfield structure but with additional elements and attributes for FRBR relationships and types. The conversion process is decomposed into a preprocessing step, a main conversion and a final postprocessing step. The tool is illustrated in figure 1 and example records are found in figure 2.

4.1   The Rule Base

The various conditions, rules and other data that are needed to define the conversion for a specific catalogue is stored in a database. The purpose of this is to support reuse of the tool across catalogues and to facilitate consistency across the many rules that are used in the conversion. The database schema is illustrated in figure 1 and consists of an entity_mapping table that contains the variable data for the various occurrences of entities. For each kind of entity occurrence different rules need to be defined, and this table will for this reason contain a number of entries (e.g. different entity types for works identified by respectively 130, 240, 245, 600$t, 630, 700$t, etc.). The attribute_mapping table defines the mapping between MARC and FRBR attributes for each entity occurence type and the relationship_mapping contains the relationship types that can exist for an entity occurence, the conditions for when a relationship exists and an expression for what entity occurence(s) to relate to.

The rule base is used to generate XSLT templates. One template is created for each entry in the mapping_entities table. Each template follows the same control structure and includes the subcode needed to test for the presence of an entity, select and copy attributes and test for and create possible relationships. A simplified example of such a template is illustrated in figure 2.

4.2   Preprocessing

The first step in the actual conversion is a preprocessing that is introduced to enable different kinds of processing that more conveniently is applied in advance rather than during the actual frbrization. Some formats may for example use features that are different from what is commonly found in other MARC-formats,

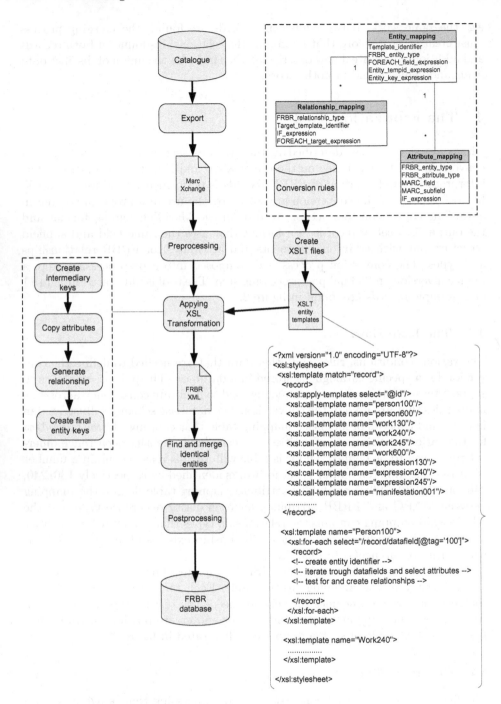

Fig. 1. The conversion tool outlined

```
<record id="pratchettterry" type="person">
  <datafield tag="100">
    <subfield code="a" type="name">Pratchett, Terry</subfield>
  </datafield>
  <relationship rel="has created" target="work" href=""pratchettterry#discworld"/>
  <relationship rel="has created" target="work" href="pratchettterry#reaperman"/>
</record>

<record id="pratchettterry#reaperman" type="work">
  <datafield tag="241">
    <subfield code="a" type="title">Reaper man</subfield>
  </datafield>
  <relationship rel="is created by" target="person" href="pratchettterry"/>
  <relationship rel="is realized through" target="expression" href="pratchettterry#reaperman#v:eng"/>
  <relationship rel="is realized through" target="expression" href="pratchettterry#reaperman#v:nob"/>
  <relationship rel="is part of" target="work" href="pratchettterry#discworldseries"/>
</record>
```

Fig. 2. Sample output FRBRXML records

and by converting these features in a separate step, a more generic solution can be applied for the main part of the conversion. Additionally we have chosen to convert the position-based control fields into a datafield/subfield structure that is easier to process using XSLT and XPATH.

4.3   The XSL Transformations

The main part of the conversion to FRBR is based on the use of the generated XSLT templates in combination with a few general purpose templates. The transformation tool iterates over all the records in the source file and applies all entity templates. If the condition for an entity occurrence is satisfied the template produces a record that includes the available datafields and relationships for this entity occurrence.

The output of this part of the conversion is a set of interrelated FRBR records for each initial MARC record. The identifiers generated in this step are based on the use of template names and field positions and are only valid in the context of a single source MARC record. To support normalization of FRBR entities across all MARC records, there is a need for identifiers that can be used to find out if one entity record describes the same entity as another record. For this purpose we do a second transformation of the records that consists of creating descriptive keys based on those fields that are most likely to contain the same information in equivalent records. We then replace all occurrences of a temporary identifier with the corresponding key. This replacement is performed for all FRBR records that are created from the same MARC record in order to maintain correct relationships.

The generation of the descriptive keys is determined by XPATH expressions defined for each kind of entity occurrence in the entity_mapping table. This expression defines what data to include in the key from the record and the ordering of fields. Additionally the creating of keys includes simple text processing operations to remove white spaces and punctuation characters. Because some entity keys include a key from another entity, the sequence of generation and replacement needs to be in an order that maintains dependencies; keys for persons and corporate bodies are created before work keys, expression keys after work keys etc.

4.4   Finding and Merging Records

Records that have equal keys are considered to represent the same entity and are merged to produce a single record that contains all the unique data fields and relationships from the initial records. Due to the inconsistent use of many MARC subfields, the use of entity keys needs to be supplemented with appropriate key matching algorithms in order to find entities that have comparable but not identical keys. Currently the tool only supports simple string matching due to the database that is used for looking up and storing records, but better algorithms for this purpose is considered to be important in the further development of the tool.

4.5   Postprocessing

The final stage of the conversion includes additional processing needed to create the required output. This may include the adding of additional information to support the indexing and presentation of records or cleaning up the data in different ways. Example records from the conversion are listed in figure 2.

4.6   Conclusions and Further Work

The work presented in this paper is the first step towards a generic approach to the conversion of MARC to FRBR. This work shows that it is possible to generalize into a common scheme the complex set of conditions and rules that governs the conversion of MARC to FRBR and in this way support different projects with a tool for converting a MARC-based catalogue.

The tool itself does not define how to interpret a MARC record but enables researchers and developers to apply a conversion based on the rules they define. Due to the level of similarity between MARC formats a large number of rules may be reusable across catalogues. The information in certain records may be sparse and it is of course not possible to directly identify other entities than the ones that are evident from the information in the records. For example the possibility to identify the correct entities and relationships for added entries will depend on the use of relator codes and indicators for these entries.

The conversion tool has been used in the FRBRization of the BIBSYS bibliographic database[1] that uses the BIBSYS-MARC format. The tool is nevertheless

---

[1] The BIBSYS FRBR project was a cooperation between BIBSYS – a Norwegian service center for libraries, the Norwegian University of Science and Technology and the National Library of Norway. The project was funded by the Norwegian Archive, Library and Museum Authority.

```xml
<xsl:stylesheet xmlns:xsl="http://www.w3.org/1999/XSL/Transform" version="2.0">
<xsl:template name="Work130">
 <xsl:for-each select="/record/datafield[@tag='130']">
  <xsl:variable name="fieldnr" select="position()" />
  <record>
  <xsl:attribute name="tempid" select="concat(/record/@tempid, ':', @tag, ':work130:', $fieldnr)" />
  <xsl:attribute name="type" select="'Work'" />

  <xsl:for-each select="/record/datafield[@tag='130'][$fieldnr],
                        /record/datafield[@tag='045' and subfield/@code = ('a')],
                        /record/datafield[@tag='658' and subfield/@code = ('a')],
                        /record/datafield[@tag='792' and subfield/@code = ('k','m','t')]">
   <xsl:copy>
   <xsl:call-template name="copy-field" />
   <xsl:for-each select="subfield">
    <xsl:choose>
     <xsl:when test="../@tag= 130 and @code='a'">
      <xsl:copy>
       <xsl:call-template name="copy-field"><xsl:with-param name="type" select="'Tittel'" /></xsl:call-template>
      </xsl:copy>
     </xsl:when>
     <xsl:when test="../@tag= 130 and @code='b'">
      <xsl:copy>
       <xsl:call-template name="copy-field"><xsl:with-param name="type" select="'Tittel'" /></xsl:call-template>
      </xsl:copy>
     </xsl:when>
     <!-- additional attribute rules ....... -->
    </xsl:choose>
   </xsl:for-each>
   </xsl:copy>
  </xsl:for-each>

  <xsl:for-each select="/record/datafield[@tag='800']">
    <xsl:variable name="target_fieldnr" select="position()" />
    <relationship rel="is part of" target="Work">
    <xsl:attribute name="href" select="concat(/record/@tempid, ':', '800', ':', 'work800', ':', position())" />
    </relationship>
  </xsl:for-each>
   <xsl:for-each select="/record/datafield[@tag='130']">
     <xsl:variable name="target_fieldnr" select="position()" />
     <xsl:if test="$target_fieldnr=$fieldnr">
      <relationship rel="is realized in" target="Expression">
      <xsl:attribute name="href" select="concat(/record/@tempid, ':', '130', ':', 'expression', ':', position())" />
      </relationship>
     </xsl:if>
  </xsl:for-each>
  <xsl:for-each select="/record/datafield[@tag='600']">
   <xsl:variable name="target_fieldnr" select="position()" />
   <xsl:if test="not(exists(subfield[@code = ('t')]))">
    <relationship rel="is about" target="Person">
     <xsl:attribute name="href" select="concat(/record/@tempid, ':', '600', ':', 'person600', ':', position())" />
    </relationship>
   </xsl:if>
  </xsl:for-each>
   <xsl:for-each select="/record/datafield[@tag='600']">
    <xsl:variable name="target_fieldnr" select="position()" />
    <xsl:if test="subfield/@code = 't'">
     <relationship rel="is about" target="Work">
     <xsl:attribute name="href" select="concat(/record/@tempid, ':', '600', ':', 'work600', ':', position())" />
     </relationship>
    </xsl:if>
  </xsl:for-each>
  <!-- additional relationship rules ....... -->

  </record>
 </xsl:for-each>
</xsl:template>
</xsl:stylesheet>
```

Fig. 3. Sample template for creating work entity records for 130 fields

able to support all the structural aspects of MARC-based formats such as the use of indicators, relator codes and field linking.

The tool can be improved in different ways. The use of better performing keys and key matching algorithms is an important topic in the further development of the tool and we are currently looking at the use of external services for retrieving information that can be added in the preprocessing step to improve the quality of the conversion. Additional future work includes the conversion to other formats than the ad-hoc XML format used in the project and the use of more formal identifiers for FRBR types. Particularly the use of RDF combined with a formal FRBR ontology e.g. in OWL will be explored.

References

1. Marie-Louise Ayres. Case studies in implementing Functional Requirements for Bibliographic Records [FRBR]: AustLit and MusicAustralia. *ALJ: the Australian Library Journal*, 54(1):43–54, February 2005.
   http://www.nla.gov.au/nla/staffpaper/2005/ayres1.html.
2. Knut Hegna and Eeva Murtomaa. *Data Mining MARC to Find : FRBR?* BIBSYS/HUL, 2002. http://folk.uio.no/knuthe/dok/frbr/datamining.pdf.
3. Thomas B. Hickey, Edward T. O'Neill, and Jenny Toves. Experiments with the IFLA Functional Requirements for Bibliographic Records (FRBR). *D-Lib Magazine*, 8(9), September 2002.
   http://www.dlib.org/dlib/september02/hickey/09hickey.html.
4. International Organization for Standardization TC46/SC4. Information and Documentation : MarcXchange. Draft standard ISO/CD 25577, ISO, 2005.
   http://www.bs.dk/marcxchange/.
5. Christian Mönch and Trond Aalberg. Automatic conversion from MARC to FRBR. In *Research and Advanced Technology for Digital Libraries, ECDL 2003*, number 2769 in Lecture Notes in Computer Science, pages 405–411. Springer-Verlag, 2003.
6. OCLC. Fictionfinder. http://fictionfinder.oclc.org/.
7. OCLC. FRBR work-set algorithm.
   http://www.oclc.org/research/projects/frbr/algorithm.htm.
8. IFLA Study Group on the functional requirements for bibliographic records. *Functional requirements for bibliographic records : final report*, volume 19 of *UBCIM Publications : New Series*. K. G. Saur, Munich, 1998.
   http://www.ifla.org/VII/s13/frbr/frbr.pdf.
9. Bemal Rajapatirana and Roxanne Missingham. The Australian National Bibliographic Database and the Functional Requirements for the Bibliographic Database (FRBR). *ALJ: the Australian Library Journal*, 54(1):31–42, February 2005.
   http://www.nla.gov.au/nla/staffpaper/2005/missingham3.html.
10. The Library of Congress' Network Development and MARC Standards Office. FRBR Display Tool.
    http://www.loc.gov/marc/marc-functional-analysis/tool.html.
11. The Library of Congress' Network Development and MARC Standards Office. Functional analysis of the MARC 21 bibliographic and holdings formats.
    http://www.loc.gov/marc/marc-functional-analysis.
12. VTLS Inc. Virtua integrated library system.
    http://www.vtls.com/Products/virtua.shtml.

Metadata Spaces: The Concept and a Case with REPOX

Nuno Freire, Hugo Manguinhas, and José Borbinha

National Library of Portugal, Campo Grande, 83, 1741-081 Lisboa, Portugal
nuno.freire@bn.pt
INESC-ID, Rua Alves Redol, 9, Apartado 13069, 1000-029 Lisboa, Portugal
mangas@bn.pt
INESC-ID, Rua Alves Redol, 9, Apartado 13069, 1000-029 Lisboa, Portugal
jlb@ist.utl.pt

Abstract. This paper describes REPOX, an XML infrastructure to store, preserve and manage metadata sets. This infrastructure is designed accordingly to the requirements of the OAIS - Reference Model for an Open Archival Information System. It can play the role of a broker or other specific service in a Service Oriented Architecture, aligned with an Enterprise Architecture model, to manage, transparently, data sets of information entities in digital libraries, independently of their schemas or formats. The main default functions of this service are submission, storage, long-term preservation and retrieval. The case is demonstrated with a deployment at the National Library of Portugal, using data collections from two information systems and four schemas: bibliographic and authority metadata from a union catalogue and descriptive and authority metadata from an archive management system.

1 Introduction

This paper proposes the concept of Metadata Space, defining its main properties and functions. The paper presents also a proof of that concept in the design and deployment off a solution at the National Library of Portugal (BN). This solution, named REPOX, is more than a simple proof of concept, representing already a stable service, providing effective support to key business processes and activities in a real organization.

A concept of "metadata space" has been proposed in [13], but such was defined in a specific scenario of metadata retrieval. Although sharing the same designation, our concept is different, closer to the concept of "dataspace" as defined in [3]. We prefer here the term "metadata" instead of "data" because we intend to stress our focus in the business area of digital libraries, where the term as already a special meaning. We must recognize that in information systems the term metadata is not used usually to refer to information entities, but to the information need to describe the models and schemas of these information entities, as it is considered by the ISO/IEC 11176 [10]. However, in digital libraries metadata has been a term used often with a different meaning, to refer to the instances of specific class of information entities, recording information about the digital library information objects.

S. Sugimoto et al. (Eds.): ICADL 2006, LNCS 4312, pp. 293–302, 2006.

In this scope, we start by defining a Metadata Space as a service that manages, transparently, large amounts of data structures, independently of their schemas or formats. These data structures are information entities related to a specific business process or activity, so the relevance of the Metadata Space will be in its properties of preservation and persistent reference. In this sense it is related with the functional requirements of the OAIS Reference Model [5], and not intended to replace any functional property of a common database management system.

In a generic sense, our concept of Metadata Space is defined aligned with the concept of Enterprise Architecture (EA[1]) and the emerging of computing environments deployed as Service Oriented Architectures (SOA)[2]. At BN, for example, this is already part of a new strategic technological view for its digital library's architecture.

This paper follows with a more detailed discussion of the concept of Metadata Space. This is followed by the description of the design and deployment of a Metadata Space at BN. Finally, we present some conclusions and describe the future work.

2   The Concept of Metadata Spaces

When a business environment changes we must also expect that its supporting information systems might have to change. This is happening everywhere in all the kinds of organizations and business areas, and there is no reason to think that it would be different for libraries, archives, documentation centres, museums, and all those cases that we can include informally under the scope of "digital libraries". It is with this in mind that we want to stress here the relevance of the concepts of Enterprise Architecture (EA) and Service Oriented Architecture (SOA).

The ANSI/IEEE 1471-2000 standard[3] defines architecture as "the fundamental organization of a system, embodied in its components, their relationships to each other and the environment, and the principles governing its design and evolution." In this sense, the concept of EA emerges to help organizations understand their business, structure and processes. An EA must provide a map of the organization and a plan for its business and technology continuous change. This is not a new concept, as it can be tracked to a long time ago.

Meanwhile a new world arrived with the technology associated with the World Wide Web, XML and the concept of SOA. The most important keyword here is flexibility! Under this model the design and development of information systems builds on a global view of the world in which services are assembled and reused to quickly adapt to new tasks and business needs. This means that the configuration of an information system might have to change at any moment, removing, adding or replacing services on the fly. This flexibility has been driving the way of how new information systems are being built. But although SOA addresses many of the traditional problems of integrating disparate business processes and applications, deploying systematic service-based applications introduces new requirements.

---

[1] http://en.wikipedia.org/wiki/Enterprise_Architect
[2] http://en.wikipedia.org/wiki/Service-oriented_architecture
[3] http://standards.ieee.org/reading/ieee/std_public/description/se/1471-2000_desc.html

In an organization with a well designed EA, the separation between the information and the information system has to be clear. The re-engineering of the information architectures according to this requirement has been an important concern in the organisations during the last twenty years. However, strangely this has not been widely recognized in the area of digital libraries, where, in a large number of cases, the business processes, the information structures and the applications, have been all mixed in the same overall sets of requirements and solutions.

In this sense, we define a Metadata Space as <u>a networked service for preservation and retrieval of information entities, with the following requirements</u>:

- Schema Registration: This comprises services for the registration of any data schema that can be expressed in XML or in a related way (this registration is only for the purposes of identification, to support naming schemas in internal processes and interoperability, as a Metadata Space should not be confused with a Metadata Registry, even if it follows in its design and implementation the terminology and the basic concepts defined by the ISO/IEC 11176).
- Submission: This comprises services for the submission of data records of any data schema previously registered. This comprises also the services for synchronisation with the external data sources, or the data provenience, independently of the technology for creating or exporting it.
- Unlimited Storage: The management of the storage space, including in its capacity, should be an internal property of the Metadata Space, and in any case its possible limitations should be a concern of the external services.
- Persistency: This implies the ability to assure the persistency of the data records (long-term preservation) and of their identifiers. It means that once a record is submitted, its later retrieval must be always assured. It includes the management of the versioning of the records, and accordingly the unique identification of each instance. Therefore, the functions of update and delete are not supported, as only new versions can be submitted.
- Retrieval: This comprises services for the retrieval of the metadata records by their identifiers (assuring therefore external persistent linking).

Ultimately, we would like to propose this concept as a new primitive service for digital libraries reference models. We are aware that its usefulness and opportunity needs to be better proved, so this paper is also a step in that sense.

3   The REPOX Model

REPOX is an implementation of our concept of a Metadata Space. The way the records are coded and managed in REPOX addresses the preservation requirements in OAIS [5], as also in [1] and [2], namely by providing platform free and non proprietary tools for the management of the preservation processes, it is robust, flexible, provides mechanisms for self-description and validation of digital resources.

The data model actually defined for REPOX is shown in the Fig. 1, and the main components of the related information system are depicted in Fig. 2.

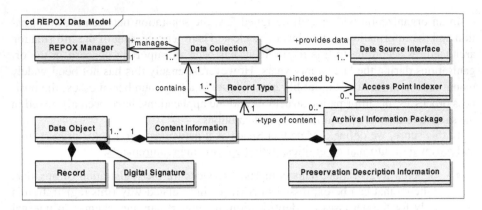

Fig. 1. The REPOX data model

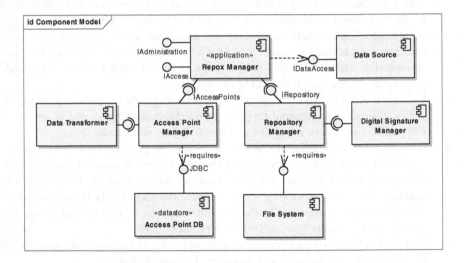

Fig. 2. The REPOX component diagram

According to the data model, each data collection must have at least one data source. Also, each data source is associated with one interface. These interfaces are software components responsible for obtaining the records, check or coding them according with their XML schema, and delivering them to REPOX. The harvesting of records may occur with any periodicity, defined in the configuration of the data collection (in the deployment at BN the most common are harvests in each 24 hours).

Each data collection can be associated to one or more record types. These represent the entities that will be collected from the data source in a XML record representation and managed by REPOX. The records of these entities are the simplest unit of data managed by the system. Their only characteristics that REPOX is aware of are their identifiers within the data collection and their XML schema.

Alternative access points can enable the retrieval of the records by more then only their identifiers. For that purpose, access point indexers (API) can be associated to record types, to define how to process the information pertinent. These API are used by the access point manager (APM) to collect the relevant data from each record and build the respective indexes (which can be maintained in a relational database for efficiency, as they are not part of the fundamental model). The APM has a default set of API defined according to the Dublin Core elements (DC)[4], but additional access points may be created for any other schema. The default APM supports a data transformation component that can be easily configured to convert any metadata schema to DC. Although nowadays this component explicitly implements the transformations, we expect that in the future, with the availability of metadata registries, this component might be able to implement these data transformations more transparently.

Each record managed by REPOX is wrapped in an Archive Information Package (AIP), defined as in the OAIS model [5]. It is coded in XML according to the AIP schema and is stored in a file, thus assuring that its storage remains independent of any particular storage system. These AIP objects contain all the information about the provenance and history of the record and of each of its versions. Therefore, REPOX maintains a URN namespace[5] for the identification of each version of the records, as also for each collection, record types and AIP.

Authenticity is another important requirement in our problem. The case of assuring long term authenticity of electronic records has been studied in [6] and [7]. In REPOX the records are stored as simple XML files, in the local file system. File systems security against changes in the files is not enough to guarantee the level of authenticity that we need, so we designed a Digital Signature Manager component, responsible for signing the records and checking their integrity. The authenticity of the records is checked periodically, but the on-demand verification is also possible. A possible point of failure in this authenticity infrastructure can occur if we need to preserve both the digital signature and the validation function, as recognized in [0]. REPOX addresses this problem by following the W3C XML-Signature Syntax and Processing recommendation [9], and also by providing mechanisms for the integration of future digital signature algorithms with migration of the existing digital signatures.

4 The REPOX Architecture

The main component of the REPOX infrastructure is the REPOX Manager. Fig. 3 shows an example of the actual deployment of this component as a Java EE[6] application implementing the model already described in the previous section.

The REPOX Manager harvests the records from the data sources via the data source interfaces. The records are digitally signed by the Digital Signature Manager, are wrapped in an AIP, and are archived in the file system. After that, the Access Point Manager creates and stores the indexes of the access points in a MySql database.

Human end-users can use a web interface for searching, navigation and access records individually, showing all the existing information. Command line tools allow a system's administrator to create, update or eliminate access points; to export records; to manually trigger the execution of a data collection harvest, etc. Similar services are available for machines, by a web services interface.

---

[4] http://dublincore.org/
[5] http://www.w3.org/TR/uri-clarification/
[6] http://java.sun.com/javaee/index.jsp

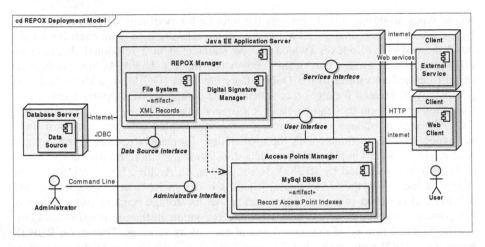

Fig. 3. A REPOX deployment at BN

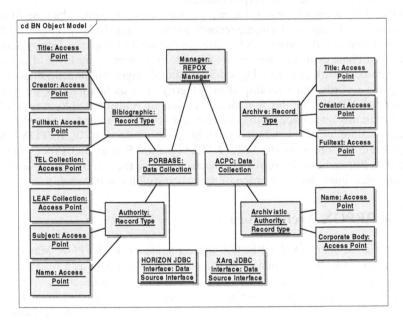

Fig. 4. The BN data collections

5   REPOX in Use at BN: The Data Collections

The REPOX infrastructure deployed at BN has been supporting two data collections: PORBASE and the Archive of the Contemporary Portuguese Culture.

PORBASE – Base Nacional de Dados Bibliográficos[7], is the national bibliographic union catalogue in Portugal. It is the largest bibliographic database in the country,

---

[7] http://www.porbase.org

with collections from nearly 200 libraries. A central library management system stores the data in a Sybase database management system (DBMS). PORBASE is an important source of information whose potential has not been fully explored, a problem that BN wants to tackle by developing new services based on REPOX. The security and preservation of the PORBASE is also an important issue to be tackled.

PORBASE is maintained by a proprietary information system designed to support the traditional cataloguing and searching processes. The database schema of this system is tuned for its own processes, therefore not always compatible with the requirements of the new services. Besides that, the possible utilization of the same server used for the cataloguing and searching by the general public would overload it with tasks that usually could be executed on a different server. Finally, there is a need to assure the data replication, coded under an open schema and stored in an open infrastructure, fulfilling the requirements for a more generic security and preservation.

Fig. 4 depicts the instantiation of the two data collections from BN in the REPOX data model. For the PORBASE data collection, two types of records are managed: UNIMARC[8] bibliographic and UNIMARC authority.

For the bibliographic records, there exist access points for titles, authors, identifiers (ISBN, ISSN, call numbers, legal deposit number, etc.), as well as for other specific cases required by the services using the repository. For the authority records, there are indexes for names of persons, names of corporate bodies, subjects, dates, etc.

The data of the PORBASE information system is stored in a Sybase DBMS. The data source interface for that extracts the bibliographic and authority records by means of a direct connection using JDBC. The records, structured in UNIMARC (the main format for exchanging bibliographic records in Portugal, and therefore in PORBASE), are extracted daily and coded in XML following the MarcXchange schema [4]. This counts actually more than 3 million records (including both bibliographic and authority records), performing 26 GBytes when coded in XML.

Both types of records are organized in collections by a collection access point. Examples of collections for the bibliographic records are those built for each library member of the PORBASE network (one collection for each library). Other examples are the collections created for TEL – The European Library[9], using the criteria defined for that purpose. Other collections exist for other purposes, based on queries by subjects, places, dates, languages, etc. For this data collection the actual system maintains a total of 33 access points and manages 21 collections of bibliographic records and 4 collections of authority records.

The other relevant data collection managed by the REPOX instance at BN is the Archive of the Contemporary Portuguese Culture[10] (ACPC). The ACPC manages the literary archives of writers and other personalities of special relevance in the Portuguese history and culture. This data source is managed by its own information system (named X-Arq), supported by a Microsoft SQL Server. It contains archival records in a format that follows the ISAD(G)[11] rules, and also authority records according to the

[8] http://www.unimarc.info
[9] http://www.theeuropeanlibrary.org/
[10] http://acpc.bn.pt
[11] http://www.ica.org/biblio/cds/isad_g_2e.pdf

ISAAR(CPF)[12]. The REPOX interface for this data source is also assured by JDBC. The archival records are coded in EAD[13] (version of 2002), and the authority records, in EAC[14].

6   REPOX in Use at BN: The External Services

A high number of services at BN are already in stable production using REPOX. In this moment, those services are using only data from PORBASE, as there are no cases yet of stable services using data from ACPC. These are:

- **URN.PORBASE.ORG - Access to PORBASE by Unique Identifiers** (http://urn.porbase.org): this is a very simple but effective service that makes available records from PORBASE to other libraries in several formats via an HTTP interface. Both bibliographic and authority collections are available. The records can be retrieved by several unique identifiers (ISBN, ISSN, legal deposit number, call number, etc.), whose resolution is supported by access points in REPOX. Besides the native format UNIMARC, the records are also made available in other structural formats, such as Dublin Core, as also in several coding formats (XML, HTML, plain text, ISO 2709, etc). These formats are generated in runtime by applying XSLT transformations to the XML records retrieved from REPOX. This service has proved to be very useful to interoperate with external services, especially library management systems which by this way can import records directly for local cataloguing.
- **Qualicat**: This is an internal service assuring the daily quality control of the bibliographic records, according to the requirements of the UNIMARC format, the Portuguese Cataloguing Rules, and also to the specific rules of PORBASE.
- **OAI-PMH[15] Service** (http://oai.bn.pt): This is a generic OAI service that makes available the records from PORBASE to cooperation projects. The OAI server gets the records from REPOX in sets that are maintained by the collection managers. A regular client of this service is the portal TEL - The European Library, where the central host harvests regularly the records from PORBASE and makes them available for searching and access (the records are obtained in MarcXchange and transformed into the TEL format by a XSLT transformation).
- **Google Scholar[16]**: PORBASE is one of the bibliographic databases pioneers in providing its data to Google Scholar for indexing, which is built over REPOX. Users of Google Scholar can see now links to the OPAC of PORBASE when their searches hit related records.
- **IRIS**: This service supports the update in PORBASE of the databases of its co-operating libraries. It supports a specific workflow and provides special features of quality control, automatic correction of errors in records, detection of duplicates, report and automated integration of bibliographic and holdings records.

---

[12] http://www.ica.org/biblio/isaar_eng.html
[13] http://www.loc.gov/ead/
[14] http://eprints.rclis.org/archive/00000316/01/pitti_eng.pdf
[15] http://www.openarchives.org/
[16] http://scholar.google.com

- **Daily Reports**: This service reports about cataloguing activity in PORBASE. It notifies the users of the system by email of all operations performed on the records during the previous 24 hours. The data is retrieved after-hours from REPOX, after its daily synchronization with PORBASE.

7 Conclusions and Future Work

REPOX started its operation with PORBASE on the 1st of October of 2005, followed by the implementation of related new services and the re-engineering of existing ones. Immediately afterwards, it was noticeable the increase in the availability and performance of access to the data, carried out by several departments of the National Library and the cooperating libraries. Also, the proprietary library management system was freed from serving many accesses to the records originated from other automated systems that were overloading it considerably. Other factor of great relevance was the backup copy of the data, expressed in XML and by this way preserved independently of any specific software or hardware.

Future developments will focus on a mechanism to support global queries for the retrieval of the record across multiple types and data sources. To better address the authenticity issues, we will implement the XML Advanced Electronic Signatures W3C recommendation [12]. We are also planning the development of services for cross-maps of metadata schemas stored in REPOX, such as to retrieve Dublin Core or MARC21 records created "on the fly" from original UNIMARC records. This will be a generalisation of the concept of the actual service URN.PORBASE.ORG (which serves only authority or bibliographic UNIMARC records from PORBASE).

Another important service will be an OpenURL[17] resolving service, a long awaited achievement by BN that will be now easy to develop in the scope of this new SOA environment. We are also following the work on the Long-term Archive Protocol [11] and its possible relevance for REPOX.

Finally, services are being developed to provide detailed statistics, quality control (including of the semantics of the records), as well as the study of data warehousing to support general data mining services to support management decision processes.

References

1. Electronic Resource Preservation and Access Network (ERPANET): Urbino Workshop: XML for Digital Preservation (2002) http://eprints.erpanet.org/archive/00000002/01/UrbinoWorkshopReport.pdf
2. Boudrez, F.: XML and electronic record-keeping (2002) http://www.expertisecentrumdavid.be/ davidproject/ teksten/XML_erecordkeeping.pdf
3. Franklin, M., Halevy, A., Maier, D.: From Databases to Dataspaces: A New Abstraction for Information Management. ACM SIGMOD Record (2005)
4. MarcXchange. MARC Records XML Schema: http://www.bs.dk/marcxchange/
5. Consultative Committee for Space Data Systems. OAIS - Reference Model for an Open Archival Information System (2002)

---

[17] http://www.niso.org/committees/committee_ax.html

6. Gladney H.M.:Trustworthy 100-Year Digital Objects: Evidence After Every Witness Is Dead. ACM Transactions on Information Systems, Vol. 22, No. 3 (2004) 406–436.
7. Waugh, A., Wilkinson, R., Hills, B., Dell'oro, J.: Preserving Digital Information Forever. Proceedings of the fifth ACM conference on Digital libraries (2000)
8. Boudrez, F.: Digital signatures and electronic records (2005) http://www. expertisecentrumdavid. be/docs/digitalsignatures.pdf
9. W3C Consortium: XML-Signature Syntax and Processing http://www.w3.org/TR/ xmldsig-core/#sec-SignatureAlg
10. ISO/IEC 11179, Information Technology - Metadata Registries (MDR). http://metadata-standards.org/11179
11. Blazic, A.J., Sylvester, P., Wallace, C.: Long-term Archive Protocol (LTAP) (2006) http://www.ietf.org/internet-drafts/draft-ietf-ltans-ltap-01.txt
12. W3C Consortium: XML Advanced Electronic Signatures (XAdES) http://www.w3.org/ TR/XAdES/
13. Wason, T., Wiley, D.: Structured Metadata Spaces. Metadata and Organizing Educational Resources on the Internet, NY: Haworth Press (2001) http://opencontent.org/docs/ metadata_spaces.pdf

Extending Greenstone for Institutional Repositories

David Bainbridge[1], Wendy Osborn[2], Ian H. Witten[1], and David M. Nichols[1]

[1] Department of Computer Science
University of Waikato
Hamilton, New Zealand
{davidb, ihw, dmn}@cs.waikato.ac.nz
[2] Department of Mathematics and Computer Science
University of Lethbridge
Lethbridge, Canada
osborn@cs.uleth.ca

Abstract. We examine the problem of designing a generalized system for building institutional repositories. Widely used schemes such as DSpace are tailored to a particular set of requirements: fixed metadata set; standard view when searching and browsing; pre-determined sequence for depositing items; built-in workflow for vetting new items. In contrast, Fedora builds in flexibility: institutional repositories are just one possible instantiation—however generality incurs a high overhead and uptake has been sluggish. This paper shows how existing components of the Greenstone software can be repurposed to provide a generalized institutional repository that falls between these extremes.

1 Introduction

Institutional repositories are a popular form of digital library. Although many software systems exist to support them, widely used ones (such as DSpace [1]) are tailored to particular requirements. They assume a certain metadata set and present readers with a fixed view of the collection when searching and browsing the repository. Depositing an item involves a pre-determined sequence of steps; the presentation of the pages in the sequence is difficult to customize; and the workflow involved in reviewing new items is built-in. Although with sufficient programming effort one can circumvent such restrictions—existing institutional repository systems do provide some hooks to facilitate a limited degree of personalization—it is fair to say that they are not designed with flexibility in mind. For example, it would be hard to adapt them to use a radically different metadata set or a different sequence of operations when depositing new items.

The Fedora framework [2] is an interesting exception that has been designed expressly with flexibility in mind—an institutional repository is merely one possible instantiation. However working with such a generalized system incurs a high overhead and such manifestations have been slow to emerge. One promising development in this area is Fez [3], which we review with other institutional repository software solutions in Section 6.

S. Sugimoto et al. (Eds.): ICADL 2006, LNCS 4312, pp. 303–312, 2006.

The paper is structured as follows. First we discuss what we mean by a "generalized institutional repository." Section 3 demonstrates a minimalist example to help convey the salient features of such a resource. Then we describe how existing components of Greenstone were repurposed to give it functionality comparable to existing repository systems. Section 5 presents a second worked example to show how the new system can be configured to emulate DSpace's submission workflow. We conclude by placing the work in the context of other repository software: DSpace, GNU EPrints and Fez.

2 Background

Greenstone is a suite of software for building and distributing digital library collections [4]. It is not a digital library but a tool for building digital libraries. It provides a flexible way of organizing information and publishing it on the Internet in the form of a fully-searchable, metadata-driven digital library. Using it, a rich set of different types of collections can be formed that reflect the nature of the source documents and metadata available.

In extending Greenstone for institutional repository use our aim was to develop a software solution that transcends the limitations imposed by current solutions specifically targeted towards institutional repositories, without triggering the high startup costs of shifting to a highly generalized framework.

We want to enable librarians to turn any Greenstone collection into a repository into which new items and metadata can be deposited by authorized personnel through an ordinary web interface. But different Greenstone collections have different metadata sets, and there is no restriction on how extensive—or minimalist—such metadata can be. So when metadata is entered through a sequence of web pages, the content of these pages, the number of pages in the sequence, and the metadata items that each one requests must all be customizable. For one collection a single web form may suffice; another may require a long sequence of different forms. When the depositing user goes back to an earlier to step to correct a metadata entry this variable amount of data—which is entirely dependent on the metadata set in use—must be remembered by the web browser.

We use the following notion of "generalized institutional repository":

- *The digital library collection can use any metadata set.*
- *Depositing an item can involve any number of steps.*
- *The stages involved in depositing an item can be designed individually.*
- *Flexible workflow.*

Depending on institutional procedures librarians may have roles such as 'reviewer', 'approver' or 'editor' for deposited items [1].

3 Example of Operation

To help illustrate the core business of an institutional repository, here is a minimalist example. Imagine a Faculty of Arts that has moved to a digital solution—couched as an institutional repository—that replaces the physical photographic color slide resource that the Faculty previously provided.

Figure 1 shows the submission process, which has in fact been developed using the newly extended version of Greenstone. A single page is used to gather salient facts before an item is deposited. Only four items of metadata are requested along with a picture of the artwork: title, artist, date and notes. A real-world version would most likely request many more fields than this.

To reach this page the user has already had to log in. In Figure 1a she is selecting the destination collection (the Art History repository). In the next step (Figure 1b) she has used the file browser that is launched by pressing the "Browse ..." button to locate the artwork to submit, and entered metadata describing the items (Title: The Bower Meadow; Artist: Rossetti; Date: 1871–1872) along with notes about the painting. Along the bottom is a progress bar with a triangular marker showing the current position ("specify metadata").

Clicking on "deposit item" takes her to the next step (Figure 1c) where the new information is digested into the collection, which occurs in a matter of seconds. The final step is to view the collection, which is shown in Figure 1d where the user is browsing the Art History Repository by title. The repository is clearly in its early stages with only three items added so far, with the newest addition, *The Bower Meadow*, listed at the top.

4 Implementation

Only a modest amount of development work was necessary to extend Greenstone to support the notion of generalized institutional repository given earlier. The three enabling technologies were macros, runtime actions, and incremental building, all of which exist in Greenstone.

Greenstone macros are the key to controlling the generalized workflow. Checking form content and manipulations of form layout (adding in previous values etc.) are spliced into macros through JavaScript and DOM manipulation. To enable document submission, an existing runtime 'action' called The Collector [5], which supports the creation and building of collections through a web browser, was further abstracted and generalized. This 'action' was already able to provide a progress bar and used a database to store previously entered values from one page to the next. The new extension was to add support for multipart form file-upload with the new action called "the depositor." Incremental building using the Lucene indexer [6] is already a feature of Greenstone.

4.1 Macros

A Greenstone installation's look and feel, page structure and language interfaces, are all achieved using a simple macro language. Figure 2 shows an artificial excerpt to illustrate the syntax through which macros are defined and used. Macro definitions comprise a name, flanked by underscores, and the corresponding content, placed within braces ({ ... }).

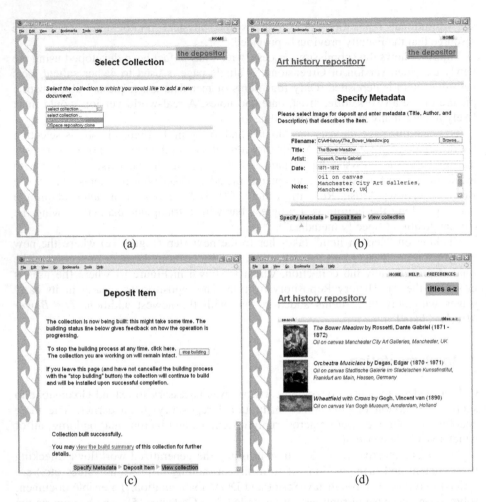

Fig. 1. A simple example (a) selecting the Art History repository (b) selecting and image and entering metadata (c) depositing the item (d) browsing the collection

Macros are grouped together into *packages*, with lexical scoping, and an inheritance scheme is used to determine which definitions are in effect at any given time. This allows global formatting styles to be embedded with the particular content that is generated for a page. For example, typical pages contain a *_header_* ... *_content_* ... *_footer_* sequence. Figure 2 shows a baseline page defined in the "Globals" package, which, in fact, is never intended to be seen. It is overridden in the "query" package below to generate a page that invites the user to enter search terms and perform a query.

Macros can include parameters interposed in square brackets between name and content. These are known as "page parameters" because they control the overall generation of a page. They are expressed as [*x=y*], which gives parameter *x* the value *y*. Two parameters of particular interest are *l*, which determines what language is used, and *v*, which controls whether or not images are used in the interface.

```
package Globals

_header_  \{ The New Zealand Digital Library Project \}
_content_ \{ Oops. If you are reading this then an error
             has occurred in the runtime system. \}
_footer_  \{ Powered by <a href="www.greenstone.org">Greenstone</a>.
\}

package query

_content_ \{ _If_(_cgiargqb_ eq
"large",_largequerybox_,_normalquerybox_)
     ... \}

# ... the macro descriptions for _largequerybox_, _normalquerybox_,
#   and other nested macros are omitted for brevity

_header_ [l=en] \{Begin search \}
_header_ [l=fr] \{D\'emarrer la recherche \}
_header_ [l=es] \{Iniciar la b\'usqueda\}

# ... and so on
```

Fig. 2. Excerpt of macro file syntax to demonstrate main features

In Figure 2 three versions of the macro *_header_* are defined within the "query" package, corresponding to the English, French and Spanish languages. They set the parameter *l* to the appropriate two-letter international standard abbreviation (ISO 639), enabling the system to present the appropriate version when the page is generated.

A precedence ordering for evaluating page parameters is built into the macro language to resolve conflicting definitions. Also included are conditional statements—an example can be seen in the *_content_* macro of Figure 2, which uses an "If" statement, conditioned by the macro *_cgiargqb_*, to determine whether the query box that appears on the search page should be the normal one or a large one. The value of *_cgiargqb_* is set at runtime by the Greenstone system (the user can change it on a "Preferences" page). Many other system-defined macros have values that are determined at runtime: examples include the URL prefix where Greenstone is installed on the system, and the number of documents returned by a search.

4.2 Controlling the Workflow

Figure 3 shows edited highlights of the macro file that produces the simple workflow shown in Figure 1. ssKey points in the file are:

- *_numsteps_*, a compulsory macro that defines the number *N* of stages in this submission process.
- *_step1content_*, *_step2content_*, ... *_stepNcontent_* is the convention used to define the page content that is displayed, along with *_stepNtext_* which controls what appears in the progress bar.
- *_step1text_* in this example is defined to be *_textmeta_*, another macro (defined at the bottom of Figure 2) which resolves through the language independence feature to "specify metadata" when viewed in English
- *_laststep_* controls how the workflow ends: for example, automatic building the collection, or going to the collection's editor for review.

```
package depositor

_numsteps_ {1}

_textstep1_ {_textmeta_}
_laststep_ {build}
_textlaststep_ {_textbuild_}


_step1content_ {

<form name="depositorform" method=post action="_gwcgi_"
  enctype="multipart/form-data">
<input type=hidden name="p" value="_cgiargp_">

<center><h2>_textstep1_</h2></center>
<p>_textimagesimpledesc_</p>

<p><table>
<tr>
  <td>Filename:</td>
  <td> <input type=file name=dauserfile value="_userfile_" size=61></td>
</tr>

<tr>
  <td>Title:</td>
  <td> <input type=text name=damd.dc.Title value="_damd.dc.Title_"
        size=74></td>
</tr>
<!-- and so on … -->
</table></p>

<!-- … -->
<p>_depositorbar_</p>
</form>
}

_textmeta_ [l=en] {Specify Metadata}
```

Fig. 3. Excerpt of macro file for producing the first step of the submission process for the Fine Arts Repository example

- _depositorbar_ is defined by the runtime system (the depositor action). It is formed by composing the information represented in _numsteps_ with _step1text_, _step2text_ and so on. _laststep_ specifies which of the predefined endings terminates the submission process (e.g. _contentbuild_ and _textbuild_). Since these two are stored in the macro files they can be refined and extended as needed.

5   Extended Example: Emulating DSpace

To demonstrate the versatility of the design, a submission workflow in Greenstone was developed that closely emulates DSpace's [1]. Since both are open source systems, much of the HTML was transferred directly. The functionality is very similar, the difference being in how a submission involving multiple files is handled—as when submitting a web page including external resources such as images. In DSpace each file must be individually specified from within the form-based submission process. Since Greenstone can already handle archive formats such as Zip and Tar, we decided to ask the user to submit multiple-file works in this form. All files that make up the work must still be identified, but this happens outside the form-based submission, and is usually easier since the files can be multiply selected in one go.

In DSpace, runtime functionality for the submission process is handled by the server. If Title metadata is compulsory this is checked when the user proceeds to the next step of the submission process. In Greenstone the analogous functionality was embedded into each web page using JavaScript. This offers more flexibility to customize the workflow and more immediate feedback to the user.

Figure 4 shows snapshots of a faculty member working their way through the Greenstone adaptation of the DSpace submission procedure. To submit an item of work the user starts by logging in, and then selects the DSpace repository clone collection. Using Greenstone's collection macro override facility, this repository provides its own tailored workflow—eight steps in all, visible at the top of the snapshots. In the simple example of Figure 1 the progress bar was located at the bottom of the page, but it is easy to move the position of the macro _depositorbar_ within the structured HTML to move it to at the top. In DSpace the progress bar is implemented as a series of images, and although we could have emulated this we chose not to because there is an existing Greenstone facility with the same function—furthermore it makes it easier to change the color scheme, fonts and wording used. (We tend to avoid textual images in Greenstone to facilitate multilingual operation.)

The scenario here is a university that uses DSpace-style submission to manage its staff's digital outputs. In Figure 4a the instructor for a Machine Learning course is at the first page of submitting a lecture on Bayesian networks. He has entered his and a colleague's name, the title of the talk and its type (a presentation). Other fields such as series, report number, and ISBN are not relevant and so he leaves them blank.

In Figure 4b the instructor has moved to the second step, which prompts for descriptive metadata: keywords, abstract, sponsors, and description. Again not every field is relevant. For each part of the form contextual help is available that describes the purpose of the field. In Figure 4c he has moved to the point where the file (in this case PowerPoint) is requested. Next (Figure 4d) information is displayed about the file transfer from submitter's computer to the server. The checksum is shown so he can check that no transmission errors occurred. This is accomplished using AJAX technology [7] to retrieve the information from the server in an extensible manner.

The fifth step (Figure 4e) provides an opportunity to review and edit all information entered so far. It is also possible to return to any previous stage by clicking the progress bar. Making the system remember existing fields—even when they support an arbitrary number of values, as with authors—is tricky in JavaScript but possible. Figure 4f shows the final user input page, where the user decides whether to grant the distribution license. If he does, the PowerPoint presentation, along with its metadata, is time-stamped and deposited into the collection area. The collection's editor will be notified by email, and/or the collection will be incrementally rebuilt, depending on the settings in the collection's configuration file.

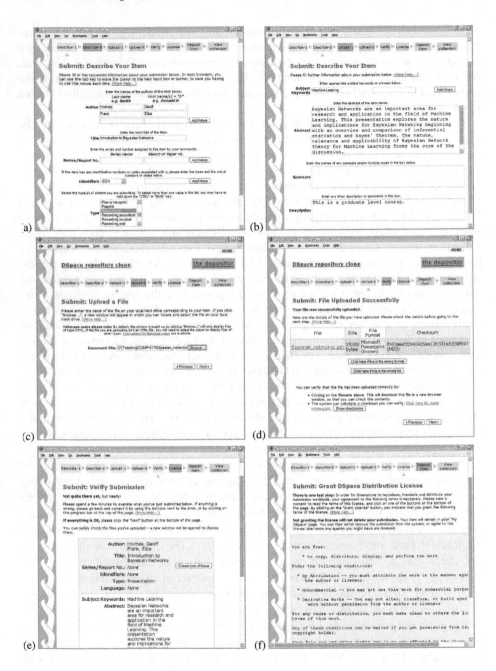

Fig. 4. Emulating the submission workflow for DSpace (a) primary metadata (b) secondary metadata (c) select file (d) check file (e) review metadata (f) choose license

6 Discussion

We now discuss the context into which this work fits by summarizing the key points to software solutions being used as institutional repositories.

DSpace is specifically designed as an institutional repository. It is a popular choice by organizations to provide a digital repository that harnesses the output of their institution. It requires an IT specialist to install, which is commensurate with the typical organizational environment in which it is used. Some customization is possible but because runtime functionality is locked up in the server it is ostensibly a fixed workflow from a librarian's perspective. Full text indexing is possible, but only limited to a small number of native file formats.

GNU EPrints [8 is another popular choice with over 200 known installations worldwide. Rather than spanning an entire organization, many EPrints installations are deployed in a niche role by an entity within the organization, although it can and is deployed in a wider context. It is easy to install and it includes configuration files that control the metadata in use and the document types supported. Ironically enough, it has been the use by niche disciplines that has driven the need to support different metadata sets rather than the unified "one shoe fits all" approach seen in DSpace; however, it lacks the notation of communities and collections, which enables a repository to be used in different ways across an organization. EPrints supports full text indexing.

Fez [3] is an emerging software solution for institutional repository use. In beta form at the time of writing, its notion of generality and configurability is more ambitious than the above two systems. It is built on top of Fedora, and is exactly the sort of development the framework is aimed at. Fez utilizes the rich complexity of the Fedora framework to deliver a system tailored for institutional repository use. It includes the concept of communities and collections, configurable workflow and metadata. While Fedora can handle full text indexing, this ability is not exposed through Fez, and there are some compatibility issues with connecting Fez with a framework that is still itself under development.

7 Conclusion

We believe that Greenstone provides the following advantages for institutional repositories: trivial to install; configurable workflow that works with any metadata set and document type; variable number of steps; collection based with support for customization; incremental building that with full text indexing across a wide range of formats include HTML, PDF, Word, PPT, email, as well as automatic metadata extraction; and language independence.

All systems we have mentioned are open source, which means that anyone wishing to evaluate them can do so freely. In practice, however, considerable effort may be needed to do a trial—installation alone is often a major stumbling block [9]. (On more than one occasion we have met library staff who have spent months trying to get a trial installation up and running.) This would be easier if developers provided a sandbox for others to try their system out (one exists for GNU Eprints). Ours is at *www.greenstone.org/ir-sandbox/*

References

1. Tansley, R., Bass, M. and Smith, M. (2003) DSpace as an Open Archival Information System: Status and Future Directions. *Proc ECDL* pp. 446-460.
2. Lagoze, C., Payette, S., Shin, E. and Wilper, C. (2006) Fedora: an architecture for complex objects and their relationships. *Int J on Digital Libraries* 6(2) 124-138.
3. Fez. *http://sourceforge.net/projects/fez* [accessed 30 June 2006]
4. Witten, I.H. and Bainbridge, D. (2003) *How to build a digital library*. Morgan Kaufmann.
5. Witten, I.H., Bainbridge, D. and Boddie, S.J. (2001) Power to the people: end-user building of digital library collections. *Proc Joint Conf Digital Libraries*, pp. 94-103.
6. Lucene. *Apache Lucene. http://lucene.apache.org/* [accessed 30 June 2006]
7. Crane, D., Pascarello E. and James, D. (2005) *Ajax in Action*. Manning.
8. Eprints, *http://www.eprints.org/* [accessed 30 June 2006]
9. Nixon, W. DAEDALUS: Initial experiences with EPrints and DSpace at the Univ. of Glasgow, *Ariadne* 37, Oct 2003. *http://www.ariadne.ac.uk/issue37/nixon/* [accessed 30 June 2006].

A Web Archiving System of the National Library of Korea: OASIS

Kyung Ho Choi and Dal Ju Jeon

National Library of Korea, Seoul, Republic of Korea
{khchoi, cityman}@nl.go.kr

Abstract. In this paper, we introduce a web archiving system called OASIS(Online Archiving & Searching Internet Sources), which was developed and has been operated by the National Library of Korea. Workflows and process of OASIS are based on the strategy that web sites and individual digital resources for web archiving are collected selectively. We mainly focus on the description of functionalities and characteristics of the system. In addition, we briefly describe the system architecture and data model.

Keywords: Archiving system, long term preservation, digital library.

1 Introduction

With the rapid development of information and communication environment, numerous intellectual works are available in digital format on the Internet, and those digital resources have disappearing tendencies soon after their appearance. Digital archiving is the long-term procedure to process, manage and preserve those digital objects, which are considered to have timeless value[1]. Since 1990's, as their long-term national projects, many countries like Australia, the United States, and European nations have progressed their online preservation efforts for digital resources led by their national libraries with cooperation from other institutions and organizations[2][3][4].

The National Library of Korea (NLK), with the change of status of libraries in digital information era, has planned an efficient national information service to the people with collection of quality online digital information and provision of public service, to preserve those intellectual records for the next generations to come.

For the opening of the National Digital Library of Korea in 2008, to collect various web contents, NLK is working on a project for online digital resource collection and preservation, OASIS (Online Archiving & searching Internet Sources). The OASIS system was developed in December 2005, to preserve online digital resource for the future generation, to collect and preserve national digital cultural heritage, and to establish standard management policies for the digital resources.

The OASIS Project, one of the five innovation brand policies by Korea's Ministry of Culture and Tourism, receives a lot of attention through the government. The government supports the project with about $1 million, in the two year period of 2005 and 2006 for its online digital resource collection and preservation process. According

S. Sugimoto et al. (Eds.): ICADL 2006, LNCS 4312, pp. 313–322, 2006.

to the current mid-to-long term strategy plan, from 2007 the government will support more systematic and developmental directions and increase the budget aiming at the National Digital Library opening in 2008 and 1 million web resource collection developments in 2010.

This paper explains how OASIS collects web resources and describes its major functions and characteristics, as well as the workflows and processes for the web archiving by OASIS. It also introduces briefly the system architecture and data model of OASIS.

2   Web Archiving Examples

Web archiving began in 1996 as experimental projects at National Library of Australia and Internet Archive, Inc. of U.S.. Over the years many other countries became interested in common standards, technologies, development of tools, and interoperation, through IIPC (International Internet Preservation Consortium) headed by France. This chapter describes developments in web archiving in Australia, U.S., and Europe, which are the most referenced countries by NLK.

2.1   National Library of Australia

PANDORA (Preserving and Accessing Networked Documentary Resource of Australia) is one of the most remarkable projects in web archiving. It has begun by National Library of Australia (NLA) in 1996. It is a basis of Australia's internet publication and includes a web digital resource collection management system, related policies, transaction processes, and technical infrastructure[6].

Currently, PANDORA collects about 15000 titles related to (or about) Australia, through PANDAS (PANDORA Digital Archiving System) with voluntary help of nine agencies. It provides services of collected resources in 15 subject areas, including Arts & Humanities, and Business & Economy.

2.2   Internet Archive

Internet Archive, Inc. of the U.S. was established in 1996 to provide researchers, historians, scholars and general public a permanently free access to digital web resources. Wayback Machine, the web robot agent by Internet Archive, Inc., is distributed online for free, and it performs periodic collection and preservation tasks on major websites around the world. The serviced data types include music, video and text. Users can view the real-time collection progress status on the website. As of now, it services about 10 billion web pages amounting to over 100 terabytes in storage.

2.3   Europe

In the U.K., UKWAC (UK Web Archiving Consortium), consisted of six key institutions including the British Library, and the National Archives, collects archive material from .uk websites. Its web archive is composed by 3067 instances and can be accessed anywhere in the world.

Some other European countries, such as France, Denmark, Finland, and Sweden, have been developing web archiving projects. IIPC provides a central role in sharing knowledge on internet content archiving and in developing collaboration tools, technologies and standards[9].

3   OASIS Approach for Web Resource Collection

This chapter describes our web archiving approach in OASIS, its target objects, policy, and procedure to take, and the numbers in the current collection by year.

3.1   Selective Collection of Web Resources

NLK's approach for web archiving is basically a selective collection. Currently we have two types of objects to collect: web sites and individual web digital resources[5][6]. They are being selectively collected by an established collection development policy. We will expand the target objects into video, image, and audio gradually.

Among the potential objects for collection, there are possibilities to have their printed versions already, but currently we keep collecting them according to the collection development policy, regardless of the potential duplicity.

3.2   OASIS Collection Target and Collection Policy

The selection of target resources was based on the utility for the current or the future information need, author's popularity, the uniqueness of information, academic contents, being up-to-date of the information, frequency of upgrading, and the accessibility.

To be selected as national preservation resources, the collection digital resource should be something important related to Korea's society, politics, culture, religion, science or economy, and authored by Koreans. Also, it should be written by those who have authorities in their expert area, such as well-known professors and researchers in the university in Korea, and they should be something that was considered to have contributed to its discipline nationally or internationally.

Examples include the digital resources considered as valuable in terms of collection and preservation based on their being up-to-date, scarcity, and utility, about the current hot issues such as national parliamentary election and the new executive capital city. They also include articles in journals that are evaluated by international organizations with reputation and authority.

3.3   OASIS Collection Steps

There are 5 steps for NLK's collection development for valuable online digital resources on the web.

The first step is the selection review process. One method is by selection policy and the other one is by the committee for digital resource collection and preservation, which consists of experts from each subject area. The second step is to process any copyright on the selected target objects, and to collect them by OASIS system. The third step is to catalog the collected digital resources by Dublin Core's basic elements such as title, URL, publisher or abstract, and subject analysis. The fourth step is to review the catalogs, to correct errors, and to make final decisions about the resource's value for preservation by subject experts. The fifth step is the preservation process where the collected digital resources are converted into preservation file format, preservation media are selected, and the collections are moved to the media.

The sixth and final step is where preparation for service to users is executed with those online digital resources of which copyright issues are resolved.

3.4 OASIS Annual Resource Collection Statistics

The collection started in 2004 and currently OASIS has 120,312 resources in total. There are 16,505 web sites including those collected in huge number for local election candidates in 2006, and 103,806 individual digital resources. The collection size is about 2 terabytes.

Table 1. OASIS Resources Collection Statistics (Number of Titles)

Type of Resources	2004	2005	30 June, 2006	Total
Individual Digital Resource	39,032	47,553	17,222	103,807
Web Site	1,064	2,706	12,735	16,505
Total	40,096	50,259	29,957	120,312

Individual digital resources were document files created by government organizations, other public institutions, research institutions, associations, and individuals. For web site resources, we collected all subject areas including sites for the new executive capital city, election sites and local festivals. The collection aims at 1 million web resources archiving in 2010, and the target areas will be expanded to video, image, and sound.

In terms of copyright agreement for collection and preservation of the collected resources, in 2005, out of 1,002 institutions asked to agree, 209 agreed at about 20% of agreement rate, while in 2006 only about 10% agreed, 45 out of 440.

Since there is lack of understanding of digital archiving and low agreement rate for copyright clearance by copyright holders, it is necessary to encourage government and other major organizations to increase their voluntary participation in national projects like digital archiving.

4   OASIS System

OASIS is a project based on proven technology and commercial software, so it is possible to archive web resources at the same time when the technical infrastructure is established.

Therefore, NLK started to collect web resources in 2004 with the early web resource collector developed in 2001. The earlier version was upgraded to OASIS version 1.0 in December 2005, and NLK has been collecting continuously web resource collecting process with the new version. Currently the second expansion upgrade is under way, and OASIS version 2.0 is being developed targeting November 2006 for its completion.

4.1 OASIS Major Functions

OASIS system consists of two major parts: One is the collection and preservation system to gather web resources on the web and to store them. The other is the public service system to provide the archived web resources to end users.

The collection and preservation system has the following functions to collect and preserve web resources on the internet.

- Collecting web resources on the internet
- Adding metadata to the collected web resources
- Verification and correction on the collected web resources
- Periodic site mirroring by schedule for specified web sites
- Managing copyright agreement for legal collection, preservation and public service

Public service system has the following functions to provide end users with the collected and preserved web resources and to protect the copyright holders of the collected web resources.

- Providing keyword searching and KDC classification search for the collection
- Providing metadata information and the contents upon search research
- Enabling self-donation from author's works and nomination for others' materials
- Managing copyright agreement documents signed by the copyright holders and their related web resources

4.2 Major Characteristics of OASIS

OASIS adopted ISO standard architecture for digital archiving. Its major characteristics are following.

4.2.1 Adoption of Digital Archiving Standard Architecture

The online digital archiving process of OASIS is based on reference model for Open Archival Information System (OAIS)[1]. OAIS was established through a long-time discussion and feedback by experts in various disciplines and related organizations and it became the ISO standard for digital archiving.

The OASIS system focused on OAIS' Ingest function and Administration function, which allow to manage internal archive data, to extract descriptive information for recording, or to generate archive information following data format or document standard.

4.2.2 Applying DCMES(Dublin Core Metadata Element Set)

To describe metadata for the collected resources, OASIS system uses 15 required metadata elements of Dublin Core Metadata, which is an international standard for data description of digital contents[7].

For digital resources, depending on data format, genre, and service, necessary metadata are different, it may be inevitable to have more than one applied metadata other than those required ones. The OASIS will continuously expand the metadata elements sets if necessary.

4.2.3 Individual Resources vs. Web Sites

The OASIS system collects, preserves, and services two kinds of web resources. One is for individual digital resources, which have informational value as a file unit such as document file and videos while the other is for web sites, of which all the resources are mirrored as a site unit.

Therefore, for individual digital resources the system collects by file unit, each file is assigned its metadata and preserved. For web sites, metadata are assigned to each site. The system then periodically revisits the site, and the whole site is archived at a given interval and in a given depth.

4.2.4 Resource Duplicity Automatic Checker

In order to prevent duplicity, OASIS is uses a method of checking values of CRC32 in files. When the system collects a resource file, its CRC32 value is obtained to compare if there any duplicated value among the existing collection. If any file with the same CRC32 value is found, the system notifies the administrator of the duplicity.

4.2.5 Site Mirroring

Site mirroring is to collect and preserve contents at a specific site to a certain depth as it is, so as time goes by, web sites at the site change. Therefore it is necessary to revisit the site and collect and preserve the contents again at a certain interval.

OASIS system periodically visits a site to collect its contents and compare the existing contents of the site in the system and show the rate of change. By examining the numbers, the administrator can easily decide whether the new collection should be preserved or not. The change rate is calculated by combination of the numbers of new resources, deleted one, and changed one against that of previously collected.

4.3 OASIS System Architecture

OASIS system architecture consists of three layers: presentation, application and data (Fig. 1).

The presentation layer is the interface between users and the application layer that provides visual display. Except for parts of OASIS web pages and interface for search, the remaining is limited to access by user privileges. The application layer consists of core applications including a web crawler, an archiving server, a server for user service, and management tools for each software tool.

The data layer is the layer to manage the information resources and the information management data including common DBMSs and search engines. Most companies provide a standard interface for this purpose.

From the perspective of servers where modules loaded, OASIS system consists of the following three servers.

- User Service Server: It has HTTP server and web application server (WAS) to process public users' requests. The application programs written in JSP/Servlet provide system management and external service.

- DB Server: It has a common DBMS and special search engines to manage data and search. It centralizes all DB data and collects files to manage them systematically.
- Collection Server: It has web robot agent, an automatic classifier and an automatic abstractor. It collects web resources upon requests, analyzes the contents, does automatic abstracting and classification and then sends the results to the DB server. The collecting server is running on a multi-server platform and currently seven collectors are gathers web resources in great quantities.

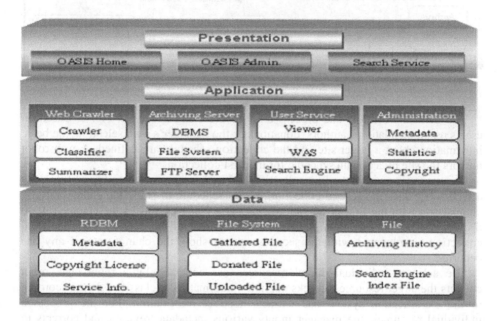

Fig. 1. OASIS Architecture

4.4   OASIS Workflow and Process

In this section, OASIS workflows and processes are described for web sites and individual digital resources respectively.

The process for web sites does not finalize with one cycle for mirroring because web sites change their contents continuously. It is necessary to collect their resources to preserve them by certain time periods. However, it is impossible for a manager to monitor numerous web sites changes manually, and it is considered a waste of resources to collect every resource unconditionally by a certain interval to preserve, for example, one month, two months, or six months.

Thse OASIS system lets collecting robots continuously collect registered sites' resources, monitor their changes, and compare the current state with the previously saved one to provide numbers for those changes. According to the number, the manager decides whether the new collection will be preserved or not.

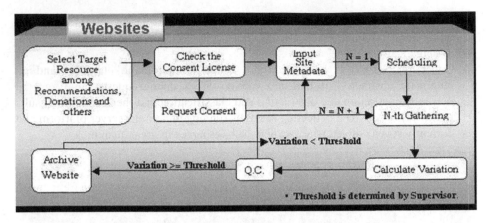

Fig. 2. Workflow for Website Archiving

The general workflow and process for web archiving is seen in Fig. 2. Based on user's recommendations, authors' donations or the manager's own selection, the basic information about a target site and the collection schedule are defined. A web robot mirrors the site by a certain schedule for the first collection.

The manager reviews the first collection and makes a preservation copy of it. Later a web robot does the second collection by the schedule to show the change rate by comparison with the first preservation copy. The manager checks the change rate to decide whether the second copy of the collection should be made or not. The third collection is compared with the second copy to show the change rate, if any has occurred.

The selected individual digital resources are collected by a robot. The robot collects the target resources, checks duplicity, automatically classifies them according to the classification system and extracts abstract information. For the processed individual resources, the manager inputs various metadata, reviews and corrects to make final catalog to preserve.

4.5 Data Model

A web site is basically represented by a URL address. However, to help web robots to collect a sub-directory's resources, which is difficult to reach technically, the manager can define multiple entrance URLs additionally.

Robots are continuously collecting resources at the web sites and upon the manager's judgment, saving the current states at a certain time to keep mirroring copies by timeline. When a mirroring copy is generated, the current URL is saved so that it facilitates the search process on the mirrored site.

The collected web documents are checked by title, URL and contents to verify any duplicity, and classified by KDC classification system to have a KDC code.

4.6 Long Term Preservation of Web Digital Resources

NLK is currently in the process of establishing strategic plans on nationwide digital information collection and preservation, for a long term preservation of web digital resources aiming for opening of the National Digital Library. OASIS uses a disk-based preservation strategy of digital resources, because the number of resources in various formats has been increasing exponentially and also because the collected resources should be easily accessible.

NLK has been monitoring researches and developments in long term storage media and preservation techniques to utilize in the future collected digital resources of the current generation.

5 Future Development Direction

The OASIS system's main users are those who are responsible for the system's collection and preservation works. Resource collection teams, subject expert librarians, and managers are working on their parts in the collection work.

In collection management, the system provides functions to collect resources, which a manager chooses on the Internet, or which are recommended or donated, and to input their metadata. It runs the system by management of mirroring, cataloging, copyright, preservation, operation, and statistics and monitors various states. The current OASIS system will be refined and upgraded continuously. The future directions are the following.

- Developing and disseminating national standard models through continuous research on the OASIS system
- Standardization of metadata by types of information resources
- Assigning a digital identification system to protect intellectual properties of the collected digital resources and to facilitate their distribution

To promote distribution of the OASIS system with budget support local centers for clustering will be formed through partnerships in disciplines and areas to decentralize the responsibility of collecting web resources.

6 Conclusion

As knowledge information resources migrate from paper to digital formats, increasing necessity is found for collection and preservation of digital knowledge information resources at the national level. Recognizing digital resources' being short-lived, the OASIS system is running at the national level led by NLK to collect and preserve valuable digital resources for the current generation to inherit to the next generation as digital cultural heritage.

To accomplish the mission, the OASIS system provides national standard models for submission of online digital resources to the authority in the future digital environment and for standardization of collection and preservation systems for online digital resources.

Major development technologies are applied to OASIS at the levels of collection, preservation, management, public service, etc. They include the development of web robot agents and techniques to use them, automatic classification and automatic abstracting and others for the collection process. For the preservation process, periodic management of recording media and backup technology should be accomplished. For public service, refinement of search technology for the copyright-cleared resources should be followed.

As a major subsystem of the National Digital Library that will be opened in 2008, the OASIS system will establish a cooperation system with related organizations led by NLK to be distributed as a standard system. The distributed system will assign web resource collection processes to each subject area.

References

1. CCSDS Recommendation for Space Data System Standards: Reference Model for an Open Archival Information System(OAIS), CCSDS 650.0-B-1 Blue Book1-2(2002)
2. PANDORA Archive : Preserving and Accessing Networked Documentary Resources of Australia; http://pandora.nla.gov.au/index.html
3. Digital Preservation Report, http://www.digitalpreservation.gov/
4. The Library of Congress, http://digitalpreservation.gov/
5. PANDORA Selection Guideline ; http://pandora.nla.gov.au/guidelines.html
6. The PANDORA Digital Archiving System (PANDAS) : managing web archiving in Australia. A refereed paper by Paul Koerbin, Supervisor, Digital Archiving Section, presented at the International Web Archiving Workshop, Bath, UK
7. Dublin Core Metadata Element Set, Version 1.1, 2004
8. Catherine Lupovici. The International Internet Preservation Consortium, IWAW 2005.

The DELOS Testbed for Choosing a Digital Preservation Strategy

Stephan Strodl[1], Andreas Rauber[1], Carl Rauch[1], Hans Hofman[2],
Franca Debole[3], and Giuseppe Amato[3]

[1] Vienna University of Technology, Vienna, Austria
http://www.ifs.tuwien.ac.at
[2] Nationaal Archief, Den Haag, The Netherlands
www.nationaalarchief.nl
[3] Consiglio Nazionale delle Ricerche (CNR), Pisa, Italy
www.isti.cnr.it

Abstract. With the rapid technological changes, digital preservation,
i.e. the endeavor to provide long-term access to digital objects, is turning
into one of the most pressing challenges to ensure the survival of our digital artefacts. A set of strategies has been proposed, with a range of tools
supporting parts of digital preservation actions. Yet, with requirements
on which strategy to follow and which tools to employ being different
for each setting, depending e.g. on object characteristics or institutional
requirements, deciding which solution to implement has turned into a
crucial decision. This paper presents the DELOS Digital Preservation
Testbed. It provides an approach to make informed and accountable decisions on which solution to implement in order to preserve digital objects
for a given purpose. It is based on Utility Analysis to evaluate the performance of various solutions against well-defined objectives, and facilitates
repeatable experiments in a standardized laboratory setting.

1 Introduction

Digital Preservation (DP) is turning into one of the most pressing challenges for any
setting handling and relying on digital objects, be it e-commerce, e-government,
or private photo collections, requiring immediate action on an international level.
With the rapid change in technology, both hardware and software, current objects will turn into uninterpretable bit-streams in relatively short periods of time,
when the original environment to interpret them correctly becomes unavailable.
Research in DP tries to mitigate this risk by devising a set of preservation strategies in order to ensure long-term access to digital objects. A number of strategies
habe been devised over the last years, the most prominent ones being (1) migration, i.e. the repeated conversion of files into different, more current or more easily
preservable, file formats (such as, e.g. to the recently adopted PDF/A standard [4],
implementing a subset of PDF optimized for long-term preservation); or (2) the emulation of either a certain hardware infrastructure, operating system, or software
functionality. All of the proposed strategies have their advantages and disadvantages, and may be suitable in different settings [13]. When implementing a digital

S. Sugimoto et al. (Eds.): ICADL 2006, LNCS 4312, pp. 323–332, 2006.

preservation strategy, the choice of the most suitable preservation solution is the most difficult part. The decision which strategy to follow and which tools and system to use is usually taken by groups of experts in the individual institution, who select the solution that seems to satisfy their requirements best. While with the profound expertise of the record managers these decisions are usually correct, it is hard to document them, to be able to later on re-establish the reasons why a certain tool was preferred over another, and why a certain parameter setting was chosen. With less expertise, or imprecise definitions of the requirements of different user groups, even the selection of a certain strategy may cause considerable difficulties. To be able to make profound, accountable decisions, an evaluation process is needed, which allows a structured and documented evaluation of available DP solutions against well-defined requirements.

The DELOS DP Testbed presented in this paper allows the selection of the most suitable preservation solution for individual requirements. It enforces the explicit definition of preservation requirements and supports the appropriate documentation and evaluation by assisting in the process of running preservation experiments. This provides a means to perform structured and repeatable evaluations of various solutions, tools and systems for a given challenge, providing a means to make informed and accountable decisions on which solution to adopt.

In this paper we describe the workflow for evaluating and selecting DP solutions following the principles of the DELOS DP Testbed. We present a tool that supports the automatic acquisition and documentation of the various requirements. Additionally, it provides a guidance for institutions having less expertise in the subtleties of DP challenges to identify core requirements that any solution should fulfill in a given setting. A set of initial case studies demonstrates the feasibility of the proposed approach.

The remainder of this paper is organized as follows: Section 2 provides some pointers to related initiatives. Following an overview of the principles of the DELOS DP Testbed in Section 3, a detailed description of the workflow is presented in Section 4. We report on a set of initial case studies in Section 5, followed by conclusions, lessons learned as well as an outlook on future work in Section 6.

2   Related Work

The increasing amount of cultural and scientific information in digital form and the heterogeneity and complexity of the digital formats make it difficult to keep the heritage accessible and usable. While libraries, archives and cultural institutions may be the primary stakeholders, other institutions such as government agencies and increasingly also large industries as well as SME's and private persons, who have increasing amounts of legally or personally important data, are facing this challenge. Thus, a number of large scale initiatives are created, that integrate digital preservation capabilities into digital repository systems [11].

During the last couple of years, a lot of effort was spent on defining, improving and evaluating preservation strategies. A good overview of preservation strategies is provided by the companion document to the UNESCO charter for the preservation of the digital heritage [13]. Research on technical preservation issues is focused on two dominant strategies, namely Migration and Emulation. Scientific results on Migration, which is at the current time the most common preservation strategy, were published for example by the Council of Library and Information Resources (CLIR) [6], where different kinds of risks for a migration project are presented. Migration requires the repeated conversion of a digital object into more stable or current file formats.

Work on the second important preservation strategy, Emulation, was advocated by Jeff Rothenberg [10], envisioning a framework of an ideal preservation surrounding. In order to make Emulation usable in practice, several projects developed it further. One of them is the CAMILEON project [2], trying to implement first solutions and to compare Emulation to Migration. More recently, the Universal Virtual Computer (UVC) has been proposed as a promising solution [3]. Emulation aims at providing programs that mimic a certain environment, e.g. a certain processor or the features of a certain operating system. The WINE emulator for example allows users to run Microsoft WORD on a Linux operating system.

Similar to the Utility Analysis based approach for identifying and documenting the objectives for a preservation endeavor [9], the Arts and Humanities Data Service (AHDS) and University of London Computer Centre started the DAAT Project (Digital Asset Assessment Tool) [12]. The aim is to develop a tool to identify the preservation needs of various digital holdings.

The approach presented in this paper basically focuses on the elicitation and documentation of the requirements (objectives), as well as running and evaluating experiments in a structured way. In order to automate the evaluation, a number of tools like JHove [1] may be employed to analyze the resulting files after applying a preservation action. PANIC [5] addresses the challenges of integrating and leveraging existing tools and services and assisting organizations to dynamically discover the optimum preservation strategy. File format repositories, such as PRONOM [8] may be used to identify specific characteristics of the digital objects at hand.

3   DELOS DP Testbed

During the last couple of years two frameworks were created for supporting the establishment of DP solutions, namely the Utility Analysis approach [9] and the Dutch testbed designed by the Dutch National Archive. The strength of the Utility Analysis is the clear hierarchical structuring of the preservation objectives, which document the requirements and the goals for a optimal preservation solution. The strength of the Dutch testbed is the detailed definition of the environment and the experiment basis. The advantages of these two were integrated and form the basis for the DELOS Digital Preservation Testbed.

3.1   Testbed Principles

Figure 1 provides an overview of the workflow of the DELOS DP Testbed. The 3-phase process, consisting of 14 steps, starts with defining the scenario, setting the boundaries, defining and describing the requirements, which are to be fulfilled by the possible alternatives. After the definition of the requirements the second part of the process is to identify and evaluate potential alternatives. Therefore, first the alternatives' characteristics and technical details are specified. Then the resources for the experiments are selected, the required tools set up and a set of experiments is performed. Based on the requirements defined in the beginning, every experiment is evaluated. In the third part of the workflow the results of the experiments are aggregated to make them comparable, the importance factors are set and the alternatives are ranked. The stableness of the final ranking is analyzed with respect to minor changes in the weighting and performance of the individual objectives using Sensitivity Analysis. The results are finally considered by taking non-measurable influences on the decision into account. After this consideration a clear and well argumented accountable recommendation for one of the alternatives can be made.

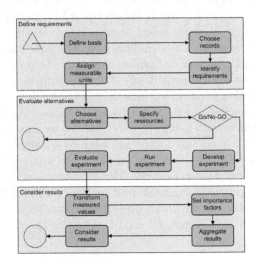

Fig. 1. Overview of DELOS Digital Preservation Testbed's workflow

To simplify the process, to guide users and to automate the structured documentation a software tool is introduced[1]. It implements the workflow of the DELOS DP Testbed, supporting the documentation of the various steps performed. Results may be stored centrally on a server or exported to an XML file.

4   Testbed Workflow

The detailed workflow consists of fourteen steps as shown in Figure 1, which are described in the following section.

---

[1] http://ifs.tuwien.ac.at/dp

Step 1 - Define basis

The testbed process starts with defining the basis. This is a semi-structured description including (i) the required types of records to be considered (e.g. E-Mail correspondence or immigration records), (ii) a description of the environment in which the testbed process takes place (e.g. governmental archive, a university library), and (iii) information on the amount of files or records which are expected to be preserved with the chosen alternative.

Step 2 - Choose records

In order to be able to evaluate the DP solutions, sample records are needed to run the experiments. In this step sample records are chosen. There exist several efforts to provide file repositories where well described files in many different formats and types can be downloaded, e.g. [7]. Alternatively, representative files from the collection to be preserved can be chosen with respect to the variety of document characteristics. The result of this stage is a set of characteristic records containing between 5 and 20 files, which are later used for evaluating the alternatives.

Step 3 - Define requirements

In order to decide which preservation solution is most suitable for a given setting, detailed requirements have to be specified in a structured and well-documented way. Requirements definition is thus a decisive step and usually the most time-consuming. The goal of this step is to clearly define the requirements and goals which should be fulfilled by the preservation solution. In the so-called objective tree, different goals and requirements, high-level as well as detailed ones, are collected and organized in a tree structure. Generally, there are two ways to define the objectives. The bottom-up approach collects a list of basic attributes (such as character encoding, font color representation or hardware costs), and aggregates them on a higher level (such as the preservation of the look and the accountability of costs). The opposite is done in the top-down approach where general aims such as record characteristics or cost structure are defined and gradually broken down into increasingly fine-granular objectives.

A synthesis of these two approaches is probably the best solution, combining high-level aims with basic requirements. While the resulting objective trees usually differ from preservation setting to preservation setting, some general principles can be observed. At top level, the objectives usually can be organized into four main categories, namely:

- *File characteristics*: In this part of the tree all objectives are mentioned that describe the visual and contextual experience a user has by dealing with a digital record. Subdivisions may be "Appearance", "Content", "Structure" and "Behavior", with lowest level objectives being e.g. color depth, image resolution, forms of interactivity, macro support, embedded metadata.
- *Record characteristics*: Here the technical foundations of a digital record are described, the context, the storage medium, interrelationships and metadata.
- *Process characteristics*: The third group are those objectives that describe the preservation process. These include usability, complexity or scalability.

– *Costs*: The last group of objectives, which have a significant influence on the choice of a preservation solution, are costs. Usually, costs may be divided in technical and personnel costs.

The objective tree is usually created in a workshop setting with experts from different domains contributing to the elicitation of requirements. These trees document the individual preservation requirements of an institution and for a given partially homogeneous collection of objects. Examples include scientific papers and dissertations in PDF format, historic audio recordings, video holdings from ethnographic studies. Typical trees may contain between 50 to several hundred objectives, organized in usually 4-6 levels of hierarchy.

Step 4 - Assign measurable units

In order to be able to objectively measure and compare the performance of the various preservation solutions with the set of requirements, units of measurement need to be defined for each objective, i.e. each leaf of the tree. Wherever possible, these objectives should be objectively (and, preferably, automatically) measurable (e.g. seconds per object, Euro per object, dots-per-inch resolution, bits of color depth). In some cases, (semi-)subjective scales will need to be employed, e.g. degrees of openness and stability, support of a standard, diffusion of a file format, number of access tools available for a specific object type.

Step 5 - Choose alternatives

In order to find the most suitable preservation solution, different alternatives need to be identified which can subsequently be evaluated in the DELOS DP Testbed. Alternatives may come from all different preservation strategies, such as specific emulators, tools to migrate digital objects from one format to another (version of the same or a different) format, put data into a computer museum, etc. Descriptions of these alternatives should be detailed enough to allow later re-evaluation of the analysis. Thus they should describe the specific tools used, including their release version, which operating system they are being run on, and which parameter settings are being used. An example is "Migration from MS Word to PDF" using Acrobat 7.0 Distiller running on WIN XP (SP2) with a documented list of the parameter settings.

Step 6 - Specify resources

In order to assess the resources that are need to run the evaluation, for each potential alternative the amount of work, time and money is estimated. The input for this step is the list of the alternatives. For every alternative a project and work description plan is developed, where the amount of work, time and money required for testing these alternative are estimated. The effort and workflow for building or installing such a process is determined, the knowledge of the required personnel set and the duration for the whole process estimated.

Step 7 - Go/No-Go decision

This stage considers the resources and requirements definition to determine if the proposed alternatives are feasible at all and whether one may proceed with the process as planned (Go), if revisions to the design or the strategy are needed before the process can go on (Provisional-Go), if the suggested strategy should be delayed for a specified period or until a specified event, such as the availability of additional research results, occurs (Deferred-Go), or if the strategy should not be considered any longer (No Go).

Step 8 - Develop experiments

In order to run repeatable tests, a documented setting is necessary, which includes the workflow of the experiment, software and system of the experiment environment and the mechanism to capture the results. All of the items needed for the experiment will be developed and/or installed and tested, including copies of all the objects needed for the experiment, software packages and programs needed, and mechanisms for capturing the results and the evaluation.

Step 9 - Run experiments

An experiment will test one or more aspects of applying a specific preservation solution to the previously defined sample objects. Running an experiment will produce results, e.g. converted computer files, revised metadata, etc., that will be evaluated in the next step.

Step 10 - Evaluate experiments

The results of the experiment will be evaluated to determine how successfully the requirements were met. Therefore, the leaf objectives defined in the objective tree are evaluated with the defined unit of measurement.

Step 11 - Transform measured values

The measurements taken in the experiments all have different scales (such as time in seconds, costs in Euro, resolution in dots-per-inch). In order to make these comparable they are transformed to a uniform scale using transformation tables. The subjectively measured objectives on a uniform scale, e.g. 0 to 5, can be used directly as comparable numbers. The objectively measured ones are transformed to the same uniform scale. Experience so far has shown that a performance scale of 1 to 5 is a reasonable approach. On several occasions the definition of a special performance level 0 (or "not acceptable", "n/a") turned out to be helpful. If the measures for a certain objective are below a certain threshold, this value will be assigned, serving as a drop-out criterion for that alternative no matter how well it performs in all other aspects. The threshold values cannot be generally defined, but have to be individually specified for every implementation. After applying the transformation functions we obtain a list of comparable values per alternative. These values form the input to the aggregation and final ranking.

Step 12 - Set importance factors

The objective tree consists of many objectives. Not all of them are equally important, and we may decide to accept different degrees of conformance of a solution in different objectives. Thus importance factors, also referred to as weights, are assigned to each node in the tree to explicitly describe which objectives play a major or minor role for the final decision. In a top-down manner, relative importance factors between 0 and 1 are assigned to all the children of a given node. These weights depend largely on individual requirements. While there are different ways of assigning the weights, practice has shown that group decision processes result in stable evaluations of the relative importance of the various objectives. The weights of the single leaves can be obtained by multiplying their value by the weights of their parent nodes, summing up to one for the whole tree. The software implementation supports sets of weights from different users, which are further used for the Sensitive Analysis of the evaluation. For the normal evaluation of the alternatives an average value of the weights assigned by different users is used. The result of this stage is an objective tree with importance factors assigned to each objective, representing their relative relevance with respect to the overall goals.

Step 13 - Aggregate results

In this step the performance measures for the individual objectives are aggregated to one single comparable number for each alternative. The measured performance values as transformed by the transformation tables and multiplied with the weighting factor. These numbers are summarized to a single comparable number per alternative. We thus obtain aggregated performance values for each part of the objective tree for each alternative, including, of course, an overall performance value at the root level. A first ranking of the alternatives can be done based on the final values per alternative.

Step 14 - Perform Sensitivity Analysis

In the last step a ranking of the performance of the various alternatives is created based on the overall degrees of fulfillment of the objectives. This ranking forms the basis for a documented and accountable decision for the selection of a specific solution to the given preservation challenge based on the requirements specified. In addition to the ranking, some Sensitivity Analysis may be automatically performed by analyzing, for example, the stableness of the ranking with respect to minor changes in the weighting of the individual objectives, or to minor changes in performance. This Sensitivity Analysis results in a stability value for each alternative and objective, which may further influence the final decision. Additionally, some side effects can be considered, which are not included in the numerical evaluation. Such effects could be relationships with a supplier, expertise in a certain alternative, or individual assessment that one or the other solution might become the market leader within a couple of years. All of these effects will of course need to be carefully documented if used to influence the final solution. The result of this analysis process is a concise, objective, and well-documented ranked list of the various alternative solutions for a given preservation task considering institution-specific requirements. By providing both overall as well as detailed performance measures, stemming from a standardized and repeatable experiment setting, it forms the basis for sound and accountable decisions on which solution to implement.

All the stages of the experiment will be considered to make recommendations for the refinement and enhancement of future experiments, to propose further experiments, and to provide input into the evaluation of the testbed.

5   Case Studies

To evaluate the potential of the presented approach, a set of case studies was performed with different partner institutions.

– Video Files of the Austrian Phonogrammarchiv
  The Austrian Phonogrammarchiv is re-considering its appraisal regulations
  for video files, specifically with respect to most suitable source format standards to migrate from. So a case study took place to evaluate the performance of potential migration tools and source formats. The defined target
  format was MPEG2000 and DPS, by considering all occurring input formats (Std DVm Digi-Betam PAL-VHS, SVHS, U-Matic, Beta Cam, MPEG,
  NTSC-VHS, DPS, Hi8). In a one day workshop an objective tree was created with around 200 objectives. These were strongly focused on detailed
  technical characteristics. The subsequent experiments and the evaluation of
  the preservation solutions took about 3 weeks. The results revealed that the
  preservation solutions differ in only few objectives, such as signal representation, color proofness and stereo quality.
– Document records of the Dutch National Archive
  The Dutch National Archive is responsible for storing all information generated by the Dutch government. The case study tried to define the objectives
  for the preservation of different kinds of documents, such as video and audio
  documents, focusing particularly on the record characteristics. The resulting
  objective tree contains around 450 objectives.
– Migration of a database to XML
  This case study was done in cooperation with the Italian National Research
  Council (CNR). The starting point was a legacy database that contains
  descriptive meta data of a small library, consisting of books, registered users,
  information about lending, order of books, content (field, review) and the
  budget for new books. The data of the database was to be converted in XML
  for archiving and further application using e.g. a native XML database. In
  this case study we tried to reduce the number of objectives, focusing on the
  critical characteristics. The resulting objective tree contained approximately
  70 nodes with a maximum depth of 6 layers.

6   Conclusions

The proposed DELOS DP Testbed provides a means to make well-documented,
accountable decisions on which preservation solution to implement. It enforces
the explicit definition of preservation requirements in the form of specific objectives. It allows to evaluate various preservation solutions in a consistent manner,
enabling informed and well-documented decisions. It thus helps to establish and
maintain a trusted preservation environment.

While many of the processing steps are automated, a significant amount of
work is still involved in the evaluation of the results of applying a preservation
action in order to acquire the measures for the various objectives. Integrating
tools for file analysis as well as adding further measurements during the experiment runs is needed in order to reduce this workload.

Furthermore, a significantly larger series of case studies will need to be performed in order to establish a solid basis of best practice models for different

institutions and different types of digital objects. This may later on even lead to a kind of recommender process, where – upon specifying e.g. the type of institution and the type of objects concerned – a pre-defined objective tree, or at least a set of building blocks, is proposed by the system.

Acknowledgements

Part of this work was supported by the European Union in the 6. Framework Program, IST, through the DELOS NoE on Digital Libraries, contract 507618.

References

1. Harvard University Library. Jhove - jstor/harvard object validation environment. Website, 2005. `http://hul.harvard.edu/jhove`.
2. M. Hedstrom and C Lampe. Emulation vs. migration. do users care?,. *RLG DigiNews*, Dec. 2001, Vol. 5, No. 6, 2001.
3. J.R. Hoeven, R.J. Van Der Diessen, and K. Van En Meer. Development of a universal virtual computer (uvc) for long-term preservation of digital objects. *Journal of Information Science,*, Vol. 31 (3), 2005.
4. *ISO/CD 19005-1, Document management - Electronic document file format for long-term preservation - Part 1: Use of PDF 1.4 (PDF/A)*, 2004.
5. Sharmin Choudhury Jane Hunter. PANIC - An integrated approach to the preservation of composite digital objects using semantic web services. In *Proc. 5th Int. Web Archiving Workshop (IWAW05)*, Vienna, Austria, September 2005.
6. G.W. Lawrence, W.R. Kehoe, O.Y. Rieger, W.H. Walters, and A.R. Kenney. Risk management of digital information: A file format investigation,. CLIR, 2000.
7. Virginia Ogle and Robert Wilensky. Testbed development for the Berkeley Digital Library Project. *D-LIB Magazine*, July/August 1996. URL http://www.dlib.org.
8. Jo Pettitt. *PRONOM - Field Descriptions*. The National Archives, Digital Preservation Department, 2003. URL http://www.records.pro.gov.uk/-pronom.
9. Carl Rauch and Andreas Rauber. Preserving digital media: Towards a preservation solution evaluation metric. In *Proceedings of the 7th International Conference on Asian Digital Libraries, ICADL 2004*, pages 203–212. Springer, December 2004.
10. J Rothenberg. Avoiding technological quicksand: Finding a viable technical foundation for digital preservation. CLIR, 1999.
11. Mackenzie Smith. Eternal bits: How can we preserve digital files and save our collective memory? *IEEE Spectrum*, 42(7), July 2005.
12. ULCC. DAAT: Digital asset assessment tool. Website, 2004. `http://ahds.ac.uk/about/projects/daat/`.
13. UNESCO, Information Society Division. *Guidelines for the preservation of digital heritage*, October 2003. URL http://www.unesco.org/webworld/mdm.

Text Image Spotting Using Local Crowdedness and Hausdorff Distance

Hwa-Jeong Son, Sang-Cheol Park, Soo-Hyung Kim, Ji-Soo Kim,
GueeSang Lee, and DeokJai Choi

Department of Computer Science, Chonnam National University,
300 YongBong-Dong, Buk-Gu, Gwangju 500-757, Korea
{sonhj, sanchun, kimjisoo}@iip.chonnam.ac.kr
{shkim, gslee, dchoi}@chonnam.ac.kr

Abstract. This paper investigates a Hausdorff distance, which is used for measurement of image similarity, to see whether it is also effective for document image retrieval. We proposed a method using a local crowdedness algorithm and a modified Hausdorff distance which has an ability of detection of partial text image in a document image. We found that the proposed method achieved a reliable performance of text spotting on postal envelops.

1 Introduction

Text spotting in a document image is to find the locations of all the texts in the document which are identical to the given query text. The query text is usually provided as a sequence of ASCII character codes, but our concern here is the query in a form of image. An efficient solution for this image-based text spotting problem has many useful applications, such as language-independent document image retrieval in digital libraries, postal automation, signature verification, and so on.

A sub-image matching is the most basic operation for the text spotting which is defined as follows: given a query image Q and a document image D, locate a sub-image Q' of D which looks similar to Q, and produce a degree of similarity between Q and Q'. If D has nothing related to Q, the similarity value would be quite low or zero.

Many studies on the similarity measure have been widely investigated in applications of image retrieval or object detection [1-6]. Most of them, however, are applicable to natural images containing various objects and use color and texture of the objects which are not available for document images. Some approaches to spotting a keyword have been mainly studied on English and Chinese text documents in the past years [7-10]. In most cases, they generally recognize all characters using a commercial software OCR or their own classifiers after segmenting words in the document. Here we propose an approach to search the query image of Korean document without the requirements of word segmentation and recognition.

In this paper, a local crowdedness algorithm [11] and a Hausdorff distance measure [3] is used as a feature extraction and a similarity measurement, respectively. The Hausdorff distance which is generally used in a sub-image matching does well on searching corresponding region between two images but takes much time to process.

S. Sugimoto et al. (Eds.): ICADL 2006, LNCS 4312, pp. 333–339, 2006.

By extracting the robust feature using the local crowdedness algorithm we can efficiently reduce the processing time maintaining the accuracy of the similarity measure. The proposed method is compared with two well-known similarity measures, a binary correlation (BC) and a modified Hausdorff distance (modified HD). Experimental results show whether the proposed method can be effective for text spotting.

2 Similarity Measures for Sub-image Matching

Let Q be a bi-level image for query text and D be a bi-level image for a document. Our purpose is to find a sub-image Q' of D (Q'⊆D) which looks similar to Q and has the maximum possible similarity with respect to Q. The result differs depending on the similarity measure adopted.

2.1 BC Method

The BC [12] is one of the most typical functions to compute the similarity between two images, D of size $X \times Y$ and Q of size $M \times N$, by using their correlation defined as Eq. (1) ($-M \le x \le X$, $-N \le y \le Y$). The summation is taken over the image region where D and Q overlap. The location (x, y) where the value of C is the maximum is the best match of the two images.

$$C(x, y) = \frac{1}{M \times N} \sum_{m=1}^{M} \sum_{n=1}^{N} D(m+x, n+y)Q(m, n) \cdot \tag{1}$$

The correlation can be computed efficiently by using the following relationship:

$$D(x, y) \circ Q(x, y) \Leftrightarrow D_F(u, v)Q_F^*(u, v), \tag{2}$$

where '∘' denotes the correlation, $D_F(u, v)$ is a Fourier transform of $D(x, y)$, and $Q_F^*(u, v)$ is a complex conjugate of $Q_F(u, v)$ which is a Fourier transform of $Q(x, y)$. The above equation indicates that the correlation of two functions in a spatial domain can be obtained by taking an inverse Fourier transform of the product $D_F(u, v)Q_F^*(u, v)$ in a frequency domain. For more efficiency, we can use a fast Fourier transform (FFT) algorithm.

2.2 Modified Hausdorff Distance Method

The Hausdorff distance (HD) [3] is the degree to which two images differ from one another when they are overlapped so that their origins coincide. Since a binary image can be regarded as a set of black pixels, for two finite points extracted by an edge operator, that is $D = \{d_1, d_2 \dots d_m\}$ and $Q = \{q_1, q_2 \dots q_n\}$, the HD is defined as

$$H(D, Q) = \max(h(D, Q), h(Q, D)), \tag{3}$$

where

$$h(D, Q) = \max_{d_i \in D} \min_{q_j \in Q} \| d_i - q_j \| . \tag{4}$$

Here $\|\cdot\|$ is the norm of a vector connecting two points; in this paper, the cityblock norm is used. To get $h(D, Q)$, we first compute every distance from $d_i \in D$ $(1 \le i \le m)$ to its nearest neighbor in Q, and then choose the maximum distance among them. $h(Q, D)$ is computed similarly, and the larger one of $h(D, Q)$ or $h(Q, D)$ is regarded as $H(D, Q)$. Therefore, $H(D, Q)$ indicates the degree of mismatch between two sets Q and D. The HD can be defined as a function of translation. If we allow Q to move, the minimum value of the HD under the translation can be described as

$$H_T(D,Q) = \min_t H(D, Q \oplus t), \tag{5}$$

where $\oplus$ is the Minkowski sum and $Q \oplus t = \{q + t \mid q \in Q\}$. Hence $H_T(D, Q)$ can be smaller than $H(D, Q)$ if there is a translation t that can place a point of Q near to some point of D. However alternative measurements such as a partial HD and a modified HD have been proposed since the HD is easily sensitive to noises or outliers due to the maximum operation. In this paper, we select the modified HD instead of the HD.

Dubussion and Jain [2] presented the modified HD by employing an average over all distances from $d_i \in D$ $(1 \le i \le m)$ to their nearest neighbors in Q, rather than choosing the maximum:

$$h_{MHD}(D,Q) = \frac{1}{m} \sum_{i=1}^{m} \min_{q_j \in Q} \|d_i - q_j\|. \tag{6}$$

2.3 Proposed Method

The method of modified HD referred above can find the corresponding location between two images more correctly than the BC method, but it is time-consuming since it investigates all pixels of the query image by translating one pixel at a time over all pixels in the document image. To speed up the keyword matching process using the HD measure, the local crowdedness algorithm is applied before finding the similar region of the two images. Originally, the local crowdedness algorithm presented by Shiku [11] treats a segment as an operation unit instead of a pixel. However it is easily affected by a noise or various distortions because of a thinning operation used to extract the segments. In this paper, thus, we use the original pixel points instead of the segments in the feature extraction step. After the feature extraction, the modified HD is used on the feature point set to evaluate the similarity between two images. The proposed method is more insensitive to various distortions in the text image than other methods and also meets the requirement of fast processing simultaneously.

The local pixel crowdedness $D(x, y)$ is defined as

$$D(x, y) = \sum_{i=1}^{N} e^{-\frac{d_i^2}{2\sigma^2}}, \tag{7}$$

where N is the number of pixels included in the circular region of radius r $(= 3\sigma$; Here $\sigma = 1.5$ in our experiments) from the point (x, y), and $exp(-d_i^2/2\sigma^2)$ is a weight of the i-th pixel to which a distance from point (x, y) is d_i $(0 \le exp(-d_i^2/2\sigma^2) \le 1)$. Weights for all points within r from the point (x, y) are summarized. The degree of $D(x, y)$ shows how many black pixels are gathered around specified circular region. Some points with high crowdedness are selected as features according to a threshold. Fig. 1 shows examples of feature extraction process. The modified HD is applied on the extracted feature to detect a similar location of the two images.

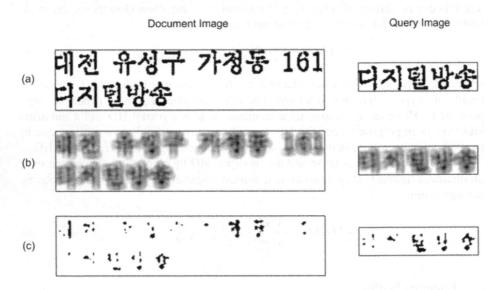

Fig. 1. Examples of the local pixel crowdedness feature for query and document images: (a) input image, (b) local pixel crowdedness, (c) extracted feature

3 Experimental Results

For the experiment we have prepared a set of Q-D pairs, where Q is a query image and D is a document image. We assume that all images to be used in this paper are deskewed in a pre-processing step, and so there is no concern with a rotational variation. Both Q and D are collected by scanning envelops of postal mails. There are two classes of Q-D pair: *class_1* is for the pair where D includes Q, while D in *class_2* has nothing related to Q. The data set consists of 380 Q-D pairs – 190 pairs of *class_1* and the other 190 pairs for *class_2*. Fig. 2 shows some example pairs of *class_1*. We partitioned the *class_1* data into four types: one is the type where Q is almost the same size as D, while Q's in the other types are about 70%, 50%, and 30% of D, respectively. The numbers of pairs are 50, 38, 58, and 44, respectively. A half of the data is used for training, and the other half is used for testing.

To evaluate the effectiveness of the similarity measures using the set of 380 Q-D pairs, we have analyzed the accuracy of classification of each pair into one of the two classes. For each similarity measure, we estimate the probability distributions of the two classes using the training data and classify each pair in the test data by using a

Document Image   Query Image

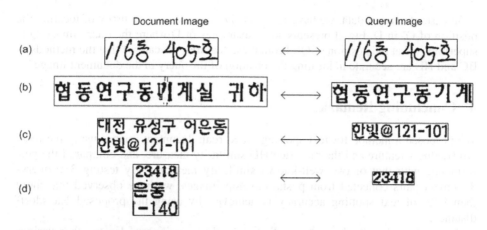

Fig. 2. Examples of sub-image pair: (a) the query contains about 100% of the image, (b) the query contains about 70% of the image, (c) the query contains about 50% of the image, (d) the query contains about 30% of the image

Bayesian decision rule. There are two types of error in the classification: type-I error is a mis-classification of a pair in *class_1* into *class_2*, and type-II error is a mis-classification of a pair in *class_2* into *class_1*. Classification accuracies along with the error ratio and the processing time are summarized in table 1. The proposed HD measure outperforms the others by from 2.7 to 9.0 percents.

Table 1. Accuracy of classification of Q-D pairs

Method	Accuracy (%)	Type-I error (%)	Type –II error (%)	Processing time (sec/image)
BC	84.2	14.7	1.1	1
Modified HD	90.5	0	9.5	10
Proposed HD	93.2	2.1	4.7	3

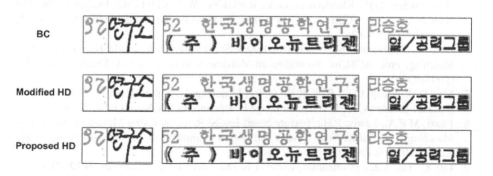

Fig. 3. Examples of overlap images resulting from three methods

In case of *class_1* data, we have additionally examined the accuracy of locating the position of Q' in D. Fig. 3 presents some examples of D where the query image Q is superimposed at the position of Q'. From these features, we can see that the methods of BC and HD are accurate in locating the position of the query in the document image.

4   Concluding Remarks

We proposed a method for text spotting on Korean document images using the local crowdedness feature and the modified HD similarity measure, and compared the performance with that of two well-known similarity measures. By testing 380 query-document pairs collected from postal envelop images, we have observed that more than 93% of text spotting accuracy is achieved by using the proposed Hausdorff distance.

The proposed method can be applied not only to mails but also to other various kinds of document images including multi-language, such as journals, newspapers, letters, and historical documents. Our future work will concentrate on how to cope with the scaling and font variations in the various document images.

Acknowledgement

This research was supported by the Program for the Training of Graduate Students in Regional Innovation which was conducted by the Ministry of Commerce, Industry and Energy of the Korean Government.

References

1. Chen, Y., Wang, J.Z., Krovetz, R.: Content-Based Image Retrieval by Clustering, Proc. ACM SIGMM Int. Workshop on Multimedia Information Retrieval, Berkeley, California (2003) 193-200
2. Dubuisson, M.P., Jain, A.K.: A Modified Hausdorff Distance for Object Matching, Proc. Int. Conf. Pattern Recognition, Jerusalem, Israel, Vol. 1 (1994) 566-568
3. Huttenlocher, D.P., Klanderman, G.A., Rucklidge, W.J.: Comparing Images Using The Hausdorff Distance, IEEE Trans. on Pattern Analysis and Machine Intelligence, Vol. 15, No. 9 (1993) 850-863
4. Luo, J., Nascimento, M.A.: Content Based Sub-Image Retrieval via Hierarchical Tree Matching, Proc. ACM Int. Workshop on Multimedia Databases, New Orleans, LA, USA (2003) 63-69
5. Sim, D.G., Kwon, O.K., Park, R.H.: Object Matching Algorithms Using Robust Hausdorff Distance Measures, IEEE Trans. on Image Processing, Vol. 8, No. 3 (1999) 425-429
6. Fauzi, M.F.A., Lewis, P.H.: Texture-based Image Retrieval Using Multiscale Sub-image Matching, Proc. SPIE Conf. Image and Video Communications and Processing, Santa Clara, California (2003) 407-416
7. Lu, Y., Tan, C.L.: Information Retrieval in Document Image Databases, IEEE Trans. on Knowledge and Data Engineering, Vol. 16, No. 11 (2004) 1398-1410
8. Lu, Y., Tan, C.L.: Chinese Word Searching in Imaged Documents, Int. Journal of Pattern Recognition and Artificial Intelligence, Vol. 18, No. 2 (2004) 229-246

9. Rath, T.M., Kane, S., Lehman, A., Partridge, E., Manmatha, R.: Indexing for a Digital Library of George Washington's Manuscripts: A Study of Word Matching Techniques, Technical Report of the Center for Intelligent Information Retrieval, University of Massachusetts (2003)

10. Srihari, S.N., Shi, Z.: Forensic Handwritten Document Retrieval System, Proc. Int. Workshop on Document Image Analysis for Libraries, Palo Alto, CA, USA (2004) 188-194.

11. Shiku, O., Kawasue, K., Nakamura, A.: A Method for Character String Extraction Using Local and Global Segment Crowdedness, Proc. Int. Conf. Pattern Recognition, Brisbane, Australia, Vol. 2 (1998) 1077-1080

12. Gonzales, R.C., Woods, R.E.: Digital Image Processing, 2nd ed. Prentice Hall (2002)

Effective Image Retrieval for the M-Learning System

Eunjung Han[1], Anjin Park[1], Dongwok kyoung[1],
HwangKyu Yang[2], and Keechul Jung[1]

[1] HCI Lab., School of Media, College of Information Technology,
Soongsil University, 156-743, Seoul, S. Korea
{hanej, anjin, kiki227, kcjung}@ssu.ac.kr
[2] Department of Multimedia Engineering, Dongseo University, 617-716, Busan, S. Korea
hayang88@hanmail.net

Abstract. In this paper, we propose augmented learning contents (ALC) with the *blended learning* on mobile devices. It augments on-line contents by indexing the corresponding off-line contents using traditional pattern recognition method, which results in a minimize of labors for conversion. Among the pattern recognition method marker-based is one of most general approach. However it must reconstruct the off-line contents with pattern markers. To solve both drawbacks that use of the pattern markers and difficulty of the color-based image retrieval by means of a low-resolution PDA camera, we used for a shape-based system. CBIR based on object shapes is used instead of pattern markers to link off-line contents with on-line, and shapes are represented by a differential chain code with estimated new starting points to obtain rotation-invariant representation, which is suited to low computational resources of mobile devices. Consequently, the ALC can provide learner with a fast and accurate multimedia contents (video, audio, text) on static off-line contents using mobile devices without space limitation.

Keywords: Contents recycling, Mobile learning, Multimedia education contents, Shape-based image retrieval, Mobile vision, DTW.

1 Introduction

A rapid growth of telecommunications wants unceasing changes and developments of knowledge and information societies. To fulfill this growth, education environments are evolving from a variety of existing education contents to learner-oriented ones [1-2]. Traditional off-line contents can be preserved for a long time and can guarantee a historicity over different media, but it is difficult to provide various contents such as a multimedia because those have only static 2D information. Hence learner-oriented e-learning educations using various technologies instead of traditional teacher-oriented face-to-face educations are spreading, and settling down as an alternative education [1]. However, the existing e-learning contents not only have restriction of space due to the use of the computer but also would be considerably expensive by means of very intensive labors to convert the original off-line contents to on-line contents.

S. Sugimoto et al. (Eds.): ICADL 2006, LNCS 4312, pp. 340–349, 2006.

M-learning and *blended learning* conceptions have appeared to solve these drawbacks. *M-learning* provides the education environment in anytime and anywhere by transforming existing education environment into mobile one [2]. Mike et al. [3] developed self-directed education contents on mobile devices. *Blended learning* is one of education concepts to prepare for education media in ubiquitous computing age, and provides education environments combining on-line contents with off-line ones [4]. Billinghurst [5] developed *MagicBook* for learners to experience 3D virtual environments on off-line contents with markers. Chen et al. [6] proposed contents including two concepts which are *m-learning* and *blended learning*. A proposed system captures butterfly images using a high-resolution digital camera, and provides learners with information relative to the captured butterfly images using a color-based image retrieval technique. Anne [7] provides how problem-based learning principles guided the design and implementation of mobile applications development. KTF [8] in Korea released new connection service for wireless Internet on mobile devices, which is not education contents, and this service links mobile contents or commerce sites when users capture *hot code* using his/her mobile camera. The previously mentioned education method using *blended learning* [5] must reconstruct the existing off-line contents with pattern markers because it uses pattern markers to recognize pages and contexts. KTF can provide users with services in only places with *hot code*. Chen et al. [6] and Yu et al. [9] provide the on-line contents by recognizing real images instead of pattern markers and *hot code*, but it is difficult to perform the color-based image retrieval on mobile devices having low-resolution cameras.

In this paper, we propose augmented learning contents (ALC) on mobile devices, including both on-line and off-line contents, to provide learner with multimedia information displayed on the PDA screen on off-line contents. To solve both drawbacks that use of the pattern markers and difficulty of the color-based image retrieval by means of a low-resolution PDA camera, we used for a shape-based system. It applicable sources of information that can be used to measure the similarity are a set of line drawings or the edges of the objects in the image. Shape-based retrieval based techniques had been developed to measure similarity according to such sources [10-13]. Yang [14] developed an elastic matching technique by constructing a self-organizing map (SOM) neural network to match two sets of feature points. But, this SOM application will show down the speed and take long processing time, and it not able to solve the PDA camera, that represent shape-based retrieval of object based on the rotation and scale.

Our proposed solution, perform the image retrieval based on shapes of figure regions of off-line contents instead of insufficient colors without pattern markers, and use a chain code that suited to the low computational resources of the PDA to represent the shapes. Although the chain code has a significant drawback which is different representations according to rotation and scales of objects, but we can obtain rotation-invariant representation using a differential chain code with new estimated starting point and compensate scale-variations using dynamic time warping (DTW), which are major issue in shape-based retrieval. Consequently, the ALC can provide learner with a fast and accurate multimedia contents (video, audio, text) on static off-line contents using mobile devices without limitation of space. The rest of the paper is organized as follows. Section 2 describes the entire system overview, and shows a shape-based image retrieval method to fast and accurate execute the ALC. In section 3, we describe an experiment about how much colors can be lost and how exactly features can be extracted on a variety of orientation and scales of the PDA. Section 4 concludes this paper.

2 Image Retrieval Method for ALC

ALC is an education system to extend the scope of existing off-line contents providing static 2D information, and can combine a variety of multimedia information with dynamic interactions using camera-equipped PDAs. Fig. 1 shows the system overview of ALC. ALC system mainly consists of an image retrieval model and a database. The image retrieval model extracts a feature from the image captured by a PDA camera, and provides a learner with multimedia contents based on the feature matching between the feature of the captured image and features within the database. We apply ALC to an English dictionary for children, and ALC provides three kinds of multimedia education contents: an English spelling, an audio stream and a video stream.

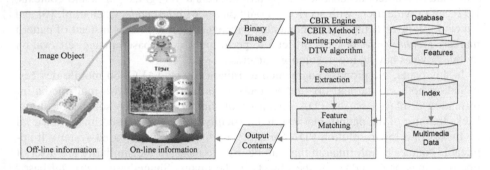

Fig. 1. System overview of ALC

Color-based image retrieval has fast computational time in any image sizes due to simple computation, but can not be performed with lack of colors (e.g. colors captured by the low-resolution PDA camera). Texture-based image retrieval has high recognition rates in images with homogeneous patterns such as a cloth, a tile and a wall, but it is not sufficient for images without any homogenous patterns used in our implementation. Therefore, we use shape-based image retrieval fitted to the PDA camera having insufficient color grabbers to recognize the image regions of off-line contents. In shape-based image retrieval, a chain code has been widely used to encode the boundary for its simplicity and low storage requirement, but the traditional chain code varies with the scaling and rotation. To resolve this problem, existing methods use Fourier descriptor or skeletons of an object [15], but need much computational time on mobile devices which do not have float-computational resources. In order to quickly execute the ALC by avoiding complex computation, we use a differential chain code with new estimated starting points which can obtain orientation-invariant features and DTW which compensates for the scale variations.

2.1   Object Extraction

We implement an object extraction as a preprocessor of the feature extraction. The preprocessor consists of three steps: making a binary image using thresholding, cutting a partial image in input image in order to resolve a camera distortion, and extracting biggest component as a main. Fig. 2 shows the stage of the preprocessor to extract the object using a connected component analysis. In Fig. 2, (a) are the input images, (b) are the binary images with gray color rectangle which includes the central region to avoid the camera distortion and gray color boundary of the object, and (c) show results of the object extraction.

(a)   (b)   (c)

Fig. 2. The results of object extraction: (a) input images, (b) binary images including the central region and the boundary of object, (c) object extraction

2.2   Object Recognition

After the user captures the image to activate the ALC, ALC retrieves the stored image corresponding to the selected image. To represent the shape of images in the regions of images which is segmented at the previous step, we use a chain code of the boundary of the region. The chain code represents regions using the direction of the boundary at each edge, and directions are quantized into one of eight.

The chain code can not only preserve lossless boundaries but also permit compact storage, but can have different descriptions according to rotation and a scale of objects [16]. To make rotation-invariant descriptions, we determine a starting point and use differential chain code based on the determined starting point. The starting point is chosen by using a closest boundary pixel (Eq. 3) from a centroid of the *region* (Eg. 2) calculated by 2D moment (Eq. 1). X_b and Y_b are sets of boundary pixels, x_{bi} and y_{bi} are i^{th} boundary pixels, x and y are coordinates, and *regions(x,y)* is a value extracted by preprocessor of coordinates of x and y.

$$M_{pq} = \sum_{x=1}^{width} \sum_{y=1}^{height} x^p y^q region(x, y) \tag{1}$$

$$C_x = \frac{M_{10}}{M_{00}}, C_y = \frac{M_{01}}{M_{00}} \tag{2}$$

$$StartPint = \arg\max_{x_{bi} \in X_b, y_{bi} \in Y_b} \sqrt{(x_{bi} - C_x)^2 + (y_{bi} - C_y)^2} \tag{3}$$

Fig. 4 shows extracted objects (Fig. 4(a,e)) and images with a boundary of objects, the centroid(black rectangle) and the starting point (gray rectangle)(Fig. 4(b-d),(f-h)). As shown in Fig. 4(e-h), our method has false results when the closest boundary pixel is on circular shapes. To resolve this problem, we obtain the starting points using the closest three pixels from the centroid[1] (Fig. 5).

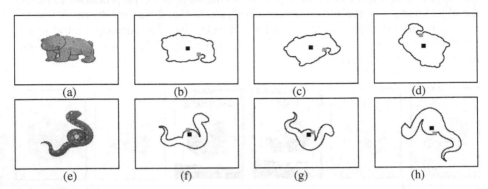

(a)   (b)   (c)   (d)

(e)   (f)   (g)   (h)

Fig. 3. The centroids and starting points: (a,e) extracted objects, (b-d,f-h) images with boundaries of objects, the centroids and the starting points

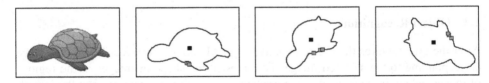

Fig. 4. The starting points based on the closest 3 pixels from the centroid

In real environments, almost all input images have different length of boundaries of objects. Therefore, we need algorithm compensating the different length between two features to measure similarity, and use DTW algorithm based on dynamic programming. If input features and reference features are $A=\{a_1,a_2,...,a_I\}$ and $B=\{b_1,b_2,...b_J\}$ respectively, similarity between two features is obtained by using (Eq. 4), and different similarity by means of the length of input features is solved by using a normalization (Eq. 5).

$$\gamma(i,j) = \min\{\gamma(i,j-1)+d(a_i,b_j), \gamma(i-1,j-1)+2\times d(a_i,b_j), \gamma(i-1,j)+d(a_i,b_j)\} \qquad (4)$$

$$DTW\ (A,B) = \frac{\gamma(I,J)}{I+J} \qquad (5)$$

Where $d(a_i,b_i)$ is distance between two points, and is calculated by Euclidean distance. We obtain the most similar index by comparing all features within the DB and the closest three features, and provide multimedia based on the index.

---

[1] In our implementation, the ALC shows the correspondence of the starting points on all test images used in our implementation when we use 3 starting points.

3 Experimental Results

We divide the experimental results into three sub-subjects. First, we analyze weakness of extracting color-information using PDA cameras to indicate the problem of performing the color-based image retrieval on mobile devices. Second, we describe an experiment results for orientation and scale variation of objects in input images, which is the problem to be solved in shape-based image retrieval. Third, we describe an analysis of a user study based on an experience of users.

3.1 Analyzing Color Information of PDA Camera

We analyze the weakness of extracting color information using the PDA camera by comparing ordinary digital cameras with PDA camera. In our implementation, the digital camera is an Olymus C-8080WZ model, and CCD is 800K pixels. The PDA is Pocket PC-2003 based POZ x301 with the camera having 30K pixels.

Fig. 5(a) shows an image capturing blue, cyan, yellow and white colors using both the digital camera and the PDA camera. Colors captured by the PDA camera have lower quality than colors captured by the digital camera, and show significant difference compared with natural colors. Therefore, we use shape-based image retrieval instead of color-based one. Fig. 5(b) shows an image to analyze a camera distortion of outer regions of input images, and is a graph showing a difference between natural colors and colors captured by the PDA camera based on Fig. 5(a). We perform object extractions within a central 260×180 region to fast execute on the PDA by avoiding a complex computation.

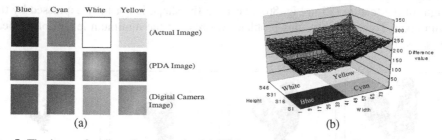

Fig. 5. The image for distortion analysis: (a) PDA camera input image, (b) actual image and difference value of (a)

3.2 Experiments for Orientation and Scale Variation of Object

Shape-based image retrieval must have high recognition rates in various variations of orientation and scales [15]. Fig. 6 shows an example of test images to analyze variation of orientation. Fig. 7 shows images expressing differential chain codes with new estimated starting points. Figs. 7(a-c) show the chain code starting from upper pixel without considering estimated starting point, and Figs. 7(d-f) show the chain code considering an estimated starting point. In Fig. 7(d) and 7(e), two chain codes are similarly expressed because the starting point of Fig. 6(d) is accidentally identical with one of Fig. 6(e) on a cat's tail.

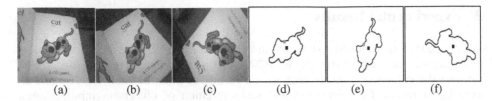

Fig. 6. Example of orientation variation: (a-c) input images, (d-f) images with boundary of objects, centroid and closest starting point

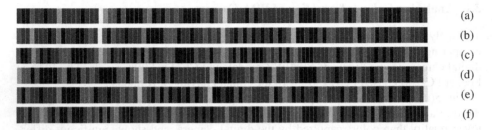

Fig. 7. Differential chain codes using Figs 11(d-f): (a-c) without considering the estimated starting points, (d-f) considering the estimated starting points

Fig. 8 shows features (Figs. 8(e-h)) based on extracted objects (Figs. 8(a-c)) to analyze scale variations. Fig. 8(b) is an ordinary scale of extracted features in DB, and the length of extracted feature is 175~200. Figs. 13(a-c) are almost similar features, but Fig. 8(d) shows an ambiguous feature. This is a problem, generated by the short length of the feature (75 in Fig. 8(d)) because the shape is not fully expressed by the chain code. To easily solve this problem, we restrict the minimum length of the feature to be 100.

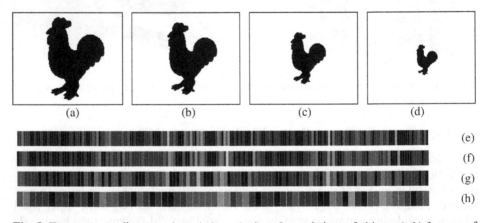

Fig. 8. Features according to scale variations: (a-d) scales variations of objects, (e-h) features of objects

3.3 ALC System

Fig. 9 shows ALC executed on a screen of the mobile devices. Each learner is ALCe to take a different English book page on images using his/her camera (Fig. 9(a)), ALC transfers each image to the database, and retrieves the stored on-line information corresponding to the captured image. After the ALC retrieves the image, ALC provides learner with multimedia information (Fig. 9(b)).

(a)   (b)   (c)

Fig. 9. The result of image retrieval: (a) a learner interacting with the ALC, (b) image retrieval, (c) augmented on-line contents

Table 1 shows an average processing time and recognition rates based on 50 images which are the total number of off-line contents used in our implementation. As shown in Table 1, the ALC has high recognition rates about text image including scale and orientation variation. Moreover, though user have about 7 seconds when users manually find a scanned image of the book on mobile devices, the ALC only has about 700 milliseconds. Consequently, the ALC has a fast and accurate output due to a content-based image retrieval using the camera attached to the mobile device.

Table 1. Average running time and recognition rate

Average running time (ms)				Recognition rate (%)
Object Extraction	Feature Extraction	Recognition	Total	
100	150	500	750	92

3.4 User Study

We implement a questionnaire to gain useful feedback from the users. Our study involved 30 subjects between the age of 8 and 13, of which fifteen were males and fifty were males. The subjects are divided into two groups that first group (A) uses only off-line contents and second group (B) uses the ALC with off-line contents. We give subjects an examination consisting of reading, writing and listening to evaluate efficiency of learning, and give again subjects the examination 21 days later to evaluate how long do they remember (Table 2). In Table 2, A group (13.6) shows higher averages than B group (9.9), and shows high averages in reading (5.0) and listening (5.3). Besides, we can take information about how long do subjects can remember

(A:9.9→4.3, B:13.6→12.6). In this test, the ALC shows effects improved in reading and listening through iterative learning of listening to pronunciations of the native speaker, and children remember for a long time due to the video stream.

Table 2. Result of user study

Contents	Date	Reading	Writing	Listening	Total
Only Off-line	1, Oct.	2.9	4.3	2.7	9.9
Contents (A Group)	22, Oct.	1.6	1.7	1	4.3
With ALC	1. Oct.	5.0	3.3	5.3	13.6
(B Group)	22. Oct.	4.5	3.3	4.8	12.6

4 Conclusion

In this paper, we proposed the augmented learning content with a *blended learning* concept which combines off-line contents with various multimedia on mobile devices (*m-learning* concept). Existing methods to combine two concepts use pattern markers and high-resolution cameras to recognize the off-line contents. We use image regions of off-line contents instead of pattern markers and shape-based image retrieval instead of color-based image retrieval requiring high-resolution cameras. To represent the shape, we use a chain code, and a differential chain code with new estimated starting points and DTW to resolve problems about variations in orientation and scaling of image. In our implementation, this method has high recognition rates in various orientation and scales. However, we have two problems yet. First, our method is sensitive to the light and surrounding environments. Second, it is difficult to perform the ALC in real-time due to low computational resources of the PDA.

To resolve these problems, we will use a Client/Server architecture using wireless communication modules of the PDA, and Server will perform the complex algorithm to exactly extract the objects, and will provide much more contents.

Acknowledgement. This work was supported by Korea Research Foundation Grant (KRF-2004-042-D00183).

References

1. Eunjung. H., Keechul. J., Chungjae. I.: E-learning Self-Directed Contents Development for Multimedia. Proceedings of Information Society, Vol.21, No.1, (2005) 1019-1022
2. ERICSSON, From e-learning to m-learning, http://learning.ericsson.net/leonardo (2002)
3. Sharples. M., Corlett. D., Westmancott. O.: The Design and Implementation of a Mobile Learning Resource. Personal and Ubiquitous, Vol. 6, Issue 3 (2002) 220-234
4. http://www.contentsmedia.com/
5. Billinghurst, M., Karo. H., Poupyrev. I.: The MagicBook: A Transitional AR Interface. Computer Graphics (2001) 745-753
6. Chen. Y. S., Kao. T., Sheu. J.: A Mobile Butterfly-Learning System for Supporting Independent Learning. IEEE International Workshop on Wireless and Mobile Technologies in Education (2004) 11-18

7. Anne. P. M.: Design, Development, and Assessment of Mobile Application: The Case for Problem-Based Learning. IEEE Transactions on Education, Vol.49, No.2 (2006) 183-192
8. KTF, http://www.ktf.co.kr
9. Yu. G. J., Chen. Y. S., Shih K. P.: A Content-based Image Retrieval System for Outdoor Ecology Learning. Proceedings of International Conference on Advanced Information Networking and Application, Vol. 2 (2004) 112-115
10. D. Doermann.: The indexing and retrieval of document images: A survey, Computer Vision and Image Understanding, Vol. 70, No.3 (1998) 287-298
11. R. Mehrotra and J. E. Gary.: Similar-shape retrieval in shape data management. IEEE Computer, Vol.28, No. 9 (1995) 57-62
12. Li. S., Lee. M. C., Adjeroh, D.: Effective Invariant Feature for Shape-based Image Retrieval. Journal of the American Society for Information Science and Technology, Vol. 56, Issue 7. (2005) 729-740
13. A. Sajjanhar and G. Lu.: A comparison of techniques for shape retrieval. Proceedings of-International Conference on Computational Intelligence and Multimedia Applications, pages (1998) 854-859
14. Yang H.C.: Shaped-based Image Retrieval by Spatial Topology Distances. Proceedings of theACM workshops on Multimedia: multimedia information retrieval (2001)38-41
15. Shapiro. L. G., Stockman. G. C.: Computer Vision. Prentice Hall, Upper Saddle River, New Jersey (2001)
16. Sake. H., Chiba. S.: Dynamic Programming Algorithm Optimization for Spoken Word Recognition. IEEE Transactions on Acoustic, Speech, and Signal, Vol. 26, No. 1 (1978) 43-49
17. Veltkamp. R. C., Tanase. M.: Content-based Image Retrieval Systems: A Survey. Technical Report, UU-CS-2000-34 (2000)

Language Translation and Media Transformation
in Cross-Language Image Retrieval

Hsin-Hsi Chen and Yih-Chen Chang

Department of Computer Science and Information Engineering
National Taiwan University
Taipei, Taiwan
hhchen@csie.ntu.edu.tw, ycchang@nlg.csie.ntu.edu.tw

Abstract. Cross-language image retrieval facilitates the use of text query in one language and image query in one medium to access image collection with text description in another language/medium. The images with annotations are considered as a trans-media parallel corpus. In a media-mapping approach, we transform a query in one medium into a query in another medium by referencing to the aligned trans-media corpus. From the counterpart of results of an initial retrieval, we generate a new query in different medium. In the experiments, we adopted St. Andrews University Library's photographic collection used in ImageCLEF, and explored different models of language translation and media transformation. When both text query and image query are given together, the best MAP of a cross-lingual cross-media model **1L2M** (one language translation plus two media transformations) achieve 87.15% and 72.39% of those of mono-lingual image retrieval in the 2004 and the 2005 test sets, respectively. That demonstrates our media transformation is quite useful, and it can compensate for the errors introduced in language translation.

1 Introduction

For systematic construction of digital libraries and digital museums, large scale of images associated with captions, metadata, and so on, are available. Users often use their familiar languages to annotate images and express their information needs. Cross-language image retrieval (CLMR) becomes more practical. CLMR, which is some sort of cross-language cross-media information retrieval (CL-CM-IR), allows users employ text queries (in one language) and example images (in one medium) to access image database with text descriptions (in another language/medium). Two languages, i.e., query language and document language, and two media, i.e., text and image, are adopted to express the information needs and the data collection. Both language translation and media transformation have to be dealt with.

Cross-language information retrieval (CLIR) facilitates the uses of queries in one language to access documents in another language. It touches on the multilingual aspect only. Language unification is the major issue in CLIR. Either query translation or document translation can be considered. In the past, dictionary-based, corpus-based and hybrid approaches have been proposed [3][11]. Dictionary-based

S. Sugimoto et al. (Eds.): ICADL 2006, LNCS 4312, pp. 350–359, 2006.
© Springer-Verlag Berlin Heidelberg 2006

approach exploits bilingual machine-readable dictionaries. Translation ambiguity, target polysemy and coverage of dictionaries are several important issues to tackle. Target term selection strategies like *select all*, *select N randomly* and *select best N*, and selection level like *words* and *phrases* have been presented. Corpus-based approach exploits a bilingual parallel corpus, which is a collection of original texts and their translations. Such a corpus may be document-aligned, sentence-aligned or word-aligned. Corpus-based approach has been employed to set up a bilingual dictionary, or to translate a source query to a target one. Dictionaries and corpora are complementary. The former provides broad and shallow coverage, while the latter provides narrow (domain-specific) but deep (more terminology) coverage of the language.

Compared with CLIR, image retrieval touches on medium aspect rather than multilingual issue. Two types of approaches, i.e., content-based and text-based approaches, are usually adopted in image retrieval [8]. Content-based image retrieval (CBIR) uses low-level visual features to retrieve images. In such a way, it is unnecessary to annotate images and transform users' queries. However, due to the semantic gap between image visual features and high-level concepts [7], it is still challenging to use a CBIR system to retrieve images with correct semantic meanings. Integrating textual information may help a CBIR system to cross the semantic gap and improve retrieval performance.

Recently several approaches tried to combine text- and content-based methods for image retrieval. A simple approach is: conducting text- and content-based retrieval separately, and merging the retrieval results of the two runs [2][9]. In contrast to the parallel approach, a pipeline approach uses textual or visual information to perform initial retrieval, and then uses the other feature to filter out irrelevant images [1]. In these two approaches, textual and visual queries are formulated by users and do not directly influence each other. Another approach, i.e., transformation-based approach, mines the relations between images and text, and uses the mined relations to transform textual information into visual one, and vice versa [10].

In this paper, we will consider how to utilize a trans-media parallel corpus to integrate textual and visual information for cross-language image retrieval. In contrast to a bilingual parallel corpus, a trans-media parallel corpus is defined to be a collection of images and their text annotations. An image is aligned to its text description. Section 2 will present a media-mapping approach. Section 3 will specify the experimental materials, i.e., St. Andrews University Library's photographic collection used in the 2004 and the 2005 ImageCLEF [4][5]. Sections 4 and 5 will show and discuss the experiments. Finally, Section 6 will conclude the remarks.

2   A Media-Mapping Approach

A media-mapping approach transforms a query in one medium to a query in another medium using a trans-media parallel corpus. Figure 1 sketches the concept. A visual query is submitted to a content-based information retrieval (CBIR) system. The IR system reports a set of relevant images. Since an image and its text description are aligned, the corresponding text descriptions of relevant images are also reported.

Different term selection methods like high frequency terms, statistically significant terms, *etc*. proposed in multilingual text retrieval [6] can be explored.

Figure 1 shows two possible media transformations, including textual query to visual one (i.e., Q1 ⇨ Q3) and visual query to textual one (i.e., Q4 ⇨ Q5). Here, X ⇨ Y denotes a translation or a transformation from X to Y. Besides media transformation, Q1 can also be translated into Q2, a textual query in target language.

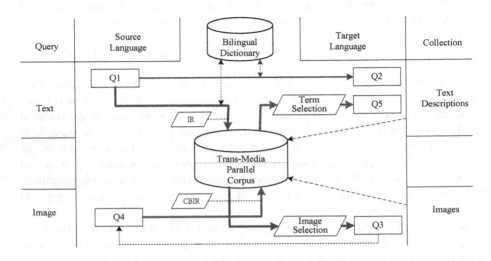

Fig. 1. A Media-Mapping Approach

Figure 2 shows a model called **1L1M**, i.e., (Q1 ⇨ Q2) and (Q4 ⇨ Q5), including one language translation and one media transformation. The overall architecture consists of a textual run, an initial visual run, and a relevance feedback run. The original textual query initiates a textual run. Its procedure is the same as a traditional CLIR system. A source textual query is translated into a target textual one, and then the target query is submitted to a text-based IR system. A set of relevant text descriptions is reported along with their images.

In an initial visual run, a visual query is transformed into a textual one through the media-mapping approach. Then, the textual query is sent to a text-based IR system to retrieve the relevant text descriptions, and, at the same time, the relevant images. This procedure is similar to traditional relevant feedback except that the feedback comes from another media, i.e., text, rather than the original media, i.e., image. This is because the performance of content-based IR is usually worse than that of text-based IR.

The results generated by the textual run and the visual run are merged together. The similarity scores of images in the two runs are normalized and linearly combined by weighting.

In Section 4, we will consider an alternative model called **1L2M** which includes one language translation (Q1 ⇨ Q2) and two media transformations (Q1 ⇨ Q3) & (Q3=Q4' ⇨ Q5). Here Q3=Q4' means the retrieval results Q3 of Q1 are considered as new query Q4'.

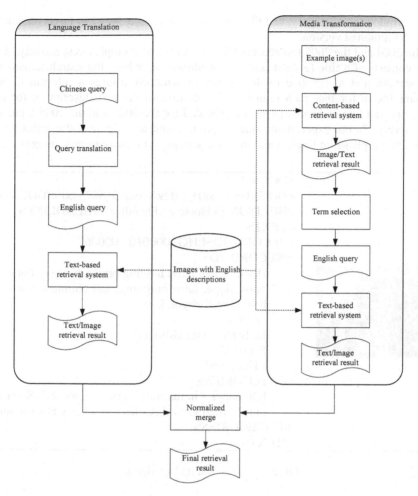

Fig. 2. A 1L1M Cross-Language Image Retrieval System with Media Mapping

3 Experimental Materials

In the experiments, we adopt the 2004 and the 2005 ImageCLEF test sets [4][5]. The image collection consists of 28,133 photographs from St. Andrews University Library's photographic collection, which is one of the largest and most important collections of historic photography in Scotland. The majority of images (82%) in the St. Andrews image collection are in black and white. All images are accompanied by a caption written in English by librarians working at St. Andrews Library. The information in a caption ranges from specific date, location, and photographer to a more general description of an image. Figure 3 shows an example of image and its caption in the St. Andrews image collection. The text descriptions are semi-structured and consist of several fields including document number, headline, record id, description text, category, and file names of images in a 368×234 large version and 120×76 thumbnail version.

The 2004 and the 2005 test sets contain 25 topics and 28 topics, respectively. Each topic consists of a title (a short sentence or phrase describing the search request in a few words), and a narrative (a description of what constitutes a relevant or non-relevant image for that each request). In addition to the text description for each topic, one and two example images are provided for the 2004 and the 2005 topic sets, respectively. In our experiments, queries are in Chinese. Figure 4 illustrates a topic of the 2005 topic set in English and in Chinese along with two example images.

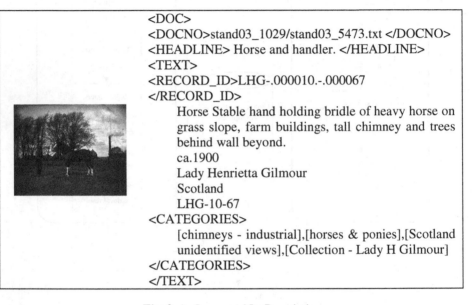

```
<DOC>
<DOCNO>stand03_1029/stand03_5473.txt </DOCNO>
<HEADLINE> Horse and handler. </HEADLINE>
<TEXT>
<RECORD_ID>LHG-.000010.-.000067
</RECORD_ID>
        Horse Stable hand holding bridle of heavy horse on
        grass slope, farm buildings, tall chimney and trees
        behind wall beyond.
        ca.1900
        Lady Henrietta Gilmour
        Scotland
        LHG-10-67
<CATEGORIES>
        [chimneys - industrial],[horses & ponies],[Scotland
        unidentified views],[Collection - Lady H Gilmour]
</CATEGORIES>
</TEXT>
```

Fig. 3. An Image and Its Description

4 Experiments

At first, we consider text query only. For each Chinese query term, we find its translation equivalents by using a Chinese-English bilingual dictionary. If a query term has more than one translation, the first two translations with the highest occurrences in the English image captions are considered as the target language query terms. Assume queries Q0 and Q2 are human translation and machine translation of a text query Q1, respectively, in Figure 1. Table 1 shows the mean average precision (MAP) of retrieval using Q0 and Q2. It is trivial that monolingual IR using Q0 is better than crosslingual IR using Q1⇨Q2. The MAPs of the latter are 69.72% and 60.70% of those of the former on the 2004 and the 2005 topic sets, respectively. Compared to the 2004 topic set, the MAP of using the 2005 topic set is decreased to 0.3952. It confirms that the 2005 topic set containing more general and visual queries is more challenging than the 2004 topic set [5].

```
<top>
<num> Number: 1 </num>
<title> aircraft on the ground </title>
<narr>Relevant images will show one or more airplanes
         positioned on the ground. Aircraft do not have to be
         the focus of the picture, although it should be
         possible to make out that the picture contains
         aircraft. Pictures of aircraft flying are not relevant
         and pictures of any other flying object (e.g. birds)
         are not relevant. </narr>
</top>
<top>
<num> Number: 1 </num>
<title> 地面上的飛機 </title>
<narr>相關圖片應顯示一架或多架地面上的飛機。飛機
         不需要在圖片中央，但是圖片上應該可以看到飛
         機。飛行中的飛機和其他飛行物體（例如：鳥）
         不算相關。 </narr>
```

Fig. 4. Topic Number 1 of the 2005 Topic Set in English and in Chinese

Table 1. Performance of monolingual (Q0)/cross-lingual information retrieval (Q1⇨Q2)

Model	2004 topic set	2005 topic set
Q0	0.6304	0.3952
Q1⇨Q2	0.4395	0.2399

Next, we consider image query only. Compared with Table 1, Table 2 shows that scontent-based IR is much worse than monolingual IR and crosslingual IR. Because example images (i.e., image queries) are in the data set, they are often the top-1 and the top-2 images reported by the content-based IR system for the 2004 and the 2005 topic sets, respectively. To evaluate the real performance, we consider two cases: the data sets with and without the example images. It is trivial that the MAPs of the former (0.0672 and 0.0725) are better than those of the latter (0.0149 and 0.0259).

Table 2. Performance of content-based information retrieval (CBIR)

	Keep Example Images		Remove Example Images	
	2004 topic set	2005 topic set	2004 topic set	2005 topic set
CBIR	0.0672	0.0725	0.0149	0.0259

With the media-mapping approach, we generate a text query Q5 from the text description counterparts of retrieved images by using Q4, shown in Figure 1. Table 3 illustrates the performance of Q5 when all the words are selected from the text descriptions of the top-*n* retrieved images. Comparing Tables 2 and 3, media transformation from image to text is better than CBIR directly.

Table 3. Retrieval performance of text query transformed from image query (Q4⇨Q5)

Top-*n* Images↓	Keep Example Images		Remove Example Images	
	2004 topic set	2005 topic set	2004 topic set	2005 topic set
1	0.4991	0.2109	0.0704	0.0582
2	0.3922	0.3409	0.0486	0.0434
3	0.2994	0.2912	0.0451	0.0441
4	0.2380	0.2004	0.0450	0.0436
5	0.2231	0.1588	0.0429	0.0450

Now, we consider both text and image queries. At first, we set up two baselines, i.e., merging the results of monolingual/cross-lingual IR and CBIR directly. The latter is one language translation and zero media transformation (**1L0M**). Table 4 shows the performance on two different topic sets. The weights for models Q0∪Q4 and (Q1⇨Q2)∪Q4 are (0.9, 0.1) and (0.7, 0.3), respectively. $X \cup Y$ means merging results of X and Y. When example images are removed from the test collection, the naïve merging model cannot even outperform text query only model (see Table 1).

Table 4. Naïve merging of monolingual IR (Q0)/cross-lingual IR (Q1⇨Q2) and CBIR (Q4)

	Keep Example Images		Remove Example Images	
	2004 topic set	2005 topic set	2004 topic set	2005 topic set
Q0∪Q4	0.6241	0.4354	0.5439	0.3770
(Q1⇨Q2)∪Q4	0.4622	0.2697	0.4265	0.2365

We consider the 1L1M model shown in Figure 1 next. Query Q1 is translated into Q2 by language translation, i.e., Q1⇨Q2. Query Q4 is transformed into Q5 by media transformation, i.e., Q4⇨Q5. In this way, all words from the text counterparts of images retrieved by Q4 form a text query Q5. Finally, we merge the retrieval results of Q2 and Q5 with weights 0.7 and 0.3. Table 5 depicts the experimental results of one language translation and one media transformation. No matter whether the examples are kept in or removed from the test collection, the 1L1M model (Q1⇨Q2)∪(Q4⇨Q5) is better than the 1L0M model (Q1⇨Q2)∪Q4.

Table 5. Performance of 1 Language Translation and 1 Media Transformation Using ALL

Top-*n* Images↓	Keep Example Images		Remove Example Images	
	2004 topic set	2005 topic set	2004 topic set	2005 topic set
1	0.5220	0.2930	0.4542	0.2440
2	0.5243	0.3194	0.4476	0.2410
3	0.5184	0.3207	0.4508	0.2497
4	0.5097	0.3139	0.4484	0.2526
5	0.4985	0.3030	0.4519	0.2526

We further introduce the 1L2M model to integrate text and image queries. This model, denoted by (Q1⇨Q2)∪((Q1⇨Q3 selected by Q4)⇨Q5), consists of one language translation, and two media transformations. In the first media mapping, the system employs Q1 to select 1,000 text descriptions, then Q4 to re-rank the 1,000 image counterparts, and finally reports re-ranking results Q3 as retrieval results of Q1. Because Q1 filters out most of the irrelevant images, and the search scope is narrowed down, it is more probable to select relevant images by using Q4. In the second media mapping, the re-ranking result Q3 is considered as new image query Q4', and transformed into Q5. Textual terms in Q5 are selected from the relevant text counterparts of a content-based image retrieval using Q4'. Finally, we merge the results of two monolingual text retrieval using Q2 and Q5 with weights 0.7 and 0.3.

Table 6 shows the performance of the new model when all words in the text descriptions are selected. Compared with Table 5, the performance is improved when example images are removed from test collections. We employ another alternative – say, Chi-Square, to select suitable terms to form query Q5. Table 7 shows the performance of the 1L2M model on the test collection without example images. The best MAPs are 0.4740 and 0.2729 for the 2004 and the 2005 topic sets, respectively, which are 87.15% and 72.39% of the performance of the mono-lingual image retrieval Q0∪Q4 (refer to Table 4). Compared with 1L0M model (Q1⇨Q2)∪Q4, the improvement of 1L2M model using χ^2 is verified as significant by a Wilcoxon signed-rank test with a confidence level of 95%. The boldface in Table 7 denotes the cases passing the significant test.

Table 6. Performance of 1 Language Translation and 2 Medial Transformations Using ALL

Top-n Images↓	Keep Example Images		Remove Example Images	
	2004 topic set	2005 topic set	2004 topic set	2005 topic set
1	0.5218	0.2917	0.4522	0.2628
2	0.5131	0.3191	0.4552	0.2659
3	0.5028	0.3210	0.4648	0.2621
4	0.4921	0.3252	0.4700	0.2625
5	0.4864	0.3091	0.4699	0.2654

Table 7. Performance of 1 Language Translation and 2 Medial Transformations Using χ^2 (Remove Example Images)

n↓	2004 topic set				2005 topic set			
m→	10	20	30	40	10	20	30	40
1	0.4494	0.4532	0.4519	0.4524	**0.2586**	**0.2628**	**0.2656**	**0.2640**
ss2	0.4424	0.4445	0.4493	0.4530	**0.2659**	**0.2625**	**0.2649**	**0.2635**
3	**0.4737**	0.4568	0.4537	0.4607	**0.2629**	**0.2624**	**0.2610**	**0.2586**
4	**0.4727**	0.4622	**0.4740**	**0.4718**	**0.2649**	**0.2729**	**0.2666**	**0.2636**
5	**0.4580**	**0.4567**	**0.4618**	**0.4600**	0.2727	0.2684	0.2662	0.2630

5 Discussion

We examine the retrieval results of the best model, i.e., two medial transformations, to see why the performance is improved. The following list three possible cases.

(1)   Image query compensates for the translation errors of text query. Consider a query "四輪馬車", which is translated into "four wheel horse car" instead of "cart" or "coach". The text retrieval returns candidate images containing "horse" at first, image retrieval then selects the most similar images from candidates by using example image, and finally the terms "cart" or "coach" in the reported images are suggested for retrieval. Similarly, query "建築物上飄揚的旗子" is translated into "building on aflutter flag". Image retrieval re-ranks those images containing "flags", and contributes the concept "flying".

(2)   The translation is correct, but the text description is not matched to the translation equivalent. For example, query "蘇格蘭的太陽" is translated into "Scotland Sun" correctly, however, the corresponding concepts in relevant images are "sunrise" or "sunset". The first media transformation proposes those images containing "sun", and the second media transformation suggests the relevant concepts, i.e., "sunrise" or "sunset".

(3)   The translation is correct, and the text description of images is exactly matched to the translation equivalent. For example, query "動物雕像" is translated into "animal statue" correctly. Here, "statue" is enhanced, so that those images containing the concept are re-ranked to the top.

To sum up, in the two media transformation model, the first media mapping (i.e., text→image) derives image query to capture extra information other than text query. The second media mapping (i.e., image → text) generates text query for more reliable text-based retrieval other than content-based retrieval. These two procedures are complementary, so that the model results in good performance.

6 Concluding Remarks

Cross-lingual IR achieves 69.72% and 60.70% of mono-lingual IR in the two topic sets used in this paper. Content-based IR gets much less performance, i.e., it achieves only 2.36% and 6.55% of text-based IR. Naïve merging the results of text and image queries gain no benefit. It would be doubt if integrating content-based IR and text-based IR was helpful for cross-language image retrieval under such a poor CBIR system.

Compared to content-based IR, the generated text query from the given image query using media-mapping approach improves the original performance from 0.0149 and 0.0259 to 0.0704 and 0.0582 in the best setting. When both text and image queries are considered, the best cross-lingual image retrieval model (i.e., the 1L2M model using χ^2 term selection), which achieves the MAPs of 0.4740 and 0.2729, are significantly better than the baseline cross-lingual image retrieval model (i.e., 0.4265 and 0.2365), and 87.15% and 72.39% of the baseline mono-lingual image retrieval model (i.e., 0.5439 and 0.3770).

Enhancing text-based IR with image query is more challenging than enhancing image-based IR with text query. The use of image query to re-rank the counterpart image results of a text-based IR in the first media mapping, the transformation of the re-ranked images to text queries in the second media mapping, and the employment of final text queries bring into full play of text and image queries.

In the current experimental materials, most of the images are in black and white. We will extend our models to the web, where plenty of color images are available, and various genres of annotations can be explored.

Acknowledgements

Research of this paper was partially supported by National Science Council, Taiwan, under the contracts NSC94-2213-E-002-076 and NSC95-2752-E-001-001-PAE.

References

1. Baan, J., van Ballegooij, A., Geusenbroek, J.M., den Hartog, J., Hiemstra, D., List, J., Patras, I., Raaijmakers, S., Snoek, C., Todoran, L., Vendrig, J., de Vries, A., Westerveld, T. and Worring, M.: Lazy Users and Automatic Video Retrieval Tools in the Lowlands. In: Proceedings of the Tenth Text Retrieval Conference (2002) 159-168.
2. Besançon, R., Hède, P., Moellic, P.A. and Fluhr C.: Cross-Media Feedback Strategies: Merging Text and Image Information to Improve Image Retrieval. In: Proceedings of 5th Workshop of the Cross-Language Evaluation Forum LNCS 3491 (2005) 709-717.
3. Chen, H.H., Bian, G.W. and Lin, W.C.: Resolving Translation Ambiguity and Target Polysemy in Cross-Language Information Retrieval. In: Proceedings of 37th Annual Meeting of the Association for Computational Linguistics (1999) 215-222.
4. Clough, P., Sanderson, M. and Müller, H.: The CLEF 2004 Cross Language Image Retrieval Track. In: Proceedings of 5th Workshop of the Cross-Language Evaluation Forum LNCS 3491 (2005) 597-613.
5. Clough, P., Müller, H., Deselaers, T., Grubinger, M., Lehmann, T., Jensen, J. and Hersh, W.: The CLEF 2005 Cross Language Image Retrieval Track. In: Proceedings of 6th Workshop of the Cross-Language Evaluation Forum LNCS (2006).
6. Davis, M.W. and Dunning, T.: A TREC Evaluation of Query Translation Methods for Multi-lingual Text Retrieval. In: Proceedings of TREC-4 (1996) 483-498.
7. Eidenberger, H. and Breiteneder, C.: Semantic Feature Layers in Content-based Image Retrieval: Implementation of Human World Features. In: Proceedings of International Conference on Control, Automation, Robotic and Vision (2002).
8. Goodrum, A.A.: Image Information Retrieval: An Overview of Current Research. Information Science 3(2) (2000) 63-66.
9. Jones, G.J.F., Groves, D., Khasin, A., Lam-Adesina, A., Mellebeek, B. and Way, A.: Dublin City University at CLEF 2004: Experiments with the ImageCLEF St. Andrew's Collection. In: Proceedings of 5th Workshop of the Cross-Language Evaluation Forum LNCS 3491 (2005) 653-663.
10. Lin, W.C., Chang, Y.C. and Chen, H.H.: Integrating Textual and Visual Information for Cross-Language Image Retrieval. In: Proceedings of the Second Asia Information Retrieval Symposium LNCS 3689 (2005) 454-466.
11. Oard, D.W.: Alternative Approaches for Cross-Language Text Retrieval. In: Working Notes of AAAI-97 Spring Symposiums on Cross-Language Text and Speech Retrieval (1997) 131-139.

A Surface Errors Locator System
for Ancient Culture Preservation

Yimin Yu, Duanqing Xu, Chun Chen, Yijun Yu, and Lei Zhao

College of Computer Science, Zhejiang University,
310027 Hangzhou, Zhejiang, P.R. China
yuyym@yahoo.com.cn, xdq@zju.edu.cn, chenc@cs.zju.edu.cn,
yijunyu@mail.hz.zj.cn, zhlzhao@yahoo.com.cn

Abstract. We present a novel system to find the surface errors for preservation and reappearance of cultural relic image better. Our approach firstly transforms images to HSL color space in accord with human vision and deal with the lightness of color conveniently. Next we use color cluster method to increase the locator accuracy. Finally we apply features analysis to find the error automatically. This procedure is consist of two phases: the Lightness of error detecting and the Adaptive detection filtering. Our technique can be applied to many areas, especially our ancient culture preservation, such as the renaissance of the costly fresco of Dunhuang, which is urgently desiderated protection. Experiments show the effects of our technique and its application foreground is attractive.

1 Introduction

Image completion, which is often named as region completion, is a challenging issue in image and graphics processing, and has been emerged to be a high level understanding task of low level vision content. Image completion plays a key role in a variety of research areas, including photo-editing, artwork-repairing, movie postproduction, etc. The procedure of completing missing content in images is the kernel task of image completion in this paper. The main idea of our approach is often the principle of good continuation, which consists of adding content with the information from the outside of the area to be restored.

Recently there have been a number of research works that bring forward some methods to solve the problem of image completion. However, most of these methods require that the portion identification should be restored with user interaction, namely users have to handle images manually, high scene complexity in interactive process. This is a tedious process when the database is very large. Instead, our method automatically detects most damages based on several filters, and acquires high efficiency.

Since it is difficult to select errors on most video frames, video completion uses motion estimation, shape features, and Kokaram's model [3] to detect errors on video. However, most existing methods can not be used directly in blemish detection of a single image. Thus, we propose an approach to detect photo errors and optimize the finding of errors in random color textures [10]. In this paper, we propose a novel

S. Sugimoto et al. (Eds.): ICADL 2006, LNCS 4312, pp. 360–369, 2006.
© Springer-Verlag Berlin Heidelberg 2006

approach to automatic detect image error and mark the specified color in it for addressing image renaissance by means of texture propagation afterwards. The goal of this paper is to accurately detect and localize errors in images.

The main contribution of this paper can be summarized as follows:

(1) The strategy is similar but different from color image segmentation [11] to find foreground objects. Our method learns to find the distinction of lightness variation and makes errors detection automatically.

(2) This paper is also devoted to an extension of the current features and takes advantage of shape information presented in the image in order to detect specific errors.

The remaining part of this paper is organized as follows: Firstly, section 2 introduces our research background of this paper. Secondly, section 3 presents a brief overview of the entire technique and the error detection algorithm in detail. Experimental results of our method are shown in section 4. Finally we give concluding remarks in section 5.

2 Research Background

The above work is being developed in the context of the National Grand Fundamental Research 973 Program of China. This project has two target applications, a virtual heritage reconstruction and automobile appearance display project. In the following sections, we describe these applications and discuss the first results of the system in use.

We briefly discuss a selection of the most relevant computer graphics/vision approaches for data capture and display. We then present a rapid overview of previous work related to the chosen application domains. The goal of our project is to reconstruct the heritage site called HEMUDU which can let the user to understand how the ancients live. The user also can participate into the virtual environments to experience the life of the ancients about 7000 years ago.

2.1 Model Reconstruction

The premise of our modeling approach is the creation of realistic 3D scenes by different methods that can be displayed in VHEs. In computer graphics, a number of Image-Based Modelling and Rendering techniques have been developed (e.g., [6], [8]). Despite recent advances (e.g., [4]), these techniques usually require special purpose display methods. Such approaches can be hard to integrate into traditional VR systems, which have numerous software components to handle the complexity of the hardware platform (stereo, tracking, different devices etc.), and are usually created with standard scene-graph APIs such as OpenGL Performer. As a result, the application of such techniques into an integrated VHE is rare. We have chosen to use a modelling-from-scanner approach (e.g., [6], or from image, ImageModeler from REALVIZ. Other forms of manual modeling using modern modeling software could potentially be used for some of the applications we examine; each approach has different tradeoffs. In the context of situated activity in a VHE, we believe that the simplicity and cost of capture from photographs, and the quality of the resulting models justifies our choice. This does not hold true for all applications (for example, where millimeter precision is required). In the long run, we believe that combinations of several different acquisition techniques should be used. For the display of vegetation, we use a mixed point-based/polygon rendering technique which allows us to handle complexity efficiently.

2.2 Display and Interaction

As VR technology becomes commonplace, there has been a proliferation of VR in fields such as design, education, and entertainment or, in other words, areas where VR applications are more easily available to and accessible by the general public. In the field of education, VEs have been developed to help teach concepts that are hard to learn [2], [9] or difficult to visualize otherwise. In design, VR has been used where conventional media are ill-suited to represent the work processes in ways that make them easy to visualize. In both cases, VR, with its immersive and interactive properties, can offer possibilities and solutions that are otherwise very difficult to obtain. For these reasons, we have chosen two application domains that relate to learning and working in VR, an archaeological reconstruction and automobile appearance display project.

Our choice has been motivated by the fact that both tasks are real-world projects that are currently in progress and in need of high-level tools and presentation means that will speedup and facilitate the work or help in better dissemination of their cause. In the first case, the Society of DUNHUANG Studies has been involved for years in display frescos and the Grottoes on which the frescos are drawn, reconstructing the archaeological site in order to make it more accessible to visitors, Additionally, the grotto-like environments can be used in a cultural heritage museum. The automobile designer, who has undertaken the development of the automobile, wishes to thoroughly evaluate the effects of the automobile on the virtual environment. Automobile appearance display can be used in designing of automobile industry, which can be reduce the cost of designing since the designer can find the bug instead of producing. We use cubic display environments called CAVE to display the frescos of DUNHUANG. These frescos are scanned form real wall of DUNHUANG, which consists of huge points data and high detail texture. For the second application, we display an outdoor complex scenes which consists of lot of objects, this objects can be from scanner or photograph or triangle model. The observer can interact with the virtual environments through a data gloves, the user can take a harpoon to fish. We use FOB(The Flock of Birds) to track the position of eyes and hand. FOB is a six degrees-of-freedom measuring device that can be configured to simultaneously track the position and orientation of multiple sensors by a transmitter. Each sensor is capable of making from 20 to 144 measurements per second of its position and orientation when the sensor is located within ± 4 feet of its transmitter. We use Cybe-Grasp to track the action of the finger, and the user can get force feedback form the objects of scenes by wearing the Cybe-Force device. By introducing viewpoint dependent display techniques the user also observe the relic in near distance.

3 Error Detection

Most existing image problem techniques depend on user interaction to select error region for location. However, user interactions initially only provide rough information and iterative interactions are needed to provide high efficiency. Thus when the image database is very large, the manual work is very tedious. Regarding this problem, we propose a error detection algorithm in this section. Given an input image with much defects or errors, our algorithm can be used to detect the error region, and remark it in a specified color. The detection procedure can be described as follows:

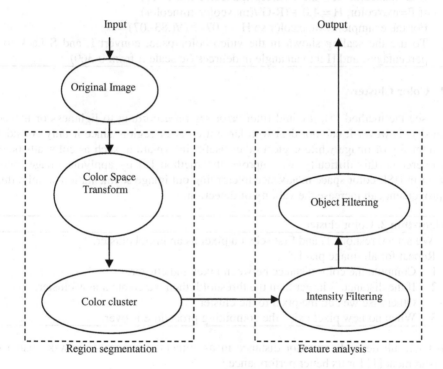

Fig. 1. Error Detection in Image

3.1 Color Model Selection

In our system, we use HSL color space instead of commonly used RGB color space since HSL is more adaptive to human being and has the consistency with human vision. Referring to [7], the conversion between the two color space is as follows:

Algorithm 1. RGB to HSL conversion
1   Convert the RBG values to the range 0-1
Example: from the video colors page, colorbar red has R=83%, B=7%, G=7%, or in this scale, R=.83, B=.07, G=.07
2   Find min and max values of R, B, G
In the example, maxcolor = .83, mincolor=.07

3	If the max and min colors are the same (ie the color is some kind of grey), S is defined to be 0, and H is undefined but in programs usually written as 0
4	Otherwise, L = (maxcolor + mincolor)/2
	For the example, L = (.83+.07)/2 = .45
5	Test L.
	If L < 0.5, S=(maxcolor-mincolor)/(maxcolor+mincolor)
	If L >=0.5, S=(maxcolor-mincolor)/(2.0-maxcolor-mincolor)
	For the example, L=0.45 so S=(.83-.07)/(.83+.07) = .84
6	If R=maxcolor, H = (G-B)/(maxcolor-mincolor)
	If G=maxcolor, H = 2.0 + (B-R)/(maxcolor-mincolor)
	If B=maxcolor, H = 4.0 + (R-G)/(maxcolor-mincolor)
	For the example, R=maxcolor so H = (.07-.07)/(.83-.07) = 0
7	To use the scaling shown in the video color page, convert L and S back to percentages, and H into an angle in degrees (ie scale it from 0-360)

3.2 Color Cluster

Let's see the method [5], it could filter error region according to lightness or named intensity, however it can not deal with large area error region, since it only consider the intensity of image while neglect other useful information, such as color attribute. To overcome this difficulty, we improve the method [5] by applying image color cluster in HSL color space in advance to carrying out image segmentation simply, this improvement can increase the validity of detection.

Algorithm 2. Color cluster
We set a threshold T, and first select a pixel as an initial cluster.
Repeat for all image pixels:
1   Compute the color distance between pixel and cluster.
2   If the distance is larger than the threshold, then we create a new cluster. Otherwise we add the pixel to the cluster.
3   When no new pixel exist, the computing procedure is over.

Cluster result depends on color distance measurement. We use Minkowski distance measurement [1] for its better performance.

$$d(i, j) = (|H_i - H_j|^a + |S_i - S_j|^b + |L_i - L_j|^c)^{\frac{1}{d}} \qquad (1)$$

Where a=3, b=2, c=1, d=3/(a+b+c).

In Equation 1, we set the weight of color information H and S large to the one of lightness L due to the importance of color information H and S in cluster procedure.

3.3 Features Analysis

After image cluster above, we shrink the area of location. Then we can perform image features analysis in each region for locating the image errors. We adopt the method [5] to achieve our purpose. The detail algorithms to find the possible minimal region of an error are shown as follow:

Algorithm 3. Lightness of error detecting

Input: image W

Output: error of image intensity R

Maximum length of a continuous curve $k(k \geq 5)$

Threshold of difference of pixel T (initially $=100$)

Amount of pixel N ($N=100$)

1   Convert image W to HSL color space

2   Compute the number of pixels, w.r.t each L variation; let P_i represents the number of pixels in the ith L variation, where $1 \leq i \leq 255$

3   Compute $\Delta P_i = (P_i - P_{i-1})$, if $\Delta P_i < T$, store i in an index list Q

4   Search Q and store the consecutive elements in set S, $S_i = \{R, M_i\} \in S$; where R is the start intensity of consecutive elements, and M_i is the length of the ith consecutive elements

5   Find S_i with the maximal length M_i in the set S, where the consecutive elements have M_i less than or equal to k

6   If no $M_i < k$ then $T = T + N$, goto 3; else return R

Algorithm 4. Adaptive detection filtering

A set of objects O; $O_j = \{A_j, B_j\} \in O$, A_j and B_j are the area size and boundary of object O_j

A percentage threshold of object size $\Omega(50\%)$

A threshold of number of pixels μ (5 or 10)

A decreasing intensity of amount ε (10)

1   Store initial objects obtained from color segmentation in set O

2   Remove small objects form set O if the area of object size $A_j < \mu$

3   Use filter Opening(Closing(C)) to remove isolated objects in O

4   Copy set O to a new set Q; Let n be the number of objects in Q; Let s= δ be an initial intensity value(from the defect intensity detector)

5   Intensity Iteration: Repeat till n has no change
        For each object O_i in Q do

                If A_i decreases $> \Omega$ from last Intensity Iteration and O_i is not split then

                        remove O_i from Q and update n

                Sets = s —ε

6   For each element O_j in set O not removed in Q
        Mark O_j in image C

In the algorithm above, we describe the lightness of error detection which is the preprocessing of our image completion approach. We use the intensity and shape of image errors instead of color attribute since an image usually include much variety of colors and it is difficult to use color contents for our purpose.

4 Experimental Results

Users can apply our method to their own private photos. In our experiments, we have applied this method to the image of Mogao Grottoes of Dunhuang of Chinese culture relic. We set the threshold of object size to 10 pixels. Of course there will be some error region left not detected.

We have been making the digitization of No.158 Mogao Grotto of Dunhuang of China. There are three sculptures in this grotto. The length of the biggest is 15.70 meter, and the other two is about 5 meter. The 3D model of the cave and sculptures were scanned by a 3PrdPTech Deltasphere 3000 laser range scanner. The adopted texture images in the experiment were acquired by a KODAK DCS 660C camera. A 14 mm, a 35 mm and a 60 mm lens had been used.

We show some original acquired images of a painted sculpture's head and the detected results in figure 3. At first we select the face of the sculpture as our test region in order to make our detection more precisely, however we exclude the eyes and the mouth which are detected. The error areas in the face are marked with red color. The upper row presents original texture images, and the lower row presents the detected texture images. We can see our approach is effective from the contrast between both of them. And we also set 5 groups of images with different point of view to be compared for better reference.

The final digitization results of those three sculptures using our detection approach and image inpainting processing are shown in figure 3. The laying sculpture has a gray color appearance, so we render this model with lighter illumination to achieve a

Fig. 2. Results of Error Detection of a Sculpture's Head

Fig. 3. Effect of Three Sculptures

good visual result. We can discover that the faces of the sculptures of Buddha are very clean and there is no error to destroy the whole effects.

Combining our method proposed in this paper with our image completion algorithms, the texture images are inpainted very well, and our work is appreciated by persons who gain strong impressions by the effect of the project. The 3-dimension scene of Mogao Grottoes of Dunhuang containing the three sculptures of Buddha is shown as figure 4:

Fig. 4. Results of Our Project

5 Conclusion

We know there are many nice algorithm of image completion, however, those algorithms need user to select the error region to dispose, which will lead to neglect some small errors. In this paper, we have presented an automatic approach to detect the error area for image completion. However, if the image is more complexity, we can split the photo into multiple portions before the regions containing errors are detected, and then apply our method to each portion individually.

Our algorithm was validated to be practical. With the assistance of this algorithm, we are able to restore many rarity photos of cultural relic, such as the photos of Dunhuang above. As for some very old photos, our algorithm also gives an effective way to solve it.

Acknowledgement

We would like to thank all that offer assistance to us. This research is supported by the National Grand Fundamental Research 973 Program of China (2002CB312106).

References

1. H.Abdi, "[1] ((2007). Distance. In N.J. Salkind (Ed.): Encyclopedia of Measurement and Statistics. Thousand Oaks (CA): Sage.".
2. S. A.BARAB, K.HAY, M. G.BARNETT: Virtual solar system project: Building understanding through model building. In Annual Meeting of the American Educational Research Association (Montreal, Canada,April 1999), AERA. 2, 8
3. Vittoria Bruni and Domenico Vitulano, "A generalized model for scratch detection," IEEE Transactions on Image Processing, 13(1), January 2004, pp. 44-50.
4. C.BUEHLER, M.BOSSE, L.MCMILLAN, S. J.GORTLER, M. F.COHEN: Unstructured Lumigraph Rendering, SIGGRAPH 2001, Computer Graphics Proc.2001, Annual Conference Series, pp. 425–432. 1, 2

5. Rong-Chi Chang, Yun-Long Sie, Su-Mei Chou and Timothy K. Shih, " Photo defect detection for image inpainting," the IEEE International Symposium on Multimedia (ISM '05) , 12-14 Dec. 2005, pp. 403-407.
6. P.DEBEVEC, C.TAYLOR, J.MALIK: Modeling and rendering architecture from photographs: A hybrid geometry- and image-based approach. In Proc.SIGGRAPH 96 (August 1996), pp. 11–20. 1, 2, 3, 4
7. James D. Foley, Andries van Dam, Steven K. Feiner, and John F. Hughes. Fundamentals of interactive computer graphics. Addison-Wesley, 2 edition, 1994.
8. S. J.GORTLER, R.GRZESZCZUK, R.SZELISKI, M. F.COHEN: The lumigraph. In SIGGRAPH 96 Conference Proc. (Aug. 1996), Annual Conference Series, pp. 43–54. 1, 2
9. M.ROUSSOS, A. E.JOHNSON, T. G.MOHER, J.LEIGH, C. A.VASILAKIS, C. R.BARNES: Learning and building together in an immersive virtual world. PRESENCE journal 8, 3 (June 1999), 247–263. 2
10. K. Y. Song, J. Kittler and M. Petrou, "Defect detection in random colour textures," Image and Vision Computing, 14(9), october 1996, pp. 667-683.
11. Swee-Seong Wong and Wee Kheng Leow, "Color segmentation and figure-ground segregation of natural images," in Proceedings on International Conference on Image Processing, ICIP'02, 2002, pp. 120-123.

Emotional Descriptors for Map-Based Access to Music Libraries

Doris Baum and Andreas Rauber

Department of Software Technology and Interactive Systems
Vienna University of Technology
Vienna, Austria
http://www.ifs.tuwien.ac.at/mir

Abstract. Apart from genre- and artist-based organization, emotions are one of the most frequently used characteristics to describe and thus potentially organize music. Emotional descriptors may serve as additional labels to access and interact with music libraries. This paper reports on a user study evaluating a range of emotional descriptors from the PANAS-X schedule for their usefulness to describe pieces of music. It further investigates their potential as labels for SOM-based maps for music collections, analyzing the differences for labels agreed upon by a larger group of people versus strictly personalized labellings of maps due to different interpretations by individual users.

1 Introduction

The most prominent and dominant ways of organizing and describing music collections usually follow genre- or artist-based structures. Yet, music is also commonly described as carrying special emotions, evoking specific feelings. Quite frequently people listen to a wide range of musical styles, picking the specific type of music at a given situation according to their mood. Thus, automatically describing music according to emotional characteristics constitutes an interesting challenge to assist in interfacing with large electronic music repositories in diverse manners.

Yet, emotions are neither easily agreed upon, nor consistently assigned to music by different people. Research in emotions has a long and diverse history, and in spite of considerable efforts, no unanimous set of emotions to describe music has been agreed upon (a situation that emotions share with genres as class labels for music or even text documents). Worse, and again similar to the more conventional genre setting, emotions are not consistently assigned by different people to the same piece of music. Even more strongly than with musical genres, the attribution of certain emotional characteristics to a piece of music depend strongly on personal aspects, preferences, and - quite likely - on the emotional situation when the actual assignment task is being performed.

In spite of this highly volatile characteristic of emotions, they still seem to merit closer inspection to identify, in how far they may be used to support other, more conventional concepts in order to characterize music. We thus report on a user study which addresses three different aspects of emotions for music

S. Sugimoto et al. (Eds.): ICADL 2006, LNCS 4312, pp. 370–379, 2006.

characterization, namely (1) in how far do people agree when assigning emotions to a given set of pieces of music; (2) in how far are the similarities between pieces of music assigned to the same emotional categories reflected in the respective feature representation, i.e. do the features we use to describe music for tasks like genre-based organization also support an emotional organization; and (3) while different people may assign different emotional attributes to a given set of music, may these personal labels still be used to describe an organization of music automatically using these emotional labels. Ten subjects took part in the study, labeling music from the benchmark collection created by George Tzanetakis according to emotions from the PANAS-X schedule [17]. These were then analyzed with respect to inter-indexer consistency, as well as interpreted as labels mapped onto a self-organizing map (SOM) [6] trained on these pieces of music using the SOMeJB music digital library system [10,12,2].

The remainder of this paper is structured as follows. Section 2 describes some related work in the fields of emotion analysis for music, and particularly its use in music information retrieval. The details of the user study performed are outlined in Section 3, followed by an analysis of the results in Section 4. The main results as well as an outlook on ongoing work resulting from this study conclude the paper in Section 5

2   Related Work

Conventionally, music collections are structured according to artist- and genre-style organizations, be it manually assigned such as in most current web shops or on-line portals, or automatically created via classification systems. The latter are mostly oriented towards western-style music, but there is increasing interest in similar organizations specifically targeted to traditional native music styles, such as e.g. for a Korean music digital library [7].

The relation between music and emotions has been addressed psychologically as early as 1936 by Hevner [5], who also created an "adjective circle" with 8 emotion categories. Since then, a lot of studies have been devoted to the emotional aspects of music, a substantial number of them summed up by Gabrielsson and Juslin [4]. However, as Gabrielsson and Juslin conclude, there still is no universally accepted set of adjectives or other characterizations for classifying music according to emotion. Thayer proposed one of the psychological models for emotion: Thayer's Model of Mood [15]. Therein, emotion is not defined as groups of adjectives but rather as a two-dimensional scale of Energy (calm - energetic) and Stress (happy - anxious).

The work of Tellegen, Watson, and Clark [14] led to the development of the PANAS-X schedule [17], which combines a dimensional scale of Positive and Negative Affect with adjective groups for a number of emotions.

Based on the vast pool of studies on emotional aspects of music, numerous groups have turned to different emotional models in the context of automated analysis of music. A set of emotional interpretations of certain parts of the Rhythm Pattern feature set is presented in [9]. The resulting *Weather Charts* were used to describe, i.e. label areas of the Islands of Music maps, clustering pieces of music according to perceived sound similarity. Apart from pure frequency spectra characteristics, such as *low frequencies dominant*, emotional aspects such as *non-aggressiveness*, based on the ratio of low-frequency amplitude modulations in the lower bark bands, were used to characterize certain areas on the map.

Li and Ogihara [8] use thirteen adjective groups – Farnsworth's [3] ten groups, which were in turn derived from Hevner's, plus three their test user created – to classify emotion in music with Support Vector Machines.

Yang and Lee [18] use the Positive and Negative Affect dimensions and the emotion categories of the PANAS-X schedule [17] and the Russel [13] and Tellegen-Watson-Clark [14] models. They extract 12 standard low-level features from the audio sources, generate 12 more features by genetic algorithms, and apply Support Vector Machine regression to them. Also, the lyrics of the songs are taken into account to disambiguate the emotion of the song.

Cunningham, Downie, and Bainbridge in [1] analyze the rather neglected area of dislike, even disgust, for music pieces. From 395 responses to a survey on "the worst song ever", they extracted, with a grounded theory approach, the most commonly named reasons why songs are "bad". Among these are the quality of the lyrics or voice, the "earworm effect", a dislike of the corresponding music video, perceived pretentiousness of the song, over-exposure to the music, and unpleasant personal experience associated with the piece.

3   User Study

3.1   Music Collection

The music used in this study was based on George Tzanetakis' benchmark collection [16]. It consists of mp3s with 30 second extracts of songs from ten different genres: Blues, Classical Music, Country, Disco, Hiphop, Jazz, Metal, Pop, Reggae and Rock. From the full benchmark collection of 1000 songs, 20 from every genre were selected randomly to make up a collection of 200 songs. They were all named uniformly so as to not give any hints concerning the genre. The ordering of the songs was randomized when presenting them to the test subjects during a form-based evaluation session to further prevent any bias.

3.2   Emotions

As previously discussed, there have been a number of studies on music and emotions, but no standard set of emotions seems to have been established. Thus, a set of emotions had to be selected, which should be founded in psychology and would prove useful in the study. The emotional categories were taken from The PANAS-X Manual for the Positive and Negative Affect Schedule - Expanded Form by Clark and Watson [17]. This may later allow us to bring together adjective groups and two-dimensional scales, as a Positive/Negative Affect axis together with an Arousal / Activation level can form a two-dimensional model

Table 1. Adjectives assigned to emotional categories, based on [17]

Category	Adjectives	Category	Adjectives
Fear:	scared / nervous	Attentiveness:	determined / alert
Hostility:	angry / disgusted	Shyness:	timid / shy
Guilt:	guilty / ashamed	Fatigue:	tired / sleepy
Sadness:	sad / lonely	Serenity:	calm / relaxed
Joviality:	happy / cheerful	Surprise:	surprised / astonished
Self-Assurance:	proud / strong	don't know	other /unassignable

similar to Thayer's. The categories in the the PANAS-X Manual are: fear, hostility, guilt, sadness, joviality, self-assurance, attentiveness, shyness, fatigue, serenity and surprise. Each category was represented in the test questionnaires by two adjectives listed in Table 1 which the subjects could associate with the music.

3.3 Study Set-Up

Ten subjects took part in the study, all between 20 and 40 years old, 6 male and 4 female, 9 of them with academic background (university students or graduates). Their musical expertise varies from amateurs to experts with theoretical background knowledge, playing instruments, singing, or even writing their own music. The subjects also showed a rather diverse range of preferred musical styles. Obviously, the small number of participants does not allow a purely quantitative evaluation, but requires a qualitative evaluation.

The study was conducted via a form-based on-line questionnaire. While data collection via the Internet form was basically open to the general public, most participants, and specifically the ones that the results in this paper are based upon, were selected to participate in the study. The home-page contained an explanation of the study for the subjects and provided a possibility to listen interactively to the individual pieces of music while ticking the check-boxes of the appropriate emotional characteristics. PHP scripts were used to automatically generate an individual music rating questionnaire for each test subject. A different randomized ordering of the songs was produced to prevent any potential bias introduced by the sequence of the pieces of music as well as the duration of the evaluation session.

The results of the study were analyzed in several different manners. First of all, the variation of emotions assigned to the various titles was analyzed to obtain a feeling for inter-indexer consistency, i.e. in how far the test subjects agreed with each other when assigning emotions to music.

Secondly, the pieces of music were clustered on a self-organizing map (SOM) [6] using Rhythm Pattern features [11]. It groups the music according to sound similarity as expressed by the feature space on a two-dimensional map display in such a way that similar pieces of music are located next to each other. The resulting map was then labeled both with the respective genre labels as well as the emotional labels in order to see in how far consistent regions could be identified in both visualizations, which do not necessarily have to coincide. The PlaySOM software [2] was used for the subsequent evaluations and visualizations.

Table 2. Number of songs in the emotion categories, regarding all users, with 50% and 70% agreement required

EMOTION	50%	70%
fear	4	0
hostility	22	7
guilt	0	0
sadness	25	3
joviality	41	18
self-assurance	36	19
attentiveness	9	3
shyness	2	0
fatigue	9	3
serenity	45	19
surprise	0	0

4   Results

4.1   Variations in Emotional Labeling

Overall, users were surprisingly consistent in assigning emotional labels to pieces of music, with half of the users agreeing on at least one emotional category in 76% of the rated songs. A list of how many songs were placed in each category is presented in Table 2. The first column lists the number of songs assigned to each emotional category, where at least 50% of the study participants agreed on it as its most dominant emotional category. If one requires that at least 70% of the test users agree on an emotion, 35% (70) of the songs can be labeled, as listed in column 2. It seems that in such a (relatively small) group, there always will be some disagreement on the emotions connected with a song but that the majority of users can agree on at least one emotion for a high number of songs.

If one were to look at the emotion categories that received more than 50% of the votes (but did not require the emotion to be the highest rated of all emotions), 153 songs would be labeled, 63% (97 songs) of which in one category, 33% (50 songs) in two categories and 4% (6 songs) in three categories.

In this case, the most highly correlated classes are: sadness/serenity, which appear in 29% (16 times); hostility/self-assurance, which appear in 23% (13 times); and joviality/self-assurance, which appear in 16% (9 times) of 56 songs in two or more classes together.

4.2   SOM for All Users

To visualize the results of the study, a SOM [6] was trained on the Rhythm Pattern features [11] of the whole music collection (1000 songs). As only 200 of the songs were rated in this study, the rest were tagged as "unknown". For the "All Users" evaluation, the music pieces were put into one or more of the emotion categories: A song was assigned the emotions most voted for if the emotions had at least 50% of the votes (that is 5 or more users agreed on the respective emotion). That is, if Song X was rated as "sad / lonely" by 5 users, as "scared / nervous" by 7 users, and as "timid / shy" by 7 users, it was assigned

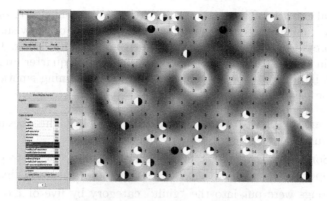

Fig. 1. Screen-shot of the SOM Viewer Software displaying serenity for all users

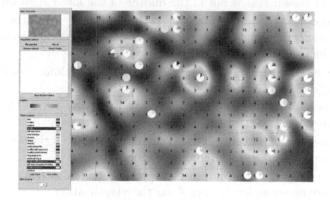

Fig. 2. Screen-shot of the SOM Viewer Software displaying joviality for all users

the categories "fear" and "shyness". Of the labeled songs, 92% (140 songs) were assigned one category, and 8% (12 songs) were assigned two categories.

Of the 200 rated songs, those that were not put into at least one and at most two classes were also tagged as "unknown" to keep the visualizations concise and readable. In total, 152 songs were labeled with one or two emotions and 848 as "unknown". This shows that at least 50% of the users agreed on at least one emotion category for more than 76% of the rated songs.

The SOM was then visualized with the SOMLib Viewer software, displaying for each emotion class which SOM units had a song of that class mapped onto it. Figure 1 provides an example visualization for the emotion class "serenity" for all users. It displays the SDH Visualization [9], revealing the sound similarity cluster structure as Islands of Music. On top of these the black pie charts show the fraction of songs on the respective unit with the class label serenity, plus, obviously, the fraction of remaining unlabeled songs in the complete data collection on those units. Quite a large number of songs (45) were assigned to this emotional category. They end up sub-divided into a big cluster on the lower border and a smaller cluster on the upper central border of the visualization.

Figure 2 provides the same visualization for the "joviality" class. These songs concentrate in two distinct areas, namely the upper left quarter and the right-hand border, indicating two loose clusters. For the remaining emotions, the locations can be briefly summarized as follows:

Fear: There are very few (4) songs marked with this label. This does not warrant any conclusion on the distribution of "fear".

Hostility: Songs that are put in the category "hostility" seem to concentrate in the upper right region of the visualization and form small clusters.

Guilt: No songs were put into the "guilt" category by five or more users, so there are no songs for "guilt" on the visualization.

Sadness: Songs in this category seem to concentrate in the lower right area, and a tight cluster stands out in the middle of the lower right quarter.

Self-Assurance: Songs in the category "self-assurance" are rather scattered, but their concentration is much higher in the upper half of the visualization. One can imagine loose clusters there.

Attentiveness: Songs in the category "attentiveness" almost exclusively appear on the right-hand border.

Shyness: There were only two songs marked with this label. This does not warrant any conclusion on the distribution of "shyness".

Fatigue: Songs in this category are few, there seems to be a cluster in the lower left quarter and a few scattered ones in the right half.

Surprise: No songs were put into the "surprise" category by five or more users, so there are no songs for "surprise" on the visualization.

Figure 3 contains a (manually produced) overview on where one can detect clusters of emotions. It is just a rough sketch, rather than a density estimation, but it nonetheless permits some conclusions: The emotions cannot be separated completely, but they overlap – as is to be expected if one takes into account that feelings mix and music carries a lot of emotional information. However, it seems that the calmer and quieter emotions come to lie in the lower half of the visualization and the more aroused feelings can be found in the upper half – with the exception of the "serenity" cluster in the upper half. On the right-hand edge there seems to be an area of strong and cheerful music – the overlapping clusters of the right "joviality" cluster and the attentiveness area. The lower "serenity" cluster encompasses "fatigue" and "sadness", and "self-assurance" overlaps with or encloses "joviality", "serenity", "hostility", and "attentiveness".

Thus it may indeed be possible to generally derive the emotion connoted with a piece of music, though the classes, the classification procedure, and the data collection probably could be improved.

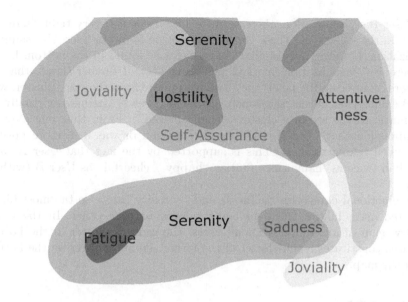

Fig. 3. Rough map of the distribution of the emotions on the SOM SDH visualization

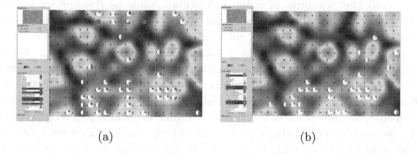

      (a)   (b)

Fig. 4. Screen-shot of the SOM Viewer Software displaying serenity for (a) User A and (b) User B

4.3 SOM for Individual Users

This section describes an interesting point found by comparing visualizations of individual user ratings. It shows how much the appraisal of music can differ between different people. Again, only songs in one or two emotion categories were used, thus, for the ten user results, between 195 and 78 songs have been assigned an emotion class in the visualizations.

Emotional appraisal can differ through individual mood or character. Comparing two users, called "User A" and "User B" here, User B has classified a lot more songs as "sad / lonely" than User A: See Figure 4(b) for User B's distribution of 36 sad songs. User A on the other hand has only rated 3 songs as "sad / lonely", which come to lie on the bottom border of the respective visualization.

In User B's visualization, there seem to be one or two very tight "sadness" clusters in the lower half. These clusters cannot be found in User A's "sadness" visualization, however, very similar clusters can be found in the bottom half of the "serenity" visualization, marked on Figure 4(a). It further shows, that the two users disagree on the labels they assign to music from the same cluster, with User B calling that music "sad/lonely", whereas User A attributes virtually the same music to the serenity cluster ("calm/relaxed"). From this, one may get the impression that User A is a "happier" person or was in a more positive mood when taking the test. This is supported by the fact that User A rated more than twice as many songs (86) as "happy / cheerful" as User B (with 33 songs).

The emotional categories "sadness" and "serenity" are also the most highly correlated ones, hinting at them being related to each other. In the global overview map of all emotions for all users, the sadness cluster in the bottom right area constitutes a sub-cluster of the larger serenity cluster on the bottom half of the map.

5   Conclusions

We analyzed the potential of using emotional labels as descriptors for map-based access to music libraries. Emotional categories from the PANAS-X Manual were used to label pieces of music, yielding a high consistency in labels assigned by different users. Furthermore, in a parallel process, the music was clustered according to psycho-acoustic features extracted from the audio files using a SOM. It showed a high consistency with respect to the labels assigned, i.e. clusters of different emotions appear on the SOM visualization, showing sensible correlation between emotions for music in the various regions. Emotions perceived as related are also located in neighboring map regions. Thus, emotions may be derivable in an automatic way by training classifiers. We are currently investigating in how far this automatic classification can achieve acceptable performance using a set of state of the art machine learning algorithms.

Still, the emotion categories from the PANAS-X Manual need to be re-thought and adapted according to the needs of the music listeners. For example, it might not be necessary to include categories such as "guilt" or "surprise" if the listeners do not use them or if different users do not agree on what is to be placed in those classes.

Different users associate different feelings with a given piece of music, but for quite a lot of songs the majority of users agree on the connoted emotions. Also, not all emotions can automatically and reliably be derived from the features used, but for some emotions the features give a good idea of which emotional categories the song could be placed in.

Finally, with something so subjective as emotion, it might be more promising to build individual emotion classifiers for each listener than to try and derive a general notion of what song belongs to which emotional class.

References

1. Sally Jo Cunningham, J. Stephen Downie, and David Bainbridge. "the pain, the pain": Modelling music information behavior and the songs we hate. In *Proc. 6th Intl. Conf. on Music Information Retrieval (ISMIR 2005)*, pages 474–477, London, UK, September 11-15 2005.
2. M. Dittenbach, R. Neumayer, and A. Rauber. Playsom: An alternative approach to track selection and playlist generation in large music collections. In *Proc. 1st Intl. Workshop on Audio-Visual Content and Information Visualization in Digital Libraries (AVIVDiLib 2005)*, pages 226–235, Cortona, Italy, May 4-6 2005.
3. Paul R. Farnsworth. *The social psychology of music.* Dryden Press, 1958.
4. Alf Gabrielsson and Patrik N. Juslin. Emotional expression in music. In Richard J. Davidson, Klaus R. Scherer, and H. Hill Goldsmith, editors, *Handbook of Affective Sciences*, pages 503–534. Oxford University Press, 2002.
5. Kate Hevner. Experimental studies of the elements of expression in music. In *American Journal of Psychology*, volume 48, pages 246–268, 1936.
6. T. Kohonen. *Self-Organizing Maps*, volume 30 of *Springer Series in Information Sciences*. Springer, Berlin, 3rd edition, 2001.
7. Kang-Kue Lee and Kyu-Sik Park. Robust feature extraction for automatic classification of Korean traditional music in digital library. In *Proc. 8th Intl Conf. on Asian Digital Libraries (ICADL 2005)*, pages 167 – 170, Bangkok, Thailand, December 12-15 2005. Springer.
8. Tao Li and Mitsunori Ogihara. Detecting emotion in music. In *Proceedings of the 4th Intl. Conf. on Music Information Retrieval (ISMIR 2003)*, Baltimore, Maryland (USA), October 26-30 2003.
9. E. Pampalk, A. Rauber, and D. Merkl. Content-based organization and visualization of music archives. In *Proc. of ACM Multimedia 2002*, pages 570–579, Juan-les-Pins, France, December 1-6 2002. ACM.
10. A. Rauber and M. Frühwirth. Automatically analyzing and organizing music archives. In *Proc. 5th Europ. Conf. on Research and Advanced Technology for Digital Libraries (ECDL 2001)*, Darmstadt, Germany, Sept. 4-8 2001. Springer.
11. A. Rauber, E. Pampalk, and D. Merkl. The SOM-enhanced JukeBox: Organization and visualization of music collections based on perceptual models. *Journal of New Music Research*, 32(2):193–210, June 2003.
12. Andreas Rauber. Creation and exploration of musical information spaces. In *Proc. Intl Conf on Digital Libraries (ICDL2004)*, pages 741–748. TERI, 2004.
13. James A. Russell. Core affect and the psychological construction of emotion. *Psychological Review*, 110(1):145–172, January 2003.
14. Auke Tellegen, David Watson, and Lee Anna Clark. On the dimensional and hierarchical structure of affect. *Psychological Science*, 10(4):297–303, July 1999.
15. Robert E. Thayer. *The Biopsychology of Mood and Arousal.* Oxford University Press, 1989.
16. G. Tzanetakis, G. Essl, and P.R. Cook. Automatic musical genre classification of audio signals. In *Proc. Intl Symp. on Music Information Retrieval (ISMIR)*, pages 205–210, Bloomington, Indiana, October 15-17 2001.
17. David Watson and Lee Anna Clark. *The PANAS-X Manual for the Positive and Negative Affect Schedule - Expanded Form.* The University of Iowa, 1994. http://www.psychology.uiowa.edu/faculty/Clark/PANAS-X.pdf
18. Dan Yang and WonSook Lee. Disambiguating music emotion using software agents. In *Proc. 5th Intl Conf. on Music Information Retrieval (ISMIR 2004)*, Barcelona, Spain, October 10-14 2004.

Role of Naive Ontology in Search and Learn Processes for Domain Novices

Makiko Miwa[1] and Noriko Kando[2]

[1] National Institute of Multiomedia Education, 2-12 Wakaba, Mihama-ku, Chiba, Japan
[2] National Institute of Informatics, 2-1-2 Hitotsubashi, Chiyoda-ku, Tokyo, Japan

Abstract. In this paper we propose to see the information seeking behaviour of domain novices as search and learn processes. We explore the concept of naïve ontology as the bases for designing browsing/navigation interface of search and learn for domain novices of digital libraries. Naïve ontology is a type of information access interface which allows domain novices to refine their knowledge interactively by acquiring information chunk-by-chunk as they encounter it in digital libraries. Through elicitation and analysis of search and learn processes of domain novices in history and geography, we identified several implications for designing naïve ontology.

Keywords: knowledge acquisition, search and learn, naïve ontology, information access interface, browsing.

1 Introduction

Literature in information seeking behaviour (ISB) informs that searchers are learning while they are looking for information bit by bit as they encounter during their search processes. Literature in education posits such type of learning within the framework of self-regulated learning (SRL) or problem-based learning.

Ever flourishing digital libraries (DLs) seem to have left some groups of people from ready access to networked digital resources. The phenomenon of digital divide has been claimed as the major cause of such a disadvantage. In addition, the level of domain knowledge held by users might be another source of handicapped access to rich resources held by DLs. This is because a general understanding of the conceptual structure of the domain is considered as indispensable in generating an adequate search strategies with acceptable terminology, as well as in comprehending and making sense out of search results. Hence people cannot function at all in physical and cognitive world without the ability to categorize [1].

We use the concept of "naïve ontology" in order to identify and establish a conceptual framework of information access interface which facilitates search and learn processes of domain novices. The naïve ontology we propose is a type of information access interface which allow domain novices to refine their knowledge interactively by acquiring information chunk-by-chunk as they encounter it in DLs [2].

S. Sugimoto et al. (Eds.): ICADL 2006, LNCS 4312, pp. 380–389, 2006.

We conducted a series of small-case studies involving seven college students as participants to identify their knowledge building processes while searching on the Web on topics related to history and geography. We interviewed them while showing the recorded search process with eye-movements, and elicited their thoughts, feelings, and reasoning of each "view". Data analysis lead us to develop a taxonomy of knowledge modification which identified that searchers are structuring their knowledge interactively through their search and learn processes. Participants' impressions of sites, reflections of their search processes, as well as the taxonomy provided some practical implications of the design of naïve ontology, as well as theoretical and methodological implications for research in search and learn. Based on these findings, we propose a new framework of "naïve ontology" which allows reconstruction of knowledge through interaction.

2 Conceptual Framework

Human information seeking behaviour is currently the focus of research in various fields, which lead to serious terminological confusion. To avoid such confusion, we will define three key terms below to introduce the conceptual framework of this research.

2.1 Search and Learn

The concept of search and learn has been built upon two research traditions of information seeking behaviour (ISB) and self-regulated learning (SRL). The former demonstrates how people's information needs is evolved through interaction with a variety of information sources. The latter informs how active and self-motivated learners cognitively engage in learning tasks.

Bates [3] described the evolving nature of information seeking processes in her berrypicking model, using the analogy with picking hackberries in the forest: The model suggests that searchers initiate their information seeking with one aspect of a broader question, and each new piece of information they encounter gives them new ideas and directions to further the process. This model suggests that searchers may identify useful information bit by bit at each stage of the processes, rather than obtaining all the necessary information at the one stage from a single information source. Based on the berrypicking model, Bates suggested a variety of design features for information retrieval systems.

Through a study of information seeking processes of secondary school students who were writing papers for class assignment, Kuhlthau [4] developed a model of the Information Search Process (ISP). Built upon the Kelly's [5] personal construct theory, the ISP model depicts the constructive nature of students' information seeking processes.

These two models of ISB not only describe the evolving nature of information seeking behaviour, but also suggest that people are learning bit by bit while looking for information from a variety of sources.

Self-regulated learning (SRL) refers to the type of learning that occurs largely from the influence of learners' self-generated thoughts, feelings, strategies, and behaviors, which are oriented toward the attainment of goals (Zimmerman, 1998). Corno and Mandinach [6] posited SRL as an effort to deepen and manipulate the associative network in a particular area in order to monitor and improve the deepening process. Rogers and Swan [7] explored the applicability of Corno and Mandinach's SRL model to Internet searching and found that the components of the model describe and predict the behaviors of searchers being engaged in learning from resources on the Internet. Thus, the framework of SRL seems to be adequate in describing how people learn while searching information on the Internet.

Both ISB and SRL seem to be useful in describing search and learn behaviour of domain novices. They are also useful in positing learners' self-generated information seeking on the Web as a type of e-learning activity.

2.2 Information Access Interface

The term "information access interface" describes the interface that mediates between information resources and users. It provides aids for users in accessing or using information resources stored on electronic media. The information interface may include metadata, question answering systems, navigation systems, and virtual agents that intend to support optimal interaction between searchers and information objects.

2.3 Naïve Ontology

The increasing availability and accessibility of Internet resources to the general public allow the domain novices to interact with unfamiliar document collections. In response to such trends, the main role of ontology seems to be shifting from a search aid to a navigation tool. "Naïve ontology" is a type of information access interface that allows domain novices to refine their knowledge interactively by acquiring information chunk-by-chunk as they encounter in digital environments. Specifically, this is a kind of navigation tool that supports browsing and searching by domain novices throughout their information seeking processes. We propose to use the term "naïve ontology" to advocate the needs for domain specific DLs to offer such navigation tools to help them build their basic knowledge of the domain.

3 Case Study

We designed and conducted a series of experiment in a case study to identify characteristics of search and learn processes as well as taxonomy of knowledge modification during the processes in order to develop a conceptual framework of naïve ontology. We chose the concept of "time and space" and posit the domain of history and geography as an instantiation to explore the domain novice's search and learn processes. So far, we invited a total of seven participants in a series of two studies.

3.1 Method

We followed the procedure as described in Figure 1. We used slightly different methods in data collection in each of these two studies.

Questionnaire: Participants were requested to complete a short questionnaire that asked them the frequency of their Internet usage, favorite browsers and search engines, topics chosen at the college entrance examination, whether they were planning to get a teacher's certificate, and topics of interest in history and geography.

Search Stimulation: Two studies differed in the stimulus given at the initiation of search and learn processes. For the first study, each participant was invited to the lab individually and given two vignette scenarios prepared by the researcher. The first scenario asked the participant to conduct a web search to prepare for teaching a middle school history class on a particular topic. The second scenario asked the participant to conduct a web search to prepare for visiting a world heritage site. For the second study, we invited a pair of participants together and asked them to discuss their topic of interest in history and geography in order to let them choose two topics for web search, one for each participant, a history and geography topic. The modification in the procedure was introduced because each of three participants in the first study was tense and nervous since they had to wear unfamiliar devices (eye-tracker) and sit alone in the lab environments while being observed by two researchers and a research assistant. This was also because one participant was unable to make progress in her search and learn because of the confusion caused by encountering incomprehensible information.

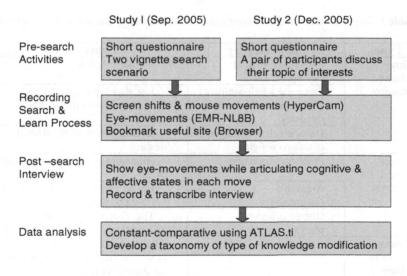

Fig. 1. Procedure

Recording of Search and learn Processes: During the search and learn processes, screen shifts, mouse movements and participants' eye movements were captured using an eye tracker (EMR-NL8B). Each session took about 15-20 minutes.

Post-Search Interview: After each search and learn processes, an interview was conducted where the recorded search process was displayed, and the participant reported why she made a particular move (e.g., typing, mouse click, browsing) and what she thought, felt, and expected at each moment throughout the process. The interview was recorded and transcribed in detail. The transcribed data were analyzed using ATLAS.ti following a bottom-up strategy with the constant comparative technique. The unit of analysis is "a view" which represents a span of attention of a participant at each move, or what a participant articulate as seeing at each move in visual perception as well as in her cognitive world [10].

3.2 Results

In the post-search interview, participants articulated what they thought, felt, expected, and intended to do at each point of movement, either voluntarily or in response to the interviewer's inquiries. From their communication, we identified several characteristics of knowledge acquisition in search and learn processes.

Representation and Modification of Knowledge
Participants' expressions of the concepts of time and space, as embedded in their communication, were categorized into three types: time-related concepts; space-related concepts; and concepts embracing time and space, as presented in Table 1.

Table 1. Representation of the Concepts of Time and Space. (*translated from Japanese)

Type	Sub-Category	Expressions*
Time-related concepts	Solely time-related concepts	13th Century; 1600s
	Temporal relationships with some well-known incidents	...just after Japan opened trade He came to Japan during the seclusion.
	Dates in relation to ages of a famous figure	...an anniversary of Beethoven's death
Space-related concepts	Place/country names	Alhambra is located in Granada, Spain
	Areas of a place/country	Basho travelled around the north-eastern region in Japan.
	Distances between places	The distance between the north and south ends of Israel is 500 km.
Concepts embracin g time and space		Alhambra was first built in the *post-Umayyad* era and expanded in the *Nasrid dynasty*.

Participants' knowledge has been modified during their search and learn process. A taxonomy of modification of knowledge with six types are developed as described in Table 2 with some examples.

Table 2. Types of Knowledge Modification in Search Processes (*translated from Japanese)

Type	Definition	Example of Expressions*
Adding	Acquire novel information to increase knowledge	Alhambra is located in Spain. I found a picture of Qumran in which the Dead Sea Scrolls were hidden. I was surprised how they could hide it in a place like this.
Correcting	Clear up a misunderstanding	The area he travelled was not all over Japan, but in the north-eastern region.
Limiting	Narrow down the scope of the concept	The site deals with present leisure in Israel, which is not what I'm looking for.
Relating	A concept is related with another concept.	The Taj Mahal was influenced by Humayun's tomb, which is some distance from Taj Mahal in terms of time and space.
Specifying	A concept is narrowed by increasing specificity.	Alhambra is located in Spain =>Granada, Spain.
Transformi ng	A concept is expressed in a different framework.	He lived in *Genroku* or *Kasai* (Japanese era). => He lived in the 1600s.

Characteristics of Search and learn Processes

Participants' general searching behaviour tended to begin with typing one or two known keywords representing relatively broad concepts. They then browse the search results by checking links to the sites from the top of the list. If the contents of the first few sites were relevant to the topic of the search, they scanned the contents of each site one by one, quickly looking at basic information such as description, chronology, and glossary to acquire general framework of the topic of the search.

When participants encountered sites highly relevant to their topic of the search, they read texts in detail and looked at visual information such as pictures of interest and graphics representing correlation among relevant people, places and incidents. When they encountered sites of interests, such as free wallpapers, historical quizzes, and advertisements for TV programs with popular actors, they interacted with these sites intensively even though these sites are not fully relevant to the topic of the search. When they encountered unexpected information, they articulated their surprise and tried to obtain further information for comprehension.

Participants acquired or used the following knowledge on the functions of the information access interface during the search processes.

- One participant indicated that the first three items in Yahoo search results are advertisements for businesses. She sometimes avoided clicking on these items because of that knowledge.
- One participant changed the color of texts when she had difficulty reading because of a high density of text.

- One participant found a button to enlarge the size of pictures displayed on the screen when she was browsing a site with high-quality pictures.
- One participant learned of the availability of a free online translation service from her partner when she encountered a site written in German, a foreign language to her, and used that service to obtain information she was looking for.

These behaviour indicates that searchers modify not only domain knowledge but also knowledge on a variety of functions embedded in the information access interface during their search and learn processes.

Reflections on Search Processes
At the end of the post-search interview, the interviewer asked each participant to comment on her own search process. All the participants said that the eye movements shown on the screen pointed to the actual place of the screen they were looking at, and some of them said that watching their own eye movements helped them recall their search and learn process including their thoughts and feelings. It should be noted that watching their own eye movements helped participants recall their search and learn processes. If so, the reliability of data elicited, and eventually the reliability of the study, should have been increased. Thus, the method of using the eye tracker in capturing search and learn processes and showing the eye movement during the post-search interview may be recommended in collecting reliable data for search and learn processes on the Web. In addition, the notion of "view" as expanded to the cognitive world and chosen as the unit of analysis for this study was found to be adequate for analyzing search and learn processes on the Internet; searchers' visual perception tended to be focused on a part of the screen or a "view".

3.3 Implications

The case study provided us with useful information for designing naïve ontology, while offered some theoretical implications to increase our understanding on the search and learn processes. The study also provided us with some methodological implications for capturing search and learn processes.

Implications for the Information Access Interface
Results of elicitation and analysis of novice searchers' search processes lead us to suggestions for the naïve ontology as reported in the previous chapter and synthesized in Table 3. These implications are expected to be expanded and elaborated through progress of the research project.

Some of the functionalities proposed in the Table 3 have been reflected in recently proposed navigation tools that combine browsing and searching functions in a seamless manner. The Flamenco system allows searchers to browse a large collection of architectural images using hierarchically faceted metadata. Searchers of the system can navigate without disturbance of their thought processes [8]. The JuNii+, an information access interface for the shared portal of the Japanese academic community, incorporates ontology-based and content-based retrieval for ranking web documents. The system intends to provide a seamless switching between searching and browsing [9]. As demonstrated in these examples, information access interface is expected to be naturalistic for searchers so that they can follow their own "view" of the world during search processes without being disturbed by the mandatory use of unfamiliar ontology intended for domain experts.

Table 3. Implications for Naïve Ontology

Aspect	Implications
Browsing	browse time and space simultaneously or interchangeably
	browse time and space from broad to specific
	trace and overview historical transitions among cultures, people, and religions of each geographic area or country
	choose pictures from among thumbnails to see high-quality pictures
Contents	provide high-quality pictures and visual images
	provide information on the genre of contents
	represent correlations between people and incidents using graphics
	provide a glossary of technical terms
	provide a dictionary of historical figures and events
	use colour to categorize texts
	present the content in a simple manner
Navigation	allow switching between different calendar systems
	provide links to contemporaneous figures and incidents
	provide historical and geographic frameworks for figures and incidents
	provide links to free online translation services

Theoretical Implications for Knowledge Building in Search and Learn Processes
Domain novices acquire general knowledge of the topic of the search bit by bit as they encounter through search processes. Participants used basic knowledge obtained from previous browsing to generate keywords or query and progress their search and learn using their own judgments. This finding verifies the berry-picking model [3] and may lead to the improvement of search results using interim search results.

Searchers learn the functions of the information access interface through search and learn processes. Participants' articulations indicated that they learn not only domain knowledge but also functions embedded in the interface. Thus, search and learn processes of novice searchers modify not only their domain knowledge but also knowledge and skills for using various functions available on the Web.

Methodological Implications for Capturing the Search and Learn Processes
Use of eye tracker in data collection and use of "view" as the unit of data analysis is recommended. First of all, we were convinced that the use of "view" as the unit of analysis captured the dynamically changing knowledge structure of searchers during their search and learn processes. In the post-search interviews, participants reported what they thought, felt and had done in relation to what they saw on the screen with their eye movements. They said the eye movements shown on the screen pointed to

the exact places that they were looking at and that watching their own eye movements helped them recall their search and learn processes. Thus, the method of using eye trackers in data collection of Web search processes and showing the recorded eye movements during the post-search interviews is recommended for future studies, not only to identify what searchers are looking at rather than what data are shown on the screen, but also to increase the reliability of data elicitation from searchers, which eventually increases the reliability of research findings.

In a series of two studies, we used a slightly different data collection procedure. In the first study, we invited three participants individually and asked each of them to conduct two Web searches following different vignette scenarios prepared by the researcher. During the post-search interviews, participants articulated reasoning of their behaviour, but seemed to hesitate to articulate their thought and feelings. In the second study, we invited four participants in two pairs. They discussed their interests with the researcher and picked up topics of interests to conduct Web search. Each participant chose one topic either on history or geography. During the search process, one participant conduct the search and the other gave suggestions. At the post search interview, the participant who conducted the search articulated what she did, thought, and felt, while the other participant of the pair shared her own perspectives. We found that the procedure used for the second study helped participants articulate their thought and feeling more freely and provided more detailed data on their search processes compared to the first study. This was probably because conversations between two participants lead to more naturalistic articulation than one to one interviewing between the researcher and a participant.

We identified that the use of vignette scenarios may introduce the processes unnatural behaviour stimulated by artificial goals, while allowing participants to choose topics lead them to more naturalistic searching behaviour. Some participants of former design also suffered from incomprehensible information resulting from completely unknown search topics. Participants of the latter design may stray from the initial search and learn goals set by themselves due to the much greater freedom that they have, but have some advantages to use the initial knowledge on the topic of the search. The latter design seems to be more advantageous in obtaining deeper understanding on search and learn processes by collecting more naturalistic data.

4   Conclusion

A case study of a series of Web searching was conducted by inviting volunteer college students. Through this study, we explored naïve ontology that allow domain novices to refine their knowledge interactively by acquiring information chunk-by-chunk as they encounter. We proposed to capture the evolving nature of information seeking behaviour of domain novices using the concept of search and learn, built upon the two research traditions of information seeking behaviour (ISB) and self-regulated learning (SRL).

We obtained useful implications for naïve ontology in the aspects of browsing, contents, and navigation, as shown in Table 3. The study provided us with some methodological suggestions for capturing search and learn processes: the use of eye-tracker in capturing the processes and showing eye movements to the participants in the post-search interviews helped them recall the physical and cognitive processes, which improve reliability; the paring of participants help them freely articulate their thought and feelings that helps to elicit rich and thick description of the processes.

What we have described above are results of two small studies conducted at the initial stage of the research project. Up to the present, we discovered that users are interactively structuring their domain knowledge, and identified taxonomy of knowledge modification. Based on these findings, we propose a new framework of "naïve ontology" which allows re-construction of knowledge through interaction. We will continue the study by recruiting additional participants in order to expand and elaborate the taxonomy. We hope to attain the goal of this research by designing an information access interface for novice users of DLs in the near future.

Acknowledgement

This research was funded by the National Institute of Informatics joint research grant. We wish to thank Dr. Barbara Kwasnik at Syracuse University for her helpful suggestions and the notion of "view" she proposed as the unit of analysis for browsing.

References

1. Lakoff, G..: Women, fire and dangerous things: what categories reveal about the mind. Chicago: University of Chicago Press (1987)
2. Miwa, M., Kando, N.: Naïve ontology for concepts of time and space for searching and learning. To be presented at the Information Seeking in Context 2006, Sydney, July 19-21
3. Bates, M.J.: The design of browsing and berrypicking techniques for the online search interface. Online Review, 13 (5), 407-424 (1989)
4. Kuhlthau, C.: Seeking meaning: A process approach to library and information sciences (2nd edition). Westport, CT: Libraries Unlimited (2004)
5. Kelly, D., Teevan, J.: Implicit feedback for inferring user preference: a bibliography. *SIGIR Forum*, *37*, 18–28 (2003)
6. Corno, K., Mandinach, E.: The role of cognitive engagement in classroom learning and motivation. Educational Psychologist, 18(2), 88-108 (1983)
7. Rogers D., Swan, K. Self-regulated learning and Internet searching. Teacher College Record, 106(9), 1804-1824 (2004)
8. Hearst, M., English, J., Shinha, R., Swearingen, K., Yee, P.: Finding the flow in web site search. *Communications of the ACM*, *45*, 42–49 (2002).
9. Kando, N., Kanazawa, T., Miyazawa, A.: Retrieval of web resources using a fusion of ontology-based and content-based retrieval with the RS vector space model on a portal for Japanese universities and academic institutes. *Proceedings of the 39th Hawaii International Conference on System Science*, Kauai, HI (2006) [CD-ROM]
10. Kwasnik, B.: A descriptive study of the functional components of browsing. In J. Learson & C. Unger (Eds.), *Engineering for Human–Computer Interaction, Proceedings of 5th IFIP Working Conference on User Interfaces*. Ellivouri, Finland, Aug. 10–14 (1992)

Kikori-KS: An Effective and Efficient Keyword Search System for Digital Libraries in XML

Toshiyuki Shimizu[1], Norimasa Terada[2], and Masatoshi Yoshikawa[1]

[1] Graduate School of Informatics, Kyoto University
shimizu@soc.i.kyoto-u.ac.jp, yoshikawa@i.kyoto-u.ac.jp
[2] Graduate School of Information Science, Nagoya University
terada@dl.itc.nagoya-u.ac.jp

Abstract. Identifying meaningful document fragments is a major advantage achieved by encoding documents in XML. In scholarly articles, such document fragments include sections, subsections and paragraphs. XML information retrieval systems need to search document fragments relevant to queries from a set of XML documents in a digital library. We present Kikori-KS, an effective and efficient XML information retrieval system for scholartic articles. Kikori-KS accepts a set of keywords as a query. This form of query is simple yet useful because users are not required to understand XML query languages or XML schema. To meet practical demands for searching relevant fragments in scholartic articles, we have developed a user-friendly interface for displaying search results. Kikori-KS was implemented on top of a relational XML database system developed by our group. By carefully designing the database schema, Kikori-KS handles a huge number of document fragments efficiently. Our experiments using INEX test collection show that Kikori-KS achieved an acceptable search time and with relatively high precision.

1 Introduction

Large number of documents in digital libraries are now structured in XML. An XML document is a text marked up by using tags. Document fragments in an XML document are identified by using tags and may have nested document fragments. Identifying meaningful document fragments is a major advantage achieved by encoding documents in XML. In scholarly articles, such document fragments include sections, subsections, and paragraphs.

XML information retrieval (XML-IR) systems need to search document fragments relevant to queries from a collection of XML documents in a digital library. As the number of scholarly articles are increasing sharply, effective search systems are required. XML-IR systems can meet the growing demand for browsing only document fragments, such as sections or paragraphs, relevant to a certain topic.

There are several forms of queries for XML-IR systems. "XQuery 1.0 and XPath 2.0 Full-Text"[1], being developed by W3C, is an XML query language with full-text search capabilities. This form of query assumes users know XML

S. Sugimoto et al. (Eds.): ICADL 2006, LNCS 4312, pp. 390–399, 2006.
© Springer-Verlag Berlin Heidelberg 2006

specific query languages, such as XPath [2] or XQuery [3], and the XML schema of documents. Although such an assumption is valid for a limited number of advanced users, we should consider many other end-users of XML-IR systems unfamiliar with XML query languages or XML schemas. As demonstrated by Web search engines, a set of keywords is a simple, intuitively understandable, yet useful form of queries, especially for unskilled end-users. Queries represented by a set of keywords are also versatile in that they can be issued against XML documents with heterogeneous schemas or without schema. In this paper, we present Kikori-KS, an XML-IR system for scholarly articles. Kikori-KS accepts a set of keywords as a query and returns document fragments in relevance order.

Developing an XML-IR system is a challenging task in many ways. Unlike conventional IR systems, XML document fragments, which are the search results of queries, can be nested each other. This feature raises an issue in the design of the user interface. We have developed a new user-friendly interface for Kikori-KS called the *FetchHighlight retrieval interface*. Because scholarly articles are an important granule, the FetchHighlight retrieval interface displays articles in relevance order, then for each article it shows document fragments in document order. The underlying database schema was designed to meet the requirements of the new user interface.

Furthermore, there are usually more document fragments than there are documents. For example, there are 16,080,830 document fragments against 16,819 documents in the XML collection used in our experiments. XML-IR systems need to process queries efficiently against a huge number of document fragments. Kikori-KS was implemented on top of a relational XML database system developed by our group [4]. In addition to tables as an XML database system, the database schema includes information on term weight. The system automatically translates sets of query keywords into SQL queries. We have designed a database schema specially tuned for fast query processing. Experiments show Kikori-KS returns query results, on average, 7.2 times faster than our previous method [5].

The rest of the paper is organized as follows. Section 2 explains the user interfaces we developed. Section 3 describes a conceptual database schema used in Kikori-KS, and we discuss how the database schema was refined and queries were processed to meet the requirements of the user interface. Section 4 presents the retrieval model used in Kikori-KS. Section 5 contains experimental results on retrieval precision and query processing time. Finally, Section 6 concludes the paper and presents future works.

2   User Interfaces

The granule of search targets for an XML-IR system are document fragments, which may be nested each other. This feature raises an important new issue when designing a user interface to browse search results. By considering users' needs for the output of a search, the INEX 2005 project [6] defined the following three strategies for element retrieval :

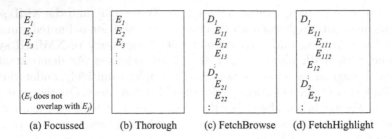

(a) Focussed   (b) Thorough   (c) FetchBrowse   (d) FetchHighlight

Fig. 1. Interfaces for each strategy

- **Focussed retrieval strategy**
  The system retrieves only focussed elements (i.e. non-overlapping elements) and ranks them in relevance order.
- **Thorough retrieval strategy**
  The system simply retrieves relevant elements from all elements without considering nestings and ranks them in relevance order.
- **Fetch and browse retrieval strategy**
  The system first identifies relevant documents (the fetching phase), and then identifies relevant elements within a fetched document (the browsing phase). The retrieved documents are initially ranked on the basis of their relevance, and then, the retrieved elements within a document are ranked in their relevance order. In the rest of this paper, we call this strategy the *FetchBrowse retrieval strategy*.

Figure 1 (a)-(c) show a naive and intuitive user interface image for each strategy. In the *Focussed retrieval strategy* (Figure 1 (a)) and the *Thorough retrieval strategy* (Figure 1 (b)), elements are displayed in descending order of their scores, i.e. element E_i is ranked higher than element E_j iff the score of E_i is higher than that of E_j. Additionally, in the Focussed retrieval strategy, E_i does not overlap with E_j for any E_i and E_j. In the FetchBrowse retrieval strategy (Figure 1 (c)), document D_i is ranked higher than document D_j iff the score of D_i is higher than that of D_j, and within the same document D_d, element E_{di} is ranked higher than element E_{dj} iff the score of E_{di} is higher than that of E_{dj}.

The three retrieval strategies of INEX were designed to evaluate XML-IR systems and were not necessarily intended to be used in designing user interfaces. From a practical point, we consider displaying search result elements aggregating by an XML document , which is a scholartic article in the case of INEX, is an effective display style for a user interface to have. The *FetchBrowse retrieval interface* is of that style. We also consider that displaying the search result elements in their document order (i.e. the occurrence order of start tags) is useful especially for document-centric XML. Taking this consideration into account, we have designed a new user interface, which we call the *FetchHighlight retrieval interface*. In the FetchHighlight retrieval interface, XML documents are first sorted in their relevance order, then relevant elements within the XML document are displayed in document order. Figure 1 (d) shows a conceptual image for the *FetchHighlight retrieval strategy*. Elements are indented in accordance with their depth in the XML tree.

In addition, to facilitate user browsing and specify the position of the relevant document fragments easily, *outline elements* are output even if the score is 0, which have particular structural information that the administrator defined, together with relevant document fragments. Such outline elements in scholarly articles are sections, subsections and so on.

Figure 2 shows an example of the FetchHighlight retrieval interface. This example shows the search results for the keyword set "ontologies case study", which is one of the topics in INEX 2005. The anchor texts corresponding to document fragments with a high score are indicated by using a larger font. Users can easily recognize highly relevant document fragments even if the document score is not so high by browsing search results using the FetchHighlight retrieval interface (lower part in Figure 2). In addition, as the search results are ordered in document order, users can recognize the parts in the documents with many high relevant document fragments clustered. Users can browse the content of the document fragment highlighted within the document by clicking the corresponding anchor text (Figure 3).

We developed not only the FetchHighlight retrieval interface but also the *Thorough retrieval interface* and the *FetchBrowse retrieval interface*, which are the interfaces for the Thorough retrieval strategy and the FetchBrowse retrieval strategy, respectively. We did not implement the Focussed retrieval strategy because users lose some possible benefits of XML-IR [7]. The naive interface for the Focussed retrieval strategy is considered to be equivalent to the Thorough retrieval interface. However, the FetchHighlight retrieval interface can be regarded as a more user-friendly interface for the Focussed retrieval strategy because users can easily identify focussed elements using the FetchHighlight retrieval interface.

3   Implementation of Keyword Search on Relational Databases

3.1   Conceptual Database Design

We show how to store XML documents and term weight information, which is explained in Section 4, in a relational XML database system developed by our group [4]. Note that the granule of search targets for an XML-IR system are document fragments, which are elements or attributes. In this paper, we regard only elements as a document fragment for the sake of simplicity. The table schema of [4] is independent of the logical structure of XML documents. Kikori-KS uses the following schema:

- Element (<u>docID, elemID</u>, pathID, start, end, label)
- Path (<u>pathID</u>, pathexp)
- Term (<u>term, docID, elemID</u>, tfipf)

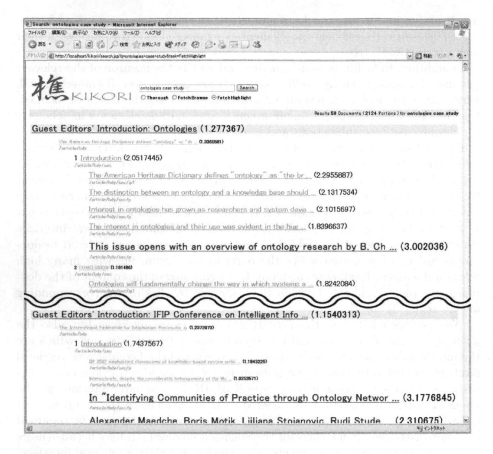

Fig. 2. FetchHighlight retrieval interface

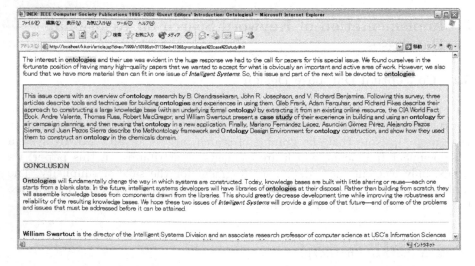

Fig. 3. Highlighted document fragment

The docID, elemID, and pathID are identifiers that identify a document, an element, and a path, respectively. A pair of docID and elemID can uniquely identify an element in a whole XML document set. The start and end are the byte positions of the element and are used to clip the document fragment. The value of the label attribute is a short text representing the element. In scholarly articles, for example, section titles are used for the label values of the elements corresponding to sections. The label value is used as an anchor text in the user interface. The pathexp is the path expression from the root node and used when we want to take the structural information into account. The term weight in the element, whose detail is explained in Section 4, is stored in the tfipf attribute in the Term table.

3.2   Schema Refinement

We refined the conceptual relational database schema by considering the requirements of the user interfaces described in Section 2. The basic policy was to reduce query processing time by storing data redundantly.

1. Materialized view
   The search results in Kikori-KS need information across the Term, Element, and Path tables. Increasing speed of query processing is possible by creating a materialized view which is the result of joining these three tables.
2. Partition of Term table
   The Term table has vast amounts of rows. By partitioning the Term table with each term, we can access only the tables that a query really needs, and therefore achieving efficient query processing.

For each term, a table that has the following schema is constructed. We can identify the table using the table name with the term value. For term "xyz", the table name is Term_xyz.

– Term_xyz (docID, elemID, tfipf, start, end, label, pathexp)

In addition, in the case of the FetchHighlight retrieval strategy, we need outline elements. The system administrator predefines outline elements in such a way as selecting path information. Although outline elements can be retrieved dynamically during searches, we can process queries efficiently by selecting outline elements and constructing an Outline table in advance. We can also apply join operations in advance to the Outline table.

– Outline (docID, elemID, start, end, label, pathexp)

3.3   Query Translation

The input keyword set is translated into an SQL statement, and the system then calculates the score of each relevant element. The Kikori-KS system can automatically translate keyword sets into SQL statements to enable each retrieval strategy.

For each term in the keyword set, the system retrieves the corresponding `Term` table, then calculates the scores on the basis of the model described in Section 4. The FetchHighlight retrieval strategy and the FetchBrowse retrieval strategy need document scores. We considered that a document score is equivalent to the score of the root node in the document. In addition, the FetchHighlight retrieval strategy needs outline elements. The system retrieves the outline elements from the `Outline` table, then returns the union of the relevant elements and outline elements.

In addition to searching by simple keyword sets, Kikori-KS supports term restrictions by using mandatory term and negation. We can specify a mandatory term by using a "+" sign preceding the term and a negation by using a "-".

Kikori-KS appropriately arranges the results of SQL queries that perform the retrieval strategy the user selected and constructs a corresponding user interface.

4　Ranking Model

We explain the ranking model and term weighting method used in Kikori-KS in this section. The term weights are calculated in advance for fast query processing during searches.

The search results of the XML-IR systems should be ranked with scores that reflect relevance to the query. We used a *vector space model*, a model widely used for calculating scores. The score this model produces is the degree of similarity between the query vector and the document vector (element vector in the case of XML-IR) represented in a term space. We can use the dot product of query vector Q and element vector E for the degree of similarity.

$$Sim(Q, E) = \sum_{t \in Q, E} weight(t, Q) * weight(t, E) \qquad (1)$$

We can use the term frequency of t in Q as the weight of the term in query ($weight(t, Q)$). As for $weight(t, E)$, which is the weight of term t in element E, *tf-idf*, which is the product of *tf* (term frequency) and *idf* (inverse document frequency), is an effective weighting scheme for unstructured documents. For structured documents, such as XML, several variants of *tf-idf* have been proposed [8,9,10]. The specificity of a term is calculated within the elements with the same *Category* in [9]. In the implementation of [9], *Category* is defined based on the path information from the root node. We call this method *ipf* (inverse path frequency) and use it in Kikori-KS. In addition, we adapted the method in [11] to XML documents and used the following formula for $weight(t, E)$.

$$weight(t, E) = \frac{ntf}{nel} * ipf \qquad (2)$$

$$ntf = 1 + ln(1 + ln(tf)) \qquad (3)$$

$$nel = \left((1 - s) + s * \frac{el}{avgel_p} \right) * (1 + ln(avgel_p)) \qquad (4)$$

$$ipf = ln\frac{N_p + 1}{ef_p} \tag{5}$$

where ntf is the normalized term frequency (tf) of t, nel is the normalization factor that reflects the element length of E, and ipf is the specificity of term t within elements that share path p. Here, el is the number of terms in element E, p is the path of E from the root node, $avgel_p$ is the average el of elements that share path p, N_p is the number of elements that share path p, ef_p is the number of elements that term t occurs in the elements sharing path p, and s is a constant parameter and is usually set to 0.2 [11].

5 Experiments

We used the XML documents provided by INEX [6]. INEX is also developing topics, which are queries for XML document collection, and relevance assessments. We used the INEX-1.9 document collection, which is about 700 MB. INEX provides two types of queries: Content Only (CO) queries and Content And Structure (CAS) queries. We used 40 CO queries of INEX 2005 in our experiments. The experimental setup used is as follows: CPU: Intel Xeon 3.80 GHz (2 CPU), Memory: 4.0 GB, OS: Miracle Linux 3.0, and RDBMS: Oracle 10g Release1.

5.1 Effectiveness

We examined the precision of the search results using the Thorough retrieval strategy and the FetchBrowse retrieval strategy of Kikori-KS. Note that although the main focus of the Kikori-KS interface is the FetchHighlight retrieval interface, the precision of the FetchHighlight retrieval strategy cannot be directly measured using the INEX test collection. However, the precision of the FetchHighlight retrieval strategy is considered to be equivalent to the FetchBrowse retrieval strategy because the only difference between the strategies is the appearance of the user interface.

Many research groups in INEX are evaluating the effectiveness of each XML retrieval system. Although many metrics have been proposed and used for evaluations, we used precision/recall graph because it seems to be general one. Figures 4 and 5 show the results of Kikori-KS with ones by other INEX participants. The position of Kikori-KS is relatively high especially using the FetchBrowse retrieval strategy (Figure 5) and so using the FetchHighlight retrieval strategy as well.

5.2 Efficiency

We examined the processing time of SQLs translated from 40 CO queries and measured the average time for the Thorough retrieval strategy, the FetchBrowse retrieval strategy, and the FetchHighlight retrieval strategy. We retrieved only the top 1,500 results as stipulated by INEX.

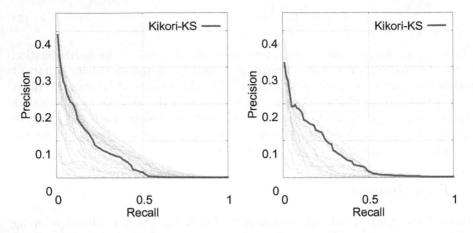

Fig. 4. Precision/Recall of Thorough   **Fig. 5.** Precision/Recall of FetchBrowse

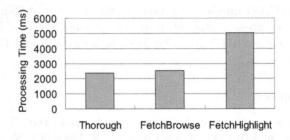

Fig. 6. Processing time

Kikori-KS achieved a processing time of about 2.5 seconds for the Thorough retrieval strategy or the FetchBrowse retrieval strategy and about 5.0 seconds for the FetchHighlight retrieval strategy. We consider this an acceptable search time.

An efficient top-k query processing method for XML-IR was proposed in [12]. The method's main focus is CAS queries and whose target is increasing speed of searches using the Thorough retrieval strategy. In the case of CAS queries, we can use structural information to narrow down candidate results, and process faster than CO queries. The processing time indicated in Figure 6 is the time when we retrieved the top 1,500 results. The processing time of Kikori-KS is comparable with the time of [12]. Kikori-KS can handle the FetchBrowse retrieval strategy with a comparable time using the Thorough retrieval strategy.

The FetchHighlight retrieval strategy needs a union with the outline elements, and the processing time is about as twice as that for the Thorough retrieval strategy or the FetchBrowse retrieval strategy. If outline elements are not needed, the processing time is equivalent to that of the FetchBrowse retrieval strategy.

6   Conclusions

We introduced Kikori-KS, a system which we can use to search XML documents by using a set of keywords. This system allows us to browse search results with a user-friendly FetchHighlight retrieval interface. XML documents and their term weight information were stored in a relational XML database system, and the schema was refined for increasing speed of query processing. Using an INEX test collection, we confirmed that Kikori-KS can handle a keyword set query in an acceptable time and with relatively high precision.

Future work includes developing storage schema and weighting methods for phrase searches and introducing content and structure (CAS) searches.

References

1. W3C: XQuery 1.0 and XPath 2.0 Full-Text (2006)
   http://www.w3.org/TR/xquery-full-text/.
2. W3C: XML Path Language (XPath) Version 1.0 (1999)
   http://www.w3.org/TR/xpath.
3. W3C: XQuery 1.0: An XML Query Language (2006)
   http://www.w3.org/TR/xquery/.
4. Yoshikawa, M., Amagasa, T., Shimura, T., Uemura, S.: XRel: a path-based approach to storage and retrieval of XML documents using relational databases. ACM Transactions on Internet Technology 1 (2001) 110–141
5. Fujimoto, K., Shimizu, T., Terada, N., Hatano, K., Suzuki, Y., Amagasa, T., Kinutani, H., Yoshikawa, M.: Implementation of a high-speed and high-precision XML information retrieval system on relational databases. In: Advances in XML Information Retrieval and Evaluation. Volume 3977 of Lecture Notes in Computer Science., Springer-Verlag (2006) 254–267
6. INEX: INitiative for the Evaluation of XML Retrieval (2005)
   http://inex.is.informatik.uni-duisburg.de/2005/.
7. Clarke, C.L.A.: Controlling overlap in content-oriented XML retrieval. In: Proceedings of the 28th Annual International ACM SIGIR Conference on Research and Development in Information Retrieval, Salvador, Brazil (2005) 314–321
8. Cohen, S., Mamou, J., Kanza, Y., Sagiv, Y.: XSEarch: A semantic search engine for XML. In: Proceedings of the 29th International Conference on Very Large Data Bases, Berlin, Germany (2003) 45–56
9. Grabs, T., Schek, H.J.: ETH Zürich at INEX: Flexible information retrieval from XML with PowerDB-XML. In: Proceedings of the First Workshop of the INitiative for the Evaluation of XML Retrieval, Schloss Dagstuhl, Germany (2002) 141–148
10. Amer-Yahia, S., Curtmola, E., Deutsch, A.: Flexible and efficient XML search with complex full-text predicates. In: Proceedings of the 2006 ACM SIGMOD International Conference on Management of Data, Chicago, USA (2006) 575–586
11. Liu, F., Yu, C.T., Meng, W., Chowdhury, A.: Effective keyword search in relational databases. In: Proceedings of the 2006 ACM SIGMOD International Conference on Management of Data, Chicago, USA (2006) 563–574
12. Theobald, M., Schenkel, R., Weikum, G.: An efficient and versatile query engine for TopX search. In: Proceedings of the 31st International Conference on Very Large Data Bases, Trondheim, Norway (2005) 625–636

Supporting Efficient Grouping and Summary Information for Semistructured Digital Libraries*

Minsoo Lee[1], Sookyung Song[1], Yunmi Kim[1], and Hyoseop Shin[2],**

[1] Department of Computer Science and Engineering
Ewha Womans University, Seoul, Korea
mlee@ewha.ac.kr, happymint@ewhain.net, cherish11@ewhain.net
[2] Department of Internet and Multimedia Engineering
Konkuk University, Seoul, Korea
hsshin@konkuk.ac.kr

Abstract. XML is the most popular platform-independent data expression language which is used to specify various digital content such as web content, multimedia content, bio-chemical data, etc. These various forms of XML data are continuously increasing by a large amount and there is a strong demand on effectively managing such data in digital libraries or archives. The most popular query language to search and retrieve information from such semi-structured XML digital libraries is XQuery. XQuery has a very powerful syntax which allows users to iterate over data items and perform calculation, string matching, and output formatting. However, it lacks a simple and easy way to group and provide summaries on vast amounts of XML data. This grouping and summary function is especially important for large digital archives where users like to obtain an overview or summary of the contents in the digital library. Our work is focused on providing an easy way for grouping in XQuery at the query language level. We provide several cases where this can be considered to be effective. We have also implemented an XQuery processing system with grouping functions based on the eXist Native XML Database.

1 Introduction

XML(eXtensible Markup Language) is increasingly becoming popular as a data expression and exchange language on the Web as well as a specification language for various multimedia content due to its flexibility and platform-independence[1]. Large amounts of digital content represented in XML format are becoming increasingly available and there is strong demand to provide digital libraries and archives for such XML data. The W3C has already adopted XML as a standard and there have been several languages devised to query XML data. Among such query languages XQuery is now considered the standard[2]. The XQuery language uses a FLWR(For-Let-Where-Return) syntax to devise queries. XQuery uses XPath[3] expressions to specify

---

* This work was supported by the Korea Research Foundation Grant (KRF-2004-041-D00572) and also partially supported by the second stage of the BK21 program.
** Corresponding author.

S. Sugimoto et al. (Eds.): ICADL 2006, LNCS 4312, pp. 400–409, 2006.
© Springer-Verlag Berlin Heidelberg 2006

hierarchical relationships, and has powerful iteration capabilities as well as convenient calculation and formatting functions.

However, the current XQuery provides very poor functionality regarding grouping and summary (i.e., aggregation) capabilities on XML data. This is especially important in large digital libraries, where users would frequently ask for an overview or summary on the large amount of XML data stored in digital libraries. Because XQuery requires users to specify their grouping and aggregation queries as multiple nested structures and join operations, it is hard to express and understand such complex query statements. In this paper, we propose a way to extend XQuery at the language level to enable such grouping and aggregation queries to be much more easily formulated. Considering various cases for grouping in semistructured data, we extend the EBNF of XQuery to incorporate a group by clause. In addition, we extended the eXist native database system[4] to implement our idea and validate the usefulness of our approach.

The organization of the paper is as follows. Section 2 discusses related research on grouping support for queries on XML data. Section 3 gives an overview of our XQuery extension to support the groupby clause as well as several cases where this could greatly benefit query construction in digital libraries. Section 4 deals with the implementation of our system based on the eXist native database and gives an explanation on how the grouping and aggregation is processed in our system. Section 5 gives the conclusion and discusses future work.

2   Related Research

Grouping on data requires restructuring of the original data and enables related data to be treated together as a group, thus allowing aggregations to be computed on the groups. Research on grouping data is still an issue in relational databases. Especially in data warehouses complex analytical queries containing various grouping conditions are issued. Therefore, users need a way to easily specify the grouping methods. Several new operators for grouping have been suggested in the data warehouse research area [5,6].

Grouping in XML documents is a much more serious issue yet it is considered as a more difficult problem due to the semistructured nature of the XML documents. There has been some work that helped understanding the difference between relational and XML data in terms of grouping and provided insight on proposing grouping operators for XML[7]. In this work, they have focused on providing binding variables for a set of tuples instead of individual tuples and devised a GApply operator that can be integrated into existing relational database engines. The Lore semistructured database system[8] does not support the groupby clause and requires a complex query to be formulated to perform grouping tasks. The TIMBER project[9] defined a tree algebra called TAX to internally identify the grouping information and used it to transform a nested XQuery into a TAX grouped query. Deutsch et al.[10] extend tree pattern queries into Group-by Normal Form Tree Pattern(GNFTP) queries, which are nested, perform arbitrary joins, and freely mix bag and set semantics. They describe a subset of XQuery, called OptXQuery and provide a normalization algorithm that rewrites any OptXQuery into a GNFTP query. The algorithm detects and eliminates redundant navigation within and across nested subqueries and it unifies and generalizes prior solutions for tree pattern minimization and group-by detection. Beyer et al.[11] provide a proposal for extending the XQuery FLWOR expression with explicit syntax for grouping and for numbering of results. In this work, they show that these new XQuery constructs not only simplify the construction and evaluation of queries requiring grouping and ranking but also enable complex analytic queries such as moving-window aggregation and rollups along dynamic hierarchies to be expressed without additional language extensions.

3   Extension of XQuery with Groupby Clause

This section explains the XQuery extension to incorporate the groupby clause. We show how our approach is consistent with the syntactic and semantic specification of XQuery by first giving the EBNF(Extended Backus-Naur Form) that includes the groupby clause and then discussing the specific query types that could benefit from the use of the groupby clause. Figure 1 shows only the extended EBNF part of the XQuery language specification including the groupby clause.

```
FLWGRExpr   ::= (ForClause|LetClause)+ WhereClause?
                   groupbyClause? "return" ExprSingle
ForClause   ::= <"for" "$"> VarName TypeDeclaration? PositionalVar? "in" ExprSingle
                  ("," "$" VarName TypeDeclaration? PositionalVar? "in" ExprSingle)*
LetClause   ::= <"let" "$"> VarName TypeDeclaration? ":=" ExprSingle ("," "$" VarName
                  TypeDeclaration?":=" ExprSingle)*
WhereClause ::= "where" ExprSingle
groupbyClause ::= <"groupby"> groupbySpecList
groupbySpecList ::= ( NgroupbySpec | SgroupbySpec )
SgroupbySpec ::= "[" groupbySpec ("," groupbySpec)* "]"
NgroupbySpec ::= groupbySpec ("," groupbySpec)*
groupbySpec  ::= ExprSingle
```

Fig. 1. EBNF including groupby in XQuery

The following subsections show 4 types of queries that could benefit from the use of the groupby clause in XQuery and are based on the XML example data shown in Figure 2.

3.1 XQuery Type 1: Group by with Single Binding Variable

XQuery Type 1 is a basic example for using group by with a single binding variable. Using the XML in Figure 2, the following query which groups according to the "author" information could be easily formulated with a groupby clause extension.

● Type 1: Output the book *titles* grouped by the *author* who published the book.

```
<?xml version="1.0" encoding="utf-8"?>
<bib>
    <book year="1994">
        <title>TCP/IP Illustrated</title>
        <author>Stevens W.</author>
        <publisher>Addison-Wesley</publisher>
        <price>65.95</price>
    </book>
    <book year="1992">
        <title>Advanced Programming in the Unix environment</title>
        <author>Stevens W.</author>
        <author>Abiteboul Serge</author>
        <publisher>Addison-Wesley</publisher>
        <price>65.95</price>
    </book>
    <book year="2000">
        <title>Data on the Web</title>
        <author>Abiteboul Serge</author>
        <author>Buneman Peter</author>
        <author>Suciu Dan</author>
        <publisher>Morgan Kaufmann Publishers</publisher>
        <price>39.95</price>
    </book>
    <book year="1999">
        <title>The Economics of Technology and Content for Digital TV</title>
        <editor>CITI</editor>
        <publisher>Kluwer Academic Publishers</publisher>
        <price>129.95</price>
    </book>
</bib>
```

Fig. 2. Example XML data

XQuery Type 1: Without groupby	XQuery Type 1: With groupby
``` <results> { let $a := doc("bib.xml")//author ⓐ for $author in distinct-values($a/text()) return <result> <author>{ $author }</author> <titles> { ⓑ for $b in doc("bib.xml")/bib/book where some $ba in $b/author satisfies ($ba/text() = $author) return $b/title } </titles> </result> } </results> ```	``` <results> { for $b in doc("bib.xml")/bib/book, $a in $b/author group by $a return <result> { $a } <titles> { $b/title } </titles> </result> } </results> ```

Fig. 3. Comparison of XQuery Type 1 with and without groupby clause

When using the current XQuery syntax to devise such a query it becomes very complex and requires a nested XQuery to obtain the desired result. However, by including a group by clause it becomes very easy to formulate such a query. Figure 3 shows this difference in formulating the query.

3.2 XQuery Type 2: Group by Used with Aggregation Function

XQuery Type 2 applies aggregation functions on the grouped data. Using the XML in Figure 2, the following query calculates the "total number of books" in the groups.

- Type 2: Output the book *titles* and *total number of books* grouped by the *author* who published the book.

Again, when using the current XQuery syntax, a nested XQuery is needed to obtain the desired result. A group by clause can simplify the query. Figure 4 shows the difference when using the current XQuery without the groupby clause and when using the extended XQuery with the groupby clause to express such a query.

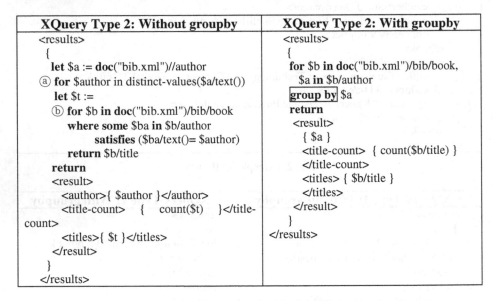

XQuery Type 2: Without groupby	XQuery Type 2: With groupby

<results>
  {
   let $a := **doc**("bib.xml")//author
  ⓐ **for** $author in distinct-values($a/text())
   let $t :=
  ⓑ **for** $b in **doc**("bib.xml")/bib/book
    where some $ba in $b/author
      satisfies ($ba/text()= $author)
   return $b/title
  return
   <result>
    <author>{ $author }</author>
    <title-count>   {   count($t)   }</title-count>
    <titles>{ $t }</titles>
   </result>
  }
  </results>
	<results>
	  {
	   for $b **in doc**("bib.xml")/bib/book,
	    $a **in** $b/author
	   <u>**group by**</u> $a
	   return
	    <result>
	     { $a }
	     <title-count> { count($b/title) }
	     </title-count>
	     <titles> { $b/title }
	     </titles>
	    </result>
	  }
	  </results>

Fig. 4. Comparison of XQuery Type 2 with and without groupby clause

3.3 XQuery Type 3: Group by with Two or More Binding Variables

XQuery Type 3 groups the XML data based on two or more binding variables. The following query is an example using the XML data shown in Figure 2.

- Type 3: Output the book *titles* grouped by the *author* who published the book and the *year* in which the book was published.

The current XQuery syntax requires a deeply nested XQuery to obtain the desired result, whereas a group by clause enables it to be expressed in a single level query. Figure 5 shows this difference.

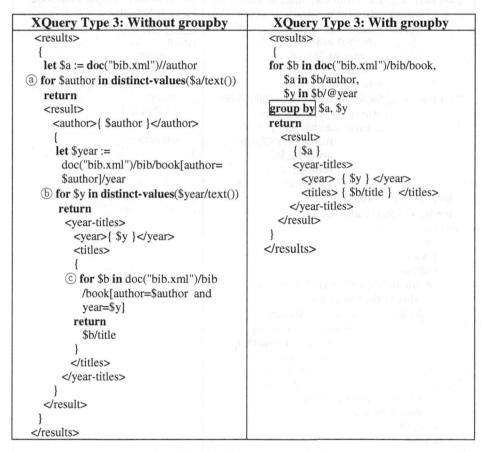

XQuery Type 3: Without groupby	XQuery Type 3: With groupby
| ```
  {
  let $a := doc("bib.xml")//author
ⓐ for $author in distinct-values($a/text())
  return
  <result>
    <author>{ $author }</author>
    {
    let $year :=
    doc("bib.xml")/bib/book[author=
    $author]/year
ⓑ for $y in distinct-values($year/text())
    return
      <year-titles>
        <year>{ $y }</year>
        <titles>
        {
        ⓒ for $b in doc("bib.xml")/bib
          /book[author=$author  and
          year=$y]
        return
          $b/title
        }
        </titles>
      </year-titles>
    }
  </result>
  }
``` | ```
  {
  for $b in doc("bib.xml")/bib/book,
    $a in $b/author,
    $y in $b/@year
  group by $a, $y
  return
    <result>
    { $a }
    <year-titles>
      <year> { $y } </year>
      <titles> { $b/title }  </titles>
    </year-titles>
    </result>
  }
``` |

Fig. 5. Comparison of XQuery Type 3 with and without groupby clause

3.4   XQuery Type 4: Group by with Binding Variable Composed of Set of Values

XQuery Type 4 groups the XML data based on a binding variable that represents a set of values. Using the example XML data shown in Figure 2, the following query could be easily formulated with a groupby clause extension.

● Type 4: Output the book *titles* grouped by the *set of authors* who published the book.

This kind of query will take into consideration "a set of elements" instead of individual values and use it to group other information. Figure 6 shows the difference when using the current XQuery without the groupby clause and when using the extended XQuery with the groupby clause to express such a query.

XQuery Type 4: Without groupby	XQuery Type 4: With groupby

`<results>`
`{`
① **let** $au1 := ⓐ **for** $b1 **in doc**("bib.xml")/bib/book
    where exists($b1/author)
    return `<author-set>` {
        for $a1 in $b1/author
        order by $a1
        return $a1 }
        `</author-set>`
② **let** $au2 := ⓑ **for** $b2 **in doc**("bib.xml")/bib/book
    where exists($b2/author)
    return `<author-set>` {
        for $a2 in $b2/author
        order by $a2
        return $a2 }
        `</author-set>`
③ **let** $au3 := union($au1, $au2)
ⓒ **for** $au4 in $au3/author-set
  return
    `<result>`
      { $au4 }
      `<titles>` {
      ⓓ **for** $b **in doc**("bib.xml")/bib/book
        where exists($b/author)
        let $au := ⓔ **let** $au5 := $b/author
            return `<author-set>` {
            for $a3 in $b/author
            order by $a3
            return $a3 }
            `</author-set>`
        where deep-equal($au,$au4)
        return $b/title }
      `</titles>`
    `</result>`
`}`
`</results>`
	`<results>`
	`{`
	for $b **in doc**("bib.xml")/bib/book
	let $a := $b/author
	group by [$a]
	return
	  `<result>`
	    `<author-set>` { $a }
	    `</author-set>`
	  `<titles>`
	    { $b/title }
	  `</titles>`
	  `</result>`
	`}`
	`</results>`

Fig. 6. Comparison of XQuery Type 4 with and without groupby clause

4 Implementation of XQuery Processor Supporting Groupby Clause

We have implemented a prototype query processor that supports XQuery with the group by clause extension to demonstrate the feasibility of our approach. Performance issues will be pursued in future work. The prototype is implemented using the eXist native database system[4]. The development environment is as follows. For the server, eXist 1.0 was used, and jEdit 4.2 was used as the client. Eclipse SDK 3.0.2 was used as the Integrated Development Environment(IDE). JDK 1.4.2 and XQuery 1.0 were used. The overall architecture of the system is shown in Figure 7. The

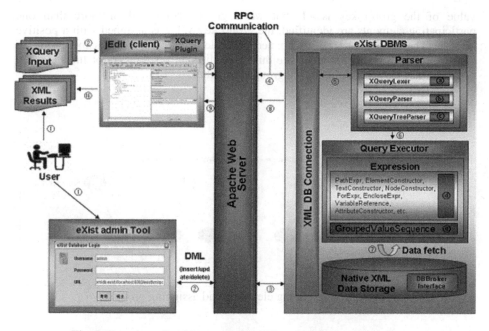

Fig. 7. Overview of architecture of the XQuery with group by processor

XQueryLexer, XQueryParser, XQueryTreeParser, and various parts of the Query Executor of the eXist system, shown as (a)-(e) in Figure 7, were modified.

Figure 8 gives a high-level overview on processing the grouping and aggregation queries. The query is first parsed and then executed and an initial XML DOM tree result without the grouping is obtained. The grouping elements are then searched and group keys are assigned to each group element. Afterwards, the XML DOM tree is restructured according to the grouping information and output format. During this step the aggregation values are also computed. The final XML result is then returned to the user.

A simple example of the three major steps are shown in Figure 9. The first step is identifying the grouping elements and assigning the group key elements. The initial

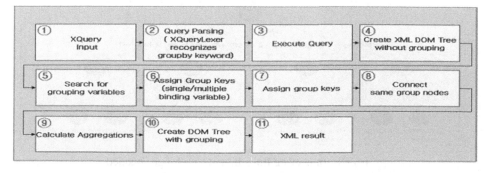

Fig. 8. Overview of processing XQuery with group by feature

value of the group key is −1, but when groups composed of more than one participating elements are identified, the group key value is assigned with a positive integer. The second step is to connect the elements within the same group to restructure the XML DOM tree. The third step disconnects those prior links that are no longer needed after elements are grouped together.

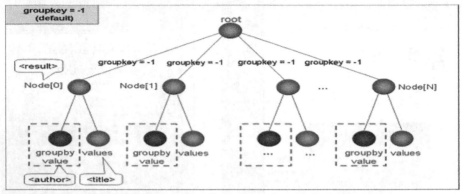

(a) Identifying grouping elements and assigning group keys

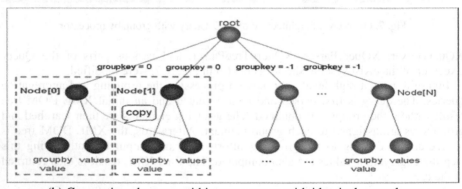

(b) Connecting elements within same group with identical group keys

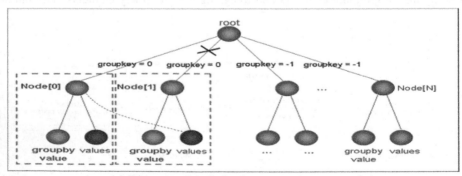

(c) Disconnecting links that are no longer needed

Fig. 9. Three major steps in processing groups in XQuery

5   Conclusion

In this paper, we have proposed an extension to the XQuery language to effectively support grouping and summaries on XML data. This work enables users of semi-structured digital libraries to easily formulate queries that provide overview or summary information for a large size digital library. We have also implemented the processing of XQuery with the groupby clause on the eXist native database system. The contribution of our paper is that with this extension to XQuery, the complex and nested equivalent queries would be reduced to simple XQueries using this groupby clause. Some comparisons on other work are shown in Table 1. Future work include performing extensive query optimization with group information and identifying more flexible semantics in group concepts regarding the semistructured nature of XML.

Table 1. Comparison of XQuery groupby support with other systems

	Lore	Timber	GApply	XQuery with groupby
Native XML support	△	○	×	○
XQuery support	×	△	×	○
Explicit group by support	×	△	○	○
Single group by variable support	×	○	○	○
Group by with aggregation support	×	×	×	○
Multiple group by variable support	×	○	○	○

○   full support   △   partial support   ×   no support

References

[1] XML(eXtensible Markup Language), http://www.w3.org/XML/
[2] XQuery (XML Query Language), http://www.w3.org/XML/Query/
[3] XML Path Language (XPath) 2.0, http://www.w3.org/TR/2005/WD-xpath20-20050404/
[4] eXist(An Open Source Native XML Database), http://exist.sourceforge.net/
[5] D. Chatziantoniou and K. A. Ross, "Querying multiple features of groups in relational databases," VLDB, 1996
[6] D. Chatziantoniou and K. A. Ross, "Groupwise processing of relational queries," VLDB, 1997
[7] S. Chaudhuri, R. Kaushik and J.F. Naughton, "On Relational Support for XML Publishing: Beyond Sorting and Tagging", SIGMOD, 2003
[8] J. McHugh, S. Abiteboul, R. Goldman, D. Quass, and J. Widom, "Lore: A Database Management System for Semistructured Data", SIGMOD Record, 26(3):54-66, September 1997
[9] H. V. Jagadish, Shurug Al-Khalifa, Adriane Chapman, Laks V.S. Lakshmanan, Andrew Nierman, Stelios Paparizos, Jignesh M. Patel, Divesh Srivastava, Nuwee Wiwatwattana, Yuqing Wu and Cong Yu. "TIMBER: A Native XML Database", VLDB Journal, Vol. 11, Issue 4, 2002
[10] Alin Deutsch , Yannis Papakonstantinou , Yu Xu, "Minimization and Group-By Detection for Nested XQueries", Int'l Conference on Data Engineering (ICDE) , pp. 839, 2004
[11] Kevin Beyer, Don Chamberlin, Latha S. Colby, Fatma Ozcan, Hamid Pirahesh, Yu Xu, "XML query, update, and search: Extending XQuery for analytics", Proceedings of the 2005 ACM SIGMOD Int'l Conference on Management of Data, pp. 503-514, June 2005

Accessing Japanese Digital Libraries: Three Case Studies

Maureen H. Donovan

Ohio State University Libraries, Columbus OH, USA
donovan.1@osu.edu

Abstract. Digital Libraries make Japan's rich cultural heritage available world-wide for the first time, opening new areas for scholarship. Nonetheless, access, discovery and navigation challenges abound. This paper presents case studies of three formats (poetry, company histories, *manga*) characteristic of Japanese print publishing, identifying specific support structures that are evolving to enhance scholarly access to and use of these resources in digital libraries. In particular, the role of researchers in design and construction of access resources is explored. Better awareness and understanding of the role of access resources in digital libraries has implications for information literacy programs and other kinds of instruction.

1 Introduction

Japanese digital library projects underway at libraries, universities, government agencies, non-profit organizations, for-profit corporations, associations and other institutions at all levels of Japanese society are providing resources for academic research on Japanese culture at an unprecedented level. The effect has been dramatic in some cases. With ubiquitous availability on the Internet, researchers all over the world who previously had access only to personal collections, now can use digitized copies of fabulous resources that not long ago were available only in Japanese rare book libraries. This has the potential to open up the field to a very large extent. At the same time, since digital libraries comprise materials that differ from those previously collected in research libraries, scholarship can expand in unforeseen directions as well. As others have noted, this is true of digital library development in general and is not particular to the Japanese case [6]. While it is too early to take full stock of the impact this changed environment is having on the field of Japanese studies, some changes are already visible.

This paper surveys access resources for three kinds of primary research materials, poetry, company histories and cartoons (*manga*), which are characteristic of Japanese publishing and also have considerable research value. Each format is comparatively well-defined. The focus here is on access resources, often created by scholars themselves, which assist researchers in identifying and using materials in Japanese digital libraries. Carole L. Palmer's research has drawn attention to the important role that access resources such as indexes, directories, bibliographies, databases and other reference works play in the cycle of scholarly communications by providing an

S. Sugimoto et al. (Eds.): ICADL 2006, LNCS 4312, pp. 410–418, 2006.
© Springer-Verlag Berlin Heidelberg 2006

infrastructure that makes searching and gathering raw materials for research possible [24]. Prior to the digital age, the value placed on such works was evident in successive compilations of guides to reference works in this field over many years. Are Japanese digital libraries incorporating similar access resources that facilitate discovery, navigation and use of their contents? Do scholars participate in their development? These questions are pursued with regard to the three kinds of research material, thereby zeroing in on the usability of digital libraries for research in specific fields.

The purpose of the study is to highlight the value added by support structures, portals and other subject-oriented access resources that help researchers use digital libraries for specific research purposes. As a preliminary study, it covers only a limited number of the many Japanese digital libraries.

A subject focus was chosen because it best represents the stance of the researcher. At the same time it allows investigation of the silo effect of digital libraries constructed independently of each other. Digital library development happens within institutions, often based on local collections of print materials which are accessed through tools specific to a particular digital library. By contrast, researchers have become accustomed to integrated databases that list resources held by many institutions.. To what extent are researchers' experiences impeded by arbitrary boundaries (silos) fragmenting the Japanese digital library landscape?

2 Case Study: Poetry

Access to the considerable body of Japanese poetry and songs in their many forms (*waka, kayo, uta, Kanshi, renga, haikai, senryu, kyoka, tanka, haiku, kindaishi, gendaishi*, etc.) has long been a challenge. Pre-modern poetry studies emphasize Imperial anthologies and other famous compilations of poetry and songs, although a much larger body of works survives. As for modern and contemporary poetry, many new works are published each year in Japan, but only the most prominent among them draw attention. Accordingly, Japanese collections in research libraries tend to be especially selective with regard to poetic works. However, poetry is popular in Japan, both as a scholarly endeavor and as a hobby in which many people participate. Further, foreigners studying Japanese enjoy reading or composing poems as a way of focusing their attention on particular words while gaining deeper understanding of Japanese culture. English language newspapers in Japan sometimes publish poetry columns. Thus, on the one hand vast areas of Japanese poetry have yet to receive scholarly attention, and on the other it has broad popular appeal. Therefore, it is an area in which improved access through digital libraries is particularly welcome.

Japanese poetry flourishes on the web. A spectrum of organizations including poetry clubs in schools, local poetry groups, national organizations, scholarly societies, and research libraries is contributing to what is available, which ranges from digitized copies of national treasures, to self-publishing by teenagers, to poems celebrated at the annual New Year's Imperial Poetry Readings (*Utakai Hajime*). Where can one turn for help in navigating and using these resources? What kinds of aids have been developed to facilitate and enhance research in this field?

a) Nippon Decimal Classification and Other Classifications

Among the modes of access that facilitate use are classification schemes. Nippon Decimal Classification (NDC) is used by two large digital libraries of modern Japanese texts, Aozora Bunko [2] and Kindai Digital Library (National Diet Library)[17], to promote browsing of digitized texts. NDC is also used for classifying web sites at general purpose portals such as Dnavi (National Diet Library)[9], Index to Resources on Internet (University of Tokyo Library)[13], and Database Shusei[7]. In these and other sites using NDC, poetry works or links related to poetry are found under: **Literature (900) -- Japanese Literature (910) -- Poetry and Songs (911)**. Following these links opens up a wide range of resources selected and classified by individuals.

The Japanese Text Initiative (University of Virginia) [15] provides general categories of Poetry, Fiction, Other Prose and Drama under broad chronological headings, thereby inviting similar access to its resources.

Digital Archive Portal (DAP) [8] of the National Diet Library also presents NDC as a search option. DAP provides cross-indexing of metadata from digital libraries, repositories, databases, catalogs, indexes, and archives of the National Diet Library along with cooperating libraries and archives. Of the resources mentioned above, Aozora Bunko, Kindai Digital Library and Dnavi are all included in DAP, so searches in DAP can be limited to these digital libraries. Use of the cross-indexing portal, though, reveals that Aozora Bunko's implementation of NDC differs from that of the National Diet Library, therby impeding the use of this search in the portal context. A general search on keywords provides better access across the digital libraries included in DAP, mitigating the "silo effect" caused by variant implementations of NDC.

b) Subject-Specific Access Aids: Chronological and Season Word (Kigo) Search Indexes

Providing enhanced access to its substantial databases of Japanese poetry, the International Research Center for Japanese Studies (Nichibunken) web site features two special access resources – one by the time period in which poems were composed[28], and the other by *kigo*, the "season words" (for example, cherry blossoms and frogs in spring; red leaves and migrating birds in autumn) that are characteristic of haiku [16]. These searches work across three separate databases: Renga Database (197,228 renga including all renga collections), Waka Database (190,423 waka including all Imperial anthologies and other major collections), and Haikai Database (25,652 haiku from major collections, including Basho and Buson), all compiled by Professor Katsuhiro Seta of Nara National College of Technology. The chronological search provides a time period scroll that can be clicked to drill down to select a particular time period. The *Kigo* Search indexes 35,811 season words across the three databases simultaneously and can also be used independently. Traditionally reference books known as *saijiki* listed season words along with examples from famous poets. This practice has been expanded and enhanced in this Nichibunken database.

Season word access is also available in the Japanese Text Initiative's Topical Haiku Dictionary[32], the Modern Haiku Association's Modern Haiku Database [11] and Zouhai (Zōshoku Suru Haiku Saijiki Kensaku)[33], as well as other in many other haiku resources on the web. Of course, individual *kigo* can also be used as keywords in database or portal searches. Overall, it seems that the availability of a season word search appears to be almost normative already among access resources for Japanese poetry.

In Japan, then, at least in the case of haiku resources, digital libraries of poetic works are enhanced by access tools that make navigating and using these materials more convenient than print resources. Given the major role that poetry has always played in Japanese culture, at both elite and popular culture levels, it is not surprising that this is an area of innovation in the development of digital tools.

3 Case Study: Company Histories

Publication of corporate histories (*shashi, kaishashi,* or *nenshi*) is a common practice at Japanese companies, and many scholars find these sources useful for research. Technically a kind of "grey literature," since they are privately published and are not distributed through normal channels, *shashi* sometimes are dense with data about the company and its industry, as well as intersections with society and the business world of the period covered. Often the works are heavily illustrated and include numerous tables and graphs. They tend to be published at regular intervals (every 10 years is common) and used within companies for training new employees, fostering team-work, and encouraging productivity by instilling awareness of the values of the company's founders. Also, they are exchanged among business partners and within industrial groups.

a) Printed Company Histories

Since company histories are published as books and cataloged into library systems, it is not hard to locate them, as long as one knows the name of the company and/or the title of its company history. However, these works are published outside of the main-stream of commercial publishing, so additional effort is needed first to collect them, and then to bring their availability to the attention of scholars. Several libraries with collections of Japanese company histories in Japan and in the United States have made web sites to facilitate use, often providing additional access by industry sector as well as by company name. Such resources are designed to increase the visibility of these valuable primary research resources that might have gone unnoticed when in-corporated into large bibliographic databases.

Library Collections of Shashi Include:

Kanagawa-kenritsu Kawasaki Toshokan (the largest collection):
        http://www.klnet.pref.kanagawa.jp/kawasaki/cole.htm
Kobe University:
        http://www.rieb.kobe-u.ac.jp/liaison/mokuroku/gyousyu.html

National Diet Library
>   http://www.ndl.go.jp/jp/data/theme/theme_honbun_102077.html
Ohio State University Libraries:
>   http://pears.lib.ohio-state.edu/dbase/DbaseHP.php
>   http://eas.lib.ohio-state.edu/ShashiDB/
Ryukoku Daigaku (Nagao Bunko):
>   http://opac.lib.ryukoku.ac.jp/nb/nagao/index.html
Shibusawa Eiichi Shiryokan:
>   http://www.shibusawa.or.jp/english/center/shashi/shashi01.html#01
University of Hawaii:
>   http://www.hawaii.edu/asiaref/japan/company/index.htm
University of Kansas:
>   http://www.lib.ku.edu/eastasia/shashi_bib.shtml

Tracking newly published company histories is a challenge, but online access to Japanese newspapers, including those covered in Factiva (Dow Jones & Reuters)[10], helps enormously with regard to learning about *shashi*, especially those that receive publicity at the time of publication (often in conjunction with special commemorative events). A cycle of actions is followed by groups of librarians in Japan (under the auspices of the Japan Special Libraries Association) and in the United States (coordinated by the Japanese Company History (*Shashi*) Interest Group) who search out information about these publications, contact companies for donations of the books, and then promote their availability for research through special listings arranged by industry sector on web sites. The latter activity creates what Palmer calls a connective structure, thereby extending and mediating "the path of information beyond a given item to other potentially relevant documents, helping the flow and exchange of information among scholars."[24]

b) Digital Company Histories and Archives

In addition to printed copies of their histories, some companies have made their histories available on their web sites, including Canon [4], Honda [12], Murata [22], Panasonic [25], Sharp [29], Shiseido [30], and others [21]. In some cases (such as Honda) the complete work is available in digital format, while in others only an outline along with collections of photographs is published. A small number of digitized copies of early shashi are included in Kindai Digital Library [17] as well, for example, the ten-year history of Iyo Agricultural Bank, *Iyo Nogyo Ginko junenshi* (Matsuyama, 1908), and the two-volume 50-year history of the opening of the port of Yokohama, *Yokohama Kaigyo Gojunenshi* (Yokohoama, 1909).

Digital access to corporate archives is also available in a few cases. The Resource Center for the History of Entrepreneurship of the Shibusawa Eiichi Memorial Foundation [26] maintains links to corporate archives as part of its company history project. The Business Archives Association [3] coordinates activities of its members, including links to their web-based exhibits and archive portals. One of the best sources related to business history on the web is included in the archives section of the National Institute of Japanese Literature's web site, namely the image database of works collected by the industrialist Shibusawa Eiichi's heirs in the 1930s-1940s for a museum of the history of Japanese industry, focusing on the Tokugawa and Meiji periods, that was never realized [23].

Newspaper clippings relevant to business and industry, including company histories, during the period 1912-1940 are available in a digital archive at Kobe University's Research Institute for Economics & Business Administration [18]. Based on scrapbooks compiled under the leadership of Professor Yuzo Sakanishi during that period, the archive is noted as bearing the imprint of selection and classification "performed with the viewpoint of a specialist researcher." This type of resource, produced by a scholar, is one that Palmer distinguishes from those generated through institutional efforts (such as commercial indexing and abstracting services) as taking a more focused and selective approach, reflecting expertise and judgment of the authors, and being "subject to a greater degree of social shaping by the scholarly communities"[24].

Although only a few companies have made their histories available on the web thus far, and no specific digital library has been constructed (probably due to copyright issues), web-based access resources make it easier for scholars to access these materials.

4 Case Study: *Manga*

The dramatic spread of *manga* around the world as part of a global youth culture is well known. A grassroots phenomenon, *manga* confronts the Japanese studies field with its immediacy. Students flock to these Japanese comics and cartoons to learn the Japanese language and study what fascinates them about Japanese popular culture.. This widespread awareness of *manga* and *anime* is promoted through web-based services. More recently, scholarly efforts have also been begun to provide structure and help to humanities scholars and social scientists who are using these materials as research materials.

a) *Anime/Manga* Community Resources

Anime News Network (ANN) [1] serves as a basic reference for English-speaking fans of *manga* and *anime*. An encyclopedia section of the web site contains extensive bibliographies, indexes, chronologies, links to recent news about the work or creator, user ratings, statistics and other kinds of data. Although this access resource reflects the information needs of the fans who contribute to it (under the direction of ANN's editorial staff) and the global youth culture they represent, nonetheless it is an example of a scholarly communication infrastructure of resources that assist users to identify, find and collect publications.

In her study Palmer notes that access to people and their expertise for consultation is an important part of scholarly communication. [24] ANN makes those linkages easy for its fans through interactive forums, chat rooms, contests, polls, blogs, as well as correspondence, including consultation with an expert (Answerman). Many of the news posts present opportunities to meet with other fans, industry leaders, authors (mangaka), voice actors, and others at conventions or other venues, thereby supporting the ongoing development of this global culture.

Another fan-oriented access resource is Tezuka Osamu @ World [31], a web site created by Tezuka Productions. With all resources available in both Japanese and English, the web site functions as a virtual encyclopedia about Tezuka Osamu, whom many credit with establishing the foundation on which the current *anime* and *manga* industries developed. The site includes a complete and authoritative bibliography of Tezuka's works, along with an index of the characters he created, and many other resources.

However, neither ANN nor Tezuka Osamu @ World is technically a digital library. Rather they serve as portals to guide fans with authoritative bibliographic information about what has been published or released in English and/or Japanese, who was involved in the production and publication, and other background information. They serve as guides to the "legal" copies of manga and anime that were issued under appropriate copyright laws.

A shadow digital library does exist, however, in the form of illegal copies of Japanese manga posted on the Internet. Of particular interest are "scanlated" (scanned + translated) copies that make episodes of popular manga available worldwide almost as soon as they have been released for sale in Japan, although with a noticeable drop in production quality[27]. The effect of scanlating is that fans around the world no longer suffer a time lag in keeping current with the latest in Japanese popular culture. This practice also creates pressure on publishers who have begun providing a legal option of fee-based, legal access to online manga in some case. This contributes to timely availability as well.

b) Scholarly Resources for Manga Studies

As with fan-oriented resources, digital library development for manga studies is severely restricted due to copyright limitations. Only a few early manga and predecessors of manga have been digitized, such as the twelfth century scroll, *Choju Jinbutsu Giga* [5] and a few manga in the Kindai Digital Library [17].

The Japan Society for Studies in Cartoon and Comics (Nihon Manga Gakkai) was founded in 2001 responding to a need to "actively encourage the organization and maintenance of historical documents, the collection and exchange of relevant information, and the creation of an environment for interaction among a variety of individuals, including researchers from abroad," and with a goal of creating a forum for people who have posed the following question to themselves, 'What has manga meant to us in the past, what is it to us now, what will it become in the future?"[14]

The society offers two databases to promote manga studies. Its Search Engine for Books about Manga [19] provides bibliographic searches for the titles of reference works and books about manga held by twelve research libraries in Japan, while Database of Manga Magazines [20] is a periodical index to thirty-five manga magazines held by the same libraries. These databases support scholarly access to *manga* at an unprecedented level. While manga themselves sometimes remain in print for an extended period or time or are reissued, works about manga go out of print quickly and subsequently are hard to obtain. Further, manga magazines are routinely discarded, so even issues that once were available in millions of copies are now scarce. Since not all the catalogs of these twelve libraries are available online, and popular culture materials are not routinely collected by academic libraries, the contribution of these two bibliographic resources has truly opened up the field to scholarly research, even without the availability of digital libraries per se.

Since *manga* and *anime* were not collected by libraries – or even museums – until fairly recently, neither were they indexed or cataloged as scholarly materials. Only with the advent of digital networks is this literature coming under some kind of control.

5 Conclusion

This study has shown considerable variation among the kinds of access resources being constructed, although only three fields were surveyed. Poetry resources are so abundant as to be overwhelming, although access resources created by scholars are starting to bear common characteristics, such as the availability of season word indexes. The company history field is more fragmented, with most materials still in printed format and access resources reflecting that situation. Finally, although copyright restrictions appear to have created insurmountable impediments to digital library growth for manga studies, neither fans nor scholars have been deterred by the limitations and have constructed useful access resources even in the absence of true digital libraries. The trend to make fee-based access to online manga available is emerging with a robust support structure already in place that will continue to facilitate access.

Digital library development in Japan is now at a stage when scholars are active in constructing access resources. Carole L. Palmer calls for research libraries to "provide services to assist researchers in these activities and integrate the digital resources they create in the new complex of digital access" [24]. To some extent this also has started to happen in Japan, with the databases of Professor Katsuhiro Seta at the International Research Center for Japanese Studies, the newspaper scrapbooks of Professor Yuzo Sakanishi at Kobe University, the images databases of resources collected by Eiichi Shibusawa's heirs in the digital archives of the National Institute of Japanese Literature, and the search engines created by the Japan Society for Studies in Cartoon and Comics.

While resources in Japanese digital libraries are available for access, bibliographers and reference librarians have roles to play in bringing attention to these resources through web sites and bibliographic instruction. In particular, awareness of scholarly access resources reveals new and improved ways of doing research. The major investment of time and money undoubtedly goes into the actual digitization of resources, but in some cases the provision of effective access resources constructed with input from scholars is what makes the digital library usable, opening up its treasures for scholars around the world.

References

1. Anime News Network: http://www.animenewsnetwork.com
2. Aozora Bunko: http://www.aozora.gr.jp/index.html
3. Business Archives Association: http://www.baa.gr.jp/files/06.html
4. Canon: Kyanon Kamerashi. http://www.canon.co.jp/Camera-muse/history/canon_story/f_index.html
5. Choju Jinbutsu Giga: http://akituya.gooside.com/choujyu_allall.htm
6. Crane,G.: What Do You Do with a Million Books? D-Lib Magazine 12:3 (March 2006). http://www.dlib.org/dlib/march06/crane/03crane.html
7. Database Shusei: http://www.ne.jp/asahi/coffee/house/DB/
8. Digital Archive Portal (National Diet Library): : http://www.dap.ndl.go.jp/home
9. Dnavi (National Diet Library) : http://dnavi.ndl.go.jp
10. Factiva (Dow Jones & Reuters): http://www.factiva.com
11. Gendai Haiku Detabesu (Modern Haiku Association): http://www.haiku-data.jp/
12. Honda Giken: Kataritsugitai Koto Charenji no Gojunen: http://www.honda.co.jp/50years-history/
13. Index to Resources on Internet (University of Tokyo Library): http://resource.lib.u-tokyo.ac.jp/iri/url_search.cgi?S_flg
14. Japan Society for Studies in Cartoon and Comics (Nihon Manga Gakkai)http://www.kyoto-seika.ac.jp/hyogen/gaikoku/English.htm
15. Japanese Text Initiative (University of Virginia):http://etext.lib.virginia.edu/japanese/
16. Kigo Search Engine (International Research Center for Japanese Studies)http://www.nichibun.ac.jp/graphicversion/dbase/kigo_e.html
17. Kindai Digital Library (National Diet Library):http://kindai.ndl.go.jp/BISmplSearch.php
18. Kobe Daigaku Senzenki Shinbun Keizai Kiji Bunko Detabesu (Kobe University): http://www.lib.kobe-u.ac.jp/sinbun/e-index.html http://www.lib.kobe-u.ac.jp/sinbun/e-gaiyou.html
19. Manga Kanren Shoseki Kensaku (Japan Society for Studies in Cartoon and Comics): http://ww1.yes.ne.jp/akitanet/shosekikensaku.htm
20. Manga Zasshi Detabesu (Japan Society for Studies in Cartoon and Comics): http://ww1.yes.ne.jp/akitanet/Default.htm
21. Murahashi, Katsuko. Shashi no kenkyu. Tokyo: Diamond, 2002.
22. Murata Shashi: http://www.murata.co.jp/company/enkaku/index.html
23. Nihon Jitsugyoshi Hakubutsukan Setsuritsu Junbishitsu Kyuzo Kaiga Detabesu (National Institute of Japanese Literature): http://archives2.nijl.ac.jp/jkdb-index.htm
24. Palmer, C. L.: Scholarly Work and the Shaping of Digital Access. JASIST 56:11 (September 2005), 1140-1153. (DOI: 10.1002/asi.20204)
25. Panasonic Shashi: http://panasonic.co.jp/company/history/index.html
26. Resource Center for the History of Entrepreneurship (Shibusawa Eiichi Memorial Foundation): http://www.shibusawa.or.jp/center/shashi/shashi05.html
27. Scanlation. Wikipedia http://en.wikipedia.org/wiki/Scanlation (accessed 07/01/2006)
28. Search Engine for Chronological Data(International Research Center for Japanese Studies): http://www.nichibun.ac.jp/graphicversion/dbase/jidai_e.html
29. Sharp Shashi:http://www.sharp.co.jp/corporate/info/history/h_company/index.html
30. Shiseido Monogatari: http://www.shiseido.co.jp/story/html/index.htm
31. Tezuka Osamu @ World: http://en.tezuka.co.jp/home.html
32. Topical Haiku Dictionary (University of Virginia)http://etext.lib.virginia.edu/japanese/haiku/saijiki/
33. Zouhai (Zoshoku Suru Haiku Saijiki Kensaku): http://zouhai.com/kigo.html

Towards Ontology Enrichment with Treatment Relations Extracted from Medical Abstracts

Chew-Hung Lee[1], Jin-Cheon Na[2], and Christopher Khoo[2]

[1] DSO National Laboratories,
20 Science Park Drive, Singapore 118230, Singapore
LChewHun@dso.org.sg
[2] Division of Information Studies, School of Communication & Information,
Nanyang Technological University,
31 Nanyang Link, Singapore 637718, Singapore
{tjcna, assgkhoo}@ntu.edu.sg

Abstract. In this paper, we present the results of experiments identifying the drug treatment relation and drug treatment attributes like dosage, treatment frequency and duration from abstracts of medical publications using linguistic patterns. The approach uses an automatic linguistic pattern construction algorithm after the dataset has been semantically annotated. The automatically constructed patterns were able to identify treatment relations and their attributes with varying success. We observe that the simple (or naïve) treatment patterns performs much better than the non-naïve treatment patterns in identifying sentences with drug treatment relationship in both cancer and non-cancer drug therapy domain. However the drug dosage, frequency and duration patterns performed much better in the identification of relationships in the cancer drug therapy domain than the non-cancer drug therapy domain.

1 Introduction

Treatment is an important causal relation in medicine describing the therapeutic effects of various regimes.Automatically acquiring this knowledge and organizing it into a digital library would help medical practitioners to keep abreast of new treatments reported in the literature. It would also facilitates the discovery of novel treatments like the linkage between migraine and the lack of magnesium [1].

An ontology as a formal specification of knowledge is a means of organizing the medical information in the digital library. However, building an ontology for a medical digital library is not a trivial task, requiring a significant amount of time and effort [2,3]. A reasonably sized ontology would contain thousands of concepts and relationships in addition to the set of axioms [4].

Our proposal for reducing the efforts in building an ontology is to start with a small (or seed) ontology and enrich it with concepts and semantic relations acquired from text. Our objective in this study is to develop a method where treatment information can be identified and extracted from medical abstracts.

S. Sugimoto et al. (Eds.): ICADL 2006, LNCS 4312, pp. 419–428, 2006.

Besides data mining approaches [5,6], researchers have also suggested using a linguistics-based approach [7]. Linguistics-based research studies the natural language structure of the textual source, identifying syntactic elements (e.g. nouns, verbs, etc.) in the sentences and their dependencies with each other. The semantic class of some of these elements can also be identified through a linguistics study.

A linguistic pattern like "@Drug is @Verb to @Disease" contains fragments of a sentence, syntactic tags (e.g. verbs) and semantic classes (e.g. drug, disease). A sentence matched by a pattern might contain the semantic relation associated with the pattern. In this paper, we focus on producing linguistic patterns for identifying and extracting the drug treatment relation and drug treatment attributes like dosage, treatment frequency and duration using our implementation of the WHISK algorithm [8].

The WHISK algorithm has been designed to work with structured, semi-structured (e.g. rental ads, medical records) as well as free text (corporate annoucements). The performance of WHISK varies in the free text domain depending on how varied is the context surrounding the phrases of interest (e.g. drugs, diseases). It is not clear if the drug therapy domain would yield high quality patterns or if the drug therapy patterns from one disease domain can be reused in a different disease domain.

The rest of the paper is organized as follows. The experimental setup as well as the research approach are briefly sketched in Section 2. The linguistic patterns constructed from one domain (breast cancer) are successively applied to more generic domains (cancer, non-cancer) and the results of these experiments are presented in Section 3. In Section 4, we present our conclusion and also highlight the future directions for this study.

2   Research Approach

Our study begins with annotating the abstracts of medical publications. The abstracts are first segmented into sentences and the syntactic elements (e.g. nouns, verbs) identified using linguistic analysis. Next, we combine and tagged the syntactic elements with semantic classes derived from the concepts and relations in the seed ontology. Next, the annotated sentences and the terms to be identified are passed to the WHISK algorithm for the pattern construction phase. The set of patterns constructed by WHISK from the annotated sentences are subsequently pruned using a validation set. Patterns with a Laplacian error above a pre-determined threshold are dropped from the final pattern set. The Laplacian error metric is defined as

$$L = \frac{Num_{err} + 1}{Num_{ext} + 1}$$

where L is the Laplacian error, Num_{err} is the number of errors in the matches and Num_{ext} is the number of matches. A pattern with the most number of matches and the least number of errors has the lowest Laplacian error.

In this study, we constructed five sets of patterns in the domain of breast cancer therapy using the training data sets listed in Table 1.

Table 1. Training data sets

Training Data Set	Domain of Identification Patterns	Total No. of Sentences	Remarks
1	Drug Treatment	112	Abstracts from Breast Cancer Drug Therapy
2	Drug Dosage	169	Abstracts from Breast Cancer Drug Administration
3	Drug Treatment Frequency	167	Abstracts from Breast Cancer Drug Administration
4	Drug Treatment Duration	97	Abstracts from Breast Cancer Drug Administration

The first training data set is used to construct two sets of drug treatment patterns, one set containing simple (or naïve) patterns and the other set containing more complex patterns. The remaining training data sets are used to construct three sets of patterns identifying different aspects of drug therapy, namely the drug dosage, frequency and duration of the drug treatment.

Table 2 lists the data sets used in evaluating the effectiveness of the breast cancer drug therapy patterns in more general domains. The first test data set is in the domain of cancer drug therapy. As there are not enough sentences describing drug dosages, frequency and duration of treatments, a second test data was created from the abstracts of drug administration articles. In addition, we constructed two additional test data sets (test data set 3 and test data set 4) using the abstracts of medical publications from the drug therapy and drug administration of four different diseases (asthma, dementia, heart attack and migraine).

Table 2. Test data sets

Test Data Set	Domain	Total No. of Abstracts	Remarks
1	Cancer Drug Therapy	30	Used to test treatment patterns
2	Cancer Drug Administration	30	Used to test treatment attribute patterns
3	Non-cancer Drug Therapy	60	Asthma (15), Dementia (15), Heart Attack (15), Migraine (15) Used to test treatment patterns
4	Non-cancer Drug Administration	60	Asthma (15), Dementia (15), Heart Attack (15), Migraine (15) Used to test treatment attribute patterns

3   Experiments

3.1   Treatment Patterns

The WHISK algorithm constructed four linguistic patterns from the training set 1. These patterns and the computed Laplacian error metric are shown in Table 3.

Table 3. Top WHISK patterns for treatment

Pattern	Template	Lap. Error	Cov.
(@Drug)(@Disease)*	Tr {Drg $1} {Dis $2}	0.01	68
(@Disease)(@Drug)*	Tr {Dis $1} {Drg $2}	0.02	42
*advanced (*) using*inhibitor (*).*	Tr {Dis $1} {Drg $2}	0.5	1
*of (*) changes*treatment in (*) .*	Tr {Drg $1} {Dis $2}	0.5	1

Note: In the linguistic patterns constructed by the WHISK algorithm, '*' is used as wildcard that matches any number of text characters including white spaces (e.g. tab character, space character). The brackets '(' and ')' marks a match boundary that is used to fill a slot as defined in the template. The '@' character indicates the usage of a semantic class. The Perl Back References $1 and $2 indicates the first slot value marker and the second slot value marker

The first pattern "*(@Drug)*(@Disease)*" matches a sentence like "The rise of @Drug[aromatase inhibitors]Drug changes our habits in hormonal treatment in @Disease[breast cancer]Disease ." where a drug precedes a disease. "@Drug[", "]Drug", "@Disease[", "]Disease" are annotations added to the sentence to mark phrases with either the semantic class of "Drug" or "Disease". Likewise, the second pattern "*(@Disease)*(@Drug)*" matches a sentence where a disease precedes a drug. In total, these two patterns covers 110 out of 112 training sentences or 98% of the training data set suggesting that the naïve approach of identifying a treatment relation solely by the presence of a drug and a disease in the sentence is sufficient.

In addition, we also constructed a set of linguistic patterns without the two naïve patterns for comparison. The top five patterns with the lowest Laplacian error from this new set are shown in Table 4. The new set of patterns was more varied and emphasizes the context surrounding the drug used in the treatment of a disease. For example, the semantic class of "Drug" can be used to describe a treatment ("@Drug[docetaxel]Drug treatment", "@Drug[taxane]Drug -based chemotherapy").

Table 4. Top five non-naïve WHISK patterns for treatment

Pattern	Template	Lap. Error	Cov.
(@Drug) is(@Disease)*	Tr {Drg $1} {Dis $2}	0.06	16
(@Drug) treatment(@Disease)*	Tr {Drg $1} {Dis $2}	0.1	14
*(@Disease)*with (@Drug) -based*	Tr {Dis $1} {Drg $2}	0.25	3
BACKGROUND: (@Drug) ,, (@Disease) ,*	Tr {Drg $1} {Dis $2}	0.3	2
*(@Drug)*recurrent and (@Disease) *	Tr {Drg $1} {Dis $2}	0.3	2

The two sets of patterns (naïve and complex treatment) were applied to test data set 1. The results are shown in Table 5 and Table 6. It can be seen from these results that the naïve set of patterns performed much better in identifying sentences with treatment relationship than the non-naïve set of patterns.

Table 5 shows the result of applying the patterns to individual sentences in the test data sets while Table 6 shows the result of applying the patterns to pairs of consecutive sentences in the test data sets. As the pairs of consecutive sentences also contains single sentences that are matched by the patterns, we discount these matches and only report matches that span two sentences. There are 326 individual sentences and 294 pairs of consecutive sentences in the test data sets. 33 individual sentences and 50 pairs of the consecutive sentences contain the treatment relationship.

We measure the effectiveness using the precision, recall and F measures. Precision is computed as the percentage of the matching sentences that have treatment relationship. Recall is computed as the percentage of the sentences in the test data set with treatment relationship that are found in the matching sentences. The F-measure is defined simply as

$$F = \frac{2 * p * r}{p + r}$$

where p is the precision measure and r is the recall measure. The higher the F measure, the better is the pattern set in indentifying sentences with the treatment relationship.

Table 5. Application of Treatment Patterns on Cancer Drug Therapy Sentences (Single Sentence)

Pattern Set	No. of Sentences	No. of Treat Sentences	No. of Matches	No. of Correct Matches	Precision (%)	Recall (%)	F
Naive Treat	326	33	31	31	100	93.9	0.969
Non-naïve Treat	326	33	3	3	100	9.1	0.167

Table 6. Application of Treatment Patterns on Cancer Drug Therapy Sentences (Sentence Pair)

Pattern Set	No. of Sen. Pairs	No. of Treat Sen. Pairs	No. of Matches	No. of Correct Matches	Precision (%)	Recall (%)	F
Naive Treat	294	50	63	49	77.8	98	0.867
Non-naïve Treat	294	50	6	4	66.7	8	0.143

As the drug described in one sentence may not be used in the treatment of a disease in a different sentence, the patterns have lower precision when applied to consecutive sentences as compared to single sentences. From Table 6, we can see that the naïve patterns produce some wrong matches (14 out of 63) supporting this observation. As we have only low number of matches for the non-naïve patterns, using the precision measure for comparison may not be effective. For example, in Table 6, each wrong match for the non-naïve patterns is a difference of 16%. Using the F-measure to balance the precision measure with the recall measure would be a fairer comparison.

Figure 1 shows a graph of the F-measure from Table 5 and Table 6. It can be seen that the F-measure of the naïve treatment patterns is much higher in each of the experiments than the non-naïve treatment patterns. We observe from this result that the set of naïve treatment patterns were better in identifying sentences in the domain of cancer drug therapy with the treatment relationship.

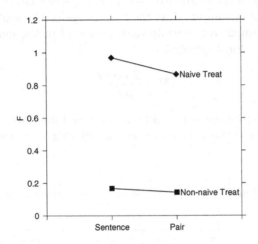

Fig. 1. F-measure of Treatment Patterns

3.2 Treatment Attribute Patterns

Dosage Patterns. The WHISK algorithm was applied to a set of sentences selected from the abstracts of medical publications relating to breast cancer drug administration (training data set 2) in order to create a set of patterns for identifying sentences with the dosage of drug administration. These sentences contain a phrase indicating the dosage of the drug administration (e.g. 500 mg / m2, medium-dose) and the drug that was administered.

The top five patterns with the lowest Laplacian error are shown in Table 7. This table shows that dosage is indicated by a number followed by the unit of measurement for dosage (e.g. mg per metres squared). The top two patterns are very similar, differing only in the presence of a space. This illustrates a weakness of the WHISK algorithm. While the WHISK algorithm is good at constructing the context surrounding the matches for the slots, it is poor at constructing a regular expression to be used as a match in the slot. This would lead to a myriad of patterns that differ only by a trivial presence or absence of spaces.

Table 7. Top five WHISK patterns for drug treatment dosages

Pattern	Template	Laplacian Error	Coverage
(@Drug)(@Num mg / m2)*	DA {Drug $1} {Dose $2}	0.04	20
(@Drug)(@Num mg/ m2)*	DA {Drug $1} {Dose $2}	0.17	57
(high-dose)(@Drug)*	DA {Dose $1} {Drug $2}	0.25	3
(@Drug)(@Num mg/ kg)*	DA {Drug $1} {Dose $2}	0.33	14
(@Drug)(@Num U)*	DA {Drug $1} {Dose $2}	0.33	2

Frequency Patterns. The WHISK algorithm was also applied to a different set of sentences selected from the abstracts of medical publications relating to breast cancer drug administration (training data set 3) in order to create a set of patterns for identifying sentences with the frequency of drug administration. These sentences contain a phrase indicating the frequency of the drug adminis-tration (e.g. weekly, once daily) and the drug that was administered.

The top five patterns with the lowest Laplacian error are shown in Table 8. These patterns show that drug treatment frequency are often indicated by words of time (e.g. daily, weekly, yearly) and words indicating frequencies (e.g. once, twice). Although the second pattern is a generalisation of the fourth pattern, WHISK considers the two patterns as unique as WHISK does not use regular expression to define the match in a slot. Hence a match of "weekly" is considered different from a match of "biweekly".

Table 8. Top five WHISK patterns for drug treatment frequencies

Pattern	Template	Lap. Error	Cov.
(@Drug)(twice daily)*	DA {Drug $1} {Freq $2}	0.03	26
(weekly)(@Drug)*	DA {Freq $1} {Drug $2}	0.16	82
(@Drug)(once weekly)*	DA {Drug $1} {Freq $2}	0.2	4
(biweekly)(@Drug)*	DA {Freq $1} {Drug $2}	0.25	3
to (@Drug)(daily)*	DA {Drug $1} {Freq $2}	0.25	3

Duration Patterns. The WHISK algorithm was also applied to a different set of sentences selected from the abstracts of medical publications relating to breast cancer drug administration (training data set 4) in order to create a set of pat-terns for identifying sentences with the duration of drug administration. These sentences contain a phrase indicating the duration of the drug administration (e.g. six cycles, 2 months) and the drug that was administered.

The top five patterns with the lowest Laplacian error are shown in Table 9. The patterns for duration of treatment were more varied. Besides words of time (e.g. weeks, months, years), there are other words like "cycles" used to indicate durations. In addition to the use of numerals (e.g. 6) for indicating the quantity of time, words were also used (e.g. six). There are also patterns like "*consisted of (*) of*(@Drug)*" where the context is more prominent as well as patterns like "*@Disease received (@Drug)*for (*).*" where semantic classes are found in the context.

Table 9. Top five WHISK patterns for drug treatment duration

Pattern	Template	Lap. Error	Cov.
(@Drug)(@Num cycles)*	DA {Drug $1} {Dur $2}	0.25	7
(@Num cycles)(@Drug)*	DA {Dur $1} {Drug $2}	0.25	11
(@Drug)(@Num months)*	DA {Drug $1} {Dur $2}	0.25	3
(@Num years)(@Drug)*	DA {Dur $1} {Drug $2}	0.33	14
(six cycles)(@Drug)*	DA {Dur $1} {Drug $2}	0.33	5

4   Comparing Cancer and Non-cancer Drug Therapy Domains

The results of identifying sentences with drug treatment relationship and drug treatment attributes are plotted in Figure 2. The first two sets of drug treatment patterns were applied to test data set 1 (cancer) and test data set 3 (non-cancer) to determine the effectiveness of patterns constructed from the breast cancer domain in identifying sentences with the drug treatment relationship from other cancer and non-cancer domains. Similarly, the last three sets of drug treatment attributes patterns were applied to test data set 2 (cancer) and test data set 4 (non-cancer) to determine the effectiveness of patterns in identifying sentences with the drug treatment attributes (dosage, frequency and duration).

From this graph, we can see that the five set of patterns were more suitable for the cancer drug therapy domain. However, the naïve treatment patterns were just as effective for the cancer drug therapy and the non-cancer drug therapy domain. On the other hand, the drug therapy duration patterns performed very badly on the non-cancer drug therapy domain.

4.1   Error Analysis

An error analysis of the wrong matches shows that the some patterns are too generic to be applicable for identifying sentences with treatment attributes. For example, in the patterns used for identifying the duration of the drug therapy, we have a pattern "*after (*) of*(@Drug)*" identify the sentence "AIM OF THE PRESENT STUDY: to evaluate the headaches occurring after administration of therapeutic dose of @Drug[sublingual nitroglycerin]Drug , in migraineurs and controls." as a sentence containing the duration of the drug therapy. As we

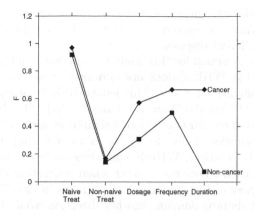

Fig. 2. Comparison of Cancer and Non-Cancer Drug Therapy Domains (Single Sentence)

can see, often the phrase found between "after" and "of" does not describe the duration of the drug therapy but rather describes the administration or initiation of the treatment. In another example, a sentence matched by the pattern "*(@Drug)*(@Num years)*" is "ACIP emphasized that the @Disease[influenza]Disease @Drug[vaccine]Drug was safe for breastfeeding mothers and their infants and that household contacts of children aged<@Num[2]Num years also should be vaccinated.". In this case, "@Num years" is not the period of the treatment but rather it is the age of the patients involved in the medical study.

One possible way of improving the patterns is to combine the two patterns. This will add a time period to the patterns with a wildcard in the match for the duration slot and a context to the time period in the other patterns. For example, we can combine the patterns "*after (*) of*(@Drug)*" and "*(@Drug)*(@Num years)*" to produce "*after (@Num years) of*(@Drug)*". Applying this combination approach applied to the patterns used to identify duration of the drug therapy of sentences in the non-cancer drug administration domain resulted in a precision of 20% and a recall of 16%. The computed F-measure score is 0.17, a slight improvement over the current result of 0.074. The patterns would need to be further improved for subsequent experiments.

5 Conclusion

In this study, the linguistic patterns constructed by the WHISK algorithm were able to identify treatment relations and their attributes with varying success. The WHISK algorithm was able to construct both naïve patterns (e.g. "*(@Drug)*(@Disease)") as well as more complex patterns (e.g. "*to (@Drug)* (daily)*"). The WHISK algorithm was sensitive to the context where the matches (or user-defined tags) were situated. Most of the patterns show that the context does not contribute to the identification of the relationships. However, some patterns include words from the context for more accurate identification of relations. The results also indicate that the drug therapy domain is closer to the ideal domain where the patterns constructed by WHISK have high precision and recall across different diseases.

A possible future direction for this study is to improve the WHISK algorithm. We have noticed that WHISK does not generate or use regular expression in the definition of matches for a slot. This led WHISK to generate patterns that are similar (e.g. "*(@Drug)*(@Num mg / m2)*" and "*(@Drug)*(@Num mg/ m2"). The inclusion of regular expression in definition of matches for a slot would enable WHISK to consider more closely the context during the construction of the patterns. At the moment, WHISK considers similar patterns as dissimilar and unique, thus would ignore the context when generating these patterns.

Given the weakness of the current set of patterns in identifying relationships in non-cancer drug therapy domain, another direction would be to augment the set of identication patterns with patterns that are constructed from non-cancer drug therapy domain. Another approach would be to combine the existing set of patterns, merging the matches for the slots in some patterns with the context in other patterns. Besides this, we can also construct patterns for other forms of therapy like radiation treatment and surgery, each with its own treatment attributes.

References

1. Swanson, D.R.: Migraine and magnesium: Eleven neglected connections. Perspectives in Biology and Medicine **31**(4) (1988) 526–557
2. Hartel, F.W., de Coronado, S., Dionne, R., Fragoso, G., Golbeck, J.: Modeling a Description Logic Vocabulary for Cancer Research. Journal of Biomedical Informatics **38**(2) (2005)
3. Golbeck, J., Fragoso, G., Hartel, F., Hendler, J., Parsia, B., Oberthaler, J.: The National Cancer Institute's Thesaurus and Ontology. Journal of Web Semantics **1**(1) (2003) 75–80
4. Hahn, U., Schulz, S.: Building a very large ontology from medical thesauri. In: Handbook on Ontologies. Springer-Verlag, Berlin (2004) 133–150
5. Kavalec, M., Svátek, V.: Relation labelling in ontology learning: Experiments with semantically tagged corpus. In: Proceedings of the EKAW 2004 Workshop on the Application of Language and Semantic Technologies to support Knowledge Management Processes, Heidelberg, Germany, Springer-Verlag (2004)
6. Lee, C.H., Na, J.C., Khoo, C.: Ontology learning for medical digital libraries. In: Proceedings of the 6th International Conference on Asian Digital Libraries (ICADL), Heidelberg, Germany, Springer-Verlag (2003) 302–305
7. Aussenac-Gilles, N., Biébow, B., Szulman, S.: Revisiting ontology design: A method based on corpus analysis. In: Proceedings of the 12th International Conference on Knowledge Engineering and Knowledge Management (EKAW 2000). (2000) 172–188
8. Soderland, S.: Learning information extraction rules for semi-structured and free text. Machine Learning **34**(1-3) (1999) 233–272

Use and Linkage of Source and Output Repositories and the Expectations of the Chemistry Research Community About Their Use

Panayiota Polydoratou

Imperial College London
South Kensington Campus
London SW7 2AZ, UK
p.polydoratou@imperial.ac.uk

Abstract. This paper presents findings from a questionnaire survey that aimed to identify the issues around the use and linkage of source and output repositories and the expectations of the chemistry research community about their use. In the context of the StORe project (http://jiscstore.jot.com/ WikiHome), which sought to develop new ways of linking academic publications with repositories of research data, thirty eight (38) members of academic and research staff from institutions across the UK provided valuable feedback regarding the nature of the research that they conduct, the type of data that they produce, the sharing and availability of research data and the use and expectations of source and output repositories.

1 Introduction

The StORe: Source-to-Output Repositories project (http://jiscstore.jot.com/ WikiHome), funded by the Joint Information Systems Committee (JISC, http://www. jisc.ac.uk/) is a collaboration between seven universities across the UK and the Johns Hopkins University in the USA, who are focusing on seven disciplines, including chemistry. The project sought to develop new ways of linking academic publications to repositories of research data. One of the project deliverables are published surveys of researchers that identify workflows and norms in the use of source and output repositories, including common attributes across disciplines, the functional enhancements to repositories that are considered to be desirable and perceived problems in the use of repositories.[1]

This paper presents findings from an online questionnaire survey that aimed to identify the issues around the use and linkage of source and output repositories and the expectations of the chemistry research community about their use and is relevant to the above mentioned deliverable of the StORe project. The respondents to the questionnaire survey provided feedback about how useful or not they considered the linking of research data to publications, the types of data they produced and

---

[1] StORe project description. Available at: http://jiscstore.jot.com/WikiHome (Last accessed 04/09/2006).

S. Sugimoto et al. (Eds.): ICADL 2006, LNCS 4312, pp. 429–438, 2006.
© Springer-Verlag Berlin Heidelberg 2006

the formats they are saved, the level of metadata that is considered important and the assignment of metadata. Furthermore they indicated perceived barriers and advantages in the sharing and access of their data and their preferred routes of searching at output repositories.

2 Definitions

Several terms were used in the questionnaire survey and throughout this paper. They are defined as:

- **Repository.** A repository is a store where electronic data, databases or digital files have been deposited, usually with the intention of enabling their access or distribution over a network.
- **Source repository.** A database that contains primary research data on which a publication will eventually be based.
- **Output repository.** A database that contains research publications, the published outcome of the research. Output repositories can function at an institutional, regional, or global level. They maybe organized accordingly to publication type (theses, working papers, post prints, etc.). They may include the commercial repositories maintained by publishers, since it can be argued that online journal services such as ScienceDirect qualify as output repositories.[2]

3 Literature Review

"The most comprehensive and reliable source of chemical and physical property data is the chemistry literature. In many cases a literature search may be the best option for finding this type of data" (NIST Data Gateway, http://webbook.nist.gov/chemistry/faq.html). Several studies had identified the extensive use that chemists make of the literature and as a research community they are considered to be those with the highest reading rates among scientists (Tenopir & King, 2002). Chemistry is a science with a long and established history. Some of the characteristics of chemistry research include its interdisciplinary nature, the production of vast amounts of data that lead to a comprehensive literature in which the relevance of the articles does not decline over the years, and the use of information technology to conduct research.

Despite this, there is a generalization that has followed chemists over the years, citing that in general they are reluctant in using information systems. More than 10 years ago, Philip and Cunningham in a British Library Research and Development study, surveyed chemists across the UK to find out about the availability and the use of automated chemical information systems. The study found that more than half of the respondents who did not make use of chemical information systems claimed this was because they did not have a need for them. Those that were thought to make the most extensive use of automated chemical information were theoretical chemists, for whom it was noted that *although some physical chemists would have need for*

---

[2] StORe Q. Screenshots of final draft. Available at: http://jiscstore.jot.com/WikiHome/SurveyPhase/StORe%2BQ.ppt?revision=1#256,1,StORe Q (Last accessed 04/09/2006).

information based on chemical structures, the majority would not, as their information would be suited to alpha-numeric format".

Developments that the e-science programme (http://www.rcuk.ac.uk/escience/) initiated since its inception in 2001 have been well documented in the literature, in particularly for chemistry by the eBank project (http://www.ukoln.ac.uk/projects/ebank-uk/) which addressed the role of repositories in linking research data to peer reviewed papers and how such a service has an impact in the scholarly communication and publication (Lyon, 2003; Lyon et al, 2004). Coles and colleagues (2006) described how the UK National Crystallography Service has developed the eCrystals repository in which electronic files that are produced in the process of the crystal structure determination are captured and validated and also are assigned relevant metadata that is automatically generated and aim to support publication and dissemination of the information. Other relevant projects that were initiated by the e-science programme were the Comb-e-Chem (http://www.combechem.org/) and the ECSES (http://www.it-innovation.soton.ac.uk/research/grid/comb_e_chem.shtml). They both run by the iT Innovation research centre (http://www.it-innovation.soton.ac.uk/) at the University of Southampton and aimed to *"develop an e-Science testbed that integrates existing structure and property data sources within a grid-based information-and knowledge-sharing environment".*[3]

4 Methods

The StORe project (http://jiscstore.jot.com/WikiHome) employed two methods to gather information about the use and the linkage of source and output repositories, with regard to researchers working in seven scientific domains. These methods were: a) an online questionnaire survey and b) interviews with members of academic staff from institutions across the UK. This paper presents the results from the questionnaire survey among chemistry researchers.

The questionnaire survey was launched on the 13th March and closed on 21st April 2006. It was publicized among 728 members of the chemistry research community at the following universities: Imperial College London, Bristol University, Cambridge University, Southampton University, University of Durham, University of Oxford, and University College London. The target group included academic and research staff engaged in chemistry research and wherever the information was available, postgraduate research students were also contacted.

For the purpose of this study the areas identified in the 2001 RAE assessment in the field of chemistry were used to identify members of staff and students conducting research in each field. The intention was to obtain, if possible, representative examples of research patterns from all chemistry research fields. Thirty eight people responded to the questionnaire survey representing 10% of the overall response that the questionnaire received and 5.2% within chemistry itself. The low response has been attributed to several factors such as survey fatigue, the timing of the survey which coincided with the exam period and then the Easter holiday and the fact that

---

[3] CombeChem. About CombeChem. Information available at: http://www.combechem.org/about.php (Last accessed 04/09/2006).

academic community did not appear to be familiar with JISC, digital repositories or repositories in general.[4]

5 Results

The online questionnaire comprised four sections that are discussed below. These were preceded by an introductory section that aimed to gather information relevant to demographic characteristics of the researchers, such as the scientific domain they represented, their employing organisation, their occupation and contact details, if they wished to provide them. Almost half of the response (47%) came from postgraduate research students. 40% of the responses came from academic staff and the remaining 13% represented responses by postdoctoral researchers, research assistants and contracted researchers. Undergraduate students were not targeted as a group and therefore there was no response received from them. Also, there was no response from any independent researchers. Analytically the response is presented in the following table.

Table 1. Response to the questionnaire survey by role of the respondents

Role:	Number of respondents	%
Academic staff	15	**39.5**
Research Assistants	2	**5.3**
Postgraduate students	18	**47.3**
Undergraduate students	0	**0**
Contract Researchers	1	**2.6**
Independent Researchers	0	**0**
Other (*please insert*)	2	**5.3**
Total	**38**	**100**

5.1 Section A. The Need for Linking Repositories

The first part of the questionnaire comprised questions that aimed to identify the need for linking source and output repositories. The respondents were invited to indicate how advantageous it would be for their research if they had the ability to link from primary research data to their published outputs and vice versa. Some examples of potential future use included the ability to count actual papers' downloads and therefore argue that the impact of a research paper had been increased. Also, the ability to track the timeline in the process and outcome of a given set of research data. Or even link a data set to researchers that had downloaded and used it for their own research.

The majority of the chemistry respondents noted that the ability to link from the published outcome of the research to the primary research data would be either a significant advantage to their work (57%) or a useful feature (29%). Only one of the respondents replied that they were not sure of the point of the survey as they had only

---

[4] Pryor, Graham. Linking research papers and research data: possibilities for a generic solution. Presentation at the DRP Workshop - StORe at WWW06. http://jiscstore.jot.com/WikiHome/DisseminationPages/WWW06-SSVY.ppt (Last accessed 04/09/2006).

recently commenced their doctoral studies and they were unable to judge the significance such a facility would have for their research. The reverse of this facility, to be able to link from a source repository to the published outcome of the research was greeted by almost half of the respondents (41%) as a significant advantage. Another third (33%) indicated that this option would be useful for them but not of major significance (Figure 1).

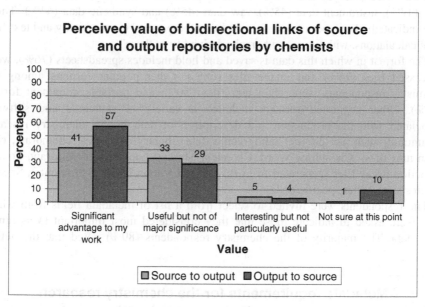

Fig. 1. Perceived value of bidirectional links of source and output repositories – Chemistry research

More than half of the chemists that were surveyed (65%) had not used a repository before and they were not familiar with the idea of open access repositories in general. They noted thought that they thought the ability to be able to link from the primary research dataset to the published outcome of the research could be either a significant advantage for their work or useful but not of major significance. Those who had used a source or output repository on a frequent basis or on several occasions thought again that it would be a significant advantage for their work. In general, academic staff although they considered the use of bidirectional links between repositories as either significant or useful for their research they tended to specify mainly for application and use by their students rather than themselves.

5.2 Section B. Research Data and Source Repositories

The second part of the questionnaire aimed to gain some understanding about the type of data that chemists produce and the formats in which it is stored. Such information could prove useful to people working in the set up of repositories in general as it provides useful insight of data types produced and could indicate software requirements for the deposition and retrieval such information. The questionnaire respondents were also asked to denote what metadata is assigned to their data and at what stage. The respondents to the questionnaire were invited to select from a range of different types of source data that they generate in their research field. The dominant types of data in the chemistry domain were SPECTRA (84%) and drawings and plots (84%). Other types of data that were noted by almost half of the respondents were images (61%), text based data (47%), instrument data (45%), raw data (45%) and synthetic data (44%). Those who indicated other types of data specified that these were "mainly binary and text files from calculations, with figures and graphs derived from these".

The format in which this data is saved and held includes spreadsheets (76%), word processed files (74%) and image files (68%). Other popular formats among the chemistry respondents were plain text files (50%) and portable document format (42%). Other suggested formats included a variety of standards and software associated with the production and description of data in the chemistry research community such as: .cif (crystallographic data), binary data files, chemdraw, cdx. xwin nmr files, Chemdraw Word, Chemical Markup Language, corel draw, Fourier induction decay files (generated from Bruker and Varian NMR instruments), Spectra are in spectrometer specific code.

The respondents were invited to select from a list of metadata fields from which they were asked to indicate those that they considered most important to assign to their data. The majority of the chemistry respondents (89%) noted that the author

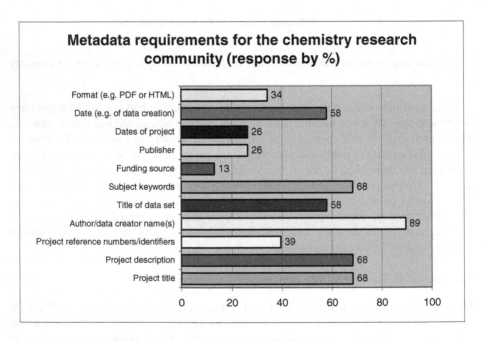

Fig. 2. Metadata requirements for chemistry researchers

and/or creator's name was the most significant metadata element for their data. Other important metadata elements were the project's description (68%), the project's title (68%) and the assignment of subject keywords (68%). The date and the title of the data set (each at 58%) were equally important. The least important metadata was considered to be the funding source of the project (13%).

The respondents were invited to indicate at what stage metadata is assigned to a resource as part of their own processes and practices, by making selections from key stages identified in the questionnaire. The responses to this question were fairly evenly spread across the options offered, which may indicate that the respondents were not familiar with the concept and the practice of assigning metadata to their resources. More than one third of the chemistry respondents (37%) noted that metadata is assigned to resources during file saving which indicates the involvement of software for automatic assignment of metadata. The second most popular choice was that metadata is assigned prior to data creation (26%) while one quarter of the respondents noted that metadata is either assigned as part of the indexing process for source files (24%) or no metadata is assigned (24%). Few of the respondents (8%) noted that metadata is assigned at a later stage, usually after the submission of the data to the repository and another the smallest group of respondents (5%) indicated that they were not sure when metadata is assigned.

More than half of the chemistry respondents (53%) noted that they themselves decide both on the terms to use and the assignment of metadata. Almost a third (29%) of the respondents replied that they were unaware of who assigns the metadata to their resources, which again complements the finding in the previous section that showed a spread in the way chemistry respondents' assigned metadata to their resources. The remainder of the responses was divided between those who replied that metadata is automatically generated (16%), metadata is assigned by research colleagues (11%), by research support staff (8%) and repository administrators (8%). One of the respondents noted that no one decides nor assigns metadata to their resources.

5.3 Section C. The Accessibility and Sharing of Primary Research Data

The aim of the third part of the questionnaire was to gather some understanding about the perceived advantages and barriers in making research data available, and where researchers do so, to find out if they apply any restrictions on how it may be accessed. The respondents were invited to indicate what measures they normally use to control access to their data by other researchers. All respondents indicated a variety of measures. The majority of the responses from the academic staff indicated storage of their data on a private network/intranet (21%) as the main measure to control access. The same measure was also employed by a large proportion of the postgraduate research students (32%) as well. All of the contracted researchers noted that they use authentication of ID and passwords for controlling access to their data. The research assistants indicate that they tend to select storage of their data on standalone computers (16%) as the main measure for controlling who has access.

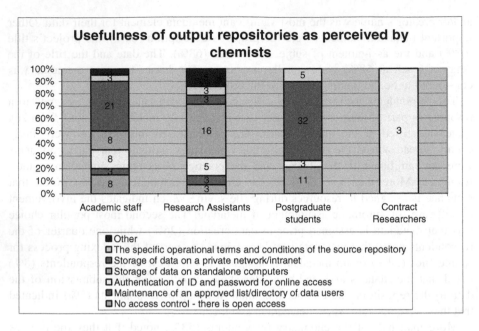

Fig. 3. Usefulness of output repositories for chemistry researchers

5.4 Section D. Output Repositories

The fourth section of the questionnaire aimed to gather some information regarding the repositories that the respondents have used for their research and for teaching purposes. In addition, they were asked to indicate how they usually search repositories for information, the amount of support they have been given (and from whom) and how much they would have liked to receive. The majority of output repositories that chemists tend to use are those in the commercial sector, set up and managed by publishers. Academic staffs are the group who indicated that they used the widest range of repositories, including institutional, discipline based and publisher repositories. Few of the academic staff replied that they do not use any repositories at all. Half of the postgraduate research students replied that they use publisher repositories for their research and the other half of the response is divided between institutional and discipline repositories. This pattern is similar to the repository usage indicated by contracted researchers as well. The research assistants also replied that they tend to use many different repositories such as institutional and publisher repositories and a few of them also noted that they do not use any repositories in particular.

Although, the majority of the chemistry respondents to the questionnaire replied that they preferred to use the simple search option when they visited both source and output repositories, the response is quite spread again according to the different types of repositories. The majority of those who tend to use the publishers repositories prefer to search employing simple methods. The use of subject specific thesauri and the use of Boolean logic are only mentioned in the searching of institutional and discipline repositories.

The respondents to the questionnaire survey were invited to indicate their preferred ways of accessing repositories. They were provided with a list of options that included access: Via a known repository's URL, Via an Open URL resolver, Via a library catalogue that links directly to an article in a repository, Via a library subject page, Through a publisher's online service (e.g. ScienceDirect), Directly through a specific journal's own web site, Through an author's personal web page, From a link provided in an e-mail, CD-rom, USB drive etc., From an Internet search engine (e.g. Google), Through a subject portal service (e.g. Entrez), I have no normal or preferred routes and Other. Half of the respondents replied that they preferred to search from an Internet search engine and from a publisher's online service. Other popular routes were via a library catalogue that links directly to an article in a repository (45%), directly through a specific journal's own web page (42%) and via a known repository's URL (39%). The least preferred route was via an Open URL resolver (11%). A small number indicated that they do not have a preferred route for accessing repositories. Few of the respondents (5%) indicated other than those prescribed routes and they specified "Web of Knowledge, SciFinder, or that they had only recently started their research, so they do not have any preferred routes of accessing a repository yet".

6 Conclusions

This paper presents results from an online questionnaire survey, undertaken as part of the StORe project, aiming to identify the issues around the use and linkage of source and output repositories and the expectations of the chemistry research community about their use. From the questionnaire survey response the following conclusions can be made:

- There is some indication from the questionnaire survey that the concepts of source and output repositories, as well as the model of open access, is not yet widely known and accepted in the chemistry research community as more than half of the chemists that were surveyed (65%) had not used a repository before and they were not familiar with the idea of open access repositories in general.
- In spite of this, bidirectional links between repositories and in particular, a bidirectional link between a source and output repository has been perceived as something that would be either a significant advantage or useful for the research conducted in the chemistry domain.
- Academic staff indicated a preference of linking from the primary research data to the published outcome of the research while PhD students and postdoctoral researchers were more interested in navigating from the published outcome to the primary data sets.
- There are many variations in the type of data produced, their recording and storage and also in the perceived value of repositories. The most common type of data produced among chemists is SPECTRA data that it is represented in drawings, spreadsheets and image files.

- Although the majority of the respondents denoted that they use a simple search when they visit a publishers' repository, the use of subject specific thesauri and Boolean logic is used when they navigate institutional or discipline repositories.
- In general it was felt that the availability of a prototype that would illustrate the aims of the StORe project to developing a facility that can link source and output repositories, would have made it easier for the respondents to understand and comment upon advantages and barriers to use.

References

1. Philip, G and *Cunningham*, F P (1995). Availability and use of automated chemical information systems by academic chemists in the United Kingdom. British Library. *Research* and Development Department. BLRD Report; 6184 1995, 63p
2. Lyon, Liz. (2003). "eBank UK: Building the links between research data, scholarly communication and learning", Ariadne (Issue 36), Available at: http://www.ariadne.ac.uk/issue36/lyon/intro.html (Last accessed 05/09/2006)
3. Lyon, L., Heery, R., Duke, M., Coles, S J., Frey, J G., Hursthouse, M., Carr, L. and Gutteridge, C. (2004). eBank UK: linking research data, scholarly communication and learning. In, *eScience All Hands Meeting*. Swindon, UK, Engineering and Physical Sciences Research Council. Available at: http://eprints.soton.ac.uk/8183/ (Last accessed 05/09/2006)
4. Tenopir, C., & King, D.W. (2002) Reading behavior and electronic journals.Learned Publishing, 15(4), 259–266.
5. Coles, S., Frey, J., Hursthouse, M., Milsted, A, Carr, A., Gutteridge, C., Lyon, L., Heery, R., Duke, M., Koch, T. and M. Day (2006). Enabling the reusability of scientific data: Experiences with designing an open access infrastructure for sharing datasets. Presented at the, Designing for Usability in e-Science. International Workshop, Edinburgh, Scotland, 26-27 January, 2006. Available at: http://www.ukoln.ac.uk/ukoln/staff/e.j.lyon/publications.html (Last accessed 05/09/2006)

Functional Composition of Web Databases

Masao Mori[1], Tetsuya Nakatoh[2], and Sachio Hirokawa[2]

[1] Department of Informatics, Kyushu University.
6-10-1 Hakozaki, Fukuoka, 812–8581, Japan
masa@i.kyushu-u.ac.jp
[2] Computing and Communications Center, Kyushu University.
6-10-1 Hakozaki, Fukuoka, 812–8581, Japan
{nakatoh, hirokawa}@cc.kyushu-u.ac.jp

Abstract. This paper proposes the architecture of the functional composition of Web databases (WebDBs). Unlike a general search engine which receives keywords and returns a list of URLs, a WebDB receives a complex query and returns a list of records. The complex query specifies the condition of each field of the records. The process of composing Web-DBs is described as a script, where a user chooses the target WebDBs and describes how to connect the output from one WebDB to the input of another WebDB and how to generate outputs. The novelty of the proposal is that both the WebDBs and output formats are considered as components of the same level and that the reuse of new keywords is represented as a connection (CGI links). Once the process is described as a script, the user can use the script for a new WebDB of his own.

1 Introduction

An increasing number of search engines are available on the Web besides general search engines such as Google. There are also databases with a Web interface. We can obtain high-quality information for a particular purpose from these databases.

However, information on these Web databases (WebDBs) cannot be indexed by general search engines and cannot be referred to directly because they are referred to only by the page that is generated dynamically from the database according to the user's query. Because of that, these databases are called by such names as Invisible Web [13,12], Deep Web [1] and Hidden Web [4,5].

We developed a system **DAISEn** [15] which performs a metasearch for such databases on the Web. Conventional metasearch engines integrate a fixed number of particular general search engines. The goal of DAISEn is the dynamic integration of an arbitrary set of databases on the Web.

On the other hand, there is a new trend of databases on the Web for a user to send a complex query. The queries are not just simple keywords; instead, they are the keywords which specify each field of the records that the user wants to retrieve from a database. For example, Amazon.com returns a list of book information which consists of the author, the title, the publisher, the price, ISBN,

S. Sugimoto et al. (Eds.): ICADL 2006, LNCS 4312, pp. 439–448, 2006.

and so on. kakaku.com returns a list of prices of PCs and other electric products. Travelocity.com returns a list of hotel information for a specified location.

When we survey a specific subject with such WebDBs, we do not stop searching with a single trial. We usually keep searching until we have enough information. In many cases, we obtain new keywords during the search process and use them for the next step of the search. For example, we can get a list of local restaurants by a search and then collect information about the menu and price of each restaurant. People who want to buy a used car can collect and compare detailed information on the cars obtained by a search. Those searches are performed by the same WebDB repeatedly, or are performed by different WebDBs. Some keywords in the output can be used as input for the next step of the search. If an attribute of the output data of a WebDB is "NAME", it can be connected to the input of another WebDB which receives the name as a search keyword.

When an author name and a keyword are sent to a WebDB of scientific journal articles, the result is not a list of Web pages but a list of articles with the author, the title, the magazine name and the publication year. When investigating papers exhaustively, even if the first search result is obtained, the investigation is not finished. The search is further continued based on the obtained information. As an example, we consider the following search.

– Are there any other articles written by the same author?
– Are there any articles written by the coauthors?
– What kind of articles does the article cite?
– How is the paper cited?
– What are the important keywords in related research?
– Where are the authors' home pages?
– Is there any related project?

We have proposed architecture to realize a search engine that combines several WebDBs. A large listing of such WebDBs is available at Dnavi, a Database Navigation service provided by the National Diet Library, Japan[1]. We confirmed that there are 2,800 WebDBs in Dnavi and proposed a method to estimate the query form automatically [10]. And, we reported the current situation of Web databases with a complex query and the possibility to guess the input metadata from the output metadata [9]. Furthermore, we proposed the algorithm which extracts items of each record from an HTML source of an output result [11].

In this paper, we discuss the co-operation between WebDBs. The script language which we propose describes the data flow between WebDBs as components with input and output metadata. Furthermore, the special component which specifies the output format can be treated similarly. The system constructs a CGI from the script and performs a semantic metasearch using the target WebDBs. To demonstrate the feasibility of this approach, we show a personal WebDB that connects four WebDBs of major Japanese IT related journals.

There are many previous works, such as TSIMMIS [2], that have examined information integration on the Web. However, in those studies, there is a requisite

---

[1] http://dnavi.ndl.go.jp/

that a developer must offer a conversion program to a common data format or detailed information of the database. The technique of this paper obtains the required information only from the Web interface of each WebDB, and can realize results independently of the system of each site.

Kitamura *et al.* [6] proposed the script language MetaCommander for extracting and unifying information from the Web. The extraction of the information needed is attained by describing the procedure as a script. However, a user needs to describe the script which extracts or converts data from HTML documents. Therefore, a semantic description such as "extracting the element of authors from the list of the outputted book" cannot be performed in MetaCommander.

Information extraction from Deep Web, WISE-Integrator [3] and SE-LEGO [14] are known; in these, the metasearch to WebDB is built automatically. The architecture of the present paper is not a simple metasearch that integrates the outputs of heterogeneous WebDBs but a creation of a new WebDB from several WebDBs as its components.

The works by Knoblock *et al.* [7,8] consider the construction of a personal information gathering tool with the integration of agents. Their goal is similar to ours. In order to define the connection between WebDBs, our system uses the script and, therefore, is more comprehensive. Moreover, we also propose the mechanism of the gathering information repeatedly by interaction with the user.

2   Composition of WebDBs

WebDBs can be considered as functions for which complex queries are input via Web interfaces and they output search results. Essentially, complex queries are a list of pairs of an attribute and instance. Similarly, search results essentially consist of a list of pairs of an attribute and instance. For example, when we make use of the WebDBs of electric journals, we provide some keywords into the query boxes. The WebDB shows the search results in browsers; these results can be a table of journals with title, author and coauthors, research keywords, etc. Each of the query boxes in the input form and each of the attributes of the table in the output data correspond to the input and output channels, respectively. In our architecture WebDBs are called *components* and their input and output interfaces are called *channels*. Composition is realized by passing data from output channels to input channels between WebDBs. We call the pairs of output and input channels *connections*.

Our architecture is characterized by the generation of CGI programs and executing them for each individual purpose. From the Web interface of our system, users give a statement of the WebDBs (called *components*) and define the connections of the components. Our architecture consists of three parts:

1. Components,
2. Composition of components, and
3. Personal output forms.

In this section we introduce the idea of components and their composition. In Section 3, the output components will be discussed.

2.1   Components

A WebDB is described as a *component* with input channels and output channels. Those channels are named with data *types*. A set of instances of these types is called a *record*. A component inputs and outputs a list of partial records: a tuple of instances in the form of a subset of types (Fig. 1). Note that "to output" is not meant as output for browsers. We consider the input and output user–interface as components.

Start component. The *start component* is a component with no input channels. It only outputs queries from users.

WebDB component. The components are equipped with wrappers and labeled with the names corresponding to the WebDBs. As WebDBs vary in their formats of input and output, wrappers of the components unify their formats.

Output component. This is the interface to the users. Input data to the user component are shown to the users. Users choose something which is output data that become queries for the next search.

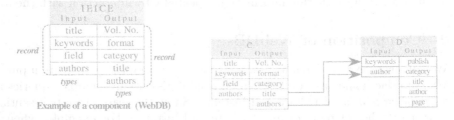

Fig. 1. Structure of a component   **Fig. 2.** Connection between components

2.2   Composition of Components

Suppose that a component C with output channels $o_1, \cdots, o_p$ and a component D with input channels $i_1, \cdots, i_q$ are given. A pair

$$\langle C.(o_{p_1}, \cdots, o_{p_k}),\quad (i_{q_1}, \cdots, i_{q_k}).D \rangle$$

of component channels denotes a *connection* from C to D through the corresponding channels $o_{p_l} \rightarrow i_{q_l}$. For $l = 1, \cdots, k$, each output channel o_{p_l} pipes the data to input channel i_{q_l} (Fig 2). If the sets of channels are singular, the connection is denoted by an abbreviated mode such as $\langle C.author, keywords.D \rangle$. The components and their connections forms a directed graph called a *connection graph* with components as nodes and connections as directed edges.

Cycles are allowed in a connection graph under the condition that at least one *CGI link* edge is included. CGI link edges are introduced in Section 3.2.

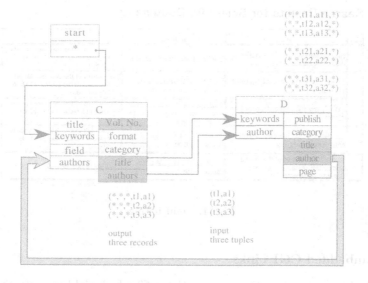

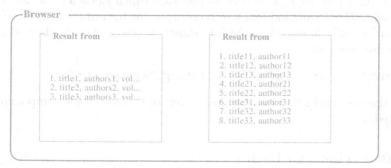

Fig. 3. Display channels

3   Output Components

Output components are interfaces to users with functions for arranging the search results. We introduce three functions which users can combine to give output forms.

3.1   Displaying Channels

Given a connection graph, the set of output channels, called *displaying channels*, is selected to display several outputs on the browser screen. In Fig 3, it contains the two output forms $C.\{volno, title, authors\}$ and $\{title, author\}.D$, which generate two listings separately on the browser screen.

Search Results for Scientific Documents

num	title	authors	source
1	Active Information Gathering by Making Use of Existing Databases	TuanNam Tran , Masayuki Numao	Transactions of the Japanese Society for Artificial Intelligence,Vol. 17 No. 5 pp.622–629 (2002)
2	A Kernel–based Account of Bibliometric Measures	Takahiko Ito, Masashi Shimbo, Taku Kudo , Yuji Matsumoto	Transactions of the Japanese Society for Artificial Intelligence,Vol. 19 No. 6 pp.530–539 (2004)
3	Social Network Extraction from the Web information	Yutaka Matsuo, Hironori Tomobe, Kôiti Hasida, Hideyuki Nakashima , Mitsuru Ishizuka	Transactions of the Japanese Society for Artificial Intelligence,Vol. 20 No. 1 pp.46–56 (2005)
4	Calculating Cross–Ontology Similarity for Web Services Discovery	Sasiporn Usanavasin, Shingo Takada , Norihisa Doi	Transactions of the Japanese Society for Artificial Intelligence,Vol. 21 No. 3 pp.231–242 (2006)
5	An Automatic Method of the Extraction of Important Words from Japanese Scientific Documents	Makoto Nagao, Mikio Mizutani, Hiroyuki Ikeda	IPSJ, Vol.16 No.0 英文誌

Fig. 4. Plain listing

3.2 Embedded CGI Links

In Fig 3, there is an edge $\langle D.author, authors.C \rangle$ which yields a cycle. Such edges are called *CGI links* and indicate parameters passing toward the next search step. The third record "3. title13, author13" shown in the browser as the result from C, is represented as

3. title13, `<a href="http://..../**.cgi">` author13 `</a>`.

When the user clicks this link, the next step of the search hit component C is activated.

3.3 Basic Filters for Listing

The format of search results are unified by each wrapper of WebDB components. For example, in Fig 4 the search results for the query "Scientific Documents" are shown by simply listing the items from the WebDB components. Each author name has a CGI link which is a filter to obtain the coauthor list (Fig 5).

By clicking the author name "Makoto Nagao" in the fifth line, for instance, the coauthors table in Fig 5 appears as a histogram listing the articles for each coauthor. This filter is useful not only for the coauthor list, but also for previous results, e.g., the table of writers and the number of their articles associated with the keyword.

4 Example

In this section, we explain the prototype of the system which gathers information by composing a WebDB. It collects information about the papers from the WebDB of each of the following academic societies in Japan.

Makoto Nagao

num	title	authors	source
1	A System for the Analysis of Aerial Photographs and Their Preprocessing	Makoto Nagao, Yasushi Fukunaga, Masatoshi Kawarazaki	IPSJ, Vol.16 No.0 英文誌
2	An Automatic Method of the Extraction of Important Words from Japanese Scientific Documents	Makoto Nagao, Mikio Mizutani, Hiroyuki Ikeda	IPSJ, Vol.16 No.0 英文誌
3	Analysis of Japanese Sentences by Using Semantic and Contextual Information (II)-Contextual Analysis	Makoto Nagao, Jun-Ichi Tsuji, Kazutosi Tanaka	IPSJ, Vol.16 No.0 英文誌
4	Analysis of Japanese Sentences by Using Semantic and Contextual Information (I)-Semantic Analysis	Makoto Nagao, Jun-Ichi Tsuji, Kazutoshi Tanaka	IPSJ, Vol.16 No.0 英文誌
5	PLATON – a New Programming Language for Natural Language Analysis	Makoto Nagao, Jun-Ichi Tsuji	IPSJ, Vol.15 No.0 英文誌
6	A Description of Chinese Characters Using Sub-patterns	Toshiyuki Sakai, Makoto Nagao, Hidekazu Terai	IPSJ, Vol.10 No.0 英文誌
7	Grammar Writing System (GRADE) of Mu-Machine Translation Project and its Characteristics	Jun-Ichi Nakamura, Jun-Ichi Tsuji, Makoto Nagao	IPSJ, Vol.8 No.2 欧文誌 (1981)

Coauthor Index

1	Jun Ibuki	[8]
2	Toshiyuki Sakai	[6]
3	Kazutosi Tanaka	[3]
4	Jun-Ichi Nakamura	[7]
5	Mikio Mizutani	[2]
6	Yasushi Fukunaga	[1]
7	Hidekazu Terai	[6]
8	Hiroyuki Ikeda	[2]
9	Masatoshi Kawarazaki	[1]
10	Masako Kume	[8]
11	Jun-Ichi Tsuji	[3], [4], [5], [7], [8]
12	Kazutoshi Tanaka	[4]

Fig. 5. Complex listing; coauthors list(the rest of article list from no.8 are omitted)

- IPSJ (Information Processing Society in Japan) [2]
- IEICE (The Institute of Electronics, Information and Communication Engineers)[3]
- JSAI (The Japanese Society for Artificial Intelligence) [4]
- JSSST (Japan Society for Software Science and Technology) [5]

This system mainly consists of the following three functions.

1. The function to search simultaneously to two or more WebDBs, and to show the user the integrated result. This is what is called a metasearch.
2. The function which extracts and lists authors in the result.
3. The function to offer the next search using the listed author as a keyword.

The mimetic diagram of the data connection of this system is shown in Fig. 6. We publish this system in http://matu.cc.kyushu-u.ac.jp/whirler/.

---

[2] http://www.bookpark.ne.jp/ipsj/
[3] http://search.ieice.org/bin/search.php
[4] http://tjsai.jstage.jst.go.jp/
[5] http://www.jstage.jst.go.jp/browse/jssst/

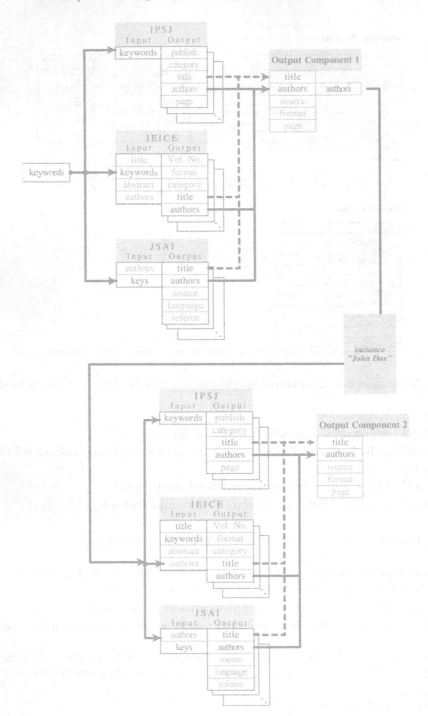

Fig. 6. Channels and connection graph

5   Conclusion

We proposed an architecture of the *functional composition of WebDBs* that aggregates WebDBs for an individual user's purpose. A user specifies the target WebDBs and how he uses them. The user's purpose is described as a script that consists of the list of WebDBs, the connection information which shows how the input and output are connected between WebDBs, and the list of display formats. Some fields of the output are shown as *CGI links* that are used as parameters for the next search step. As an output format, the user may write a sorted list of data, a histogram of some selected fields, and other filters as well as a plain listing of the records. Once the process is described as a script, the user can use the script as a new WebDB of his own.

In this paper, the authors considered the realistic situation that a user uses 5 or 6 WebDBs in his daily work and that he knows and can describe how he is using them. He only has to describe his search process as a script. Automatic selection of WebDBs will be necessary for a large pool of WebDBs. We assumed a wrapper for each WebDB. The automatic generation of such wrappers is indispensable and is an important problem for our architecture.

References

1. BrightPlanet, *The Deep Web: Surfacing Hidden Value*, BrightPlanet White Paper, 2000.
2. S. Chawathe, H. Garcia-Molina, J. Hammer, K. Ireland, Y. Papakonstantinou, J. Ullman and J. Widom, *The TSIMMIS Project: Integration of Heterogeneous Information Sources*, In Proceedings of IPSJ Conference, pp. 7-18, Tokyo, Japan, October 1994.
3. H. He, W. Meng, C. Yu, Z. Wu, *WISE-Integrator: A System for Extracting and Integrating Complex Web Search Interfaces of the Deep Web*, Proceedings of the 31st International Conference on Very Large Data Bases (VLDB2005), Trondheim, Norway, August 30 - September 2, 2005. pp.1314- 1317.
4. P. Ipeirotis, L. Gravano and M. Sahami, *PERSIVAL Demo: Categorizing Hidden-Web Resources*, JCDL2001, 2001.
5. P. Ipeirotis, L. Gravano and M. Sahami, *Probe, Count, and Classify: Categorizing Hidden-Web Databases*, ACM SIGMOD 2001, 2001.
6. Y. Kitamura, T. Noda and S. Tatsumi, *Single-agent and Multi-agent Approaches to WWW Information Integration*, Multiagent Platforms, Lecture Notes in Artificial Intelligence, Vol. 1599, Berlin et al.: Springer-Verlag, 133-147, 1999.
7. C. A. Knoblock, S. Minton, J. L. Ambite, N. Ashish, I. Muslea, A. G. Philpot, and S. Tejada, *The Ariadne Approach to Web-Based Information Integration*, International Journal of Cooperative Information Systems, vol.10, no.1-2, pp.145-169, 2001.
8. C. A. Knoblock, *Deploying Information Agents on the Web*, IJCAI-03, Proceedings of the Eighteenth International Joint Conference on Artificial Intelligence, Acapulco, Mexico, August 9-15, 2003. pp. 1580-1586.
9. T. Nakatoh, K. Ohmori and S. Hirokawa, *A Report on Metadata for Web Databases*, IPSJ SIG Technical Reports, 2004-ICS-138(17), pp. 95-98, 2004.

10. T. Nakatoh, K. Ohmori, Y. Yamada and S. Hirokawa, *COMPLEX QUERY AND METADATA*, Proc. ISEE2003, pp. 291-294, 2003.
11. T. Nakatoh, Y. Yamada and S. Hirokawa, *Automatic Generation of Deep Web Wrappers based on Discovery of Repetition*, Proc. of the First Asia Information Retrieval Symposium (AIRS 2004), pp.269-272, 2004.
12. P. Pedley, *The invisible web*, ASLIB, 2001.
13. C. Sherman and G. Pric, *The Invisible Web*, Information Today, Inc., Medfore, New Jersey, 2001.
14. Z. Wu, V. Raghavan, C. Du, K. Sai C, W. Meng, H. He and C. Yu, *SE-LEGO: creating metasearch engines on demand*, Proceedings of the 26th annual international ACM SIGIR conference on Research and development in information retrieval (SIGIR '03), 2003.
15. *Project DAISEn: Directory Architecture for Integrated Search Engines*, http://daisen.cc.kyushu-u.ac.jp/

Integration of Wikipedia and a Geography Digital Library*

Ee-Peng Lim, Z. Wang, D. Sadeli, Y. Li, Chew-Hung Chang,
Kalyani Chatterjea, Dion Hoe-Lian Goh, Yin-Leng Theng,
Jun Zhang, and Aixin Sun

Nanyang Technological University, Singapore

Abstract. In this paper, we address the problem of integrating Wikipedia, an online encyclopedia, and G-Portal, a web-based digital library, in the geography domain. The integration facilitates the sharing of data and services between the two web applications that are of great value in learning. We first present an overall system architecture for supporting such an integration and address the metadata extraction problem associated with it. In metadata extraction, we focus on extracting and constructing metadata for geo-political regions namely cities and countries. Some empirical performance results will be presented. The paper will also describe the adaptations of G-Portal and Wikipedia to meet the integration requirements.

Keywords: Web-based encyclopedia, geography digital libraries, integration.

1 Introduction

G-Portal is a digital library that supports learning of geography based on publicly available web information[1, 4, 5]. In G-Portal, we treat geography related web pages and other types of web objects as content resources. Metadata records of these web objects are created and stored in a database server, and can be shared by different learning projects. G-Portal also provides the map-based and classification-based interfaces to view and query metadata records.

Wikipedia represents a very appealing source of information to G-Portal as it contains many entries related to geography in addition to its many interesting features mentioned earlier. Wikipedia has 44 sub-categories under the *geography* category, and at least another 600 sub-categories at the next level. Each geography entry or article is jointly authored and edited by a group of Wikipedians from different parts of the world, and hence is of quality generally much better than the other non-reviewed web pages. With so much knowledge embedded in Wikipedia, it is interesting to explore how the Wikipedia resources can be utilized in research and education.

Since Wikipedia is not a digital library, it lacks several important features that are essential to digital library users. At present, metadata of Wikipedia entries

---

* The project is funded by Centre for Research in Pedagogy and Practice, National Institute of Education with Project ID "CRP25/04 LEP".

S. Sugimoto et al. (Eds.): ICADL 2006, LNCS 4312, pp. 449–458, 2006.

are very basic and it does not provide sufficient information for searching and browsing at metadata level. Wikipedia has strong system features for users to edit entries, while digital libraries have better support for tracking information of interest to each user or a group of users. For example, G-Portal allows metadata records to be selected into different groups known as *projects*, and each project is designed for the learning needs of one or more user.

There are clearly many benefits accrued from integrating Wikipedia and G-Portal. Firstly, the addition of Wikipedia metadata to G-Portal will not only enlarge the latter's metadata collection, but also create a special web content resources that are of high quality and are constantly updated with the latest information. Secondly, users can now exploit the use of G-Portal features to access the metadata of Wikipedia entries and to further organize them for different learning purposes. For example, one can create a G-Portal project consisting of metadata of both Wikipedia and non-Wikipedia content for some geography learning activity.

In this research, we have therefore investigated different approaches to integrate Wikipedia and G-Portal. On one extreme is a tightly coupled integrated system with a single user interface supporting a combined set of functions based on a single database. On the other extreme is a loosely coupled system with Wikipedia and G-Portal retaining their original user interfaces, functions and databases. For the practical reason of keeping each system autonomous, we have chosen the latter integration approach. This approach minimizes changes to Wikipedia and G-Portal so that both can continue to service their own existing users. Nevertheless, the loosely coupled integration still poses some technical challenges, namely identifying relevant Wikipedia entries, and extracting metadata attribute information from the entries.

Our work focuses on constructing the metadata for geo-political regions such as countries and cities. Geo-political regions form a basic but significant and important set of entries in Wikipedia (and also important to geography in general). The descriptions of these regions are usually very comprehensive in Wikipedia and they often serve as the background context for discussing other geography concepts.

We aims to develop new extensions to G-Portal to make it easy to invoke G-Portal from Wikipedia with the requested metadata record shown prominently in its user interface. At the same time, G-Portal's metadata embeds links to access Wikipedia entries.

2   System Architecture for the Integrated System

The essential system modules of Wikipedia and G-Portal, together with those modules for integrating them are shown in Figure 1.

Wikipedia itself is implemented using a server engine known as MediaWiki that maintains a large collection of entries in a MySQL database[7]. To display a Wikipedia page in a web browser, MediaWiki retrieves the user requested entry from the database, formats it in HTML and returns the formatted HTML page[3].

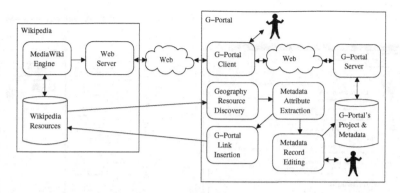

Fig. 1. System Modules for the Integration of Wikipedia and G-Portal

G-Portal, on the other hand, maintains its metadata and project information in its own database implemented on an XML database system and another relational database system. G-Portal has a server module that handles retrieval and updates of its database. Upon user request, G-Portal client obtains metadata records under the selected project from the server and displays them.

To support a two-way integration framework, a user viewing a Wikipedia entry using a web browser should be able to invoke G-Portal client whenever required to display the metadata record of the Wikipedia entry. On the other hand, a user of G-Portal should be able to view the metadata records of geography-related Wikipedia entries using the G-Portal client.

The metadata records of geography-related Wikipedia entries are constructed by two modules, namely the geography resource discovery and metadata element extraction module as shown in Figure 1. Geography resource discovery involves scanning through the Wikipedia entries in the database and finding those that are related to the various geography topics.

Once the relevant Wikipedia entries are found, their metadata records have to be constructed by extracting metadata attributes and their values from the Wikipedia page content. This metadata creation process can be a painstaking task for large collection of entries if it is done manually. In many cases, even with automated metadata attribute extraction, the metadata records still have to be further manually edited before they can be imported into G-Portal.

As new metadata records are constructed and added to G-Portal, the Wikipedia pages need to be modified to have the links to G-Portal Client inserted. These links will allow Wikipedia users to invoke the G-Portal Client which displays the corresponding metadata record.

3   Identification of Relevant Wikipedia Articles

3.1   Organization of Wikipedia Entries for Geo-political Regions

Every Wikipedia entry is associated with an article that contains the entry description and this also applies to geo-political regions entries. In addition to

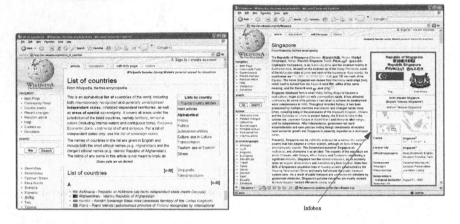

(a) List of Countries" page   (b) "Singapore" page

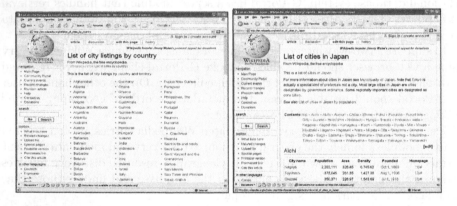

(c) "List of Cities by Country"   (d) "List of Cities in Japan" page
page

Fig. 2. Wikipedia Pages

having an article to describe each geo-political region (e.g., country, state, city, etc.), Wikipedia also supports some *List_of_⟨region⟩* entry that enumerate all articles of some ⟨region⟩ type. We call these the *list-type* pages. For example, a list of countries covered by Wikipedia can be found at: "http://en.wikipedia.org/wiki/List_of_countries" as shown in Figure 2(a). The link of each country leads to a Wikipedia article about the country as shown in Figure 2(b).

A list-type page also exists for cities grouped by countries (see Figure 2(c)). This page provides the link to a list of cities page for each country. For example, the list-type page for the cities of Japan is shown in Figure 2(d). Every city of Japan can be found by navigating the links from this page.

The existence of such list-type pages simplifies the task of identifying geo-political regions covered by Wikipedia and extracting the corresponding entries. Nevertheless, there are still some complications caused by the nature of Wikipedia:

- The links to country entries in the "List_of_countries" article are formatted manually and there are other links in the article not linked to country entries.
- The city entries in the "List_of_cities_in⟨country ⟩" also demonstrate a wide variety of formats across different countries complicating the way they can be identified. For example, the way Japan cities are formatted in the "List_of _cities _in_Japan" entry is different from those formatted in the "List_of_cities _in_China" entry.
- Some regions may not be covered by Wikipedia but their links may still exist in the list-type entry. A city name may appear in the "List_of_cities_in_China" entry but there is no corresponding Wikipedia entry.

While the above observation of list-type entries were made on geo-political entries, we also found similar style of organizing entries in other subject domains, e.g., list of mathematics topics, list of songs. This suggests that our methods developed for geo-political entries can be adopted for entries of other domains.

3.2   Entry Link Extraction Algorithm for List-Type Pages

In this section, we proposed an algorithm to extract the links to entries for geo-political regions. We focus on the extraction of links to country and city entries since they are the ones with list-type pages.

Our algorithm makes the following assumptions:

- For each geo-political region type (say, city), there is a single root list-type page that provides the links to the correspoding entries either directly or indirectly via a set of other intermediate list-type pages (e.g., List_of_cities_by_country page). This root page serves as the input to our algorithm.
- A set of region names are available for training purpose. Very often, names of some well known regions are already known in the public domain. For example, a set of countries and cities are available at ESRI's website. These training sets may not be able to cover all countries and cities in Wikipedia[1], they serve as useful information for training our extraction patterns.

To avoid developing different extraction algorithms for list-type pages in Wiki-Text and HTML, our algorithm first represents a WikiText or HTML page as a DOM tree. The DOM tree consists of leaf nodes each representing a basic text segment and internal nodes each representing a tagged document element in the WikiText or HTML page. The children of an internal node represents a

---

[1] The coverage of countries is usually much better than that of cities in the training set.

set of text segments or document elements nested within the parent document element.

As shown in Algorithms 1 and 2, our algorithm first collects a set of tag paths (*PathSet*) for the training regions found in the DOM tree. The tag paths are then used to extract all the region names by traversing the DOM tree as shown in Algorithm 2. Due to space constraint, we will leave out the experimental results of these algorithms. In general, they performed reasonably well in finding the country and city regions from the list-type pages.

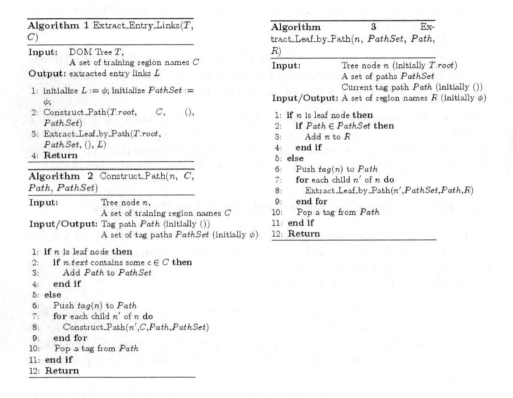

Algorithm 1 Extract_Entry_Links(T, C)

Input: DOM Tree T,
      A set of training region names C
Output: extracted entry links L

1: initialize $L := \phi$; initialize $PathSet :=$
   ϕ;
2: Construct_Path($T.root$, C,   (),
   $PathSet$)
3: Extract_Leaf_by_Path($T.root$,
   $PathSet$, (), L)
4: **Return**

Algorithm 2 Construct_Path(n, C, $Path$, $PathSet$)

Input: Tree node n,
         A set of training region names C
Input/Output: Tag path $Path$ (initially ())
         A set of tag paths $PathSet$ (initially ϕ)

1: **if** n is leaf node **then**
2:   **if** $n.text$ contains some $c \in C$ **then**
3:     Add $Path$ to $PathSet$
4:   **end if**
5: **else**
6:   Push $tag(n)$ to $Path$
7:   **for** each child n' of n **do**
8:     Construct_Path($n',C,Path,PathSet$)
9:   **end for**
10: Pop a tag from $Path$
11: **end if**
12: **Return**

Algorithm   3   Extract_Leaf_by_Path(n, $PathSet$, $Path$, R)

Input: Tree node n (initially $T.root$)
         A set of paths $PathSet$
         Current tag path $Path$ (initially ())
Input/Output: A set of region names R (initially ϕ)

1: **if** n is leaf node **then**
2:   **if** $Path \in PathSet$ **then**
3:     Add n to R
4:   **end if**
5: **else**
6:   Push $tag(n)$ to $Path$
7:   **for** each child n' of n **do**
8:     Extract_Leaf_by_Path($n',PathSet,Path,R$)
9:   **end for**
10: Pop a tag from $Path$
11: **end if**
12: **Return**

Fig. 3. Algorithms for Identifying Geo-political Entries

4   Extraction of Metadata Attributes

Instead of taking a text extraction approach looking for possible metadata attributes and values from Wikipedia pages, we examine the *infoboxes* commonly found in the Wikipedia entries. An infobox is essentially a table included in articles with a common subject, e.g. country, city, etc.. Infobox templates are also available for the tables to have a common look in different Wikipedia articles. An example of a country infobox is shown in Figure 2(b) where the infobox contains information about the capital, largest city, official language, government, and others. It turns out that many country and city articles in Wikipedia contain good quality metadata attribute information in infoboxes. Infoboxes are also widely used for representing metadata attributes of Wikipedia entries from other domains (e.g., science, technology, arts and entertainment, etc.).

The task of extracting metadata attribute information from infoboxes consists of two parts: (i) identifying the existence of infoboxes (as not all infoboxes contain the metadata information, and some pages may not even contain a relevant infobox); and (ii) extracting the metadata attributes and their corresponding attribute values. To tackle the task, we adopted a set of training metadata attributes for recognizing the relevant infoboxes, as well as for recognizing their formats. The set of training metadata attributes for country (denoted by $A_{country}$) was first obtained by manual inspection from the relevant infobox of USA Wikipedia page while the training metadata attributes (A_{city}) was obtained from the Beijing Wikipedia page in a similar way. We chose them because of their rich sets of metadata attributes in the infoboxes. There were 15 attributes in $A_{country}$ (namely, Motto, Anthem, Capital, Largest city, Official languages, Government, Independence, Constitution, Area, Population, GDP, Currency, Time Zone, Internet TLD, and Calling Code), and 17 attributes in A_{city} (namely, Origin of name, Administration type, CPC Beijing Committee Secretary, Mayor, Area, Population, GDP, Major nationalities, City trees, City flowers, Country-level divisions, Township-level divisions, Postal code, Area code, Licence plate prefixes, ISO 3166-2, and Official website).

To identify the relevant infobox from a Wikipedia page, the infoboxes in the page are ranked by the numbers of metadata attributes from $A_{\langle region \rangle}$ found in them. The highest ranked infobox is chosen for the second sub-task of metadata extraction where columns in the infobox are further ranked by the number of metadata attributes. The column with the highest rank will be assumed to contain the metadata attribute names while the other columns are treated as attribute values. Each metadata attribute value pair is then extracted from the row corresponding to the metadata attribute.

5   Modification of G-Portal Client and Wikipedia Entries

The access to G-Portal metadata from Wikipedia allows Wikipedia users to easily switch from the web browser's page-based view of a resource to the G-Portal's map-based and category-based views of the corresponding metadata record together with the metadata records of other Wikipedia resources. This switch is extremely useful when one wishes to visualize different Wikipedia resources on a map or in a hierarchy of categories.

To provide access to G-Portal metadata from Wikipedia, there are some modifications to be made to both G-Portal and Wikipedia, namely: (a) Automatic login for Wikipedia project; (b) Parameterized record centric display for G-Portal's map-based interface; and (c) Insertion of G-Portal client links into Wikipedia resources. The first two affects the design of G-Portal while the last involves some changes to Wikipedia articles.

5.1   Automatic Login

G-Portal users are usually required to manually log in with their user names and passwords before they are allowed to view the metadata of selected projects. In contrast, Wikipedia supports public access and passwords are not required. Furthermore, G-Portal users are also required to select the specific project for viewing metadata. For Wikipedia users to directly access G-Portal metadata without having to worry about logging in and selecting projects, G-Portal has to be modified to receive login and project parameters upon invocation. This is done by extending the G-Portal client applet to take the above input parameters. A PHP script (known as "gportal.php") is also generated for Wikipedia users to invoke G-Portal client applet and passing to the latter the user ID, password and name of the corresponding project. In our case, there is so far only one project created for Wikipedia resources and it is known as "Wiki Project". Note that the above mechanism can be easily extended for other G-Portal projects whenever automatic login and project selection are required.

5.2   Parameterized Metadata Centric Display

G-Portal, in its original user interface design, displays the full extent of the map of a project before the user starts browsing the metadata within the project. This design assumes that the user has no specific metadata record to view at the beginning. This assumption however does not hold when we integrate G-Portal with Wikipedia since Wikipedia users access G-Portal from some Wikipedia resources and it is necessary to show clearly where the metadata of these resources are located in the map interface. A simple solution to this is to highlight a selected metadata record in the map interface but this method suffers from some shortcomings. Firstly, there may be many other metadata records located nearby. A full map extent display thus will not be able to display the highlighted

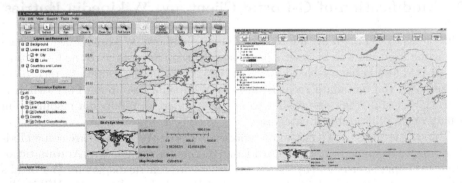

(a) London at the center   (b) China in the map interface

Fig. 4. G-Portal's map interface with computed bounding rectangle region

one clearly. Secondly, metadata records on the map are of different shape and sizes, it is visually unpleasant to show a highlighted metadata record using the same zoom level.

We address the above issues by making G-Portal client display the map region with the selected metadata record at the center and at the appropriate zoom level. We have extended G-Portal client to accept a geographical region defined by a bounding rectangle as another input parameter. To provide this input to the G-Portal client, the G-Portal script "gportal.php" (for invoking the G-Portal client) has been further modified to (1) take resource id of the metadata record; (2) retrieve the spatial shape of the record from the G-Portal's database; and (3) compute the bounding rectangle containing the record at the center with the appropriate zoom level. For point represented metadata, the point location and a pre-defined zoom level is used to determine the bounding rectangle (see Figure 4(a)). For polygon or line represented metadata, the script computes the bounding box containing the shape (see Figure 4(b)).

5.3   Insertion of G-Portal Client Links into Wikipedia Resources Using Reverse Proxy

For Wikipedia users to directly call on G-Portal, it is necessary to insert links to G-Portal client (or more accurately, the links to the G-Portal PERL script which invokes the client) within the Wikipedia resource web pages. The insertion can be automated by having a program editing the content of Wikipedia pages. Nevertheless, this insertion will inevitably modify the operational Wikipedia entries and affect the use of Wikipedia. To minimize changes to Wikipedia, we have chosen to implement a reverse proxy[9] for Wikipedia. Our reverse proxy is a virtual mirror of Wikipedia which takes a URL request for Wikipedia page and forwards it to real Wikipedia server so as to receive the corresponding HTML page. As part of the proxy, we developed a filter to add appropriate G-Portal links to the received HTML page if the request concerns a country or city entry before the page is further returned to the client of reverse proxy. Furthermore, the filter modifies all links in the HTML page by their proxy links so as to ensure that further browsing from this page will also involve the reverse proxy.

6   Conclusion

Interoperability among digital libraries has been an very active area of research. There are standardization efforts for metadata representations such as Dublin Core[2], and protocols for sharing and querying metadata records, e.g., OAI[6], Z39.50[8]. The work however focuses more on the integration among different digital libraries as opposed to between digital libraries and non-digital libraries. We have also observed that the ongoing development of Wikipedia has very much on content construction and content review activities instead of integrating with digital libraries. The research issues related to integrating Wikipedia with digital libraries are therefore very much unexplored.

In this paper, we therefore studied the task of finding and extracting metadata from Wikipedia articles. We specifically focused on the metadata of Wikipedia articles of geo-political regions. Our experiments have shown that our proposed extraction algorithms performed quite well on country and city articles. This paper also reports how G-Portal and Wikipedia have to be modified to support the proposed integration. Interested users can try out G-Portal's Wiki Project at http://gportal.cais.ntu.edu.sg/GPortal/index.htm.

References

1. Chew Hung Chang, John Hedberg, Yin-Leng Theng, Ee-Peng Lim, Tiong-Sa Teh, and Dion Hoe-Lian Goh. Evaluating G-Portal for Geography Learning and Teaching. In *ACM/IEEE Joint Conf. on Digital Libraries*, Denver, USA, June 2005.
2. Makx Dekkers and Stuart Weibel. Dublin Core Metadata Initiative Progress Report and Workplan for 2002. *D-Lib Magazine*, 8(2), 2002.
3. Wikimedia Foundation. http://www.mediawiki.org/wiki/mediawiki.
4. Dion Hoe-Lian Goh, Aixin Sun, Wenbo Zong, Dan Wu, Ee-Peng Lim, Yin-Leng Theng, John Hedberg, and Chew Hung Chang. Managing Geography Learning Objects Using Personalized Project Spaces in G-Portal. In *European Conf. on Research & Advanced Technology for Digital Libraries*, Vienna, September 2005.
5. Ee-Peng Lim, Dion Hoe-Lian Goh, Zehua Liu, Wee-Keong Ng, Christopher Soo-Guan Khoo, and Susan Ellen Higgins. G-Portal: A Map-based Digital Library for Distributed Geospatial and Georeferenced Resources. In *ACM/IEEE Joint Conference on Digital Libraries*, Portland, July 2002.
6. Xiaoming Liu, Kurt Maly, Mohammad Zubair, and Michael L. Nelson. Repository Synchronization in the OAI Framework. In *ACM/IEEE Joint Conf. on Digital Libraries*, Houston, May 2003.
7. MySQL. www.mysql.com/.
8. Michalis Sfakakis and Sarantos Kapidakis. Expression of Z39.50 Supported Search Capabilities by Applying Formal Descriptions. In *European Conf. on Research and Advanced Technology for Digital Libraries*, Vienna, September 2005.
9. Wikipedia. Reverse proxy — wikipedia, the free encyclopedia, 2006. [Online; accessed 19-June-2006].

Impact of Document Structure on Hierarchical Summarization

Fu Lee Wang and Christopher C. Yang

[1] Department of Computer Science, City University of Hong Kong,
Kowloon Tong, Hong Kong
flwang@cityu.edu.hk
[2] Department of Systems Engineering and Engineering Management,
Chinese University of Hong Kong,
Shatin, Hong Kong
yang@se.cuhk.edu.hk

Abstract. Hierarchical summarization technique summarizes a large document based on the hierarchical structure and salient features of the document. Previous study has shown that hierarchical summarization is a promising technique which can effectively extract the most important information from the source document. Hierarchical summarization has been extended to summarization of multiple documents. Three hierarchical structures were proposed to organize a set of related documents. This paper investigates the impact of document structure on hierarchical summarization. The results show that the hierarchical summarization of multiple documents organized in hierarchical structure outperforms other multi-document summarization systems without using the hierarchical structure. Moreover, the hierarchical summarization by event topics extracts a set of sentences significantly different from hierarchical summarization of other hierarchical structures and performs the best when the summary is highly-compressed.

1 Introduction

Many automatic summarization models have been proposed previously [1, 3, 4]. Traditionally, summarization systems consider a document as a sequence of sentences. The system calculates the significance of sentences to the document. The most significant sentences are then extracted and concatenated as a summary. Research of automatic summarization has been extended to multi-document summarization [6, 10]. Multi-document summarization system provides an overview of a topic based on a set of related documents. It is very useful in digital libraries.

It has been shown that the document structure is important in both automatic summarization [12] and human abstraction [2]. Hierarchical summarization model was proposed based on the hierarchical structure of documents [15]. Experiment results have shown that hierarchical summarization is a promising summarization technique. Nowadays, many digital libraries have begun to provide summarization service. Many documents exhibit a hierarchical structure, such as, books, websites, newsgroups, etc. Hierarchical summarization can effectively extract the most

S. Sugimoto et al. (Eds.): ICADL 2006, LNCS 4312, pp. 459–469, 2006.
© Springer-Verlag Berlin Heidelberg 2006

important information from the documents with hierarchical structures. It provides an important tool for digital libraries.

In most digital library systems, a collection of related documents are returned for a query. However, there is not a trivial way to organize a large collection of documents into a hierarchical tree structure. Three hierarchical structures were proposed to organize a collection of documents into a tree structure [13]. This paper investigates the impact of different hierarchical structures on the summarization technique. Experiments have been conducted to study how the extraction of information is affected by the hierarchical structures.

The results show that the hierarchical summarization of multiple documents outperforms other multi-document summarization without using the hierarchical structure. Moreover, the hierarchical summarization by event topics extracts a set of sentences significantly different from hierarchical summarization of other hierarchical structures and performs the best when the summary is highly-compressed. It is shown that the hierarchical summarization system can extract the critical information effectively among a large collection of documents.

2   Hierarchical Summarization Model

The information overloading problem can be solved by the application of automatic summarization. A number of automatic summarization techniques have been developed [1, 3, 4]. The hierarchical summarization model was proposed to summarize a large document based on the hierarchical structure and salient features of the document [15]. Experimental results have shown that the hierarchical summarization model is a promising summarization technique.

Traditional automatic text summarization is the selection of sentences from the source document based on their significances to the document [1, 4]. The selection of sentences is conducted based on the salient features of the document. The thematic, location, and heading are the most widely used summarization features.

- The thematic feature is first identified by Luhn [4]. Edmundson proposed to assign the thematic weight to keyword based on term frequency, and the sentence thematic score as the sum of thematic weight of constituent keywords [1]. Nowadays, the *tfidf* (Term Frequency, Inverse Document Frequency) method is the most widely used method to calculate the thematic weight of keywords [11].
- It is believed that the topic sentences tend to occur at the beginning or the end of documents or paragraphs [1]. Edmondson proposed to assign positive weights to sentences as location score according to their ordinal position in the document.
- The heading feature is proposed based on the hypothesis that the author conceives the heading as circumscribing the subject matter of the document. When the author partitions the document into major sections, he summarizes them by choosing appropriate headings [1]. A heading glossary is a list of words, consisting of all the words in headings, with weights. The heading score of sentence is calculated by the sum of heading weight of its constituent words.

Typical summarization systems select a combination of features [1, 4], the sentence significance score is calculated as sum of feature scores. The sentences with sentence significance score higher than a threshold value are selected as summary.

A large document has a hierarchical structure with several levels, chapters, sections, subsections, paragraphs, and sentences. Related studies have shown that the document structure is very useful for human abstraction process [2] and automatic summarization [12]. Hierarchical summarization model was proposed to generate summary based on the hierarchical structure and salient features of the document [15]. The original document is partitioned into range blocks according to its document structure. The document is then transformed into a hierarchical tree structure, where each range block is represented by a node. The system calculates the number of sentences to be extracted according to the compression ratio. The number of sentences is assigned to the root of tree as the quota of sentences. The system calculates the significance score of each node by summing up the sentence scores of all sentences under the nodes. The quota of sentences is allocated to child-nodes by propagation, i.e., the quota of parent node is shared by its child-nodes directly proportional to their significance scores. The quota is then iteratively allocated to grandchild-nodes until the quota allocated is less than a threshold value and the node can be transformed to some key sentences by traditional summarization methods.

3 Hierarchical Summarization for Multiple Documents

Multi-document summarization techniques have been developed for flat-structured documents. However, a collection of related documents may exhibit a much more complicated structure. As it was shown that the document structure is important in summarization, three hierarchical structures were proposed to organize a collection of news stories [13].

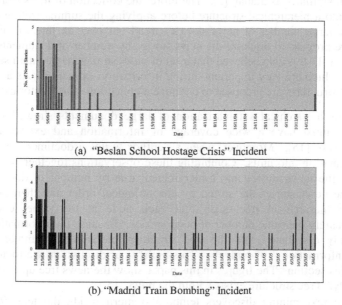

(a) "Beslan School Hostage Crisis" Incident

(b) "Madrid Train Bombing" Incident

Fig. 1. Distribution of News Stories vs. Time

Multi-document summarization systems have been developed in the past [6, 10]. Typically, the summarization systems consider a collection of documents as a set of individual documents with flat-structure. Given a set of documents, some summarization systems extract concepts and their relationships, and then integrate the extracted information as a summary [10]. Alternatively, some systems segment the documents into some small text units. They compute the similarities among the text units [6]. Then, the text units are extracted based on their similarity measurement to generate summaries. However, a collection of related documents exhibit a more complicated structure. At the initial step, we investigate the summarization of a collection of news stories related to an incident. Each news story is associated with a time stamp. Moreover, the news stories can be classified into event topics [14]. Current summarization system cannot capture the above information. As a result, a multi-document summarization system for structured document is required.

In order to have a better understanding of news stories related to an incident, two incidents have been analyzed. Related news stories have been collected from the CNN.com. The first incident is the "Madrid Train Bombing". The second incident is the "Beslan School Hostage Crisis". In the figure of distribution of news stories against time, obvious peaks can be identified at the beginning (Fig 1). The peaks correspond to the burst of the incidents. Then, the number of news stories decreases as time goes by. As shown in the Fig. 1, the "Madrid Train Bombing" has a more long-term impact. Therefore, there are more news stories and last for a longer period.

There is a large collection of news stories related to an incident. It is difficult for a human to view all the information without a structure. When a human professional writes a document about an incident, he partitions the information into chapters and then sections. As human is the best summarizer, a high quality summarization system should work similarly as human [2]. Therefore, the collection of news stories must be organized into a hierarchical structure before applying the summarization techniques. In Fig. 1, a large number of news stories spread out over an interval of time. By intuition, we propose to organize the news stories by number of documents as well as by time interval. It is also believed that a set of news stories may contain several event topics [14], which are very important during information extraction. As a result, three hierarchical structures are proposed to organize a collection of news stories.

– Results of hierarchical summarization of large documents showed that a good summary must have a wide coverage of information and extract information distributively [15]. Moreover, when an author writes a document, he distributes the information into units. Combining these observations together, we propose to organize the news stories into a hierarchical tree by number of documents (Fig. 2a). The news stories are sorted by chronological order and then organized as balanced hierarchical tree, such that each node at the same level contains approximately the same number of news stories. Because the information contents are evenly distributed into the tree structure, hierarchical summarization will extract information distributively. To simplify our discussion, we focus on binary tree in this section. The figures in this paper show the news tree up to news stories level only. Tree structure exists within the news story.

– Temporal text mining discovers temporal pattern inside the text [7]. Similar technique has been used in multi-document summarization [6], summarization of news stories are generated for fixed number of days, then an overall summary is generated. Therefore, we propose the hierarchical structure by time interval (Fig 2b). The news stories are organized into a hierarchical structure such that each child node represents an equal and non-overlapping interval. Unlike the hierarchical structure by number of documents, the hierarchical structure by time interval is an unbalanced tree structure. Therefore, the information is not evenly distributed into node blocks.

- It is believed that a collection of news stories may contain several event topics, the detection of event topics is very important in information retrieval [14]. Recent research in automatic summarization proposes to classify the documents into document sets before summarization [9]. Therefore, we propose the hierarchical structure by event topics (Fig 2c). Because the accuracy of event topic detection affects the performance of the summarization directly, the news stories are

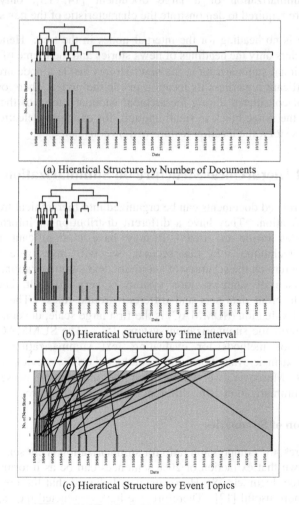

(a) Hieratical Structure by Number of Documents

(b) Hieratical Structure by Time Interval

(c) Hieratical Structure by Event Topics

Fig. 2. Hierarchical Structure of "Beslan School Hostage Crisis" Incident by Event Topics

clustered into event topics by qualified human professionals in our experiment. Each event topic is represented as a child node under the root node. The news stories under the event topics are then the child nodes of events. The hierarchical structure by event topic is not a balanced tree.

Hierarchical summarization is applied to summarize the news stories with different hierarchical structures. The system generates a summary for each range block, and then the summaries of range blocks are concatenated as an overall summary for the collection of news stories. When the number of news stories inside a range block is too large, iterative partition of range block into sub-range blocks is required and the hierarchical summarization technique will be applied to summarize the range blocks. The hierarchical summarization for multiple documents is very similar to the hierarchical summarization of a large document [14, 15], only some minor modifications are required to demonstrate the characteristic of the news stories.

- Firstly, there is no heading for the internal nodes in the tree. Hence, the heading feature considers only the headings of news stories and the theme of the incident.
- Unlike traditional summarization, the news stories inside a node are considered as equally significant regardless its location inside the node. Therefore, the location feature is not considered during hierarchical summarization of the tree structure. However, if the range block is small enough, for example, selection of sentences within a news story, the location feature will be considered.

4   Impact of Hierarchical Structure on Summarization

A collection of related documents can be organized into hierarchical tree structures by different classification. They have a different distribution of information contents among the nodes inside the tree. It may have a significant impact on the summarization technique. In this section, we will investigate the impact of hierarchical structure on the accuracy of automatic text summarization.

The comparison of summarization system is very difficult, because different research uses different data sets and different ground-rules. The TIPSTER Text Summarization Evaluation (SUMMAC) is the first large scale, developer-independent evaluation of automatic summarization systems [5]. The SUMMAC has identified two categories of methods for evaluating text summarization. Both intrinsic evaluation and extrinsic evaluation will be conducted on the previous two incidents in our experiment. Moreover, we will analyze the intersection of sentences in the summaries by summarization using different hierarchical structures.

4.1   Intersection of Summaries

In most literatures, the compression ratio for summarization is chosen as 25% because it has been shown that extraction of 20% sentences can be as informative as the full text of the source document [8]. However, it is believed that the highly-compressed abstracting is more useful [12]. Therefore, we have conducted the experiments from 5% to 25% for each interval of 5%. The intersections of summaries by summarization of different hierarchical structures are analyzed.

Table 1. Intersection Percentage of Summaries (Compression Ratio = 5%)

		By Event Topic	By No. of Document			By Time Interval		
			Deg. 2	Deg. 3	Deg. 4	Deg. 2	Deg. 3	Deg. 4
By Event Topic		-	44.3%	44.3%	41.6%	47.0%	43.8%	47.6%
By No. of Document	Deg. 2		-	84.1%	85.6%	67.8%	77.5%	79.1%
	Deg. 3			-	82.9%	66.1%	73.2%	76.4%
	Deg. 4				-	64.5%	76.6%	78.2%
By Time Interval	Deg. 2					-	69.3%	69.9%
	Deg. 3						-	86.6%
	Deg. 4							-

In our previous discussion, the number of children (degree) of a tree is limited to two for hierarchical tree by number of documents and by time interval. However, there may be a large number of children in the hierarchical tree by event topics. The number of children nodes will significantly affect the distribution of information. In order to have a fair comparison, we have conducted the experiment to summarize hierarchical tree with different degrees for these two hierarchical structures. For a fixed compression ratio, the summaries have an equal number of sentences. We calculate the intersection of two summaries as the number of sentences which appear in both summaries. The intersection of summaries with 5% compression ratio is reported in Table 1. As shown in the table, the intersection for summarization by event topics to another two hierarchical structures is not high. The intersection for summarization by number of document and summarization by time interval is higher. Moreover, the summarization of hierarchical structure of same classification with different degree has a high level of intersection.

Table 2. Average Intersection Percentage of Summaries

Compression Ratio	5%	10%	15%	20%	25%
Intersection Percentage	65.0%	59.5%	72.2%	74.7%	79.5%

Table 2 shows the impact of compression ratio on intersection of summaries. As the compression ratio increases, the intersection of summaries for summarization with different hierarchical structures increases. Because extraction of 20% sentences can be as informative as the full text of the source document [8], when the compression ratio is large, summarization of different hierarchical structures can extract the common set of essential information from source documents. Therefore, intersection percentage is high. However, the intersection of summaries cannot show the performance of summarization. Therefore, intrinsic evaluation and extrinsic evaluation will be conducted in next two subsections.

4.2 Intrinsic Evaluation of Summarization

Intrinsic evaluation is the most straight forward method to measure the quality of system summaries. It judges the quality of summaries by direct analyses in terms of some set of norms. One of the most common approaches is to match a system summary against an ideal summary.

Because highly-compressed abstracting is more useful [12] and there are a huge number of sentences within a collection of related news stories, user evaluation are conducted only at 5% compression ratio to reduce the workload of human abstractors. The collection of news stories is presented to human professionals, and they are asked to compose a covering summary for the incident. In order to have a fair comparison between the system summaries and the human abstract, the human professionals are asked to select specific number of most important sentences among the news stories as indicated by the compression ratio.

Table 3. Precision of Summaries with Different Degrees by Gold Standard

	By Even Topic	By No. of Documents			By Time Interval		
		Deg. 2	Deg. 3	Deg. 4	Deg. 2	Deg. 3	Deg. 4
Precision	77.1%	60.4%	57.7%	62.1%	57.7%	61.0%	57.3%
		60.1% (Mean)			58.7% (Mean)		

The system summaries are compared with human abstracts to measure the quality of summaries by gold standard [3]. The precision are shown in Table 3. The ANOVA shows that there is no significant difference among the precisions of summaries of one hierarchical structure with different degrees. Therefore, the mean of precision of one hierarchical structure with different degrees is taken as the precision of the hierarchical structure. One-way ANOVA reveals a significant difference between different document structures ($p < 0.002$). The t-test shows that the hierarchical summarization by event topics outperforms the hierarchical summarization by number of documents and the hierarchical summarization by time interval at 88% and 92% significance levels respectively. There is no significant difference identified between the hierarchical summarization by number of documents and the hierarchical summarization by time interval.

The precision of hierarchical summarization by event topics is significantly higher than the other two structures (Table 3). It can be explained by that news stories organized by event topics gives a more natural segmentation. When an author writes a large document with a lot of information, he groups similar information into same sections. Therefore, classification of news stories into event topics simulates the process of an author writing a large document. It is the most human-like classification of news stories. The other two structures partition the news stories by brute force, therefore, the themes among stories are not preserved. In conclusion, the hierarchical structure by event topics is the most natural partitioning of news stories. The hierarchical summarization is developed based on the hierarchical structure of document, and it does summarization in the similar way as a human abstractor. Therefore, it is perfectly matched with the document tree by event topics.

The intrinsic evaluation is based on human abstraction. However, it is very time-consuming for a human professional to compose an abstract. Therefore, it is extremely difficult to conduct the intrinsic evaluation with different parameter of settings. A more comprehensive experiment of extrinsic evaluation will be conducted in the next subsection.

4.3 Extrinsic Evaluation of Summarization

The extrinsic evaluation judges the quality of the summarization based on how it affects the completion of some other tasks. Among the extrinsic evaluations, the question-answering task is to find the "informativeness" of a summary, namely, the degree to which it contains answers found in the source document to a set of topic-related questions [5]. The question-answering task has been proved as a promising method for automated evaluation of summarization [5]. The quality of summaries will be measured by question-answering task in our study.

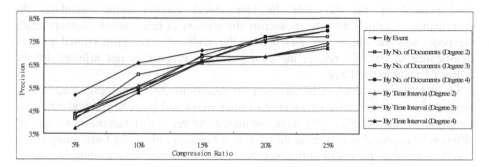

Fig. 3. Recall of Summaries in the Q&A Task for All Hierarchical Structures

Given a collection of news stories, human professionals are requested to prepare a set of topic-related questions and the answer keys using a common set of guidelines. These questions cover some essential information that is provided in any of the news stories. We have conducted experiments on the previous two incidents. The recall of the summarization is defined as the percentage of answers that can be found in the system summaries [5]. In the question-answering task, the set of questions and their answer keys can be used for evaluation at different compression ratios. Therefore, it is feasible to conduct experiments with different settings without increase in the workload on the human professionals. We have conducted experiments from 5% to 25% for each interval of 5% (Fig. 3).

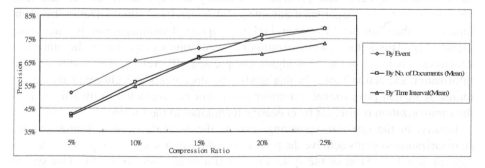

Fig. 4. Average Recall of Summaries in Q&A Task for Three Hierarchical Structures

In the intrinsic evaluation, no significant difference is identified among the precisions for the hierarchical trees with different degrees. For the extrinsic evaluation, we have also compared the recall of summarization of hierarchical trees with different degrees by ANOVA. It further confirms that there is no significant difference between different degrees. As a result, we take the mean of recalls of one hierarchical structure with different degrees as the overall recall of the hierarchical structure (Fig 4). The results in intrinsic and extrinsic evaluation have shown that the degree of a hierarchical tree will not affect the accuracy of hierarchical summarization. Similar observation is identified in the intersection analyses. It could be explained by the fact that the hierarchical summarization calculates the significance score of a node by measuring the amount of information contents inside the node, and the quotas are assigned to the nodes directly proportional to their significance score. Therefore, the summarization process is not affected by the degree of a hierarchical tree.

In the intrinsic evaluation, hierarchical summarization by event topics outperforms hierarchical summarization by number of documents and by time interval when the compression ratio is 5%. We have compared the recalls of summarization using different hierarchical structures at different compression ratios. By t-test analysis, we find that there is no major difference between the hierarchical summarization by number of documents and by time interval. However, we find that hierarchical summarization by event topics outperforms hierarchical summarization by number of documents and by time interval at 90% significance level, when the document is highly compressed, i.e., 5% and 10% compression ratio. However, as compression ratio increases, the recall increases and the difference diminishes. When the compression ratio is 15%, hierarchical summarization by event topics outperforms hierarchical summarization by number of documents, but there is no difference between hierarchical summarization by event topics and hierarchical summarization by time interval. When the compression ratio further increases, there is no significant difference identified among three hierarchical structures.

Because extraction of 20% sentences can be as informative as the full text of the source document [8], when the compression ratio is higher than 20%, most of the summarization systems can produce a summary as informative as the full text. Therefore, there is no significant advantage for hierarchical summarization by event topics over the other two. However, highly-compressed summarization is much more useful [12]. Hierarchical summarization by event topics outperforms the other two structures, when the summary is highly compressed. Therefore, it provides a useful information extraction tool. In this study, the documents are clustered into event topics by human professionals. Further study will be conducted to investigate how the summarization is affected by clustering techniques in the future.

Finally, in the question-answering task of the SUMMAC, it is found that the summarization systems achieve the peak value of recall when the compression ratio is 35% to 40% [5]. Most of the system recorded a recall about 60% [5]. Our system achieves a recall of 60% when the compression ratio is 10%, and a recall of 70% when the compression ratio is 20%. Hierarchical summarization of news stories organized in tree structure outperforms the participants in the SUMMAC. The results show that our system is a promising system for multi-document summarization.

5 Conclusion

Multi-document summarization is very useful to extract information from a large collection of news stories.   Three hierarchical structures have been proposed. Experimental results show that the hierarchical summarization of multiple documents organized in a hierarchical structure outperforms significantly the multi-document summarization without using hierarchical structure.   It also showed that hierarchical summarizations by event topics outperform the other two hierarchical structures when the summary is highly-compressed.   As there is a large volume of information related to an incident, a highly-compressed summarization is more desired.   This novel technique extracts essential information from a large number of documents effectively.

References

1. Edmundson H. New methods in automatic extraction. J. ACM, 16(2) 264-285, 1968.
2. Endres-Niggemeyer B. et al., How to implement a naturalistic model of abstracting: four core working steps of an expert abstractor. Info. Proc. & Manag., 31(5) 631-674, 1995.
3. Kupiec J. et al., A trainable document summarizer. SIGIR'95, 68-73, 1995.
4. Luhn H.P. The automatic creation of literature abstracts. IBM J. R&D, 159-165, 1958.
5. Mani I. et al., The tipster SUMMAC text summarization evaluation. 9th conference on European chapter of the Association for Computation Linguistics, 1999.
6. McKeown K. et al., Tracking and summarizing news on a daily basis with columbia's newsblaster. Human Language Technology Conference, 2002.
7. Mei Q. et al., Discovering evolutionary theme patterns from text: an exploration of temporal text mining. ACM SIGKDD, 198-207, 2005.
8. Morris G. et al., The effect and limitation of automated text condensing on reading comprehension performance. Information System Research, 17-35, 1992.
9. Nobata C. et al., A summarization system with categorization of document sets, Third NTCIR Workshop, 2003.
10. Ou S. et al., Development and evaluation of a multi-document summarization method focusing on research concepts and their research relationships, ICADL, 2005, 283-292.
11. Salton G. et al., Term-weighting approaches in automatic text retrieval.   Info. Proc. & Manag., 24, 513-523, 1988.
12. Teufel S. et al. Sentence extraction and rhetorical classification for flexible abstracts, AAAI'98 Spring Sym., Stanford, 1998.
13. Wang F. et al., Multi-document summarization for terrorism information extraction, IEEE ISI-2006, 2006.
14. Yang Y. et al., Learning approaches for detecting and tracking news events. Intelligent Information Retrieval, 32-43, 1999.
15. Yang C. et al., Fractal summarization: summarization based on fractal theory, SIGIR, 2003.

Wavelet-Based Collaborative Filtering for Adapting Changes in User Behavior

Hyeonjae Cheon, Hongchul Lee, and Insup Um

Department of Industrial Systems and Information Engineering
Korea University, 136-701 Seoul, South Korea
{slash, hclee, uis27}@korea.ac.kr

Abstract. Recommendation systems help users find the information, products and services they most want to find. Collaborative filtering is the method of making automatic predictions about the interest of a user by collecting interest information from many users, which has been very successful recommendation technique for recommendation systems in both research and practice. However, the traditional collaborative filtering is slow to detect the interest of a user changing with time as a case of user behavior and to adapt the changes, because the traditional collaborative filtering uses Pearson's correlation coefficient between users with the numerous values of property. In this paper, we apply the wavelet analysis to collaborative filtering in order to reveal the trends hidden in the interest of a user and propose the wavelet-based collaborative filtering for adapting changes in user behavior. The results of the performance evaluation show that the proposed wavelet-based collaborative filtering makes the improvement in the personalized recommendations.

Keywords: Recommendation system, Collaborative Filtering, User Behavior, Wavelet analysis.

1 Introduction

According as online services become various and grow, recommendation systems are have been made use of suggesting products to their users and providing users with information that help them decide which products they purchase in E-commerce sites. Collaborative filtering [4] systems work by collecting user feedback in the form of ratings for items in a given domain and exploit similarities and differences among profiles of several users in determining how to recommend an item, which has been very successful recommendation technique for recommendation systems in both research and practice. A variety of collaborative filtering algorithms have previously been reported in the world [5]. However, most algorithms have not considered the interest of a user changing with time as a case of user behavior although it is important to provide the recommendation services for customers in E-commerce sites. In this paper, we present a unique approach that the recommendation system automatically detects the interest of a user changing with time and adapts the changes in order to improve its performance.

S. Sugimoto et al. (Eds.): ICADL 2006, LNCS 4312, pp. 470–473, 2006.
© Springer-Verlag Berlin Heidelberg 2006

2 Wavelet-Based Collaborative Filtering

2.1 Item-to-Item Similarity

One critical step in our method is to compute the similarity between items for an active user u_a. The similarity between two items is computed by the Pearson's correlation coefficient [6]. We analyze the item-to-item similarities for an active user u_a using wavelet method [3] in order to detect the interest of a user changing with time.

2.2 Prediction

The prediction in our wavelet-based collaborative filtering is computed by (1).

$$prediction = \overline{u}_a + \frac{\sum_{i=1}^{n}(corr_{ai}) \times (r_i - \overline{r}_i) \times WT_i}{\sum_{i=1}^{n}|corr_{ai}|} \tag{1}$$

where $WT_i (1 \leq WT_i \leq 2)$ is the weight value for user u_i. High WT_i value means that u_a's interest is similar to u_i's interest at the same time period. WT_i is computed by the following steps:

1. Rearrange all items for an active user u_a with time.
2. Compute the item-to-item similarities between items.
3. Apply discrete wavelet (haar) transform [1] to the similarity signal.
4. Detect the recent time period t_a when u_a's interest changes (See Figure 1).
   - t_a is determined by the presence of high-frequency information (a sudden change or discontinuity around 64th item) in the approximation at level 5.
5. Select user u_i's items $\{I_1, \cdots, I_k\}$ from the items that both u_a and u_i rated during the time period t_a.
6. Construct a matrix W_i as (2), and compute AW_i, $\overline{AW_i}$ and WT_i as (3), (4) and (5).

$$W_i = \begin{array}{c} \begin{matrix} I_1 & I_2 & I_3 & \cdots & I_{k-1} & I_k \end{matrix} \\ \begin{bmatrix} w_{11} & w_{12} & 0 & \cdots & 0 & 0 \\ 0 & w_{22} & w_{23} & \cdots & 0 & 0 \\ \vdots & \vdots & \vdots & \cdots & \vdots & \vdots \\ 0 & 0 & \cdots & w_{k-2k-2} & w_{k-2k-1} & 0 \\ 0 & 0 & \cdots & 0 & w_{k-1k-1} & w_{k-1k} \end{bmatrix} \end{array} \tag{2}$$

$$AW_i = \begin{bmatrix} w_{11} & (w_{12} + w_{22}) & \cdots & (w_{k-2k-1} + w_{k-1k-1}) & w_{k-1k} \end{bmatrix} \tag{3}$$

$$\overline{AW_i} = \frac{w_{11} + (w_{12} + w_{22}) + \cdots + (w_{k-2k-1} + w_{k-1k-1}) + w_{k-1k}}{k}$$

$$= \frac{\sum w_{all}}{k}, -1 \le \overline{AW_i} \le 1 \tag{4}$$

$$WT_i = 1 + \overline{AW_i}, \quad if \ 0 < \overline{AW_i} \le 1$$

$$WT_i = 1, \quad\quad if \ \overline{AW_i} \le 0 \tag{5}$$

where each w is the half of item-to-item similarity derived from both adjacent items .
For example, $w_{11} = w_{12} =$ (item-to-item similarity between item I_1 and item I_2)/2. $\overline{AW_i}$
is the average of the sums of the columns except for 0 in (2).

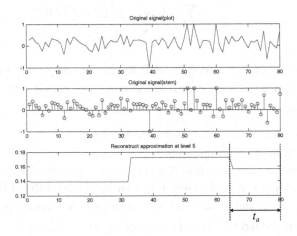

Fig. 1. Wavelet analysis (original signals and approximation at level 5)

3   Performance Evaluation

In order to evaluate the performances of our wavelet-based collaborative filtering, we
simulated the proposed system using data from MovieLens(http://movielens.umn.
edu). The data set consists of 100,000 ratings (1-5) from 943 users on 1682 movies.
411 users with more than 80 ratings are selected from the data set and are divided into
80% training set and 20% test set. Also, we used Mean Absolute Error (MAE) as a
metric for evaluating our algorithm and the traditional CF algorithm because it is most
commonly used and easiest to interpret directly. MAE between ratings and
predictions evaluate the accuracy of a system by comparing the numerical
recommendation scores against the actual user ratings for the user-item pairs in the
test data set.

We evaluated the traditional collaborative filtering (CF) and wavelet-based
collaborative filtering (WBCF) with training set and test set.

Table 1. Comparison of prediction quality of CF and OLBF

Neighborhood size(N)	5	10	15	20	25	**30**	35	40
WBCF	0.843	0.822	0.774	0.762	0.757	**0.739**	0.740	0.739
CF	0.841	0.824	0.782	0.767	0.769	**0.761**	0.759	0.758

Table 1 shows the MAE of both algorithms according to the neighborhood size. The size of the neighborhood is a important factor in the recommendation quality [2]. In this experiment, we varied the neighborhood size (N) from 5 to 40 with step 5. When the neighborhood size is 30, the related MAE of both algorithms is smaller than others. We determined the neighborhood size as $N = 30$. Also, it is observed that the prediction quality of wavelet-based collaborative filtering is better than that of the traditional collaborative filtering on the whole.

4 Conclusion

In this paper, we present a unique approach that the recommendation system automatically detects the interest of a user changing with time and adapts the changes in order to improve its performance. We proposed the wavelet-based collaborative filtering for recommendation system and compared it with the traditional collaborative filtering. Our results showed that our wavelet-based collaborative filtering held the promise of allowing collaborative filtering to adapt changes in user behavior and at the same time produced good performance.

Acknowledgments. This work was supported by the Brain Korea 21 Project in 2006.

References

1. Chui, C. K.: An Introduction to Wavelets. Academic Press, San Diego (1992)
2. Herlocker, J. L., Konstan, J.A., Riedl, J.: An algorithmic framework for performing collaborative filtering. In Proceedings of the ACM SIGIR '99. ACM Press (1999) 230-237
3. Mallat, S.G.: A theory for multiresolution signal decomposition: The wavelet representation. IEEE Transactions on Pattern Analysis and Machine Intelligence, Vol. 11 (1989) 674-693
4. Resnick, P., Iacovou, N., Suchak, M., Bergstrom., Riedl, J.: GroupLens: an open architecture for collaborative filtering of netnews. In Proceedings of the ACM CSCW '94. ACM Press (1990) 175-186
5. Sarwar, B. M., Karypis, G., Konstan, J. A., Riedl, J.: Analysis of Recommendation Algorithms for E-Commerce. In Proceedings of the ACM EC '00 Conference on Electronic Commerce, Minneapolis (2000) 158-167
6. Sarwar, B. M., Karypis, G., Konstan, J. A., Riedl, J.: Item-based Collaborative Filtering Recommender Algorithms. In Proceedings of the 10th International World Wide Web Conference (WWW10), Hong Kong (2001) 285-295

Activity-Based Query Refinement
for Context-Aware Information Retrieval

Shun Hattori, Taro Tezuka, and Katsumi Tanaka

Department of Social Informatics, Graduate School of Informatics, Kyoto University
Yoshida-Honmachi, Sakyo-ku, Kyoto 606-8501, Japan
Tel.: +81-75-753-5385; Fax: +81-75-753-4957
{hattori, tezuka, tanaka}@dl.kuis.kyoto-u.ac.jp

Abstract. Mobile Web search will gain more importance. This paper proposes a novel method for query refinement based on real-world contexts of a mobile user, such as his/her current geographic location and the typical activities at the location which are extracted by Blog mining. Our method enhances location-awareness and even further context-awareness to the existing location-free keyword-based Web search engines.

1   Introduction

With the exponentially growing amount of information available on the Web and the advances in wireless and mobile computing environments, we have been able to access information anywhere at any time in our daily life. Mobile Web search engines will increase their significance in the future. It is remarkably crucial to refine better the retrieval results in mobile computing environments, because mobile devices have poorer I/O user interfaces and we have little time for browsing information slowly while moving or doing some activities in the real world. However, mobile users' original queries are often so short and ambiguous that mobile Web search engines cannot guess their information demands accurately and thus would present too many and too noisy retrieval results.

There exist various approaches proposed for the so-called "mismatched query problem" in IR (Information Retrieval): query modification such as query expansion [1], query relaxation or query substitutions [2], automatic classification and visualization of the retrieval results by clustering, and written or spoken natural language querying [3]. Our work also relates very much to the research fields of Mobile IR [4, 5] and Context-Aware IR [6, 7, 8] for mobile and ubiquitous/pervasive computing environments.

In this paper, we propose a novel method for query refinement based on real-world contexts of a mobile user, such as his/her current geographic location and the typical activities at the location which are extracted by Weblog mining techniques. For instance, when a mobile user in a bookstore issues ["da vinci"] as an original query, our system would infer from his/her original query and current place-name as a real-world context that he/she is requesting information about not a movie but a book of "da vinci code", and offer or retrieve automatically by ["da vinci code" AND "book" AND "buy"] as one of its alternatives.

S. Sugimoto et al. (Eds.): ICADL 2006, LNCS 4312, pp. 474–477, 2006.

2   Query Refinement Based on Real-World Contexts

Our proposed method for refining a mobile user's original query based on real-world contexts, that consist of (1) the place-names which are obtained from his/her current geographic location and (2) the typical activities at the location which are extracted by Weblog mining techniques, executes the following flows.

Step 0. Query Inputted by Mobile User:
   A mobile user at certain location issues his/her original query q.
Step 1. Sensing Real-World Contexts:
   Obtain the user's current geographical coordinates (latitude and longitude or altitude) by receiving GPS or the user's current place-names by reading real-world embedded RFID tags linking location information.
Step 2. Translating Contexts into Contextual Words:
   Convert the above real-world contexts into "contextual words" that are place-names by using a GIS with data from residential maps and the typical activities (object-names and action-names) at the location of each place-name by mining blog data [9].
Step 3. Assigning Weight to Contextual Word:
   Assign to each contextual word c_i such as names of place, object and action, the weight $W(c_i; q)$ that evaluates its usefulness for expanding the query q. We will describe "context weighting" in detail in the last half of this section.
Step 4. Enforcing Query Refinement:
   Generate alternative queries that consist of the original query and the contextual word with higher weight and let the user select from among them, or presents the results retrieved by the alternative query with highest weight.

The advance of sensor technologies such as GPS or RFID allows mobile users to obtain their numerous real-world contexts. All of those information are, however, not always useful for query refinement to match their information demands. Therefore, it is very necessary to assign some sort of weight based on their original query to each real-world context, in order to classify whether or not it is useful for query refinement. We define the importance $W(c; q)$ of a contextual word c with regard to a user's original query q as follows. It is defined based on the proportion of the local probability $Pr(c|q) = \frac{DF(c \wedge q)}{DF(q)}$ of the contextual word c in the retrieval documents by the user's original query q to the global probability $Pr(c) = \frac{DF(c)}{N}$ of the contextual word c in the whole documents of the target corpus,

$$W(c; q) = \frac{Pr(c|q)}{Pr(c)} = \frac{DF(c \wedge q)}{DF(c)} \cdot \frac{N}{DF(q)} \simeq \frac{DF(c \wedge q)}{DF(c)} \cdot \alpha, \qquad (1)$$

where $DF(q)$ stands for the number of searched documents by submitting a query q to a search engine, N stands for the total number of documents in the corpus of the search engine, and α stands for the certain constant value when given the query. In this paper, we calculate each importance $W(c_i; q)$ where $\alpha = 1$ by using Google Blog Search [10] as the corpus.

3   Experimental Results

We have carried out some experiments, in order to justify that our method can improve the retrieval results by refining an original query by its related contextual words such as names of place, object and action. Table 1 shows each weight $W(c; q)$ of contextual word to "da vinci code" as a mobile user's original query. Because "da vinci code" has some subtopics such as "book" and "movie", we expected that the top 4 names of each subtable for Places, Objects and Actions have higher weight. Table 1 shows almost the same results as our expectation with respect to Places and Objects, but has some undesirable results with respect to Actions. Table 2 shows that our method can improve the approximate precision in the top 20 web pages googled [11] by adding each contextual word such as name of place, object or action to "da vinci code" as an original query. For mobile users, precision is generally more important than recall.

Table 1. Weight of Place/Object/Action-Name c to "da vinci code" as User Query q

Place	W(c;q)		Object	W(c;q)		Action	W(c;q)	
"bookstore"	(3)	0.00620	"book"	(4)	0.00940	"buy"	(7)	0.00116
"library"	(6)	0.00246	"novel"	(1)	0.03808	"order"	(3)	0.00156
"movie theater"	(1)	0.01059	"movie"	(3)	0.01163	"read"	(1)	0.00347
"theater"	(5)	0.00462	"film"	(2)	0.01429	"see"	(2)	0.00175
"church"	(2)	0.00891	"dvd"	(6)	0.00234	"climb"	(10)	0.00105
"hotel"	(10)	0.00094	"comic"	(5)	0.00425	"drive"	(8)	0.00109
"museum"	(4)	0.00516	"magazine"	(7)	0.00207	"learn"	(9)	0.00108
"restaurant"	(8)	0.00145	"game"	(8)	0.00156	"sell"	(6)	0.00126
"station"	(7)	0.00157	"drug"	(10)	0.00090	"swim"	(5)	0.00136
"university"	(9)	0.00142	"food"	(9)	0.00147	"walk"	(4)	0.00151

Table 2. Approximate Precision of the Top 20 Web Pages by Refining Query

Original/Refined Query	book (dvc)	movie (dvc)	both	others
"da vinci code"	0.50 (0.50)	0.30 (0.30)	0.05	0.15
"da vinci code" & "bookstore"	0.75 (0.70)	0.15 (0.15)	0.00	0.10
"da vinci code" & "book"	0.60 (0.55)	0.05 (0.05)	0.05	0.30
"da vinci code" & "novel"	**0.85 (0.80)**	0.00 (0.00)	0.05	0.10
"da vinci code" & "buy"	0.55 (0.50)	0.15 (0.15)	0.00	0.30
"da vinci code" & "read"	0.50 (0.45)	0.10 (0.10)	0.00	0.40
"da vinci code" & "theater"	0.00 (0.00)	0.65 (0.65)	0.10	0.25
"da vinci code" & "movie"	0.05 (0.05)	**0.80 (0.80)**	0.05	0.10
"da vinci code" & "film"	0.05 (0.05)	0.60 (0.60)	0.00	0.35
"da vinci code" & "see"	0.10 (0.10)	0.45 (0.45)	0.00	0.45

The number followed by '(' is the precision of web pages about the books or movies of "Leonardo da Vinci", and the number placed between '(' and ')' is the precision of web pages about the book or movies of "The Da Vinci Code".

4   Conclusion and Future Work

In this paper, we proposed a method for query refinement based on real-world contexts of a mobile user, such as his/her current geographic location and the typical activities at the location which are extracted by Weblog mining techniques, aiming to enhance location-awareness and even further context-awareness to the existing location-free keyword-based Web search engines. In the near future, we plan to develop and evaluate a prototype system based on our method, and then we would like to challenge to utilize not only current real-world contexts but also history of continuous past ones and/or prospective ones.

Acknowledgments. This work was supported in part by the Japanese MEXT the 21st Century COE (Center of Excellence) Program "Informatics Research Center for Development of Knowledge Society Infrastructure" (Leader: Katsumi Tanaka, 2002–2006), and the Japanese MEXT Grant-in-Aid for Scientific Research on Priority Areas: "Cyber Infrastructure for the Information-explosion Era", Planning Research: "Contents Fusion and Seamless Search for Information Explosion" (Project Leader: Katsumi Tanaka, A01-00-02, Grant#: 18049041).

References

1. Xu, J., Croft, W.B.: Query Expansion Using Local and Global Document Analysis. In: Proc. of the 19th Annual International ACM SIGIR Conference on Research and Development in Information Retrieval. (1996) 4–11
2. Jones, R., Rey, B., Madani, O., Greiner, W.: Generating Query Substitutions. In: Proc. of the 15th International Conference on WWW. (2006) 387–396
3. Chang, E., Seide, F., Meng, H.M., Chen, Z., Shi, Y., Li, Y.C.: A System for Spoken Query Information Retrieval on Mobile Devices. IEEE Transactions on Speech and Audio Processing **10** (2002) 531–541
4. Kawai, H., Akamine, S., Kida, K., Matsuda, K., Fukushima, T.: Development and Evaluation of the WithAir Mobile Search Engine. In: Proc. of the 11th International Conference on World Wide Web (WWW'02), Poster-ID:102. (2002)
5. Jose, J.M., Downes, S.: Evaluation of Mobile Information Retrieval Strategies. In: Proc. of the 5th ACM/IEEE-CS Joint Conference on Digital Libraries. (2005) 411
6. Jones, G.J.F., Brown, P.J.: Context Aware Retrieval for Ubiquitous Computing Environments. In: Proc. of the Mobile HCI 2003 International Workshop on Mobile and Ubiquitous Information Access, LNCS Vol.2954. (2004) 227–243
7. Yau, S.S., Liu, H., Huang, D., Yao, Y.: Situation-Aware Personalized Information Retrieval for Mobile Internet. In: Proc. of the 27th Annual International Computer Software and Applications Conference (COMPSAC'03). (2003) 638–645
8. Rhodes, B.: Using Physical Context for Just-in-Time Information Retrieval. IEEE Transactions on Computers **52** (2003) 1011–1014
9. Kurashima, T., Tezuka, T., Tanaka, K.: Blog Map of Experiences: Extracting and Geographically Mapping Visitor Experiences from Urban Blogs. In: Proc. of the 6th International Conference on WISE, LNCS Vol.3806. (2005) 496–503
10. Google Blog Search: http://blogsearch.google.com/.
11. Google: http://www.google.com/.

Retrieval Technique with the Modern Mongolian Query on Traditional Mongolian Text

Garmaabazar Khaltarkhuu and Akira Maeda

Graduate School of Science and Engineering, Ritsumeikan University
1-1-1, Noji Higashi, Kusatsu, 525-8577 Shiga, Japan
garmaabazar@gmail.com, amaeda@is.ritsumei.ac.jp

Abstract. This paper will discuss possibilities to create a digital library on traditional Mongolian script. Also we will introduce system architecture of a digital library that will store materials of historical importance written in traditional Mongolian which contain history of over 800 years. Specifically, we will propose a technique that will enable digital library system to allow users to search traditional Mongolian texts with keywords in modern Mongolian Cyrillic characters. To accomplish this goal, we will use Greenstone digital library system and it will be based on a traditional Mongolian dictionary.

Keywords: Traditional Mongolian Script, Digital library, Unicode.

1 Introduction

The main purpose of this research is to develop a technique to keep over 1,000 years old historical records written in traditional Mongolian script for futures use, to digitize all existing records and to make those data available for public screening.

We believe that the most efficient way to keep and protect old historical materials is to digitalize and create a digital library. This paper will introduce some ideas to build Mongolia-specific digital library for traditional Mongolian script documents.

2 Traditional Mongolian Script and Mongolian Language

The main purpose of this paper is to explore opportunities to build a traditional Mongolian script digital library. One of the biggest problems is that the traditional Mongolian script differs from the modern Mongolian language.

At present, people use dictionaries between the traditional Mongolian written words and modern Mongolian words. Mongolia introduced a new writing system (Cyrillic) in 1946. This has been a radical change and alienated the traditional Mongolian language. The traditional Mongolian script character code set has been placed in Unicode at the range of 1800-18ff [10]. But it is not enough to solve problems in processing information in Mongolian. The traditional Mongolian script is written vertically from top to bottom in columns advancing from left to right. This directional pattern is unique among existing scripts.

S. Sugimoto et al. (Eds.): ICADL 2006, LNCS 4312, pp. 478–481, 2006.

3   Traditional Mongolian Script Digital Library

3.1   Overview

In this section we will introduce traditional Mongolian script digital library with Cyrillic interface. We choose Greenstone Digital Library (GSDL), developed by New Zealand Digital Library (NZDL) Consortium at the University of Waikato[1]. The basic structure of our system is shown in Fig. 1.

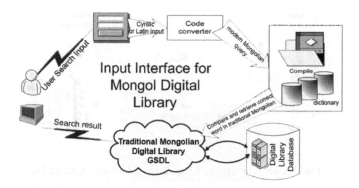

Fig. 1. Traditional Mongolian script digital library system. General architecture consist of user search input interface, converter, compiler, dictionary, GSDL core and display interface.

3.2   Architecture

3.2.1   Cyrillic and Latin Code Converter

One of the main functions of a digital library is the search engine. Input Method Editor (IME) is not available for traditional Mongolian script text input. On the other hand, text input in Cyrillic is available. If we take into account that in Mongolian it is relatively easy to find Cyrillic and Latin IME, these scripts should be used in our digital library's search engine. User will input keyword(s) in Cyrillic or in Latin alphabet. Since we have chosen GSDL as the base system, the user interface have to be web-based. An example of converting result is provided below.

Fig. 2. Cyrillic or Latin code converter interface. JavaScript is used to convert character sets as interface is web based.

After the conversion is complete, the system will search using converted text and display the results.

---

[1] http://www.greenstone.org

3.2.2   Code Conversion in Unicode for Display Interface

Mongolian characters are written in succession, meaning that depending on where the letter is placed in a word, it may have different forms. Unicode standard included only the basic character sets, special punctuation symbols and numerals, but does not explicitly encode the variant forms or the ligatures. In our case only basic characters will be stored in Digital library database. If we store letter's variant forms, indexing and searching functions will become complicated. Therefore we will use code converter to display already stored basic characters correctly. Example is shown in Fig. 3.

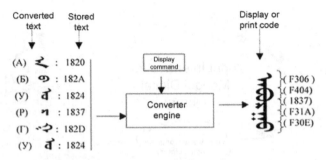

Fig. 3. Converter engine for traditional Mongolian script [4]

There are control-symbols encoded that can be used to resolve ambiguities in few cases where the context rules are inadequate. These control-symbols can also be used to override the default forms if it is required. We will develop an algorithm to display the traditional Mongolian characters correctly using control characters and/or basic characters. This is one of the most important parts of traditional Mongolian script digital library.

3.3   Greenstone Digital Library Experiment

To test Greenstone digital library compatibility with traditional Mongolian script, we have created traditional Mongolian collection. Collection was created without any problem with MS Word document, HTML file and plain text file. Title list of collection is shown in Fig. 4.

Fig. 4. Greenstone collection of traditional Mongolian text

Afterwards, we have tried default search function of Greenstone digital library. Sample of text inputting is shown in Fig. 5. So far we just tested traditional Mongolian keyword search on traditional Mongolian text. In near future we will concentrate on our main research Cyrillic and Latin keyword search in traditional Mongolian text.

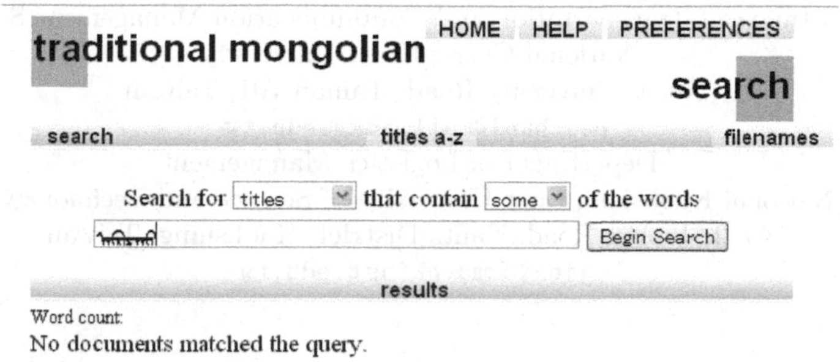

Fig. 5. Search result of traditional Mongolian collection

4   Conclusion and Future Work

In this research we introduced suitable system architecture for a traditional Mongolian script digital library. We proposed possible methods for traditional Mongolian text displaying and converting user search text that will enable digital library system to allow users to search traditional Mongolian text with keywords in modern Mongolian characters. Those are main parts of traditional Mongolian script digital library. For the purpose of creating a digital library of materials written in traditional Mongolian script, it is important to invent a way to connect the traditional Mongolian text and the modern Mongolian text.

Moreover, display character codes with control-symbols and searching on those codes still remaining as a major problem.

References

1. Mikami, Y.: A History of Character Codes in Asia. Kyoritsu publishers, Japan (2002) (in Japanese)
2. Насан-Урт, С.: Монгол хэл бичгийн сураг занги боловсруулах онол практикийн зарим асуудал. Улаанбаатар (2004) (in Mongolian)
3. Erdenechimeg, M., Moore, R., M., Namsrai, Yu.: UNU/IIST Technical Report No. 170 – Traditional Mongolian Script in the ISO/Unicode Standards (1999)
4. Man, D., Fujii, A., Ishikawa, T.: A Method for Electronizing the Traditional Mongolain Script and Its Application to Text Retrieval. The IEICE Transactions D-II Vol. J88-D-II No.10 (2005) 2102-2111(in Japanese)

Empirical Investigation on Interface Usage of Citation Database

Pei-Chun Lin[1] and Chen-Cheng Chen[2]

[1] Department of Transportation and Communication Management Science,
National Cheng Kung University,
No. 1, University Road, Tainan 701, Taiwan
peichunl@mail.ncku.edu.tw
[2] Department of Logistics Management,
National Kaohsiung First University of Science and Technology,
No. 2, Juoyue Road, Nantz District, Kaohsiung, Taiwan
jjen@ccms.nkfust.edu.tw

Abstract. This study seeks to report an investigation into the ways in which end-users perceived citation database interfaces (CDI). The investigation uses the Technology Acceptance Model (TAM) constructs of usefulness and ease of use to assess acceptance of citation database interfaces by university graduate students. A structural equation model was used to fit and validate the Citation Database Interface Acceptance Model (CDIAM) and the results indicate good fit to the data. The causal relationships between the constructs considered by the CDIAM are well supported, accounting for 95% of the total variance in the citation database interface acceptance and usage. This study concluded that usefulness and ease of use for citation database interface are proved to be key determinants of the acceptance and usage of citation database. This study may help explain human-computer interaction using MIS-proven TAM instead of traditional system usability approach.

1 Introduction

The interface design of citation databases has been dominated by the use of menus systems, with the majority of citation database interfaces relying on user interaction with menus as the main dialogue structure. Prior research in designing menu interfaces indicates that different ways of menu item organization affect user performance in terms of time, accuracy and user satisfaction, and also reveals that interface usability affects thesaurus browsing/navigation and other information-searching behaviors. Web sites are an increasingly important part of a library's service. As such, it is crucial that they are easy to navigate and deliver the required information in a clear and consistent manner. Human-computer interaction (HCI) with the design, evaluation and implementation of interactive computing systems for human use, is proved to be useful for improving the usability of traditional interactive applications [3]. Determining the psychometric properties of key constructs such as usefulness and ease of use is

S. Sugimoto et al. (Eds.): ICADL 2006, LNCS 4312, pp. 482–485, 2006.

of paramount importance in establishing the quality of user interactions with database interfaces.

This study adopts the Technology Acceptance Model (TAM) and integrates it with theoretical and empirical finding from prior usability research for information system to model the usability of database interfaces. The TAM developed by Davis, et al. [1] has received little attention among HCI practitioners and system designers. However, TAM appears to offer HCI professionals a theoretically grounded approach to software acceptability, which can be directly coupled to usability evaluation [2]. This study asked subjects recruited at National Sun Yat Sen University (NSYSU) and National Kaohsiung First University of Science and Technology (NKFUST) in Taiwan to query two popular citation databases, ABI/INFORM and Science Direct OnSite (SDOS), at university libraries. The primary research questions to be addressed in this study are as follows:

- Would perceived ease of use or perceived usefulness of citation database interface affect on its usage?
- Whether interface language would interfere the strength of perceived usefulness of citation database interface would affect its usage?
- Whether user characteristics such as gender, university would interfere the strength of perceived usefulness of citation database interface would affect its usage?

2 Research Method

Three constructs were used as acceptance indicators: ease of use, usefulness, and usage. The usefulness of the citation database interface is defined as "the students' beliefs that using a citation database interface will enhance their searching performance, efficiency, and effectiveness". Ease of use refers to "the extent to which the user expects the use of the citation database interface to be free of effort". The usage of the citation database interface is the intent to use the citation database interface. Students are likely to choose the citation database interface as a research support technology if they perceive that this technology would help them to improve their searching effectiveness and efficiency. Therefore, a useful citation database needs a suitable interface. CDIAM is TAM applied to the citation database interface, therefore the basic TAM hypotheses are to be verified. The first hypothesis tests the relationship between citation database interface ease of use and usefulness. The ease of use is postulated to affect the usefulness of the citation database interface. Accordingly, the following hypothesis is proposed.

H1. The ease of use of a citation database interface significantly affects its usefulness.

A citation database interface that is easy to use is likely to be well accepted and used. The second hypothesis tests the relationship between ease of use and the acceptance and usage of the citation database interfaces. The ease of use is postulated to affect the usage and acceptance of the citation database interfaces. Accordingly, the second hypothesis is proposed.

H2. The ease of use of a citation database interface significantly affects its usage and acceptance.

If students perceive the interface of a citation database as useful, then they are likely to find it acceptable for future usage. Accordingly, the following hypothesis is proposed:

H3. Usefulness is important in predicting the citation database usage. The usefulness of citation database interface usefulness positively affects its usage.

This study hypothesizes that a user's perceptions of usefulness to his usage and acceptance of citation database interface does not vary according to the interface language, gender and university.

H4. Perceptions of usefulness of a citation database interface influence usage and acceptance by both Chinese and English interfaces equally.

H5. Perceptions of usefulness of a citation database interface influence usage and acceptance by both male and female students equally.

H6. Perceptions of usefulness of a citation database interface influence usage and acceptance by graduate students at NSYSU and NKFUST equally.

3   Hypothesis Testing

The Structural Equation Modeling was utilized to examine the full CDIAM and evaluate its goodness of fit. The modification indices recommended by AMOS 5.0 were adopted, and the standardized residuals were verified. The path coefficients for three measurement subsystems were all above 0.7. The χ^2 value indicates that the CDIAM fitted the collected data ($\chi^2 = 11.179$, p-value $= 0.083 > 0.05$, and χ^2/degree-of-freedom$=1.863$). The GFI and AGFI values were 0.973 and 0.906 also indicating a good fit. Furthermore, the RMR value of 0.049 was within the acceptable levels. The explained variance of citation database interface usefulness was 33%. The CDIAM as a whole explains 95% of the variance in the acceptance of citation databases interfaces.

The direct path {CDI ease of use $\rightarrow$ usefulness} is significant since the regression coefficient is 0.501 with $p < 0.0001$. Therefore, the hypothesis **H1** is supported, which implies that the ease of use of a citation database interface significantly affects its usefulness. Although the path {CDI ease of use $\rightarrow$ usage} has insignificant direct effect on the usage and acceptance, it has significant indirect and total effects on the usage and acceptance via usefulness. The bootstrap approximation obtained by constructing two-sided bias correlation confidence intervals demonstrated that the unstandardized indirect effect and total effect of CDI ease of use were significantly different from zero at the 0.01 level ($p=0.001$, two-sided). Therefore, the hypothesis **H2** is supported, which indicates that the ease of use of the citation data-base interfaces significantly affects its usage and acceptance. The unstandardized total effect of the ease of use of the citation database interface on the usage and acceptance of citation database interface was 57%. The third hypothesis **H3** is accepted because the direct path {CDI usefulness $\rightarrow$ usage} is significant, having a regression parameter of 1.09 with $p < 0.0001$. The results indicated that CDI usefulness had the strongest direct impact on CDI usage and acceptance, and that CDI ease of use had a significant direct impact on CDI usefulness, whereas the CDI ease of use had a smaller direct effect on CDI usage and acceptance.

This study then applied the "Manage Models" and "Manage Groups" dialog built into AMOS 5.0 to test hypotheses 4, 5 and 6. The hypothesis **H4** is supported, which means that a user's perceptions of usefulness of a citation database interface influences his usage and acceptance of both Chinese and English interfaces equally. The hypothesis **H5** is supported, which means that a user's perceptions of usefulness of the citation database interface influences usage and acceptance equally among both male and female users. However, the hypothesis **H6** is not supported, which means a user's perceptions of usefulness of the citation database interface influences her or his usage and acceptance more strongly for graduate students at NSYSU than at NKFUST. This result is possibly due to the different focus of the two universities. NSYSU is much more research orientated than NKFUST.

4 Conclusions

The purpose of this study was to investigate the acceptance of citation database interfaces as research tools in higher education institutions as perceived by university first-year graduate students. The causal relationships among the constructs were well supported. The CDIAM analysis indicates that the perceived usefulness of citation database interfaces has a significant direct impact on the usage and acceptance of citation database interface. Ease of use significantly affects the students' perceived usefulness directly and the acceptance indirectly through the usefulness of mediating construct in citation database interface.

This study shows how first-year graduate students who are unfamiliar with the ABI/INFORM and SDOS citation databases rated their perceptions of interface usage after conducting several queries. TAM provides a theoretically sound and parsimonious method for evaluating the citation database interface. By gathering user perceptions of a citation database interface's usefulness and ease of use, developers can accurately assess whether systems will ultimately be accepted by users and design a user-centered interface. Future study should incorporate the design of the user interface to increase the usability of citation database system.

References

1. Davis, F. D., Bagozzi, R. P. and Warshaw, P. R.: User acceptance of computer technol-ogy: a comparison of two theoretical models, Management Science, Vol. 35(8), 982-1003 (1989)
2. Morris, M. G., Dillon, A.: How user perceptions influence software use?, IEEE Software, Vol. 14(4), 58-65 (1997)
3. Schmidt, C. T.: The systemics of dialogism: on the prevalence of the self in HCI design, Journal of the American Society for Information Science, Vol. 48(11), 1073-1081 (1997)

Adding SOMLib Capabilities to the Greenstone Digital Library System

Rudolf Mayer and Andreas Rauber

Institute of Software Technology and Interactive Systems
Vienna University of Technology, Vienna, Austria
mayer@ifs.tuwien.ac.at, rauber@ifs.tuwien.ac.at
http://www.ifs.tuwien.ac.at/~[mayer,andi]

Abstract. Many conventional digital library systems offer access to their collections only via full text or meta-data search, or by browsing-access via a hierarchy of categories. With the increasing amount of digital content available, alternative methods to access the content seem necessary. The SOMLib system, which is based on using Self-Organizing Maps (SOMs), has been used to automatically organize documents of a digital library by their content. In this paper, we present an integration of this system into the popular open-source digital library system Greenstone, combining searching and explorative browsing through the thematically organized content using the map. We present the system on a demo collection consisting of the abstracts of papers and posters from the last 5 years from the JCDL, ECDL and ICADL conferences.

1 Introduction

Digital library systems provide a uniform way to organize, maintain and access collections of digital objects, may they be text, images, audio, or others. However, many conventional digital library systems have shortcomings on providing the user with ways to access and retrieve their content. This is due to many of the systems offering access to their collections only via full text or meta-data search or browsing-access via simple ordered lists or a hierarchy of categories.

The SOMLib system [1], which is based on using Self-Organizing Maps (SOMs) [2], has been successfully used to automatically organize documents of a digital library by their content. The user can explore the thus generated map, as she is used to exploring a conventional geographical map. However, this approach can only be understood as an addition to traditional ways of retrieving the information. Therefore, integrating both traditional ways like full text or meta-data search and explorative search via the SOMLib map is necessary.

In this paper, we present a system that integrates SOMLib features into the popular digital library system *Greenstone*. The system thus created combines full text or meta-data search with explorative browsing through the thematically organized content. This is achieved by visualizing the search results on the map, and by including map-selections into the list of results. This way, users can easily find documents which are similar in content to their search result

S. Sugimoto et al. (Eds.): ICADL 2006, LNCS 4312, pp. 486–489, 2006.

and may therefore be relevant to them, but were not retrieved by conventional search methods. With an advanced SOMViewer interface, additional means of interaction become possible.

The remainder of this paper is organized as follows. In Section 2 we will give an introduction into retrieval capabilities offered by conventional digital library systems, based on the example of Greenstone. Section 3 shortly describes the Self-Organizing Map and the SOMLib digital library system, and presents the integration of SOMLib and Greenstone. We give conclusions and an outlook on future work in Section 4.

2   The Greenstone Digital Library System

Greenstone is a popular open-source digital library system for constructing comprehensive document collections [3]. As other systems, Greenstone supports the generation of indices of various kinds of media (e.g. text, images, audio and video). Documents of any kind can further be described by a set of additional meta-data information. Greenstone offers two widely used ways to locate documents within the collection: full text and meta-data based *search*, and *browsing*.

Search: The full text and meta-data search allows for proximity search and exact phrase search. Additionally, a fielded search is provided, which allows the user to combine searching on different indices at the same time. Although a very powerful tool, especially compared to conventional libraries, searching inherits a few problems: First, broadly formulated queries may lead to huge result lists. Although the documents the user is looking for will probably be part of the result list, it is quite unlikely that she will look through the whole list to find them. Another problem is known as the vocabulary problem: the same object or action may be named differently by different people, resulting in a low recall when query terms differ from the terms used in the documents.

Browsing: Browsing offers an (ordered) list of the documents in the collection, built on meta-data. Greenstone offers browsing by providing a simple scrollable list of the documents, ordered according to a given meta-data field. Moreover, Greenstone offers a hierarchical classication, which allows to define an arbitrary number of levels of hierarchies. However, the meta-data hierarchy has to be defined separately by the user. The quality of the meta-data is crucial for the meta-data based searching and browsing. If some meta-data is not available for a document, the document can not be easily found through that search or browsing list. Another problem is inconsistency, for example two documents having the same author might have different meta-data due to different spellings of the name, or different ordering of name and surname.

Some of the mentioned disadvantages can be solved by the proposed integration of the SOM into a digital library system.

3   A Self-Organizing Map for Greenstone

Self-Organizing Maps and SOMLib

The Self-Organizing Map [2] is a well known and widely used neural network model based on unsupervised learning. The SOM provides a mapping from a high-dimensional input space to a lower dimensional output space. In this mapping, the SOM preserves the topology of the input space, i.e. input patterns that are located close to each other in the input space will also be located closely in the output space, while dissimilar patterns will be mapped on to opposite map regions. In our application, the input space is formed by a vector-space representation of the documents of the digital library collection. The features of the vector are selected according to their document frequency, and the weights are computed using a standard $tf \times idf$ weighting scheme.

The SOMLib digital library system [1] creates maps of a document collection. A rich desktop client application allows interactive exploration of the data space by zooming into and selecting areas of documents. The system can organize any kind of objects that can be represented numerically by feature vectors, such as text, images and music [4].

Greenstone Integration

Greenstone offers in its current version 3 an open architecture that allows developers to provide additional services to a Greenstone collection. We make use of this plug-in architecture to provide our own service as an extension, based on the existing query services. That way, the user can still use all the basic functionality provided by Greenstone. Additionally, she will be able to use the wealth of additional information the SOM mapping provides about the documents matching the query results and the whole collection itself.

The map can be used in two different ways. First, results of the Greenstone search will be highlighted on the map: map nodes that contain at least one of the documents matched by the query are indicated by a white circle. With this visualization of the search results, the user can immediately see which documents have a topical similarity - these documents will all be located close to each other and form a cluster on the map. Additionally, outliers become visible as isolated spots on the map.

Secondly, the user can explore the map - she can select nodes, upon which the documents lying on that nodes will be added to the result list of the Greenstone search. Documents that have been matched both by the map selection and the search result will be marked especially. The user can get additional information on the content of the collection by just moving over a node of the map with the mouse, upon which a pop-up will display terms that describe the documents on that node the best. This is achieved by utilising the LabelSOM algorithm [5].

Figure 1 depicts the standard search interface of Greenstone, extended by the SOM map on the top-right corner. The collection used in this example consists of the abstracts of the accepted papers and posters of the three major conferences on digital libraries during the last years: JCDL (2001-2005), ECDL (2001-2005), and ICADL (2002-2005). It contains 1051 documents. In the given example,

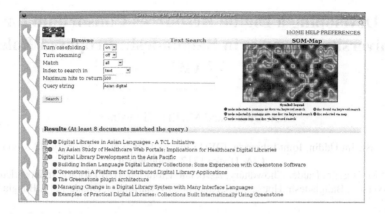

Fig. 1. Enhancing the traditional Greenstone query search with a SOMLib map

the user has issued a query 'Asian digital', wanting to search for documents dealing with Asian digital libraries, and got 3 hits. However, manually inspecting the map on the search hits, the user however is possible to detect five more documents. Of those, one deals with an Indian digital library, and two others deal with international digital libraries and may be relevant for her.

4   Conclusion and Future Work

In this paper we presented an integration of a SOM map into a conventional digital library system such as Greenstone. This combination allows the user to use both traditional search and browsing with a wealth of new exciting possibilities to exploratively search in the digital library's content. Future work will focus on increasing the level of interaction with the map, as it is already now possible in the desktop application (e.g. zooming functionality).

References

1. Rauber, A., Merkl, D.: The SOMLib digital library system. In: European Conference on Digital Libraries, Paris, France (1999) 323–342
2. Kohonen, T.: Self-Organizing Maps. Volume 30 of Springer Series in Information Sciences. Springer, Berlin, Heidelberg (1995)
3. Witten, I.H., Bainbridge, D., Boddie, S.J.: Greenstone: Open-source digital library software. D-Lib Magazine **7** (2001)
4. Neumayer, R., Dittenbach, M., Rauber, A.: PlaySOM and PocketSOMPlayer: Alternative interfaces to large music collections. In: Proceedings of the Sixth International Conference on Music Information Retrieval (ISMIR 2005), London, UK (2005) 618–623
5. Rauber, A., Merkl, D.: Text mining in the SOMLib digital library system: The representation of topics and genres. Applied Intelligence **18** (2003) 271–293

Developing a Digital Resources Consortium for University Libraries in Bangladesh: Proposed Role of UGC

M.N. Uddin[1] and M.H.H. Chowdhury[2]

[1] Md. Nazim Uddin, Joint Librarian, EWU Library, East West University, 43 Mohakhali C/A, Dhaka 1212, Bangladesh
[2] M. Hossam Haider Chowdhury, Associate Librarian, IUB Library, Independent University, Bangladesh, House no. 6, Road no. 14, Baridhara, Dhaka 1212, Bangladesh

Abstract. University Grants Commission (UGC) of Bangladesh has taken an initiative to form a Digital Resources Consortium for the university libraries in Bangladesh for sharing integrated library systems and computer databases, collection development, purchasing of electronic journals, and digital resources. As of today there is no formal platform of consortium is established in Bangladesh. This paper attempt to analyze the suitability of formation of consortium in Bangladesh based on the requirement and usage of digital information and gives some overview of progress in developing a consortium for academic libraries in Bangladesh, with an emphasis on the role of UGC Bangladesh.

Keywords: Digital libraries, Consortia, Information services, Information technology, Bangladesh.

1 Preamble of Consortium in Bangladesh

The University Grants Commission (UGC) of Bangladesh [1] initiated Digital Resources Consortium in Bangladesh would unveil enormous opportunities in the field of education and research. In order to provide the current literature to academia, UGC has initiated for formation of Digital Resources Consortium in Bangladesh. A 4-member Committee has already been assigned at UGC to draft a concept paper on forming a consortium in Bangladesh.

2 Methodology

In order to provide a detailed analysis of the literature on digital resources consortium for university libraries in Bangladesh, many webliographic sources were consulted. We attended meetings, which were conducted by the UGC Bangladesh. We also participated in the discussion of UGC meeting, exchanged views, shared opinions, and finally submitted a concept paper on Consortium of University and Research

S. Sugimoto et al. (Eds.): ICADL 2006, LNCS 4312, pp. 490–493, 2006.

Libraries in Bangladesh (CURLB) to the UGC. The draft concept paper was developed by the authors of this article and other two authors. Current situation of consortium in Bangladesh, documentary sources and direct observations are the major methods of this article.

3   Local Librarians' Initiative for Consortium

About a year back a small group of local librarians including the author of this article working at private university libraries discussed many issues on the development of academic libraries including information resources sharing in the line of reducing journals' prices, inter-library cooperation, jointly acquiring new resources at a great savings, and strengthening professional relationship among universities. The co-author of this article informed us that he has already started subscription to very expensive e-journals through Balani-Infotech, New Delhi, India, who is the sole agent for some e-resources of this region. Two Librarians (author and co-author of this article), in charge of East West University and Independent University, Bangladesh shared opinion each other on inter-library cooperation as the university management wants to have the best services from their libraries but at the reduced cost. In the month of August 2005, Mr. Nirmal of Balani-Infotech came to Bangladesh for exploring new institutional subscribers. Mr. Nirmal held some meetings with the local librarians and also held a meeting with the member of UGC, where the local university librarians participated. As a result an overview paper was prepared for forming a consortium in Bangladesh [3]. About three months back, the local librarians particularly four major top private university librarians of North South University (NSU); Independent University, Bangladesh (IUB); BRAC University (BU); and East West University (EWU), sat together, floated ideas and exchanged views with each other on library resources for sharing what the universities don't have. After a few months, Dr. Javed I. Khan, Fulbright Senior Specialist, Kent State University, USA, visited Bangladesh and expressed his interest to guide for formation of Research and Education Network (REN) and Bangladesh Digital Library Consortium (BDLC). He has recently submitted a draft proposal to the UGC. Recently Bangladesh Association of Librarians, Information Scientists, and Documentalists (BALID) organized a seminar on Impact of Digital Libraries for Higher Education and Research in Bangladesh where Mr. S.I. Khan presented a keynote paper [4].

4   Present Scenario of Consortium in Bangladesh

At present, there is no library consortium in Bangladesh. In the past, UGC had taken many initiatives for sharing information resources of different universities for the benefits of the universities. Since, 1980s' there have been a number of attempts by UGC to unify the library catalogue systems and even to arrange some form of cooperative journal subscription for sharing resources. However, it is yet to be realized due to financial constraints. None of the public universities, including the largest research and technical universities Open University (OU) and Bangladesh University of Engineering and Technology (BUET) can provide access to any electronic journal to its students or faculty. Few private universities provide access to limited collections namely DOAJ, AGORA, HINARI, OUP, eGrannary, EMERALD, ACM, IEEE, and JSTOR. Not a single institution in Bangladesh could afford the institutional membership to any major medical, engineering, or technology collections; such as ACM, IEEE, Elsevier, Academic Press journals, and proceedings [2]. After 1992 Private University Act, many private universities particularly some top ranking universities came forward and emphasized to establish an automated modern library in respective premises with all IT facilities i.e. computer network, Internet, and email, etc. Out of 54 private universities, two or three of them have their own VSAT.

In 1998, there were a networking attempt called Bangladesh National Scientific and Library Information Network (BANSLINK). This Project was initiated by the Bangladesh National Scientific, Technical and Documentation Centre (BANSDOC). It ventured to connect libraries across the country by setting up a network with 15 libraries- 6 out of Dhaka and 9 in Dhaka via dial-up links. The initiative fell apart due to administrative reorganization at the top and subsequent lack of appreciation [2].

We are not highly ambitious for formation of consortium in Bangladesh at this moment, because of our limited infrastructure facilities and resources. But we are very much interested to form this consortium for the greater interest of our own existence in the global village. Proposed Consortium may be divided into three phases. In 2003, UGC recommended in the light of the National Conference of Inter-University IT Professionals in Bangladesh that "a common library for all Universities is required"[5]. We all must admit that the problems were too hard and too expensive for libraries to undertake alone. Both private and public university libraries will achieve great benefits from this form of co-operation (please see the table).

Table 1. Beneficiaries of the Proposed Consortium

Types	Institutions
Public Universities	20
Private and International Universities	54
Public Medical and Dental Colleges	14
Private Medical and Dental Colleges	17
Open University	1
National University	1
Research Instituites/Centres	58
Research Academy	3
Total Universities and other Institutes	168

5   Implementation Plan for Formation of Consortium

UGC of Bangladesh will act as a coordinating agency to implement the project. UGC will engage all universities to draw, design, and prepare a work plan for implementation of the said project. UGC, Donor Agency, and participant university partners will work together. However, administration of the project will be run by the UGC. Three phases implementation plan may be made for formation of Consortium -

Phase 1. Consortium may be launched immediately by the university libraries, which are already connected with Internet and having basic IT facilities. Interested Research Organizations which have basic IT facilities in Bangladesh may join this proposed Consortium in phase 1. Which institutions do not have those facilities, they should join in phase 2 plan.

Phase 2. Draft proposal submitted to the UGC by Dr. Javed I. Khan may be considered for implementation in phase 2. Dr. Khan has given some guidelines for formation of Bangladesh Digital Library Consortium in his proposal. That proposal will be considered as a national project. Participants of phase 1 consortium may take part in dialogue for sharing their experiences gained in phase 1. E-Journal Consortium project may be upgraded in phase 2. Prepare recommendations for implementation of project in phase 3.

Phase 3. Phase 1 and phase 2 plan may be implemented in phase 3 with all IT facilities and ensure dissemination of information through the consortium with reduced cost but maximum benefit. Keep an eye on the project, review it and take steps for further improvement, if required.

6 Conclusion

Bangladesh being a developing country should form a body among the university libraries to catch the new opportunity to make her people competent for the world. UGC's initiative for formation of Consortium would develop facilities for making suitable environment for higher education and research by which the country will be benefited ultimately.

References

1. University Grants Commission of Bangladesh: [Got access on 18 March 2006, http://www.ugc.org/ugcb.htm]
2. Khan, Javed I.: A Global Perspective on University Libraries and a Roadmap for Bangladesh Digital Library Consortium (Draft). Department of Computer Science, Kent State University, Kent (2006) 6-7
3. Abdussattar, M., Chowdhury, M.H.H.: Overview on Consortium as Background Paper of Forming Consortium with the University Libraries of Bangladesh. Dhaka (2005) [The Paper submitted to UGC by the authors]
4. Khan, M.S.I., Nazim Uddin, M.: Impact of digital library on higher education and research in Bangladesh. Dhaka (2006) [a paper presented at the Seminar on Impact of Digital Library on Higher Education and Research in Bangladesh organized by Bangladesh Association of Librarians, Information Scientists, and Documentalists (BALID), held in Planning Academy Auditorium, Nilkhet, Dhaka, Bangladesh, on 05 May 2006]
5. Bangladesh University Grants Commission: Development of University Libraries in Bangladesh. UGC Annual Report 2003, Dhaka (2004) 125-7

Speech Audio Retrieval Using Voice Query

Chotirat Ann Ratanamahatana and Phubes Tohlong

Dept. of Computer Engineering, Chulalongkorn University, Bangkok 10330 Thailand
ann@cp.eng.chula.ac.th, Tohlong@hotmail.com

Abstract. Multimedia data has increasingly become a prevalent resource in Digital Library system; this includes audio, video, and image archives. However, each type of these data may need specific tools to help facilitate effective and efficient retrieval tasks. In this paper, we focus on retrieval of speech audio collection, which includes audio books, speech recordings, interviews, and lectures. Currently, most of the audio retrieval systems are based on keyword/title/author search typed into the system by users. The system then searches for particular keywords and gives a list of entire audio files that potentially are relevant to the query. Nonetheless, browsing audio content for particular section of the audios without knowing the actual content is yet a very difficult task. Moreover, since audio transcription or keyword annotation is very labor intensive and becomes infeasible for large data, we introduce here a preliminary framework that locates subsections of the audio that correspond to the voice query made by a user. We demonstrate a utility of our approach on query retrieval tasks in various types of audio recordings. We also show that this simple framework can potentially help retrieve and locate the voice query within the audio accurately and efficiently.

Keywords: Audio retrieval, time series, query by example, voice search.

1 Introduction

Speech processing has established itself in research communities since 1950s. However, it still has many unsolved problems and remains a very challenging and active area of research nowadays due to its exceptionally complex nature of the problem itself. Many speech processing techniques have been proposed for speech audio retrieval [1][6][7]. In spite of this, none of them have really solved a problem of searching the actual content within large retrieved audio files. Instead, the search processes usually are text-based or voice query, searching for entire audio files according to provided titles, authors, and keywords [1][3]. Some system may need manual transcription of the speech/audio into text before searching can be performed. It would be very helpful and more convenient if we can search *any* part of the speech audio using our voice as a query without having to do the transcription. This paper proposes a preliminary alternative to textual annotations, which is based on time series features extracted from the raw speech data.

S. Sugimoto et al. (Eds.): ICADL 2006, LNCS 4312, pp. 494–497, 2006.
© Springer-Verlag Berlin Heidelberg 2006

1.1 Motivation

Our motivation started from an attempt to search the recorded lectures archived in the digital library collection. At this point, we can generally search for audio files as a whole, based on keywords, titles, and authors. However, if the retrieved audio file is very long, it is still extremely hard to browse or locate the exact content within the audio, when we are interested only in some parts of the recording; it is more likely that a user would like to only hear subsections within the audio file instead of having to listen to the whole audio from the beginning.

This work is based on a query-by-example (QBE) technique, where users provide voice/speech examples of the word or phrase they seek. Some may argue that this query-by-example approach has a major limitation when the users really want to search for semantic concepts rather than the "exact" word or phrase; rather, query by keyword approaches may be more appropriate. Since these types of research have been a research of interest within speech communities for years and still have not been considered a completely solved problem, we are taking this opportunity to explore an alternative in approaching the problem without using the full speech processing techniques. We would like to be able to search *inside* each audio file to locate the exact content that we want based on a given voice query.

2 Time Series Representation for Voice Searching

More complex analysis of the speech audio cannot be achieved by looking at the raw audio plots alone. To get some information about the frequency distribution, harmonics, and others, some signal processing such as Fourier analysis is needed. In this work, we propose a simple approach to approximately represent audio features using time series representation, an approach recently used in query by humming system [4][5]. Note that by looking at the raw audio plot (.WAV file), we can extract several features, such as volume from the amplitude and the "timbre" of the voice. However, these characteristics are irrelevant to the task of differentiating one word from another. Instead, we propose to simply use the frequencies information as approximations of words in the audio. Note that the effectiveness and accuracy of this approach essentially depend on the nature of the spoken languages themselves as well. In this work, we test our method in Thai language, a tonal language with 5 tones.

We start off with acquiring the Thai digital audio recording in WAV file format. In our experiment, all recordings are originally recorded at the sampling rate of 22,050 Hz, but we decide to downsample the data to only 2,000 Hz (16 bits mono) to significantly speed up the search process and make sure that we do not lose too much of important features during the reduction and calculation. In speech community, such sampling rate is considered unacceptably low; however, our proposed work has one big difference in the algorithm in that we process the speech in *word level*, instead of *phoneme level* as typically being done in speech processing. This in turn allows us to easily process a 1-hour audio which almost seems unfeasible if we were to employ a traditional automatic speech recognition process.

We then preprocess the data by transforming a raw audio into a frequency domain using Fast Fourier Transformation (FFT), which gives the frequency distribution information about the spoken word or subsequence of the recording. This is a time series to be later used in similarity search in our framework. In addition, to further remove noise and outlier, we also apply some smoothing and z-score normalization to all datasets in our work before utilizing a Dynamic Time Warping distance measure (DTW) to locate the K-nearest neighbor query word within the given recording.

The algorithm is simply a subsequence matching using a sliding window of the size of the query window. Starting from the beginning of the recording until the end, it looks for the one with best match using a similarity measure. To simplify the implementation, a Euclidean distance metric could be used. However, we believe that a more sophisticated similarity measures, such as Dynamic Time warping [2][8], could significantly improve the accuracy of the result since it could gracefully resolve the problem of discrepancies or minor time variation in the time series, where we could intuitively map the time series query to the appropriate section of the recording.

3 Experimental Evaluation

We have put together a collection of various audio recordings for our experiment; some are audio books, and some are real lectures with both male and female speakers. Each one is approximately 45 to 60 minutes in length, with word content ranging from 6,000 to 9,000 words. We have chosen some words from each recording and exclusively removed those occurrences from the recording to avoid getting an exact match during the search. To evaluate the retrieval's effectiveness, we calculate the Precision, Recall, as well as the F-Measure to compare results among various parameter settings and approaches.

3.1 Experiment Results and Discussions

At this preliminary stage of our work, the evaluation process must be done manually. After the query words are selected, we have to actually listen to the whole recording and mark all the actual occurrences of each word within the recording, since there is no transcription available. The main contribution of our work is an ability to perform a voice search within a large audio file, where speech processing community may still have difficulties with. We demonstrate our utility by querying a word in an hour-long audio then measure the retrieval effectiveness both by looking at the precision/recall as well as the running time. Up to this point, we have demonstrated that Dynamic Time warping distance measure always outperforms the classic Euclidean distance metric in terms of the accuracy but with the price of higher time complexity.

In addition, we also consider another approach using Mel Frequency Cepstral Coefficients or MFCC that is regularly employed in speech processing to see if its superiority still holds for voice search in the word level. We first compare its time complexity with the Euclidean and Dynamic Time Warping distance measures. With exactly the same parameters and settings, MFCC measure is running 30 times slower

Table 1. Comparison of results between FFT with DTW and MFCC measures, showing that DTW gives more accurate results

Approach	Precision	Recall	F-Measure
FFT with DTW	80%	75%	77.42%
MFCC	61.11%	68.75%	64.71%

than Euclidean distance and about 5 times slower than the Dynamic Time warping. The retrieval's effectiveness between the two approaches is shown in Table 1.

Since the MFCC's running time is larger and its F-Measure is much lower, FFT with DTW distance measure is then employed in our experiments. With speaker-dependent experiment, as expected, we get much worse results; there are many more query words that were left undetected, as well as a lot more false alarms. Ideally, we would like to minimize the number of False Negatives as much as possible, with an acceptable number of False Positives. Looking closely, we found that the results are affected across genders as well. We look at the Fourier analysis of the same word spoken by different speakers and discover that they approximately have the similar shape but relatively shifted along the frequency axis. That means the structure of the word spoken are quite similar across the speakers, but the overall speaking frequency for each person differs and can be thought of as a frequency offset.

4   Conclusions and Future Work

In this preliminary work, we have proposed a simple approach to approximately represent speech audio features using time series representation, then to locate a voice query within the audio recordings. We have demonstrated the utility of our approach on query retrieval tasks for audio recordings in Thai language, i.e., to locate a voice query within the lecture recordings. From the experiment results, we have demonstrated that this simple framework can potentially help retrieve and locate the audio according to voice query inputs, especially in the speaker-dependent situation. Since the pitch discrepancies among speakers pose a limitation in our current framework, we need to look more closely into these features and see if any normalization among various speakers could be attained. Together with a Dynamic Time Warping distance measure as well as some lowerbounding and dimensionality reduction techniques, this could potentially resolve the problem and to help speed up the overall search process.

Referenes

[1] Franz, A. & Milch, B. (2002). Searching the Web by Voice. In Proceedings of COLING.

[2] Kruskall, J. B. & Liberman, M. (1983). The symmetric time warping algorithm: From continuous to discrete. In Time Warps, String Edits and Macromolecules.

[3] Klabbhankao, B. (2000).   Online Information Retrieval Using Genetic Algorithms. NECTEC Technical Journal Vol 2, No.7. March-June.

[4] Zhu, Y., Shasha, D., & Zhao, X. (2003). Query by Humming – in Action with its Technology Revealed. ACM SIGMOD, June 9-12.

[5] Zhu, Y. & Shasha, D. (2003). Warping Indexes with Envelope Transforms for Query by Humming. ACM SIGMOD, June 9-12.

[6] Hazen, T.J., Saenko, K., La, C.-H., & Glass, J.R. (2004). A Segment-Based Audio-Visual Speech Recognizer: Data Collection, Development, and Initial Experiments. Proc. ICMI.

[7] Gutkin, A. & King, S. (2004). Structural Representation of Speech for Phonetic Classification. In Proc. 17th International Conference on Pattern Recognition (ICPR), volume 3, pages 438-441, Cambridge, UK, August 2004. IEEE Computer Society Press.

[8] Ratanamahatana, C.A. & Keogh, E. (2005). Three Myths about Dynamic Time Warping Data Mining. SIAM International Conference on Data Mining (SDM).

A Methodology for Retrieving SCORM-Compliant Teaching Materials on Grid Environments

Wen-Chung Shih[1], Chao-Tung Yang[2,*], and Shian-Shyong Tseng[1,3]

[1] Department of Computer Science
National Chiao Tung University, Hsinchu 30010, Taiwan, R.O.C.
{gis90805, sstseng}@cis.nctu.edu.tw
[2] High Performance Computing Laboratory
Department of Computer Science and Information Engineering
Tunghai University, Taichung 40704, Taiwan, R.O.C.
ctyang@thu.edu.tw
[3] Department of Information Science and Applications
Asia University, Taichung 41354, Taiwan, R.O.C.
sstseng@asia.edu.tw

Abstract. This paper proposes a methodology for acquiring the top k highest-ranking SCORM-compliant teaching materials on grid environments, for a given query. Especially, the ranking criterion combines the relevance of the document and the efficiency of transmission. This methodology consists of three steps. First, the ranking function of each Learning Object Repository (LOR) is evaluated. Next, the number of documents to be retrieved from each LOR is decided according to the Ranking Ratio. Finally, the k documents are retrieved from the grid. To verify this approach, a prototype of the retrieval system was built on a grid testbed. Experimental results showed that the proposed approach can retrieve satisfactory teaching materials for users.

Keywords: Grid Computing, Globus Toolkit, SCORM, Information Retrieval.

1 Introduction

Recently, the Sharable Content Object Reference Model (SCORM) has been widely accepted as a standard of e-learning for users to share and reuse teaching materials. Conventional e-learning systems are based on a client-server model, which is characterized by the centralized management of learning objects. In this kind of system, teaching materials are usually stored in a database, named the Learning Object Repository (LOR). However, when several LORs are built in different sites on the Internet, there exists a need to share learning objects across the Internet.

Grid computing is considered to be an inexpensive and promising alternative to parallel computing, and it extends conventional parallel and distributed computing by

---

* Corresponding author.

S. Sugimoto et al. (Eds.): ICADL 2006, LNCS 4312, pp. 498–502, 2006.
© Springer-Verlag Berlin Heidelberg 2006

utilizing computers on the Internet to compute [2]. Consequently, the rise of grid computing provides a potential solution to the e-learning. Researchers have proposed to utilize data grid technologies to share learning materials [3, 4]. However, these approaches focused on the infrastructure of e-learning platforms, and did not address the issue of SCORM-compliant content management.

In this paper, we apply the concept of performance-based grid computing to the field of e-learning. In addition, the teaching material is seen as a structured document, and is searched for and retrieved according to the structural weighting scheme. The primary original contribution of this paper is the proposal of a methodology for retrieving SCORM-compliant content packages on grid environments. To the best of our knowledge, this topic has not been addressed in previous work. Second, this methodology adopts a criterion combining efficiency and relevance to rank the LORs. Next, real-time information of network bandwidth is taken into consideration for estimation of node performance. Finally, we have built a prototype on a grid testbed.

The rest of this paper is organized as follows. First, the model of SCORM-compliant documents and ranking functions are defined in Section 2. Then, Section 3 presents the proposed methodology. Next, experimental results are described in Section 4. Finally, the concluding remarks are given in Section 5.

2   The Model of SCORM-Compliant Documents

In the SCORM standard, a Content Package (CP) is defined as a package of learning materials, and a LOR is a database where the CPs are stored. We define the LOR located in the site i of the grid as a set of CPs.

$$LOR_i = \{CP_1^i, CP_2^i, ..., CP_m^i\} \qquad (1)$$

In (1), LOR_i , $1 < i < n$, is the LOR located in the site i of the grid. CP_j^i is the jth CP in LOR_i. Also, each CP can be represented by an ordered tree as the example shown in Figure 1. In addition, we adopt the well-known Vector Space Model to represent the documents in this paper.

In the proposed methodology, a CP is summarized in a representative vector, called CP_sum. The CP_sum is evaluated by the following formula:

$$\sum_{i=1}^{l} d_i \times \bar{v}_i \Big/ \sum_{i=1}^{l} d_i \qquad (2)$$

where
– d_i is the depth of the leaf document i in the content tree;
– v_i is the feature vector of the leaf document i.

For example, the CP_sum of the content package shown in Figure 1 is <28/17, 37/17, 35/17>, which can be evaluated by (2). Also, we define LOR_sum to summarize the CPs of a LOR. The LOR_sum is defined to be the average of the

CP_sum's in the LOR. In addition, we use the conventional Cosine function as our similarity measure.

In this paper, we define the Ranking Function (RF) of a LOR to represent the score of the LOR for a given query. The higher the score is, the more desirable the LOR is. The ranking function is defined as follows.

$$RF = C_1 \times sim + C_2 \times B(L_i) \qquad (3)$$

where
- *sim* is the *cosine* similarity of the *LOR_sum* and the query;
- $B(L_i)$ is the available network bandwidth between the LOR and the user who requests the query, which can be acquired by our grid monitoring tool;
- C_1 and C_2 are normalized coefficients. The sum of C_1 and C_2 is one.

Furthermore, we define the Ranking Ratio (RR) to be the ratio of RFs between the LORs, and the RR is utilized to determine the number of CPs retrieved from each LOR.

3 Methodology

Given a query q, the top k highest-ranking CPs on the grid with respect to the given Ranking Function is that k CPs with the largest *RF* values. The Grid-based CP Retrieval problem is to find the top k highest-ranking CPs on the grid for the query.

This problem can be exhaustedly solved by searching every CP in each LOR. However, this approach will increase the response time of retrieval. Therefore, we propose an approximate method, which consists of the following steps.

First, evaluate the Ranking Function of each LOR on the grid. We use a vector, CP_sum_{ij}, to summarize a CP j in LOR i. In addition, we use a vecvor, LOR_sum_i, to summarize the CPs in the LOR i. Then, the Ranking Function of each LOR is computed according to (3).

Second, determine the value of k_i for LOR i according to the Ranking Ratio, where k_i is the number of CPs retrieved from LOR i and the sum of all k_is are k. After the evaluation of Ranking Functions, the Ranking Ratio is obtained according to the ratio of RFs. Then, k_i, the number of CPs to be retrieved from LOR i, is determined by $k \times RR_i$.

Third, retrieve k_i content packages from LOR i. Once the value of k_i is determined, the remaining step is straightforward. The basic idea is to retrieve k_i CPs from LOR i.

4 Experimental Results

A grid testbed has been built based on the middleware, Globus Toolkit 3.0.2 [1]. This grid consists of one portal and four domains, and its topology is shown in Figure 2. In addition, a prototype of the retrieval system has also been built and its web-based interface is shown in Figure 3.

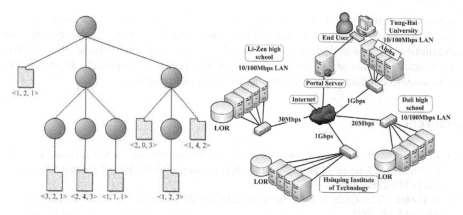

Fig. 1. The representation of a CP   **Fig. 2.** Topology of the grid testbed

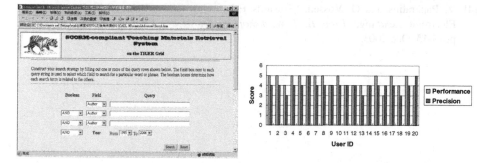

Fig. 3. Web-based interface of the prototype   **Fig. 4.** The degree of satisfaction

In the experiment, we have prepared a set of 100 articles for each site, and each set contains five specific topics: concept learning, data mining, and information retrieval, grid computing and e-learning. There are 20 articles for each topic. Also, each article is transformed into SCORM-compliant packages. Then, 20 participants are invited to use our prototype system for retrieving documents. These users include 10 students in THU and 10 students in HIT, in Taiwan. They are asked to answer two questions after they use this prototype. The first question is concerning the precision of the retrieval, and the second question is regarding the perceived performance of transmission. The results are illustrated in Figure 4. In this figure, the score given by a user ranges from one to five. "One" means "Very Unsatisfactory" and "Five" means "Very Satisfactory". This experiment shows that our system could be efficient and helpful to users.

5 Conclusion

With the rapid development of grid technology, more and more LORs are constructed and need to be connected to share the content. Efficient content retrieval can reduce the response time and thus attract more users to utilize the e-learning systems. In this paper, we have proposed a methodology to retrieve content packages on grid environments. In addition, a grid testbed was built to implement the system. Experimental results show the efficiency of the proposed approach. In our future work, we will conduct more experiments to verify our approach.

References

[1] I. Foster and C. Kesselman, "Globus: A Metacomputing Infrastructure Toolkit," *International Journal of Supercomputer Applications and High Performance Computing*, 11(2):115-128, 1997

[2] I. Foster, "The Grid: A New Infrastructure for 21st Century Science," *Physics Today*, 55(2):42-47, 2002.

[3] C. T. Yang and H. C. Ho, "An e-Learning Platform Based on Grid Architecture," *Journal of Information Science and Engineering*, vol. 21, no. 5, pp. 911-928, Sep. 2005.

[4] V. Pankratius and G. Vossen, "Towards E-Learning Grids: Using Grid Computing in Electronic Learning," *Proc. IEEE Workshop on Knowledge Grid and Grid Intelligence*, pp. 4-15, Oct. 2003.

Customising Interfaces to Service-Oriented Digital Library Systems

Hussein Suleman, Kevin Feng, and Gary Marsden

Department of Computer Science, University of Cape Town
Private Bag, Rondebosch, 7701, South Africa
{hussein, ffeng, gaz}@cs.uct.ac.za

Abstract. Digital library systems that once were mostly monolithic in construction are slowly making the transition to component-based models. However, it is not clear how best to design or construct the user interfaces to such systems - one alternative would be to create associated interface elements while another would be to create a separable interface layer. This paper discusses an attempt to do the latter by using current browser-based tools - recently named Ajax - in order to visually design the layouts, workflows and service connections of a user experience layer. Expert evaluators provided feedback during this process and the eventual level of functionality and usability of the proof-of-concept system demonstrate the inherent possibilities and relevance of the emerging Ajax technologies for not only the rendering or execution but also the design of browser-based Web applicatons, and digital library systems in particular.

1 Introduction

Current digital library (DL) systems such as DSpace, EPrints and Greenstone all require some - often non-trivial - customisation in order to fit in with the hosting organisation's Web presence. Simple changes such as HTML page titles are usually effected by the setting of parameters or variables. More elaborate changes such as integration with a university portal may require substantial (re-)programming.

In addition, users of standard toolkits may want to use a different set of services than those provided by default. This is especially relevant where a service-oriented architecture has been adopted and services can be readily added, removed or customised.

This high degree of flexibility has to be reflected in the user interface and most current DL systems do not cater for this. In contrast, the Web community has recently begun to create more flexible user interfaces using Asynchronous Javascript and XML (Ajax) [4]. Ajax is an approach to developing interactive browser-based user interfaces using a combination of Javascript and in-browser XML tools. Ajax applications are essentially Javascript applications associated with Web pages, with the added ability that they are able to send HTTP requests to Web servers and process the output in the Javascript code. Assuming

S. Sugimoto et al. (Eds.): ICADL 2006, LNCS 4312, pp. 503–506, 2006.
© Springer-Verlag Berlin Heidelberg 2006

that the response is in XML, Javascript/Ajax provides the ability to access and manipulate the DOM tree of this XML response and/or the current document in the browser window, or perform transformations on any XML fragments using XSLT. Thus Ajax can be used to provide an interactive user interface within the otherwise static Web browser.

This paper reports on an attempt to use the Ajax approach to design a customisable user experience layer that caters for both interface and service flexibility. While Ajax has typically been used for rendering of interactive user interfaces, this work has attempted to use Ajax primarily as the basis of a design tool for user interfaces.

2   Service Oriented Digital Library Systems

In designing a user experience layer, it is necessary to connect interface elements to back-end services. For this, a Service Oriented Architecture (SOA) was used, as this is arguably ideal for loosely-coupled systems that need to interconnect with other systems. Greenstone 3 [1] uses such an architecture and DSpace [7] is possibly also going to adopt this approach.

User interfaces to SOA-based systems need to submit requests (typically in XML over the Web) and parse and reformat or transform responses (typically also in XML) in order to generate portions of the Web interface. This communication is easily accomplished using Ajax.

For this work, it was necessary to use a foundation set of services provided by an existing framework. The ODL [5] tools were used because of availability at the time, but the system could just as easily be layered over Greenstone 3. The ODL toolkit is a suite of components for providing DL services such as search and browse, each of which has a simple machine interface accessible over the Web [6] [2].

3   Design of the Designing System

The user experience layer was decomposed into the following three elements, with associated sections in the Ajax-based design tool:

- Services, for specifying and configuring a list of services, each of which connects to a service endpoint of a corresponding back-end service component;
- Flows, for specifying a list of pages and assigning a flow structure for inter-page navigation; and
- Pages, for designing each page using a WYSIWYG (visual) editor.

Figure 1 shows a screen snapshot of the visual page editor. Each page is designed as a series of elements that can be selected from a toolbar and dragged within a canvas. The toolbar contains both static (e.g., text) and dynamic (e.g., forms to invoke services) elements.

The flow structure editor then ties these pages together and provides a basic system of navigation. For example, the page where a user enters search queries

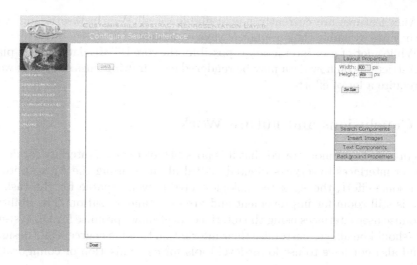

Fig. 1. User interface page layout editing

could lead to a page were search query results can be displayed. This structure is presented as a sitemap, using an approximation to a tree representation.

The services are connected into the individual pages when each page is being designed. Each service must, however, be configured in terms of the service endpoint and parameters necessary for the communication with this endpoint.

Finally, after the user experence layer has been designed, the designer can switch to the "playback" mode where the system is executed or rendered in production mode.

4   Evaluation and Analysis

The system was initially specified in a participatory design session with 3 post-graduate computer scientists, all with experience in digital library systems.

During its development, the system was subject to a two phase expert evaluation by a usability specialist and a digital library specialist. In the first phase various usability and functionality problems were identified and subsequently addressed [3]. During the second phase, it was felt that the functionality problems were largely resolved but the usability of the system could be further improved. However, the system was deemed to contain all the functionality required to customise and/or design a suitable user experience layer for a service oriented DL system.

This project has also led to some important observations about the Ajax technology:

– Javascript libraries are necessary to perform some functions that are sometimes taken for granted in traditional GUIs, such as drag-and-drop. While these libraries are readily available, they are not always easy to integrate at present.

- Ajax features are currently not available on all Web browsers, and where they are available they are not always consistent.
- While a lot of user interaction is possible, the core HTML data format places restrictions on how data may be rendered e.g., drawing lines or graphs would require a lot of effort.

5   Conclusions and Future Work

This project has demonstrated that it is possible to create an interface for designing user interfaces to service-oriented digital libraries, using the Ajax approach. With some effort, the Ajax technologies have proven capable for the task but there is still room for improvement and greater standardisation. The ability to customise user interfaces using the interface itself shows promise for DL systems - users should be able to customise their interaction to some degree while designers should also not have to use lower-level tools for customisation or configuration.

Acknowledgements

This project was made possible by funding from UCT, NRF (Grant number: 2054030), NRF-THRIP, Telkom and Siemens.

References

1. Bainbridge, David, Katherine J. Don, George R. Buchanan, Ian H. Witten, Steve Jones, Matt Jones and Malcolm I. Barr (2004), "Dynamic Digital Library Construction and Configuration", in Heery, R., and L. Lyon (eds), Research and Advanced Technology for Digital Libraries: 8th European Conference (ECDL2004), 12-17 September, Bath, UK, LNCS 3232, Springer.
2. Eyambe, Linda K., and Hussein Suleman (2004), "A Digital Library Component Assembly Environment", in Proceedings of SAICSIT 2004, Stellenbosch, South Africa, pp.15-22.
3. Feng, Fu-Yao Kevin (2006) Customisable Abstract Representation Layer for Digital Libraries, MSc Dissertation, Department of Computer Science, University of Cape Town.
4. Garrett. J. J. (2005), Ajax: A new approach to web applications, February 2005. Available http://www.adaptivepath.com/publications/essays/archives/000385.php.
5. Suleman, Hussein, and Edward A. Fox (2001), "A Framework for Building Open Digital Libraries", in D-Lib Magazine, Vol. 7, No. 12, December 2001. Available http://www.dlib.org/dlib/december01/suleman/12suleman.html
6. Suleman, H., and E. A. Fox (2002), "Designing Protocols in Support of Digital Library Componentization", 6th European Conference on Research and Advanced Technology for Digital Libraries (ECDL2002), Rome, Italy, 16-18 September 2002.
7. Tansley, Rob (2004), DSpace 2.0 Design Proposal, presented at DSpace User Group Meeting, 10-11 March, Cambridge, USA. Available http://wiki.dspace.org/DspaceTwo

Understanding User Perceptions on Usefulness and Usability of an Integrated *Wiki*-G-Portal

Yin-Leng Theng, Yuanyuan Li, Ee-Peng Lim, Zhe Wang, Dion Hoe-Lian Goh,
Chew-Hung Chang[1], Kalyani Chatterjea[1], and Jun Zhang

Nanyang Technological University, Singapore
[1] National Institute of Education, Singapore

Abstract. This paper describes a pilot study on *Wiki*-G-Portal, a project integrating Wikipedia, an online encyclopedia, into G-Portal, a Web-based digital library, of geography resources. Initial findings from the pilot study seemed to suggest positive perceptions on usefulness and usability of *Wiki*-G-Portal, as well as subjects' attitude and intention to use.

1 *Wiki*-G-Portal: Community-Based Geospatial Digital Libraries

Although geospatial digital libraries (DLs) are beginning to play key roles in education, especially in the provision of information to learners, there is a lack of systematic support in ensuring that geography resources are continually being monitored and updated. This is far from desirable, since within the classroom environment, DLs have the potential to be useful tools for active learning in which activities are characterized by active engagement, problem-solving, inquiry, and collaboration with others so that each student constructs meaning and hence knowledge of the information gained [3].

Despite these issues, the evolution of DLs from being static repositories of information in which access is limited to searching and browsing, to more subject-based DLs that offer a greater array of services, allowing users to new ways to access, interact and manipulate content including annotations, workspaces and user content contributions, has come a long way due to a growing trend in recent years towards community-based, participatory systems such as Wikipedia (http://www.wikipedia.com; retrieved 30 June, 2006) being a good example.

With so much knowledge embedded in Wikipedia, it presents an interesting test-bed for geospatial DLs such as G-Portal to investigate whether community-contributed resources like the Wikipedia can enhance geospatial DLs. The implementation issues involved in *Wiki*-G-Portal represent a very much unexplored area in interoperability. Using this reverse proxy approach (see http://en.wikipedia.org/wiki/Reverse_proxy; retrieved 30 June, 2006) in *Wiki*-G-Portal, users can create own personalized projects, and bookmark useful Wikipedia resources by creating metadata in G-Portal projects. Resources can be classified into different categories. Users can also locate geographical resources, such as cities and countries, using the map interface. Users can also define new resource types and create new resources. Further, they are free to give ratings and comments to the resources through G-Portal's review module [2].

S. Sugimoto et al. (Eds.): ICADL 2006, LNCS 4312, pp. 507–510, 2006.
© Springer-Verlag Berlin Heidelberg 2006

2 Pilot Study

The pilot study gathered initial feedback on the *Wiki*-G-Portal system to understand users' perceptions of usability and usefulness of integrating Wikipedia into G-Portal, based on the well-established Technology Acceptance Model (TAM) [1, 4] (see Figure 1). In this paper, we refer to usability as defined in ISO 9241-11 as "the extent to which a product can be used by specified users to achieve specified goals with effectiveness, efficiency and satisfaction in a specified context of use". Davis et al. [1] define *perceived usefulness* as "the degree to which a prospective user expects the target system to be free of effort". Usefulness, on the other hand, refers to measurements in reference to system specifications and the extent of coverage of end-users' tasks supported by the system, but not on end-user performance testing. Davis et al. [1] see *perceived usefulness* as "the prospective user's subjective probability that using a specific application system will increase his/her job performance".

Two sessions of three subjects each were carried out in a specially designed usability lab to provide a consistent environment for usability evaluations. Each subject was given a computer in each of the three rooms with Internet facilities to access the *Wiki*-G-Portal. The sessions took approximately two hours with the subjects carrying out six tasks. The subjects were asked to think aloud, and the sessions were captured using the Morae software (see http://www.techsmith.com/morae.asp).

The six subjects recruited were frequent Wikipedia users, and they were undergraduates at a local university, proficient in the use of the Internet and computers. A suite of six tasks was given for the subjects to work on as they used the *Wiki*-G-Portal system. After completing the tasks, the subjects were then asked to complete a survey instrument which consisted of closed questions in which users were asked to comment using a 5-point Likert scale, and open-ended questions on advantages and disadvantages.

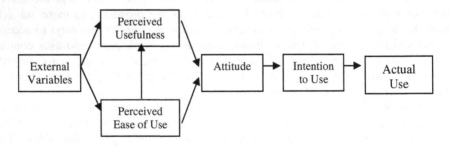

Fig. 1. Technology Acceptance Model (TAM)

3 Results and Analysis

3.1 Tool Functionality

Tool functionality refers specifically to the perceived ability of *Wiki*-G-Portal to provide flexible search and retrieval to geography resources. Positive responses indicated that *Wiki*-G-Portal was easy to use, with reasons such as: (i) it was easy to browse resources from both the map interface and the resource list; (ii) Wikipedia page URLs provided in *Wiki*-G-Portal resources were helpful to link to related Wikipedia web pages; (iii) it was easy to read resources in *Wiki*-G-Portal; (iii) the map interface was helpful in locating geographical resources (e.g. cities, countries) easily; (iv) the bookmarking was helpful and easy to use; (v) good organization of resources into categories; and (vi) the review module, showing subjects' opinions to the resources, was easy to use.

In contrast, negative responses seemed to point out that it was not easy to search a resource on the map if the resource location was not known to the user. In addition, *Wiki*-G-Portal resources were not well-organized, for example, due to an encoding problem, unrecognized characters might be contained in the resources. Another comment from an expert in geography indicated that the map interface was not an added value. The bookmarking procedure was tedious, and subjects needed to key in the attributes' values manually. It would be better if the system was able to automatically extract useful information from the bookmarked page when the URL was provided.

3.2 Intrinsic Motivation, Perceived Usefulness and Perceived Ease of Use

Intrinsic motivation refers to users' experience of "perceived helpfulness and enjoyment". Four out of six subjects agreed that *Wiki*-G-Portal was helpful for locating geography resources. They found *Wiki*-G-Portal friendly to use, and that the world map was helpful in locating geography resources. The two subjects who were "neutral" in their responses thought the map-based interface was not so easy to search for a resource on the map since the resource location might not be known to the user. All 6 subjects thought their experiences using *Wiki*-G-Portal were pleasant, as it was easy to learn to use, and they were able to find the correct way within a short time.

In general, the subjects felt that *Wiki*-G-Portal was useful and helped them to accomplish the tasks effectively and efficiently. However, subjects commented that the Wiki-G-Portal resources did not provide enough information, and they needed to refer to Wikipedia for detailed information.

Two subjects (1 "strongly agreed"; 1 "agreed") commented that it was easy getting *Wiki*-G-Portal to do what they wanted it to do during Geography study, with the other 4 subjects thought it was alright, giving a "neutral" response. In terms of learning how to use, 5 out of 6 subjects (3 "strongly agreed"; 2 "agreed") commented that they learned how to use *Wiki*-G-Portal quickly but 1 subject disagreed. However, in general, *Wiki*-G-Portal was perceived as easy to use by 5 subjects (1"strongly agreed"; 4 "agreed"), with 1 subject giving a "neutral" response.

3.3 Attitude and Intention to Use

A user's attitude is defined as his/her belief about the consequences of using *Wiki*-G-Portal. All things being equal, Davis et. al [4] argue that people form intentions to perform behaviors toward which they have a positive attitude. All 6 subjects (1 "strongly agreed"; 6 "agreed") thought it was a good idea as the experience when using the *Wiki*-G-Portal was pleasant. As for liking it enough to use *Wiki*-G-Portal for Geography study, 4 subjects (1 "strongly agreed"; 3 "agreed") indicated positively.

Two subjects giving a "neutral" response, however, thought the system could be further improved.

Finally, "intention to use" responses showed that 5 out of 6 subjects (2"strongly agreed"; 3 "agreed") would like to use *Wiki*-G-Portal for geography study in the future. However, 1 subject was willing to use *Wiki*-G-Portal in the future provided *Wiki*-G-Portal has more resources in terms of higher quantity and better quality.

3.4 Discussion on Subjects' Experiences with *Wiki*-G-Portal

Findings from the pilot study were positive in suggesting that *Wiki*-G-Portal was easy to learn and had a user-friendly graphical user interface. The map-based interface provided users a convenient access when they only roughly knew the location of a geography resource but not the resource name. Some felt that the *Wiki*-G-Portal could be developed into a more efficient tool to search for that resource when compared with Wikipedia. Many useful features in *Wiki*-G-Portal were implemented, for example, the classification module and the review module.

Our results provided good insights on subjects' positive perceptions on usefulness and usability of *Wiki*-G-Portal. As the evaluation statements were formulated based on TAM, the reasons for subjects' perceptions on usefulness and usability could also be gleaned from subjects' responses to other factors such as intrinsic motivation, tool functionality and task-technology fit. Finally, responses to "attitude" and "intention to use" were also positive.

4 Conclusion and On-Going Work

Although this was a pilot study with only six subjects, findings seemed to suggest that perceived usefulness was more important in influencing "attitude" and "intention to use", since subjects would be driven to adopt an application primarily because of the functions they performed. The ease or difficulty of getting the system to perform those functions was of secondary relevance. Further work involves carrying out a quantitative study with more subjects across different age groups for statistically-based results.

References

1. Davis, F. D., & Venkatesh, V. (2004). Toward Preprototype User Acceptance Testing of New Information Systems: Implications for Software Project Management. IEEE Transactions on Engineering Management, 51(1), 31-46.
2. Lim, E.P., Wang, Z., Sadeli, D., Li, Y., Chang, C.H., Goh, D., Theng, Y.L., Zhang, J. and Sun, A. (2006). Integration of Wikipedia and a Geography Digital Library. Accepted for ICADL2006. 27-30 November 2006. Kyoto (Japan).
3. Oldfather, P., Bonds, S., & Bray, T. (1994). Drawing the circle: Collaborative mind mapping as a process for developing a constructivist teacher education program. Teacher Education Quarterly, 21, 5-13.
4. Theng, Y.L. and Lew, Y.W. (in press). Weblogs for Higher Education: Implications for Digital Libraries. Accepted for the 10th European Conference on Research and Advanced Technology for Digital Libraries, ECDL2006, Alicante, Spain, September, 17-22, 2006.

A Peer-to-Peer Approach to Collaborative Repository for Digital Libraries

Jenq-Haur Wang[1], Hung-Chi Chang[1], Chih-Yuan Lin[1], and Lee-Feng Chien[1,2]

[1] Institute of Information Science, Academia Sinica, Taiwan
[2] Department of Information Management, National Taiwan University, Taiwan
{jhwang, hungchi, garylin, lfchien}@iis.sinica.edu.tw

Abstract. Growing amount of precious content digitized in digital libraries (DLs) could cost much digitization, backup, and restoration effort. To meet the requirements in a digital archiving system, several issues must be addressed. First, it usually requires much storage and network bandwidth for each individual DL to maintain its own backup service. Second, the manual effort makes it difficult to maintain. In this paper, we propose a peer-to-peer (P2P) approach to collaborative repository for DLs. Cooperating spiders are utilized to facilitate efficient and scalable archiving without much manual effort. The spidering-based approach can automatically keep the structure of content thus enabling simpler implementation and easier support for cross-archive applications. Preliminary experimental results show the potential of the proposed approach.

1 Introduction

Precious contents are being digitized in digital libraries (DLs), especially for cultural heritage. Building such a collection could cost much digitization effort. How to safely keep precious digitized content in storage that can persist even longer than human lives is a great challenge. Therefore, digital preservation has attracted growing attention from DL communities.

There are several functional requirements in a digital archiving system. First, data needs to be effectively and exactly archived, and later exactly recovered without any loss of fidelity. Second, data backup/restore process should be simple and easily managed. To meet these requirements, several issues should be addressed. First, it usually requires huge amount of storage and network bandwidth for each individual DL to maintain its own backup service. Second, the manual effort involved would make it difficult to maintain. There are still other concerns such as the efficiency of the backup/restore process, and so forth. In this paper, we focus on the first two issues, the *cost* and *manual effort* aspects.

We propose a peer-to-peer (P2P) approach to collaborative repository for digital libraries. Through the collaboration among DLs that have similar needs, a cost-effective way of digital archiving is possible. The spidering-based approach automatically keeps the structure of the content, thus enabling simpler implementation and easier support for cross-archive applications such as image copy detection.

S. Sugimoto et al. (Eds.): ICADL 2006, LNCS 4312, pp. 511–514, 2006.

Preliminary experiments are conducted to test the performance of the proposed approach. Further experiments are needed to investigate the load balancing and coverage issues.

2 Related Work

Backup mechanisms are necessary in all kinds of data collections. Hardware-based solutions such as RAIDs (Redundant Array of Inexpensive Disks) [4] or SAN (Storage Area Network) are commonly deployed as redundant replication of the same data. However, the very high hardware maintenance cost prohibits widespread adoption in non-profit organizations such as university libraries and public museums.

Digital preservation [1] is a major research topic that deals with long-time preservation of data under various hardware/software failures. There are some open source projects for digital repository and archiving such as Fedora [5]. Cooperative DLs such as OverCite [6] incorporate multiple DLs to host digital collections. However, preservation model that is practically useful is still not common. P2P digital preservation systems were proposed, such as LOCKSS [2]. Our approach differs from the digital preservation systems in that a group of distributed spiders were incorporated in the backup/restore process. We focus on an effective automatic way of archiving and later restoring data using existing software/hardware technologies without much human effort.

3 The Proposed Approach

We propose a distributed spidering-based approach to collaborative archiving of contents in digital libraries. In this approach, the distribution of crawling task plays the most critical role. Each DL acts as a *peer* with one or more spiders that collaborate on a common goal, i.e., archiving, which is expressed as a given set of target URLs for the spiders to crawl. The criterion for task distribution is the domain of the URL, from which we can decide the responsible peer for crawling it. The cost and resources required on each peer DL could be shared and greatly reduced.

For better scalability, a hybrid P2P architecture is adopted when designing such a distributed archiving system. It avoids the single-point-of-failure problem in centralized model and the peer selection problem in fully distributed model. There are two roles in the architecture: *general archival peer* and *super-peer* [7].

General archival peer serves as a main repository in the system. The crawling module in each peer is modified from an open source crawler Nutch [3]. For each target URL assigned to a peer, the page for the URL is first fetched, parsed, and cached in the local repository. Then, the links contained in the page are extracted and forwarded to the super-peer for dispatching to the responsible peer.

URL dispatching, the process of dispatching newly extracted URLs to the responsible peer, is the main function of *Super-peer*. That's the most critical part in making the spiders distributed. When a new URL is extracted and forwarded from a peer or fed by the user, it's dispatched to the responsible peer. Many factors could affect the performance of URL dispatching, for example, network proximity, load balancing, and storage consumption. Intuitively, a peer closer to the target URL with lower system load and storage consumption will get higher priority. In our approach, we used network proximity as the main criterion, which is estimated using the round-trip time from a peer to a given target URL.

4   Experiments and Observations

To determine the effectiveness of the proposed approach, we conducted several experiments on National Digital Archives Program (NDAP, http://www.ndap.org.tw/) archival sites, which contain data collections from various public institutions or organizations across different topic domains. To compare the performance of distributed spiders with ordinary standalone spiders, two modes of operations, *standalone* and *collaborative* modes, are incorporated in our Nutch-based spider. For standalone mode, a 17-hour crawling session was conducted where the data were automatically recorded at a constant interval of 5 minutes. For collaborative mode, one super-peer and 3 cooperating archival peers were run on machines with varying hardware capacities in a three-day crawling session.

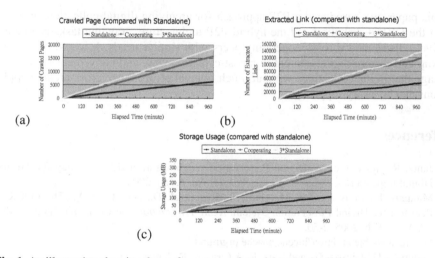

Fig. 1. An illustration showing the performances of standalone and collaborative modes, in terms of (a) the number of pages crawled, (b) the number of links extracted, and (c) the amount of storage used (in bytes)

As shown in Figure 1, the spider crawls at a steady speed in terms of the three different metrics. These metrics for collaborative mode are slightly less than three times the number for standalone crawlers. The reason could be the overhead in P2P communications and the wide variance in the computing power among peers. We argue that the overall coverage of the cooperating peers should be larger than those of the individual crawlers if they run independently. The preliminary experimental results show the potential of our proposed approach. Further experiments will be needed to investigate in larger scales.

5 Discussions and Future Work

Several issues need further discussions. First, the coverage of distributed spiders could be affected by the crawling strategy. Breadth-first search tries to explore most upper-level links before traversing the next level; while best-first search explores more in-depth pages as early as possible. Second, for better scalability and load balance, other factors should be considered in the URL dispatching process, such as CPU load, storage consumption, and hardware capability.

One potential weakness of the proposed approach is the possible security breach when multiple copies of sensitive data might be more vulnerable to unauthorized access. In future, we plan to enhance the system security, such as access control, authentication, and data integrity. Also, further experiments will be conducted to verify the effects of different crawling strategies, URL dispatching strategies, and load balance factors. Finally, cross-archive applications such as domain-specific information search and content-based image/video copy detection will be developed.

6 Conclusion

In this paper, we introduced a P2P approach for archiving digital collections in DLs. With the URL distribution and the hybrid P2P architecture, crawling tasks can be effectively distributed across cooperating peers with similar needs. It would be easy to backup and restore digital content in a cost-effective way, and convenient for DLs to manage the digital collections without much manual effort. Also, cross-archive applications can be easily supported.

References

[1] Jantz, R. and Fiarlo, M. Digital Preservation: Architecture and Technology for Trusted Digital Repositories. *D-Lib Magazine, Vol. 11, No. 6*, Jun. 2005.
[2] Maniatis, P., Roussopoulos, M., Giuli, T., Rosenthal, D., and Baker, M. The LOCKSS Peer-to-Peer Digital Preservation System. *ACM Transactions on Computer Systems, Vol. 23, No. 1*, Feb. 2005, 2-50.
[3] Nutch, available at: http://lucene.apache.org/nutch/
[4] Patterson, D., Gibson, G., and Katz, R. A Case for Redundant Arrays of Inexpensive Disks (RAID). In *Proceedings of the ACM SIGMOD1998*, 109-116.
[5] Payette, S. and Staples, T. The Mellon Fedora Project. In Proceedings of the 6th European Conference on Research and Advanced Technology for Digital Libraries (ECDL 2002). 2002, 406-421.
[6] Stribling, J., Councill, I., Li, J., Kaashoek, M., Karger, D., Morris R., and Shenker, S. OverCite: A Cooperative Digital Research Library. In *Proceedings of the 4th International Workshop on Peer-to-Peer Systems (IPTPS 2005)*, 2005, 69-79.
[7] Yang, B. and Garcia-Molina H. Designing a Super-Peer Network. In Proceedings of the 19th International Conference on Data Engineering (ICDE 2003). 2003, 49-60.

Web Page Classification Exploiting Contents of Surrounding Pages for Building a High-Quality Homepage Collection

Yuxin Wang[1] and Keizo Oyama[1,2]

[1] School of Multidisciplinary Sciences, The Graduate University for Advanced Studies
[2] National Institute of Informatics, Research Organization of Information and Systems
2-1-2 Hitotsubashi, Chiyoda-ku, Tokyo, 101-8430 Japan
mini_wang@grad.nii.ac.jp, oyama@nii.ac.jp

Abstract. We propose a web page classification method for creating a high quality collection of researchers' homepages. A method to reduce manual assessment required for assuring given precision/recall using a recall-assured and a precision-assured classifier is presented. Each classifier is built with SVM using textual features obtained from each page and its surrounding pages and tuning parameters. These pages are grouped based on connection types and relative URL hierarchy levels, and independent features are extracted from each group. Experiment results show the proposed features evidently improve classification performance and the manual assessment is significantly reduced.

Keywords: Web page classification, SVM, Quality assurance.

1 Introduction and Related Works

A web page collection with a guaranteed high quality (i.e., recall and precision) is required for implementing high quality web-based information services. However, to build such a collection demands a large amount of human work because of diversity, vastness and sparseness of the web pages. Thus, we investigate a web page classification method that assures a given high recall/precision and minimizes human assessment cost. We first target at researchers' homepages with an intention to use the collection for extending a guarantee-type scholarly information service.

For web page classification techniques, the first factor to consider is what information sources to use and the second is how to use them. Many prior works have tried to exploit, besides textual contents, various web-related information sources such as html tags [2], URLs [5], directory structure [3], anchor texts [2], contents of globally linked pages [4] and contents of surrounding pages [1, 3]. All such sources except the last one are effective to select highly probable pages. The last one, contrarily, is potentially useful to collect related information scattered over component pages and effective to gather potential entry pages comprehensively, but it is very noisy and prior works hardly exploited it. Nevertheless, since the comprehensiveness is a key for quality assurance, we mainly investigate to exploit it.

S. Sugimoto et al. (Eds.): ICADL 2006, LNCS 4312, pp. 515–518, 2006.

For reducing the noises, the features on surrounding pages are partially merged then concatenated, so that their relative locations are represented.

There are almost no prior works that assure high quality required by practical applications for web page collections. We approach to this problem with a three-way classifier built by combining a recall-assured and a precision-assured classifier.

2 Composition of the Classifiers

Fig.1 shows the scheme of the proposed method (95% recall and 99% precision are the example quality requirement for illustration). We use two component classifiers to construct a three-way classifier. The recall-assured (precision-assured) classifier assures the target recall (precision) with the highest possible precision (recall).

All pages are first input to the recall-assured classifier and its negative predictions are classified to "assured negative." The rest are then input to the precision-assured classifier and its positive predictions are classified to "assured positive." The remaining pages are classified to "uncertain," which require manual assessment.

We use the SVM-light package by Joachims with linear kernel, tuning with its options c (tradeoff between training error and margin) and j (training error cost-factor of positive examples over negative examples).

We use textual features $f_{t,v}(g,w_t)$, where t indicates a text type *plain* (plain-text-based) or *tagged* (tagged-text-based), v indicates a value type *binary* or *real*, g denotes a surrounding page group and $w_t \in W_t$ denotes a feature word. Feature sets are composed by concatenating one or more feature subsets $F_{t,v}(g) = \{ f_{t,v}(g,w_t) \mid {}^\forall w_t \in W_t \}$.

Surrounding page group: When a page (current page) is given, its surrounding pages are categorized to groups $G_{c,l}$ based on connection types c (in-link (*in*), out-link (*out*) and directory entry (*ent*)) and URL hierarchy levels l (*same*, *upper* and *lower*) relative to the current page; e.g., $G_{out,same}$ consists of out-link pages in the same directory. The current page constitutes an independent group G_{cur}. A feature set consists of G_{cur} and any number of $G_{c,l}$'s. For instance, feature set "u-1" shown in Section 3 consists of G_{cur} and $G_{*,upper}$ (surrounding page groups of upper hierarchy level) and feature set "o-i-e-1" consists of G_{cur} and $G_{*,*}$ (all surrounding page groups).

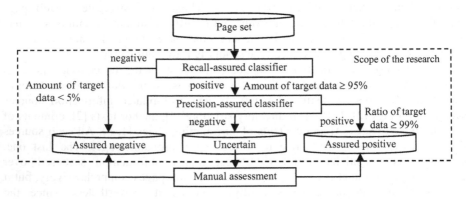

Fig. 1. Scheme of the Classification

Text type and feature word: $F_{plain,*}(*)$ are extracted from textual content excluding tags, scripts, comments, etc. We use "Chasen" to segment Japanese words. Top 2000 words with mutual information are selected as feature words W_{plain}. $F_{tagged,*}(*)$ are extracted from text segments "*text*" that match either ">*text*<" or "<img...alt= "*text*"...>" and that are not more than 16 bytes long omitting spaces. Based on our observation, we expect they contain useful information for representing a page. We use "Chasen" to segment Japanese words. Words with file frequency not less than 1% are selected as feature words W_{tagged}. A feature set is composed either using *plain* alone or using *plain* and *tagged* together.

Value type: A *binary* value $f_{*,binary}(g,w_t)$ represents presence of w_t in g. A *real* value $f_{*,real}(g,w_t)$ represents proportion of pages containing w_t within g. The *real* value is tested to see if feature word distribution within surrounding page groups is informative. The two value types are used exclusively for composing a feature set.

3   Experiments and Considerations

We manually prepared a sample data of researchers' homepages (906 positives and 20,366 negatives) from NW100G-01 [6], a 100-gigabyte web document data. Five-fold cross validation is adopted for all experiments. We mainly use precision and recall for evaluating the classification performance. For comparison, a feature set composed by $F_{plain,\ binary}(G_{cur})$ only is used as a baseline. The experiment results of well performing feature sets and the baseline are shown in Table 1. Suffix "_tag" indicates text types *plain* and *tagged* are used together and suffix "_real" indicates value type is *real*.

Table 1. Performance of well performed feature sets

Feature set	Best F-measure	Recall at 99% precision	Precision at 95% recall
o-i-e-1_tag_real	0.8865	0.2086	0.4133
u-1_tag	0.8858	0.2318	0.3322
baseline	0.8326	0.1798	0.2649

Based on the experiment results, the proposed features all together are shown to be effective not only for the general performance (in F-measure) but also for the performance of precision/recall-assured classifiers. Surrounding page groups are generally effective but their contributions vary. For precision-assured classifiers, the upper hierarchy page groups ($G_{*,\ upper}$) contribute most to the recall. It probably indicates that such pages provide contextual information, e.g., organization names and research fields, which is lacking in the current page itself but is very important for classifying them with very high confidence. For recall-assured classifiers, all surrounding page groups ($G_{*,*}$) contribute to the precision notably, despite of their noisy natures. Other experiment results not presented here have shown the followings: If we group the surrounding pages based only on either connection types or hierarchy levels, much poorer performance can be obtained; Adding tagged-text-based features consistently gained performance; Effect of value types varies depending on feature sets and its gain is marginal.

Table 2 shows estimated page numbers of classification output from the corpus at three different quality requirements for two three-way classifiers, one using baseline and the other using o-i-e-1_tag_real for both recall/precision-assured classifiers. Comparing the uncertain class sizes, o-i-e-1_tag_real significantly reduces the amount of pages requiring manual assessment, especially when the required quality is relaxed.

Table 2. Estimated page numbers of classification output from the corpus

Required quality	baseline			o-i-e-1_tag_real			reduction ratio
precision / recall	assured positive	uncertain (N_B)	assured negative	assured positive	uncertain (N_O)	assured negative	N_O/N_B
99.5% / 98%	3800	461832	1618988	9206	358207	1717187	77.6%
99% / 95%	6163	274524	1803913	11251	156782	1916567	57.1%
98% / 90%	11116	155418	1918066	15503	81157	1987940	52.2%

4 Conclusions

We proposed a web page classification method for building a high quality collection of researchers' homepages, using a three-way classifier composed by two component classifiers, recall-assured and precision-assured, in combination. We used support vector machine (SVM) with textual features obtained from each page and its surrounding pages. Applying the proposed method, the amount of pages that require manual assessment for assuring the required quality is significantly reduced.

References

1. Y. Wang and K. Oyama: Combining Page Group Structure and Content for Roughly Filtering Researchers' Homepages with High Recall. IPSJ Digital Courier, Vol. 2 (2006) 369-381.
2. A. Sun, E.-P. Lim and W.-K. Ng: Web Classification using Support Vector Machine. In: Proc. 4th International Workshop on Web Information and Data Management, McLean, Virginia (2002) 96-99.
3. A. Sun and E.-P. Lim: Web Unit Mining: Finding and Classifying Subgraphs of Web Pages. In: Proc. International Conference on Information and Knowledge Management (CIKM2003), New Orleans, Louisiana (2003) 108-115.
4. E. J. Glover, et al.: Using Web Structure for Classifying and Describing Web Pages. In: Proc. 11th International World Wide Web Conference, Honolulu, Hawaii (2002) 562-569.
5. M.-Y. Kan and H.O.N. Thi: Fast Webpage Classification using URL Features. In: Proc. CIKM'05, Bremen, Germany (2005) 325-326.
6. NTCIR Project: NTCIR-4 WEB (Web Retrieval Test Collection). http://research.nii.ac.jp/ntcir/permission/ntcir-4/perm-en-WEB.html (2006).

Managing and Querying of Videos by Semantics in Digital Library – A Semantic Model SemTTE and Its XML-Based Implementation[*]

Yu Wang, Chunxiao Xing, and Lizhu Zhou

Department of Computer Science and Technology, Tsinghua University

Abstract. Managing video data and providing semantic-based retrieval mechanism is an indispensable part of digital library. However, most exiting digital library systems only provide the functionality of retrieving video data by meta-data which can not fulfill users' requirements. This is due to the lack of appropriate video semantic model and powerful query interface. In this paper, we will first briefly introduce our video semantic model SemTTE and its query language VSQL, then show how they can be implemented based on XML technologies and how strategies of mapping and optimization are chosen.

1 Introduction

In most current digital library systems, video data can only be queried by meta-data, which is too limited to satisfy users. In order to query videos by semantics, an appropriate semantic model is needed. We summarized properties of video semantics into two aspects and designed a video semantic model SemTTE by considering them [12, 13] and implement it based on XML.

- *Typed events*: events in video can be abstracted to a finite set of types and the video can be viewed as a sequence of instances of these types.
- *Temporal structures*: the occurrences of events are temporally ordered from the beginning to the end of a video. Each event is related to a video segment.

2 Video Semantic Model: SemTTE

This paper will only present the main idea of SemTTE, for details please refer to [13], and for more about its constraint mechanism, please refer to [12].

Schema of SemTTE is composed of type definitions for entities and events. Instance is composed of entity instances and event trees. Figure 1 is an example of entity instances in NBA domain. Figure 2 is an example of event tree. Each node represents an event instance and the rectangle represents the video file.

---

[*] Supported by the National Natural Science Foundation of China under Grant No. 60473078 and 973 Program Under Grant No. 2006CB303103.

S. Sugimoto et al. (Eds.): ICADL 2006, LNCS 4312, pp. 519–522, 2006.

Players		
Name	age	team
YaoMing	26	Rockets
McGrady	27	Rockets
Kaman	24	Clippers

Teams		
name	year	players
Rockets	1967	{YaoMing, McGrady}
Clippers	1970	{Kaman}

Fig. 1. Entity instances in NBA domain

The query language VSQL has following SQL-like syntax:

SELECT   <target list>
FROM   <variable list>
[WHERE   <search condition>]
[GROUP BY <target list>
[HAVING   <search condition>]]
[ORDER BY <target list>]

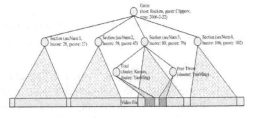

Fig. 2. Example event tree in NBA domain

3   XML-Based Implementation of SemTTE

For implementation, we map SemTTE's schema to XML DTD, SemTTE's instance to XML document, and VSQL query to XQueryn. Two strategies exist for instance mapping: attribute strategy and element strategy, which map all attributes and roles of instance into attributes and sub-elements of the corresponding elements respectively. Similarly, there are multiple XQuery queries corresponding to a VSQL query. For example, for VSQL query:

   SELECT f.*   **FROM** *Player* p, *Foul* f
   WHERE p.age <25 **AND** p **participate** f
   Following are two XQuery queries that may be generated for it:
   for $p in collection("NBA")//Player, $f in collection("NBA")//Foul
   where $p/@age < 25 AND (f/@foulerID=$p/@ID OR f/@fouledID=$p/@ID)
   return ...   (1)
   for $p in collection("NBA")//Player[@age < 25],
      $f in collection("NBA")//Foul[@foulerID=$p/@ID or @fouledID=$p/@ID]
   return ...   (2)

In (2), the sizes of the intermediate result set of variable "$p" and "$f" are much smaller than that in (1), thus will be evaluated faster. In VSQL, four kinds of conditions may be optimized: value conditions, participation conditions, temporal conditions, and composing conditions. Experiments are made to determine which mapping strategy should be taken and which condition should be optimized. The result is shown in Figure 3-6. Semantic information acquired from 125 NBA game videos are used as the testing data and the platform is Berkeley's XMLDB. For each kind of condition, four XQuery queries corresponding to attribute strategy and element strategy, optimized and no optimized are evaluated and the time used is recorded. The x-coordinates represent number of games in the database (1 grid for 5 games) and the y-coordinates represent the time used.

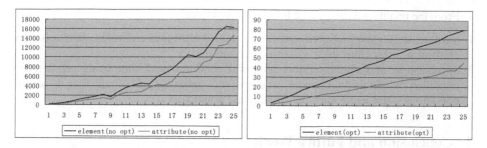

Fig. 3. Results for value condition

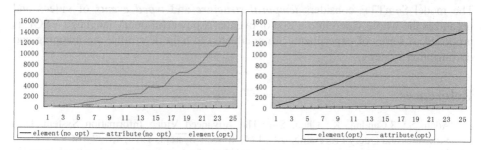

Fig. 4. Results for participating relationship condition

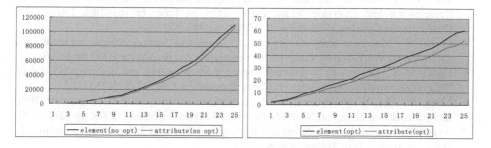

Fig. 5. Results for temporal relationship condition

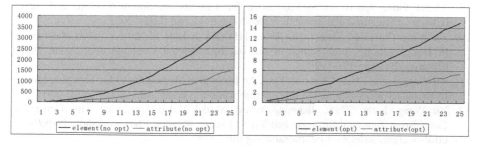

Fig. 6. Results for composing relationship condition

From the results we can get the following strategies:

1. attribute strategy is preferred, only multi-valued attributes and roles are mapped by element strategy (thus these values can be indexed);
2. optimization of value condition, temporal condition and composing relationship condition when using element strategy and optimization of all four kinds of conditions when using attribute strategy are mandatory.

4   Conclusion and Future Work

In this paper, we present a video semantic model and its XML-based implementation. The model SemTTE considers *temporal structure* and *typed events* of videos and organizes the whole video into a tree of events. A powerful query language VSQL is proposed. A series of experiments are conducted to help determine the mapping and optimization strategy.

References

1. Adah, S.; S.Candan, K.; Chen, S.-s. The Advanced Video Information System: Data Structures and Query Processing. ACM Multimedia Systems 1996, 4, 172-186
2. Tusch, R.; Kosch, H.; Boszormenyi, L. VIDEX: An Integrated Generic Video Indexing Approach; ACM Multimedia, 2000; pp 448-451
3. Tran, D. A.; Hua, K. A.; Vu, K. VideoGraph:A Graphical Object-based Model for Representing and Querying Video Data; 2000; In Proc. of the 19th International Conference on Conceptual Modeling (ER2000), pp 383-396
4. Combi, C. Modeling temporal aspects of visual and textual objects in multimedia databases; Int Workshop on Temporal Representation and Reasoning 2000; pp 59-86
5. Hacid, M.-S.; Decleir, C. A database approach for modeling and querying video data. IEEE Transactions on Knowledge and Data Engineering 2000, 12, 729-750
6. Yong, C.; De, X. Hierarchical semantic associative video model; In proc of IEEE International Conference on Neural Networks and Signal Processing, 2003; pp 1217-1220
7. Aygun, R. S.; Yazici, A. Modeling and Management of Fuzzy Information in Multimedia Database Applications; Technical Report, 2002
8. Arslan, U. A Semantic Data Model and Query Language for Video Databases; Master thesis, 2002
9. Ahmet Ekin, Sports Video Processing for Description, Summarization, and Search (Chapter 2 Structural and Semantic Video Modeling), phd thesis, 2003
10. Yu Wang, Chunxiao Xing, Lizhu Zhou, THVDM: A Data Model for Video Management in Digital Library, proceedings of the 6th International Conference of Asian Digital Libraries, 2003, pp 178-192
11. Yu Wang, Lizhu Zhou, Chunxiao Xing. An Evaluation Method for Video Semantic Models, International Workshop on Multimedia Information Systems (MIS) 2005, pp207-220
12. Yu Wang, Lizhu Zhou, Jianyong Wang. Model Video Semantics with Constraints Considering Temporal Structure and Typed Events, ICDE06 PHD workshop, http://ir.iit. edu/~waigen/icde06phd/camera/wang.pdf, 2006
13. Yu Wang, Chunxiao Xing, Lizhu Zhou. Managing and Querying Video by Semantics in Digital Library. The 10th European Conference on Research and Advanced technology for Digital Libraries 2006, Springer LNCS 4172, pp. 367-378.

RDF/XTM Ontology Construction Based on a Topic Maps-Driven Framework*

Cheng-Zen Yang[1], Ing-Xiang Chen[2], Chun-Hua Chou[3], and Meng-Chia Yang[4]

Department of Computer Science and Engineering
Yuan Ze University, Taiwan, R.O.C.
{czyang[1],sean[2]}@syslab.cse.yzu.edu.tw,
{s922303[3],s922212[4]}@mail.yzu.edu.tw

Abstract. Ontology construction plays an important role in many semantically working environments, such as knowledge management systems and digital libraries. The efficiency, quality, and comprehensiveness of the construction process highly depends on the employed development framework. In this paper, we propose a Topic Maps-driven framework, called XRVAT, to alleviate the cumbersome construction procedure and generate both RDF/XTM ontologies with an effective XTM-to-RDF translation kernel. This paper briefly presents its design and an operational example.

1 Introduction

In many semantically working environments, such as Semantic Web services (e.g. [1]), knowledge management systems (e.g. [2,3]), e-government (e.g. [4,5]), and digital libraries (e.g. [6]), ontology construction plays an important role. For example, ontology establishment is reported as the first step to create a knowledge management system for an efficient e-government [5]. In digital museums, ontologies are also a key issue in organizing and browsing knowledge [6]. Therefore, many authoring frameworks such as TM4L [7] and Protégé [8] have also been proposed to facilitate ontology construction.

Due to our recent survey, most of these authoring tools are not designed to consider RDF and Topic Maps within an integrated interface [7,8,9,10,11]. To the best of our knowledge, only the tool presented in [5] can render both RDF-based ontologies and XTM-based ontologies. However, its interface is textbox-oriented, and thus cannot provide users with a clear view about the associations. Although a topic-driven graphical ontology authoring tool has the advantages of presenting a top-down conceptual view in its nature [12] and providing meaningful associations for people [13], unfortunately, there are very few Topic Maps-driven tools [14].

In this paper, we propose a Topic Maps-driven authoring framework and have implemented a prototype called XRVAT (XTM-to-RDF Visual Authoring Tool) to facilitate RDF/XTM ontology construction. XRVAT has two major design features: (1) the Topic Maps-driven GUI can be easily employed to edit XTM-oriented ontologies; (2)

---

* This work was supported in part by National Science Council of R.O.C. under grant NSC 95-2815-C-155-019-E, and 95-2745-E-155-008-URD.

S. Sugimoto et al. (Eds.): ICADL 2006, LNCS 4312, pp. 523–526, 2006.

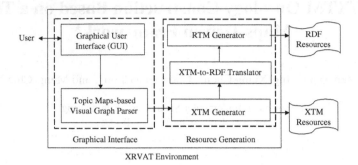

Fig. 1. The architecture of the XRVAT framework

the XTM-to-RDF translation kernel supports high interoperability for RDF-based ontology operations. Therefore, the authoring work can be benefited because the Topic Maps-driven GUI clearly presents the conceptual structures. In addition, the need of machine understandability for logical inference can be satisfied because the framework can render well-formed RDF descriptions.

2   The Topic Maps-Driven Framework

The interactive Topic Maps-driven framework is called XRVAT (XTM-to-RDF Visual Authoring Tool). Users can manipulate and describe the Semantic Web ontologies with less effort. Figure 1 shows the architecture which consists of two major modules, namely, the graphical interface and the resource-generating module. The graphical interface provides users with an interactive visual authoring interface and a graph parser to further analyze the relationships of visual components.

The resource-generating module contains three components: an XTM generator, an XTM-to-RDF translator, and an RTM generator. The XTM generator processes the Topic Maps relationships generated from the graph parser and renders the XTM-format resources. The XTM-to-RDF translator, which adopts the Ogievetsky proposal with the consideration of its semantic completeness requirement, can then be invoked to translate XTM syntax into RDF syntax [15]. The RTM generator takes the responsibility to generate RDF-based resources for interoperability.

Figure 2 shows the interface design. In the XRVAT design, six visual components, namely, Topic, Association, Occurrence, Member, Scope, and Basename, are designed to describe the semantic relationships within the Topic Maps [16]. In the XRVAT interface design, each visual component provides an interactive functionality accompanied with a pop-up form, in which users can fill in to complete the description of Topic Maps and generate well-formed XTM/RDF ontological resources.

3   Ontology Construction Examples

We have implemented an XRVAT prototype to demonstrate a Topic Maps-based visual authoring environment for RDF/XTM ontology construction. In Figure 3, a camera

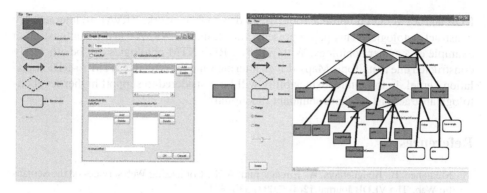

Fig. 2. The XRVAT interface and components   **Fig. 3.** An ontology example for cameras

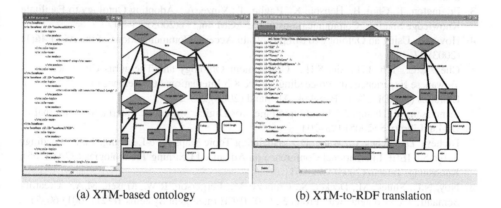

(a) XTM-based ontology   (b) XTM-to-RDF translation

Fig. 4. The automated creation of RDF/XTM ontologies

ontology is created using XRVAT to show the topics and relationships between the individual parts of a photo camera. This example is originally demonstrated in OWL on the Protégé Web site [17]. In XRVAT, the ontology construction is completed with drag-and-paste operations under the restriction of XTM syntax.

After users create the ontology, they can use XRVAT to generate the XTM-based ontology. Figure 4 (a) shows the generation result of the camera example. XRVAT can generate the corresponding RDF-based ontology for further interoperability considerations. Figure 4 (b) illustrates the automated translation of XTM to RDF and the generation of an RDF document in RTM format. The operating examples show that XRVAT efficiently facilitates the creation of both XTM and RDF documents with visual authoring functionalities.

4   Conclusion

Ontology plays an important role in knowledge management, concept modelling, and Semantic Web operations. We target on two most commonly used ontology languages,

RDF and XTM, and propose a Topic Maps-driven framework, XRVAT, to interactively construct ontologies. This paper presents the design of XRVAT and a demonstration example of a camera ontology. With XRVAT, RDF/XTM ontologies can be efficiently constructed due to its Topic Maps-driven interface and the effective XTM-to-RDF translation kernel. In the future, extensibility will be considered to support higher-level ontology abstractions for more abundant functionalities.

References

1. Medjahed, B., Bouguettaya, A., Elmagarmid, A.K.: Composing Web services on the Semantic Web. The VLDB Journal 12(4) (2003) 333–351
2. Shanks, G., Tansley, E., Weber, R.: Using Ontology to Validate Conceptual Models. Communications of the ACM 46(10) (2003) 85–89
3. Edgington, T., Choi, B., Henson, K., Raghu, T., Vinze, A.: Adopting Ontology to Facilitate Knowledge Sharing. Communications of the ACM 46(11) (2003) 85–90
4. Hovy, E.: Using an Ontology to Simplify Data Access. Communications of the ACM 46(1) (2003) 47–49
5. Chen, C.C., Yeh, J.H., Sie, S.H.: Government Ontology and Thesaurus Construction: A Taiwanese Experience. In: Proceedings of the 8th International Conference on Asian Digital Libraries (ICADL 2005), Bangkok, Thailand (2005) 263–272
6. Srinivasan, R., Huang, J.: Fluid Ontologies for Digital Museums. International Journal of Digital Library 5 (2005) 193–204
7. Dicheva, D., Dichev, C., Wang, D.: Visualizing Topic Maps for e-Learning. In: Proceedings of the 5th IEEE International Conference on Advanced Learning Technologies (ICALT'05), Kaohsiung, Taiwan (2005) 950–951
8. Noy, N.F., Sintek, M., Decker, S., Crubezy, M., Fergerson, R.W., Musen, M.A.: Creating Semantic Web Contents with Protégé-2000. IEEE Intelligent Systems 16(2) (2001) 60–71
9. The TM4J Project: (http://tm4j.org/)
10. Ramalho, J.C., Henriques, P.R., Librelotto, G.R.: TM-Builder: An Ontology Builder based on XML Topic Maps. CLEI Electronic Journal 7(2) (2004)
11. Pietriga, E.: IsaViz: A Visual Environment for Browsing and Authoring RDF Models. In: Proceedings of WWW 2002, the 11th World Wide Web Conference (Developer's day), Honolulu, Hawaii, USA (2002) Also in http://www.w3.org/2001/11/IsaViz/.
12. Vatant, B.: Ontology-driven Topic Maps. In: Proceedings of XML EUROPE 2004. (2004)
13. Chen, I.X., Yang, C.Z., Hsu, T.L.: Design and Evaluation of a Panoramic Visualization Environment on Semantic Web. Information and Software Technology 48(6) (2006) 402–409
14. Ramalho, J.C., Librelotto, G.R., Henriques, P.R.: Ontology Driven Websites with Topic Maps - TUTORIAL. In: Proceedings of the 3rd International Conference on Web Engineering. (2003)
15. Ogievetsky, N.: XML Topic Maps through RDF glasses. Markup Languages: Theory & Practice 3(3) (2001) 333–364
16. Pepper, S., Moore, G.: XML Topic Maps (XTM) 1.0. Specification, TopicMaps.Org, http://www.topicmaps.org/xtm/ (2001)
17. XFront OWL Tutorial: camera.owl. http://protege.stanford.edu/plugins/owl/owl-library/(2006)

Building an Arabic Digital Collection: The IIUM Library's Experience

Sarifah binti Abdullah

Library, International Islamic University Malaysia (IIUM)
Jalan Gombak, 53100 Kuala Lumpur, Malaysia
sarifah@iiu.edu.my

Abstract. The IIUM Library's mission is to be an excellent information centre providing information to meet the learning, teaching, and research needs of its customers. The Library gives special attention to Islamic studies and its information resources are predominantly in English and Arabic. To make the resources readily accessible "anytime" and "anywhere" heavy investments were made in a digital library system that implements the latest ICT advancement. The need for Arabic language capabilities has always been one of the Library's major requirements. This paper shares the Library's experience in implementing a digital library system, focusing on the challenges in handling Arabic language information resources.

1 IIUM Digital Library

The IIUM digital library is called Media on Demand (MOD) system. It comprises of the video on demand (Quick Video on Demand), content management and taxonomy management (Multimedia Object Manager (MOM)), Web application (eQUIP) and security and access management (Membership Management) systems. The MOD system runs on three IBM servers (IBM XSeries 365 with 2GB RAM, 80GB hard disk and 2X Intel Xeon 2.4 Processor).

Digital Resources: MOD acts as a repository for all types of digital material and provides public access to the digitized collections through web-based search and browsing facilities. Due copyright issues, the Library decided to focus and digitize the University's resources including theses, exam papers, videos, books, articles, manuscripts and contents pages.

Workflow: All resources are processed in accordance with the set standard workflow which are digitization (scanning, conversion to PDF format, book marking, water marking and security setting), optical character recognition (OCR) processes, metadata creation, quality checking and publishing through the web. These tasks are carried out by the Digital Library Services department.

Taxonomy: The library has decided to establish a corporate taxonomy, since we are forecasting the current digital library system as the university's repository knowledge bank. The taxonomy is being built in stages and currently we have established the body of knowledge which covers all core subjects taught in the university.

Access Management and Security: The Library has decided that only registered members are allowed to access the digital library system. A library portal has been developed by using the eQUIP system. The Membership Management system is used to control access to the digital library. For example, users are allowed to access the

S. Sugimoto et al. (Eds.): ICADL 2006, LNCS 4312, pp. 527–528, 2006.

metadata and first 24 pages of theses through any PCs in the campus. The full text can only be viewed through specified PCs in the Library and its branches.

2   Challenges in Handling Arabic Materials

Research and development on Arabic digital library is behind that of non-Arabic resources. The IIUM library is taking the challenge to implement its digital library which incorporates the Arabic resources.

Arabic Scripts: The Arabic scripts is different from other scripts. First, it is written from right to left while most other scripts are written from left to right. Second, Arabic text is written in many type of fonts or calligraphies such as Tsuluts, Naskhi, and etc. Third, the big difference between the nature of Arabic text and English or other languages is cursiveness. Character overlap on top of each other, either in one solid form or overhanging form. In addition, characters may vary their shapes depending on their position within a word, which implies a larger pattern classes to be recognized relating to English and other languages. It is important to point out that there are some Arabic characters, which are highly ambiguous in shape, particularly when OMNI font is considered. Typical examples are some middle shape characters of *sad, mim, ain*. There is considerable confusion among these characters in different fonts. Arabic human reading, however, relies on language experience for disambiguation among these characters.

Staff: To develop an Arabic digital library, it needs staff who has knowledge and expertise in the Arabic language and cataloguing and also with basic ICT skills.

Optical Character Recognition (OCR): To OCR Arabic documents, the Library is using SAKHR and Open Office software. Sakhr is the only OCR software available at the time we started the project. It was found that there were a lot of words it could not recognize. The staff has to do a lot of editing and this task is very time consuming. This problem is still not fully resolved at this point. When the RTF file is opened in windows, the character direction was not displayed from right to left. After sometime, we found the solution by opening the RTF file through Open Office. Then, the characters direction are displayed correctly from right to left. Since then, we set a procedure that all Arabic RTF files should be opened through the Open Office. The Sakhr software may support many types of fonts, but due to lack of understanding and lack of local support , the above problem is still not resolved.

Content Management System: Content management system offered by the vendor was IBM Content Manager with DB2 database. However, in the middle of project we found that the system does not sufficiently support Arabic documents as required. We could not create metadata and index Arabic materials. This problem delayed the implementation of the project. To fulfill the requirement, the vendor developed their own content management system namely Multimedia Object Manager (MOM).

3   Conclusion

The implementation of the digital library in IIUM Library is timely. The existing system needs further improvement especially in speeding up the digitization process, portal layout and incorporation of Arabic version in order to allow the Middle East community to also surf the site. We hope with the knowledge and expertise that we have gained, our University will involve us in a big way in the establishment of the University's institutional repository/memory.

Access to E-Journals: Need and Impact of Users Training

Prakash Chand, Nishy P, and G Mahesh

National Institute of Science Communication and Information Resources
14-Satsang Vihar Marg, New Delhi 110 067
prakashc@niscair.res.in, pchand_insdoc@yahoo.com

Abstract. The paper presents an analysis of feedback taken from participants of trainers training programme of Council of Scientific and Industrial Research (CSIR), India, for 38 national R&D laboratories/institutions of CSIR. The study reveals the need of distribution and display of publicity material at prominent places of user institutions; training to end users requires repetitive and dynamic order; and library portal be the linking hub of all the information resources. The paper also covers web based monitoring and common search interface system developed for control and user friendliness.

1 Introduction

To arrest the declining information base of CSIR, a consortium based access to 4000+ international journals from eleven publishers has been enabled. To maximize the usage of these resources, a trainer's training program was organized at six locations in the country inviting 3 to 4 persons from all 38 laboratories during July and August, 2005. Users without wide experience and confidence tend to rely on a limited set of tools, exclude all others and resultantly low usage of available resources [1]. The training, experience and relevant qualifications enhance the search power of users and it can alter the achievement of an effective search [2]. A number of studies have emphasized the importance of training and many have discussed the outcomes of such training programmes [3-7]. At the culmination of the programme, feedback of all the 93 participants was obtained through a structured questionnaire for analysis.

2 Analysis

Out of 93 participants, 75 (80.6%) were LIS professionals and 18 (19.4%) scientists. The participants represent all specific subject areas like building research, toxicology, environmental engineering, food science, mining, electro chemistry, leather science, oceanography, road research etc. The break-up of participants in five broad areas are: 30 (32.3%) were from engineering sciences, 19 (20.4%) each from biological and chemical sciences and 15 (16.1 %) & 10 (10.8 %) from information sciences and physical sciences respectively. Analysis shows that 51(54.8 %.) participants had more than 5 years experience of online searching, 37 (39.8%) participants had 1 to 5 years experience and only 5 participants (5.4%) had less than one year experience of online search; 43 (46.2%) participants performed more than 25 searches, 37 (39.8 %)

S. Sugimoto et al. (Eds.): ICADL 2006, LNCS 4312, pp. 529–530, 2006.
© Springer-Verlag Berlin Heidelberg 2006

performed between 6 and 25 and 10 (10.8 %) carried out less then 5 searches in a month. 68 (73.1 %) participants do searches for self and others both, 16 (17.2 %) for others, and only 8 (8.6 %) exclusively for themselves. This shows that in spite of having desktop access, users still prefer to get the searches done by the LIS experts. Predominantly free text 66 (70.9 %) searches to retrieve full text of articles have been employed. A Common Search Interface and Web based Monitoring system developed allows the users click on any icon of publisher and register complaints. 89(95.698%) participants were of the opinion that it is a very useful. 95% of the participants recommend such training workshops in dynamic & recurrent order.

3   Conclusion

The participants' suggestions and views in brief were as: 1 the publicity material likes- pamphlets, posters be displayed on notice boards and other prominent locations of all the laboratory, 2 extensive and repetitive training to actual end users required to understand their requirements, problems and accordingly will help to evolve mechanism, 3 Institutions should have link to consortium home page for visibility of facility, quick and planned access, 4 Infrastructural facilities and manpower in library to be adequate.

References

1. Janet, Guinea.: Building Bridges: The Role of the Systems Librarian in a University Library. Library Hi Tech, **21** (2003) 325-332.
2. Constantine, M.: Nyamboga. Information Skills and Information Literacy in Indian University Libraries. Program: Electronic Library and Information System **38** (2004) 232-239
3. Nadia, Caidi. Building "Civilization Competence": a New Role for Libraries? Journal of Documentation **62** (2006) 194-212
4. Penny, Garrod. Staff Training and End-User Training Issues within the Hybrid Library, Library Management **22** (2001) 30-36.
5. Glen, Mynott., Stella, The bridge., Michael, Shoolbred.: A Distance Learning Course in Research Skills for Public Librarians – an Evaluation , New Library World **101** (2000) 315-324.
6. Shelda, Debowski. Wrong Way: Go Back! An Exploration of Novice Search Behaviors While Conducting an Information Search , The Electronic Library **19** (2001) 371-382.
7. Jacqueline, M. Roberts: Faculty Knowledge about Library Services at the University of the West Indies, New Library World **96** (1995) 14-22.

Reskilling Staff for Digital Libraries

Naicheng Chang[1] and Alan Hopkinson[2]

[1] General Education Center,Tatung University, 40, Sec.3 ChungShan N. Rd. Taipei, Taiwan
ncchang@ttu.edu.tw
[2] Library Systems and Bibliographic Services, Middlesex University,
Hendon, London NW4 4BT, UK
a.hopkinson@mdx.ac.uk

Abstract. In academic libraries, the digital library world has had a profound impact on staffing. Academic libraries are facing huge pressure on their staffing levels at a time when digital libraries are being introduced. Digital libraries cannot be divorced from ordinary libraries. What skills do traditional librarians need? There is little in the literature on training for staffing for digital libraries. Consequently, evidence from a recent PhD gleaned from research interviews of these digital libraries case studies is included in this paper. This research uncovered a variety of different management and organizational issues and revealed the large cost of personnel in the implementation and maintenance of digital libraries

1 Introduction

As part of a study on the impact of XML (Extensible Markup Language) in digital library development, studies were undertaken on three digital library initiatives, which were chosen because of their size and being examples in the global digital library community. These studies included research interviews conducted during visits in September 2002 to three projects which were in different types of library. The Perseus Digital Library (PDL) was selected as an example of a research and development testbed. The University of Michigan Digital Library Services (DLS) represented an academic library (In June 2003 the DLS was renamed Library Information Technology). Its mission is to support a virtual learning environment and preserve campus-wide materials for long-term access. The Library of Congress (LC) National Digital Library Program (NDLP) was taken as an example of a national library project.

2 Expectations for Digital Library Staff

There is much more to digitization than scanning data. The non-technical challenges encountered by digital library developers are proving to be elusive, complex and profound. Institutions are not looking for people doing routine work but for those who have knowledge of future trends in their professions. Therefore, our view is that librarians in general, following the lead of those in the Library of Congress, are wise to see the future in XML. The results of our investigations of real world library posts discussed in the following paragraphs support our vision of this.

We did an investigation using Web job listings in the UK, the US and Taiwan. We targeted academic librarian jobs and computing jobs in the academic sector. Further-

S. Sugimoto et al. (Eds.): ICADL 2006, LNCS 4312, pp. 531–532, 2006.
© Springer-Verlag Berlin Heidelberg 2006

more, we investigated whether in those three countries XML was part of the curriculum in library schools and if there were reports or activities related to XML from the library associations in the three countries.

We found few jobs in librarianship compared with computing mentioned XML as a requirement.

We discovered that library schools have not recognized the need for XML skills. According to their course descriptions, in the UK, only one out of 8 library schools provided an XML course; in the US, two out of 50 library schools provided an XML course; in Taiwan, one out of 9 library schools provides an XML course. On the other hand, the concept of XML has been introduced into courses, such as Electronic Publishing, Document Engineering, and Technologies in Web Content Management.

As far as professional associations are concerned, in the UK, the Chartered Institute of Library and Information Professionals (CILIP) has been announcing more training workshops on library and information technology in which XML-related initiatives such as markup language, schema, Resource Description Framework (RDF) are among the topics. In the US, since 2000 the Library and Information Technology Association at ALA has selected XML related initiatives such as MARC XML as annual top technology trends. The Library Association of the Republic of China in Taiwan provides irregular XML training courses.

To conclude our investigation, although XML has not been recognized as a core skill in library jobs or as part of the core programme in library schools, nevertheless, library associations with their responsibility for professional development have identified XML as an important technology trend that needs to be monitored carefully. We suggest that it would be advantageous for librarians to have knowledge of XML even if they do not work directly with XML; and library schools could provide selective courses on XML.

Staff retention is important and it is necessary to have a good career structure in place, which is going to be difficult in most environments where academic digital libraries are being developed.

XML is a new technology for the Web likely to play its part in every library operation. Librarians in the future will play a mediating role between the computing professions and users. Knowledge of current standards and newly emerging technology trends such as XML will be a beneficial skill for librarians while looking for jobs either in the library sector or information-related sectors. Library schools could therefore contribute to the acquisition of this professional knowledge by covering these subject materials in their curriculum. As Hey suggested, librarians should be aware of the technological trends and be prepared, in order to compete and survive in the ever-changing environment.

3 Future Studies

The studies were all of libraries in the US since when we began our research there were few developments elsewhere. We have detected from personal experience in the UK and Asia that in some areas there is opposition in various levels of the profession to librarians becoming more involved in the management and technical activities associated with digital libraries. Senior librarians may feel deskilled in face of a digital library whether it be in developing it or being a user of it or assisting library users to use it. So, there are many reasons why this may have resulted in other groups such as computing professions stepping in. Clearly, there is ample material for a further study.

Institutional Repositories in India: A Case Study of National Aerospace Laboratories

Poornima Narayana[1], B.S. Biradar[2], and I.R.N. Goudar[1]

[1] Information Center for Aerospace Science & Technology,
National Aerospace Laboratories
Bangalore 560 017, India
[2] Chairman, Department of Library and Information Science
Kuvempu University, Shankarghatta
Shimoga – 577 451 Karnataka, India

Abstract. This paper traces the history and developments in Open Archives Initiatives including open access journals, e-print archives and Institutional repositories. The setting up of NAL's Institutional Repository using OSS GNU Eprints, document types with statistical analysis, country wise statistics of full text download, levels of accessibility and technologies used in building the Institutional Repository have been discussed at length.

Keywords: Institutional Repository, Open Access Initiatives, India, NAL.

1 Institutional Repositories in India

Institutional Repositories are digital archives of intellectual products created by the faculty, staff and students of an institution or group of institutions accessible to end users both within and outside the institution. Metadata harvesting services index OAI-compliant IRs. India has adopted the Open Access much ahead of other developing countries. More than 130 peer reviewed open access journals are being published out of which 94 titles are by 6 major publishers like INSA, IAS, MedInd, MedKnow, Indianjournals.com and Kamala-Raj enterprises.

Registry of Open Access Repositories (ROAR) lists 22 Indian IRs including Institution based ones like those of IISc, NAL, RRI, INFLIBNET, IIMK, IITD, IISB, NITR, NCL, NIO etc; subject specific like LDL and MedInd(http://www.archives.eprints.org). Four Metadata Harvesting Services known so far use PKP harvester. Open J-Gate (*www.openj-gate.org*), covers more than 3,500 open access academic, research and industry journals world over of which > 1,500 are peer-reviewed scholarly journals with 0.3 million new articles added every year.

2 NAL- Institutional Repository (http://nal-ir.nal.res.in/)

NAL, a constituent of CSIR has made very significant contributions to Indian aerospace programmes, especially in designing and developing small and medium size civil aircrafts in India.

S. Sugimoto et al. (Eds.): ICADL 2006, LNCS 4312, pp. 533–534, 2006.
© Springer-Verlag Berlin Heidelberg 2006

The Information Centre of NAL (ICAST), an ISO-9001: 2000 Certified Centre serves as the National Information Centre for Aerospace Science and Technology.

ICAST initiated setting up of its own repository during 2003 using, the then most popular open source software Greenstone Digital Library (GSDL) with more than 300 papers. In 2004, the NAL-IR adopted GNU E Prints for archiving and managing the digital collections. More than 1500 items have been added to this Institutional Repository covering journal articles, conference papers, technical reports, presentation/lectures, preprints, thesis, images etc. of which Technical Reports account for 63.61% followed by Journal Articles and Conference Papers with 29.34% an 5.74% respectively. More than 15,000 downloads to the full texts of NAL-IR have been recorded for about 340 documents, of which United States accounts for 33.6% followed by India 23.61%, United Kingdom 9.48%, Canada 3.63%, Japan 3.2%, China 1.65%, Germany 1.37%, Netherlands 1.21% and so on. More than 33% of the documents uploaded have been downloaded till date. Three documents have been downloaded more than 200 times followed by 8 documents between 100-200; 13 documents between 50-100 and so on.

The level of accessibility includes fully open on Internet with or without full text; only on institute's Intranet with or without full text, accessible only to concerned Heads of the departments and project leaders. The IR facilitates browsing by year of publication, author, concerned department, subject category and document type. One can also search documents by author, title, subject, publisher using simple and advanced search features with many options.

NAL-IR runs on GNU EPrints open archive software (revision EPrints 2.3.6) and powered by MySQL for database, Apache Web server, scripting language PERL5, XML standard for retrieving, the Document Object Model (DOM) platform- and language-neutral interface that allow programs and scripts to dynamically access and update the content, structure and style of documents, ParaCite for both reference parsing and location. The IR Supports OAI-PMH for effective interoperability, VLit for electronic locations (URLs), Valid XHTML and Valid CSS for checking Cascading Style Sheets for display.

Remarks: The concept of Institutional Repository in India has made a tremendous progress compared to other developing countries. More and more institutions are setting up their digital repositories. NAL plans to add other documents in its collection and adopt Dspace for archiving shortly. The Metadata harvesting facility, still in experimental stage, aims to extend at CSIR (40 laboratories) and Aerospace areas.

The Digital Divide in Developing Countries: With Special Reference to Bangladesh

Md. Anisur Rahman[1], Mahmudun Nahar[2], Md. Azharul Islam[3], and Razina Akhter[4]

[1] Lecturer (Part-time)
Post graduate Diploma in Library and Information Science Program
Darul Ihsan University, Dhaka 1209, Bangladesh
anisdacca@gmail.com
[2] Palli Karma-Sahayak Foundation (PKSF), Dhaka 1207, Bangladesh
mnahar@pksf-bd.org
[3] SAARC Meteorological Research Centre, Dhaka 1207, Bangladesh
aim71@hotmail.com
[4] Bangladesh Shishu (Child) Academy, Old High Court Area, Ramna
Dhaka 1000, Bangladesh
raginaakhter@yahoo.com

Abstract. There is a digital divide between developed and developing countries. The digital divide around the world is usually measured through statistical indices such as the number of telephone lines, personal computers, websites and Internet users and their ratio to the total population. This paper reviews scholarly published books, articles, newspapers, journals and conference proceedings that address the issues related to digital divide that is affecting so many citizens in developing countries especially in Bangladesh and the factors that alienate people from enjoying the benefits of ICT. The authors tried to discuss the overall situation and recommends possible strategies that can be implemented in developing countries to reverse the widening gap of digital divide.

Keywords: Digital divide, Information technology, Communications Technology, Internet.

1 Introduction

Computers, modern telecommunication and the Internet all reduce communications costs and break down geographical borders. Information and communication technologies serve as powerful tools for empowering people, benefit business and virtually link people around the world to share their views, ideas and innovation.

2 Digital Divide

Developed countries are getting much benefit from the advancement of ICT. So, there is a digital divide between developed and developing countries. Digital divide is "a gap, which tends to deepen, is produced between those individuals that can access new information and communication tools such as phones, TV sets or the Internet, and those who are too poor to get them between the have's and the have nots." The digital divide around the world is usually measured through statistical indices such as the number of stationary telephone lines, personal computers, websites and Internet users and their ratio to the total population.

3 ICT Status in Bangladesh

Uses of Computer in Bangladesh started with a mainframe computer in 1964. The Internet came in Bangladesh in 1993 and IP connectivity in 1996. In April 2000, the Government withdraws taxes on VSAT after that the use of Internet scenario of the country has been changing rapidly. Presently, there are nearly 120 ISPs serving for accountholders-based connectivity with more than 500,000 users. The ICT Act 2003, based on the United Nations Commission on International Trade Law (UNCITRAL) has been drafted by the Ministry of Law, Justice and Parliamentary Affairs and is now being reviewed, while the Copyright (Amendment) Act 2005 has been passed to protect intellectual property rights, including computer equipments like software, hardware and patent.

South East Asia-Middle East-West Europe (SEA-ME-WE-4) is a submarine cable consortium connecting 14 counties at 16 landing stations. Bangladesh joined the consortium and signed a MoU on 4 September 2002 at Bali in Indonesia. On 21 May 2006, the Prime Minister of Bangladesh inaugurated this submarine cable connecting with Bangladesh. The total length of the cable is 22,000 km (approx.), where the Bangladesh landing station is 1,260 km away from the Cox's Bazar seashore. According to the Project Director, the Submarine Cable Implementation Project "...initially Bangladesh would get the opportunity to transmit data 10 gbps which are equivalent to 100,000-voice channel". Meanwhile, many ISPs in Dhaka have already started using the submarine cable although an appropriate cable infrastructure is yet in place. They are providing speed up to 2 mbps.

4 Conclusion

The digital divide is increasing notably between advanced and developed countries. A collective action approach is required both within countries and among countries to achieve this target. Within countries, collaboration of government, private sector and NGOs is required, while among countries, advanced and developing countries should cooperate, the former advancing financial and technical support.

References

1. The Independent (Internet ed.). June 7 2006 (issue 1521)
2. Rahman, Md. Anisur & Akhter, Razina.: The role of libraries and librarians in Information literacy: an overview (Paper accepted for Poster Presentation in ICDL 2006, 5-8 December, New Delhi, India)

The Design and Implementation of Chinese Rural Studies Database

Jianhua Wu[1], Fang Lin[1], Haiyan Chen[1], Xian Zhang[1], Jing Wang[2], and Li Li[1]

[1] Library of Central China Normal University, Wuhan, 430079, P.R. China
[2] Center for Chinese Rural Studies, Wuhan, 430079, P.R. China
{wujh, linfang, chenhy, zhangx, lili}@mail.ccnu.edu.cn,
wangjinghs@sohu.com

1   Introduction

CASDP is one of CALIS's programs during the10th 5-year plan, it tries to build a group of subject databases characterized with China feature, local feature, high education feature or document resources feature, serving both teaching and research of high education and economic development. Since 2003, 75 subject databases from 61 universities have become members of the program. A Portal is being built to integrate all metadata and provide access to the whole world.

CCRS(Center for Chinese Rural Studies) is a comprehensive academic research institution on rural problems characterized with politics. CCRS's research is insisting on "face to society, face to the countryside, face to grass roots" and making deep investigation and experiment in a long-term. CCRS has set up nearly 100 investigation and study bases in China. The investigations and researches undertaken by CCRS have been providing reliable reference for the government's decision-making and the legislation work.

CRSD is a subject database characterized with both discipline and document features relying on CCRS. It became a member of CASDP in 2004. CRSD aims at serving scholars of CCRS and other institutes, policy and decision makers from government at all levels, and interested publics.

CRSD is a representative of these subject databases and will meet the common issues that other subject databases will encounter.

Choosing a proper subject is the first step to construct a database. The key to this step is to start with "characteristic". With the advantages of leading position in rural studies and rich investigation data in CCRS, Chinese rural studies is an ideal subject for constructing a subject database.

To ensure the quality and value of the database, demands and data sources are analyzed thoroughly. Following suggestions of CCRS scholars, monographs, papers, investigation reports, case studies, chorography, statistical data, and other materials have been chosen.

2   Developing Platform

It is vital to choose a proper developing platform for subject database. It took one and half a year to choose a platform to develop CRSD, and 5 software had

S. Sugimoto et al. (Eds.): ICADL 2006, LNCS 4312, pp. 537–538, 2006.
© Springer-Verlag Berlin Heidelberg 2006

been used for trial. Two criteria are mapped out to guide the choice. First, the software must accord with CALIS's standards completely. Secondly, it is able to provide an integrated environment to develop and run a digital library.At last, TRS is chosen. TRS is the first Chinese full text retrieval system in China ,it takes a leading position in the fields of Internet searching, content management, and information mining.

3   Functions and Standards

The whole database is parted into 8 sub-databases, they are: "laws and policies", "books", "journal navigations", "papers", "case studies", "statistical materials", "specialists and scholars", and "center library". These 8 sub-databases are interconnecting and linked with outside databases. For example, records of books are linked to the library's OPAC system, journal records are linked to CNKI and VIP. The "specialists and scholars" links with the "papers"and the "books".

Up to June 5, 2006,there are over 40,000 records in CRSD,73% records are full-text. Simple, advanced, and full-text search are all available. It is noteworthy that this database provides cluster search. Clicking on a single knowledge point, records related to this point will be listed.

Metadata and some full-text data such as laws and policies are open to everyone. Copyrights protection is applied in two ways. First, the campus network users are authorized to access the full text by limiting the IP addresses. Secondly, a third-party digital viewer is used,in which the users' operations are limited.

CASDP's major standards basis is "CADLIS Technical Standards and Specifications" and "CALIS Subject Database Program Local System Technical Specifications".To ensure that all subject databases are accord with the uniform standards and specifications, CALIS tested and certified 8 software. Only the software passed the test are recommended to members of CALIS.

4   Future Development

Before CRSD is going to be finished, a meeting was held to survey scholars' attitudes. After the meeting,a decision was made to build a more comprehensive Chinese rural studies database, with CRSD as the foundation. The new CRSD will become one of the 10 humanities and social science databases of the Ministry of Education in it's 11th 5-year plan, which will be sponsored as a key project. The aim of the new CRSD is to become the largest and most comprehensive database about Chinese rural society, the best one, and a unique one.

The content of CRSD will be expanded. The collections of the new CRSD should be rich and unique. Plentiful fact data, data collected from surveys, such as project "100 villages in 10 years" will be included. A countryside digital museum will be constructed, which is open to the public.

Functions of CRSD will be improved too. Evaluation function will be added and a 5-level membership system will be set up.

Digital Library Service of the National Diet Library

Toshiyasu Oba

Digital Library Division, Kansai-kan of the National Diet Library,
8-1-3- Seikadai, Seika-cho, Soraku-gun, Kyoto, 619-0287, Japan
oba@ndl.go.jp

Abstract. The National Diet Library (NDL) is Japan's only national deposit library and also the country's parliamentary library. Timed with the opening of the Kansai-kan of the NDL in 2002, it has expanded its electronic library services.

The NDL has been actively working on digitization of its collections. The "Digital Library from the Meiji Era" (http://kindai.ndl.go.jp/), which was opened to the public in 2002, carries full-text digital images of about 127,000 volumes of 89,000 titles of the books published in the Meiji era (1868-1912). In addition, it has been promoting copyright clearance and digitization of most of the books published in the Taisho era (1912-1926).

The NDL offers the "NDL Gallery" (http://www.ndl.go.jp/en/gallery/index. html) as an online exhibition under the general title "Memories of Japan," on specific themes, and introduces unique materials held by the NDL with descriptions and commentaries. Nine exhibitions are available so far, including the "Birth of the Constitution of Japan" and "Portraits of Modern Japanese Historical Figures." We will sequentially add new contents.

The "Web Archiving Project (WARP)" (http://warp.ndl.go.jp/) is a project to preserve information gathered from the Internet for the sake of future generations. We have collected selected Internet resources with license agreements, and provided about 1,500 online periodicals and 1,900 websites.

These services are available to anyone via the NDL's website (http://www.ndl.go.jp/).

Long-term digital preservation has become a significant issue. The NDL has conducted research on case examples of foreign countries and long-term preservation for packaged electronic publications since 2002. We will continue these studies to find practical application of migration and emulation.

Based on the research results, the NDL has been working on construction of the NDL Digital Archive System which preserves and provides the digital information heritage of Japan for a long period. This system conforms to the Open Archival Information System (OAIS). We are also planning to construct a portal site for digital archives in Japan and are already providing the prototype (http://www.dap.ndl.go.jp/).

S. Sugimoto et al. (Eds.): ICADL 2006, LNCS 4312, p. 539, 2006.
© Springer-Verlag Berlin Heidelberg 2006

Institutional Repositories in Japan

Yuko Murakami and Jun Adachi

National Institute of Informatics,
2-1-2 Hitotsubashi, Chiyoda-Ku Tokyo 101-8430 Japan
{murakami, adachi}@nii.ac.jp

Abstract. This report describes the growth of institutional repositories in Japan and NII's support projects since 2004. The characteristic features of the process were: (1) the diversity of the partner universities (2) the collaboration between universities and NII, and (3) the fast localization and installation with limited budget.

Keywords: Institutional repository, universities in Japan, open access.

1 Introduction

The National Institute of Informatics (NII) was founded in April 2000 as an inter-university research institute. It not only conducts comprehensive research on informatics, but develops and provides an advanced infrastructure for disseminating scholarly information.

Its cyberscience infrastructure (CSI) initiative aims at providing industrial and social contribution as well as international cooperation on scientific research.

The initiative includes the following projects:

- SINET. NII provides 100M network infrastructure shared among academic institutions in Japan.
- NAREGI. NII promotes a research grid middleware to enhance supercomputing in scientific research.
- UPKI. NII collaborates with universities to construct interuniversity public key infrastructure.
- Next-generation content services[1]. Infrastructure for scholarly information resources is under construction on the basis of existing scholarly content services that were established by collaboration between NII and universities.

In this report, we focus on the content services. They are to integrate its existing content services, which cover the disciplines of science, technology, and medicine as well as humanities and social sciences. NII-CAT provides bibliographical information which has been developed in collaboration with universities in Japan. The portal GeNii offers an integrated search of the following databases: the citation information database (CiNii), the bibliographical information database with

---

[1] The project information is available at http://www.nii.ac.jp/irp/index-e.html (last accessed on September 4, 2006).

S. Sugimoto et al. (Eds.): ICADL 2006, LNCS 4312, pp. 540–549, 2006.

an associative search (Webcat Plus), the database of research projects funded by Japan Society for Promotion of Science (KAKEN), and the database of scientific databases (NII-DBR). A secure access to e-journal articles is established by collaboration between NII and the Japan Association of National University Libraries (JANUL). NII's e-journal repository (NII-REO) has archived e-journal back numbers published by Oxford university press and Springer as far back as 1849. JANUL members with the consortium contract can access the articles.

2   NII's Projects for Institutional Repositories: 2004-2005

NII launched projects for institutional repositories (IR) in 2004. They are considered components of the CSI initiative in 2005. Detailed information is available in [1].

2.1   Backgrounds: Governmental Reports on Dissemination of Academic Information

In 2003, the Subdivision on Science in the Council for Science and Technology at Ministry of Education, Culture, Sport, Science and Technology (MEXT) of Japan published a report[2] that emphasized the role of university libraries in the dissemination of academic information, in particular in the areas of humanities and social science.

Since then, the idea of an institutional repository has formed. On June 28, 2005, the MEXT Council published an interim report[3] on university libraries to explicitly state the significance of institutional repositories in the dissemination of academic information resources.

2.2   2004: Experimental Implementation

After the 2003 report, university libraries stepped forward to realize the system for disseminating scholarly information. In 2004, NII collaborated with six universities to introduce institutional repositories to Japanese universities. Those universities summarized their experiences in manuals: (1) the installation and localization of institutional repository software, (2) policy making for the entire university, and (3) copyright processing.

2.3   2005: Pilot Implementation

In 2005, NII started a collaborative experiment with 19 university libraries. The project's purpose was the deployment and coordination of institutional repositories in Japan. By June 2006, 17 institutional repositories were running; these repositories hold a total of 62,423 items (as of June 28, 2006). The list of participant universities appears in the appendix.

2.4 Problems Found in 2004 and Solved in 2005

Most of the problems are commonly observed in universities throughout the world in the launching and the operating phases of institutional repositories, such as the following problems which we faced in our activities in 2005.

Getting University-wide Support at the Launching Phase. For effective operation of an institutional repository, a university-wide agreement is crucial because an institutional repository belongs to the whole university, not just to the university library.

In 2005, two approaches were taken: bottom-up and top-down. In the bottom-up approach, a university library takes the initiative to spread the idea of an institutional repository to the whole university. Hokkaido University and Chiba University took this approach. On the other hand, in the top-down approach, the decision is made first by the university management level. The University of Tokyo and Tokyo Institute of Technology took this approach.

Practical Structure. In 2005, the departments in charge of running their institutional repositories, such as libraries and computing centers, used one of the three structures listed below to launch the project. and computing centers, used one of three structures to launch the project.

1. Special project. Hiroshima University launched its institutional repository by appointing two librarians specialized for the project.
2. Additional loads. Most universities launched institutional repositories without changing the departmental structure. The tasks were added to the ordinary routine. This approach seems difficult to maintain in the long term because it burdens the staff in charge.
3. Integrated workflow. Tasks concerning the institutional repository were integrated into the library's standard workflow. This approach has the most potential for the future. In 2005, Keio University attempted this approach.

Collection Policy. Institutional repositories should emphasize the strength of each university. Collection policies, which thus reflect the diversity of the universities, are roughly classified into two categories. IRs in the first category mainly collect journal articles based on the open access (OA) movement. Hokkaido University emphasizes influences of IR on impact factors and focuses on green journal articles. IRs in the other category collect any scholarly data to make the repository into a showcase of institutional achievements. Chiba University extended its IR to accept factual data in addition to articles and e-books.

Registration and Permission Process. Researchers were found to be reluctant to self-archive their achievements, while libraries tried to facilitate the process. Most universities introduced proxy registrations of items and proxy copyright permissions in 2005.

Copyright Permission. JANUL collected copyright policies from publishers in Japan. A database of the policies should be launched. Nevertheless, most academic societies and publishers in Japan do not have explicit and clear copyright policies in written form. Each publisher should implement an effective legal basis of copyright contracts.

System Localization. There are specific problems in Japan or other countries with 2-byte character codes. Following the experiment in 2005, various approaches were taken for choosing and constructing institutional repository systems.

- Bootstrap the system setup using an open source. This requires the least cost, but it is risky because the staff in charge can be replaced. In national universities, staff members are usually replaced in every two or three years to move to another university library. In private universities, staff members may not stay in the library but can move to other administrative offices.
- Rely on commercial vendors by purchasing a software package or commissioning the setup of open source software. This can be costly. A vendor eventually put a relatively high price tag (3.3 million JPY, or 28 thousand USD) on a localization package of DSpace in 2006.

Two tasks are imperative for the future efforts: delineating criteria for selecting the system and providing information to universities who plan to introduce institutional repositories.

3   NII's IR Project in the Promotion Phase: 2006-2007

The installment of institutional repositories to all universities in Japan requires an enormous amount of effort; there are 726 universities in Japan (87 national universities, 86 municipal universities, 553 private universities, and 4 private correspondence education colleges) in the academic year 2005. Their backgrounds are diverse and the library systems are not uniform. Nevertheless, NII stepped forward to install IR at many universities as quickly as possible.

In 2006, the CSI initiative put more emphasis on the content services. NII began working jointly with 57 universities in the construction of a next-generation scientific information resources infrastructure. The goal in the promotion phase is twofold. First, it aims to triple the number of OA repositories in Japan; the country has 19 currently functional repositories. Second, it supports the research and development activities that help facilitate the dissemination of scholarly contents.

The partner universities are expected to share their experiences and project deliverables with the whole academic community as well as the academic contents in their IRs.

The budget for the 2006 academic year amounts to 300 million JPY (2.6 million USD). The project period is from August 1, 2006 to March 31, 2008.

The 57 universities were selected from the 77 that applied for funding, replying to NII's request for proposals. Of the 57, 47 were national universities. Those with matching funds were appreciated.

The method was historically significant, since the request for proposals was the first announcement in Japan for university libraries to call for external competitive fundings. It caused cultural changes throughout university libraries; universities recognized their libraries' potential for procurations of external fundings; some universities announced the acceptance of the project proposal as a top news of their university website.

3.1 Projects Commissioned

The following projects were commissioned in 2006 to solve the problems found in 2005.

Supports for IR Management. Chiba and Mie Universities are collaborating to develop a system for analyzing access statistics. The system will provide a basis of evaluation for IRs together with progress management tools.

Copyright Policy Database. Tsukuba University and JANUL have been working together to construct copyright policies for Japanese publishers. Unclear copyright policies and ad hoc custom for copyright processing have been apparent problems among publishers in Japan. Most publishers are small and they need information. NII has supported the academic societies by using its society village service to have their academic information disseminated. Its annual meeting for the service participants now includes information sessions on copyright policies.

Connections to Other Systems. Connections between IRs and other systems inside and outside of universities have a great marketing value. Among them, the connection to a researcher's performance database is expected to alleviate the paperwork load from researchers. The Tokyo Institute of Technology is constructing a system to make it easy to register materials. An authority directory is indispensable for connecting an IR system with the faculty performance database. Nagoya University is in charge of developing this feature. Connections to open course ware (OCW) systems are also of interest.

Okayama University has constructed the *Digital Okayama Encyclopedia* with the Okayama Prefectural library which is to be integrated with the institutional repository of the university.

In 2005, some universities began providing their metadata via OAI-PMH to service providers that are attractive to users. Chiba University began to collaborate with Scirus. Google, OAIster and JuNii+ are other prospective providers. In addition, some systems were developed that accommodate with link resolvers that guide users to adequate and available contents.

Some users want to register various contents on IRs, such as fact data and multimedia contents. Metadata extension is required to accept them. Nagoya University is in charge of developing this feature.

Content Recruitment and Marketing Practices. All repository construction, content extension, and utilization promotion require marketing that suits their target consumers. In 2005 during the launching phase, practices were accumulated for marketing toward librarians, library managers, and university executives, as well as toward researchers for the long term. Nevertheless, this is hard in Japan because few subject librarians exist for historical reasons. Hokkaido University has tackled the problem and made various attempts. From meeting in the library, the staff found that many researchers did not accept their invitations, so they changed their strategy: librarians now go to departmental meetings and researcherfs offices to explain the significance of IRs.

Special Purpose IRs. Some universities are developing institutional repositories for special purposes. Waseda, Hiroshima, and Nagasaki Universities are working toward institutional repositories as a platform of in-house journals and overlay journals. The Tokyo University of Foreign Language is actualizing a multilingual institutional repository which can deal with documents in Arabic as well as those in Japanese and European languages. Kyoto University is launching an institutional repository which focuses on articles in mathematics in cooperation with the Hokkaido and Tokyo Universities. Hiroshima University collaborates with the Stockholm International Peace Research Institute (SIPRI) to collect Japanese translations of articles on peace study. Education universities are also working to disseminate educational material such as classroom practices and course materials.

3.2   NII's Supports for Institutional Repositories

While partner universities carry out their projects, NII provides supports not only for partners but also for other universities in Japan that are interested in institutional repositories.

Community Enhancement and Information Exchange. NII invites librarians in charge of institutional repositories to its mailing lists to share their experiences. NII also provides an information website, which bears the manuals and reports on institutional repositories in Japan, such as installation manuals and reports of library visits outside of Japan.

Moreover, NII provide translated material on institutional repositories published by organizations and institutions such as JISC and SPARC. Although most Japanese librarians can read English, it is much easier if they can access information in Japanese. The articles include: "The Case for Institutional Repositories: A SPARC Position Paper" by Raym Crow, "A Recipe for Cream of Science: Special Content Recruitment for Dutch Institutional Repositories" by Martin Feijen and Annemiek van der Kuil, and "Concretizando o acesso livre a literatura cientifica : o repositorio institucional e a politica de auto-arquivo da Universidade do Minho" by Eloy Rodrigues.

Supports for Content Building. As mentioned in the introduction, NII has built databases for academic information in collaboration with universities, which are accessible via GeNii and the other existing content services of NII. Moreover, it has also digitalized university journals. To support universities in building their initial contents for their own institutional repositories, NII has decided to release the data created by universities directly to them via FTP and CD-ROM upon request.

Workshops and Conferences. NII holds workshops and conferences for various levels. Some workshops concentrate on technical issues, while some conferences are for conceptual discussions on open access, advocacy, and policy. An international conference for digital repositories is to be held on December 18-19, 2006 in Tokyo.

Training and Education. Most partner universities in the 2006 project just began to introduce their own repositories at the beginning of the project period, during which time a typical partner university is given 2 million JPY (about 17,000 USD). They could not afford the DSpace commercial localization package as mentioned. NII thus made an effort to encourage the universities by presenting several models to establish the implementation of institutional repositories within such a limited budget.

NII held a workshop for system selection and implementation with open source software. The most stressed point in the workshop was that it is not wise to spend money and time on systems; content recruitment has priority. Suggested open source software included XooNIps in addition to DSpace. XooNIps is an extension of Xoops with library modules, still under further development by a joint project between Keio University and RIKEN. XooNIps already accommodates Japanese characters and offers a one-click installation package for Windows PC.

As mentioned, DSpace in Japanese universities requires localization. Hokkaido University and Kanazawa University lead a user community in Japan to exchange information on the installation and operation as a part of their commissioned project from NII.

NII has updated its 3-day training session's existing curriculum on library portals. The sessions are held twice a year as a part of NII's education and training programs for librarians, to emphasize the practical aspects of institutional repositories. The new curriculum includes a general introduction, trends in the world, case studies, system implementation, marketing strategies, copyright permission procedures, and writing a proposal for a mimic presentation for researchers and university executives.

Related Project: JuNii+ as a National Portal with Federated Search. NII is building a portal for Japanese institutional repositories, called JuNii+. It will harvest metadata from institutional repositories to provide for a federated search. While each university may make contracts with other portal services and search engines such as Google and Scirus, NII supports the national portal to allow world-wide users to access academic information created in Japan.

4   Features of the Projects and Further Problems

The diversity of the projects comes out from the spontaneity of the partner universities on the projects. The project also has dimension. The number of IRs in Japan has tripled every year since 2004. The speed of installation is getting faster little by little, since the community has exchanged practical information.

The JANUL-NII report[2] on open access (OA) showed that only 29% of researchers in national universities recognize OA, while most understand the significance when explained. Comparing to the Swan's reports ([8], [9]), those researchers in Japan behave similarly to those without knowledge of OA in the UK. Most are concerned with copyright issues; further information on the issue as well as the concept of OA is still to be distributed.

Alleviating the costs to introduce and run the repository is urgent. Information on the development and maintenance of the repository must be shared in the user communities and open source software must be distributed.

Long-term preservation and disaster plan is to be considered immediately in spite of the limited budget. Most IRs currently lack secure backup system. International collaboration is expected.

5   Conclusion

There are two aspects of the conceptual relationship between digital library at universities and the institutional repository. First, the institutional repository embraces the concept of a digital library. The information assets, particularly those accumulated in the digital library, amount to identity of the academic institution; moreover, up-to-date information of scholarly accomplishments enhances the productivity of the institution. Academic achievements are advertised via the IR to underscore the strength and competency of information management of the institution.

The second aspect is that the institutional repository is a component to realize the very idea of the digital library. The interoperability and prospective integrated search via the open access initiative protocol of metadata harvesting (OAI-PMH) emphasize the usability of the digital library.

Thus, the growth of institutional repositories embodies the idea of the digital library in the context of academia. It facilitates the dissemination of scholarly information to promote scientific research. Although this report focuses on the situation in Japan, the whole system of the dissemination of scholarly information should spread throughout the world; international collaboration and cooperation are expected to pursue the truth.

Acknowledgements. We thank our colleagues at National Institute of Informatics for their supports and valuable comments; Kazunobu Konishi, Koichi

---

[2] The summary appears at http://www.nii.ac.jp/sparc/doc/oa_report_summary_en.pdf and the report is available at http://www.nii.ac.jp/sparc/doc/oa_report_en.pdf (both is last accessed on September 4, 2006).

Ojiro, Hideyuki Yamanishi, Mitsushi Kikuchi, Haruo Asoshina were especially helpful. In particular, Koichi Ojiro took the time to read our draft. We are grateful as well to librarians in the project partner universities who have shared their experiences. Without those assistances, this report would not appear.

References

1. National Institute of Informatics, *Gakujutu kikan repository kochiku software jisso jikken project hokokusho (In Japanese. Report of experimental installation of institutional repository software).* http://www.nii.ac.jp/metadata/irp/NII-IRPreport.pdf

2. Ministry of Education, Culture, Sport, Science and Technology, *Jinbun shakai kagaku no shinko ni tsuite (In Japanese. On promotion of humanity and social science)* http://www.mext.go.jp/b_menu/shingi/gijyutu/gijyutu4/toushin/020601.htm (last accessed on September 8, 2006.)

3. Ministry of Education, Culture, Sport, Science and Technology, *Gakujutu joho kiban to shiteno daigaku toshokan to no kongo no seibi no arikata ni tsuite (In Japanese. On further development of university libraries and other facilities as infrastructure of scholarly information)* http://www.mext.go.jp/b_menu/shingi/gijyutu/gijyutu4/toushin/05071402.htm (last accessed on September 8, 2006.)

4. Japan Association of National University Libraries, *Daigaku toshokan ni okeru chosakuken mondai Q and A (In Japanese. Q and A on copyright issues at university libraries).* March 2006. Available at http://wwwsoc.nii.ac.jp/janul/j/documents/coop/copyrightQA_v5.pdf (Last accessed on August 28, 2006)

5. Japan Association of National University Libraries, *Denshi-toshokan kinou no koujika ni mukete 2 (In Japanese. Toward digital library of higher level)* June 2006. Available at http://wwwsoc.nii.ac.jp/janul/j/projects/si/dc_chukan_hokoku_2.pdf (Last accessed on August 28, 2006)

6. Japan Association of National University Libraries and National Institute of Informatics, *Kenkyu katsudo oyobi open access ni kansuru chosa hokokusho (In Japanese. Research report on research activities and open access).* March 2006. Available at http://wwwsoc.nii.ac.jp/janul/j/projects/isc/sparc/oa_chosa.pdf (Last accessed on August 28, 2006)

7. Japan Association of National University Libraries, *Chosakuken no toriatsukai ni kansuru anketo, kekka sokuho (Preliminary report on the result of inquiries on copyright policies of Japanese academic societies)* March 2006. Available at http://www.tulips.tsukuba.ac.jp/ir/ (Last accessed on August 28, 2006)

8. Swan, Alma and Sheridan Brown (2004) Report of the JISC/OSI open access journal authors survey. Available at http://www.jisc.ac.uk/uploaded_documents/JISCOAreport1.pdf (last accessed on September 4, 2006).

9. Swan, Alma and Sheridan Brown (2005) Open access self-archiving: an author study. Available at http://www.keyperspectives.co.uk/openaccessarchive/reports/Open%20Access%20II%20(author%20survey%20on%20self%20archiving)%202005.pdf (last accessed on September 4, 2006).

A   Partner Universities

The following list is the 57 project partners in 2006. The 19 universities in italics were also our partners in 2005.

Hokkaido Univ.	Obihiro Univ. of Agriculture and Veterinary Medicine
Asahikawa Medical College	Kitami Institute of Technology
Hirosaki Univ.	*Tohoku Univ.*
Yamagata Univ.	Fukushima Univ.
Tsukuba Univ.	Gunma Univ.
Saitama Univ.	*Chiba Univ.*
Univ. Tokyo	Tokyo Univ. of Foreign Studies
Tokyo Gakugei Univ.	*Tokyo Institute of Technology*
Ochanomizu Univ.	Hitotsubashi Univ.
Yokohama National Univ.	Niigata Univ.
Kanazawa Univ.	Shinshu Univ.
Gifu Univ.	*Nagoya Univ.*
Mie Univ.	Shiga Univ. of Medical Science
Kyoto Univ.	*Osaka Univ.*
Osaka Kyoiku Univ.	Hyogo Univ. of Teacher Education
Kobe Univ.	Kyoto Institute of Technology
Nara Univ. of Education	Nara Women's Univ.
Yamaguchi Univ.	Shimane Univ.
Okayama Univ.	*Hiroshima Univ.*
Kochi Univ.	*Kyushu Univ.*
Saga Univ.	*Nagasaki Univ.*
Kumamoto Univ.	Oita Univ.
Kagoshima Univ.	Ryukyu Univ.
JAIST	*Keio Univ.*
Toyo Univ.	Hosei Univ.
Waseda Univ.	Kanto Gakuin Univ.
Doshisha Univ.	Kansai Univ.
Kwansei Gakuin Univ.	Kochi Univ. of Technology
Ritsumeikan Asia Pacific Univ.	

Introduction to the National Archives of Japan Digital Archive Service

Shohei Muta

National Archives of Japan
3-2 Kitanomaru Park, Chiyoda-ku, Tokyo 102-0091, Japan
smuta2@archives.go.jp
http://www.archives.go.jp, http://www.jacar.go.jp

Abstract. National Archives of Japan provides two digital archive projects; Japan Center for Asian Historical Records (JACAR) and National Archives of Japan Digital Archive (NAJDA). This presentation provides outline of these two projects focusing at their common technical specifications such as EAD/XML, Dublin Core, and Z39.50.

Keywords: Digital Archive, EAD/XML, Encoded Archival Description 2002, Dublin Core, Z39.50, SRW, OAI-PMH.

1 Introduction

National Archives of Japan provides following two digital projects:

- Japan Center for Asian Historical Records (JACAR) started in 2001 as a precursor to the National Archive of Japan Digital Archive (NAJDA). It provides digital images of government records in modern Japanese history from 1880's to 1945. As of 2006/09, it provides 840,000 searchable records and over 12 millions of digital images on the Internet. JACAR database system is scheduled to be renewed on October 2006 (as of this writing) sharing technologies which had been developed for and adopted by the National Archive Digital Archive (NAJDA). Therefore, this paper will concentrate mostly on NAJDA's technical specifications.
- National Archives of Japan Digital Archive (NAJDA) was started its Internet service in April 2005. NAJDA is consisted from two services:
  - ➢ Digital Archive System, which provide catalog search service of more than 2.6 million records with 3 million digital images of government records and other historical materials such as 430 thousands records from former Cabinet Library Materials. The system provides various search methods such as layered or keyword search. With the protocol such as Z39.50 and SRW, NAJDA database is linked with other institutions such as the National Diet Library (NDL) and the National Institute for Informatics (NII);
  - ➢ Digital Gallery, which provides 375 items (520 images) of Important Cultural Properties, large-sized materials, colorful scrolls, and posters that are difficult to have access to original ones. The Gallery provides search by region, category or A-Z.

S. Sugimoto et al. (Eds.): ICADL 2006, LNCS 4312, pp. 550–555, 2006.

Fig. 1. Top page image of National Archive of Japan Digital Archive

2 Key Concepts of Designing National Archive Digital Projects

Prior to the establishment of the NAJDA, the National Archives of Japan adopted the "Outline for Promoting Digital Archive Projects 2004." It states that the main aim of the projects is to provide both catalog search services and browsing digitalized images

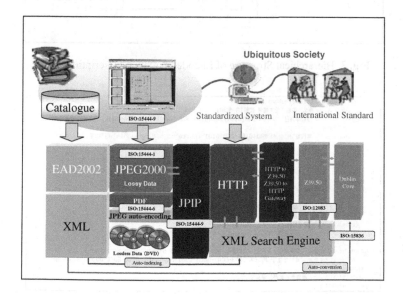

Fig. 2. System Outline of the National Archive of Japan Digital Archive

on the Internet, making accessible to anyone, from anywhere, at anytime and free. Characteristics of the projects are to use either internationally standardized or open source formats and technologies such as EAD2002 (Encoded Archival Description 2002), XML, and Unicode for database; JPEG 2000 for main image format; Dublin Core, Z39.50, SRW for sharing metadata among various databases operated by other institutions such as NDL and NII.

The search system provides various finding tools for varieties of users, professional researchers or ordinary people such as the layered search operated by the EAD based database system allowing users to look into the database following the hierarchical structure of archival materials.

3   Technical Information

JPEG 2000 (ISO 15444-1) was selected from various image formats because of its multiple functions and standardized definition which satisfied requirements in one

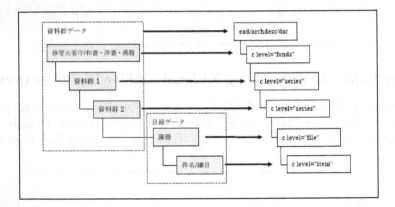

Fig. 3. Hierarchical Structure of Encoded Archival Description 2002

```
<unitid>C04015151300</unitid>
<unittitle label="件名">表紙「公文備考 臨艦13 巻38」</unittitle>
<unitdate label="作成年月日" normal="20010101/20010101" era="ce" calendar="gregorian">大正15年2月13日
     </unitdate>
<unitdate label="年代域" normal="20010101/20010101" era="ce" calendar="gregorian">昭和2年</unitdate>
- <physdesc>
     <extent>5</extent>
  </physdesc>
<origination label="作成者名称">海軍省</origination>
- <langmaterial>
     <language langcode="jpn">ja</language>
  </langmaterial>
<container label="電子媒体ボリューム名">/c0250326011</container>
<container label="電子媒体フォルダ名">/koubun_0020</container>
<container label="電子媒体ファイル名">/0001_01</container>
<materialspec label="目録種別">3</materialspec>
<materialspec label="データ種別">03</materialspec>
<materialspec label="簿冊キー">海軍省-公文備考-大正15年 昭和元年-S1-049</materialspec>
<materialspec label="資料整理コード">CA-0003-0001-0003-0001-0000-0049-0000-0000-0000</materialspec>
</did>
<bioghist altrender="組織歴／履歴">海軍省</bioghist>
- <scopecontent>
```

Fig. 4. EAD data sample

```
<dc>
    <Identifier>御30168100</Identifier>
    <Title>日本国憲法・御署名原本・昭和二十一年・憲法一一月三日</Title>
    <Date>1946</Date>
    <Creator>内閣</Creator>
    <Language>01:日本語</Language>
</dc>
```

Fig. 5. Dublin Core data sample: 日本国憲法 (Constitution of Japan)

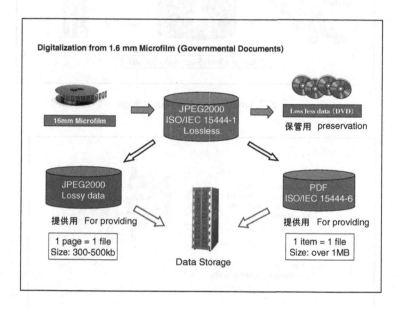

Fig. 6. Digitalizing governmental documents

format from both users' convenience and long term stability. The NAJDAS uses lossless format of JEPG 2000 for preservation and lossy format for proving images through the Internet. The material images vary in type and size. There are manuscripts, books, drawings, maps, and scroll paintings. One of the largest map is 4m x 5m and longest scroll painting is 24m long. Data size also varies from 1 MG to 9 GB for lossless images for preservation and 300 KB to 300 MG for lossy images.

4   New Task for the Digital Archives

In 2001, Japanese government initiated 'e-Japan Strategy' to create IT based society. Under the strategy, the government decided to realize an e-government, which handles

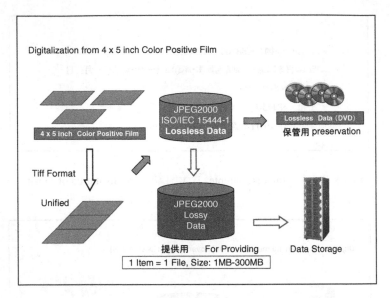

Fig. 7. Digitalization of large maps

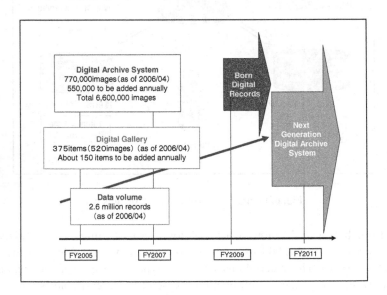

Fig. 8. Future projection of NAJDA

electronic information in the same manner as paper-based information. However, there is little consideration of long term preservation of born digital records. In order to meet this challenge, the National Archives of Japan, working closely with government ministries and agencies concerning record keepings, conducts researches for long term preservation of born digital records and next generation of digital archive system, which is able to handle born digital records transferred to the National Archives for permanent preservation.

References

1. ISAD (G) official site http://www.ica.org/biblio.php?pdocid=1
2. Dublin Core official site http://www.dublincore.org
3. EAD official site http://www.loc.gov/ead/
4. National Archives EAD definition
   http://www.digital.archives.go.jp/howto/pdf/naj_ead107.pdf
5. e-Japan Strategy official site http://www.kantei.go.jp/foreign/policy/it/enkaku_e.html

The Development of Digital Library Projects in Taiwan

Hsueh-hua Chen

No. 1, Sec. 4, Roosevelt Road, Taipei, 10617 Taiwan
Professor, Department of Library and Information Science, National Taiwan University
Director, National Taiwan University Press
Co-PI, Applications & Services Division, National Digital Archives Program
Co-PI, Institutional Project of National Taiwan University, National Digital Archives Program
sherry@ntu.edu.tw

Abstract. The development of the national level digital library projects in Taiwan began in 1998. The initiate project -- Digital Museum Project (DMP, 1998~2001), sponsored by the National Science Council (NSC), included several topic-based projects and technical support projects. The outcomes of DMP was quite successful, however, the scale and budget (only $130 million NTD, ca. US$4 million) of DMP was not big enough to cover the whole picture of cultural heritage in Taiwan. For this reason, NSC proposed a five-year's National Digital Archives Program (NDAP) in the year of 2002 as a sub-project of e-Taiwan.

The main goal of the National Digital Archives Program is to promote and coordinate content digitization and preservation at leading museums, archives, universities, research institutes, and other content holders in Taiwan.

The goals of NDAP are compounded the ultimate mission of preserving and sustaining the culture and civilization of mankind in Taiwan. They are:

1. To preserve national cultural collections.
2. To popularize fine cultural holdings.
3. To revitalize cultural heritage and cultural development.
4. To invigorate cultural, content, and value-added industries.
5. To promote knowledge and information sharing.
6. To enhance research, education, and life-long learning.
7. To improve literacy, creativity and quality of life.
8. To embrace collaboration and international community.

The organization and functions of the NDAP includes three components: Program Office, Institutional Projects and Non-solicited Projects.

There are five divisions in the Program Office: Content Development Division, Research and Development of Technology Division, Applications & Services Division, Training & Promotion Division, and Operations Management Division. These divisions will jointly carry out the overall planning organized by the Program Office, build common infrastructures and establish general content processing guidelines and specifications for all participating institutions and non-solicited projects.

S. Sugimoto et al. (Eds.): ICADL 2006, LNCS 4312, pp. 556–558, 2006.

The Institutional projects are conducted by major content holders and providers of digital resources in Taiwan. There were nine participating institutions, including the Academia Historica, the Academia Sinica, and the Council for Cultural Affairs, the National Central Library, the National Museum of History, the National Museum of National Science, the National Palace Museum, the National Taiwan University and the Taiwan Historica. These institutes hold national cultural heritage and collections, and take leadership position in different areas. Digitizing these archives can not only preserve the cultural treasure, but also improve the applications of collections and cultural holdings. Each institute of NDAP has their tasks and missions.

The Non-solicited Projects are those selected from proposals submitted to open Request-for-Proposal (RFP) announcements. From 2002 to 2006, 282 projects were selected, including: 90 for digital content development, 51 for technology research and development, 55 for e-learning application, and 86 for various applications of digital archives.

	2002	2003	2004	2005	2006	Total
Digital content development	6	8	22	25	29	90
Technology research and development	5	6	10	17	13	51
E-learning application	N/A	N/A	10	25	20	55
Various applications of digital archives	16	15	25	16	14	86
Total	27	29	67	83	76	282

In order to make the NDAP work more efficiently, the Program Office has set up 16 thematic groups for content to provide coordination, technical support and personnel training, including Anthropology, Archaeology, Architecture, Archives, Artifacts, Botany, Calligraphy & Painting, Chinese Classics Full-text Database, Geology, Journalism & Mass Media, Linguistics, Maps & Remote images, Rare Books, Stone & Bronze Rubbings, Video, Zoology. These thematic groups provide a coordination mechanism to solve problems arising in digitizing and managing collections among different institutions in the respective areas.

The NDAP budget for the first five years is $339, $368, $530, $638 and $645 million NTD, respectively, (approximately $10.3, $11.2, $16.2, 19.5 and 19.7 million USD). The second phase of NDAP will start in 2007 and covers the period 2007 to 2011. It is estimated that the budget for the second phase will be higher than the first phase.

Although the main goals of NDAP are to preserve national cultural collections, to enhance research, education, and life-long learning, as the sizes and varieties of cultural digital archives have been growing dramatically, an industry that is built around the construction and applications of digital archives is gradually coming into shape. It's also very important for NADP to identify the business models for the cultural digital archives industry.

References

[1] National Digital Archives Program, Taiwan. *National Digital Archives Program*. Retrieved Sep. 1, 2006 from http://www.ndap.org.tw/index_en.php
[2] Council of Economic Planning and Development (2002). *Challenge 2008—National Development Plan*. Retrieved Sep.1, 2006 from http://www.gio.gov.tw/taiwan-website/5-gp/glance/ch11.htm
[3] *National Science Council Digital Museum Project (In Chinese)*. Retrieved Sep.1, 2006 from http://aps.csie.ntu.edu.tw/museum.html

Kyoto International Manga Museum

Masaharu Sekiguchi

Kyoto Seika University Trust Planning department 137 Kino-cyo, Iwakura, Sakyo, kyoto
606-8588
kyotomm@kyoto-seika.ac.jp

Abstract. In November, 2006, Kyoto Seika University establishes the Kyoto International Manga Museum where 200,000 items of Manga materials are exhibited. Its research department is to work on such projects as theoretical analysis of the changes in presentation styles of Manga, and sociological study of Manga. It is also to study how to expand the use of Manga to digital contents or educational materials in collaboration with industries, and to consider Manga in terms of intellectual property and how to protect its copyright. In addition, the Digital Archives (Manga Archives) made public on the Internet are going to be built. In preparation for information exchange with concerned institutions by metadata management of information, and with a view to development of the Mangapedia: Manga-Encyclopedia in the future, the system will be created based on the OAI-PMH (Open Archives Initiative Protocol for Metadata Harvesting), the ISO23950 (Z39.50) which is the international standard for cross search function, and the JPEG2000 which is the international standard for the digital image.

1 Introduction

Kyoto Seika University, which has been engaged in the study and education of Manga since it launched the unique Manga curriculum in 1973, is starting remarkable new projects in 2006 with a view to bringing together its performances and accomplishments of the last 33 years and presenting them worldwide. Firstly, it established the Faculty of Manga last April, which was the first one as such in Japan, to enhance its function to teach and study Manga that constitutes a considerable part in the contents industry Japan boasts to the world. Moreover, it is going to open the Kyoto International Manga Museum in November as a joint project with Kyoto City, which will be the first comprehensive institution for Manga in Japan. The Kyoto International Manga Museum uses a renovated building of an elementary school which is located right in the center of Kyoto. This good location will make it easy for a lot of people to visit it.

2 Outline of the Kyoto International Manga Museum

In the Kyoto International Manga Museum, Nishiki-e and Ukiyo-e, Western caricatures, Bande Dessinées (cartoons seen mainly in Belgium and France), comic

S. Sugimoto et al. (Eds.): ICADL 2006, LNCS 4312, pp. 559–560, 2006.
© Springer-Verlag Berlin Heidelberg 2006

books, weekly Manga magazines, supplements to Manga magazines and so on from the end of Edo Period, when the Manga started to be printed in mass duplication, to the present day are collected and organized. Such Manga materials will amount to 200,000 items in number and be presented to visitors in a form of exhibitions resourcefully planned from various viewpoints.

The museum will also have a research department, where both domestic and foreign researchers will be engaged in such projects as theoretical analysis of the changes in presentation styles of Manga and sociological study of Manga. They will also study how to expand the use of Manga to digital contents or educational materials in collaboration with industries, or consider how to protect the copyright of cartoonists against pirated copies or secondhand bookstores which sell new books as used ones, and the way Manga should be in terms of intellectual property.

The greatest characteristic of the Kyoto International Manga Museum is in that it is a visitor-participation-type museum. The museum is going not only to offer its Manga materials to visitors but also to gather information about visitors' reading experiences of Manga and analyze them, the result of which will be reflected in its exhibition plans and so on. By examining and exhibiting each Manga content while examining the variety of Manga experiences (the ways Manga is read and understood), it will try to make an approach to the Manga content as a whole and the whole Japanese pop culture.

3   Outline of the Manga Archives

The Kyoto International Manga Museum is going to establish the Manga Archives available on the Internet, in order to present its materials and study developments publicly and to offer the information system infrastructure with education and research functions. The Manga Archives are digital archives which are planned to be developed and established in two years after the opening of the museum. They will consist of the information of the books, the magazines, the works in them, and the image information of the materials that belong to the museum; the information about the Manga collections of domestic and foreign facilities; and the information of Manga character goods. The Manga Archives also have a view of development of the Mangapedia: the Manga-Encyclopedia provided on the Internet.

Because Manga contents contain various kinds of information and expression, the metadata management of retrieval information will be implemented, which makes possible the search beyond publishing forms like books or magazines. In addition, in preparation for information exchange with concerned institutions, the system is to be built based on the OAI-PMH (Open Archives Initiative Protocol for Metadata Harvesting) and the ISO23950 (Z39.50) which is the international standard for cross search function. Its aim is to make up the basis for realization of Manga knowledge sharing by making it possible to access the Archives by way of information services of various institutions. Furthermore, Manga content itself, when its copyright issues are cleared, is going to be presented publicly, and for this purpose the JPEG2000 which is the international standard for the most advanced digital image is adopted.

Building the National Digital Library of China for Global Users

Qi Xin and Sun Wei

Digital Library Administration Division, National Library of China
qixin@nlc.gov.cn, sunw@nlc.gov.cn

Abstract. National Digital Library of China Project is the biggest digital library system in China. The article presents the background of NDLCP and describes the architecture of the system. The article also presents the big challenge in NDLCP and the solutions.

Keywords: NDLCP, digital library, preservation, challenge.

1 General Information

1.1 National Digital Library of China Project (NDLCP)

a. Digital Library in NLC

Digital library is a significant symbol to estimate the development of national information infrastructure and the important power to promote the development of knowledge economy. With the great support of the government, China's digital library got a rapid growth. In China, many libraries began the innovation and construction of digital library. At present some projects has been launched such as National Library Project, Chinese National Science Digital Library, China Academy library and Information System, and Party of Socialism Digital Library.

Since 1995, NLC realized the digital age was coming and began to pursue international digital library research. The main program is listed as bellow:

1997   State Development Planning Commission Project: Chinese Pilot Digital Library
        NLC, Shanghai Library, Shenzhen Library, Sun Yat-Sen Library of Guangdong Province, Liaoning Provincial Library, Ministry of Culture

1998   863-306 Project "Knowledge Grid- Digital Library System"
        Institute of Computing Science CAS, NLC

2000   863-300 Project "China Digital Library Application System
        Ministry of Science and Technology, NLC

1999   "Zhongguancun Science Park– Digital Library Cluster" Project
        NLC, Peking University Library, Tsinghua University Library, Library of Chinese Academy of Science

S. Sugimoto et al. (Eds.): ICADL 2006, LNCS 4312, pp. 561–567, 2006.

2002   "China Digital Library Standard" Project
National Science and Technology Library, Library of Chinese Academy of
Science, NLC

b. National Digital Library of China Project

The National Library of China Phase II & National Digital Library of China Project
was set up with an approval of the China State Council in 2002. On October 11th 2005,
National Development and Reform Commission approved the preliminary design and
investment of National Digital Library Project. The total investment is 1.2 billion
RMB. The National Digital Library Project has been launched in 2005, and will be
completed in 2008. The project is listed as the key item in the Tenth Five-Plan of China.
The center of National digital library will be located in the new building of the National
Library, which plays an important role of demonstration during the construction of
China digital library.

1.2 Resources in the National Library of China

a. Traditional Resources

The total of collections in NLC has reached 25,049,236(volumes/items), which is 5th
biggest in the world and is developing 0.6-0.7 million every year. Our collection is vast.
It covers every information format from manuscripts of 1500 years ago, oracles of 3000
years ago to audio,   video, and other electronic collection。

Table 1. Statistics of open stack collections (Volumes/Items)

	Books	Periodicals	Newspapers	Others
Total in main library	1,516,781	715,488	283	141,106
Total in branch	173,008	5,328	130	0
Total	2,552,124			

b. E-Resources

Since 1980s, NLC has begun to collect E-resources. As the beginning, NLC made the
Chinese catalogue database in 1987. At the same year, NLC began to purchase the
E-resources in CD-ROM. Since 2000, NLC got extra funding from the government and
began to digitize the collection.

NLC has established a digital portal website depending on the rich collections and
digital resources on the Internet.

In addition, different databases and information services are customized for the
government and legislatures. NLC also provides real-time information and digital
reference services.

Table 2. Statistics of digital collections (Items)

Collection Catalogue	3.57 million
Regulation Data	0.7 million
Bibliography Data	2.75 million
Full-text images	80 million
Audio	0.40 million
Video	13 thousand
Purchased Electronic Resources	
Chinese Database	28
Foreign Language Database	102
DIALOG Database	600+
Foreign Language Electronic Publication	1,000+
Audio and Video	0.1 million

2   The Target of NDLCP

At the end of 2007, National Library of China will offer 30 million items of catalogue and Bibliography, and 200TB digital resources in uniform portal of National Digital Library.

From 2008 to 2015, NLC will finish the bibliography database offering the retrieval to the names of books, serials, and newspaper and contents records. The characteristic databases of NLC will be also finished, including oracle, Dunhuang, Chinese doctoral dissertations, Sinology. The Chinese Internet resources database will be built to preserve the important Chinese websites and web pages.

As the national library, NLC will collect and preserve Chinese digital resources, including the online massive Chinese digital resources. As the professional leader in China library community, NLC will make a complete digital resource process workflow. NLC will offer the large-scale Chinese digital resources to Global World. NLC will be the Biggest Chinese digital resources preservation and service center in the world and important national information infrastructure of China. A big digital library technical platform will be established to collect, process and preserve digital resources.

System requirements:

1.   Digitization:
     Digitization from paper: 300,000 items/ year
     Digitization from microfilm: 3,000,000 images/ year
     Abstract record processing: 90,000 items/ year
2.   Repository:
     Online storage $\geq$ 60TB
     Long-term preservation $\geq$ 340TB (including online and offline)
3.   Service:
     6000 computers access to Internet in the new building of NLC
     Wireless Internet Access in NLC (11M/ second or 108M/ second)
     Digital resources service $\geq$ 1000GB/ day
     Internet access $\geq$ 3G/S

Support retrieval in 200 million metadata records
Response to 100,000 retrievals/ minute, 10,000 retrievals/ second in MAX
Support full-text retrieval in 100 million pages
Support retrieval n rare books

3 Architecture of NDLCP

3.1 Digital Resource Collection

a. Internet Resources

The collection of Internet resources is an important part of digital collection. Since 2004, NLC has begun the test of online resources preservation. The catalogue regulation of Internet resources and database is in research. 193 websites were collected and classified as subjects, such as Sinology, Olympics Games, media report about NLC, digital library development. Now NLC is cooperating with Internet Archive and Peking University to collect the online resources before 2004. As the first step of large-scale web harvesting, NLC began to preserve over 20,000 government websites of China. We plan to harvest the content once a week. These websites are in four main network providers in China, including China Telecom, CNC China CERNET, China Science and Technology Network. The bandwidths between them are very narrow. If NLC only have access to one single network provider, it is impossible for us to harvest all the websites in a week. NLC have to build 4 LAN access to 4 different providers for web harvesting. (See Fig.1.)

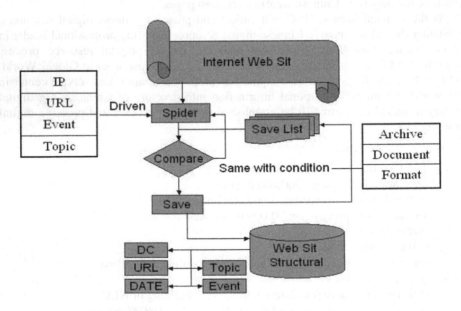

Fig. 1. Overview of Internet Resources Repository

b. E-resources Deposit

In 1996, National Copyright Administration of China issued Notice about Electronic Publication Deposit. The notice regulated that all the electronic publications after 1st January, 1996 should deposit to National Copyright Administration of China, Copyright Library of China (located in Beijing) and NLC. In January 2 1997, State Council of the People's Republic of China established No.210 Publication Administration Byelaw regulated legal deposit to NLC. Now the e-resources deposit includes two parts. The first is the e-resources from press. As the negotiation with Chinese digital content providers, NLC will collect the all their resources just for preservation. CD-ROM or hard disk will deliver the resources. Another part is the doctoral dissertations. NLC will develop an online doctoral dissertation deliver system. The system will support the deposit not only from single person but also form institutions such as China Science Digital Library. (See Fig. 2.)

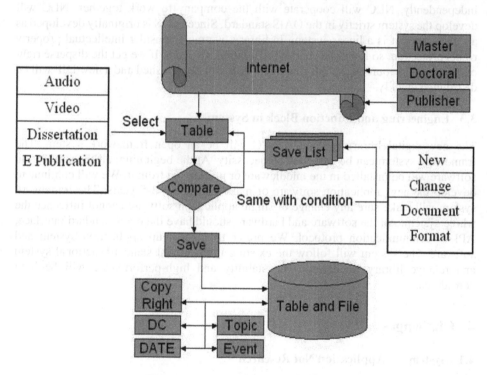

Fig. 2. Overview of E-Deposte Services

3.2 Long-Time Preservation

a. Preservation Strategy

First is to confirm what kind of resources will be preserved. According to the function of national digital library, the digital resources will be divided into 3 levels:

Long-time preservation: the resources will be preserved and offered persistently.
Short-time service: NLC will own the access and offer to library users.
Mirror and link service: NLC will only offer the mirror or URL of the resources.

Long-time Preservation is facing the technical, budget challenges, but also the challenges of how to preserve both the knowledge and physical features of the document. NLC has a big amount of rare books and manuscripts. The format of rare books is also an important part of Chinese culture. On the other hand, all the digital resources are depending on the special operation and application system. The system will be updated in 3-5 years. If any digital resource cannot be immigrant to the new platform, we will print the resource into paper format and then digitized again to make sure the digital format will be always available.

b. OAIS Model

OAIS model is the key part of digital library preservation system. NLC will develop the system cooperating with an IT company or research institute. Since seldom Software Company knows OAIS very well and NLC is also not able to develop the system independently, NLC will cooperate with the company to work together. NLC will develop the system strictly in the OAIS standard. Since OAIS is originally developed as a GIS system, it is a linear system. In library, we must consider intellectual property rights protection, so it will be changed as a circular system. If we get the disperse right of any digital resources, the information in AIP will be refreshed and a new DIP will be distributed quickly.

3.3 Engineering and Function Block in System

The new digital library system in NLC will be an open framework system. The framework system can be extended by necessity. At the beginning, all the application software will be installed in the middleware or uninstalled from it. We will continue to develop the new application software or make updates in 3-5 years. The framework system will make sure any change of single application software cannot influence the whole system. All the software and hardware should have the open standard interface, API or communication protocol. We prefer the grown up application system and software. The system will follow the existing international standard, national system and relative library regulation. The stability and high-performance will be both considered.

4   Challenges

4.1 System for Application Not Research

NDLCP is not a research program any more. The project is under the supervision of National Development and Reform Commission, Ministry of Culture, Ministry of Finance. The project time limit and performance index is firm. On the other hand, most digital library programs are designed for universities, the target and scale is quite different. That means we have little experience for reference.

4.2 Limited Budget and Massive Data

At the end of 2005, 103 million pages have been scanned into full-text images in NLC. The system will also post the links to other institutions, such as Peking University library. The NDLCP investment cannot support the federated full-text retrieval to all the library digital resources. The system can support the retrieval to content record. Only the rare book full-text retrieval is supported.

4.3 Persistent Digital Library System (Data Warehouse)

As NDLCP is completed, NLC will become the biggest Chinese digital resources database in the world. The massive data management and preservation is a big challenge to NLC. We will use the data warehouse and Virtual Memory technique to insure the secure of the data.

4.4 System Extend and Maintenance

NDLCP is a five years program, but the system will run a long time. We must consider the maintenance and development after NDLCP in advance. Because NDLCP is a government investment project, the system is a public production. We expect the system becomes the model for all the Chinese public libraries. Every library can use the software free of charge. The system should be flexible, and can be easily extended or reduced. Since the budget of most libraries is limited, the system will be fit for the PC server, which is easy for maintenance.

4.5 Intellectual Property Limitation

Intellectual property management is the important component of digital resources service. Due to the limitation, most of the digital resources in NLC cannot offer to the readers. Many e-resources and database only can be used in the library intranet. NLC is trying to find a way to solve the Intellectual property problem. We will note the detailed Intellectual property status to the reader. Under the term of "Fair Use", NLC is digitizing the documentation out of protection period primarily. In cooperating with some professional communities such as Music Copyright Society of China, NLC will authorize them to process the intellectual property.

5 Conclusion

The NDLCP is a big chance for NLC, and also a big challenge. The target of NDLCP is not only to build a digital library system. NLC wish to improve the evolution of NLC from Traditional Library to Modern library. The NDLCP is the update for both the equipment and the idea of NLC. NLC will be more open and friendly. The Chinese digital resource will serve the global users.

Author Index

Lecture Notes in Computer Science

For information about Vols. 1–4210

please contact your bookseller or Springer

Vol. 4253: B. Gabrys, R.J. Howlett, L.C. Jain (Eds.), Knowledge-Based Intelligent Information and Engineering Systems, Part III. XXXII, 1301 pages. 2006. (Sublibrary LNAI).

Vol. 4252: B. Gabrys, R.J. Howlett, L.C. Jain (Eds.), Knowledge-Based Intelligent Information and Engineering Systems, Part II. XXXIII, 1335 pages. 2006. (Sublibrary LNAI).

Vol. 4251: B. Gabrys, R.J. Howlett, L.C. Jain (Eds.), Knowledge-Based Intelligent Information and Engineering Systems, Part I. LXVI, 1297 pages. 2006. (Sublibrary LNAI).

Vol. 4249: L. Goubin, M. Matsui (Eds.), Cryptographic Hardware and Embedded Systems - CHES 2006. XII, 462 pages. 2006.

Vol. 4248: S. Staab, V. Svátek (Eds.), Managing Knowledge in a World of Networks. XIV, 400 pages. 2006. (Sublibrary LNAI).

Vol. 4247: T.-D. Wang, X. Li, S.-H. Chen, X. Wang, H. Abbass, H. Iba, G. Chen, X. Yao (Eds.), Simulated Evolution and Learning. XXI, 940 pages. 2006.

Vol. 4246: M. Hermann, A. Voronkov (Eds.), Logic for Programming, Artificial Intelligence, and Reasoning. XIII, 588 pages. 2006. (Sublibrary LNAI).

Vol. 4245: A. Kuba, L.G. Nyúl, K. Palágyi (Eds.), Discrete Geometry for Computer Imagery. XIII, 688 pages. 2006.

Vol. 4244: S. Spaccapietra (Ed.), Journal on Data Semantics VII. XI, 267 pages. 2006.

Vol. 4243: T. Yakhno, E.J. Neuhold (Eds.), Advances in Information Systems. XIII, 420 pages. 2006.

Vol. 4242: A. Rashid, M. Aksit (Eds.), Transactions on Aspect-Oriented Software Development II. IX, 289 pages. 2006.

Vol. 4241: R.R. Beichel, M. Sonka (Eds.), Computer Vision Approaches to Medical Image Analysis. XI, 262 pages. 2006.

Vol. 4239: H.Y. Youn, M. Kim, H. Morikawa (Eds.), Ubiquitous Computing Systems. XVI, 548 pages. 2006.

Vol. 4238: Y.-T. Kim, M. Takano (Eds.), Management of Convergence Networks and Services. XVIII, 605 pages. 2006.

Vol. 4237: H. Leitold, E. Markatos (Eds.), Communications and Multimedia Security. XII, 253 pages. 2006.

Vol. 4236: L. Breveglieri, I. Koren, D. Naccache, J.-P. Seifert (Eds.), Fault Diagnosis and Tolerance in Cryptography. XIII, 253 pages. 2006.

Vol. 4234: I. King, J. Wang, L. Chan, D. Wang (Eds.), Neural Information Processing, Part III. XXII, 1227 pages. 2006.

Vol. 4233: I. King, J. Wang, L. Chan, D. Wang (Eds.), Neural Information Processing, Part II. XXII, 1203 pages. 2006.

Vol. 4232: I. King, J. Wang, L. Chan, D. Wang (Eds.), Neural Information Processing, Part I. XLVI, 1153 pages. 2006.

Vol. 4231: J. F. Roddick, R. Benjamins, S. Si-Saïd Cherfi, R. Chiang, C. Claramunt, R. Elmasri, F. Grandi, H. Han, M. Hepp, M. Hepp, M. Lytras, V.B. Mišić, G. Poels, I.-Y. Song, J. Trujillo, C. Vangenot (Eds.), Advances in Conceptual Modeling - Theory and Practice. XXII, 456 pages. 2006.

Vol. 4230: C. Priami, A. Ingólfsdóttir, B. Mishra, H.R. Nielson (Eds.), Transactions on Computational Systems Biology VII. VII, 185 pages. 2006. (Sublibrary LNBI).

Vol. 4229: E. Najm, J.F. Pradat-Peyre, V.V. Donzeau-Gouge (Eds.), Formal Techniques for Networked and Distributed Systems - FORTE 2006. X, 486 pages. 2006.

Vol. 4228: D.E. Lightfoot, C.A. Szyperski (Eds.), Modular Programming Languages. X, 415 pages. 2006.

Vol. 4227: W. Nejdl, K. Tochtermann (Eds.), Innovative Approaches for Learning and Knowledge Sharing. XVII, 721 pages. 2006.

Vol. 4226: R.T. Mittermeir (Ed.), Informatics Education – The Bridge between Using and Understanding Computers. XVII, 319 pages. 2006.

Vol. 4225: J.F. Martínez-Trinidad, J.A. Carrasco Ochoa, J. Kittler (Eds.), Progress in Pattern Recognition, Image Analysis and Applications. XIX, 995 pages. 2006.

Vol. 4224: E. Corchado, H. Yin, V. Botti, C. Fyfe (Eds.), Intelligent Data Engineering and Automated Learning – IDEAL 2006. XXVII, 1447 pages. 2006.

Vol. 4223: L. Wang, L. Jiao, G. Shi, X. Li, J. Liu (Eds.), Fuzzy Systems and Knowledge Discovery. XXVIII, 1335 pages. 2006. (Sublibrary LNAI).

Vol. 4222: L. Jiao, L. Wang, X. Gao, J. Liu, F. Wu (Eds.), Advances in Natural Computation, Part II. XLII, 998 pages. 2006.

Vol. 4221: L. Jiao, L. Wang, X. Gao, J. Liu, F. Wu (Eds.), Advances in Natural Computation, Part I. XLI, 992 pages. 2006.

Vol. 4220: C. Priami, G. Plotkin (Eds.), Transactions on Computational Systems Biology VI. IX, 247 pages. 2006. (Sublibrary LNBI).

Vol. 4219: D. Zamboni, C. Kruegel (Eds.), Recent Advances in Intrusion Detection. XII, 331 pages. 2006.

Vol. 4218: S. Graf, W. Zhang (Eds.), Automated Technology for Verification and Analysis. XIV, 540 pages. 2006.

Vol. 4217: P. Cuenca, L. Orozco-Barbosa (Eds.), Personal Wireless Communications. XV, 532 pages. 2006.

Vol. 4216: M.R. Berthold, R. Glen, I. Fischer (Eds.), Computational Life Sciences II. XIII, 269 pages. 2006. (Sublibrary LNBI).

Vol. 4215: D.W. Embley, A. Olivé, S. Ram (Eds.), Conceptual Modeling - ER 2006. XVI, 590 pages. 2006.

Vol. 4213: J. Fürnkranz, T. Scheffer, M. Spiliopoulou (Eds.), Knowledge Discovery in Databases: PKDD 2006. XXII, 660 pages. 2006. (Sublibrary LNAI).

Vol. 4212: J. Fürnkranz, T. Scheffer, M. Spiliopoulou (Eds.), Machine Learning: ECML 2006. XXIII, 851 pages. 2006. (Sublibrary LNAI).

Vol. 4211: P. Vogt, Y. Sugita, E. Tuci, C. Nehaniv (Eds.), Symbol Grounding and Beyond. VIII, 237 pages. 2006. (Sublibrary LNAI).